AMERICAN COLOSSUS

ALSO BY H. W. BRANDS

The Reckless Decade
T.R.
The First American
The Age of Gold
Lone Star Nation
Andrew Jackson
Traitor to His Class

American Colossus

THE TRIUMPH OF CAPITALISM
1865–1900

H. W. Brands

Doubleday

New York   London   Toronto   Sydney   Auckland

DD

DOUBLEDAY

Copyright © 2010 by H. W. Brands

All rights reserved. Published in the United States by Doubleday,
a division of Random House, Inc., New York,
and in Canada by Random House of Canada Limited, Toronto.

www.doubleday.com

DOUBLEDAY and the DD colophon are registered trademarks
of Random House, Inc.

Book design by Maria Carella

Library of Congress Cataloging-in-Publication Data
Brands, H. W.
American colossus: the triumph of capitalism, 1865–1900 /
H. W. Brands. — 1st ed.
p. cm.
Includes bibliographical references and index.
1. United States—Economic conditions—19th century.
2. United States—Social conditions—19th century. I. Title.
HC105.B813 2010
330.973'08—dc22   2010008538

ISBN 978-0-385-52333-2

PRINTED IN THE UNITED STATES OF AMERICA

1 3 5 7 9 10 8 6 4 2

First Edition

CONTENTS

PART THREE
GOTHAM AND GOMORRAH

PART FOUR
THE FINEST GOVERNMENT MONEY CAN BUY

PART FIVE
THE DECADE OF THE CENTURY

AMERICAN COLOSSUS

Prologue

THE CAPITALIST REVOLUTION

John Pierpont Morgan enjoyed an excellent Civil War. He didn't fight, although he was prime military material, being in his midtwenties and blessed with solid health. Instead he hired a substitute in the manner of many rich, tepid Unionists. Morgan's father was a transatlantic banker with one foot in New York and the other in London; to train his son for the business he had sent him to school in Switzerland and college in Germany. The young man's aptitude for numbers prompted one of his professors at Göttingen to suggest a post on the mathematics faculty, but he replied that he heard the family business calling, and he returned to America to become a commodities trader. In an early transaction he bought a boatload of coffee without authorization; before his astonished superiors could fire him, he unloaded the cargo for a fat profit. They appreciated the income but distrusted the audacity and so declined to make him a partner, whereupon, in 1861, he planted his own flag on Wall Street.

His timing couldn't have been better, nor his scruples more suited to the opportunities the war afforded. Hearing of a man who had purchased five thousand old carbines from an armory in New York for $3.50 each, Morgan proceeded to finance a second purchaser, who paid $11.50 per gun, rifled the barrels to improve the weapons' range and accuracy, and sold them back to the government for $22.00 apiece. The government got something for the six-fold premium it paid to repurchase its guns, but not nearly as much as Morgan did.

Morgan speculated in all manner of commodities during the war. Though he didn't shun honest risk, neither did he unnecessarily court it. He cultivated confidential informants who could tell him, a critical moment before such news became common knowledge, of the latest developments on the battlefield. His rewards were remarkable, especially for one so young. The tax return he filed in the spring of Appomattox revealed an annual income of more than $50,000, at a time when an unskilled worker counted himself lucky to get $200.

Morgan wasn't alone in profiting from the nation's distress. Andrew Carnegie had clerked on the Pennsylvania Railroad during the decade before the war; by the time the war ended he was crowing, "I'm rich! I'm rich," from his speculations in railroads, iron, and oil. John D. Rockefeller focused on oil and did even better than Carnegie, creating the company that would show America and the world what an industrial monopoly looked like and how it behaved. Jay Cooke sold more than a billion dollars of bonds for the Union and took several hundred thousand in commission for himself. Cornelius Vanderbilt lengthened his lead as the richest man in America by diversifying from steamboats into railroads. Jay Gould learned the ways of Wall Street and the weaknesses of the federal government as he prepared for a breathtaking assault on the nation's gold supply. Daniel Drew, Gould's occasional partner, summarized the mood of the entrepreneurial classes: "Along with ordinary happenings, we fellows in Wall Street had the fortunes of war to speculate about, and that always makes great doings on a stock exchange. It's good fishing in troubled waters."[1]

WHEN ABRAHAM LINCOLN honored the heroes of Gettysburg after the battle that largely decided the war, he carried his listeners back to the dawn of American freedom, to the moment when Thomas Jefferson drafted and the Continental Congress approved the Declaration of Independence. Jefferson's assertion that all men were created equal provided the basis for democracy—the government of, by, and for the people Lincoln proclaimed the Gettysburg dead had died defending.

Yet another manifesto of 1776 was beginning, by the time of the Civil War, to exert as much influence over American life. Adam Smith's *Wealth of Nations* was to capitalism what Jefferson's Declaration was to democracy; where Jefferson cited natural law to justify a politics of self-government, Smith appealed to human nature in support of an economics of self-interest. Democracy didn't spring fully formed from Jefferson's brow, nor capitalism from the brain of Smith; each required decades to evolve and mature. But nowhere did they mature more fully than in the United States, which became the world's archetype of a capitalist democracy.

Yet the dual manifestos of 1776 were also dueling manifestos. The visions limned by Jefferson and Smith were in some ways complementary, with each claiming to maximize personal freedom, the first in politics, the second in economics. But in other respects they were antagonistic. Democracy depends on equality, capitalism on inequality. Citizens in a democracy come to the public square with one vote each; participants in a capitalist economy arrive at the marketplace with unequal talents and resources and leave the marketplace with unequal rewards. Nor is inequality simply a side effect of capitalism. A capitalist economy can't operate without it. The differing talents and resources of individuals are recruited and sorted by the differential rewards, which reinforce the original differences. Inequality drives the engine of capitalism as surely as unequal temperatures drive heat engines—including the steam engines that were the signature devices of industrial capitalism.

Tension between capitalism and democracy has characterized American life for two centuries, with one and then the other claiming temporary ascendance. During the first half of the nineteenth century, democracy took the lead, as the states abandoned property qualifications for voting and the parties responded by courting the masses of ordinary men. Andrew Jackson embodied the democratic ethos, by both his humble origins and his reverence for the people as the wellspring of political legitimacy. Jackson waged political war on the pet projects of the big capitalists of his day, smashing the Bank of the United States, vetoing federal spending on roads and canals, and beating down tariff rates.

But capitalism fought back during the Civil War. Even as the Republican party freed the slaves, it emancipated the capitalist classes from the constraints imposed by Jackson and his Democratic heirs. Government became the sponsor of business rather than its foe, underwriting railroad construction, raising tariff rates, creating a national currency, and allowing the likes of Morgan to troll for fortunes in the troubled waters of the war.

And the war was just the beginning of the capitalist ascendance. Morgan's peace proved even better than his war. He never became as wealthy as Carnegie, Rockefeller, or some of the other great capitalists of the era; upon the reading in 1913 of Morgan's will, which showed an estate of $68 million (exclusive of an art collection valued at $50 million), Carnegie lamented, "And to think, he was not a rich man." Yet Morgan's power was more pervasive than the others'. Carnegie dominated steel, the industry on which modern America was, almost literally, built, and Rockefeller controlled oil, which lit, lubricated, and was beginning to power American life. But Morgan commanded money, the philosopher's stone of modern capitalism. Morgan money's reorganized the railroads, the nation's vascular system. It bought out Carnegie and fought off Rockefeller to create the largest corporation in American history to that time, the United States Steel trust. And in one telling instance, it rescued President Grover Cleveland and the federal government from financial catastrophe.[2]

In his lighter moments Morgan played at being a pirate. He cruised about in a black-painted yacht he called the *Corsair*; he read of the exploits of that other famous Morgan, the English buccaneer Henry, and wondered if they were related. But Morgan was more than a pirate. He was a revolutionary. Pirates prey on the status quo; Morgan dismantled and rebuilt it. During the decades after the Civil War, Morgan and his fellow capitalists effected a stunning transformation in American life. They turned a society rooted in the soil into one based in cities. They lifted the standard of living of ordinary people to a plane associated, not long before in America and for decades after elsewhere, with aristocracy. They drew legions of souls from foreign countries to American shores. They established the basis for the projection of American economic and military power to the farthest corners of the planet.

They didn't do this alone, of course. A secret of their success was their ability to harness the strength and skill of armies of men and women to their capitalist purposes. More than a few of these foot soldiers participated unwillingly in the revolution; many hated Morgan and his ilk and passionately opposed them. But the nature of revolutions is to sweep the reluctant along, and despite the protests of farmers, laborers, and others attuned to a different time and sensibility, the capitalist revolution surged forward.

It left not a single area or aspect of American life untouched. It roared across the South, wrenching that region from its feudal past into the capitalist present, reshaping relations of race, property, and class and integrating the Southern economy into the national economy. It burst over the West, dictating the destruction of aboriginal economies and peoples, driving the exploitation of natural resources and making the frontier of settlement a frontier of national—and global—capitalist development. It crashed across the urban landscape of the East and North, turning cities into engines of wealth and poverty, opulence and squalor, that confirmed cardinal tenets of the American creed even as it contradicted others. It swamped the politics of an earlier era, capturing one major party and half the other, inspiring the creation of a third party, and determining the issues over which all three waged some of the bitterest battles in American history. It demanded, and received, the protection of the courts, which reinterpreted the Constitution in capitalism's favor.

In accomplishing its revolution, capitalism threatened to eclipse American democracy. Morgan never ran for political office, but his mastery of finance afforded him more power than any elected official save the president, and sometimes even more than the president. No senator or governor so directly controlled the lives of so many people as Carnegie, whose hundreds of thousands of employees looked to him for the wages on which they and their millions of dependents relied. Rockefeller held whole regions hostage to his petroleum monopoly; he browbeat city governments, extorted favors from the states, and defied the federal government to rein him in. Lesser princes of the capitalist clan were hardly more accountable to the tens of millions who worked for them or purchased the goods and services they provided.

Wealth had always conferred power, but never had a class of Americans been so wealthy as the great capitalists of the late nineteenth century, and never had such a small class wielded such incommensurate power. By the century's end the imperatives of capitalism mattered more to the daily existence of most Americans than the principles of democracy. The old forms of law and politics survived, not least since the capitalists couldn't be bothered to change them. "What do I care about the law?" bellowed Cornelius Vanderbilt. "Hain't I got the power?" He did have the power, and with it he and the other capitalists dominated American life. Whether their advantage would prove more durable than democracy's earlier edge, none of them could tell. But for the time being, in the land of Jefferson the sons of Smith held sway.[3]

Part One

THE RISE OF THE MOGULS

Chapter 1

SPECULATION AS MARTIAL ART

The capitalist revolution was a matter of technique and technology. The techniques that carried the capitalists to power in the final third of the nineteenth century grew out of the methods of the merchant entrepreneurs of the eighteenth century, men like John Jacob Astor, who got his business start selling musical instruments, graduated to furs, added tea and other addictive luxuries (including opium), and topped out in real estate. The secrets of Astor's success included his acquisitive nature, his eye for a bargain (and a wife whose eye was even better than his), and the networks of buying and selling that brought his suppliers to him and him to his customers. And yet, as he was happy to admit, the most powerful secret was the one that was least secret of all: the rapid and relentless expansion of the American population, which drove property values ever upward. Shortly before his death in 1848 he was asked what he would do differently, if he could live his life over. "Could I begin life again," he answered, "knowing what I now know, and had money to invest, I would buy every foot of land on the island of Manhattan."[1]

There were other secrets of American success that, like the growth of the American population, were available to Astor imitators by the middle of the nineteenth century. The legal system of the country, adapted from the system of the English common law, secured property from arbitrary seizure by government. The financial system of the country, based on hundreds of competing state banks but no central bank (after Andrew Jackson killed the second Bank of the United States), promoted rapid economic growth, albeit at the cost of recurrent instability. The financial panic of 1837 followed Jackson from office; the panic of 1857 unnerved a country already on edge regarding slavery.

Underlying the benefits and costs of finance was the question of money. The federal government issued specie currency: gold and silver coins. But since colonial times specie had never sufficed to keep the economy moving at the pace Americans demanded, and so they turned to paper. Banks printed notes, which circulated at par (face value) near the point of issue but were discounted, for the trouble and uncertainty of redemption, the farther they traveled. The notes were convenient, but because they weren't legal tender (no one was required to accept them in payment of debts) they were no stronger than the issuing banks, which often collapsed in the recurrent panics. The discovery of gold in California in 1848 alleviated the strain on the paper system by increasing the supply of gold (it was estimated that more gold was dug from the earth in the quarter century after 1848 than in the previous 350 years), but it didn't end the demand for paper.[2]

In fact, the demand for paper grew—enormously—during the Civil War, when both sides issued paper notes by the hundreds of millions of dollars. No one took the Confederate currency seriously, which was why the Confederate government had to keep printing more of the stuff, touching off a ruinous inflation. The Union currency—printed in green ink, and so dubbed "greenbacks"—was more persuasive, but only because it was supported by series of draconian fiscal innovations. The Legal Tender Act required debtors to accept the greenbacks (an exception being the Union government itself, which insisted on hard money). The National Bank Act barred state banks from issuing notes, thus giving the government a monopoly on paper. And the Internal Revenue Act imposed a federal income tax and other levies that assured the federal government a reliable source of revenue, thereby easing the pressure to print more greenbacks.[3]

The wartime measures diminished the anarchy in the money system, but considerable uncertainty remained. The constitutionality of the Republican financial program was open to serious question. The Constitution said the federal government can "coin" money. Did that mean it could print money as well? Did the proscription against state bank notes follow from the commerce clause, from the elastic clause, or from Treasury secretary Salmon P. Chase's imagination? As for the income tax, that seemed a patent violation of the constitutional ban on "direct" taxes not proportioned to population.

Until the courts settled the constitutional questions, the postwar financial markets faced the problem of accommodating the dual money system. Gold dollars and greenbacks competed directly with each other for the affections of merchants and investors, and indirectly for the affections of everyone else. The greenbacks drove gold from domestic circulation (why pay a debt with expensive gold when cheaper greenbacks would do?), but gold was still required for international transactions (American legal tender rules didn't apply abroad) and for payments to the government. The relative prices of the two currencies fluctuated according to the laws of supply and demand, and the fluctuating attracted speculators, who tried to anticipate the direction of the market. From anticipation to manipulation was a short, tempting step.

Gold transactions took place in a special room in the neighborhood of lower Manhattan that had become the financial hub of the country. In colonial days Boston had been the center of finance, followed by Philadelphia in the early national period. But New York's central location, its unsurpassed harbor, and the ambitions of the heirs of its Dutch founders made it a worthy rival to its northern and southern neighbors. New York's traders organized themselves on Wall Street in the 1790s, gathering under a buttonwood tree to forge an agreement establishing rules for buying and selling bonds and shares of companies. The traders eventually moved indoors, gaining credibility with the growth of the city's economy, especially after the opening of the Erie Canal in 1825. The demise of the Philadelphia-based Bank of the United States (at the hands of Andrew Jackson) crippled New York's primary rival, and by the time California gold began flowing east, New York was the clear leader in American finance. The energy of its brokers, most notably Jay Cooke, in selling Union bonds during the Civil War, cemented its primacy.[4]

By that time New York's reputation and reach were international. London and Paris still did more financial business than New York, but the comparative maturity of the European economies caused bold investors to look to developing countries for higher returns. Of the developing countries, the United States appeared the most promising. The rate of return on investments in American railroads and telegraphs, for instance, outstripped that on most investments in Europe. America's periodic panics were disconcerting, but the revolutions and civil wars in Latin America and the mutinies and insurgencies in India and other parts of Asia made the United States seem quite stable in comparison with those areas. And after the revolutions that rocked Europe in 1848, it seemed more stable than several countries much closer to home. The American Civil War briefly frightened fainthearts among European investors, but long before Appomattox sealed the Union victory, the international investors had written off the Confederacy and were writing American securities back into their portfolios.

As it happened, the telegraph linked New York to the markets of Europe just as the war was ending. Samuel Morse's invention had spread across the eastern half of the United States during the 1840s and to California in the early 1860s. By detaching communication from transportation (for the first time in history, excepting the odd smoke signal and semaphore), the telegraph further consolidated American financial markets in New York. The fundamental commodity bought and sold in financial markets is information, and once information slipped the bonds of gravity and friction it tended to cluster where it was most valuable—that is, in the largest markets. The Atlantic cable extended information's reach, and, by reducing the message time from London to New York and back from several weeks to several minutes, it allowed European investors to operate in the American market almost as efficiently as brokers and speculators with offices on Wall Street itself.[5]

WILLIAM WORTHINGTON FOWLER was a grandson of Noah Webster, but where the great lexicographer's passion had been for letters, Fowler's was for numbers. With hundreds of other ambitious young men he migrated to New York during the 1850s, hoping to win his fortune among the brokers and bankers there. His timing proved unfortunate when the Panic of 1857 slaughtered the money men, yet he hung on till the Civil War made most of the survivors rich. Though his fortune never rivaled that of the great capitalists, he was a keen observer of the markets and their denizens, whom he judged worthy of serious—but not *too* serious—study.

Many Americans misapprehended Wall Street, Fowler believed. The term itself was misleading, suggesting a strip of geography when in fact it signified far more.

> To the merchant and banker it is a financial centre, collecting and distributing money, regulating the exchanges of a continent and striking balances of trade with London and Frankfort. To the outside observer and novice it is a kind of work-shop thronged by cunning artisans who work in precious metals, where vessels of gold and silver are wrought or made to shine with fresh lustre, and where old china is fire-gilt as good as new. The moralist and philosopher look upon it as a gambling-den, a cage of unclean birds, an abomination where men drive a horrible trade, fattening and battening on the substance of their friends and neighbors—or perhaps as a kind of modern coliseum where gladiatorial combats are joined, and bulls, bears and other ferocious beasts gore and tear each other for the public amusement. The brokers regard it as a place of business where, in mercantile parlance, they may ply a legitimate trade, buying and selling for others on commission. To the speculators it is a caravansera where they may load or unload their camels and drive them away betimes to some pleasant oasis. To the financial commanders it is an arsenal in which their arms and chariots are stored, the stronghold to be defended or besieged, the field for strategy, battles and plunder.[6]

The striking thing about the business of Wall Street—striking to those ordinary Americans who dealt in real goods, the actual produce of farm and shop and factory—was the degree to which the traders there dealt in ephemera. "All the principal values of commerce are in this mart represented by so many paper certificates," Fowler explained. "The goods and credit of the merchant are represented by promissory notes, which are bought and sold, and pass from hand to hand, almost like bank-bills. Cotton, pork, grain, sugar, tobacco, and a thousand other bulky and gross products are represented under the form of warehouse certificates. The wealth of banks, of railway corporations, and of many other stock companies, are floating about under the guise of certificates, and to the very gold in the vaults of the Treasury, wings are given, and coin and bullion fly in notes of yellow and green."

Precisely because everything took wing in Wall Street, because everything was reduced to paper, speculation became the predominant form of activity. The speculators were a distinctive species, yet one that crossed other lines of social demarcation. "All classes and grades are represented here—rich and poor, gentle and simple, learned and illiterate. Not unfrequently these noisy groups contain more than one white cravat, on divines who have left their lambs to graze at large, while they, the shepherds, wander among a herd of another complexion, clad in bull's or bear's clothing. A certain harmony reigns among these discordant elements. . . . The bankrupt elbows the millionaire, and asks of him the price of Fort Wayne, and the millionaire replies with the utmost suavity, 'eighty-five, sir, at the last quotation.' The broken operator takes whiskey 'straight' with the wealthy capitalist, and the puritan and blackleg exchange a sympathetic smile when they see the stocks advancing in which they are interested."[7]

To the uninitiated, the life of the speculator seemed full of ease. Fowler didn't deny that the Wall Street trader exerted himself physically rather less than the farmer threshing wheat or the mason building stone walls. "And yet what life is more trying than his?" he asked.

> Beneath his frontal sinuses, amid the convolutions of his brain, a silent, invisible struggle is going on, which if put into bodily shape, would startle the beholder. There the vulture passions are at work, led on by their generals, ambition and avarice. Pining envy, fear of an evil which always impends, rage over injuries inflicted by others, or by his own weakness and incapacity, jealousy and hatred of successful rivals, all hold carnival in the space of an hour, and are kept active and sleepless by hope which quickens them with her enchanted wings. Above him hovers, day and night, a vast, dark, formless shape, threatening ruin and penury. This is the spectre of panic. One day he is lifted to dizzy heights, the next, plunged into black depths. He is hurried through dark labyrinths through paths where a single step is destruction. He climbs on the edge of a sword to a fool's paradise, where he tastes joys brief as a dream, and in an hour is abased to the earth where he drinks the full cup of humiliation and want.

And to what could speculators look forward? "When they have once entered the street, they never leave it except in a pine box or a rosewood case, according to circumstances. If they lose money, they stay there to regain it, and if they make money, they stay there to make more."

Fowler adduced a modest taxonomy of traders, arranged by numbers and speculative weight. Most numerous were the small fry, who nibbled at the edges of the market and measured victory and defeat in the thousands of dollars. Fewer but more formidable were the serious operators, men with resources and connections to move markets and not simply respond to them, and who didn't flinch when the stakes rose to tens or hundreds of thousands of dollars. And then there were Cornelius Vanderbilt and Daniel Drew, the "central Titanic figures" of Wall Street.

These men are the Nimrods, the mighty hunters of the stock market; they are the large pike in a pond peopled by a smaller scaly tribe. They are the holders of those vast blocks of stock, the cubical contents whereof can be measured by an arithmetic peculiar to themselves; they are the makers of pools large enough to swallow up a thousand individual fortunes. Sooner or later, the money of the smaller tribe of speculators finds its way into the pockets of these financial giants.

Young men! ye "wealthy curled darlings of our nation," who are about to "put up your money in the street," let me whisper a word in your ear. Before you venture on this perilous step, go to Cornele or Uncle Daniel, and make them a free gift of all the money you are willing to risk (for into their strong boxes it will come at last), and thus you will be saved a world of wrong and trouble, entailed by that mysterious, protracted, and to you painful process which will surely end, finally, in the transfer of your money into the strong boxes aforesaid.[8]

DANIEL DREW REMEMBERED when most of Manhattan was farmland and Broadway a cattle trail. As a drover in the early decades of the nineteenth century he herded cattle the sixty miles from his home in Putnam County to the abattoirs of the Bowery. Drew was a diligent worker, of impoverished necessity. "I was rarely in those days off my horse's back," he said later. "It was all-day work riding about the country and buying the cattle, and all-night work driving them to the city." On one occasion, amid a thunderstorm, he took a blow from a lightning bolt that killed his horse and nearly killed him. The experience seems to have intensified a piety he inherited from his mother; he frequently cited Scripture in explaining his actions, and after he acquired the wealth to do so he endowed a Methodist seminary in New Jersey. Faith afforded Drew solace and moral self-confidence. A nosy interlocutor once asked if his business practices troubled his sleep. "Sir," Drew answered, "I have never lost a night's rest on account of business in my life."⁹

As the query suggested, some people thought he deserved insomnia. A story linked to Drew from his droving days captured his reputation for sharp practice. At the end of a long cattle drive, Drew arranged for the animals to be fed salt, which heightened their thirst and caused them to drink large quantities of water. This swelled their weight and fattened Drew's account when they were sold. If Drew in fact did what he was said to have done (which is doubtful, as cattle were typically sold by the head rather than the pound), he certainly didn't invent the scam (the human connection to cattle being older than commerce and almost as old as greed). But Drew *may* have been the one who introduced the term *watering stock* into the argot of Wall Street by applying the dilutionary technique to corporate stock.

He gained his opportunity after leaving the saddle for the management of the Bull's Head Tavern on Third Avenue at Twenty-fourth Street. The saloon was a favorite of the drovers and cattle buyers, who often asked Drew for credit. He complied, eventually becoming a private banker to the bovine trade. In the late 1830s he formalized his new practice and broadened it, moving downtown to Wall Street, where he established a banking and brokerage firm.¹⁰

If Drew's youth had included any formal education, the effect quickly faded. Nor did his innate intelligence particularly impress those people who knew him. But he was cunning, as everyone agreed, and utterly unscrupulous in matters pertaining to business. He would drop slips of paper on the ground, as if by accident; the unwitting discoverers exploited the intelligence the slips conveyed—only to be exploited by Drew himself, doubling back on his own apparent advice. He betrayed partners as readily as rivals, and did so time and again. "The belief that he never hesitates to sacrifice his friends, if the necessities of speculation require it, is entertained with such unanimity in the money-quarter, and is illustrated by so many anecdotes, that one is compelled to acquiesce in it," observed a contemporary who had studied the matter and who went on to remark, "This foible is the more salient on account of the genuine piety of the man. All who have heard him speak at Methodist Conferences are struck by the fine religious fervor and earnestness of his demeanor. . . . He has built churches, founded a Theological Seminary, and given away prodigally to individual charities. Yet he has the reputation of being close in the extreme. Probably the secret of this amazing contradiction between facts and opinion is to be found in the enmities which his daring, subtle, and obscure speculations have excited. He is the sphinx of the Stock Market."[11]

IF DREW WAS the Sphinx, Vanderbilt was the Colossus. Born into modest circumstances on Staten Island in 1794, Vanderbilt became the wealthiest man in America by the time of his death in 1877, the one person whose private resources could break the market and throw a large part of the American economy into turmoil.

Vanderbilt's power and fortune reflected his peculiar ability to master both the techniques and the technology of the capitalist revolution. The technological heart of the revolution was the application of steam power to transport and manufacture. Vanderbilt knew little about manufacture but a great deal about transport. At the time he was born, modes of transportation had scarcely changed in the several millennia since humans had domesticated horses, put wheels on axles, and raised sails over watercraft. Not least because he grew up on an island, Vanderbilt took to sailing as a youth. At sixteen he ferried passengers by sailboat across the Hudson River and about New York's harbor.

But by then the new age of transport had begun. In 1807 Robert Fulton bolted a steam engine onto a river packet and chugged from Manhattan to Albany. Though the novel technology was unreliable and dangerous—boilers often exploded, superstructures caught fire—the more insightful ferrymen could see their future in the black clouds that trailed behind the steamboats. Vanderbilt was as insightful as any, and he abandoned his sailboats for the steam craft. His first employer was a man whose name would attach to a landmark case in the evolution of corporate law. Thomas Gibbons operated a steam ferry out of New Brunswick, New Jersey. In crossing the Hudson, Gibbons's vessel crossed the legal path of a vessel operated by Aaron Ogden under an exclusive license from the New

York state legislature. Gibbons challenged Ogden's monopoly as infringing the commerce clause of the Constitution, which reserved to Congress the control of interstate commerce. In 1824 the Supreme Court agreed, thereby liberating capitalism from most attempts by the states to rein it in.[12]

Vanderbilt was no lawyer, but he read the court's decision for the declaration of entrepreneurial independence it was, and he promptly began building a steam fleet of his own. His vessels plied the Hudson, turning profits that attracted competitors, including Daniel Drew. Vanderbilt managed to fend off Drew by buying him out, but the purchase simply attracted greater attention to the profits to be had from moving people and products about the bustling, growing country.

Vanderbilt remained a waterman till midcentury. He launched a fleet of steamships to exploit the demand for transport to California during the days of the gold rush. The steamers carried argonauts from Boston, New York, and New Orleans to Nicaragua, which they crossed by various means; another set of steamers picked them up on the Pacific side and transported them to California. Vanderbilt's Nicaraguan venture involved him in international machinations for which he wasn't fully prepared. After some associates tried to swindle him, he responded with a terse letter: "Gentlemen: You have undertaken to cheat me. I won't sue you, for the law takes too long. I will ruin you." And so he did, although the overall experience cured him of any further desire to expand abroad.[13]

In this attitude he wasn't alone. A characteristic of American capitalism from the middle of the nineteenth century to the end was its parochialism. At a time when the capitalists of Europe were scouring the earth (including the United States, but also Latin America, Asia, and Africa) for investment opportunities, American capitalists concentrated on their home market. They had good reason, for the American market was the largest in the world, as the result of several mutually reinforcing influences. Geographically, the United States was one of the most extensive countries in the world, commanding the resources of several geologic and climatic zones. Demographically, America's population (40 million in 1870, growing to 76 million in 1900) placed it among the planet's several most populous countries. Legally, the American Constitution (as interpreted in the Gibbons and subsequent cases) made it a single arena of commerce, with no customs officials or money changers to impede transactions across the borders between the states. Politically, the defeat of secession guaranteed that all these benefits of geography, demography, and law would remain within a single set of national borders, even as emancipation, the principal side effect of suppressing the rebellion, extended the principles of market capitalism to the labor and property system of the South.

AS VANDERBILT RETURNED his attention to the United States, he couldn't ignore a growing threat to his steamboat empire. For decades the "Commodore"—a nom de guerre reflecting his exploits on water—had derided "them things that go on land," as he called railroad trains. It didn't help matters that one of his first experiences of trains ended in a wreck that nearly killed him. But despite Vanderbilt's scornful antipathy, the new technology of transport advanced. Steam-powered railcars were introduced in England's coalfields in the second decade of the nineteenth century; in the mid-1820s they began carrying passengers. The technology crossed the Atlantic a few years later, and in 1830 the Baltimore & Ohio Railroad started moving passengers and freight from the Chesapeake to points west. During the three decades till the Civil War, railroads short and longer ramified across the country from northeast to west and gradually south. Because their iron (later steel) rails could support cargoes much heavier than the mostly dirt roads of the era could accommodate, and because their steam engines outperformed horses, mules, and oxen, they soon captured most of the freight traffic on the routes they served. And because they were largely—though not completely—immune to disruptions by weather and afforded a smoother, faster ride than horse-drawn coaches, they became the technology of choice for paying passengers. The Erie Canal, which in 1825 opened the interior of the continent to inexpensive freight transport, had been operating hardly a decade when the Erie Railroad and other lines from the Atlantic to the Lakes began stealing its traffic. Railroads reached Chicago in the early 1850s and made that city the gateway to the upper Midwest. Steamboats on the Ohio and Mississippi held out against the railroads for a while longer, enjoying the advantage of natural rights-of-way. But by the Civil War the convenience of rail lines (which didn't clog with ice during the winter or know the difference between upstream and down) was prompting the shrewder among steamboat men to look for alternative employment. (Pilot Samuel Clemens, for one, went into journalism in silver-bonanza Nevada before settling on fiction as Mark Twain. In the latter guise he gave the steamboats an extended lease on life in the American imagination.)

By 1865 the railroad was a comparatively mature technology. Steam-driven locomotives pulled (occasionally pushed) heavy cars along steel rails. Coal (or, less and less frequently, wood) boiled the water that became the steam. The very rich could afford private passenger cars; others made do with less sumptuous accommodations. Change continued in track and rolling stock, but not as rapidly as before.[14]

The technique of railroads—in contrast to their technology—changed dramatically, however. Railroads were the first really large corporations in American history, employing thousands of persons spread over entire regions. They were the first to develop the methods of corporate adminis-tration that would characterize modern enterprise. Other businesses—mercantile houses, plantations, factories—had typically set supervisors over workers, but the railroad corporations set supervisors over supervisors (over supervisors) in multilayered administrations. Railroads pioneered the kind of precise management of operations that other firms would follow. Initially this was a matter of safety: more than a few early trains collided, causing injuries and death, when their schedules overlapped. Later it became a matter of corporate survival, as competition compelled the roads to utilize their personnel and rolling stock with maximum efficiency. Rail-roads were the first industry to evolve a cadre of professional managers—men who specialized in railroad administration, developed standards for measuring performance, shared and debated new ideas, and published journals. "By an arrangement now perfected, the superintendent can tell at any hour in the day the precise location of every car and engine on the line of the road, and the duty it is performing," the *American Railroad Journal* reported, regarding recent innovations on the Erie Railroad. "Formerly, the utmost confusion prevailed in this department, so much so that in the greatest press of business, cars in perfect order have stood for months upon switches without being put to the least service, and without its being known where they were. All these reforms are being steadily carried out as fast as the ground gained can be held."[15]

Railroads were also the first large corporations to be publicly traded. The capital demands of the railroads required expanding the pool from which that capital might be drawn. One way of acquiring capital was to borrow it from banks or other lenders. Railroads did borrow, but often their business plans were too risky, their collateral assets too meager, or the banks too cautious to cover all the roads' investment needs. The other technique was to sell partial ownership—that is, shares of the railroad corporation. This spread the risk among the many owners and allowed for more-rapid expansion than borrowing alone did. In the process it forced the blossoming of the financial markets of New York. On one day in 1830 the New York Stock Exchange reported a total of thirty-one shares traded; by the 1850s, after railroads discovered the stock market, tens of thousands of shares were traded each day. After the Civil War, as other industries learned from the railroads, hundreds of thousands of shares changed hands daily.[16]

The massive sale of shares led to something new in American economic history: the divorce of ownership from management. Previously, owners typically managed their firms, leaving little distance between the interests of ownership and the interests of management. But as ownership spread to hundreds and then thousands of people, the vast majority of whom had no responsibility for day-to-day management of the firm, owners and managers could develop interests that diverged and occasionally collided. In particular, owners might come to consider their shares simply a commodity to be bought and sold as prices fell and rose, regardless of the effect of such transactions on the operation of the firm. If a trader could speculate in cattle and cotton, as traders had for decades, why not in railroad stocks?

DANIEL DREW ASKED himself that question, and decided that railroad stocks were at least as promising as livestock. The New York & Harlem Railroad allowed an early test of the theory. Chartered to operate entirely on Manhattan Island, the Harlem, as it was called, later extended its lines north to Albany. Besides providing competition for steamboats on the Hudson (including Cornelius Vanderbilt's), the road for the first time allowed people who worked in Manhattan to live outside the city and commute on a daily basis. Drew purchased enough shares to have himself named to the board of directors. From this position he could influence the operation of the road; he could also manipulate the price of its shares.

Vanderbilt bought into the Harlem not long after Drew did. But where Drew, as matters soon proved, saw the road as a speculation, Vanderbilt perceived it as an investment—a property to be held and improved rather than pillaged and sold.

Vanderbilt's interest in the Harlem helped drive the share price up. The price rose further when Vanderbilt persuaded—probably through bribery, the commonest mode of persuasion in the New York politics of Tammany Hall—the city council to let the Harlem extend its line south from Union Square, its previous terminus, to Wall Street and the Battery.

As a director, Drew applauded Vanderbilt's coup, for it increased the likely profits of the Harlem considerably. As a shareholder he should have been similarly pleased, for the promise of future profits enhanced the value of his own holdings. But it was as a speculator that Drew perceived the greatest benefit, for with everyone else bidding the Harlem up, he decided to bet on a fall. He sold the company short (that is, took present payment for future delivery of shares he didn't yet own but hoped to purchase at a lower price before the delivery date). To prompt a fall in the price, he employed some persuasion of his own—again, almost certainly bribes—causing the city council to rescind the approval it had just given Vanderbilt.

The stock indeed began to fall, and Drew began counting his profits. But Vanderbilt, though new to railroads, was no innocent in the ways of speculators, and he snatched the falling Harlem stock before Drew could make good his short contracts. This left Drew in the lurch, as he had promised to deliver more shares than were now available, and reminded him of the peculiar risk in short selling: that while a person who owns stock can lose no more than the purchase price of the stock, a person who has promised to deliver stock not yet purchased can lose an indefinite amount (as there is no upper limit on how high the stock price can climb before the short seller buys it). At this point or later Drew composed a couplet intended as warning to short sellers:

> He that sells what isn't his'n
> Must buy it back or go to pris'n.

Drew avoided prison in this case by throwing himself on Vanderbilt's mercy. So convincing was Uncle Daniel, who didn't hesitate to cry when circumstances suggested that tears might soften a rival's heart or at least blur the ink on a troublesome contract, that Vanderbilt offered him a private settlement.[17]

HAVING WON CONTROL of the Harlem, Vanderbilt proved himself a good manager. He invested heavily in track, cars, and locomotives, till the line became a model of efficient passenger service. Even Horace Greeley, no flack for capitalists, remarked the favorable change in the operation of the road. "We lived on this road when it was poor and feebly managed, with rotten cars and wheezy old engines that could not make schedule time," Greeley wrote in 1867. "And the improvement since realized is gratifying."[18]

But the Harlem was simply a start for Vanderbilt. He purchased the Hudson River Railroad, whose tracks paralleled those of the Harlem, and turned his gaze on the New York Central, which ran from Albany to Buffalo. The directors of the Central sought the help of Drew, notwithstanding his recent defeat at Vanderbilt's hands and his longer record of double-dealing. Drew ran a steamboat line that ferried Central passengers from Albany to New York City, except when extreme weather made river travel risky. During these periods, the Central passengers switched to the railcars of the Hudson line, by a preexisting agreement. Vanderbilt waited till January 1867 and then abruptly canceled the agreement, leaving the Central shivering far from its Manhattan market. The directors shortly accepted Vanderbilt's terms, yielding him the dominant railroad position in the Empire State.

Yet Vanderbilt had a larger empire in mind. If he could add the Erie Railroad to his network, it would give him control of a corridor from America's primary port to its agricultural heartland. But the Erie was an elusive target, having earned a reputation as the "scarlet woman of Wall Street" for being bought and sold so promiscuously. And her main consort was Daniel Drew, who perfected his speculative gifts driving her shares prices this way and that. As the wisdom of the street put it:

> Daniel says "up": Erie goes up.
> Daniel says "down": Erie goes down.
> Daniel says "wiggle-waggle": it bobs both ways.[19]

Drew had allies, more formidable this time than in his previous bouts with Vanderbilt. James Fisk Jr. ("Jubilee Jim," the "Barnum of Wall Street") was hard to take seriously but impossible to ignore. "He is first, last, and

always a man of theatrical effects, of grand transformations, and blue fire,"
William Fowler wrote. "All the world is to him literally a stage, and he the
best fellow who can shift the scenes the fastest, dance the longest, jump the
highest, and rake up the biggest pile." Fisk had been a peddler in New
England, from a family of peddlers. "His wagon was magnificent, his four
horses sleek and mettlesome," Fowler explained. "At different points in his
triumphal progress through the rural districts, he was met by a train of his
subalterns, who filled the sheds of the country inns with their wagons, held
audience with their chief, and obeyed his orders." From peddling Fisk
turned to dry goods, and from dry goods to paper products—that is, stocks
and bonds. He opened a brokerage in New York, where he fell in with
Daniel Drew, who taught him the arts of speculation—by swindling him
out of everything he owned. "James saw his pile growing small by degrees
and beautifully less," Fowler related. "And early in 1868, as he told a friend,
he was worth not a dollar in the world."

Yet even in his poverty Fisk was magnificent. "The strong point of this
man is his physique, so robust, so hale, so free from the shadow of every
peptic derangement," Fowler marveled. "His boldness, *nerve*, and business
capacity are supplied by this physique, which also supplies him with animal spirits beyond measure. He is continually boiling over with jokes—
good, bad and indifferent." Fisk liked to recount how his father had been
accused by an elderly woman of cheating her on a piece of calico worth
twelve and a half cents. The son defended the old man to the woman. "I
don't think father would tell a lie for twelve and one-half cents," Fisk said,
"though he might tell eight of 'em for a dollar." The grammatically fastidious Fowler was reduced to fragments to characterize Fisk: "Boldness!
boldness! twice, thrice, and four times. Impudence! Cheek! Brass! Unparalleled, unapproachable, sublime!"[20]

Drew's other ally in the Erie struggle was a different sort entirely. Jay
Gould was as silent as Fisk was noisy, as thin as Fisk was full, as pallid as
Fisk was florid. He had lost his mother at four, his first stepmother in the
same year, a second stepmother not long after that. His father was a difficult man addicted to drink, whose angered neighbors took out their anger
on his son. Jay fled home as soon as close calls with typhoid and pneumonia
allowed. He taught himself surveying, then bought an interest in a tannery.
His partner committed suicide, causing some of the customers to wonder

whether Gould's increasingly evident ambition—"Look at Gould; isn't he a driver?" one said—speeded the self-destruction.[21]

Gould arrived in New York in time for the Civil War. He learned the ways of the speculators but distinguished himself for particular talents. He mastered the arcana of finance and displayed a preternatural single-mindedness. "When intensely interested in any matter," a contemporary remarked of Gould, "he devoted his whole concentration of thought upon that one thing, and would seem to lose interest in things often of greater pecuniary importance but of not so much commercial fascination. He loved the intricacies and perplexities of financial problems." His associates recognized his financial reveries by his unconscious habit of tearing paper into tiny bits, which piled around his chair like indoor drifts of snow.[22]

THE FIRST FEW years after Appomattox were a slow time for American journalism. Correspondents accustomed to reporting the victories and defeats of the battlefield found themselves—and their readers—hungry for similarly dramatic fare. New York alone had several dailies competing for the public's penny (James Gordon Bennett in the 1830s had exploited the power of steam to produce the first penny paper, the *New York Herald*, and other publishers had followed suit). Politics provided intermittent entertainment, but nothing like the daily drama of war.

Eventually, however, the New York papers perceived in the stock market a substitute for the battlefield, and when Vanderbilt tangled with Drew, Fisk, and Gould, the press promptly labeled the conflict the "Erie War." The opening salvo was a preemptive purchase by Vanderbilt and some allies of what seemed a majority of Erie stock; this was followed by a putsch against the board of directors, including Drew.

Drew again threw himself on Vanderbilt's mercy, portraying himself as an old man (he was nearly seventy, but three years younger than Vanderbilt) who required his income from the Erie directorship to keep the wolf from the door. Again Vanderbilt relented. He let Drew remain with the Erie as treasurer and added him to the Vanderbilt alliance.

Drew avowed his gratitude—but almost immediately returned to his usual tricks. "Daniel Drew could no more refrain from playing his old games in Erie than the veteran gamester can withhold his hand from cards and dice," William Fowler said. "It was play to him, but death to others." Soon Drew was speculating in Erie stock against the interests of his new sponsor. Vanderbilt's group was bulling Erie stock—conniving to push its price upward—and Drew exploited his inside knowledge of the scheme to unload some of his own shares on the group, adding to their burden but profiting at their expense. He also sold the stock short, hoping to reverse the price rise and profit still further at their expense.[23]

When Vanderbilt discovered Drew's double cross, the battle escalated. He petitioned the New York supreme court (which, despite the name, was—and is—not the august court of final appeal in the state but a modest court of original jurisdiction) to remove Drew as treasurer of the Erie and, by means similar to those he had employed with the New York city council, obtained an injunction barring Drew from issuing any new shares in the company. Drew's habit of doing precisely this was what had linked his name to the practice of stock watering, and Vanderbilt expected more of the same.

He didn't move fast enough. Drew gathered Gould and Fisk and some other Erie bears—short sellers—and all worked to drive the price down. They spread evil rumors about the company's prospects and the liquidity of its sponsors. When these efforts failed to stem the rise in Erie shares, Drew got an injunction staying Vanderbilt's injunction, and he and Gould and Fisk, operating as the executive committee of the corporation, proceeded to issue fifty thousand new shares of Erie stock. Vanderbilt discovered that the more shares he purchased, the more hit the market. Fisk, directing the production of the new stock certificates, reveled in Vanderbilt's discomfiture. "If this printing press don't break down," he said, "I'll be damned if I don't give the old hog all he wants of Erie." (Fisk later called the outcome of the Erie War a victory for the First Amendment—for "freedom of the press.")[24]

Vanderbilt summoned fresh allies, including a sheriff with a warrant to arrest the Erie trio and seize the corporate offices. But word of the lawman's approach preceded him. "There were hurryings to and fro in the Erie Railroad Office," William Fowler recorded. "A few moments later and the policeman on that beat observed a squad of respectably dressed but terrified looking men, loaded down with packages of greenbacks, account books, bundles of papers tied up with red tape, emerge in haste and disorder from the Erie building. Thinking perhaps that something illicit had been taking place, and these individuals might be plunderers playing a bold game in open daylight, he approached them. But he soon found out his mistake; they were only the executive committee of the Erie Company, flying the wrath of the Commodore and laden with the spoils of their recent campaign."25

The three didn't stop till the Hudson River separated them from Vanderbilt and his judges and sheriffs. They used some of the money they had absconded with—estimated at six to ten million dollars—to persuade the New Jersey legislature to let them incorporate the Erie in the Garden State. But they also sent Gould to Albany to purchase protection from the New York legislature. The lawmakers licked their chops. "The boys were poor and hungry after the long abstinence of the session," a journalist covering the legislature wrote. "How beautiful, then, the prospect which the Erie contest opened up to them! How they gloated over the pleasures which the fight would develop." Vanderbilt prepared to match the bribes offered by Gould, till votes on measures touching the Erie commanded more than fifteen thousand dollars each. But at the last moment Vanderbilt hesitated. "A rumor ran through Albany as of some great public disaster, spreading panic and terror through hotel and corridor," a contemporary recounted. "The observer was reminded of the dark days of the war, when tidings came of some great defeat. . . . In a moment the lobby was smitten with despair, and the cheeks of the legislators were blanched, for it was reported that Vanderbilt had withdrawn his opposition to the bill."26

He had indeed. The prize was no longer worth the price, Vanderbilt concluded, and in exchange for a large but publicly unspecified payment from Gould and Fisk (Drew having determined that his health couldn't stand such excitement and chosen to leave the company to his younger partners), he called off his campaign for control of the Erie and dropped his lawsuits against the conspirators. The scarlet woman was theirs.27

HENRY ADAMS OBSERVED the Erie War and wondered what it meant. Adams was thirty and seeking a career, having lost his bearings amid the turmoil of the Civil War and its aftermath. Had he been an Adams of an earlier generation, he would have gone into politics, as his great-grandfather John Adams and his grandfather John Quincy Adams had done with the highest distinction. He did dabble in diplomacy, acting as secretary to his father, Charles Francis Adams, during his father's service as American minister to Britain. But the partisan strife that pervaded Republican politics at the end of the war precluded a post of his own and left him at a loss as to what to do with himself. "Henry Adams could see easy ways of making a hundred blunders," he recalled, employing the self-referential third person. "He could see no likely way of making a legitimate success."[28]

Adams wandered Europe and discovered Darwin. The English naturalist had published his landmark work, *The Origin of Species*, in 1859, but not till after the Civil War did Adams have the time and attention to appreciate the revolution in human understanding Darwin had set in train. Adams was an instant convert. "He was a Darwinist before the letter, a predestined follower of the tide," Adams wrote of himself. He admitted to ignorance of the science required to appreciate Darwin's arguments in detail. "But this never stood in his way." Darwin's theory of evolution by natural selection explained much that had puzzled Adams about the world, and he embraced it with enthusiasm.[29]

At the heart of the puzzle was the historic decline of the Adams family. John Adams had been a foremost Founder: sponsor and drafter of independence, second president. John Quincy Adams had been secretary of state, president, and congressman. But even in Quincy's day the decline was apparent, for his presidency began under a cloud of scandal (when candidate Henry Clay threw his electors to Adams and received appointment as secretary of state) and it ended in political ignominy (when voters overwhelmingly rejected him in favor of Andrew Jackson). The decline continued under Henry's father. The ministry in London wasn't unimportant, especially during the Civil War, but it was nothing next to the White House or the State Department. And yet, by all evidence, it was far more than Henry himself could expect to achieve.

He had to ask whether the fault lay with him or his stars. He didn't claim special gifts, but he deemed himself reasonably competent. The trouble, he concluded, was that the world had changed. America, at least, no longer rewarded the same talents and traits it had in the glory days of the Adams clan. Henry returned across the Atlantic to trace the transformation and discovered that it was even larger than he had thought. "The last ten years had given to the great mechanical energies—coal, iron, steam—a distinct superiority in power over the old industrial elements—agriculture, handwork, and learning." The effect on society he discerned everywhere around him; the effect on himself was only a bit more subtle. "The result of this revolution on a survivor from the fifties resembled the action of the earthworm; he twisted about, in vain, to recover his starting point; he could no longer see his own trail; he had become an estray, a flotsam or jetsam of wreckage, a belated reveler, or a scholar-gipsy like Matthew Arnold's. His world was dead."[30]

The new world awaited explanation. The market for scholar-gypsies being limited in postwar America, he became the next best thing: a journalist. The dailies were dominated by men of fewer letters than Adams (like all of his family he was a Harvard man) and sharper politics (partisan detachment being a quality that promised, to that generation of publishers, little of either profit or honor). So he aimed instead for the quarterlies, among which the *North American Review*, conveniently edited by a family friend, appeared the most likely. Few people read the quarterlies, but these were the ones who could appreciate quality. And presumably they were the ones whose sense of derangement in the new order most closely paralleled Adams's.

"OF ALL FINANCIAL operations, cornering gold is the most brilliant and the most dangerous," Adams wrote in 1870. "And possibly the very hazard and splendor of the attempt were the reasons of its fascination to Mr. Jay Gould's fancy. He dwelt upon it for months, and played with it like a pet toy. His fertile mind even went so far as to discover that it would prove a blessing to the community, and on this ingenious theory, half honest and half fraudulent, he stretched the widely extended fabric of the web in which all mankind was to be caught."[31]

Adams had intended to write about the Erie War, but by the time he put pen to paper an even more spectacular scandal had rocked the American financial world. In the summer of 1869 Jay Gould evolved a scheme to drive the price of gold dramatically upward. Since the Union government began printing greenbacks during the Civil War, their price had fluctuated dramatically compared with gold, with as many as 285 paper dollars required to purchase 100 gold dollars at dire moments during the war. After Appomattox the discrepancy diminished; by 1869 the ratio had fallen to around 135 paper dollars per 100 gold dollars (for a quoted price of 135, which was often shortened to 35, as gold never dipped below par with paper). Gold was purchased for use—by merchants with international accounts and by anyone who had to pay customs duties. It was also purchased for speculation—by anyone willing to bet that the price would move one way or the other.

Gould wasn't a user of gold directly, but neither was he a mere speculator. He claimed to have become interested in gold as it influenced traffic on the Erie. The extension of railroads to the grain belt of the Midwest allowed the farmers of that region to ship their produce cheaply to the ports of the East Coast, whence steamships owned by the likes of Cornelius Vanderbilt carried the grain to Europe. In other words, for the first time American farmers competed on a world market—which meant that for the first time they needed to pay attention to the dollar's standing against other currencies, particularly gold. When gold rose, products denominated in dollars—including wheat—fell in price on the world market, making them more attractive to foreign purchasers. Gould didn't grow wheat, but he (that is, the Erie) transported wheat bound for the world market, and hence had reason to hope for a rise in gold. And although altruism wasn't his nature, he recognized that what was good for the Erie, in this case, was good for the wheat farmers, for the railroad workers, longshoremen, and sailors who moved the wheat, and for much of the American economy as a whole. This "ingenious theory," as Adams derisively called it, knowing its subsequent use, was what Gould peddled as the harvest of 1869 approached.

But bulling gold was a bigger chore than anything he had contemplated previously. By comparison, the Erie finagles were a piker's pastime. Gold touched everyone, including the government, which owned more gold than any private individual and used it to stabilize the dollar. If Gould intended to boost gold by more than a point or two, he'd have to persuade the government not to push the price back down by selling some of its gold.

As it happened, Gould knew Abel Corbin, who had recently married Ulysses Grant's spinster—till then—sister. Gould applied to Corbin to arrange an interview with the president, at which he explained his theory of gold and American prosperity and urged Grant to support, or at least allow, higher prices for the yellow metal. Grant was dubious of monetary theories and discouraging to Gould. "He remarked that he thought there was a certain amount of fictitiousness about the prosperity of the country, and that the bubble might as well be tapped in one way as another," Gould testified later. Grant asked Gould for his opinion, and he obliged. "I remarked that I thought if that policy was carried out, it would produce great distress, and almost lead to civil war; it would produce strikes among the workmen, and the workshops, to a great extent, would have to be closed; the manufactories would have to stop. I took the ground that the government ought to let gold alone, and let it find its commercial level; that, as a matter of fact, it ought to facilitate an upward movement of gold in the fall." But Grant wasn't persuaded, at least not visibly. "We supposed, from that conversation, that the President was a contractionist."[32]

Yet as the harvest progressed, bringing large crops and correspondingly low prices, Gould hoped Grant might change his mind. Meanwhile he worked on Grant's subordinates. A friend of Abel Corbin had recently been hired as assistant federal treasurer in New York, in the office that monitored the gold market and would release the government's gold if matters came to that. The Treasury's man was Daniel Butterfield, and to make him feel at home in his new post, Gould loaned him ten thousand dollars. Repayment might have been discussed, but not seriously.

At the beginning of September 1869 Gould approached Grant again. One of the president's former comrades in arms had died; Grant attended the New York funeral and stayed at the home of Abel Corbin. Gould dropped in on Corbin, encountered the president, and reiterated his argument about the value to the country of rising gold prices. This time Grant listened more carefully. "The President said then that he was satisfied the country had a very bountiful harvest; that there was to be a large surplus; that unless we could find a market abroad for that surplus it would put down prices here," Gould remembered. "And he remarked that the government would do nothing during the fall months of the year to put down the price of gold or make money tight. On the contrary, they would do everything they could to facilitate the movement of breadstuffs." Gould added that Grant appeared to have thought the question through. "It seemed to have been a matter of study with him. I was surprised at the clearness with which he seemed to comprehend the whole question."[33]

Buoyed by this conclusion, Gould ordered his brokers to buy gold. He covered his tracks, dividing his business among many brokers and shielding each from knowledge of the others' activities. He also purchased insurance, of a sort, by cutting Corbin in on the scheme, to the amount of $1.5 million. Corbin expressed appreciation but, sensitive to appearances, asked that the transaction be made in his wife's name rather than his own. Evidence indicates that Gould made a similar arrangement for Butterfield, although Butterfield later denied it.[34]

The purchase orders pushed the price of gold steadily up, from the mid-130s to 140. As it climbed, the gold bears exhibited various forms of distress, including crying to the Treasury for relief and planting rumors that their cry was being heard. The prospect of a federal rescue briefly brought the price back down to 135.

Gould intensified his efforts to forestall government intervention. He again visited Grant and again urged the president to let the markets have their way. He evidently increased Butterfield's stake in the plot and tried—unsuccessfully—to win over Grant's private secretary. And he persuaded Corbin to write Grant delineating the dire consequences to the economy if gold fell. Corbin's letter reached the president in western Pennsylvania, where he was vacationing. The courier arrived while Grant was playing croquet. He waited patiently, then impatiently, for the president to finish his game and read the letter. After Grant did, the courier asked whether there was a reply. The president said there was none. The courier rode to the nearest telegraph office and reported that the letter had been "delivered all right." But the message was garbled in transmission and reached Gould as "Delivered. All right."[35]

Yet Gould soon sensed that things weren't all right. He had never relied on Corbin to move events in the right way, only to warn him if things began to move wrong. And Corbin now began to cry warning. His wife had learned that her brother, the president, was catching on to the gold bulls' scheme. "I told Mr. Gould, at once, that I *must* go out of this matter," Corbin testified later.[36]

Gould realized the game was up. The current price of gold was unsustainable: it must either rise or fall. If the president was determined to prevent its rise, a fall was inevitable. The only question was when the plunge would occur. To delay it, Gould offered Corbin $100,000 to keep quiet. "Mr. Corbin, I am undone if that letter gets out," Corbin recounted Gould saying. Corbin refused the money but told Gould, "I am not going to publish it. . . . You need not have any anxiety of mind on that account." Gould skeptically prepared his own retreat.[37]

Suddenly Jim Fisk became useful. Gould had hesitated to bring Fisk in on the planning of the gold scheme; the Vermonter's talents notably lacked an ability to keep secrets. But he hadn't objected when Fisk noticed the rise in gold and jumped on board. Fisk's presence was felt at once, as he rollicked about the Gold Room shouting purchase orders and making side bets that gold would top 145. The gold shorts were in agony. "As the roar of battle and the screams of the victims resounded through New Street," a journalist reported, "it seemed as though human nature was undergoing torments worse than any that Dante ever witnessed in hell."[38]

Fisk remained bullish overnight, chiefly because Gould declined to share the intelligence that the government was going to break the market. Fisk and his friends celebrated the fortunes they were about to make; Gould kept to himself. "I had my own views about the market, and had my own fish to fry," he said later. "I listened to what was said, but it went in one ear and out of the other. I was all alone, so to speak, in what I did, and I did not let any of those people know exactly how I stood."[39]

The next day was Friday, September 24. The Gold Room opened at ten o'clock, but the bidding began early, and by the opening bell gold had jumped from 143 to 150. "Take all that you can get!" Fisk shouted above the tumult. The price leaped another five points to 155. The shorts were in despair. Some cut their losses and sold; others held on for precious life. Threats of mortal violence flew across the room. Fisk, utterly in his element, shouted the louder: "Take all you can get at 160." An eyewitness marveled at the tumult. "It was a desperate battle between two hosts of gamblers, whose minds were quickened by incessant plots, whose hearts were cold and their greed rapacious," he wrote. "Gold, Gold, Gold was the cry."[40]

Gould was always quiet, and so his silence this day occasioned scant notice. And Fisk was too excited to pay attention to what his partner was about. But stealthily, employing that regiment of brokers, he disposed of his gold. The price reached 162, and Gould continued to sell, pocketing millions beneath the nose of the bulls.

And then, near noon, the market collapsed. Rumors circulated that the government was going to sell gold. Minutes later came confirmation, in the form of an order from the Treasury in Washington to sell $4 million in gold. Though this amount was a small fraction of the total being traded in New York, it had a solidity those paper transactions lacked. James Fisk, queried afterward, replied matter-of-factly: "O, our phantom gold can't stand the weight of the real stuff." In the event, the real gold crashed downward with unprecedented speed and fury. "Possibly no avalanche ever swept with more terrible violence," the *New York Herald* explained. "As the bells of Trinity [Church] pealed forth the hour of noon, the gold on the indicator stood at 160. Just a moment later, and before the echoes died away, gold fell to 138."[41]

Now it was the bulls' turn to howl. Most of the gold had been purchased on margin, or highly leveraged credit; as the falling price consumed the margin, the purchasers were left naked before their creditors. Everyone knew of Fisk's role in driving the price up, and nearly everyone supposed that where Fisk went, Gould went too. Traders screamed for the Erie partners' skins. One witness to the riot asserted that their lives were in actual jeopardy. If the two hadn't gone into hiding, he said, "the chances were that the lamp-post near by would have very soon been decorated with a breathless body."[42]

Even without a lynching, that day became known as Black Friday. Fortunes evaporated in minutes; brokerages failed by the score. The tumult in the gold market spread across the street to the stock market, claiming thousands of victims who had never been tempted by currency speculation. Gould probably made money on gold, having unloaded most of his holdings before the government intervened, but the collapse of the stock market caught him by surprise and left him unprepared to meet his margin calls. Even he didn't know for months whether he came out ahead or behind in the whole affair, so tangled were the accounts and inadequate the accounting practices of the day. Scores of people were sure he had cheated them, though they couldn't say quite how. Lawsuits rained down upon him, which he countered with lawsuits of his own.

One person, strikingly, who didn't hold Gould's actions against him was James Fisk. Whether because he understood the inescapable uncertainties of speculation or because Gould quietly compensated him for his losses, the impresario of Wall Street adopted a phlegmatic view of the affair and its denouement. "It was each man drag out his own corpse," he said.[43]

SURVIVORS AND OTHER witnesses searched for meaning in the scandal. Congressman James A. Garfield, writing for the majority of the House Committee on Banking and Currency, which investigated the affair at length, expressed shock at what Gould and Fisk had nearly accomplished. "The whole gold movement is not an unworthy copy of that great conspiracy to lay Rome in ashes and deluge its streets in blood, for the purpose of those who were to apply the torch and wield the dagger," the Ohio Republican said. Calming himself somewhat, Garfield added:

> But however strongly we may condemn the conspirators themselves, we cannot lose sight of those causes which lie behind the actors and spring from our financial condition. The conspiracy and its baneful consequences must be set down as one of the items in the great bill of costs which the nation is paying for the support of its present financial machinery. For all purposes of internal trade, gold is not money, but an article of merchandise; but for all purposes of foreign commerce it is our only currency.
>
> So long as we have two standards of value recognized by law, which may be made to vary in respect to each other by artificial means, so long will speculation in the price of gold offer temptations too great to be resisted, and so long may capital continue to be diverted from enterprises which add to the national wealth, and be used in this reckless gambling which ruins the great majority of those who engage in it, and endangers the business of the whole country.[44]

Henry Adams drew a different lesson. Adams mined the Garfield committee's report and produced an interpretive summary entitled "The New York Gold Conspiracy." He liked his article immensely. "It was the best piece of work he had done," he declared. Yet Adams decided against publishing it in the *North American Review* or any other American quarterly. The American press had reported the Erie War and the attempted gold corner in great detail, and Adams wanted his masterpiece to be appreciated by unjaded eyes. "London was a sensitive spot for the Erie management," he explained, "and it was thought well to strike them there, where

they were socially and financially exposed." Adams on this point was being
naive or disingenuous. Gould and Fisk, social pariahs in America, hardly
feared the censure of Britain's respectable classes, and though English
money underwrote many American railroads, including the Erie, Gould
and Fisk never had more trouble fleecing English investors than those of
any other nationality. Adams's subsidiary explanation for seeking a British
outlet for his gold-conspiracy article was more to the point. "Any expres-
sion about America in an English review attracted ten times the attention
in America that the same article would attract in the *North American*.
Habitually the American dailies reprinted such articles in full. Adams
wanted to escape the terrors of copyright; his highest ambition was to
be pirated and advertised free of charge, since, in any case, his pay was
nothing."[45]

The piece, which appeared in the *Westminster Review* in 1870,
recounted the conspiracy as revealed by the congressional committee and
interpreted by Adams. He didn't hesitate to impeach the witnesses, including the principals. Of a long and intricate explanation by Fisk of a critical
meeting among the conspirators, Adams remarked, "There is every reason
to believe that there is not a word of truth in the story from beginning to
end. No such interview ever occurred, except in the unconfined apartments
of Mr. Fisk's imagination." Nor did Adams hesitate to render his judgment of the whole affair.

> The fate of the conspirators was not severe. Mr. Corbin went to
> Washington, where he was snubbed by the President, and at once dis-
> appeared from public view, only coming to light again before the
> Congressional Committee. General Butterfield, whose share in the
> transaction is least understood, was permitted to resign his office with-
> out an investigation. Speculation for the next six months was at an
> end. Every person involved in the affair seemed to have lost money,
> and dozens of brokers were swept from the street. But Mr. Jay Gould
> and Mr. James Fisk, Jr., continued to reign over Erie, and no one can
> say that their power or their credit was sensibly diminished by a shock
> which for the time prostrated all the interests of the country.

Yet the experience hadn't been all for the bad. Quite the contrary,
Adams said. "The result of this convulsion itself has been in the main

good. It indicates the approaching end of a troubled time. Messrs. Gould and Fisk will at last be obliged to yield to the force of moral and economical laws."

Adams wasn't so sanguine about the corporations Gould, Fisk, and the other capitalists directed. The Erie War and the gold conspiracy were evil omens for democracy.

> For the first time since the creation of these enormous corporate bodies, one of them has shown its power for mischief, and has proved itself able to override and trample on law, custom, decency, and every restraint known to society, without scruple, and as yet without check. The belief is common in America that the day is at hand when corporations far greater than the Erie—swaying power such as has never in the world's history been trusted in the hands of mere private citizens, controlled by single men like Vanderbilt, or by combinations of men like Fisk, Gould, and Lane [Frederick Lane, counsel to Fisk and Gould on the Erie], after having created a system of quiet but irresistible corruption—will ultimately succeed in directing government itself. Under the American form of society, there is now no authority capable of effective resistance.[46]

Chapter 2

ONE NATION UNDER RAILS

The same year—1869—that produced the climax of the Erie War and the weaving and unraveling of the gold conspiracy also witnessed a landmark accomplishment of American capitalism: the completion of the country's first transcontinental railroad. Participants and observers feted the Pacific railroad as a giant step in the march of technology. And so it was. Yet the techniques employed by the builders of the road were at least as important as the technology. Some of the techniques reflected improvements in the craft of construction: clever solutions devised by foremen and crews to deal with the unaccustomed challenges of distance, terrain, and weather in the West. But the really vital techniques involved the manner in which the Pacific railroad was financed—in particular, the way in which the capitalists commanding the road recruited the institutions of government to share the risk and costs of construction.

The dream of a Pacific railroad was almost as old as railroads in America. In 1832 a committee of citizens in Dunkirk, New York, agitated for the inclusion of their town on the route of a proposed railroad from the Hudson River to Lake Erie, on grounds that such a road "would be a strong and powerful link in a Railway to the valley of the Mississippi, and finally to the Pacific Ocean." Only a few weeks later a territorial newspaper in Michigan avowed a desire on behalf of all forward-thinking Americans "to unite our Eastern and Western shores firmly together . . . to unite New-York and the Oregon by a railway by which the traveller leaving the city of New-York shall, at the moderate pace of ten miles an hour, place himself in a port right on the shores of the Pacific."[1]

Serious consideration of a railroad to the Pacific awaited actual possession by the United States of Pacific frontage. Acquisition of title to Oregon in 1846 afforded the prospect of a seaport on the Columbia, linked to the East by rail. The annexation of California in 1848, at the end of the war with Mexico, shifted the attention of the transcontinentalists south to San Francisco and its incomparable bay. But it was the gold rush of 1849 and after that made a rail line to the Pacific appear both necessary and possible. The necessity was more than obvious to the hundreds of thousands of emigrants who walked from the Missouri to the gold fields and didn't want to have to walk back. The possibility reflected the likelihood that California, suddenly teeming with people, would generate enough traffic to pay for a Pacific railroad.

Yet even if it did, the payback would require decades, given the tremendous cost of construction across many hundreds of miles of desert and mountains uninhabited by potential customers. (Indigenous peoples didn't count, except as a likely expense.) In the East, rail lines traversed districts blanketed by farms and villages; the whole length of a line produced business for a road. In the West, a transcontinental line would have to support itself by the terminus-to-terminus, end-to-end traffic.

It would, that is, unless the government could be persuaded to share the cost. Government participation in "internal improvements" had a long history in America, but it had often been controversial. Counties built roads and bridges, and states pitched in, but when the roads crossed state lines and advocates argued for federal funding, strict constructionists demurred. Andrew Jackson's first veto was of a bill to fund the Maysville road to Kentucky. Old Hickory objected not to the road, merely to the federal funding. Jackson's opponents coalesced in the Whig party, which advocated internal improvements till it split over slavery. At that point a Pacific railroad became a pet project for elements of both the Democrats and the newly forming Republicans. Democrat Stephen A. Douglas of Illinois guessed that a Pacific road was coming, and he determined that its eastern anchor be Chicago, where he had friends and property. But the region west of the Missouri and east of the Sierra Nevada had yet to be organized politically, and investors required at least that modicum of protection before they'd sink their money in something as risky as a long-haul rail line. Douglas solved the organizational problem by guiding the Kansas-Nebraska Act through Congress. He conceded that his bill would "raise a hell of a storm," in that it required addressing the explosive topic of slavery in the territories, but he thought the benefit—to the country, to his party, to himself—worth the turbulence. In the event, the Douglas measure raised far more than a storm, triggering a guerrilla war in "bleeding Kansas."[2]

Among the Republicans, support for a Pacific railroad fitted a general belief that government could benefit the American people by helping American business. The railroad won a place on the Republican platform in 1856, when the presidential nominee was John C. Frémont, who had personally reconnoitered potential railroad routes, and again in 1860, when the party put forward railroad attorney Abraham Lincoln. Southern secession after Lincoln's victory gave the Republicans a new reason for sponsoring a railroad to California. Despite having entered the Union as a free state in 1850, California was predominantly Democratic and strongly sympathetic to the South; upon Southern secession, many Californians spoke of leaving the Union themselves—if not to join the Confederacy, at least to adopt a stance of pro-Confederate independence. Lincoln opposed secession of any sort, but the thought of losing California's gold made him even less likely to tolerate a western split. He had no troops to spare to hold California in the Union, but he had something more effective: the promise of a railroad. Californians' brave talk of self-sufficiency suddenly ceased when they heard the Republican offer; all they could think of was getting back home—to the civilized parts of the United States—in days rather than weeks or months.[3]

Converting the Republican promise of a Pacific railroad into legislation to fund construction required the concerted efforts of small armies of lobbyists, who spent more time fighting one another than persuading skeptics. The California crowd was led by Leland Stanford, an unlikely railroad mogul and a hardly more probable entrepreneur. A New Yorker by birth, Stanford was practicing law in Wisconsin when the discovery of gold in California lured his several brothers west. Leland resisted the temptation, preferring the steady income of the bar to the potentially larger but far less certain payoff of the mines. And when the brothers wrote home that mining wasn't all they had hoped, he congratulated himself on his conservatism and looked forward to a career in the law. But then his law office burned down, claiming his books and his records. The same fire destroyed the businesses of his best clients, leaving Stanford to wonder whether he could reconstitute his practice and to revise his estimates of the risks and rewards of life. By now his brothers had given up on mining, in favor of the dry-goods trade. They were doing a brisk business, they explained, and could use another partner. Leland would be most welcome.[4]

He decided to take the chance, arriving in San Francisco via Nicaragua in the summer of 1852. He opened a branch of the brothers' business at Cold Springs, not far from Coloma, the site of the original 1848 gold discovery. Stanford's store did well till the gold ran out at Cold Springs and his customers decamped for newer, richer claims. He followed them to Michigan Bluff, where he made more money and some friends who elected him justice of the peace. His courtroom was the local saloon; verdicts were delivered over shots of whiskey. He might have remained at Michigan Bluff, but he missed his wife, who had refused to come west to live in a raucous, rowdy mining camp. She held out till he promised to move to less boisterous Sacramento, where he built a general merchandise emporium.

In Sacramento he also joined the Republican party. For national Republicans opposition to slavery was the primary issue and a Pacific railroad a secondary concern. For California Republicans the issues were reversed. Slavery was distant, while a railroad was immediate, or would be if the federal government cooperated. A railroad would benefit all Californians but especially California's capitalists. Shipments from the East would be cheaper and more reliable; in a broader sense a railroad would spur the growth of California's population and hence of California's business activity.

The California Republicans were a lonely bunch at first. "In Sacramento, where I resided, the party at its inception was extremely limited in numbers," Cornelius Cole remembered. "No record, I venture to say, can be found of a political organization starting out with fewer adherents. There were C. P. Huntington, Mark Hopkins, Leland Stanford, Edwin B. and Charles Crocker, all personal as well as political friends of mine. There were not for some time, besides these, as many as could be counted on one's fingers." The hardy band endured the taunts of their neighbors. "The convention of nigger worshippers assembled yesterday in this city," the Sacramento *State Journal* declared during a meeting of the Republicans. And it survived a disastrous attempt by Stanford in 1859 to win the governorship of the state (he received but 10 percent of the vote). Yet after Lincoln won the presidency the following year, and after Southern secession made the Republicans the dominant party in Congress, the California Republicans prepared to claim the reward for their years in the wilderness.[5]

By this time three of Stanford's fellow Republicans from Sacramento were also his partners in a railroad venture. Charles Crocker was a blacksmith turned merchant; Collis Huntington was a former peddler who had settled down in hardware; Mark Hopkins was Huntington's associate. As the possibility that the federal government might actually build a Pacific railroad came into view, the four organized the Central Pacific Railway Company. In 1861 Stanford traveled to Washington to represent the company—and California Republicans—to the Lincoln administration. Theodore Judah, a railroad visionary long dismissed as a crank, followed Stanford to Washington to work on Congress.

Judah's methods comported with the practice of the times. One of his suitcases bulged with shares of the Central Pacific; his instructions from Stanford and the others were to employ the shares in whatever manner they might be of use. How thoroughly Judah spread the wealth became a matter of dispute. Stanford recalled that he and his partners had given Judah $100,000 in stock to take east. "I think, however, that he brought most of it back," Stanford added vaguely.[6]

While Judah was doing his part for Stanford and the Californians, other agents were busy on behalf of other hopefuls. The Pacific railroad would be built from both ends toward the middle; the eastern counterpart to Stanford's Central Pacific turned out to be a group calling itself the Union Pacific and headed by Thomas Durant, a former ophthalmologist lately linked to the Mississippi & Missouri Railroad. Durant's backers included Senator James Harlan of Iowa, a close friend of Lincoln (whose old employer, the Rock Island line, had spawned the Mississippi & Missouri).

Securing a majority for the Pacific railroad wasn't easy. Judah described a "determined and bitter warfare" in Congress. "Pamphlets were written and laid on the desks of members and Senators, absurd statements with regard to bribery, fraud, etc., were freely circulated, and every effort made to poison the minds of members against the bill." To counteract the poison, Judah and the other supporters of the railroad made a simple, straightforward argument: that without federal funding the road simply wouldn't be built. Private capital markets couldn't attract investors willing to hazard such large sums (tens of millions of dollars, at least) on such a distant payoff (at least a decade away). Complementing this bottom-line negativity was patriotic positivism: a Pacific railroad was necessary to the security of the Union and would redound to the benefit of the nation as a whole. It was a sound investment in the nation's future and therefore deserved national support. If the defenders of states' rights hadn't silenced themselves by seceding, the new anti-Jacksonians might have added that federal funding of the Pacific railroad didn't overly intrude on state prerogatives, as the great majority of the track mileage would be built on federal land.[7]

Eventually the arguments—and the bribes, which were even more lavish on the part of the Durant group than on that of Stanford—carried Congress. The Pacific Railway Act of 1862 authorized the construction of a single line from the Missouri River to California. Stanford's Central Pacific would build east, Durant's Union Pacific west. The federal government would subsidize the project with loans and grants of land. The loans were thirty-year first-mortgage bonds at 6 percent interest, in amounts that varied according to the difficulty of construction. For each easy mile at the eastern and western ends of the road, the companies would receive bonds worth $16,000. For construction on the High Plains, the Union Pacific would receive $32,000 per mile. For crossing the Sierra Nevada, the Central Pacific would get $48,000 per mile. The Union Pacific would receive the same for the steep pitches in the Rocky Mountains. In addition to the bonds, the companies would receive ten square miles (6,400 acres) of land for each mile of road constructed. The land would lie in alternating sections along the right of way.

The act represented a huge investment by the federal government in the future of the West—but also in the future of the two railroad companies. If all went well, the American taxpayers would get their bond money back, with interest, at the end of the thirty-year period. If things went poorly—and because nothing on this scale had ever been attempted in

America, there was no way of knowing whether it would go well or poorly—the taxpayers would be left holding worthless notes.

The land grants were less risky, if only because the land in question was currently worth next to nothing. Only after the railroad made it accessible would it command any price. Over the long term, the land would prove the most valuable part of the subsidy. But the American people would share the bounty, as the lands along the right of way but *not* allocated to the railroads increased in value. And the opening up of the West would provide a boon to the nation as a whole.

YET EVEN WITH the government subsidies, private investors were reluctant to get on board. The subsidies wouldn't begin until the companies had demonstrated their competence and good faith by constructing forty miles of track. This required raising large amounts of private capital, which was scarce amid the boom brought on by the war. A more serious constraint was the condition in the 1862 law that gave the government first lien on the assets of the companies. Investors considered the Pacific railroad a risky venture, and many didn't want to stand in line behind Washington in the event of default.

Construction commenced, but the reluctance of the private sector to join the project kept the pace to a crawl. Stanford and his partners in the Central Pacific borrowed all they could against their own credit but still fell short. Charles Crocker crossed the Sierra to Nevada Territory and importuned the silver barons of the Comstock. "They wanted to know what I expected the road would earn," Crocker recalled. "I said I did not know, though it would earn good interest on the money invested, especially to those who went in at bed rock. 'Well,' they said, 'do you think it will make 2 per cent a month?' 'No,' I said, 'I do not.' 'Well,' they answered, 'we can get 2 per cent a month for our money here,' and they would not think of going into a speculation that would not promise that at once."[8]

Crocker remembered those early months as downright harrowing. "I would have been glad, when we had thirty miles of road built, to have got a clean shirt and absolution from my debts. I owed everybody that would trust me, and would have been glad for them to forgive my debts and take everything I had, even the furniture of my family, and have gone into the world and started anew."[9]

So the principals returned to the public sector. Stanford, who, without diminishing his participation in the Central Pacific, had been elected governor of California on a wave of pro-Union, pro-railroad sentiment, browbeat the state legislature into putting up $15 million to get the road started. He also engineered local referendums in favor of smaller issues from counties that stood to benefit from the project. Various reports indicated that his brother Philip distributed gold coins to voters as either a sign of the prosperity to come or a token of current appreciation.[10]

In the East, the agents of the Central Pacific and the Union Pacific returned to Congress, where Representative Thaddeus Stevens provided invaluable assistance. Stevens's family and state (Pennsylvania) were both in steel, the industry that benefited most directly from railroad construction, and with other Republicans he believed that what was good for business was good for the country. Moreover, Stevens considered the Pacific railroad essential to national cohesiveness, to prevent a Western version of what the South was currently attempting. As chairman at once of the Ways and Means Committee and the Select Railroad Committee, Stevens was well placed to shepherd friendly new legislation through the House.

His right-hand man on the railroad committee was Oakes Ames, a founding member of the Republican party in Massachusetts, who had made a fortune selling shovels to miners in California and Nevada—winning him the nickname "King of Spades"—and who expected to sell more of the earth-movers to the gangs building the Pacific railroad. Ames had lately diversified into steel, intending to profit from the rails as well as the roadbed.

Stevens and Ames consulted fellow committeeman and Stanford ally Cornelius Cole of California, as well as Thomas Durant of the Union Pacific and Collis Huntington of the Central Pacific, who had taken up residence in Washington to plead their respective companies' cases. Together the capitalists and the congressmen crafted an amendment to the 1862 railroad act that was everything the corporations wanted. It doubled the land grants to the railroads, expedited the delivery of government loans, and, of greatest immediate significance, transferred first-lien rights from the government to the private investors. Now American taxpayers shouldered the largest risk.

Not every Republican rolled over for the railwaymen. Elihu Washburne was an Illinois lawyer, the chairman of the House Commerce Committee, and a lonely guardian of the public purse. "I am a friend to the Pacific railroad," Washburne declared. "That friendship has been proved by my official action in this House for the last ten years. I want to see that magnificent enterprise completed at the earliest moment, and anything the Government can properly do in this time of war to urge forward the object, I am in favor of. But because I am in favor of it, I am not going blindly for any projects that may be thrust forward by interested parties, projects that will take the means of the Government and not secure the end desired." Washburne contended that the railroads ought to stick to the original law, which they had essentially written. "Capitalists and others made their estimates and declared that the work could be successfully accomplished under that act. It embraced all the provisions asked for." But now they complained that it didn't give them enough. Amid the war, the capitalists were asserting national necessity. "I have no faith in the noisy patriotism of shoddy contractors," Washburne said, "and none in the men who in these times of trial and tribulation through which the country is passing are scheming and plotting to fill their own pockets while the nation is verging toward bankruptcy. The sublime and unselfish patriotism of our people, who stand like a wall of adamant behind the Government in its support, a people suffering, bleeding, dying for their country, is in magnificent contrast to the flaunting counterfeit everywhere to be seen."[11]

But a large majority of the House preferred the words of Hiram Price of Iowa, a former bank president and future railroad chief executive. "We want this road, stretching from the granite hills of New England to the golden sands of California," Price said. "When completed it will far outshine in importance and grandeur the famed Appian Way. It will be the greatest and most useful work done by man. It is needed, and these amendments are necessary for its success." Thaddeus Stevens guided the bill through the House and dominated the joint committee that reconciled the House measure with its Senate counterpart. At the beginning of July 1864 the bill gained the approval of Congress and shortly that of the president.[12]

THE NEW DISPENSATION signally eased the task of Stanford and the other railwaymen in drawing capital to their project. With the government now bearing most of the risk, and with the rewards promising to be even larger than before, capitalists found the railroad to be a most attractive investment. Charles Crocker would come out of the bargain with his furniture, a clean shirt, and considerably more.

Yet the liberality of Congress didn't prevent the railwaymen from manipulating the system. The original law allowed greater compensation to the railroads for track laid in the mountains, but it didn't specify where the mountains began. Stanford remembered a statement by a geologist to the effect that the Rocky Mountains could be thought of as rising out of the Mississippi River; he now supposed that something similar might be said of the Sierra Nevada vis-à-vis the Sacramento River. He commissioned a team of geologists—who, as employees of the state of California, answered to him as governor—to survey the route from Sacramento east. When they determined that the Sierra Nevada did indeed start very far down in what laymen considered the Sacramento Valley, Stanford applied to receive the mountain rate for some rather level roadbed. The federal Interior Department initially challenged Stanford's innovative geology, but the governor dispatched one of California's Republican delegation in Congress, Representative Aaron Sargent, to speak with the president. Lincoln didn't know much geology, yet he did know politics, and with a chancy election approaching he preferred to keep his allies happy. "Here you see," Sargent reported after the successful meeting, "my pertinacity and Abraham's faith moved mountains."[13]

ONCE THE PROBLEMS of funding were solved, the principal challenge of the Pacific railroad was finding the workers to construct it. Neither Stanford and his partners in the Central Pacific nor their counterparts on the Union Pacific had any good idea when the building began of the manpower required to complete the road; as in the case of financing, they made up policy as they went. Each commenced construction with the workers at hand but quickly discovered the need to supplement the locals with large numbers of laborers imported specifically for the railroad's purpose. Before they knew it, Stanford and his partners were the agents of a demographic and cultural transformation in the American West that revealed the breadth and power of the capitalist revolution of which it was a part.

The transformation had begun more than a decade earlier when, in response to the discovery of gold, Chinese started emigrating to California. The news of the gold discovery reached China, straight across the Pacific, before it reached New York or Boston, which were twice as far away, as the ship sailed, around South America. The Chinese had often been reluctant to emigrate, constrained by both filial duties, including the responsibility to tend the shrines of ancestors, and political edicts, which discouraged or forbade emigration. In the latter category was a law established in the early years of the Qing dynasty, when the new rulers feared the return of exiles from the old regime, and still on the books in the nineteenth century (and indeed until 1910), declaring that "all officers of government, soldiers, and private citizens who clandestinely proceed to sea to trade, or who remove to foreign lands for the purpose of cultivating and inhabiting the same, shall be punished according to the law against communicating with rebels and enemies, and consequently suffer death by being beheaded." In the nineteenth century the law wasn't always enforced, but even the off chance of decapitation gave pause to would-be emigrants.[14]

What this meant in practice was that only the truly determined left China. As it happened, determination levels rose dramatically during the nineteenth century. Population pressure accounted for some of the rise. China's population grew by half between the late eighteenth century and the middle of the nineteenth, with even larger gains occurring in the southeastern province of Guangdong. Simultaneously China came under assault from European imperialists. The First Opium War of 1839–42 forced China open to British merchants (including those selling opium) and burdened China with a large reparations bill. The merchants flooded the Guangdong region with foreign goods, while the reparations drained silver from the same area, throwing its economy into turmoil and displacing many thousands of merchants, artisans, and workers. The turmoil spread and magnified a few years later with the outbreak of the Taiping Rebellion, an enormous civil conflict that killed tens of millions of people and devastated a region as large as Western Europe.[15]

Under the circumstances, many Chinese, especially in Guangdong, sought an occasion to relocate. The discovery of gold in California provided just the occasion. *Gum Saan*—"Gold Mountain," as California was called—became the object of the dreams of thousands of Chinese. Ship brokers and others who hoped to profit from a trans-Pacific traffic spread the news. "Americans are very rich people," explained one pamphlet printed in Cantonese and circulated about Guangdong.

> They want the Chinese to come and will make him welcome. There will be big pay, large houses, and food and clothing of the finest description. You can write your friends or send them money at any time, and we will be responsible for the safe delivery. It is a nice country, without mandarins or soldiers. All alike: big man no larger than little man. There are a great many Chinese there now, and it will not be a strange country. The Chinese god is there now, and the agents of this house. Never fear, and you will be lucky. Come to Hong Kong, or to the sign of this house in Canton, and we will instruct you. Money is in great plenty and to spare in America. Such as wish to have wages and labor guaranteed can obtain the security by application at this office.[16]

Chinese responded by the tens of thousands to this sort of appeal. By 1851 some 25,000 Chinese had journeyed to California, and the number continued to rise. The emigration took various forms. Those with ready cash paid the forty or fifty dollars for passage east (via sailing ship till the late 1860s, when steamship service commenced); the rest traveled on someone else's money. The latter group included the credit-ticket emigrants, who borrowed the price of the ticket and repaid it from their American earnings. It also included contract laborers, who signed contracts in China committing them to fixed periods of labor in America. The contract laborers were the contemporary equivalent of the indentured servants of the American colonial and early national era. Though the practice had fallen out of favor in the American East, it represented an obvious solution to the problem of providing transport to people who couldn't pay up front.

The Chinese weren't uniformly welcomed in America. Native-born American miners demanded to know what right these foreigners had to gold dug from ground liberated from Mexico at the cost of American blood and treasure during the recent war. The California legislature passed a tax on foreign miners, designed to discourage the Chinese (and other foreigners) from entering the mining business. The law was controversial and not entirely successful. Yee Ah Tye, an emigrant from Hong Kong, the British colony at the edge of Guangdong, went into mining and succeeded so well as to hire scores of men to work in his operations along the Feather River. Though Yee avoided (or ignored) the worst of the animus against the Chinese, many of his countrymen weren't so lucky. (Nearly all the Chinese were men. As late as 1900, census takers discovered that just 5 percent of the 90,000 Chinese in the United States were women.) Chinese workers were widely distrusted as being willing to work for wages below what native-born Americans considered acceptable, and they were resented on this score. And in an age permeated by racism and ethnocentricity, they often seemed peculiarly exotic. Mark Twain described their predicament as it looked from Nevada:

> Of course there was a large Chinese population in Virginia [City]. It is the case with every town and city on the Pacific coast. They are a harmless race when white men either let them alone or treat them no worse than dogs; in fact they are almost entirely harmless anyhow, for they seldom think of resenting the vilest insults or the cruelest injuries. They are quiet, peaceable, tractable, free from drunkenness, and they are as industrious as the day is long. A disorderly Chinaman is rare, and a lazy one does not exist. So long as a Chinaman has strength to use his hands he needs no support from anybody; white men often complain of want of work, but a Chinaman offers no such complaint; he always manages to find something to do. He is a great convenience to everybody—even to the worst class of white men, for he bears the most of their sins, suffering fines for their petty thefts, imprisonment for their robberies, and death for their murders. . . . As I write, news comes that in broad daylight in San Francisco, some boys have stoned an inoffensive Chinaman to death, and that although a large crowd witnessed the shameful deed, no one interfered.[17]

Twain's was a sympathetic view. Horace Greeley, the reforming editor of the *New York Tribune*, described the Chinese immigrants as "uncivilized, unclean and filthy beyond all conception, without any of the higher domestic or social relations." Robert Louis Stevenson, visiting from Britain, found Greeley's attitude to be far more common than Twain's. "The Chinese are considered stupid because they are imperfectly acquainted with English," Stevenson wrote after a journey to California. "They are held to be base because their dexterity and frugality enable them to underbid the lazy, luxurious Caucasian." This competitive element was the crucial point, Stevenson judged, even if the Americans didn't always admit it. "The Mongols were their enemies in that cruel and treacherous battle-field of money. They could work better and cheaper in half a hundred industries, and hence there was no calumny too idle for the Caucasians to repeat and even to believe."[18]

Despite the discrimination, the Chinese held on. Some went home (as most, indeed, had planned to do), but others replaced them. And as the California economy developed beyond gold mining, they moved into other sectors. They became farmers and fisherman, houseboys and hostlers, truck farmers and nurserymen, carpenters and bricklayers. They broke into railroad construction on lines built within California during the late 1850s and early 1860s. And when the Central Pacific began advertising for workers, they prepared to push east.

The Chinese contract laborers—"coolies," in American parlance, derived from the Urdu and Tamil of South Asia, where expatriate Chinese had long worked for the British—were particularly suited to the construction work on the railroads. The Central Pacific required thousands of workers, the cheaper and more vulnerable the better. Chinese labor contractors were well positioned to deliver what the company required. The Chinese workers, once they signed their indentures, couldn't effectively complain of low wages or difficult conditions, which were issues between the contractors and the foremen hired by Stanford and his partners. The only recourse for dissatisfied workers was flight—abandonment of the labor contract and escape into the Chinese population in California and the neighboring states. This was a drastic step, in that fugitives from labor contracts, especially when Chinese, couldn't expect much sympathy from the courts if their contractors caught them and delivered their own form of exemplary justice. Yet it happened often enough (and among other nationalities as well) that the same corporate-friendly Congress that liberalized the compensation to the railroad companies wrote a law authorizing the federal government to enforce labor contracts concluded on foreign soil. Fugitives from the construction gangs who had signed such contracts henceforth had to deal not only with the contractors but with federal marshals.[19]

Beyond its other attractions to employers, the contract-labor system was ideally attuned to the requirements of strikebreaking. For all their industriousness, the Chinese weren't the first labor choice of Stanford and his associates. As a Republican candidate for governor in a largely Democratic state, Stanford had taken pains to show that while he opposed slavery, he didn't much care for people of color. "I am in favor of free white American citizens," he declared on the stump. "I prefer white citizens to any other class or race." Upon his election as governor, Stanford explicitly included Chinese in his nonpreferred category. "To my mind it is clear that their settlement among us is to be discouraged by every legitimate means. Large numbers are already here, and unless we do something early to check their immigration, the question which of the two tides of immigration meeting upon the shores of the Pacific"—the Euro-American and the Asian—"shall be turned back, will be forced upon our consideration when far more difficult than now of disposal."[20]

But Stanford knew the difference between politics and business, even if he didn't always honor it. The fact that California was the most cosmopolitan state in the Union (as a result of the gold rush) simply made white voters more susceptible to racist and xenophobic arguments, which Stanford wasn't above employing. But when some of the Irish workers the Central Pacific had imported from the East to commence the construction began complaining about pay and working conditions, Charles Crocker told his foreman to try Chinese. The foreman was skeptical. "I was very much prejudiced against Chinese labor," he admitted afterward. "I did not believe we could make a success of it." Yet the Chinese came cheap and easily. The foreman negotiated a deal with a labor contractor who delivered Chinese workers at $26 a month, compared with $30 a month plus board for white workers. The Chinese were initially assigned only the most unskilled jobs: moving dirt, hauling rocks. But as they proved their value there, they were tested on more-demanding tasks. When Irish stonemasons went out on strike, Crocker demanded that the Chinese be used as strikebreakers. His foreman complained that he couldn't make masons out of the Chinese, causing Crocker to retort, "Didn't they build the Chinese Wall?"[21]

Before long there were no jobs the Chinese weren't doing. The most difficult stretch of the road east of Sacramento rounded a cliff a thousand feet above the American River. Called Cape Horn from its steepness and inherent danger, the cliff confronted the engineers with a daunting task: to carve the roadbed from the wall of solid stone. While they were puzzling how to tackle the job, a Chinese crew chief pointed out that his people had experience of this sort of thing along the Yangtze River at home. The engineers told him to put that experience to use.

With reeds brought up from the Sacramento delta, the Chinese wove baskets large enough to hold a man. They ran ropes through eyelets at the tops of the baskets to hoists anchored at the crest of the Cape Horn cliff. By now the Chinese crews were facile in the use of black powder (a Chinese invention, some of them pointed out), and the best of the blasters were lowered in the baskets to the line of the roadbed, where they drilled holes in the rock, tamped in the powder, lit the fuses, and signaled to be pulled out of the way before the charges ignited. In time the work assumed a regular tempo, till hundreds of barrels of black powder were going up in flame, concussion, and smoke. The canyon echoed with the roar of the blasts, followed by the rumble of the freed rock as it disappeared into the depths of the gorge.[22]

Long before this stretch of the road was finished, Stanford and his partners had become convinced of the value of the Chinese. "Without them it would be impossible to go on with the work," Mark Hopkins declared.[23]

The appreciation of the Central Pacific partners for their Chinese employees had limits, though. As the work progressed, the efficiency of the Chinese crews became apparent to other employers in the West, especially operators of mines, who began to bid up the price of Chinese labor. "We have proved their value as laborers," Crocker's brother Edwin, the chief attorney for the Central Pacific, explained. "And everybody is trying Chinese, and now we can't get them." The Chinese railroad crews demanded a raise, to $40 per month, and a reduction in hours, from eleven per day to ten. Till their terms were met, they wouldn't work.

The Central partners determined not to give in. "If they are successful in this demand, then they *control* and their demands will be increased," Hopkins warned the others. Edwin Crocker put the danger differently. "The truth is," he said, "they are getting smart."

The partners were smart, too, and cunning. By now the war had ended, leaving millions of former slaves free and looking for employment. A black man in California named Yates suggested to Stanford that the Central

Pacific apply to the Freedmen's Bureau for help in transporting willing black workers from the South to California. Stanford shared the proposal with his associates, who thought it brilliant. "A Negro labor force would tend to keep the Chinese steady, as the Chinese have kept the Irishmen quiet," Hopkins asserted. As things developed, the idea never materialized. But the possibility that it might softened the demands of the Chinese even as it stiffened the resolve of Stanford and the others to resist their demands.

What broke the Chinese strike was a tactic more direct: the threat of starvation. Charles Crocker ordered the provisioners to the Chinese camps to stop supplying them with food. "They really began to suffer," Edwin Crocker recalled. "None of us went near them for a week—did not want to exhibit anxiety. Then Charles went up, and they gathered around him, and he told them that he would not be dictated to, that he made the rules for them and not they for him." The hungriest of the strikers agreed to return to work, but others vowed violence against the waverers. "Charley told them that he would protect them, and his men would shoot down any man that attempted to do the laborers any injury. He had the sheriff and posse come up to see that there was no fighting."

The show of force, combined with the empty bellies of the workers, terminated the strike. To prevent a recurrence, the Central associates brought in new gangs. "There is a rush of Chinamen on the work," Edwin Crocker wrote two weeks later. "Most of the fresh arrivals from China go straight up to the work. It is all life and animation on the line."[24]

THE PROBLEMS CONFRONTING the Union Pacific were different in kind from those facing the Central, but not in degree. Where the workers of the Central battled mountains and forests, those of the Union Pacific contended chiefly with distance. From Omaha the route stretched west across the Nebraska prairie, rising slowly onto the High Plains till it reached the Rockies in southeastern Wyoming. The construction crews were a city on wheels, supplied by the single track they left behind as they inched toward the setting sun. Nearly everything had to be imported: food, often water, fuel, even most of the building materials. When the California crews of the Central Pacific needed stone for footings or bridgework, they simply borrowed some of that which they had already subtracted from the

Sierra batholith; the Nebraska crews of the Union had to cart stone from hundreds of miles away. For the ties beneath the rails, the Central crews sawed the giant trees that had blocked their way; the Union ties grew in forests far distant from the line.

Labor at times was equally scarce. When the construction commenced, large numbers of the able-bodied males in the states east of the Missouri were off to war. Those who hadn't enlisted were in great demand with civilian employers and hence were in no hurry to head to the hardship assignment of railroad construction on the frontier. Thomas Durant and his superintendent of construction, Grenville Dodge, struggled to fill the ranks of their workforce. At one point they considered enlisting Indians who had been taken prisoner in the frontier fighting that accompanied the Civil War. Ultimately they turned to labor contractors who applied the same techniques in Ireland that the Chinese contractors employed in China. Yet perhaps because the Irish spoke the language of the American majority, because they encountered less pervasive hostility on the part of native-born Americans, or because they had a better chance of escaping their contracts and disappearing into the local population, they tended to be more rambunctious than the Chinese. "What a happy time we have been having here for the last four weeks," one of Dodge's lieutenants reported ironically during one difficult stretch. "With drunken Irishmen after their pay, I can assure you it is enough to make men crazy."[25]

The end of the war eased the labor problems of the Union Pacific, but other problems remained. The largesse of the federal government guaranteed the future of the road, but employees and contractors had to be paid in the present, and funds often fell short. "We must have five hundred thousand dollars to pay contractor's men immediately or road cannot run," a payroll officer telegraphed headquarters at a crucial moment. The funds eventually arrived, but barely in time to prevent a mutiny among the men.[26]

Under other circumstances the kink in the cash flow would simply have slowed the project; delays have been a part of construction since the Pyramids. But the legislation authorizing the railroad gave the Central Pacific and the Union Pacific strong incentives to lay track as quickly as possible. The compensation structure, of payments keyed to mileage completed, compelled the two lines to compete with each other. Every mile one company built represented so many thousands of dollars and sections of land precluded to the other. The construction became a great race, with the Central crews tearing east and the Union crews west. The competition provided the country an entertaining diversion in the years after the war, but it was hard on the nerves of the company executives, on the account balances of suppliers unable to collect their due, and on the backs of the workers driven to labor long days for months on end.

ONE PROBLEM WAS peculiar to the Union Pacific. By the middle of the nineteenth century relations between the Indian tribes living within the boundaries of the United States and the American government had reached a kind of equilibrium. Andrew Jackson and his immediate successors had driven all but a scattered remnant of the Eastern tribes across the Mississippi River to Arkansas and what would become Oklahoma, where they struggled to make a living on parcels of land far smaller and more limited in resources than their former homes. The tribes of the West, especially those of the Plains and the mountains, remained comparatively undisturbed. To be sure, diseases inadvertently introduced by traders and other travelers to the Indian country had caused devastating losses of population. But these were partially offset by the advantages of contact with the Euro-Americans, especially the acquisition of trade goods and horses. Metal knives and cooking utensils facilitated daily chores, while firearms extended the range of hunters. Horses wrought a revolution in the culture of such tribes as the Comanche and the Sioux, making them true nomads and their warriors a formidable light cavalry. The Comanches became the scourge of the southern Plains, while the Sioux grew dominant on the northern Plains.[27]

White Americans certainly knew about the Plains tribes. The Comanches were the reason the Mexican government had invited American settlers into Texas; unable to hold Texas against Comanche forces invading from the northwest, the Mexicans intended the Americans to be a buffer. In the event, the Americans made off with Texas, but not before coming to know and respect the Comanches (whom they wouldn't subdue for many years). A decade later American emigrants on the Oregon Trail encountered the Sioux, Pawnee, and other northern tribes. Historian Francis Parkman became sufficiently fascinated by the Sioux to abandon his books and spend a summer among the tribe, whom he described in *The Oregon Trail*, an account that soon became a classic. Many more Americans met the Plains tribes during the gold rush. The Indians haunted the dreams of most of the gold seekers but rarely bothered them in daylight. The emigrants greatly outnumbered the Indians, and as long as they stuck together they experienced few difficulties. From the Indians' perspective, the emigrants were less a threat than an opportunity. They didn't covet the Indians' land, lusting for faraway gold instead, and en route they made good customers. They needed meat, horses, and other items the Indians were happy to supply on a sellers' market.

The railroad was a different matter. The Indians didn't take long to realize that the iron road was a permanent presence. Already it brought small armies of construction workers and the accoutrements of civilization their presence required. Towns sprang up along the line, and soldiers guarded the towns and camps. The Indians knew from experience and hearsay that wherever the railroad went, white settlers followed. Farmers fanned out from the rail lines, plowing and fencing land the Indians had used for hunting. Already white hunters were killing the buffalo, on which the Indians depended for physical and cultural sustenance.

Anticipating these events, the Indians struck at the tip of the spear, the Union Pacific crews. In the spring of 1867 parties of Sioux and Cheyenne conducted a series of attacks against surveyors, engineers, and construction gangs. Sometimes they spared the workers, satisfying themselves with stealing or destroying their equipment and, in the case of survey markers, spoiling their work. Other attacks were more deadly. One war party surprised an engineering crew, killing a surveyor and one of the soldiers escorting the crew. Another war band ambushed a train that had reached the current end of the line; three men were killed. A party of Cheyennes tore up a section of track and killed members of the crew of the locomotive that derailed as a result. When a trainload of investors, government officials, and other distinguished individuals came out from Washington to inspect the work, a hundred Indians attacked the train and its military escort. The dignitaries escaped bodily harm, but a shudder of insecurity rippled back up the line to the national capital.

The Indian offensive threatened to stop the construction quite literally in its track. "We've got to clean the damn Indians out or give up building the Union Pacific Railroad," Grenville Dodge declared. "The government may take its choice!" Thomas Durant told Ulysses Grant at the War

Department: "Unless some relief can be afforded by your department immediately, I beg leave to assure you that the entire work will be suspended."[28]

The Indian problem was larger than the Union Pacific, though Dodge and Durant had difficulty seeing it so. And its solution took longer than they wanted to allow. But the War Department did find sufficient forces to get the construction crews past the most dangerous zones, and the locus of the heaviest fighting shifted elsewhere.

THE CENTRAL PACIFIC confronted no comparable problems with Indians, largely because the hordes of gold seekers had driven the California Indians to the edge of extinction a decade before. But the inanimate troubles it encountered almost made Stanford and the others wish for enemies of flesh and blood. The granite of the Sierra gave way to the black powder of the Chinese sappers only slowly; pressed to accelerate the excavation, the Central's engineers turned to nitroglycerin. This liquid explosive was far more potent than powder, but because it was new—having been invented in Italy just two decades earlier, and employed in large-scale construction only now—it posed peculiar challenges. It was supposed to require a detonator but occasionally ignited on its own, leaving advocates of its use to their imaginations in explaining what went wrong. A spontaneous explosion in New York City prompted one pro-nitro observer to declare, evidently with a straight face, "It is perfectly safe and harmless and simply blew up from maltreatment and in self-defense." The Central tried nitro once but gave it up after a worker killed himself and some others by accidentally striking a charge of the stuff with his sledgehammer.

Yet in early 1867, when the construction had slowed to less than a crawl deep in the granite heart of the Sierra, in what would be the longest tunnel on the route, the Central tried it again. James Strobridge brought in a Scotsman named James Howden, a chemist familiar with nitro. Howden pointed out that the liquid was eight times as powerful as powder and had the additional benefit of producing less smoke, so workers could begin clearing the rubble from explosions sooner. He trained the crews in its use, and soon it became a regular part of their arsenal. Accidents still happened, to be sure. "Many an honest John went to China feet first," one of Strobridge's engineers observed afterward. But the improvement in performance seemed worth the risk, at least to the directors. "Charles"—Crocker—"has just come from the tunnel and he thinks some of them are making three feet per day," Mark Hopkins reported. "Hurrah for nitroglycerine!"[29]

From the stony bowels of the earth, the Central crews emerged to the icy slopes of the Sierra. As numerous travelers, including the ill-fated Donner party, discovered over the years, the western slopes of California's highest range catch snow in quantities almost unimaginable to easterners. Drifts of twenty, forty, sixty feet weren't uncommon, and as warm days of approaching spring alternated with still-freezing nights, the drifts compacted to solid walls of glacial ice. Stanford later recalled a spot where sixty-three feet of snow had become eighteen feet of ice, which required pickax and blasting powder to remove.

At first Strobridge and the others thought they could beat the problem if they removed the snow before the melt-freeze cycle set in. But the drifts themselves overwhelmed the men and their machinery. On one occasion a snowplow driven by five locomotives ground to an impotent halt under hundreds of tons of the fluff. The only solution seemed to be to catch the snow before it hit the ground. The crews tested snow sheds: sloped roofs erected during the summer to keep the grade and track clear. Adjustments were required to ensure that the roofs didn't collapse under the weight of the snow, but in the end they solved the problem (and remain a feature of rail travel in the Sierra to this day).[30]

IN THE SPRING of 1868 the Union Pacific crews crossed the Rockies in southwestern Wyoming. Durant couldn't resist boasting to Stanford of the rapid progress the Union was making. "We send you greeting from the highest summit our line crosses between the Atlantic and the Pacific Oceans, 8200 feet above tidewater," Durant said. "Have commenced laying iron on the down grade westward." The Central's nitro men had finished work on their summit tunnel a few months before, and though his company's total mileage fell far short of the Union's, Stanford refused to be provoked. "Though you may approach the union of the two roads faster than ourselves, you cannot exceed us in earnestness of desire for that event," he said. "We cheerfully yield you the palm of superior elevation;

7042 feet has been quite sufficient to satisfy our highest ambition. May your descent be easy and rapid."[31]

Stanford was playing with words when he said the Sierra summit satisfied his "highest" ambition. He had no intention of letting Durant and the Union claim any more mileage than they deserved. By far the most difficult part of the Central route was now behind it, while the Union was just reaching the most technical portion of its route, between the Continental Divide and the valley of the Great Salt Lake. As the crews of the Central flew across the desert of northern Nevada and Utah, those of the Union blasted their way through the Wasatch Range. Each company enlisted Mormons to supplement its regular workforce; each spurred its crews to work as rapidly as they could. Such concerns for quality as had initially influenced corporate decisions now fell by the wayside. "Run up and down on the maximum grade instead of making deep cut and fills," Collis Huntington advised, "and when you can make any time in the construction by using wood instead of stone for culverts &c., use wood. . . . If we should have now and then a piece of road washed out for the want of a culvert, we could put one in hereafter." Mark Hopkins agreed; the overriding objective, he said, was "to build road as *fast* as possible of a character acceptable to the commissioners." Not that the commissioners—the federal agents supposedly protecting the stake of taxpayers in the project—were expected to be any obstacle, for the same favors and promises that had brought Congress aboard in the first place were now being lavished on them. "We *know* the commissioners will readily accept as poor a road as we can wish to offer for acceptance," Hopkins frankly remarked.[32]

During the late winter of 1869 the two roads raced around the northern edge of the Great Salt Lake; in April the competing crews climbed Promontory Point from opposite sides. They finally met in early May. An elaborate ceremony was scheduled to mark the meeting of East and West, the defeat of geography by the forces of American enterprise, but a problem developed when crews of the Union Pacific, impatient at the tardiness of the company in paying wages, seized the ceremonial train carrying the Union directors to Utah and held them hostage. Later evidence suggested a scam: that Union director Durant put the workers up to the kidnapping in order to ensure payment to a construction subsidiary in which he had a major interest. "Durant is so strange a man that I am prepared to believe any sort of rascality that may be charged against him," an associate remarked.[33]

In fact, a great deal more rascality would soon be charged against Durant and his partners, but in the flush of success such minor sins were overlooked. Bret Harte commemorated the completion with a poem entitled "Opening of the Pacific Railroad":

What was it the Engines said,
Pilots touching, head to head
Facing on the single track
Half a world behind each back?

Walt Whitman weighed in with "Passage to India":

I see over my own continent the Pacific Railroad, surmounting every
barrier;
I see continual trains of cars winding along the Platte, carrying
freight and passengers;
I hear the locomotives rushing and roaring, and the shrill
steam-whistle,
I hear the echoes reverberate through the grandest scenery in the
world.

Other responses were more prosaic but not less significant. A wire connected the symbolic golden spike to a telegraph line that ran to Washington, New York, and other parts of the East, as well as to San Francisco. The electric echo of the hammer blows of Stanford and Durant was followed by messages from the news correspondents present. "The last rail is laid!" the reporter for the Associated Press wrote. "The last spike is driven! The Pacific Railroad is completed! The point of junction is 1086 miles west of the Missouri River and 690 miles east of Sacramento City." The news set church bells ringing in Boston and New York, and the Liberty Bell in Philadelphia. Washington fired cannons; Chicago held a parade. San Francisco, which had jumped the gun with a party two days earlier, celebrated again, firing hundreds of cannon salutes from Fort Point on the Golden Gate and otherwise feting its deliverance from the tyranny of distance.

William Sherman, whose first trip to California, during the Mexican War, had taken 196 days, wrote congratulations to the organizers of the epic project and to the "thousands of brave fellows who have fought this glorious national problem in spite of deserts, storms, Indians, and the doubts of the incredulous" and said he hoped to travel to California again soon, and much faster.[34]

Chapter 3

THE FIRST TRIUMVIRATE

———

To many Americans of the Gilded Age, J. P. Morgan represented the ugly face of American capitalism. It didn't help matters that Morgan's face was indeed daunting. His nose was downright frightening: a "huge, more or less deformed, sick, bulbous mass in the center of his face," according to Edward Steichen, the most celebrated photographer of the era and a man who made a profession and an art of studying faces. Morgan suffered from a severe case of acne rosacea, which left his nose chronically inflamed. His eyes were terrifying in a different way. Pale hazel, almost yellow, they burned with a fury that reminded Steichen of an express train hurtling through the night. An observer transfixed by their gaze had to turn away or risk obliteration beneath their weight and power.[1]

In photographs Morgan invariably had the nose retouched, and he was said to retaliate against persons who even mentioned it. Yet he couldn't do much about the working-class children who skipped rope to the rhythm of "Johnny Morgan's nasal organ has a purple hue," and when the Russian finance minister, Count Witte, suggested surgery, Morgan responded, "Everybody knows my nose. It would be impossible for me to appear on the streets of New York without it." In one of his better moods he declared his nose "part of the American business structure."[2]

Morgan might have been too near the subject to offer an objective opinion on his nose, but no one knew more about the structure of American business than he. Even Morgan didn't always know much; the great challenge for those engaged in enterprise during the Gilded Age was to acquire the strategic intelligence they needed to conduct their affairs successfully. What made Wall Street so tempting to speculators and manipulators like Jay Gould and Jim Fisk was the veil of ignorance that shielded the operations of nearly all the firms trading there. Corporations guarded their balance sheets as the proprietary information it was; not even to shareholders did boards of directors typically reveal reliable numbers on assets, revenues, and profits. Stock was issued at whim—which was what made watering stock so tempting. Insiders held an enormous advantage over everyone else; only the boldest or most foolish investors dared to tilt with the professional speculators on their own turf.

If microeconomic intelligence (relating to individual firms) was hard to come by, macroeconomic intelligence (regarding the economy as a whole) was harder still. Gould and Fisk nearly cornered the gold market in large part because no one knew how much gold was available for sale, who owned it, or what the intentions of the owners were. The state of the broader money supply was even more unfathomable. Figures regarding overall employment, investment, inventories, imports and exports, and dozens of other essential attributes of the national economy were either notional or nonexistent. Navigating the American economy in the Gilded Age was often like venturing west from Europe during the Age of Discovery. Columbus and his fellow mariners possessed charts, but the large blank spots and the sectors labeled "Here be monsters" hardly inspired confidence in their accuracy. Similarly for the voyagers to the edge of the American economy. Newspapers provided information regarding business in the major cities, but this was usually anecdotal and episodic; meanwhile much of the rest of the country was economic terra incognita. An entrepreneur plotting a venture was reduced to the equivalent of dead reckoning—starting from a known point and pushing cautiously out from there, measuring motion forward by reference to the starting point, and preferably keeping in sight of land. Enterprises grew slowly and fitfully under these constraints; the audacious often sailed right off the edge of the economy into the abyss of bankruptcy.

As in the Age of Discovery, when accurate maps were treated like crown jewels, verifiable intelligence commanded a premium in the Gilded

Age. And no one possessed more accurate intelligence than J. P. Morgan. Other men—and the rare woman—dealt in commodities and corporate shares; Morgan dealt in these but mostly in business intelligence, which he leveraged to an extent that made him the arbiter of the nation's economy and occasionally the most powerful man in the country. Most of those who watched him—and nearly everybody in America watched him at one time or other—assumed that his power derived from his large wealth. In fact his fortune was rather modest by comparison with those of the other moguls of the era. What distinguished Morgan was what he knew and how he employed that knowledge.

He started inauspiciously enough, being born in the year of the Panic of 1837. But his grandfather capitalized on the chaos in the financial markets to purchase properties distressed to dimes on the dollar, and when the economy recovered, the elder Morgan grew wealthy. His son, Junius Spencer Morgan, diversified into commodities brokering, moving the family from Hartford to Boston and eventually to London, and multiplying the Morgan wealth in the transatlantic trade. Pierpont, as Junius's son was called, went to school in Switzerland and college in Germany before returning to America to apply the mathematics in which he excelled.[3]

In 1857 he entered the Wall Street firm of Duncan, Sherman & Company, the American agent of his father's London house. He made a promising start in commodities, displaying a shrewd grasp of what people would pay for various things and an intuitive understanding of the larger currents affecting the Atlantic economy. The Civil War disrupted much of the transatlantic trade, especially that gulf stream of cotton that flowed from Southern plantations to the mills of the English Midlands, but like Daniel Drew, Morgan learned to fish in troubled waters. He left Duncan Sherman to start his own firm, and from the day J. P. Morgan & Company opened its doors at 54 Exchange Place, it earned a reputation as one of the canniest, boldest, and most successful houses in Wall Street.

The end of the war curtailed the commodities boom, requiring Morgan to look elsewhere for the handsome profits to which he had grown accustomed. It didn't take him long to realize that the troubled waters were now swirling about the railroad industry, where the Pacific road was being completed in a frenzied grab for federal land and loans and the Erie

Railroad was being tossed up and down by Drew, Gould, Fisk, and other speculators. The signs of genius were beginning to show in Morgan, but even a dullard could discern that the rail industry would have to be restructured. Railroads, like other corporations, acquired capital for expansion (or reorganization) in two ways: by issuing equity (stock) or assuming debt (loans). The equity route left corporations at the mercy of speculators, as the Erie War had demonstrated. The debt path put the corporations in the hands of bankers. These were often better hands, in that the bankers took the long-term interests of a corporation more closely to heart than the speculators did, on account of the obvious fact that if the corporation didn't survive, the bankers would lose their loans. Anyway, by the time the speculators had watered, floated, and sunk the stock of a corporation, the equity often wasn't worth much. Debt and bankers were the last recourse.

Morgan became a serious banker in 1871 when he allied with the Drexel house of Philadelphia to form Drexel, Morgan & Company, with its main office in New York City at the corner of Wall Street and Broad. From the beginning, Drexel Morgan's reach was both transcontinental and intercontinental. Morgan's family connection to London, where his father remained a force in banking, gave him entrée to the world of the European *haute banque*, where small groups of wealthy investors collaborated to share the risks and split the profits of challenging investment opportunities. European banks had underwritten the Pacific railroad and the Suez Canal, which opened within months of each other in 1869. Their loans bolstered governments in Europe, Asia, Africa, and both Americas. Their principals had nationalities but their assets were stateless, roaming the planet in search of the most lucrative prospects and the greatest returns.

At the acme of this rarefied world was the Barings Bank of London, which had supplied the $15 million Thomas Jefferson paid Napoleon for Louisiana, before financing the indemnity France was forced to pay its vanquishers after Napoleon's fall. Barings's reach prompted the duc de Richelieu to remark, "There are six great powers in Europe: England, France, Prussia, Austria, Russia, and Baring Brothers." Britain's poet Byron called Barings and its banking kin "the true lords of Europe," whose "every loan . . . seats a nation or upsets a throne."[4]

J. P. Morgan never quite upset a throne. But he did come to conceive of himself as a lord of America, with responsibility for rectifying the mistakes of lesser mortals, and power to match.

WHILE MORGAN WAS being educated in the academies of Europe, John D. Rockefeller attended a harder school in America. His first teacher was his father, William Rockefeller, a confidence man, purveyor of snake oil, fornicator, liar, and cheat. A journalist contemporary of John D., writing about the father, aptly remarked, "He had all the vices save one—he never drank." Yet Bill Rockefeller could be utterly charming. "He was the best-dressed man for miles around," a neighbor in upstate New York remembered. "You never saw him without his fine silk hat." The ladies loved him, to their dismay. He married Eliza Davison chiefly because her father was rich and Rockefeller hoped to claim her inheritance. But he refused to leave off with his other girlfriends. He brought one of these, Nancy Brown, into his and Eliza's home as a housekeeper, and he proceeded to cohabit with both. He fathered a daughter by Eliza in 1838, and then a daughter by Nancy. In 1839 Eliza bore him a son, John Davison Rockefeller. Several months later Nancy gave him a fourth child, another girl.[5]

Eliza was too smitten to terminate this ménage, but her brothers did it for her, compelling Rockefeller to dismiss Nancy. Yet their intervention hardly curbed his lust or diminished his appetite for unconventional arrangements. His work as a traveling huckster ("Dr. William A. Rocke-feller, the Celebrated Cancer Specialist, Here for One Day Only. All cases of cancer cured unless too far gone and then can be greatly benefited") carried him far from home, often for months at a time. On one journey to Ontario, Canada, he met a trusting young woman with equally trusting parents. Without divorcing or even informing Eliza and his family in New York, he married Margaret Allen and commenced a secret, second life with her.

John D. Rockefeller (who insisted on using his middle initial from youth) knew little of his father's escapades and admitted less. The boy was more directly influenced by his mother, who suffered her husband's sins in silence and prayer. Eliza was a Baptist, a child of the Second Great Awak-ening that swept through the "burned-over district" of upstate New York during the first half of the nineteenth century. She placed her trust in God and inculcated a puritan abstemiousness in her son. "The Baptists I knew listened to their consciences and their religious instructions, and not only did not dance in public places but did not dance anywhere and did not even concede the reputability of dancing," Rockefeller remembered. "The theater was considered a source of depravity, to be shunned by conscientious Christians." On the irregular occasions when Bill Rockefeller was home, he plied the children with candy and gifts, leaving matters of discipline to Eliza. She meted out enough for any two parents. "I made my protests, which she heard sympathetically and accepted sweetly—but still laid on, explaining that I had earned the punishment and must have it," Rockefeller recalled. "She would say, 'I'm doing this in love.'" Innocence was no excuse. "Never mind," she said during one thrashing, when he convincingly complained that he hadn't done what he was being punished for. "We have started in on this whipping, and it will do for the next time." Not even heroism stayed her hand. John and his brother William went skating on the Susquehanna River despite her injunction against it; a comrade fell through the ice and would have drowned but for their quick thinking and brave action. When they got home she hailed their courage. "We thought we should be left off without punishment," Rockefeller said. "But Mother gave us a good tanning nevertheless."[6]

Rockefeller spent much of his long life in denial about his early years. As they pertained to his father, the denial was direct; years before Bill died, John D. began referring to Eliza as his "widowed mother." And the memories he related of his father were unaccountably fond. "He himself trained me in practical ways. He was engaged in different enterprises; he used to tell me about these things. . . . He taught me the principles and methods of business. . . . I knew what a cord of good solid beech and maple wood was. My father told me to select only solid wood . . . and not to put any limbs in it or punky wood. That was a good training for me." Bill Rockefeller was more candid about his pedagogy. "I cheat my boys every chance I get," he told a contemporary. "I want to make 'em sharp. I trade with the boys and skin 'em and I just beat 'em every time I can. I want to make 'em sharp."[7]

Between his mother's discipline and his father's cheating, Rockefeller learned to fend for himself. He cultivated a reserve that would persist throughout his life. One of his high school teachers described him as "the coldest blooded, the quietest and most deliberate chap." A young woman who occasionally tutored him declared, "I have no recollection of John excelling at anything. I do remember he worked hard at everything: not talking much, and studying with great industry." She added, "There was nothing about him to make anybody pay especial attention to him or speculate about his future." Yet a peer remembered something that *was* unusual: Rockefeller's preoccupation with money. "Some day, sometime, when I am a man," Rockefeller confided to this friend, "I want to be worth a hundred thousand dollars." Another friend from Rockefeller's youth was Mark Hanna, who would grow up to be a senator from Ohio and William McKinley's closest adviser. A mutual acquaintance characterized the two: "Mark was of the virile type, always active, and took part in almost all forms of athletics, while John Rockefeller was reserved, studious, though always pleasant. No matter what the excitement, John retained his quietude and smiled on all occasions." Hanna himself was quoted as saying of Rockefeller that he was "sane in every respect save one—he is money mad!"[8]

EDWIN DRAKE GAVE form to Rockefeller's madness. In 1859 Drake drilled for oil near Titusville, Pennsylvania, and struck the greasy liquid. The discovery set off a boom to northwestern Pennsylvania that paralleled the gold rush to California a decade earlier, with the difference that the "black gold" was even more mysterious than the yellow stuff and its provenance more puzzling. Humans had known of oil since antiquity, encountering it where it seeped to the surface or tainted water wells. Such seeps were what inspired Drake to drill along Oil Creek, which got its name *before* the morning of August 28, 1859, when he woke to find that his seventy-foot hole had filled with oil overnight. But he couldn't have said where the oil came from, why it was located in this place and not others, or what, precisely, it consisted of.[9]

Its usefulness was slightly better known. "Rock oil," as it was called, to distinguish it from the oils of plants and animals, had been used medicinally for millennia. Whether it cured anything was hard to say, but that didn't stop hucksters like Bill Rockefeller from making extravagant claims of its virtues or his customers from swallowing them and it. But Drake and his backers weren't thinking of medicine when they sank their money into the Pennsylvania ground; they were thinking of light. For a thousand generations men and women had gone to sleep when the sun did and waked with its first light. Gradually they learned to push back the dark with hearth fires, torches, and candles. These last, rendered from animal fat, represented the state of the illuminating art till the nineteenth century. In the early part of that century whale oil filled the lamps of the wealthy, and by the century's midpoint oil derived from coal was being similarly employed. But there were only so many fish (as Herman Melville and many others insisted on calling the cetaceans) in the sea, and coal clung tightly to its oil. If the mass of humanity depended on whale or coal oil, it would never be released from its bondage to the sun. This wasn't simply a matter of social equality—the rich affording light, the poor doing without—but an issue of economic development. Farms might operate quite well by the sun, with the short days of winter being the time when farmers had little work to do. But factories had their own imperatives, and they couldn't wait for the December sun to rise before their wheels whirred into motion. The man who provided cheap light would not merely let farmers read their almanacs after supper but allow the factory-working sons and daughters of farmers to tend looms and lathes before breakfast.

It was this property of oil that inspired the rush to Pennsylvania. Petroleum promoters broadcast its virtues. "As an illuminator the oil is without a figure," one said. "It is the light of the age. . . . Those that have not seen it burn may rest assured its light is no moonshine, but something nearer the clear, strong, brilliant light of day, to which darkness is no party. . . . Rock oil emits a dainty light, the brightest and yet the cheapest in the world, a light fit for Kings and Royalists and not unsuitable for Republicans and Democrats." Whatever oil did for the kings and royalists, those Republicans and Democrats, in their capacity as capitalists, poured themselves and their money into northwestern Pennsylvania. "The whole population are crazy almost," an early arrival wrote home. "I never saw such excitement. The whole western country are thronging here, and fabulous prices are offered for lands in the vicinity where there is a prospect of getting oil." Within months, dozens of wells punctured the landscape along Oil Creek; by the autumn of 1860 the rig count reached seventy-five. Speculators drove prices to levels unimagined just two years before. "They barter prices in claims and shares, buy and sell sites, and report the depth, show, or yield of wells, etc. etc.," an observer explained. "Those who leave today tell others of the well they saw yielding fifty barrels of pure oil a day. . . . The story sends more back tomorrow. . . . Never was a hive of bees in time of swarming more astir, or making a greater buzz."[10]

And then, quite fortuitously, a larger hive made a greater buzz that intensified the oil excitement still further. The secession of the South prompted the North to prepare for war. Besides being the light of the age, petroleum was the era's best lubricant, not as fine as sperm oil, which

would still be used in watches and delicate instruments, but far cheaper—
and much cheaper also than coal oil. To keep the pistons in the steam
engines of locomotives and factory power plants from seizing up, to prevent the bearings in push rods and wheel trucks and stamp presses from
smoking, nothing beat rock oil. Few doubted that human mettle would
ultimately determine the outcome of the war and the fate of the Union, but
most acknowledged that metal of a different sort, and the lubricants that
kept the metal sliding and rolling, would set the boundaries for the actions
of muscle and bone.

JOHN D. ROCKEFELLER observed the commotion in the oil fields
with far more enthusiasm than he did the excitement on the battlefields.
Like Morgan and other capitalists of the era, Rockefeller reckoned that his
time was worth more to himself than to the Union army, and he paid three
hundred dollars to avoid the draft. He found two partners, Maurice Clark
and Samuel Andrews, and engaged to exploit the resource that was gush-
ing from the hillsides above Oil Creek. Whether by accident or inspira-
tion, the three eschewed production for refining. The former required
talents not given to Rockefeller, who quickly proved the driving force
in the joint venture. Rockefeller lacked the gambling instinct to risk everything on wells that might turn up dry—and that might bankrupt their
owners even if they struck oil. As production soared from nil in 1859 to
three million barrels in 1862, prices plunged, leaving many producers with
nothing but blackened palms and faces for their efforts. Rockefeller's
native caution and acquired puritanism recoiled from such chaos; he was
willing to work—very hard, if necessary—but only in a field where the
rewards were less subject to wayward chance and ruinous competition.

Refining was more to his taste. Although the art of separating crude
oil into its component compounds remained as much alchemy as science, it
was an industrial process that might be rendered more efficient by the
application of sound business practices. Rockefeller prowled the floor of
the refinery the partners built in Cleveland, the urban gateway to the oil
region, and constantly searched for waste and carelessness. When a
plumber submitted a bill that seemed padded, Rockefeller decided to purchase pipe and other supplies himself. His cooper charged him $2.50 per
oak barrel; Rockefeller was sure his own men could make the barrels

cheaper, and soon they did, turning them out for less than a dollar each. Irked at having to throw away some sulfur-based byproducts of the refining process, he devised a scheme for converting the waste into fertilizer, which he then converted into cash.[11]

The more he learned about the oil refining business, the more it defined his life. His partner Clark later observed, "John had abiding faith in two things: the Baptist creed and oil." Rockefeller's sister grew tired of hearing John talk to Clark about refining. "I got sick of it and wished morning after morning that they would talk of something else," she said. An associate from this period declared, "The only time I ever saw John Rockefeller enthusiastic was when a report came in from the creek"—Oil Creek—"that his buyer had secured a cargo of oil at a figure much below the market price. He bounded from his chair with a shout of joy, danced up and down, hugged me, threw up his hat, acted so like a madman that I have never forgotten it."[12]

Rockefeller soon realized he took the business far more seriously than his partners did. Clark was a decade older than Rockefeller and resented the younger man's assertiveness; by way of warning he regularly threatened to dissolve the partnership, supposing this would keep Rockefeller in line. Instead Rockefeller arranged the support of Andrews, and the next time Clark threatened dissolution, Rockefeller readily agreed. Too embarrassed to withdraw his bluff, Clark consented to an auction of the business to the partner or partners willing to pay the most. The bidding began at $500 but quickly escalated to many times that much. "Finally it advanced to $60,000," Rockefeller recalled, "and by slow stages to $70,000. . . . I almost feared for my ability to buy the business and have the money to pay for it. At last the other side bid $72,000. Without hesitation I said $72,500. Mr. Clark then said: 'I'll go no higher, John. The business is yours.' 'Shall I give you a check for it now?' I suggested. 'No,' Mr. Clark said. 'I'm glad to trust you for it. Settle at your convenience.'"[13]

Rockefeller's timing couldn't have been better. Two months after he gained his independence, the Civil War ended, and while the war had been good for the oil business, the peace promised to be even better. Railroad construction was booming, with the Pacific railroad leading the way. The market for illuminating oil was certain to grow rapidly as more consumers discovered the convenience and value of oil-derived kerosene.

Nor could Rockefeller have improved on his location. Besides being the gateway to the oil fields, Cleveland was a place where railroads reached the Great Lakes. Petroleum arrived from the oil district in barrels (of forty-two gallons, which became and would remain the industry standard). It was refined in Rockefeller's plant and the many others that sprang up nearby. The refined lubricating oil, kerosene, and lesser products like tar and paraffin were repackaged and shipped out by train and steamer. In time the oil business would become global, but in its American infancy it was strictly regional, and Rockefeller had the good luck—and good sense—to be at the center of the oil region.

In 1867 Rockefeller brought a new partner into the business. Henry M. Flagler couldn't have been more different from Rockefeller in outward demeanor if he had been Rockefeller's father—of whom Flagler reminded many of those who knew both John D. and Big Bill. Flagler was handsome, debonair, and funny. But the inner man was Rockefeller's alter ego. He didn't drink or swear, and he took his Protestant religion as seriously as Rockefeller did—which was to say, he read his Bible religiously but kept his ledger books in a different drawer. "I had scruples about the business and gave it up," he remembered of a partnership that involved alcohol, "but not before I made $50,000." On his desk he displayed a line from a popular novel of the day, which read: "Do unto others as they would do unto you—and do it first." Like Rockefeller, Flagler saw an oily future for America and was determined to have a part in it. He brought to his partnership with Rockefeller a loan of $100,000 from a former associate, who stipulated that Flagler be made treasurer. Rockefeller tested Flagler's cost-consciousness, found it almost equal to his own, and accepted the deal.[14]

With Flagler at his side, Rockefeller set out to conquer the Cleveland market for refined oil. The first part of the campaign was easy, for in the early days of the industry persons with neither expertise nor true passion for the business often took up refining. "All sorts of people went into it," Rockefeller said. "The butcher, the baker, and the candlestick maker began to refine oil." Many of these tyros were eliminated by a combination of Rockefeller's efficiency and their own incompetence. Rockefeller relentlessly drove his costs down. He kiln-dried the wood for his barrels *before* transporting it to his refineries, to save the transport cost of the water that evaporated off. After the company switched to tin cans for kerosene, he tinkered with the equipment to reduce the number of drops of solder required to seal the cans. An employee described a Rockefeller epiphany:

He watched a machine filling the tin cans. One dozen cans stood on a wooden platform beneath a dozen pipes. A man pulled a lever, and each discharged exactly five gallons of kerosene into a can. Still on a wooden carrier, the dozen cans were pushed along to another machine, wherein twelve tops were swiftly clamped fast on the cans. Thence they were pushed to the last machine, in which just enough solder to fasten and seal the lid was dropped on each can.

Mr. Rockefeller listened in silence while an expert told all about the various machines used to save time and expense in the process. At last Mr. Rockefeller asked: "How many drops of solder do you use on each can?"

"Forty."

"Have you ever tried thirty-eight? No? Would you mind having some sealed with thirty-eight and let me know?"

The experiment was tried, and a small portion of the cans leaked. The number of solder drops was increased to thirty-nine. This time none leaked. Rockefeller had his economic savings and his moral triumph over waste.

His accountants knew he was always watching. A random check of barrel stoppers turned up a discrepancy. "Your March inventory showed 10,750 bungs on hand," Rockefeller informed the man in charge. "The report for April shows 20,000 new bungs bought, 24,000 bungs used, and 6,000 bungs on hand. What became of the other 750 bungs?"[15]

ANDREW CARNEGIE WOULD never have joined the capitalist revolution in America had his father not been a casualty of the British version. Will Carnegie was a talented artisan, a weaver of linen, but the new steam-powered looms produced cloth that, if not so fine as that of the weavers, was far less expensive. Will might have become a power-loom tender, but the mill owners favored the quick, young hands of girls who worked cheaply, arrived promptly, and accepted their fate meekly. Day after day Will searched for alternative employment; night after night he came home to the family cottage more discouraged than when he left. Half a century later, Andrew recalled the defeat in his father's voice as he said, "Andra, I can get nae mair work."[16]

Others had suffered the same problem in that part of Scotland and done what millions before them had done when life in the Old World turned bad: they fled to the New. Will's wife, Margaret, had siblings in America. "This country is far better for the working man than the old one," her brother explained in a letter home. Will wouldn't believe it, but Margaret couldn't let herself not. Her family was falling apart in Scotland; perhaps America could save it. "I'll make a spoon or spoil the horn," she vowed, in a phrase whose tone required no translating even if the particulars did (Scots stirred their porridge with spoons carved from cow horns). She borrowed the money the passage to America required. The Carnegies reached New York in the summer of 1848 and were greeted at the wharf by fellow Scots who guided them through the city and pointed the way to Allegheny, Pennsylvania, where Margaret's sister lived.[17]

Andrew was twelve years old, with four years of school behind him and none ahead. Margaret, reading the despair in her husband's eyes, understood that he'd never adjust to the new life, which meant that Andy must. He went to work at once, in a textile mill owned by a Scotsman who was happy to employ his compatriots, especially if they were young. Andy was paid $1.20 per week for tending the bobbins on the steam looms. "I have made millions since," he wrote afterward, "but none of those millions gave me such happiness as my first week's earnings. I was now a helper of the family, a breadwinner."[18]

He was also ambitious. A higher-paying job came open in a factory that made the bobbins; Andy dipped the bobbins in oil and kept the boiler stoked. He hated the work, as the smell sickened him and the responsibility for the boiler gave him nightmares about blowing up the factory and killing all the workers. But for two dollars a week he put up with it—until something better appeared. His boss had a shaky hand and required help keeping the company records. Andy seemed quick, and the man asked him if he could write a fair hand. The boy's penmanship passed the test, and he moved from shop floor to office.

He nonetheless kept looking. His uncle told him of a telegraph office in Pittsburgh, across the river from Allegheny, that required a messenger. Andy put on his one suit, crossed the water, and landed the job. His daily rounds introduced him to the leading men of Pittsburgh: the railroad managers, the factory owners, the bankers, the merchants, the lawyers. He learned their names and faces and heard their conversations. To improve his prospects still further, he taught himself Morse code, which enabled him to fill in when the regular telegraphers were sick, and to read the business correspondence that came down the wires. He soon advanced to full-time keyman, and astonished his fellows and bosses by becoming one of the first operators in the country to be able to read the incoming messages by ear (most operators transcribed them one letter at a time).

His reputation spread. Thomas Scott, a division superintendent of the Pennsylvania Railroad, offered Carnegie a job as his personal assistant. He would make thirty-five dollars a month and receive the best business education America had to offer, Scott said. He would learn accounting, marketing, scheduling, inventory control, and personnel management. Carnegie absorbed the lessons as fast as they came and missed no opportunity to expand his responsibilities. One day a derailment fouled traffic throughout western Pennsylvania. Scott was away, but Carnegie had watched him deal with similar tangles and thought he could handle it, despite the danger to persons and property if he put trains on the wrong tracks. "Death or Westminster," he told himself. "I knew it was dismissal, disgrace, perhaps criminal punishment for me if I erred. On the other hand, I could bring in the wearied freight-train men who had lain out all night. I could set everything in motion. I knew I could." And he did. He forged Scott's signature on the orders he sent up and down the line; before long, traffic was flowing normally.

Scott arrived to discover what his young assistant had done. "He looked in my face for a second. I scarcely dared look in his. I did not know what was going to happen. He did not say one word." But neither did he rescind Carnegie's orders, and soon he was boasting to his colleagues about him. "Do you know what that little white-haired Scotch devil of mine did?" he said. "I'm blamed if he didn't run every train in the division on my name without the slightest authority." An associate asked if Carnegie had run them right. "Oh, yes, all right," Scott answered.[19]

Carnegie's star rose with Scott's during the 1850s, till in 1859 he took over Scott's old post as superintendent of the western division. That same year saw the oil rush to the region north of Pittsburgh. By now Carnegie was a capitalist in his own right, having followed Scott and Scott's lieutenant Frank Thomson into a partnership with a maker of sleeping cars. The deal entailed what a later generation would deem an egregious conflict of interest, as the principal purchaser of the cars was the Penn. Even by the standards of that day, it made Scott and Thomson nervous, and so they put their shares in Carnegie's name lest someone have to take a fall. But no one complained, and within two years Carnegie's income from the venture was three times his salary from the Penn. "Blessed be the man who invented sleep," he said.[20]

Upon the discovery of oil, Carnegie determined to invest in this new industry. "Everyone was in high glee," he said of a visit to the oil region. "Fortunes were supposedly within reach; everything was booming." Carnegie invested some of his sleeping car profits in oil properties, and while several hundred thousand other men his age marched off to the Civil War, he hired a substitute and counted his money. An old friend visited him in 1863 and asked how he was doing. "Oh, Tom, I'm rich! I'm rich!" he replied. His tax return for 1863 showed just how rich: Carnegie made nearly $48,000 that year, of which only $2,400 came from his day job on the Penn.[21]

Carnegie thereupon decided to become a full-time capitalist. "Thenceforth I never worked for a salary," he said. "A man must necessarily occupy a narrow field who is at the beck and call of others. Even if he becomes president of a great corporation he is hardly his own master, unless he hold control of the stock. The ablest presidents are hampered by boards of directors and shareholders, who can know but little of the business."[22]

Seeking new fields for investment, Carnegie identified iron and steel as a likely choice. As the war ended and the postwar railroad boom began, thousands of tons of ferrous metal were being consumed as fast as the smelters and furnaces could produce them. Carnegie's initial venture was with a company that built iron bridges, including the Eads Bridge at St. Louis, the first span across the Father of Waters below the mouth of the Missouri. But before long he had moved upstream (in the business sense), into production. He organized the Union Iron Works, which became an early producer of steel rails for trains, replacing the iron rails that bent and failed under heavy usage.

The state of the art in steel production was the Bessemer process, named for English foundryman Henry Bessemer, who discovered that blasting air through molten iron dramatically improved alloying efficiency. Carnegie knew of the Bessemer process but didn't appreciate its potential till he visited the mother plant in Derby, England. Nor did he recognize his own potential till then. Carnegie had been a conventional capitalist to this point in his career, investing here and there, without passion or overall plan. But now, staring at the incandescent liquid pouring from Bessemer's furnace, he discovered his calling. "I believe the true road to preeminent success in any line is to make yourself master in that line," he later wrote. "I have no faith in the policy of scattering one's resources, and in my experience I have rarely if ever met a man who achieved preeminence in money-making—certainly never one in manufacturing—who was interested in many concerns. The men who have succeeded are men who have chosen one line and stuck to it." Carnegie decided that steel was his line, and he stuck to it the rest of his career. "My advice to young men would be not only to concentrate their whole time and attention on the one business in life in which they engage, but to put every dollar of their capital into it." This was precisely what Carnegie did. On another occasion he summarized his philosophy more prosaically: "Put all your eggs in one basket and then watch that basket."[23]

MORGAN, ROCKEFELLER, AND CARNEGIE were too busy making money to worry about the political reconstruction of the Union and the moral and constitutional issues it raised. But they couldn't ignore an event that, in its own way, marked the end of the era of the Civil War.

Jay Cooke was a Union stalwart no less valuable to the Northern cause than Ulysses Grant or William Sherman, but like Morgan, Rockefeller, and Carnegie, he confined his fighting to the economic front. At a time when bonds were something only rich folks bought, Cooke sent small armies of agents across the Northern countryside selling Union war bonds to farmers and mechanics, lawyers and merchants, wives and widows, and aunts and orphans. In all he sold more than $1 billion of bonds, and it was largely because of this that the greenbacks the Union government printed during the war didn't depreciate the way the Confederate currency did. Cooke grew rich in the bargain, earning around $1 million, but those who thought seriously about the subject accounted his services cheap at that price (which amounted to a commission of one-tenth of 1 percent).[24]

After the war Cooke devoted that same promotional zeal to underwriting railroads. He hawked $100 million in bonds for the Northern Pacific, a prospective second transcontinental, particularly targeting European investors whose knowledge of American geography was acquired chiefly from Cooke's agents. Duluth, Minnesota, at the eastern end of the line, was dubbed "the Zenith City of the Unsalted Seas." The Great Plains were an agricultural wonderland requiring only railroad access to become the breadbasket of the world. The Pacific Northwest, where the road would end, was luscious beyond imagination. "There is nothing on the American continent equal to it. Such timber—such soil—such orchards—such fish—such climate—such coal—such harbors—such rivers. . . . The empire of the Pacific Coast is to be enthroned on Puget Sound. Nothing can prevent this. . . . There is no end to the possibilities of wealth here." The rumors were even more marvelous than the printed statements. Monkeys were said to frolic in the orange groves that flanked Puget Sound. When skeptics made sport of the exaggerations, deriding the Northwest as "Jay Cooke's Banana Belt," he didn't bother to rebut.[25]

The campaign to unload the bonds might have succeeded had peace not broken out in Europe unexpectedly. The Franco-Prussian War ended sooner than anyone but Bismarck anticipated, causing world grain prices to plunge and, with them, the prospects of a new railroad to the wheat fields of the northern Plains. Then a scandal regarding the finances of the Union Pacific surfaced, prompting a federal investigation (of which more in chapter 12) and blackening the bonds of all railroads. Not even the irrepressible Cooke could overcome this double blow, and his Northern Pacific issue went begging. So far had he extended himself on the road that the failure sealed his business fate. In September 1873, in the anniversary week of Jay Gould's Black Friday, Cooke announced that he couldn't meet his obligations and would have to close his doors.[26]

The news staggered Wall Street. "Dread seemed to take possession of the multitude," the New York Tribune reported. Cooke had been a pillar of the financial community; if he could fall, anyone could. A correspondent for the Nation observed, "Great crowds of men rushed to and fro trying to get rid of their property, almost begging people to take it from them at any price." Banks trembled and collapsed; brokers issued frantic margin calls before going under themselves. One Wall Streeter called the debacle the "worst disaster since the Black Death." The governors of the stock exchange shut the system down, causing the panic to spread to Boston, Philadelphia, and even Chicago. President Grant traveled to New York, where the bankers and brokers pleaded with him to bolster the banking system by an infusion of federal cash. Grant demurred on constitutional grounds but agreed to an emergency buyback of government bonds, which had a similar, though insufficient, effect.[27]

The panic revealed the rickety nature of corporate America. Leland Stanford's railroad, it turned out, hadn't been the only company to sacrifice quality to speed in its pursuit of profit; the temptation had grown irresistible since the Civil War first stirred the waters of speculation. The failure of the financial system, starting with Cooke & Company, caused huge sections of the capitalist structure to collapse. Thousands of firms—railroads, manufacturers, merchant houses, commodity traders, law and accounting offices—went under, leaving the survivors to count their blessings and reckon that the fat days of the Civil War were finally over.

As ALWAYS, THOUGH, some people thrived on the bust, it being a tautology that for every seller there is a buyer. Jay Gould, by now recovered from the lawsuits, if not the scandal, of Black Friday and from the shocking murder—by a rival in love—of partner Jim Fisk, swooped in and snatched up a number of bargains, especially in railroads. Cornelius Vanderbilt renovated the New York Central's grand depot at Forty-second Street and Park Avenue in Manhattan with construction laborers desperate for work for any wage.

But the big winner was J. P. Morgan. Though a banker, Morgan was also a student of capitalism. When he loaned money, he insisted on knowing his borrowers. As these were typically corporations, he learned a great deal about various facets of American business. He learned, for example, that the railroad industry was badly overbuilt, with too many lines chasing too little traffic. This was what made the industry so vulnerable to bond failures like that which claimed Jay Cooke and touched off the Panic of 1873. In the wake of the panic, Morgan conceived a plan to restructure the industry—to eliminate superfluous lines and curtail competition.

He tested his plan in minor ways until a larger opportunity arose, upon the 1877 death of Cornelius Vanderbilt. To the astonishment of the financial world, Vanderbilt left almost his entire fortune to his son William, whom the Commodore had often and publicly castigated as a dolt. The younger Vanderbilt immortalized himself by declaring, in response to a question whether the public interest ought to be considered in corporate decisions, "The public be damned. I am working for my stockholders." (In the retelling, Vanderbilt's second sentence was typically omitted.) William decided he owned more of the New York Central than he needed, and he turned to Morgan to unload a quarter million shares.[28]

Morgan's fee in the transaction was $3 million, but his more important compensation was a place on the Central's board of directors, as the representative of British investors to whom he sold large blocs of the shares. This became Morgan's modus operandi in similar deals, and it was a strategy that paid off handsomely in information and influence. As director of any single company, Morgan gained privileged access to intelligence about that company; as director of multiple companies he multiplied his intelligence many-fold. Soon he knew more about the railroad industry than anyone else in the country. And because railroads touched nearly every other industry, he learned more about the economy as a whole than anyone else. His imprimatur became essential for mergers and acquisitions; his disapproval could kill otherwise promising deals. When competing rail lines, and eventually competing firms in other industries, came into destructive conflict, Morgan stepped in as arbiter and peacemaker.[29]

He played both roles—arbiter and peacemaker—in a clash between the New York Central and the Pennsylvania Railroad. The Central started the conflict by commencing a new line from Philadelphia to Pittsburgh, in the heart of Penn country. Andrew Carnegie, John Rockefeller, and other shippers applauded the increased competition for their business, but the directors of the Penn took it seriously amiss. They struck back with a foray into the Central's home territory, building a line up the Hudson. As it happened, the new road passed near Morgan's summer home, and the blasting disturbed his vacations, while the proximity of the unwashed workforce made him worry for his children.

Morgan decided the Penn–Central battle had to cease. He summoned two principals of the Penn, George Roberts and Frank Thomson, to join him and fellow Central director Chauncey Depew aboard Morgan's steam yacht, the *Corsair*. Depew, one of the great talkers of the era, harangued Roberts and Thomson on the folly of the Penn's offensive into New York; they reminded him and Morgan that the Central had invited its troubles by invading their turf. Depew suggested a truce and reciprocal retreats. Thomson, softened by Morgan's hospitality, consented, but Roberts resisted. He continued to resist as the *Corsair* passed the Palisades. He was still resisting when the craft had to turn around below West Point. His boycott held as the boat approached its Jersey City slip. Morgan directed the skipper to keep going—past the Battery, past Ellis Island, all the way to Sandy Hook. Roberts remained obdurate all afternoon; only when the boat was tying up that evening did he consent to withdraw the Penn's construction gangs.[30]

The "*Corsair* compact" provoked relief and outrage. Other railroad men were relieved, hoping that what Morgan had done to rescue the Penn and the Central from their ruinous competition could be done to save themselves similarly from themselves. Shippers and advocates of the public interest were outraged that Morgan could so blithely conspire in this blatant attempt to foster monopoly.

Both emotions—the relief and the outrage—intensified when Morgan convened a meeting of the foremost railroad association at his Murray Hill house in Manhattan. Over Morgan's food and wine and amid the smoke of his cigars, the railroad magnates heard their host appeal to their sense of self-preservation. "The purpose of this meeting is to cause the members of this association to no longer take the law into their own hands when they suspect they have been wronged, as has been too much the custom heretofore," Morgan explained. "This is not elsewhere customary in civilized communities, and no good reason exists why such a practice should continue among railroads."

The meeting wasn't an entire success. Some of the barons preferred their chances in the field. Jay Gould bolted Morgan's house and convened a counter-session of Western railroaders who thought Morgan unfairly favored the East. Yet Morgan got enough from the remaining presidents to support the lead in the next day's paper: "The New York bankers triumph."[31]

As JOHN ROCKEFELLER's refining costs fell, his price advantage over his rivals increased, allowing him to expand his market share. And as his market share expanded, he gained leverage both over the firms that supplied him his oil and over the companies that carried away his refined products. By the late 1860s Rockefeller was one of the largest shippers in Ohio, and his business meant a great deal to the railroads that connected the Great Lakes to the Atlantic. Jay Gould appreciated the implications, and during the same period when he was bulling gold to move wheat, he offered Rockefeller a rebate on oil shipped through the Erie system. Rockefeller

liked the idea so much he accepted Gould's offer and applied the principle
to other roads. Rockefeller approached the Lake Shore Railroad, an Erie
competitor, and promised to give it a huge amount of business for the
time—sixty carloads of refined oil products per day—in exchange for a discount. Because railroads, as Gould explained more than once to Ulysses
Grant, chronically suffered from seasonal swings in demand for transport,
the guarantee of a Rockefeller trainload per day, season in and season out,
was worth a lot of money. Rockefeller told the Lake Shore just how much
it was worth: 75¢ per barrel, deducted from the posted price of $2.40. The
Lake Shore agreed.

Both parties took pains to keep the arrangement secret. The Lake
Shore didn't want other shippers to know what a discount it was giving
Rockefeller; they might demand the same for themselves. Rockefeller
wasn't eager to reveal the cost structure of his business lest his competitors
gain useful intelligence and his customers discover how large his profits
were. Moreover, there was something unseemly about this kind of discount. Under English common law certain transport firms had long been
classed as "common carriers" and obliged to treat all shippers on equal
terms. The concept had crossed the Atlantic and informed American practice if not always American law. Whether the concept applied to the new
technology of railroads was a much debated issue. Not surprisingly, those
shippers who could command discounts contended that it didn't apply and
shouldn't; those with less market power held that it did and should.

Rockefeller saw nothing wrong with the rebates. Large customers
almost always got better prices than small. "Who can buy beef the
cheapest—the housewife for her family, the steward for a club or hotel, or
the commissary for an army?" he later asked rhetorically. "Who is entitled
to better rebates from a railroad, those who give it 5000 barrels a day, or
those who give 500 barrels—or 50 barrels?" In fact, Rockefeller believed it
would have been unjust for him to have been charged the same rate as
other shippers. His trainloads of oil were much cheaper for the Lake Shore
to handle, per unit volume, than the carload shipments of his competitors.
If he didn't claim some of that cost saving, he would be subsidizing his
competitors' inefficiency—a concept that offended both his business
sense and his moral sensibility. Nor was the arrangement without risk to
the Rockefeller group. He committed to ship sixty carloads whether the
demand existed for that quantity or not. As for the secrecy surrounding the

rebates, this was simply prudent business practice. "These arrangements were not, except by the academic, expected to be published, any more than the general of an army's plans are published to enable the enemy to defeat him."[32]

Regardless of their justification, Rockefeller's rebates confirmed his advantage over his rivals. Business increased apace, so that when the Rockefeller partnership was dissolved in 1870 and the enterprise was reincorporated as the Standard Oil Company, it was the largest petroleum refiner in America. And it was poised to grow still more. One of Rockefeller's business colleagues in Cleveland remembered him saying, "The Standard Oil Company will someday refine all the oil."[33]

Whether or not he truly meant this, he acted as though he did. Like Morgan in railroads, Rockefeller had no use for competition in oil refining. Competition was wasteful; competition produced the kind of anarchy one saw in the oil fields, where a barrel might be lost to spillage, fire, or overproduction for every barrel captured and brought to market. The refining of oil benefited from economies of scale—the savings that result from larger facilities and longer production runs. The big companies themselves gained from these economies, in the form of higher profits, but so did their customers, in lower prices. Rockefeller didn't consider himself a philanthropist—that would come later—but neither did he consider himself an exploiter of other people. Customers were free to purchase kerosene from Standard Oil or not; the choice was theirs. But if they did, they received a product they couldn't have purchased at any price fifteen years earlier, and at a price that kept falling every year. If this didn't constitute progress, Rockefeller didn't know what did.

And those persons who stood in the way of progress deserved what they got. Capitalist theoreticians would talk about the "creative destruction" economic development entails; Rockefeller didn't theorize but gladly took part in both the creation and the destruction. He—and Henry Flagler, who actually drafted the corporate charter—created Standard Oil, which proceeded to destroy most of the competition in the refining business.

But it didn't do so alone. As powerful as Standard Oil was, it couldn't prevent the entry of new refiners into the industry. The technology of refining remained so rudimentary that the barriers to entry—the costs of starting a business—were quite low. The result was a drastic oversupply of refining capacity. At one point in the 1870s capacity outstripped demand by as much as three to one.

To solve the problem, Rockefeller collaborated—"conspired" wasn't too strong a word, as the collaboration was closely held—with several other large refiners and a number of railroads in what was called the South Improvement Company. This cartel embodied an effort by railroads and refiners to apportion the market in a way that preserved their profits—and, not incidentally, crowded out their competitors. To Rockefeller the cartel represented the triumph of reason over the law of the jungle.

But the triumph was short-lived, for word of the cartel leaked out, angering producers who guessed that it would lead to lower prices for their crude. The producers launched what came to be called the "Oil War," pitting the thousands of producers—many of whom were full-time farmers or merchants and pumped oil part-time from a single well or two—against the handful of refiners and railroads of the South Improvement Company. The producers organized an oil embargo, hoping to starve the refiners and railroads into submission. The campaign assumed the air of a crusade, with the producers holding solidarity rallies praising their own devotion to democracy and equal opportunity and damning the refiners and railroads as plutocratic oppressors. Yet the very number of the producers was their Achilles' heel, for it was far easier for the cartel to hold its few members in line than it was for the producer's ad hoc organization to discipline its thousands.

The cartel tried to exploit this weakness, offering sweetheart deals to producers willing to break ranks. One small producer, Frank Tarbell, received an offer of $4.50 per barrel, twice the market price, for his entire year's production. Tarbell, however, spurned the offer, valuing the respect of his fellow producers (and his young daughter Ida, who would grow up to become the scourge of Standard Oil) above the cartel's cash. And in the end the producers won. Between the ill will the cartel generated and the oil it didn't receive, the South Improvement Company collapsed.[34]

Rockefeller wasn't surprised. He later claimed that the cartel wasn't his idea, that he had gone along to please the other directors of Standard Oil. Though Rockefeller was the largest shareholder in Standard, he didn't own a majority of the stock and so had to lead by persuasion rather than decree. "When it failed," he said of his thinking on the cartel scheme, "we would be in a position to say, 'Now try our plan.'"[35]

Rockefeller's plan was something at once simpler and more ambitious than a cartel. Far from curing him of the idea of industrial cooperation, the South Improvement fiasco convinced him that cooperation was more necessary than ever. If cooperation couldn't be sustained among the several big firms in the refining industry, it would have to be effected by a single firm. If Standard couldn't organize the industry, it would have to own the industry.

During the next several years Standard swallowed one competitor after another, buying up refineries and the companies that operated them. Rockefeller was a reasonably honest man and, by his own lights, a compassionate man. He didn't aim to ruin anyone. "He treated everybody fairly," recalled a rival who accepted Rockefeller's purchase offer. "When we sold out he gave us a fair price." Rockefeller paid in cash or Standard stock. He preferred to pay in stock, and nearly all those who accepted stock were happy they did, especially after the stock made some of them millionaires. Rockefeller came to believe that many of those who criticized his takeover campaign were really angry at themselves for insisting on cash and thereby missing the chance to grow rich on Standard stock.

But though Rockefeller could be kindly, he was also implacable. Those rivals who refused his offers felt the full weight of Standard's power. He cut prices to below theirs; if they answered with cuts of their own, he cut again. His lower production and transportation costs gave him an advantage over everyone else; when this advantage failed to elicit capitulation, he cut prices to below his own costs, knowing he could stand the attrition longer than they could. He and Flagler engineered shortages of railcars and bought up all the barrels in the neighborhoods of the recalcitrants.

Rockefeller was convinced he was doing the Lord's work. "I believe the power to make money is a gift from God," he told an interviewer, "just as are the instincts for art, music, literature, the doctor's talent, the nurse's, yours—to be developed and used to the best of our ability for the good of mankind. Having been endowed with the gift I possess, I believe it is my duty to make money and still more money, and to use the money I make for the good of my fellow man according to the dictates of my conscience." And Rockefeller's conscience dictated the consolidation of the oil industry. He afterward derided allegations that Standard had engaged in predatory practices in acquiring its competitors. "How ridiculous all that talk is!" he said. "It's twaddle, poisonous twaddle, put out for a purpose. As a matter of fact, we were all in a sinking ship, if existing cut-throat competition continued, and we were trying to build a lifeboat to carry us all to shore. You don't have to threaten men to get them to leave a sinking ship in a lifeboat." Warming to the memory, he described some of the companies he purchased as "old junk, fit only for the scrap heap," and declared, "The Standard was an angel of mercy, reaching down from the sky, and saying 'Get into the ark. Put in your old junk. We'll take the risks!'"[36]

Standard did take risks. Rockefeller's buying spree began during the depression that followed the Panic of 1873. He benefited from the depression prices, but he had no guarantee of when, or even if, the American economy would pull out of its slump. On occasion he had to reassure his wife—he had married in 1864—that he had made investments beyond oil and that they could survive even if Standard didn't.

THE BIGGER GAMBLE was that new sources of oil could be found. During its entire brief history, the American oil industry had depended on a single source, the oil district of northwestern Pennsylvania. The older wells there were beginning to fail, and one had to think the newer wells would fail, too. The state geologist of Pennsylvania went so far as to describe "the amazing exhibition of oil" in the producing region as "a temporary and vanishing phenomenon, one which young men will live to see come to its natural end." John Archbold, one of Rockefeller's own men at Standard, said the chances of finding another field like that of the Oil Creek district were "at least one hundred to one against." Standard might own the entire industry, but without more oil it wouldn't be an industry worth owning. Already railroads were reluctant to reinvest in equipment to handle oil shipments.[37]

Rockefeller bet that new oil would be found. He couldn't believe that God would have guided him into the oil industry only to snatch away the resource that made it all possible. Nor would God take oil away from the American people. "The whole process seems a miracle," Rockefeller said. "What a blessing the oil has been to mankind!"[38]

He continued to pour money into the business. He purchased competitors till only a handful remained, and these he let survive as a testament to his patience. When railroads refused to invest in the new technology of tanker cars, Rockefeller built the cars himself and leased them to the railroads. Besides guaranteeing Standard the most efficient means of transporting oil, this strategy gave the company a veritable stranglehold over its remaining rivals, as it now owned the cars they needed to transport their product. Not long after the tanker cars became the transport of choice, producers and others began experimenting with pipelines, which promised to be even more efficient. Rockefeller invested heavily in pipelines, again with the dual purpose of improving Standard's efficiency and placing competitors at his mercy.

Meanwhile he consolidated the Standard empire internally. Though Standard seemed solid enough to outsiders, Rockefeller knew it was an institutional hodgepodge. The companies he had acquired were purchased not by Standard itself but by its directors. This arrangement afforded camouflage; Rockefeller could deny the extent of Standard's monopoly and be technically correct. And for the time being the directors were happy to follow Rockefeller's lead. But they—or, more likely, their heirs—might not always be so complaisant, and, anyway, it was inefficient to have to persuade the multiple owners whenever Rockefeller thought the group ought to move in this direction or that. It would be far more efficient to centralize control.

To this end Rockefeller and his lawyers adapted the common-law concept of a trust—something held for someone else—to a novel purpose. The Standard Oil trust, established in 1882, held shares of the companies that formed the Standard empire, giving the nine trustees control of those companies. There was nothing especially nefarious about the arrangement; similar schemes occurred to other corporate lawyers about the same time. But neither was it something Rockefeller boasted about. In fact, he did just the opposite, covering his trail with dissimulation and denial for several years, until congressional antitrust investigators revealed the existence of the Standard trust.[39]

Though the trust arrangement increased Rockefeller's control of the corporation, it still didn't give him majority ownership. He still guided by persuasion, although now he had to persuade a smaller number of people. He avoided the first-person singular in talking about his business dealings. "Don't say that *I* ought to do this or that," he told his associates. "*We* ought to do it. Never forget that we are partners; whatever is done is for the general good of us all." His hand rested lightly on the tiller. "I have seen Mr. Rockefeller often at a meeting of the heads of the different departments of the Company, listening carefully to each one and not saying a word," one of his colleagues remembered. "Perhaps he would stretch out on a lounge and say: 'I am a little tired, but go right on, gentlemen, for I know you want to reach a decision.' He might close his eyes now and then, but he never missed a point. He would go away without saying a word but good-bye. But next day when he came down he had digested the whole proposition and worked out the answer—and he always worked out the right answer."[40]

Under Rockefeller's gentle guidance, the Standard trust extended its hold on the oil industry. Having routed the refiners—by the time the trust was created, Standard refined nine of every ten barrels processed in the United States—Rockefeller took on the producers. Standard's dependence on firms it didn't control for the oil that formed its lifeblood had always made him nervous. And as the South Improvement failure had demonstrated, he needed the producers as much as they needed him, and such dependence was something he couldn't stand.

As matters developed, the decline in the Pennsylvania fields inspired oil prospectors to look elsewhere. Like the gold prospectors who traveled from California to Nevada and other parts of the mountain West in search of new mines, they knew nothing of the genesis of the deposits they sought; like the prospectors, they simply looked for topographical and geological features that resembled those that had paid off elsewhere. Along the Ohio–Indiana border were springs that, since time out of mind, had spontaneously burst into flame; these seemed a good bet for the drillers. In the mid-1880s these Lima-Indiana fields, as they were called, began producing copiously.

Rockefeller spied his chance to break into production. Though the Lima oil stank so badly consumers wouldn't purchase the kerosene it made (drillers called the new oil "skunk juice"), Rockefeller determined to acquire as many production leases as possible. His fellow directors were skeptical; no one knew if the sulfur that caused the stink could be removed economically. "Our conservative brethren on the board held up their hands in holy terror and desperately fought a few of us," Rockefeller remembered. But he assured the skeptics that Standard's chemists could solve the sulfur problem, and they let themselves be persuaded. "Buy all we can get," he cabled his agents. They bought a great amount, even as the chemistry division worked overtime. By the early 1890s both groups had succeeded, and Standard, while retaining its refining monopoly, was America's largest producer as well.[41]

ANDREW CARNEGIE WAS less religious than Rockefeller but no less convinced he was doing good by doing well. Having put all his eggs in the basket of steel, Carnegie devoted himself to becoming the master steelmaker in America. He found a few deep-pocketed partners, including Tom Scott, his old mentor, and built a cutting-edge steel mill on the field south of Pittsburgh where British general William Braddock had died in the battle that started the French and Indian War a century earlier. Besides being close to Carnegie's home, the Pittsburgh site combined access to coal and transport, the latter by three rivers and two railroads. (The competing railroads were crucial to Carnegie's plan; having spent a dozen years on the Penn, he knew how they squeezed customers wherever they enjoyed local monopolies.) The Panic of 1873 threatened the project's funding, but Carnegie refused to let anything bar the path. At one point Scott asked for help meeting current demands. Carnegie sympathized but reckoned that affording the assistance would hinder construction on the steel plant. After what he called "one of the most trying moments of my whole life," he decided that profits came before friendship or loyalty.[42]

Carnegie's immersion in the steel business convinced him that most of those in the industry didn't know what they were doing. "I was greatly surprised to find that the cost of each of the various processes was unknown," he said. "Inquiries made of the leading manufacturers of Pittsburgh proved this. It was a lump business, and until stock was taken and the books balanced at the end of the year, the manufacturers were in total ignorance of results. I heard of men who thought their business at the end of the year would show a loss and had found a profit, and vice versa."[43]

Carnegie applied what he had learned on the Penn to track his own costs, and he employed this knowledge to his advantage. The steelmakers of Pittsburgh typically formed cartels, or pools, in bidding large contracts. Carnegie initially went along. But when one such pool allocated him the smallest share of the contract, he balked. Instead he demanded the largest share and warned that if he didn't get it he would undercut them all, since he could roll steel rails at nine dollars a ton. They surrendered, thereby confirming his belief that they hadn't the faintest idea what the cost per ton of steel production was, since his actual costs were fifty dollars a ton.[44]

They didn't stay that high. Carnegie obsessed about costs, doing everything humanly possible to bring them down. He monitored inventories constantly. "There goes that damned bookkeeper," one of his foremen groused as Carnegie walked past. "If I use a dozen more bricks than I did last month, he knows it and comes round to ask why." To unravel the mysteries of steel manufacture he hired teams of chemists, who also had orders to find uses for the byproducts of the smelting and alloying process. His engineers streamlined the path of the metal from ore to alloy, pouring ingots, for instance, on moving flatcars, in anticipation of the assembly-line methods of Henry Ford. To cut the cost of fire insurance—a major expense in the hellish business of steelmaking—he tore down his wood buildings and replaced them with iron. Whenever he heard of an innovation that promised to save money, he ordered it implemented, almost regardless of capital cost. In one instance he ripped out a three-month-old rolling mill to replace it with a more efficient model. A British steelman Carnegie met declared proudly that his company was still using equipment introduced two decades before; Carnegie answered that that was what was wrong with British industry. "It is because you keep this used-up machinery that the United States is making you a back number."[45]

Carnegie obsessed over cost because it was the one part of his business he could control. "Carnegie never wanted to know the profits," an associate said. "He always wanted to know the cost." Carnegie himself explained: "Show me your cost sheets. It is more interesting to know how well and how cheaply you have done this thing than how much money you have made, because the one is a temporary result, due possibly to special conditions of trade, but the other means a permanency that will go on with the works as long as they last."[46]

As he wrung the excess costs out of his own facilities, he sought savings elsewhere. He acquired coke ovens to control the source of his carbon and bought iron mines to ensure his ore. He purchased railroads and lake steamers lest he suffer from the inefficiencies of his transporters. And he set prices wherever he had to in order to keep the entire system running at full capacity, which maximized his economies of scale.

By the 1880s he was the undisputed champion of the steel industry, with production costs that broke the back of the competition. In a pinch he was willing to let his rivals set his prices for him. "The Union Pacific had advertised for 70,000 tons of rails, the biggest order that had been given," he explained to a congressional committee investigating the steel industry. "It was to be decided at Omaha, and all my competitors, all these agents of corporations, were out at Omaha, and those bids were to be opened. I walked over to Sidney Dillon"—the president of Union Pacific. "I was able to do the Union Pacific a favor once and I did it. I said, 'Mr. Dillon, you have had some Carnegie rails. What is the report?' 'Oh, first class; splendid rails, Mr. Carnegie.' 'I want you to do this for me: your people are out there bidding on 70,000 tons of rails. I ask you to give me those rails, and I promise to take the lowest price that is bid.'" Dillon agreed. Carnegie made a nice profit on the deal, and his competitors made nothing.[47]

As much as Carnegie learned about the manufacture of steel, and as expert as he became in the craft, he never lost a sense of wonder as to what it all entailed. In a reflective moment he summarized his life's work:

> Two pounds of iron-stone purchased on the shores of Lake Superior and transported to Pittsburgh;
>
> Two pounds of coal mined in Connellsville and manufactured into coke and brought to Pittsburgh;
>
> One-half pound of limestone mined east of the Alleghenies and brought to Pittsburgh;
>
> A little manganese ore mined in Virginia and brought to Pittsburgh;
>
> And these four and one half pounds of material manufactured into one pound of solid steel and sold for one cent.
>
> That's all that need be said about the steel business.[48]

Chapter 4

TOIL AND TROUBLE

Carnegie's recipe for steel made the metal's manufacture sound easier than it was. Carnegie's genius—for the steel master's gift was nothing less than that—was his talent for organization. Those chunks of iron ore and coal and limestone and manganese didn't migrate to Pittsburgh on their own; they were gathered by the legions Carnegie employed for the purpose. He trained his legions; he drilled them; he rewarded those officers and men who performed to his standard and dismissed those who didn't. Carnegie was no inventor; not a single technique for steelmaking was his original idea. And he was an innovator only in adopting and adapting other men's discoveries. But he was nonetheless creative, in the way Alexander and Napoleon were creative. They created political empires; Carnegie created a ferrous empire.

Rockefeller's achievement was comparable. The empire of Standard Oil reflected Rockefeller's relentless pursuit of efficiency and his ability to motivate those who worked for him to strive as hard as he did. The alchemy of oil was less impressive than that of steel; the kerosene that emerged from Standard's refineries was more obvious kin to the crude that entered the intake pipes than Carnegie's gleaming steel rails were to the rusty rock from which they sprang. Yet the magic of Standard's organization—the transforming power of monopoly—cast even Carnegie's operation in the shade. Rockefeller's regiments didn't march in lockstep; the armies of capitalism appear chaotic by comparison with regular armies. But the efforts of Standard's constituents meshed in a manner to inspire the envy of the sternest Prussian general. And they crushed the competition with an implacability that would have made Wellington proud.

For such reasons it was the more striking that Carnegie's recipe for steel included nothing about labor. He didn't mention the men who dug the iron and coal from the ground and loaded it on the ships and railcars that carried it to Pittsburgh, nor did he acknowledge those who fired the furnaces and poured the molten metal into ingots and operated the rest of the machinery that made his steelworks the most productive in the world. Carnegie's failure to acknowledge his debt to labor wasn't unusual for capitalists of his day; indeed, until the 1890s he was considered *more* aware of his workers and sensitive to their needs than most other employers. On this account it was especially significant that he ignored one of the most portentous aspects of the capitalist revolution of the late nineteenth century: the emergence of an American working class.

Of workers, America had always had many, of course—although never enough to meet the demand for labor. In fact, the historic dearth of labor was perhaps the central feature of the American economy in the seventeenth and eighteenth centuries. In Europe land was scarce but labor plentiful; in America the balance tipped the other way. This explained much of why Americans resorted to slavery (while Europe, for most domestic purposes, did not). It was also why labor was better rewarded in America (except for those slaves) than in Europe, which in turn explained much of the attraction of America to immigrants.

Until the nineteenth century, many laborers could hope to earn and save enough to become their own employers. In the countryside farm laborers could look to buy land; in the cities and towns apprentices and journeymen could anticipate becoming masters. By no means did reality always match the hopes of the laborers, but it did so sufficiently often that little in the way of class consciousness developed among workers. Wage labor was a stop on life's journey, not life's destination. Nothing intrinsic or permanent separated those who hired from those who hired out.

Things changed as the country industrialized. Many of the early textile mills favored young women, for whom the water-powered looms and spindles were a prelude to marriage and motherhood; but the heavy lifting in the coal mines and ironworks that characterized the age of steam was done by men who increasingly expected to grow old on the job. This expectation—novel for America—contributed to a sense among workers that they were a class apart from those they worked for.

"THE ENTRANCE TO the mines is from the top of a precipitous hill, which, covered with the black refuse of scores of years, bears the semblance of a mountain of coal dust," a visitor to the anthracite district of Pennsylvania wrote.

> From the doors and open windows of the colliery buildings a great cloud of dust is ever streaming, settling on everything. . . . The interior of the building is a cloud of hazy blackness, and the black silent men, as they appear and disappear in the dust, seem like so many evil genii floating in the dark storm clouds.

This mine employed three hundred workers.

> Each one had his routine to go through, and he went through it just as a steam engine or a clock. And when quitting time came each one went back to his home in the regular groove, just as the steam goes out of the boiler when its work is done, and then dropped off into sleep, his only pleasure. I have seen far more cheerful bodies of men in prison. It may be their black and dreary surroundings; it may be their knowledge of constant and terrible danger; it may be the strain of great physical labor—I know not what it is, but something there is about these mines that wears the life and soul out of the men, leaving only the weary, blackened shell.[1]

The miners indeed faced danger. In the early days of American steam power, wood and coal competed as fuels for the boilers that produced the steam. Wood had the advantage of being ubiquitous—available, for instance, along the rivers plied by steamboats, which could refuel at their convenience. But wood had the disadvantage of containing less carbon per pound than coal, which had been compressed during eons by the weight of the rocks that overlay it and effected the conversion from dead vegetation to fossil fuel. Thus in any application where fuel had to be transported more than a short distance, coal won out. And the best coal—that with the densest energy—was anthracite, the hard, black, combustible rock found most conspicuously in Schuylkill and neighboring counties in east-central and northeastern Pennsylvania.

The first mines were mere pits, holes sunk where the coal seams came to the surface of the earth. But as the miners dug into the seams, the pits and holes became shafts and tunnels. Miners worked with picks, hammers, and shovels. They broke the rock free from the face of the seam and loaded it into wheelbarrows and buckets, with which they rolled or windlassed the coal to the surface. As the mines developed, narrow-gauge tracks were laid in the drifts—horizontal tunnels—and small railcars of coal were pulled by men or mules.

During the initial decades of mining, till the middle of the nineteenth century, operations tended to be small and relatively inexpensive. Individuals and partnerships could generate the capital to develop the mines, and the mining industry was characterized by hundreds of separate enterprises. But as the easy pickings—those near the surface—were taken, mining grew more difficult, expensive, and exclusive. The first barrier was the water table. As long as they lacked the technology to delve below the natural level of underground water, many miners convinced themselves that the seams ended just below the water table. (This wishful thinking reflected not simply technological incapacity but the prevailing ignorance of how coal was produced in the first place.) But a few bold spirits thought otherwise, and those with access to sufficient capital installed pumps to depress the water table in the vicinity of their shafts. The expense of the pumps culled the ranks of the operators, and the success of the pumps required additional expenditures, to make the most of the seams now rendered accessible. Shafts drove deeper into the earth, and elaborate techniques evolved to scrape as much coal as possible from the seams. Miners excavated large "rooms" from the coal seams, leaving "pillars" of coal to support the roof (and the hundreds of feet of rock and dirt above it). But because the pillars contained marketable material, the miners, on second pass, began to excavate the pillars. This required a careful weighing of costs against benefits: the costs in danger of cave-ins against the benefits of selling more coal. Under the best of circumstances, the technique demanded the expertise of men who had learned to detect the signs of strain in the pillars and the overburden; under the worst, it claimed the lives of men crushed when insufficient pillars collapsed.[2]

Cave-ins weren't the only danger. Floods were a constant threat, should the pumps fail or a miner unknowingly break through to an underground stream. Suffocation could come from nonaqueous sources as well. Miners had names for the several gases that crept into mine shafts and displaced the oxygen that kept them alive. "Firedamp" was methane, "stinkdamp" hydrogen sulfide, "blackdamp" carbon dioxide, "whitedamp" carbon monoxide. All could kill, often without warning. Paradoxically, the most dangerous gas was oxygen, which fed the fires that were the greatest hazard of all. The engines that powered the mines ran hot, and sparks could ignite timbers or especially the coal dust that suffused the atmosphere in and around the mines. In 1869 at Avondale in Luzerne County, sparks from a furnace that drove ventilation equipment set the structure on fire. The fire spread to the timbers supporting the equipment, which crashed down the shaft even as it sealed the only exit. In minutes the fire exhausted the oxygen in the mine and spread deadly carbon monoxide among the 110 men trapped below. Everyone died.[3]

DISASTERS LIKE THAT at Avondale angered mine workers, who blamed the mine owners and operators for failing to provide such elementary safeguards as multiple exits. The anger eventually yielded results, and the Pennsylvania legislature ordered the operators to undertake basic reforms. Yet the order wasn't always enforced, and in any event the complaints of the workers went deeper than mine safety. As the demands of mining technology grew, and with them the need for larger amounts of capital, the individual operators gave way to large corporations. In some cases these corporations confined themselves to mining, but often their portfolios were more diverse. Carnegie Steel owned coal mines, as did Rockefeller's Standard Oil. During the 1870s the dominant mining company in the Pennsylvania anthracite district was in fact a railroad, the Philadelphia & Reading. The Reading and its president, Franklin B. Gowen, took the idea that started Jay Gould on the path to the gold conspiracy—that railroads could improve their profits by guaranteeing traffic—and applied it differently. The main commodity the Reading transported was coal; to ensure traffic, the Reading purchased coal mines.[4]

This served the shareholders of the Reading but placed the mine workers at a serious disadvantage. With the smaller operators, whom they typically knew by name and face, they shared certain interests, including a desire that the local economy thrive. And even where the interests of workers and operators diverged—for example, in negotiations over pay— the workers and small operators discussed their differences across a relatively level bargaining table. The operators couldn't squeeze the workers without worrying they'd go to work elsewhere. But once the Reading took over in the anthracite district, the workers no longer knew the owners, who lived elsewhere and had little attachment to the coal community per se, and they confronted an effective monopolist who left them nowhere else to work. Moreover, because the resources of the Reading transcended the anthracite region, Gowen could, if necessary, close the mines and starve the workers into submission.

Nor was this the extent of the workers' disadvantage. Since colonial times Pennsylvania had been a melting pot for immigration, but a pot in which the melting often took several generations. Benjamin Franklin, for one, had railed against the refusal of German immigrants to adopt the language and customs of the English majority (although his dissatisfaction didn't prevent him from publishing books and magazines in German). The German strain in Pennsylvania persisted into the mid-nineteenth century, when it was complemented by the large immigration from Ireland that followed the failure of the potato harvest for several years in the 1840s. The Irish landed in Boston, New York, and Philadelphia (avoiding the South for its embrace of slavery). They formed urban enclaves but also spread to rural districts that needed unskilled workers. They reached the coalfields of Pennsylvania by the 1850s. Some of their new neighbors—employers, for example, and predecessors from Ireland—were happy to see them. Others— existing mine workers, members of other ethnic groups—were not. Previous immigrants from England and Wales formed the largest group of workers in the mines, and on both cultural and economic grounds they eyed the newcomers with suspicion and dislike. They did what they could to distance themselves from the Irish, who found themselves damned as drunken, ignorant papists. Among the workers a class system developed, distinguishing "miners" from "mine workers." The former, mostly British, were the men who freed the native coal from the seam face; the latter, mostly Irish, were the ones who broke the freed coal into manageable chunks, which they loaded into cars and transported to the surface. The difference in condition between the two groups was described by a Welshman who, though a miner, sympathized with the Irish mine workers: "The miner and laborer go to work at seven o'clock in the morning and probably the miner will cut enough coal by ten or twelve o'clock. Then he will go out, leaving the poor laborer up to his waist in water and he will have to pile the lumps and fill three or four cars with coal after the gentleman has left. . . . Between five and six, the laborer, poor thing, arrives home wet as a fish." For his pains the laborer received about a third the wages of the miner.[5]

One might have expected the consolidation of the coal industry to force the different groups of employees together. (Technically the miners were not employees but independent contractors. In some cases the mine workers worked for them.) Occasionally it did, but at least equally often it intensified the differences between the groups. Miners, for instance, often blamed accidents on the alleged carelessness of the mine workers. After the Avondale fire, Welsh miners accused Irish workers of deliberately setting the fire to retaliate against perceived injuries from the Welsh. The accusation gained credence from the fact that few Irish were working when the disaster struck, most having taken the day off—ironically, to attend a funeral. Of the 110 victims, only six were Irish.[6]

For all the disadvantages of labor in the coal industry, management wasn't without its problems. The Reading was a monopolist in the small world of the coalfields, but it was one road among many in the cutthroat rail industry. And when the Panic of 1873 sent the industry reeling, the Reading was forced to reduce costs wherever it could. The alternative was bankruptcy, which would displease shareholders but devastate employees, including the mining men of the anthracite country.

Yet the cost-reduction plan was painful enough. In the autumn of 1874 the Reading announced wage cuts of up to 20 percent, with additional cuts projected in the event coal prices kept falling. Whether Gowen expected the workers to accept the cuts was open to some doubt. For years the Reading had been battling the Workingmen's Benevolent Association, the largest union in the region; Gowen seems to have been looking for a showdown. If so, he got what he wanted. The WBA rejected management's terms and called a strike.

The stoppage shut down nearly all production in the anthracite region by January 1875. This timing would have favored the union—demand for coal peaked in winter—had Gowen and the Reading not been stockpiling coal for many months, partly on account of its low price but partly in preparation for a strike. The strike elicited surprising solidarity among the workers, given their ethnic and occupational divisions. The union also enjoyed considerable support among Pennsylvanians at large. This reflected the distrust of corporations in general and railroads in particular that was beginning to characterize large segments of the American population; it also reflected, paradoxically, the success of the Reading's stockpile strategy, which prevented Pennsylvanians from shivering for lack of fuel.

The workers held out for six months, a long time in the coal industry, where strikes typically lasted no more than weeks. (The 1875 strike would often be called simply the "Long Strike.") By late spring the lack of wages was telling severely on workers and their families. One union official, later recalling the hardship of this period, testified, "Hundreds of families rose in the morning to breakfast on a crust of bread and a glass of water. . . . Day after day men, women, and children went to the adjoining woods to dig roots and pick up herbs to keep body and soul together." Finally most workers gave in, and by the beginning of July nearly all the mines were back in operation, on Gowen's terms.[7]

YET THE STRUGGLE hadn't ended. Among the Irish miners was a mysterious network of radicals calling themselves "Molly Maguires." Who they were, how many they numbered, and how closely they conspired were questions that exercised the American legal imagination at the time and the American historical imagination afterward. Without doubt the Molly Maguires drew on a tradition of radicalism with roots in the Irish countryside, where secret societies of "Whiteboys," "Ribbonmen," and "Molly Maguires" protested evictions and other attacks on the rights and privileges, as the protesters interpreted them, of ordinary folk. The protesters responded with attacks of their own, including arson, assault, and even murder. Because the evictors were often British (or Irish in league with the British) and the protesters Irish, the movement acquired ethnic, cultural, and nationalistic overtones.

The radical tradition crossed the Atlantic with some of the Irish immigrants. In America it lost its nationalistic edge, though some of the anti-British feeling remained, exacerbated by the occupational differences in the coalfields between British and Irish miners. But the primary focus of the radicals was the management of the mines, and beginning in the 1860s foremen, superintendents, and the occasional mine owner fell victim to fatal assault. For years no one knew who the murderers were, or even whether the murders were related. Yet when the period of the Long Strike produced a rash of killings—eight attributed to the Molly Maguires between October 1874 and September 1875—the Pennsylvania authorities and the mine operators made apprehending the killers their first priority.

For help they turned to Allan Pinkerton, a former Chicago police investigator who in the decade after the Civil War transformed an ordinary detective agency into the intelligence arm of capitalist management. The Reading's Franklin Gowen, writing a retainer check to Pinkerton, told him to go after the Molly Maguires by any means necessary. "What we want, and everybody wants," he said (by Pinkerton's later account), "is to get within this apparently impenetrable ring; turn to the light the hidden side of this cruel and dark body."

Pinkerton accepted the challenge and considered what was required. "It is no ordinary man that I need in this matter," he explained to Gowen. "He must be an Irishman, and a Catholic, as only this class of persons can find admission to the Mollie Maguires. My detective should become, to all intents and purposes, one of the order, and continue so while he remains in the case before us. He should be hardy, tough, and capable of laboring, in season and out of season, to accomplish, unknown to those about him, a single absorbing object."[8]

The agent he assigned to the task was a reasonable approximation to the ideal. James McParlan was a native of Ulster who had worked in a chemical factory and a textile warehouse before emigrating to America just after the Civil War. In 1871 he joined the Pinkerton agency, and two years later Pinkerton put him on the Molly Maguire case. Pinkerton arranged for McParlan to assume the identity of one James McKenna, a drifter who wended his way to the anthracite district. Evidence indicated that Patrick Dormer, a Pottsville innkeeper, might be a Molly, and so McParlan, alias McKenna, made Dormer's inn a haunt. He treated the house to drinks, which pleased the proprietor as well as the customers, and he let slip that he was on the run from the law for counterfeiting—"shoving the queer," he called it—and murder. When his new friends insisted, he showed them samples of his handiwork, which looked just like the real money it was.

Pinkerton helped McParlan establish credibility by sending around detectives asking about him. McParlan helped his own case by striking up a romance with Mary Ann Higgins, the sister-in-law of another suspected Molly, Jimmy Kerrigan; the wooing gave McParlan an excuse for spending time around the Kerrigan house. Before long he had insinuated himself among what seemed to be the leadership of the secret organization.

Yet the closer he got, the greater the compulsion he felt to join. He accepted initiation into the Ancient Order of Hibernians, the Irish fraternal group to which all the Mollies seemed to belong. And he was drawn into planning for some of the attacks on the Reading management. At this point he faced the mole's dilemma: whether to inform the intended victim and thereby risk being discovered or to keep silent in the interest of the continuing investigation and perhaps let the victim die. By Pinkerton's account, McParlan sent warning in the case of at least one man targeted for death, who then escaped (temporarily). By his own admission, in another case McParlan failed to give effective warning, and people died.[9]

Though McParlan thought he knew the men behind some of the murders, he realized there was much he didn't know. And neither he nor Pinkerton had any confidence that what he did know would stand up in court. The Irish were famously loyal, one to the other, and amid a strike they stuck even closer together. Pinkerton doubted that any jury in the coal country would convict an Irish mine worker for killing a manager, almost regardless of the evidence. Those who didn't sympathize with the defendants would be intimidated by those who did.

So Pinkerton suggested an application of that standby of frustrated citizens, vigilante action. He circulated a handbill around the coal country. "The followings are the FACTS for the consideration of the Vigilance Committee of the Anthracite Coal Region, and all other good citizens who desire to preserve law and order in their midst," the handbill began. It proceeded to recount the late murders and attempted murders, and it listed the names of those it said were responsible for the crimes. Some of the men named were under arrest; others were at large. Pinkerton never acknowledged printing the bill, but textual evidence—misspellings consistent with misspellings in agency documents—pointed his way.

Pinkerton had reason to cover any connection to the handbill after masked men burst at night into the Wiggans Patch home of one of those on the list. The homeowner managed to escape, but another of those listed was murdered in the most brutal fashion. More shocking to many was the killing, apparently by mistake in the dark, of the wife of the homeowner.

The Wiggans Patch murders jolted everyone touched by the coalfield violence. The Catholic Church, which till now had equivocated on the Molly Maguires, was forced to take a stand. The local bishop excommunicated the Mollies. "Beware of the Molly Maguires," his right-hand priest explained. "If you have a brother among them, pray for his repentance but have nothing further to do with him—and remember that he is cut off from the Church."

Shortly thereafter the trials of three men previously arrested as Mollies began. The prosecution chose to try the cases separately, starting with the least sympathetic suspect. The state summoned 122 witnesses, who built a powerful circumstantial case against Michael Doyle. To the astonishment of nearly all observers, the defense didn't call a single witness, instead merely pointing out weaknesses in the prosecution's argument. The jury— which, tellingly, and by the prosecution's successful design, included no Irish—returned a guilty verdict. Three weeks later the judge sentenced Doyle to be hanged.[10]

As the prosecution had hoped, this initial verdict prompted reflection in the remaining prisoners. One, Jimmy Kerrigan, the kin of James McParlan's sweetheart, decided to turn state's evidence; he implicated several more Mollies, who were arrested shortly.

The trials continued. The second defendant, Edward Kelly, was convicted in April 1876 and sentenced to join Doyle on the scaffold. Jimmy Kerrigan got off in exchange for his testimony, but the prosecution of the other prisoners proceeded. As the evidence against these men was less convincing than that against Doyle and Kelly, the state's attorneys pressed Pinkerton to make McParlan take the stand. McParlan was predictably unhappy at having to reveal himself; he'd be useless for similar work in his chosen field, assuming he survived the likely assassination attempts by the Mollies or their friends. But McParlan's identity was leaked to the defense, apparently by a Catholic priest who differed with his bishop on the culpability of the Mollies, and McParlan had no choice but to testify.[11]

By this time the Molly Maguire prosecution was national news. Correspondents arrived from all over the country to report the trial. McParlan was the star witness for the prosecution, portraying the Mollies as a conspiracy dedicated to ruling the coal country by violence and intimidation.

The defense strove to impeach McParlan's testimony. It portrayed him as an agent provocateur, demanding to know why he hadn't tried to save the men targeted for death. "Why did you not go over yourself, from Columbia House, five miles to save the life of a man you knew was going to be assassinated?" the defense counsel asked.

"I was afraid of being assassinated myself," McParlan replied.

"You would not take that risk to save the life of John P. Jones?"

"I would not run the risk of losing my life for all the men in this Court House."

"You were playing the part of a detective and yet you would not take that much trouble to walk five miles?"

"Walking the five miles was nothing. I would walk twenty. . . . It was the saving of my own life I was looking to."[12]

McParlan's honesty apparently appealed to the jury, which seemed ready to convict the prisoners until one of jurors fell ill with pneumonia and died. The judge was compelled to declare a mistrial.

In the court of public opinion, however, the Mollies had already been convicted. "When the inner history of the Molly Maguires shall have been written," the *Philadelphia Inquirer* predicted, "it will embody the harrowing details of a conspiracy such as the world has rarely known. This history has been making itself through years of lawlessness, bloodshed, plunder and general anarchy." The Irish terrorists had done their best to blight the Commonwealth of Pennsylvania. "What Providence intended for a harvest of peace and plenty, the devilish ingenuity of banded cut-throats turned into a harvest of death and rapine. . . . Capital was fettered, honest labor held by the throat, and Red-Handed Murderers, Reeking with the blood of their victims, held high carnival over the prostrate form of Justice, blind and bleeding." The *New York Times* was slightly less wroth but no less convinced that the guilty must pay: "The Pennsylvania authorities owe it to civilization to extirpate this noxious growth, now that its roots have been discovered."[13]

New trials began and continued through the autumn of 1876 and into the new year. Beyond the men charged with murder, many others were prosecuted for conspiracy. Earlier fears of jury intimidation diminished as the jurors delivered one guilty verdict after another. By the beginning of June 1877, ten men had been convicted and sentenced to death for the coalfield murders.

The executions were scheduled for June 21. Six of the condemned would hang at Pottsville, four at Mauch Chunk. The sheriff at Pottsville initially wanted to dispatch all six of his prisoners at once, for maximum exemplary effect, and even had a special scaffold built. But for reasons unclear, he changed his mind and decided to execute them by pairs. Thousands of people gathered about the yard where the execution would take place. Some came for vicarious vindication; others wept for the doomed prisoners. A letter to one of the prisoners, James Roarity, from his father back in Ireland was printed in the local papers:

> *Dear Loving Son:*
>
> *I sit to write you the last letter that I'll ever write. . . . Don't be afraid to meet your doom or your Judge. If you are going to suffer innocent, I'm sure God will spare your soul, and it's far better to suffer in this world than in the world to come. . . . Before you die, declare to your Judge and to the world whether you are guilty or innocent. . . . And when your dear wife sees you, and the children, give them good encouragement, and keep yourself up. Certainly we are sorry, but what is the use? I did not tell your mother about it so far.*

The first two men carried roses to the scaffold. When the boards swung away beneath their feet and the ropes snapped tight about their necks, the scarlet petals scattered upon the ground. The next two, including James Roarity, proclaimed their innocence as the hangman prepared to repeat his work; then they also had their necks broken by the noose. Thomas Duffy had been kept till the last; the prosecutors apparently had less confidence in his conviction than in the others, and they wanted to leave open the possibility that a scaffold confession by one of the others would clear him. But none of them obliged, and he and the sixth prisoner went to their grim fate, too.

The Mauch Chunk executions were held indoors. The prisoners were manacled and hooded before the nooses were placed around their necks. Attending priests led them in prayer till the last moment, when the floor fell away beneath them all simultaneously. Two had their necks snapped cleanly; the others struggled before falling unconscious and finally strangling.

After the executions the Reading Railroad provided special trains to transport the bodies, packed in ice, to their homes for burial, and to take friends and relatives to the memorial services. The Catholic bishop, having proscribed the Molly Maguires, relented so far as to allow the executed men to be buried in consecrated ground. He wished he hadn't when the relatives of at least one of the men held a traditional Irish wake, of the pre-Christian sort the Church had been trying to stamp out in the old country for centuries. Far into the night the keening that had sent ancient Gaels into the afterlife drifted down the blackened valleys of the anthracite district.[14]

"THE STRUGGLE IS OVER," the *Miners' Journal* lamented in the wake of the coalmen's strike against Franklin Gowen and the Reading. "The war between Capital and Labor is ended, and Labor is not victor. It is not even the drawn battle signified by compromise; it is an unconditional surrender, a capitulation of all the army, and relinquishment of all the claim for which it fought." A miners' minstrel put the outcome to verse:

Well, we've been beaten, beaten all to smash
And now, sir, we've begun to feel the lash,
As wielded by a gigantic corporation,
Which runs the Commonwealth and ruins the nation.[15]

A few unions, though, lived to fight on. The Brotherhood of Locomotive Engineers represented drivers, brakemen, and other operating personnel on various railroads. The Reading, the Penn, the Erie, and the Baltimore & Ohio, after slashing one another with rate cuts following the Panic of 1873, called a halt to the competition in a series of secret meetings during the spring of 1877. "The great principle on which we all joined to act was to earn more and spend less," Hugh Jewett of the Erie reported to an approving J. P. Morgan. The greater earnings would come from customers, who would be compelled by the cartel's new rate structure to pay more; the lesser spending would come from the railroads' employees, who would be forced to accept pay cuts.[16]

The engineers on the Reading were the first to respond when the owners announced the cuts. In April 1877 the engineers' brotherhood called a strike, and half the drivers walked off the job. But Franklin Gowen, flushed with his victory over the miners and the Molly Maguires, quickly struck back. He ordered his managers into the cabs and cabooses and paid bonuses to those regular engineers who stayed at work. When short-staffed trains derailed and wrecked, he blamed the brotherhood for sabotage and persuaded various editors to print his explanation. Within weeks the strike collapsed, breaking the union on the Reading and demoralizing its members elsewhere. The pro-management *New York Times* applauded the result. "The Brotherhood is destroyed as a dictatorial body," the paper proclaimed. "Neither railroad nor engineer will fear it henceforth or regard its ukases."[17]

Yet the Reading was a small fish in this particular pool. The whale was the Penn, which had outgrown the state of its name to become a transportation empire, with tracks that ran from the Atlantic to the Mississippi and from the Great Lakes to the Ohio. Capitalized at nearly $400 million, it was the largest corporation in America. Tom Scott, its president, had won political friends for the line during the Civil War by moving Union troops swiftly and surely; after the war he remembered his friends and they him.

But Scott had to contend with John Rockefeller, who was currently launching his revolution of oil transport. Rockefeller was starting to purchase pipelines; Scott warned him to stick to refining and let the shippers handle the carrying trade. When Rockefeller ignored the warning, Scott fired a larger shot across his bow by having a Penn ally, the Empire Transportation Company, enter the field of refining. This succeeded in getting Rockefeller's attention. He went straight to Scott and demanded that he desist. The Empire had no business in refining, Rockefeller said. He added that Scott had a choice: immediate withdrawal or industrial war. Scott refused to back down, and America's biggest railroad and its largest oil company locked in combat. Rockefeller canceled his contracts with the Penn and transferred his business to Scott's railroad rivals. To help them handle the shipments he placed a rush order for six hundred new tank cars. He closed his refineries in Pittsburgh, a Penn-dominated city, and increased production in Cleveland, controlled by the Penn's competitors. He undercut the Empire in every market where that company sold kerosene. The effect was dramatic. Between the shrunken traffic and the lost sales, the Penn began hemorrhaging cash. By the beginning of June 1877 it had bled a million dollars.[18]

Prudence suggested that Scott capitulate, but he was too proud and stubborn. Instead he called a June 4 meeting with a delegation from the engineers' union. He described the dire condition of the company and explained the need for cost savings. The shareholders had done their part, he said; dividends had been cut 40 percent. It was only fair for the workers to accept a cut. So far the workers had given back a mere 20 percent; surely they could give a bit more. Otherwise they all—Scott included himself here—might be out of jobs.

Scott hadn't risen to the top of the railroad industry without possessing skills of persuasion, and the workers' committee left this meeting accepting Scott's argument, if reluctantly. They managed to get the leaders of most of the local chapters of the union to join them. But longshoremen at the Penn's docks in New York, suffering from a recent pay cut that put their hourly wage at thirteen and a half cents (down from twenty cents before the cutting began), staged a wildcat strike.

The stoppage didn't last. Scott offered to restore a half cent to the wage even as he ordered other company workers to fill in for the striking dockers. Between the promise and the threat, the longshoremen felt compelled to take the half penny and return to work.[19]

Scott's success inspired other railroads to institute similar cuts and to require workers to sign "yellow dog" contracts banning unions. "I do agree to keep out of all combinations of men encouraging strikes, and in case of strikes or combinations, will work faithfully for the company's interest," a typical contract read. But the cuts and the contractual duress caused the resentment against the railroads to fester and grow. Penn workers in Pittsburgh formed a new organization, the Trainmen's Union, that aimed to unite all railroad workers against the companies. Several hundred men signed up at once, despite infiltration by company spies and orders by company executives to fire any workers who joined the new union.[20]

At Martinsburg, West Virginia, workers on the Baltimore & Ohio who had recently been recruited to the Trainmen's Union reacted to the pay cuts by seizing a cattle train, detaching its locomotives, and stranding the cars on the main east-west line. The mayor of Martinsburg called out the police, but the townspeople, who had long chafed at their dependence on the railroad, sided with the workers, hoisting the brakeman who had initiated the stoppage to their shoulders and parading him heroically about the town.

Company officials appealed to the governor of the state, Henry Mathews, for protection of their property. Mathews weighed the votes of the workers and their friends against the money and influence of the railroads and chose the latter. He summoned the militia and ordered it to ensure the safety of the trains and the freedom of commerce. A special train carrying the state troops approached Martinsburg, where it was surrounded by a jeering mob. One of the strikers had thrown a derail switch; as the train slowly approached, an armed soldier leaped down and tried to restore the switch to its safe position. The striker fired a pistol at the soldier, who shot back, hitting the man in the head but miraculously not killing him. Other soldiers, however, opened fire, fatally wounding the striker.

Within minutes reports of the shootings flew east and west along the telegraph wires that flanked the rail line. Governor Mathews grew alarmed and appealed to President Rutherford Hayes for help. "Owing to unlawful combinations and domestic violence now existing at Martinsburg and at other points along the line of the Baltimore and Ohio railroad, it is impossible with any force at my command to execute the laws of the State," Mathews wrote. "I therefore call upon your Excellency for the assistance of the United States military." The head of the B&O, John Garrett, seconded the appeal. "This great national highway," Garrett told Hayes, referring to the railroad, "can only be restored for public use by the interposition of the U.S. forces." Garrett warned that the fate of the nation hung in the balance: "Unless this difficulty is immediately stopped, I apprehend the gravest consequences, not only upon our line, but upon all the lines in the country which, like ourselves, have been obliged to introduce measures of economy in these trying times."[21]

Hayes had dealt with the insurrection of the South during the Civil War, when he served as major general in the Union army. After the war, as governor of Ohio, he had deployed his state's militia to counter a coal miners' strike there. Now, as leader of the party of business and the recipient of campaign donations from Tom Scott and other railroad executives, he acted with equal decisiveness in ordering federal troops from the arsenal at Washington and from Fort McHenry at Baltimore to Martinsburg.[22]

The federal force quelled the uprising in West Virginia, which had begun to dissipate on its own. But the troubles leapfrogged the troop train to Baltimore. Maryland's first city was reeling from the depression; industrial workers, who constituted perhaps a third of the labor force, had suffered job reductions and pay cuts that were, if anything, worse than those afflicting the railroad engineers. "The working people everywhere are with us," one rail unionist told a reporter. "They know what it is to bring up a family on ninety cents a day, to live on beans and corn meal week in and week out, to run in debt at the stores until you cannot get trusted any longer, to see the wife breaking down under privation and distress, and the children growing sharp and fierce like wolves day after day because they don't get enough to eat."

As a result, when Baltimore rail workers struck the B&O in July 1877, a friendly populace applauded them. "There is no disguising the fact that the strikers in all their lawful acts have the fullest sympathy of the community," the *Baltimore Sun* reported. Even the *un*lawful acts evoked substantial support. When the governor summoned the state militia to keep the strikers in line, Baltimore erupted in riot. Workers heaved rocks and bricks at the militiamen, who responded with rifle fire. Members of the crowd— which the vice president of the B&O called "the fiercest mob ever known in Baltimore"— produced firearms of their own, and the streets of the city became shooting galleries. One part of the crowd cornered a regiment of militia in the railroad station while others began destroying rail stock. Three men (or boys: to some witnesses they looked quite young) commandeered a locomotive, built up a full head of steam, opened the throttle, and jumped off to watch with glee as the engine crashed into some railcars before taking out a loading platform, shattering a dispatcher's office, and overturning itself with its wheels still spinning.

The terrified militiamen effected their escape by charging through the crowd with leveled bayonets. The crowd retreated but continued its destruction of railroad property, ripping rails from the ties, breaking windows, and setting trains alight. When firemen arrived to battle the blaze, the rioters cut their hoses and sabotaged their pumps.

Nightfall brought the calm of exhaustion and a reckoning of the casualties. At least ten people were dead, all of them members of the crowd. Additional dozens, including several militiamen, were wounded. Property damage was impossible to estimate so long as some of the fires still burned.[23]

THE VIOLENCE SPREAD to Pittsburgh. The depression had hammered the steel city, and though the steel industry was slowly recovering, the plants were operating far below capacity. Millworkers were restive and willing to lend support to their fellows of the rails. "We're with you," a steelman told the local of the Trainmen's Union. "We're in the same boat. I heard a reduction of ten per cent hinted at in our mills this morning. I won't call employers despots; I won't call them tyrants. But the term capitalists is sort of synonymous and will do as well."

The labor solidarity spooked the guardians of the status quo. The *Pittsburgh Leader* reported what it deemed the ravings of a "representative workingman" who had declared that the recent events "may be the beginning of a great civil war in this country, between labor and capital." The union man told the governor not to bother calling out the militia. "The laboring people, who mostly constitute the militia, will not take up arms to put down their brethren," he predicted. Should President Hayes send in the army, the federal troops would be "swept from our path like leaves in the whirlwind." America belonged to its people. "The workingmen of this country can capture and hold it, if they will only stick together." The capitalists might win a round or two, but the workers would finally "have our revenge on the men who have coined our sweat and muscle into millions for themselves."[24]

The local militia commander braced for the worst. Having orders to keep the peace but distrusting the Pittsburgh militiamen to fire on their neighbors, he requested reinforcements from Philadelphia. He prepared for their arrival by mounting two cannons above a road crossing of the Penn tracks. As the troop trains from Philadelphia approached the crossing, hundreds of workers and their supporters clogged the road and the track. The crowd pelted the trains with epithets, rocks, and paving stones. Rifle barrels ominously emerged from the train windows. But to the obvious relief of most and the apparent disappointment of some, no one fired. The trains inched slowly through the crowd to the downtown depot.

There the six hundred militiamen debarked from the cars and got ready to return to the crossing to clear the crowd. A Pittsburgh steel manufacturer, James Park, warned Alexander Cassatt of the Penn against hasty action. It was Saturday afternoon, and most of the steelworkers had started their weekend, which meant they were drinking and were available to join the rail workers. "I think I know the temper of our men pretty well," Park told Cassatt. "You would be wise not to do anything until Monday." He added that Cassatt didn't have enough militia. "If there's going to be firing, you ought to have at least ten thousand men, and I doubt if even that many could quell the mob that would be brought down on us."

Cassatt closed his ears. "We must have our property," he declared. "We have lost an hour and a half's time."

The militia moved out, shouldering rifles and pulling two Gatling guns. At the head of the column were the sheriff and more than a dozen deputies, carrying warrants for the arrest of eleven workers alleged to be instigators of the strike.

By now the crowd at the crossing numbered several thousand. They shouted at the soldiers and cursed the sheriff and the deputies. Many of the militia felt torn. One of their officers later observed, "Meeting an enemy on the field of battle, you go there to kill. The more you kill, and the quicker you do it, the better. But here you had men with fathers and brothers and relatives mingled in the crowd of rioters. The sympathy of the people, the sympathy of the troops, my own sympathy, was with the strikers. . . . We all felt that those men were not receiving enough wages." But the officer had his job, and his orders. "The tracks must be cleared," he said.

The men leveled their bayonets and pushed into the crowd. Those persons closest to the troops started to move away, but the wall of flesh behind them prevented escape. Some turned and tried to wrest the rifles from the soldiers' grasp. Meanwhile members of the crowd farther away began hurling stones and chunks of coal at the troops. A witness recalled that one soldier "had the whole side of his face knocked off by a brick."

The crowd taunted the soldiers: "Shoot, you sons of bitches, why don't you shoot?" Firecrackers left over from Independence Day, just two weeks earlier, began exploding. Someone fired real shots—perhaps one of the soldiers, frightened for his life, perhaps a member of the crowd. The militia officers later denied having given the order to fire, but several said they would have done so if the firing hadn't started on its own. In the time it took the crowd to realize that guns, and not firecrackers, were the source of the popping sounds heard over the general tumult, more than a dozen people were killed or fatally wounded. The casualties included women and children. A four-year-old girl's knee was shattered by a rifle bullet, and the leg had to be amputated.

The militia gained control of the crossing but in the bargain lost the city. "It was evident," one reporter asserted, "that the whole labor interest of Pittsburgh was about to fight the Pennsylvania Railroad." The crowd that abandoned the crossing regathered at the Penn rail yards three blocks away. Individuals began torching freight cars, and then cars containing coke for the steel mills, and then anything else that would burn. To spread the fire some of the strikers rolled the flaming cars downhill and deliberately derailed them, spilling their fiery contents across the tracks and grounds. A roundhouse caught fire. Meanwhile a second wing of the mob attacked a federal arsenal nearby, seizing its weapons, including some cannons; when firemen arrived to extinguish the roundhouse blaze, the rioters trained a cannon on them and forced them to let the building burn. New fires broke out in several places around the city, obviously set separately. Looters followed the arsonists and didn't confine themselves to railroad property. During all of Saturday evening and into Sunday morning a general conflagration threatened the city.[25]

Sunday newspapers weren't common in the 1870s, but the events in Pittsburgh that weekend prompted publishers in several cities to print special editions. "Pittsburgh Sacked," a typical headline read. "More Bloodshed!" The publishers doubtless believed they were doing their civic duty in reporting the breaking news; they certainly also appreciated the windfall profits the special editions generated. Not since the Civil War had papers sold so fast. The profit incentive trickled down to the newsboys who hawked the special editions on the street. "Strikers' war!" they shouted. "Bloody battle in Pittsburgh!"

Most editors condemned the violence, but a few of the Pittsburgh papers (in those days most cities had several papers) sided with the strikers. One called the ongoing events "the Lexington of the labor conflict." Another, with a large working-class readership, asserted, "There is tyranny in this country worse than anything ever known in Russia. . . . Capital has raised itself on the ruins of labor. The laboring class cannot, will not stand this any longer. The war cry has been raised. . . . The principle that freed our nation from tyranny will free labor from domestic aggression."[26]

This hope of the workers was precisely the fear of the capitalists—and of many Americans with no such distinct class affiliations. Since the multinational revolutions of 1848, the "specter of communism," as Karl Marx and Friedrich Engels then put it, had been haunting Europe and the capitalist strongholds of America. But a more recent memory had a larger impact. In 1871 socialists in Paris had taken control of the French city, establishing a "commune," a nascent workers' republic that denied the primacy of capital and challenged existing property relations. The Communards employed lethal violence against their class enemies, who eventually rallied the army and crushed the socialist experiment. The corpses of tens of thousands of revolutionaries and their kin littered the streets of Paris.

Every capitalist in America knew about the Paris Commune, and most had congratulated themselves that such anarchy wasn't possible in America. But the events in Pittsburgh smacked hard of anarchy. "War between labor and capital has begun in earnest," the *New Orleans Times* asserted. "America's first experience in communism is now the most significant episode of the most extraordinary year in our political history." The *Pittsburgh Leader*, in the article reporting the labor radical's declaration of civil war between labor and capital, concluded, "It will be seen that he is really a communist." The *New York Times* decried the "tyranny of trades-unionism" and the "reign of mob law." The *New York World* wondered succinctly in a headline: "Riot or Revolution?"[27]

THE STRIKE NOW spread across the country as tens of thousands of rail workers walked off the job. Many engaged in violence similar to that in Baltimore and Pittsburgh. In Buffalo an angry crowd besieged a militia regiment protecting a roundhouse of the Erie Railroad. Rocks rained down on the troops, who prepared to fire on their assailants. The crowd, painfully aware of the events at Pittsburgh, scattered—only to regroup at the yards of the New York Central. William Vanderbilt, who had learned some lessons himself from the Pittsburgh rioting, declined to challenge the strikers or fuel their arson. He simply suspended all New York Central traffic to Buffalo. The mob, eventually discerning Vanderbilt's strategy, returned to the Erie yards, where they seized trains and manhandled their replacement crews. When a train arrived carrying militia reinforcements, the crowd fired on and stormed the cars, provoking the soldiers to return fire. Several rioters were killed and a comparable number of the soldiers wounded. As Buffalo was less friendly to workers than Pittsburgh, the sheriff had little difficulty deputizing some three hundred citizens, who supplemented the regular Buffalo police force. The latter, armed with riot sticks, caught up with a small crowd burning some New York Central rolling stock Vanderbilt hadn't managed to extricate. The police captain gave the order to charge. "Like lightning the clubs ascended and descended," an appreciative reporter explained. "Every stroke hit a new head whose owner went solid to the ground or bowled in continued somersaults. The officers seemed to put their whole souls into this commendable work. . . . Those who did not get hit fled as fast as legs could carry them. . . . A howling chorus of pain could be heard at the high trestle more than a mile way. The rout was complete and final."

At Reading, Pennsylvania, rail workers and sympathizers sacked the depot of Franklin Gowen's Reading Railroad. Lest they be fingered by company spies, the rioters painted their faces with coal dust before tearing up track, derailing and burning cars, and smashing equipment. They then marched to an iron-and-wooden bridge that spanned the Schuylkill River at the edge of town, soaked the timbers with coal oil, and set the structure ablaze. The bridge burned against the night sky till, to the cheers of the crowd, it crashed sizzling into the stream. Other rioters clashed with imported militiamen (some of whom came from the anthracite district, which they had patrolled on the day of the Molly Maguire hangings, to foil rescue attempts). Rocks and pistol fire struck the militiamen, who fired back at their assailants. Nearly a dozen persons were killed outright or mortally wounded.[28]

Railmen in Ohio halted trains there, although they didn't have to try very hard as the shutdown farther east kept most trains from entering the state. A crowd in Cincinnati burned a bridge and might have burned other railroad property but for a drenching rain that kept putting out the fires they started. Serious trouble in Toledo was averted only after the police commissioner expressed his support for the strikers. "You are not slaves, gentlemen," he said. "And I am glad to see you assert your manhood." In Newark, a would-be strikebreaker was confronted by a striker shaking a fist, missing three fingers, in the man's face. One of the striker's comrades declared, "This is the man whose place you are taking. This is the man who works with a hand and a half to earn a dollar and a half a day, three days in the week, for his wife and children. Are you going to take the bread out of his mouth and theirs?" The strikebreaker changed his mind and left.

In Chicago, memories of the Great Fire of 1871 made everyone nervous about arson. Strikers seized trains of the several lines that converged at the city, while the police and militia girded for battle and the city elders decried the challenge to the rule of law. "As God lives and my soul lives," the pastor of the Unity Church declared, "I would rather die in twenty minutes in defense of order and of our houses, against these men, than to live twenty years of as happy a life as I have lived all these fifty years."

When a squadron of police encountered a large crowd of rioters, batons and bullets felled the rioters by the dozen. "The blood and brains were oozing down his neck," a reporter said of one rioter clubbed while trying to flee. "But buoyed by the unnatural excitement, he managed to continue with the others for quite a distance without falling. When he did fall, he was borne away by his comrades." Another rioter wasn't so lucky. "He fell with a bullet through the base of his uncultivated brain and lay like a log upon the pavement."

The strike continued to spread—to St. Louis, which saw the spectacle of German-born radicals singing the French "Marseillaise" in symbolic solidarity with workers everywhere; to Galveston, which witnessed an alliance of African American and white workers; to Omaha, where the threat of violence compelled the management of the Union Pacific to rescind a recent pay cut; to San Francisco, where a large crowd cheered the burning of a wharf of the Pacific Mail Steamship Line, a subsidiary of the Central Pacific Railroad. (The San Francisco crowd completed the evening in customary California fashion, by rampaging through Chinatown.)[29]

THE GREAT STRIKE, as it was called as soon as its magnitude became apparent, was an artifact of the industrial era in one obvious way and one less patent. The obvious aspect was that workers felt themselves confronting a capitalist monolith. To be sure, the railroad corporations competed among themselves, but they acted alike toward their workers. When one cut wages, the rest did. When one hired Pinkertons and planted spies, the others followed. From a worker's perspective, the salient characteristic of the modern age was consolidation. The railroads grew bigger and more powerful, by honest means and corrupt. The only hope for the workingman was offsetting consolidation. Labor unions were the first line of defense; where these needed to be supplemented by non-union workers and auxiliary crowds, perhaps armed with rocks and matches, more than a few unionists were willing to accept the help.

The less obvious aspect of the Great Strike was that it would not have been possible—that is, it would never have metastasized the way it did— without modern communications technology. The strike spread with the speed of telegraphy; San Francisco was rioting within days of the first battle in Pittsburgh. Had eastern rail workers walked off the job a generation earlier, the West wouldn't have heard about their action for weeks, not till the exhausted Pony Express rider dropped his saddlebags in Sacramento.

And by then it would have been too late. After the outbreak of urban warfare in Pittsburgh, President Hayes felt enormous pressure to send federal troops to the rescue, as he had in Martinsburg. Railroad officials joined state and local authorities in pleading for the kind of muscle only the army of the Union could supply. But no sooner had Pittsburgh called than similar demands arose from Buffalo and Chicago and St. Louis. Even if he had wanted to accede to the demands, Hayes didn't know where he'd get the troops. The huge Union army of the Civil War had long since dwindled to a force that could barely guard the frontier against Indians. If the president hoped to answer all the requests for troops, he'd have to ask for volunteers. But doing so would sound alarmist. The country was nervous enough already; Hayes wanted to calm things, not stir them up. "Tell the President a call for volunteers will precipitate a revolution," a correspondent from Cincinnati wrote John Sherman, Hayes's secretary of the Treasury. "Tell him I speak advisedly." Besides, as the man who had just ended the military occupation of the South, Hayes hardly wanted to be known as the one who initiated the occupation of the North.[30]

So he bided his time. And as he did, the strike began to run out of steam. To some extent it was a victim of its own success. By now the strike had stopped or slowed traffic on perhaps two-thirds of the nation's 75,000 miles of track. But because the strike had no central leadership, there was no way to coordinate the actions of all the strikers. Moreover, because most of the strikers belonged to no union, they lacked strike funds or other reserves that might have enabled them to survive without paychecks for more than a few weeks.

The railroads, by comparison, had very deep pockets. Even those that were in financial trouble had cash reserves that dwarfed anything the strikers could command. And though the railroads were less than united among themselves, their far smaller number than the strikers afforded them a decisive organizational advantage. By offering modest concessions here and there, they could hope to entice the most desperate workers back to the job and break the will of the rest.

They received crucial assistance from the courts. Some of the insolvent railroads had gone into receivership, making them wards of the federal courts. Clever lawyers for the railroads contended that this meant that obstructers of the operation of those railroads could be held in contempt of court, and sympathetic judges agreed. Federal arrest warrants against the leaders of the strike supplemented warrants approved by local courts.[31]

Against this opposition, the strikers were forced to retreat, then capitulate. Within weeks of its start, the Great Strike of 1877 was over. Conventional wisdom held that the strikers had lost, and in the near term they had. The workers were forced to accept most of the pay cuts that had started the whole affair. But labor learned from its failures. The conditions that gave rise to the strike hadn't disappeared, and the next time the workers went out, they would be better prepared.

Nor were they the only ones who learned from the experience. "The strikes have been put down by *force*," Hayes wrote in his diary in early August. "But now for the *real* remedy. Can't something be done by education of the strikers, by judicious control of the capitalists, by wise general policy to end or diminish the evil? The railroad strikers, as a rule, are good men, sober, intelligent, and industrious." To a friend he wrote, "If anything can be done to remove the distress which afflicts laborers, and to stimulate enterprises, I am ready and not afraid to do my share towards it."[32]

Part Two

FRONTIERS OF ENTERPRISE

Chapter 5

THE CONQUEST OF THE SOUTH

———

Booker T. Washington never forgot the moment of his emancipation. "Freedom was in the air, and had been for months," he wrote later. Washington was a boy of five or six—like many slaves, he didn't know precisely when he had been born—and was living on a plantation in Franklin County, Virginia, as the Union army approached. "Deserting soldiers returning to their homes were to be seen every day. Others who had been discharged, or whose regiments had been paroled, were constantly passing near our place. The 'grape-vine telegraph' was kept busy night and day. The news and mutterings of great events were swiftly carried from one plantation to another." The anticipation increased, and acquired a distinctive tone.

As the great day drew nearer, there was more singing in the slave quarters than usual. It was bolder, had more ring, and lasted later into the night. Most of the verses of the plantation songs had some reference to freedom. True, they had sung those same verses before, but they had been careful to explain that the "freedom" in these songs referred to the next world, and had no connection with life in this world. Now they gradually threw off the mask, and were not afraid to let it be known that the "freedom" in their songs meant freedom of the body in this world.

The night before the eventful day, word was sent to the slave quarters to the effect that something unusual was going to take place at the "big house" the next morning. There was little, if any, sleep that night. All was excitement and expectancy. Early the next morning word was sent to all the slaves, old and young, to gather at the house. In company with my mother, brother, and sister, and a large number of other slaves, I went to the master's house. . . .

The most distinct thing that I now recall in connection with the scene was that some man who seemed to be a stranger (a United States officer, I presume) made a little speech and then read a rather long paper—the Emancipation Proclamation, I think. After the reading we were told that we were all free, and could go when and where we pleased. My mother, who was standing by my side, leaned over and kissed her children, while tears of joy ran down her cheeks. She explained to us what it all meant, that this was the day for which she had been so long praying, but fearing that she would never live to see.[1]

THE FIRST TASK of American democracy after the Civil War was to determine how the Union would be reconstructed. Secession and the war had upset the balance crafted and maintained during the previous several decades; to what extent the balance would be restored, and what would supplant the part of it that wasn't, were the most obvious questions facing the federal government, the states, and the American people at the war's end.

Had the fighting somehow ceased before 1863, political readjustments might have been the total of reconstruction. But emancipation added other, more complicated dimensions. The transformation of four million slaves into four million free men, women, and children was the most dramatic change in the history of American society. How the South and the nation as a whole would accommodate this change became the pressing issue as the war ended. Would the South and the nation move forward, toward a more comprehensive equality between blacks and whites? Or would the country accept something less, perhaps a caste-based system of peonage for African Americans? The Northern president had proclaimed emancipation in his role as commander in chief, and Northern troops enforced his proclamation as they defeated and occupied the South. But the president's war powers would diminish with the end of the war, and the troops would eventually go home. What they would leave behind was anyone's guess.

Inseparable from the social consequences of emancipation were the economic ramifications. Before slavery became an institution of social control, it had been a system of labor mobilization. The Southern economy in 1860 rested on the bound labor of African Americans. Emancipation compelled Southern planters and other consumers of labor in the South to find new methods of mobilizing the labor force. Many Northerners assumed that the labor system that worked in the North—the market-based exchange of labor for money—could be reproduced in the South. Most white Southerners doubted that such a system could work in Dixie or that it should if it could. As for the freed men and women, they had their own ideas, which didn't accord neatly with the thinking of the whites of either camp.

Even as capitalism revolutionized life within the South, it transformed the role of the South in the nation at large. Until the Civil War the semi-feudal Southern economy had stood apart from the rest of the national marketplace. Connections existed, of course; Southerners sent cotton north and brought manufactured goods south. But investors and especially immigrants preferred the North and the West, where the rewards to labor were more attractive and the laws of property less peculiar. The end of slavery made the South a new frontier for capitalist expansion, a frontier to be integrated, with ease or difficulty, into the booming postwar economy.

WILLIAM SHERMAN HAD been about as unradical on the race question when the war began as a man could be and not own slaves himself. He was belligerently apolitical, having conceded the political role in his family to his younger brother John, a Republican congressman from their home state of Ohio. William Sherman's antipathy to politics reflected his belief that every issue was being reduced to what he called "the nigger question," and he warned John to "avoid the subject as a dirty black one." He told his foster brother Thomas Ewing (who was also his brother-in-law): "I would not if I could abolish or modify slavery. . . . I don't know that I would materially change the actual political relation of master and slave. Negroes in the great numbers that exist here"—Sherman happened to be writing from Louisiana—"must of necessity be slaves."[2]

Sherman's attitude was unexceptional in the North before the war, and it remained unexceptional after the fighting began. Yet it afforded Sherman's political enemies an opening for attack, and it allowed the Radical Republicans—those members of the governing party most committed to broader rights for African Americans—to press their case at Sherman's expense. "While almost every one is praising your great march through Georgia, and the capture of Savannah," Chief of Staff Henry W. Halleck wrote from Washington at the end of December 1864, "there is a certain class having now great influence with the President, and very probably anticipating still more on a change of cabinet, who are decidedly disposed to make a point against you. . . . They say that you have manifested an almost *criminal* dislike to the negro, and that you are not willing to carry out the wishes of the Government in regard to him, but repulse him with contempt!" The Radicals' complaint against Sherman was that he hadn't done enough to liberate slaves on his march across Georgia and South Carolina. Halleck said he understood why Sherman had not welcomed large numbers of fugitive slaves into his lines—"because you had not the means of supporting them, and feared they might seriously embarrass your march"—but he thought Sherman ought to know what was being said about him, and he wondered if now that Sherman had reached the coast, where supplies were no longer a problem, he might reconsider his policy.[3]

About this time, Sherman received a visit from Secretary of War Edwin M. Stanton. Sherman distrusted Stanton, an ally of the Radicals, as much as he distrusted most politicians (conspicuous exceptions being his brother and Lincoln). But he suppressed his suspicions and bore the visit as best he could. "Mr. Stanton seemed desirous of coming into contact with the negroes to confer with them, and he asked me to arrange an interview for him," Sherman recounted. Sherman complied, inviting dozens of black leaders from the vicinity of Savannah, mostly Baptist and Methodist preachers, to sit down with the war secretary. Twenty appeared, and these chose Garrison Frazier as their spokesman. Stanton asked the group if they knew about the Emancipation Proclamation. Frazier said they certainly did. "All the slaves in the Southern states should be free, henceforth and forever," he paraphrased.

Stanton asked how Frazier and the others conceived of slavery and freedom. Frazier answered, "Slavery is receiving by irresistible power the work of another man, and not by his consent. The freedom, as I understand it, promised by the proclamation, is taking us from under the yoke of bondage and placing us where we can reap the fruit of our own labor, and take care of ourselves and assist the government in maintaining our freedom."

Stanton asked whether the blacks preferred to live among whites or by themselves. "I would prefer to live by ourselves," Frazier said, "for there is a prejudice against us in the South that will take years to get over." But Frazier added that on this point he could speak only for himself. "I do not know that I can answer for my brethren."

Sherman had been present at the interview till now. Stanton asked him to leave, as he wished to probe the freedmen's opinion of the general, especially as it related to their emancipation and future condition. Sherman heard the answer later. "We looked upon General Sherman, prior to his arrival, as a man, in the providence of God, specially set apart to accomplish this work," Frazier said. "And we unanimously felt inexpressible gratitude to him, looking upon him as a man who should be honored for the faithful performance of his duty. Some of us called upon him immediately upon his arrival, and it is probable he did not meet the secretary with more courtesy than he did us. . . . We have confidence in General Sherman, and think what concerns us could not be in better hands."[4]

Frazier and the other black leaders shortly had their judgment confirmed. Sherman was one of the many Northerners—starting with Lincoln and running far down the chain of command—whose views on the race question changed dramatically during the course of the war. His prewar hostility to blacks had less to do with the blacks themselves than with the fact that their condition was the cause of the rupture of the Union. But once the rupture occurred, Sherman's anger found a new target: the secessionists. And blacks became potential allies in defeating and punishing the rebels. Even more than Lincoln, Sherman viewed emancipation as an act of war. Slavery had caused the war; emancipation would help end it. Emancipation would destroy the Southern economy—more thoroughly than his own march from Atlanta to the sea had done—and would thereby terminate the ability of the South to carry on the war. And it would prevent the South from starting any more wars.

Yet for emancipation to be real, it had to be followed by measures to make the former slaves independent of their erstwhile masters. To this end Sherman issued an order in January 1865 that had enormous symbolic impact and made him the improbable embodiment of Radical

Reconstruction. "The islands from Charleston south," Special Field Order 15 stated, "the abandoned rice-fields along the rivers for thirty miles back from the sea, and the country bordering the St. John's River, Florida, are reserved and set apart for the settlement of the negroes now made free by the acts of war and the proclamation of the President of the United States." The order continued: "On the islands, and in the settlements hereafter to be established, no white person whatever, unless military officers and soldiers detailed for duty, will be permitted to reside; and the sole and exclusive management of affairs will be left to the freed people themselves, subject only to the United States military authority, and the acts of Congress." On the lands reserved to the freedmen, heads of families might claim parcels as their own. "Each family shall have a plot of not more than forty acres."[5]

Sherman later directed that confiscated mules be made available to the black settlers. Special Order 15, together with this decision, became the basis for the slogan "Forty acres and a mule" that served as a beacon to black hopes and the battle cry of the Radical Reconstructionists. In the process it confirmed Sherman's reputation among Southern whites as the devil incarnate.

GERTRUDE THOMAS WAS among those who uttered a prophylactic prayer when they heard Sherman's name. The daughter of one Georgia planter and the wife of another, Gertrude Thomas was living in Augusta when Sherman's army swept through and wreaked havoc on her family's property. She seethed with indignation at Sherman's violation of the accepted rules of warfare, and in her anger she imagined herself writing a letter to Ellen Sherman, the general's wife. A message from Mrs. Sherman to her husband had found its way into Southern papers recently, and it provided the literary stimulus to Gertrude Thomas's response.

> *Mrs. General Sherman. . . . I, a rebel lady, will give you some infor-mation with regard to General Sherman's movements. Last week your hus-band's army found me in the possession of wealth. Tonight our plantations are a scene of ruin and desolation. You bade him "God speed" on his fiendish errand, did you not? You thought it a gallant deed to come amongst us where by his own confession he expected to find "only the shadow of an army." A brave act to frighten women and children! desolate homes, violate the sanc-*

tity of firesides and cause the "widow and orphan to curse Sherman for the cause." And this you did for what? To elevate the Negro race.

Mrs. Sherman must know what the elevation of the Negro entailed.

> *Enquire of General Sherman when next you see him who has been elevated to fill your place. You doubtless read with a smile of approbation of the delightfully fragrant ball at which he made his debut in Atlanta? Did he tell you of the Mulatto girl for whose safety he was so much concerned that she was returned to Nashville when he commenced his vandal march? This girl was spoken of by the Negroes whom you are willing to trust so implicitly as "Sherman's wife."*
>
> *Rest satisfied, Mrs. Sherman, and quiet the apprehension of your Northern sisters with regard to the elevation of the Negroes. Your husbands are amongst a coloured race whose reputation for morality has never been of the highest order. And these gallant cavaliers are most of them provided with "a companion du voyage."*

Perhaps Mrs. Sherman felt sorry for those whose homes and lives her husband wrecked. She shouldn't bother.

> *As your brave husband considers a southern lady a fair object to wage war against, and as I do not yet feel fully satisfied that there is no danger of a clutch from his heavy hand upon my shoulders, I will only add that, intensely Southern woman that I am, I pity you.* [6]

Gertrude Thomas did not mail this letter. Even if postal operations hadn't been disrupted by the war, she was too much the gentlewoman to intrude on another gentlewoman's private life. She prided herself on the manners she had learned at the Wesleyan Female College of Macon, Georgia, and she took pains to display them as the mistress of one of Augusta's most distinguished households.

Until Sherman brought the war to Georgia, the Thomas household had comprised Gertrude; her husband, Jefferson; their four children; and several slaves. The family property included the house in Augusta and various farms outside the town, with the many slaves that worked the farms. Sherman's soldiers ravaged the farms and encouraged the field hands to flee. Gertrude's situation would have been discouraging under any circumstances, but that she was pregnant again rendered her predicament even more dismaying. "I make no plans for the future," she wrote in her journal, despite the fact that she dearly wished to know where and under what circumstances her baby would be born. "During the first months of pregnancy I am always sadly depressed, and, the body acting upon the mind, my whole nature is affected. This time I was congratulating myself that I was going through the terrible ordeal in better style, but thanks to General Sherman . . . my nervous system received a shock which was terrible. I was made really sick by the combined prospect of Sherman's visit and the burning cotton." Like most prospective mothers she looked to the time of her delivery with some trepidation. The recent events doubled her distress. "I have been so sad, unusually low spirited. . . . I have thought of my dying when the hour of trial comes. . . . If I do die, I hope that my baby will die with me."[7]

The following weeks brought word of Lee's surrender at Appomattox. "The war is over, and I am glad of it," Gertrude wrote. For many months she and her neighbors had known the South would lose; the only question was how badly. "What terms of agreement may be decided upon, I cannot say, but if *anything* is left us—if we can count with certainty upon enough to raise and educate our children—I shall be grateful."

One thing was clear: the Thomas family would not be left their slaves. Gertrude and the other whites had learned of the Emancipation Proclamation at the time of its publication, but only after Union forces occupied Augusta did emancipation become real for them and their slaves—and even then not entirely so. "This morning a large force of Yankees came marching into Augusta, the drums beating and colours flying, surrounded by a large crowd of Negroes," Gertrude wrote on May 7. She deliberately slept late in a silent attempt to snub the invaders. "I felt no particular emotion as I looked at them through the closed blinds." She picked up the morning paper and read an order regarding labor relations under the occupation. "The impression is general that *slavery* is *abolished*, that *the negroes are free*." But, surprisingly, it was only an impression.

The next day she learned a bit more of the new reality. "Mr. Thomas and I were out riding in the buggy. Pinck and Cora"—a neighbor and his wife—"in his buggy overtook us and enquired if we had seen the order from General Smith with regard to free labor, viz: that the Negroes were to be subsisted, paid six months wages in advance and half the crop made to be divided among them. Contracts to be made between negro and Planter—there, I have followed the Yankee fashion of naming the Negro first and the Master last. A failure to plant will cause the land to be confiscated."

Gertrude Thomas felt that her world had been turned upside down. "We can count with certainty upon nothing. Our Negroes will be freed, our lands confiscated, and imagination cannot tell what is in store for us." Yet though her husband was "utterly spirit-broken" by the recent events, Gertrude felt an odd ambivalence. "I cannot say 'Why art thou cast down, oh my soul?' for indeed I am not cast down. On the contrary, I am not the person to permit pecuniary loss to afflict me as long as I have health and energy. As to the emancipation of the Negroes, while there is of course a natural dislike to the loss of so much property, in my inmost soul I cannot regret it. I always felt that there was a great responsibility. It is in some degree a great relief to have this feeling removed."

All the same, she felt no gratitude toward those who were the occasion of her relief. "For the Negroes I know that I have the kindest possible feeling," she wrote. "For the Yankees who deprive us of them I have no use whatever."[8]

As GERTRUDE AND Jefferson Thomas learned from their neighbors, the emancipation of the slaves was wrapped closely in concern for their future subsistence and employment. Sherman's policy of forty acres and a mule—which was applied, with modifications, in certain other parts of the South on other properties confiscated from the rebels—provided one model for the future of the former slaves. Sherman's approach had the advantage of being self-sustaining, or at least promising to be. The former slaves possessed farming skills, honed in years of bondage but now employed on their own behalf. As property owners they would respond to, and benefit from, the same incentives that had motivated farmers in the North for generations.

But Sherman's plan had serious drawbacks. The first was political. The Republicans were the party of free labor, but they were also a party of respect for private property, and to confiscate and redistribute large amounts of property cut against their political grain. The second drawback was constitutional. Sherman's order could be justified as a wartime measure, but once the war ended, peacetime interpretations of the Constitution would again apply, and these didn't appear to countenance the wholesale redistribution of land by the federal government.

The third drawback was economic. Emancipation by itself disrupted the Southern economy; if emancipation was followed by the confiscation and redistribution of land, the disruption would be many times as severe. Disruption, of course, was precisely the point of Union policies while the war lasted, but once the war ended the emphasis shifted diametrically, to reconstruction and revitalization. The most vindictive of the Radicals might be happy for the South to starve, but more responsible types recognized an obligation to rebuild the Southern economy, if only because a languishing South would burden the country as a whole. Besides, any economic policy that punished the South would almost certainly punish the freedmen the most, which hardly seemed fair.

For these reasons, the redistribution of land died aborning. The forty-acre settlers found it nearly impossible to acquire title to their plots, and as the original owners returned after the war they thrust the freedmen aside, with the help of friendly sheriffs and courts and the acquiescence of the federal government. The process took more time in some places, less in others, but within a few years of the war's end the dream of black ownership on any but the most limited scale had vanished.[9]

MANY OF THE freedmen predictably felt betrayed. "We were promised homesteads by the government," declared a delegation from Edisto Island, South Carolina, to Oliver O. Howard, a decorated Union officer who headed the Freedmen's Bureau.

> If it does not carry out the promises its agents made to us . . . we are left in a more unpleasant condition than our former. We are at the mercy of those who are combined to prevent us from getting land enough to lay our fathers' bones upon. We have property in homes, cattle, carriages, and articles of furniture, but we are landless and homeless. . . . This is not the condition of really free men. You ask us to forgive the landowners of our island. *You* only lost your right arm in the war, and might forgive them. The man who tied me to a tree and gave me 39 lashes, who stripped and flogged my mother and sister and who will not let me stay in his empty hut except I will do his planting

and be satisfied with this price, and who combines with others to keep away land from me, well knowing I would not have anything to do with him if I had land of my own—that man, I cannot well forgive.

The government in Washington must know what its decisions entailed.

> This is our home. We have made these lands what they are. We were the only true and loyal people that were found in possession of lands. We have been always ready to strike for liberty and humanity, yea to fight if need be to preserve this glorious Union. Shall not we who are freedmen and have always been true to this Union have the same rights as are enjoyed by others? Have we broken any laws of these United States? Have we forfeited our rights of property in land? If not, then are not our rights as a free people and good citizens of the United States to be considered before the rights of those who were found in rebellion against this good and just government?

Was money an issue? The freedmen could deal with that. "We are ready to pay for this land." But they had to be given the opportunity to do so. "Will the good and just government take from us this right and make us subject to the will of those who cheated and oppressed us for many years? God forbid!"[10]

IF THE FREEDMEN couldn't be landowners, then, in an agrarian economy, they had to be employees of the people who were. Historically, markets take time to develop, but the South after the Civil War was allowed almost no time to develop a market for labor. The war ended amid the spring planting season, as the need for labor was peaking. But at that very moment the slaves discovered that they no longer had to work for their old masters. Theoretically the masters might have hired their former slaves, yet in practice most lacked the money. Cash flows had typically been modest under slavery, as slave labor was a capital investment rather than an operating expense. The planters might have borrowed money to pay the former slaves, but the four years of the war had used up all the available capital, and in any event emancipation destroyed their principal form of collateral, the market value of their slaves. Nor would land, the basis for borrowing by

Northern farmers, be worth anything to speak of until the labor question was answered.

During that first season the labor system evolved haphazardly. Where freedmen retained their forty acres they worked for themselves. In the rare cases where the former masters had sufficient reserves to pay their former slaves, they often tried to do so. Many of Gertrude and Jefferson Thomas's field hands had fled for freedom upon Sherman's approach, but the house slaves remained, and the Thomases hoped to keep them on. "This morning Mr. Thomas assembled the servants together, told them that numerous reports were about town, that it was extremely probable that the Yankees would free them," Gertrude wrote on May 8. Jefferson Thomas said he wished to hire them. "He would have to hire someone, and had as soon pay them wages as anyone else, and advised them to wait quietly and see what could be done." The offer appeared to elicit general acceptance. "I have seen no evidence of insubordination," Gertrude remarked. "On the contrary, they all worked very cheerfully. . . . Since his explanation there has appeared a more cheerful spirit than ever."

Yet attitudes changed as the new reality sank in. One of the former house slaves, a man named Daniel, abruptly departed. "Took off all of his clothes during the night and left without saying anything to anyone," Gertrude wrote. She felt betrayed. "He is here in town, but I have not seen him nor do I wish to do so. If he returns to the yard, he shall not enter it." The next day another slave left. "Betsey, a little servant, went for the *Chronicle* as she was in the habit of doing every day, and did not return. . . . I was really annoyed about it." Gertrude discovered that Betsey had rejoined her mother, whom Jefferson Thomas had sold earlier on suspicion of stealing food from the storeroom. Gertrude thought the departure was Betsey's loss. "She was a bright, quick child, and raised in our family would have become a good servant. As it is, she will be under her mother's influence and run wild in the street." Within two weeks more, nearly the entire staff of the house had melted away. "Out of all our old house servants, not one remains except Patsey and a little boy, Frank."[11]

J. T. TROWBRIDGE was a journalist and author who traveled through the South during the year after Appomattox. His first impression of what he called "the desolated states" was that they were indeed in a desolated state. The countryside bore deep scars of the fighting, but the cities showed the damage most starkly. "Everywhere were ruins and rubbish, mud and mortar and misery," he wrote of Atlanta. "Hundreds of the inhabitants, white and black, rendered homeless by the destruction of the city, were living in wretched hovels, which made the suburbs look like a fantastic encampment of gypsies or Indians. Some of the negro huts were covered entirely with ragged fragments of tin-roofing from the burnt government and railroad buildings. Others were constructed partly of these irregular blackened patches, and partly of old boards, with roofs of huge, warped, slouching shreds of tin, kept from blowing away by stones placed on the top." Sherman had wanted to cripple Southern commerce and industry, and by the evidence of Atlanta he had succeeded. "Every business block in Atlanta was burned, except one. The railroad machine-shops, the foundries, the immense rolling-mill, the tent, pistol, gun-carriage, shot-and-shell factories, and storehouses, of the late Confederacy, disappeared in flames and explosions. Half a mile of the principal street was destroyed."[12]

But life went on, haltingly. Shop owners sifted through the rubble; planters returned to their farms. Shortages of all sorts—building materials, capital, transportation—plagued the reconstruction efforts. Yet one question hung over everything. Trowbridge heard it from a dozen mouths; it took unspoken shape in the very air: "Will the freedmen work?"

The answers depended on who was speaking. Colonel Samuel Thomas of the Freedmen's Bureau in Mississippi was hopeful. Thomas had charge of efforts to place black farmers on lands abandoned by their owners. "I am confident there is no more industrious class of people anywhere than the freedmen who have little homesteads of their own," he said. "The colonies under my charge, working lands assigned them by the government, have raised this year ten thousand bales of cotton, besides corn and vegetables for their subsistence until another harvest."

Other officers of the Freedmen's Bureau concurred, as did many—but, interestingly, not all—of the freedmen themselves. Trowbridge toured Vicksburg with the Union commander of the Department of Mississippi, Major General Thomas J. Wood. They visited the freedmen's quarter below the center of town and together inquired what portion of the former slaves would work, and what portion would try to live without working. "We got very candid replies: the common opinion being that about five out of twenty still had a notion of living without work." Trowbridge added, perhaps with a smile, "Not one would admit that *he* was one of the five—every man and woman acknowledged that labor was a universal duty and necessity."[13]

The shiftless five—if that was indeed their number—could cite reasons for not working. An informant explained to Trowbridge the employment practices of a white landowning neighbor. "He goes by the name of 'Honest M—' all through the country," Trowbridge explained, adding parenthetically, "I omit names, for he"—Trowbridge's source—"told me that not only his property but his life depended upon the good-will of his neighbors." Trowbridge continued, of "Honest M":

> Honesty appeared to be a virtue to be exercised only towards white people; it was too good to be thrown away on niggers. This M has four hundred sheep, seventy milch cows, fifteen horses, ten mules, and forty hogs, all of which were saved from the Yankees when they raided through the country, by an old negro who run them off across a swamp. Honest M has never given that negro five cents. Another of his slaves had a cow of his own from which he raised a fine pair of oxen; Honest M lays claim to those oxen and sells them. A slave-woman that belonged to him had a cow she had raised from a calf; Honest M takes that, and adds it to his herd. He promised his niggers a share of the crops this year; but he has sold the cotton, and locked up the corn, and never given one of them a dollar. And all this time he thinks he is honest; he thinks Northern capitalists treat free laborers this way.

Trowbridge's informant was a Northerner who had come south seeking opportunity after the war (which was another reason he had to be careful of his neighbors' opinions). He had rented one of M's two plantations, as M lacked the capital to run both himself. "But he gave me notice at the start that he should take all the niggers from my plantation, and that I must look out for my own help." When the Northerner, however, in company with M, went to take possession of his rented property, all the freedmen were there.

"How's this?" he asked the owner. "I thought these people were going with you."

M explained that he couldn't persuade them to work for him. He said he had offered twenty-five dollars a month, plus board and medical attention, but they wouldn't come.

The Northerner hesitantly asked if he might try to employ them. M said he was welcome to try. After M left, the Northerner called the freedmen around. He afterward told Trowbridge what happened.

> Said I: "Mr. M offers you twenty-five dollars a month. That is more than I can afford to pay, and I think you'd better hire to him." They looked stolid; they couldn't see it; they didn't want to work for him at any price.
>
> Then I said, "If you won't work for him, will you work for me?" I never saw faces light up so in my life. "Yes, master! Yes, master!" "But," said I, "ten dollars a month is all I can afford to pay." That made no difference, they said; they'd rather work for ten dollars, and be sure of their pay, than for twenty-five dollars, and be cheated out of it.

The Northerner concluded his story happily. "They went right to work with a will. I won't ask men to do any better than they have been doing. They are having their Christmas frolic right now, and it's as merry a Christmas as ever you saw!"[14]

ANOTHER OF TROWBRIDGE'S interviews revealed something else he considered significant about attitudes in the South. Among his interlocutors was "a very intelligent young man of Chambers County" in Alabama. This young man, the son of a planter, had fought with the Confederate army but been taken prisoner and sent to Pennsylvania. At the end of the war, having heard that everything he might have expected to own back in Alabama had been destroyed, confiscated, or stolen, he decided to stay in Pennsylvania. "I had never done a stroke of labor in my life, and it came hard to me at first. But I soon got used to it." He worked on a farm for six dollars a month, then in a store for eighteen. He impressed his employer, who promoted him steadily till he was earning fifty dollars a month. "I had been a wild boy before the war," he told Trowbridge. "I had plenty of money with no restrictions upon my spending it. But I tell you, I was never so happy in my life as when I was at work for my living in that store. My employer liked me, and trusted me, and I liked the people."

In time he returned home on a visit, which was how Trowbridge came to meet him. Things weren't going well. "My relations and neighbors are very much incensed against me because I tell them plainly what I think of the Yankees. I know now that we were all in the wrong, and that the North was right, about the war; and I tell them so. I have met with the most insulting treatment on this account. They feel the bitterest animosity against the government, and denounce and abuse the Yankees, and call me a Yankee, as the worst name they can give me." Trowbridge asked how widespread this view was. The young man said it was overwhelming. "There are fifteen hundred voting men in the county, and all but about a hundred and eighty feel and talk the way I tell you. They can't be reconciled. . . . Those who are able are preparing to emigrate. A fund has already been raised to send agents to select lands for them in Mexico."

Trowbridge asked if the young man hadn't encountered similar animosity in the North toward the South. He said he had, but only a little. "And there was this difference: In the North it is only a few ignorant people, of the poorer class, who hate the South. I believe the mass of the Northern people, while they hate treason and rebellion, have only kind feelings toward the Southern people. But with us it is the wealthy and influential class that hates the North, while only the poor whites and negroes have any loyalty at heart."

An Alabama planter registered despair rather than hatred. "The country is ruined," he told Trowbridge. "The prosperity of our people passed away with the institution of slavery. I shall never try to make another fortune. I made one, and lost it in a minute. I had a hundred and fifty thousand dollars in niggers. I am now sixty years old. I'll bet a suit of clothes against a dime, there'll be no cotton crop raised this year."

This man predicted that blacks would find their freedom a mixed blessing. "Some few niggers go on, and do well, just as before; but they're might scarce." Others, especially the aged and infirm, would long for the security of the old days, when they could count on a roof over their heads and food on their tables. Already the reaction was setting in. "A nigger drayman came to me the other day and asked me to buy him. He said, 'I want a master. When I had a master, I had nothing to do but to eat and drink and sleep, besides my work. Now I have to work and think too.' When I said the law wouldn't allow me to buy him, he looked very much discouraged." (Commenting on the exchange, Trowbridge wrote, "I heard of a few such cases as this drayman's, but they were far less common than one would have expected.")[15]

JOURDON ANDERSON HAD been the slave of Colonel P. H. Anderson of Big Spring, Tennessee. Upon emancipation he went to Nashville before heading north for Ohio, where he received a letter from his old master. "I got your letter and was glad to find you had not forgotten Jourdon," he responded (with the help of a literate friend), "and that you wanted me to come back and live with you again, promising to do better for me than anybody else can." Jourdon said he had felt uneasy about the colonel since they had parted. "I thought the Yankees would have hung you long before this for harboring Rebs. . . . I suppose they never heard about your going to Col. Martin's to kill the Union soldier that was left by his company in their stable." Jourdon said he had no hard feelings, "although you shot at me twice before I left you." He sent his regards to the whole family. "Give my love to them. . . . I would have come back to see you all when I was working in the Nashville hospital, but one of the neighbors told me Henry intended to shoot me if he ever got a chance."

Jourdon explained that he was prospering in Ohio. "I get $25 a month, with victuals and clothing; have a comfortable home for Mandy (the folks here call her Mrs. Anderson), and the children—Milly, Jane and Grundy—go to school and are learning well. The teacher says Grundy has a head for a preacher." Yet Jourdon couldn't deny sometimes feeling homesick, and he couldn't rule out a return to the old plantation. "If you will write and say what wages you will give me, I will be better able to decide whether it would be to my advantage to move back again."

His wife had some doubts. "Mandy says she would be afraid to go back without some kind of proof that you are sincerely disposed to treat us justly and kindly." They had decided what sort of proof they required. "I served you faithfully for thirty-two years, and Mandy twenty years. At $25 a month for me, and $2 a week for Mandy, our earnings would amount to $11,680. Add to this the interest for the time our wages has been kept back and deduct what you paid for our clothing and three doctor's visits to me, and pulling a tooth for Mandy, and the balance will show what we are in justice entitled to. Please send the money by Adams Express, in care of V. Winters, esq., Dayton, Ohio."

Considering the matter further, Jourdon added another request. "Please state if there would be any safety for my Milly and Jane, who are now grown up and both good-looking girls. You know how it was with poor Matilda and Catherine. I would rather stay here and starve and die, if it comes to that, than have my girls brought to shame by the violence and wickedness of their young masters." And one other thing: "You will please state if there has been any schools opened for the colored children in your neighborhood. The great desire of my life now is to give my children an education, and have them form virtuous habits."

Jourdon suspected he might not be hearing from the colonel again. So he reiterated his regards for all at the old place. "Tell them I hope we will meet in the better world, if not in this. . . . Say howdy to George Carter, and thank him for taking the pistol from you when you were shooting at me."[16]

THE CONFUSION IN the labor system that first season led to the adoption of general policies in various states. These "black codes," as they came to be called, were swiftly criticized as attempts to reimpose slavery in all but name. The criticism wasn't wrong but was somewhat misleading. In certain respects the black codes were liberal documents, at least by contrast to what had gone before in the slave states. Because slaves were construed as property, they had lacked the most basic civil and human rights. The black codes sought to define some of these rights for the freedmen. "All freedmen, free negroes, and mulattoes may sue and be sued, implead and be impleaded, in all the courts of law and equity of the State," the Mississippi code declared. "Freedmen, free negroes, and mulattoes shall be competent in civil cases, when a party or parties to the suit, either plaintiff or plaintiffs, defendant or defendants; also in cases where freedmen, free negroes, and mulattoes is or are either plaintiff or plaintiffs, defendant or defendants, and a white person or white persons is or are the opposing party or parties." The rights of the former slaves extended to criminal cases as well. "It shall be lawful for any freedman, free negro or mulatto, to charge any white person, freedman, free negro, or mulatto, by affidavit, with any criminal offense against his or her person or property, and upon such affidavit the proper process shall be issued and executed as if said affidavit was made by a white person."

The black codes constructed family law for African Americans. "All freedmen, free negroes, and mulattoes may intermarry with each other, in the same manner and under the same regulations that are provided by law for white persons," the Mississippi code declared. "All freemen, free negroes, and mulattoes who do now and have heretofore lived and cohabited together as husband and wife shall be taken and held in law as legally married, and the issue shall be taken and held as legitimate for all purposes." South Carolina was more succinct—and implicitly more eloquent in marking the difference between the era of slavery and that of freedom. "The relation of husband and wife among persons of color is established," the South Carolina code stated. "The relation of parent and child among persons of color is recognized."[17]

On these points the black codes were a signal advance for African Americans. To be able to marry and have the union recognized in law, to know that one's children weren't liable to be snatched away at the whim of others, were precious rights, and made all the more precious by their absence just months before. To be able to sue and testify in court, to be able to bring criminal charges against anyone, were foundation stones of participation in civil society.

Yet there was, of course, more to the black codes than empowerment of former slaves. Slavery had been a system of labor relations, but it was also a system of social control. Slavery specified what black men and women (and children) could and couldn't do, where they could and couldn't go, with whom they could and couldn't associate. Many whites had difficulty imagining a society in which such controls were absent. They feared a footloose population of blacks roaming the countryside and deliberately or inadvertently fomenting trouble, from petty crimes to grand felonies. They assumed that since blacks had had to be coerced into working under slavery, they would have to be coerced into working under freedom. This was necessary for the survival of the Southern economy, which had been built on black labor, but it was also necessary for the welfare of blacks, who didn't know enough to care for themselves.

The black codes went to great lengths to describe and proscribe vagrancy. "All persons who have not some fixed and known place of abode, and some lawful and reputable employment; those who have not some visible and known means of a fair, reputable, and honest livelihood; all common prostitutes; those who are found wandering from place to place, vending, bartering, or peddling any articles or commodities, without a license from the district judge or other proper authority; all common gamblers, persons who lead idle or disorderly lives, or keep or frequent disorderly or disreputable houses or places; those who, not having sufficient means of support, are able to work, and do not work . . . shall be deemed vagrants," said South Carolina. (The proscribed vagrant class also included "fortune-tellers, sturdy beggars, common drunkards, those who hunt game of any description, or fish on the land of others," as well as unlicensed performers of "any tragedy, interlude, comedy, farce, play, or any other similar entertainment, exhibition of the circus, sleight of hand, wax-works, or . . . any concert or musical entertainment.") The definition of vagrancy applied to persons of any race, but the penalty was specified only for persons of color. That penalty was imprisonment and hard labor for up to twelve months. But partly because the lawmakers and their constituents didn't want to pay for the upkeep of prisoners and partly because the point of the statute was to ensure a supply of workers for the farms of the South, provision was made for the privatization of punishment. "The defendant, if sentenced to hard labor, after conviction may . . . be hired, for such wages as can be obtained for his services, to any owner or lessee of a farm for the term of the hard labor to which he was sentenced, or be hired for the same labor on the streets, public roads, or public buildings."[18]

Proscribing vagrancy was neither new nor unique to the South. Northern states had been doing it for years, and, upon the emergence of city-based manufacturing, several were stiffening their statutes. But the Southern codes went beyond outlawing vagrancy to specifying terms of employment. "Every freedman, free negro, and mulatto shall, on the second Monday of January, one thousand eight hundred and sixty-six, and annually thereafter, have a lawful home or employment, and shall have written evidence thereof," the Mississippi law declared. The evidence of a home should be a license or statement from a mayor or police board; the evidence of employment should be a contract. Length of service under labor contracts would be agreed upon by the employers and workers (officially styled "masters" and "servants" under South Carolina law) but would typically be a year. ("The period of service shall be expressed in the contract," the South Carolina law said; "but if it not be expressed it shall be until the twenty-fifth day of December next after the commencement of the service.") Failure to sign a contract would make a black person a vagrant and subject to the criminal sanctions for vagrancy. Failure to complete a signed contract would do the same and more. "If the laborer shall quit the service of the employer before expiration of his term of service, without good cause," the Mississippi law stipulated, "he shall forfeit his wages for that year up to the time of quitting."[19]

Predictably, the reaction to the black codes diverged dramatically. A North Carolina planter considered them useful guides to the self-improvement of the former slaves. "If they cannot (as they never can) occupy the places of legislators, judges, teachers, &c., they may be useful as tillers of the soil, as handicraftsmen, as servants in various situations, and be happy in their domestic and family relations. . . . It is our Christian duty to encourage them to these ends." Governor Benjamin G. Humphreys of Mississippi considered his state's code humane and just. If anything, it erred on the side of liberality in the legal privileges accorded blacks. But this was a small price to pay for the greater good. "The question of admitting negro testimony for the protection of their persons and property sinks into insignificance by the side of the other great question of *guarding them and the State* against the evils that may arise from their sudden emancipation." What were these evils? "The answer is patent to all—vagrancy and pauperism, and their inevitable concomitant crime and misery."[20]

The former slaves took a decidedly different view. A group of Mississippi freedmen petitioned Humphreys in complaint of the code. "We do not want to be hunted by negro runners and their hounds unless we are guilty of a criminal crime," they said. The new law would punish honest and hardworking African Americans, upon whom the future of the state depended. "If every one of us colored people were removed from the state of Mississippi, our superiors would soon find out who were their supporters. We the laborers have enriched them, and it is as much impossible for them to live without us as it is for we to be removed from them."[21]

A visitor to the South observed that times had changed since the days of slavery, but more for the masters than for the slaves. "Although the former owner has lost his individual right of property in the former slaves," he said, "the blacks at large belong to the whites at large."[22]

BOOKER WASHINGTON MET capitalism at the mouth of a West Virginia salt mine. After the war he moved with his mother and brother to Malden, where his stepfather and other former slaves dug salt from the ground and refined it for household and industrial use. Booker earned his first wages working at the mine's furnace, which boiled water away from the salt. He didn't like the work and was happy to leave it for school when the local community of freedmen hired a teacher to impart basic literacy to young and old. But Booker didn't stay in school long: his stepfather determined that the family couldn't spare his lost wages and called the boy back to the furnace. As he grew older and stronger he graduated to the coal mine next door that supplied the fuel to the furnace. The pay was better but the job was hard, dirty, and dangerous. "There was always the danger of being blown to pieces by a premature explosion of powder, or of being crushed by falling slate," he remembered. "Accidents from one or the other of these causes were frequently occurring, and this kept me in constant fear." It also kept him on the constant lookout for an escape from the mine.[23]

One day he overheard two miners talking about a fancy school for blacks in Virginia. "This was the first time that I had ever heard anything about any kind of school or college that was more pretentious than the little coloured school in our town. In the darkness of the mine I noiselessly crept as close as I could to the two men who were talking. I heard one tell the other that not only was the school established for the members of my race, but that opportunities were provided by which poor but worthy students could work out all or a part of the cost of board, and at the same time be taught some trade or industry." He eventually caught the name of the school, Hampton Normal and Agricultural Institute. "I resolved at once to go to that school, although I had no idea where it was, or how many miles away, or how I was going to reach it."

He worked a few months more in the mine, steeling his nerve and saving what he could of his pay. Finally he made his escape, with the clothes on his back, a few items in a cheap satchel, and a kiss from his mother. Washington had discovered that Hampton was about eighty miles southeast of Richmond, and about five hundred miles from Malden. He rode a stage coach part of the way, the only black passenger among several whites. They were civil enough, but the white landlord of the hotel where the stage stopped for the night refused him food and lodging. "This was my first experience in finding out what the colour of my skin meant," he recalled. In particular it meant he spent the night cold and hungry, walking about to keep warm amid the mountains.

When his money ran out he walked and hitched rides with friendly farmers. In time he reached Richmond, exhausted, famished, and dirty. "I had never been in a large city, and this added to my misery. . . . I had not a single acquaintance in the place, and, being unused to city ways, I did not know where to go. I applied at several places for lodging, but they all wanted money, and that was what I did not have. . . . I passed by many food-stands where fried chicken and half-moon apple pies were piled high and made to present a most tempting appearance. At that time it seemed to me that I would have promised all that I expected to possess in the future to have gotten hold of one of those chicken legs or one of those pies."[24]

He slept under the wooden sidewalk and next morning found work with the white captain of a boat loading pig iron on the James River. He worked days on the river and slept nights under the sidewalk, till he had saved enough for the final leg of his journey to Hampton, which he reached with fifty cents to spare.

His application interview consisted of a single task. The head teacher took him to an empty recitation room and told him to sweep it. Washington was overjoyed, for in his last months at Malden he had lived in the house of a man whose wife instructed him in the fine art of housecleaning. "I swept the recitation room three times. Then I got a dusting cloth and I dusted it four times. All the woodwork around the walls, every bench, table, and desk, I went over four times with my dusting cloth." He moved the furniture and dusted underneath. He swept and dusted the closets. In time he told the teacher he was done. She inspected thoroughly. "She was a Yankee woman who knew just where to look for dirt. She went into the room and inspected the floor and closets; then she took her handkerchief and rubbed it on the woodwork about the walls, and over the table and benches. When she was unable to find one bit of dirt on the floor, or a particle of dust on any of the furniture, she quietly remarked, 'I guess you will do to enter this institution.'"[25]

Hampton transformed Washington's life. The education there was practical as well as academic. Instruction began with basic hygiene. "The use of the bath-tub and of the tooth-brush, as well as the use of sheets upon the bed, were all new to me." Clothes had to be clean and shoes polished. Washington was one of the youngest students; his classmates included men and women of middle age, all earnestly striving to better themselves. More than a few came from circumstances even less promising than Washington's. "Many of them had aged parents who were dependent upon them, and some of them were men who had wives whose support in some way they had to provide for."

Washington worked as a janitor to pay his boarding expenses of ten dollars per month. But the annual tuition of seventy dollars was beyond his means. The director of the school, General Samuel Armstrong, found him a sponsor, a resident of New Bedford, Massachusetts, who supported African American education from afar and who paid Washington's tuition. Washington borrowed books and wore hand-me-downs sent in barrels from the North.

He spent three years at Hampton, imbibing the ethos of self-help on which its educational philosophy was based. "For the first time, I learned what education was expected to do for an individual," he wrote. "Before going there I had a good deal of the then rather prevalent idea among our people that to secure an education meant to have a good, easy time, free from all necessity for manual labour. At Hampton I not only learned that it was not a disgrace to labour, but learned to love labour, not alone for its financial value, but for labour's own sake and for the independence and self-reliance which the ability to do something the world wants done brings."

He also learned that the payback from education didn't come at once. "I was completely out of money when I graduated."[26]

MONEY WAS ON every mind in the South after the war. In a school run by the Freedmen's Bureau in Kentucky, a teacher quizzed his pupils. "Now, children," he asked rhetorically, "you don't think white people are any better than you because they have straight hair and white faces?"

"No, sir," the children responded.

"No, they are no better, but they are different," the teacher continued. "They possess great power; they formed this great government; they control this vast country. . . . Now what makes them different from you?"

The children replied with a unanimous shout: "Money!!"[27]

What the Kentucky children knew, and what Booker Washington learned at Hampton, was one of the most lasting lessons of reconstruction for the South: that money mattered as it had never mattered before. Before the war, a large segment of the Southern population—namely the four million slaves—had spent their daily lives beyond the capitalist economy. Slaves weren't responsible for buying their food and clothing; they didn't pay rent for their accommodations. And, needless to say, they didn't receive wages for their work. Had Booker Washington remained a slave, he never would have learned the value of an education, or its monetary cost. Absent emancipation, those Kentucky schoolchildren would have discovered a different set of distinctions between themselves and white folks.

The extension of the capitalist economy compelled dramatic changes in mindset among the people of the South. "The old system is gone up," an Alabama planter acknowledged. This man had fired his overseers. "They can't learn to treat the freedmen like human beings," he said. And now he lectured his black workers on the new dispensation:

> Formerly, you were my slaves. You worked for me, and I provided for you. You had no thought of the morrow, for I thought of that for you. If you were sick, I had the doctor come to you. When you needed clothes, clothes were forthcoming; and you never went hungry for lack of meal and pork. You had little more responsibility than my mules.
>
> But now all that is changed. Being free men, you assume the responsibilities of free men. You sell me your labor, I pay you money, and with that money you provide for yourselves. You must look out for your own clothes and food, and the wants of your children. If I advance these things for you, I shall charge them to you, for I cannot give them like I once did, now I pay you wages. Once if you were ugly or lazy, I had you whipped, and that was the end of it. Now if you are ugly or lazy, your wages will be paid to others, and you will be turned off, to go about the country with bundles on your backs, like the miserable low-down niggers you see that nobody will hire. But if you are well-behaved and industrious, you will be prosperous and respected and happy.[28]

Whatever the unfamiliarity of their new responsibilities, most blacks welcomed the changes, preferring the uncertain rewards of freedom to the assured oppression of slavery. As an African American minister told his Louisville flock, "It is better to work for Mr. Cash than Mr. Lash." This minister went on to predict even better things as capitalism erased the distinctions slavery had rested on. "A black man looks better now to the white man than he used to. He looks taller, brighter, and more like a man. The more money you make, the lighter your skin will be. The more land and houses you get, the straighter your hair will be."[29]

For a time the operation of Southern capitalism fulfilled the expectations of its advocates and its prospective beneficiaries. As planters scrambled to find hands to till their fields, they bid up the price of labor, putting former slaves in the unprecedented position of holding the balance of negotiating power. "They are constantly striking for higher wages," one Georgia employer complained. "They will not stick to a contract; they are fickle; they are constantly expecting to do better; they will make a contract with me today for twelve or fifteen dollars a month, and in a few days somebody will come along and offer a dollar or two more, and they will quit me—never saying anything to me, but leave in the night and be gone."

Blacks shared intelligence regarding pay and working conditions. "The Negroes have a kind of telegraph by which they know all about the treatment of the Negroes on the plantations for a great distance around," a Florida planter remarked. Entire states acquired bad reputations. A Mississippi planter desperate for workers went to New Orleans and engaged a black labor contractor to find workers, offering five dollars a head. The contractor refused and said he wouldn't send workers to Mississippi for a hundred dollars a head. "And why?" the astonished planter recounted afterward. "All because the sassy scoundrel said he didn't like our Mississippi laws."[30]

Obviously those New Orleans workers had other options. At times the competition for labor was fierce. A traveler at Natchez marveled at the way prospective employers—planters from Mississippi and Louisiana— descended upon a regiment of African American soldiers being mustered out of the Union army. "The negro was king," he explained. "Men fawned upon him; took him to the sutler's shop and treated him; carried pockets full of tobacco to bestow upon him; carefully explained to him the varied delights of their respective plantations. Women came too—with coach and coachmen—drove into the camp, went out among the negroes, and with sweet smiles and honeyed words sought to persuade them that such and such plantations would be the very home they were looking for."[31]

The driving force of the higher returns to black labor was increased productivity. Under slavery, African Americans had no reason to work harder than was absolutely necessary, and every reason not to. Under capitalism, the incentives were reversed. The result was striking. "I never knew, during forty years of plantation life, so little sickness," a Sea Island planter said. "Formerly, every man had a fever of some kind; and now the veriest old cripple, who did nothing under secesh rule, will row a boat three nights in succession to Edisto, or will pick up the corn about the corn-house. There are twenty people whom I know were considered worn out and too old to work under the slave system, who are now working cotton, as well as their two acres of provisions; and their crops look very well."[32]

This, of course, was precisely how a capitalist market in labor was supposed to work, encouraging and rewarding diligence and ambition. But Southern planters hadn't adopted the capitalist approach to labor voluntarily and, not surprisingly, they attempted to subvert it. Some simply refused to believe that blacks would respond to the kind of incentives that worked for whites. "I know the nigger," a Mississippi planter told an official of the Freedmen's Bureau. "The employer must have some sort of punishment. I don't care what it is. If you'll let me tie him up by the thumbs, or keep him on bread and water, that will do. . . . All I want is just to have it so that when I get the niggers on to my place, and the work is begun, they can't sit down and look me square in the face and do nothing."[33]

When it became clear that the old methods of physical coercion would not be allowed, Southern employers adopted other methods of controlling labor. The black codes placed the force of law on the side of employers, severely limiting the mobility and alternatives of blacks and hence their bargaining power. The black codes were eventually repealed as the Radical Republicans in Congress, outraged over such measures, seized control of Reconstruction; by that time Southern employers had borrowed a page—and occasionally personnel—from their capitalist colleagues in the industrial North. "I'm hiring now to a Northern man, who gives me three thousand," a former overseer explained.

A Northern man will want to get more out of the niggers than we do. Mine said to me last night, "I want you to get the last drop of sweat and the last pound of cotton out of my niggers," and I shall do it. I can if anybody can. There's a heap in humbuggin' a nigger. I worked a gang this summer, and got as much work out of 'em as I ever did. I just had my leading nigger, and I says to him, I says, "Sam, I want this yer crop out by such a time; now you go a-head, talk to the niggers, and lead 'em off right smart, and I'll give you twenty-five dollars." Then I got up a race, and give a few dollars to the men that picked the most cotton, till I found out the extent of what each man could pick; then I required that of him every day, or I docked his wages.[34]

But wage labor represented a false start in reconstructing the plantation economy. Too few planters commanded the cash to pay workers regular wages, and too many workers resisted the slavelike discipline of gang labor in the fields. After a couple of seasons of experimentation, a system emerged that solved the planters' cash-flow problem and the workers' problem with old-style field labor.

Sharecropping was based on a partnership of landowners and laborers in the production of cotton and other commercial crops. The owners—who might or might not live on the property, or even in the state—provided the land, seed, and tools necessary to produce a crop. The sharecroppers—who might be poor whites as well as blacks—provided labor and expertise. At the harvest the two parties divided the crop. Often the split was down the middle; sometimes the ratios differed.

Partnerships had been a feature of economic life since before the emergence of capitalism. Sometimes the partnerships were symmetric, as when several investors contributed cash toward the purchase of a cargo of trade goods to be sent to some distant market. Sometimes they were asymmetric, as when an artisan found a sponsor to stake him to a start in his craft. A characteristic of partnerships (and of the publicly traded corporations that were their successors) was the sharing of risk. If the cargo ship sank, the investors shared the loss; if the artisan attracted no business, the sponsor suffered as well. In this regard sharecropping made eminent sense, as agriculture has often been a high-risk undertaking. If the crop thrived, owners and sharecroppers both benefited; if the crop failed (as it did every third or fourth year in the South), both bore the loss.

But though partnerships tend to align the interests of the partners, they rarely make those interests identical, and a common theme of partnerships is the effort by one or more parties to shift the risks to the others. In the case of Southern sharecropping, the landowners did most of the shifting. They persuaded state legislatures to pass crop-lien laws that gave the landowners first right to the crops. In a bad year, when revenues from the crops failed to cover an owner's expenses, the croppers came up empty-handed. The crop-lien laws also allowed the owners to dictate which crops would be produced—commercial cotton, for example, rather than corn, which in lean times could be eaten as well as sold. The owners typically wrote contracts requiring the sharecroppers to purchase food and other provisions from the owners, at prices and interest rates set by the owners.

Croppers were almost always financially unsophisticated and were frequently illiterate, which placed them at a singular disadvantage with respect to the owners, whose natural tendency was to protect themselves. Some owners were dishonest and deliberately preyed on the croppers; other owners were honest but simply ungenerous.[35]

Whether from law or contract, fraud or neglect, many of the sharecroppers became virtual serfs on Southern plantations. They were not chattel: they couldn't be bought and sold. But neither were they free to come and go as they pleased. Each year they found themselves deeper in debt to the owner of the property they worked, with little choice but to work another year under the same discouraging circumstances.

Chapter 6

LAKOTA'S LAST STAND

The most obvious geographical consequence of the Civil War was the reattachment of the South to the North, but a result scarcely less significant was the cementing of the West to the East. More than a few Northerners might have bid the South good riddance in 1861 had the South's departure not threatened to carry away the West as well. Since the eighteenth century American leaders had understood that whoever controlled the lower Mississippi controlled the West. Benjamin Franklin said as much when he rejected a Spanish proposal that would have restricted American use of the lower Mississippi. "A neighbor might as well ask me to sell my street door," Franklin explained. Thomas Jefferson reiterated this view when he declared, "There is on the globe one single spot the possessor of which is our natural and habitual enemy. It is New Orleans." Andrew Jackson acted on the same principle in treating the British attack on New Orleans in the War of 1812 as precisely what it was: the opening thrust of an attempt to sever the American West from the American East. Since then railroads had revised but hadn't repealed the laws of gravity and precipitation that made the Ohio, Mississippi, and Missouri rivers highways of commerce. When a relieved Lincoln declared, after Grant took Vicksburg, that "the Father of Waters again goes unvexed to the sea," he meant that the West would remain with the Union.[1]

Besides ensuring the political attachment of the West to the Union—an attachment reinforced, for the Far West, by the Pacific railroad—the Northern victory removed a principal hindrance to Western development. For four decades every effort to organize a Western territory or admit a Western state had run afoul of the slavery controversy. From the political fight over Missouri in the 1810s to the guerrilla war in Kansas in the 1850s, potential settlers had had to ask themselves whether, in addition to the normal hazards of life on the frontier, they wished to take on the slavery dispute. After the Civil War they didn't have to.

In American history the West had always been a comparative concept. At the midpoint of the eighteenth century the West began fifty miles from Philadelphia; by the early nineteenth century it started just across the Appalachians. At the end of the Civil War the West consisted, for the most part, of the region beyond the 100th meridian, the line that runs roughly from Laredo to Bismarck.

Distance from the center of population had always characterized the West, and still did; but more salient than the remoteness of the postwar West was its dryness. With the exception of a strip along the Pacific, where ocean breezes moderated the regional drought, and the crests of the highest interior ranges, which caught what little moisture escaped the Cascades and Sierra Nevada, the new West was a desert. Nearly everything about preexisting American society and culture (and their European forerunners) had supposed ready access to water. Adjusting to desert life required new techniques and technology, to stretch the limited resource, and a new frame of mind, to stretch the received society and culture.

Settling the new West also required answering the Indian question more definitively than ever. Since the seventeenth century, English and then American policy toward the aboriginal peoples had supposed a relatively empty district to the west of the moving frontier of white settlement, to which the tribes might be lured or driven. By the late nineteenth century, the frontier had reached the Pacific, and there was nowhere left to move the Indians to. Moreover, the supposition had rested on the further premise that the Western territory allowed to the Indians would never attract much white interest. But the capitalist revolution overturned that premise, along with so much else. Railroads opened the plains and mountains of the postwar West to white hunters, miners, ranchers, and farmers. The Indians resisted this latest encroachment, with a desperation born of the knowledge that they were making their last stand. The fighting didn't end until the Indians lacked the capacity to resist anymore.

The capitalist revolution shaped much else about the new West. To a far greater degree than in the East, settlement in the West reflected the influence of corporations and other institutions of capitalism. Eastern farms had rarely been self-sufficient; almost from the beginning, American farmers produced for market. But Western farms carried the commercial imperative to an extreme, in many cases becoming outdoor factories, specializing in particular crops with all the single-mindedness of the most highly organized Eastern mill. Eastern towns had been sited by God, as it were, where rivers joined, went over falls, or grew too shallow for ocean-going vessels. Western towns were sited by railroad corporations, along lines where their surveyors said the grading would be easiest and their accountants predicted the operation would be most profitable. Westerners were rugged individualists chiefly in their dreams (and the dreams of their Eastern and foreign admirers); in real life they were likely to draw paychecks for digging in corporate mines, plowing corporate fields, or chasing corporate cattle.

The settlement of the postwar West brought the frontier experience in America to an end. To those who applauded this latest conquest of nature and indigenous peoples, it seemed a triumph of American values. And so it was. But the values that mattered most by the waning years of the nineteenth century, and that figured most prominently on this final frontier, were the same capitalist values that were conquering the rest of the country.

IN 1865 the Sioux nation was somewhat more than a century into its own economic and social revolution, one triggered by the arrival of the horse. The western Sioux had split off from their eastern cousins, who occupied the forests of Minnesota, sometime before the beginning of the eighteenth century, largely in response to pressure from the neighboring Ojibwa, who in turn felt pressure from their own eastern neighbors and from whites. The western Sioux, also called Lakota, were a pedestrian people when they emerged onto the plains of the upper Missouri River. They traveled on foot and hunted on foot, devising elaborate strategies for killing the largest animal species they encountered, the bison, or buffalo. A favorite strategy entailed setting fire to the grassland behind a herd and then channeling the resulting stampede toward a cliff. Most of the herd would stop short, but a few beasts would fall or be pushed over the edge by those behind. Some of these would break their legs, and the Sioux hunters would dispatch them with arrows and spears.[2]

The Sioux encountered the horse about the time they reached the plains. The Spanish had reintroduced the horse to the Americas in the early sixteenth century (equines had roamed the Americas before the last Ice Age). Some escaped or were stolen; the descendants of these made their way north in the company of various Indians and on their own. The initial impact of the horse on the Sioux was modest. The horse increased their semi-nomadic range, but not till the mid-eighteenth century did they become an equestrian people.

The slow adoption of the horse resulted in part from the friction that attends any cultural transformation. Besides acquiring the animals, the Sioux had to learn how to train them, breed them, and care for them. All this took time. But the long lag probably also reflected an understanding that, in adopting horses, the Sioux were giving up other things. The Cheyennes told a story about their own adoption of horses, from the Comanches, and though the myth was peculiar to them, the lesson must have applied more broadly. According to this story, the Cheyennes' god spoke to them through the oldest priest of the tribe:

> If you have horses, everything will be changed for you forever. You will have to move around a lot to find pasture for your horses. You will have to give up gardening and live by hunting and gathering, like the Comanches. And you will have to come out of your earth houses and live in tents. . . . You will have to have fights with other tribes, who will want your pasture land or the places where you hunt. You will have to have real soldiers, who can protect the people. Think, before you decide.

Almost certainly the Cheyenne story showed the wisdom of hindsight, which may or may not have helped the Sioux appreciate what they were getting into. In any case the Sioux were riding seriously by the 1750s, when their own census records counted horse-borne warriors among their men of military age.[3]

At that point the Sioux might have become full nomads, following the buffalo herds for most of the year. But something else slowed the transition. From before the arrival of Europeans and Euro-Americans, the Sioux, like every other people in North America, were tied into various trade networks. Trade carried dried salmon from the Pacific Northwest across the mountains to the interior of the continent; trade brought turquoise from Mexico and flint from the Ozarks. And trade brought the first aspects of European civilization to the Sioux: horses from the Spanish lands to the south; knives, tobacco, and guns from the French and English to the east.

To pay for what they imported, the Sioux trapped beaver, which the Europeans and Americans coveted. The beaver trade employed the Sioux for generations after they acquired horses; as late as the 1790s a French trader saw the Sioux as trappers first of all. "The Sioux tribes are those who hunt most for the beaver and other good peltries of the Upper Missouri," he said. "They scour all the rivers and streams. . . . They carry away every springtime . . . a great number of them, which they exchange with the other Sioux situated on the St. Peter's"—Minnesota—"and Des Moines Rivers."[4]

But the beaver declined from overtrapping, and the Sioux shifted more and more to the buffalo. The buffalo furnished meat for food, robes for clothing, hides for shelter, tendons for bowstrings, and horns for containers. Yet the buffalo was never solely an item of subsistence; it was also a commodity for commerce. The Sioux traded buffalo robes, buffalo pemmican, and buffalo tongues to their Indian neighbors and later to white merchants at the trade fairs that formed a regular feature of life on the plains from the eighteenth century till the middle of the nineteenth. In the spring of 1832 at Fort Pierre on the upper Missouri, George Catlin encountered a band of Sioux who unceremoniously dumped fourteen hundred fresh tongues on the ground of the fort, taking in exchange several gallons of whiskey, which they immediately consumed.[5]

The buffalo trade was competitive, and the Sioux and the other tribes didn't confine themselves to competing on price and quality. From the late eighteenth century well into the nineteenth, the Sioux engaged their neighbors in a long series of conflicts that were, at their heart, economic wars. The Sioux sought to expand production by monopolizing the best hunting grounds; they tried to protect their markets by physically driving their rivals away from the trade fairs.

They achieved a success that would have made any robber baron proud. During the first half of the nineteenth century the Sioux established their dominance over the large region from the Minnesota River in the east to the head of the Yellowstone in the west, and from the Missouri in the north to the Republican River in the south.[6]

Their success owed to their ruthlessness—they destroyed entire villages of their enemies and made vassals of the survivors—and their mastery of the horse, but it also reflected an element of chance. As the Europeans and Euro-Americans did everywhere else in the Western Hemisphere starting in the fifteenth century, they unintentionally introduced exotic diseases among the indigenes of the North American interior. Smallpox, in particular, ravaged one community after another. In some cases the casualties were almost total; epidemics in the 1780s and 1790s killed almost 90 percent of the Arikaras and roughly the same proportion of Mandans and Hidatsas.

The Sioux, however, proved less vulnerable. The scattered nature of their camps and villages inhibited the spread of disease, and by the 1830s their American trading partners brought doctors to vaccinate them. As a result, while the population of nearly every other tribe was diminishing, slowly or swiftly, the Sioux numbers actually increased. By some estimates the Sioux population quintupled between 1800 and 1850, albeit to only 25,000.[7]

Until midcentury, the Sioux expansion had little effect on citizens of the United States. As the effort to vaccinate them indicated, at least some Americans saw the Sioux as allies. Yet others warned that the Sioux were getting too strong. "The day is not far off when the Sioux will possess the whole buffalo region, unless they are checked," the federal agent to the Pawnees predicted in 1838. As this forecast came true, federal officials attempted to neutralize the growing Sioux power. The mass emigration of gold seekers to California in 1849 and after brought large numbers of Americans to the Sioux country for the first time, and although few attacks on the emigrants took place, the intrusion sufficiently disturbed the politics of the region that American officials felt obliged to call a peace conference at Fort Laramie in 1851.[8]

It was a grand event. Dozens of tribes sent representatives, and perhaps ten thousand Indians attended; their horses stripped the grass for miles in every direction. But no one, either Indian or white, doubted that the Sioux were the dominant force among the indigenes. The conference produced an exchange of gifts and promises of friendly relations, yet its more important result was to let the Sioux and the Americans take the measure of each other. When the American officials tried to persuade the Sioux to stay north of the Platte—the main emigrant route west—Black Hawk, an Oglala Sioux, refused. His people, he said, had conquered the territory from which the Americans wanted to keep them, as fairly as the Americans had conquered much of the rest of the continent. "Those lands once belonged to the Kiowas and the Crows, but we whipped those nations out of them," Black Hawk said. "In this we did what the white men do when they want the lands of the Indians." The conference broke up peaceably, but neither the Americans nor the Sioux, on parting, doubted that they would be fighting for control of the northern Plains, perhaps soon.[9]

THE FIGHTING MIGHT have started at once had the Americans not become distracted by their own internal troubles. But though the squabble over slavery in Kansas postponed the conflict over the region farther north and west, the discovery of gold in Colorado in 1858 refocused attention on the lands still held by the Sioux and the other Plains Indians. The Pikes Peak and Denver gold rushes weren't as large as the rush to California, but they were more threatening to the indigenes, in that while the earlier argonauts had been passing through, these intruders came to stay. In 1861 the federal government created the Territory of Colorado, with a governor and other apparatus of permanent occupation.

The Indians responded to the new invasion variously. The Sioux launched raids against wagon trains, stagecoach roads, and isolated settlements, while the Cheyennes and Arapahos, less confident of their military prowess vis-à-vis the whites, generally acquiesced.

Yet their complaisance won them no protection. The Colorado governor, John Evans, and the commander of Colorado volunteers, Colonel John Chivington, contended that the Indians must be driven from Colorado. This view drew support from many whites, including those who had joined the Colorado volunteers to avoid the draft into the Union army. When the Cheyennes and Arapahos expressed their desire for peace with the whites, Evans balked. "What shall I do with the Third Colorado Regiment if I make peace?" he demanded of an officer who thought the governor ought to accept the Indians' proposal. "They have been raised to kill Indians, and they must kill Indians." Chivington was even more emphatic. "Kill all the Indians you come across," he ordered his soldiers. Nor did he except women and children. "Nits make lice," he explained to a Denver audience.[10]

Chivington's troops carried out his orders in late November 1864 on the banks of Sand Creek in eastern Colorado. After an overnight ride, during which the soldiers fortified themselves against the cold—and evidently against their consciences—with whiskey, the regiment attacked a camp of Cheyennes and Arapahos. The camp comprised mostly women, children, and old men, as the young men were away hunting. This circumstance was perfectly clear to the soldiers, as an eyewitness later explained. "I saw five squaws under a bank for shelter," he said. "When the troops came up to them they ran out and showed their persons to let the soldiers know they were squaws and begged for mercy." But mercy didn't appear. "The soldiers shot them all. . . . There were some thirty or forty squaws collected in a hole for protection. They sent out a little girl about six years old with a white flag on a stick. She had not proceeded but a few steps when she was shot and killed. All the squaws in that hole were afterwards killed. . . . I saw quite a number of infants in arms killed with their mothers." Death afforded no protection. "Every one I saw dead was scalped. I saw one squaw cut open with an unborn child, as I thought, lying by her side. . . . I saw one squaw whose privates had been cut out." Chivington's own soldiers confirmed the atrocities. "I did not see a body of man, woman, or child but was scalped," one said, "and in many instances their bodies were mutilated in the most horrible manner—men, women, and children's privates cut out, &c.; I heard one man say that he had cut out a woman's private parts and had them for exhibition on a stick. . . . I also heard of numerous instances in which men had cut out the private parts of females and stretched them over the saddle-bows and wore them over their hats while riding in the ranks."[11]

The Sand Creek massacre—or rather the response to it—revealed an abiding theme in American policy and attitudes toward Indians. For generations a sympathy gradient had existed regarding Indians, with greater sympathy emerging the farther one traveled east from the frontier. And so it did now. Many Westerners actively applauded Chivington and his men; the *Rocky Mountain News* asserted, "Colorado soldiers have again covered themselves with glory." Other Westerners, with slightly more conscience, were willing to overlook the atrocities the militia committed, as necessary to the advance of civilization. But Easterners grew queasy at the reports and many expressed outrage. Eastern editors decried the massacre; Congress launched an investigation. Yet even the Easterners had a limited attention span for Indian affairs. In the final winter of the Civil War, other matters intruded and the investigation proceeded slowly.[12]

Meanwhile the Indians took matters upon themselves. The Cheyennes and Arapahos joined the Sioux in a general assault on white outposts and settlements in Colorado. In January 1865 the allies attacked the town of Julesburg, killing indiscriminately, scalping the victims, and setting the buildings on fire. They tore out telegraph wires and closed the road to Denver, threatening Colorado's capital with starvation.[13]

Leading the Sioux was Red Cloud, a war chief of the Oglala band, who subscribed to a Sioux version of Manifest Destiny. "The Great Spirit raised both the white man and the Indian," he explained. "I think he raised the Indian first. He raised me in this land and it belongs to me. The white man was raised over the great waters, and his land is over there. Since they crossed the sea, I have given them room. There are now white people all about me. I have but a small spot of land left. The Great Spirit told me to keep it."

Red Cloud served notice of his vision at a council called by American officials during a lull in the fighting. The Americans hoped to negotiate rights for a road across the Sioux lands to Bozeman in Montana Territory, where gold had been discovered in 1862. Red Cloud attended the council but denounced the road as a pretext for further land grabs. "The white men have crowded the Indians back year by year until we are forced to live in a small country north of the Platte," he said. "And now our last hunting ground, the home of the People"—the Sioux—"is to be taken from us. Our women and children will starve, but for my part I prefer to die fighting."[14]

The whites went ahead with the Bozeman road, building forts along the route. Red Cloud gathered warriors from his fellow Sioux and from the Cheyennes and Arapahos. During the summer and autumn of 1866 Red Cloud's men harassed federal soldiers who were traveling the road, cutting trees for construction, and provisioning the forts.

Red Cloud's most active lieutenant was a young Oglala named Crazy Horse, who delighted in taunting the whites and drawing the unwary into ambushes. In late December Red Cloud and Crazy Horse laid a trap. A small company of Cheyennes, Arapahos, and Sioux struck a wagon train on the Bozeman road. They did enough damage to anger the soldiers stationed at Fort Phil Kearny, where the second in command was Captain

William Fetterman, a Civil War hero who couldn't believe Indians could fight nearly as effectively as the Confederates he had defeated. "A single company of regulars could whip a thousand Indians," he boasted. "A full regiment could whip the entire array of hostile tribes." On another day he declared, "With eighty men I could ride through the Sioux nation."[15]

With eighty-one men Fetterman galloped forth in pursuit of Crazy Horse and the Indian raiders. Fetterman's explicit orders were to halt at Lodge Trail Ridge, several miles from the fort, lest he outrun reinforcements. But he ignored the orders, intent on crushing the savages. Just beyond Lodge Trail Ridge waited two thousand Arapahos, Cheyennes, and Sioux; as Fetterman rode past they sprung their trap, cutting off the federals' retreat. Though Fetterman's men, better armed than the Indians and now fighting for their lives, put up a desperate resistance, they were annihilated. Not one escaped. Fetterman's body was found with a bullet through the temple; powder burns indicated that it was fired at close range, either by himself or by a fellow officer, in order that the captain not be taken alive. Many of the bodies were mutilated.[16]

Till William Sherman was nine he went by his middle name, Tecumseh, chosen by a father who admired the Shawnee chief responsible for the best organized and most nearly successful counteroffensive—in the early 1810s—in the history of the long struggle between whites and Indians for mastery of North America. Even after his father died and his mother adopted him out to a family that insisted on employing his Christian name, Sherman was "Cump" to his friends. If he noted the irony, after he inherited command of the war against the Indians of the Plains, he never let on.

Sherman could have entered politics at the end of the Civil War. In the celebrations that marked the Union victory he was the hero second only to Grant, and not always second. "The acclamation given Sherman was without precedent," a reporter covering the Washington review of the Union army declared. "The whole assemblage raised and waved and shouted as if he had been the personal friend of each and every one of them. . . . Sherman was the idol of the day." Happiness had never come easily to Sherman; depression trailed him for years. His brooding, even scowling, demeanor put people off. But now that he was the vindicator of liberty his sternness simply made him more appealing. Young women rushed to kiss his red-bearded cheek; he gained a reputation as "the great American soldier who whipped every foeman who stood before him and kissed every girl that he met." The young ladies couldn't vote, but their husbands and fathers could, and, by all evidence, many would have been delighted to vote for the man who drove Dixie down.[17]

But Sherman knew himself well enough to realize he wasn't meant for politics. He didn't suffer fools, and crowds made him testy. "At first he was affable," an observer at one of Sherman's ceremonial outings recalled. "Then he grew less cordial as the crowds crushed. He pushed down the steps, step by step, and refused proffered hands, finally exclaiming, 'Damn you, get out of the way, damn you!'" A voice called out asking whether Sherman would lead an army against French forces then occupying Mexico. Sherman shouted back, "You can go there if you like, and you can go to hell if you want to!" On another occasion he explained his political philosophy to a reporter: "When I speak, I speak to the point, and when I act in earnest, I act to the point. If a man minds his own business, I let him alone, but if he crosses my path, he must get out of the way."[18]

Sherman's admirers refused to be discouraged, and his disavowals of interest in politics merely titillated popular feeling. But meanwhile he accepted a new assignment from his old commander, Ulysses Grant. General orders issued in June 1865 divided the United States into nineteen departments and five divisions; Sherman received command of the Division of the Mississippi, comprising the Departments of the Ohio, Missouri, and Arkansas. The Ohio department was soon transferred to another division, and Sherman's command was renamed the Missouri Division, leaving him responsible for the entire West north of Texas.

From his headquarters in St. Louis he observed with concern the escalating hostilities on the Plains. Sherman initially blamed the white settlers, who wanted the army to "kill all the Indians," as he explained to Grant in the summer of 1866. The Indians, he said, were "pure beggars and poor devils more to be pitied than dreaded." Sherman determined to resist the white pressure for an army offensive. "I will not permit them to be warred against as long as they are not banded together in parties large enough to carry on war."[19]

Sherman was imposing an impossible condition. The Sand Creek massacre demonstrated that the Indians couldn't rely on the goodwill of whites for their survival (many of those killed at Sand Creek had huddled beneath a flag of the United States), and so they had little choice but to band together. Yet Sherman declared this unacceptable.

And after the destruction of Fetterman's force, he responded as might have been expected of the avenging angel of the Union army. "We must act with vindictive earnestness against the Sioux, even to their extermination: men, women, and children," he told Grant. The power of the Plains tribes must be broken. "Both the Sioux and the Cheyennes must die, or submit to our dictation."[20]

Sherman delivered his ultimatum personally to the Indians at a council at the forks of the Platte in September 1867. President Andrew Johnson had appointed a "peace commission" to seek an end to the fighting on the northern Plains. Johnson offered the Sioux a reservation consisting of the western half of the modern state of South Dakota. In addition the Sioux would receive hunting grounds along the Powder River, and the federal government would abandon the Bozeman road. Finally, the government would supply the Indians with rations and money payments for thirty years.

Sherman warned the Sioux to accept the president's offer. "If you don't choose your homes now," he said, "it will be too late next year." The Indians might drive the white soldiers back momentarily, but the soldiers would be followed by white settlers. "You can see for yourselves that travel across the country has increased so much that the slow ox wagons will not answer the white man. We will build iron roads, and you cannot stop the locomotives any more than you can stop the sun or the moon." The Great Father at Washington wanted to assist his Indian children. "Choose your homes and live like white men, and we will help you," Sherman said. Yet the Great Father's kindness was matched by his strength. "Our people in the East hardly think of what you call war out here, but if they make up their minds to fight, they will come out as thick as the herd of buffaloes, and if you continue fighting you will all be killed."[21]

The Sioux leaders refused to heed his advice, and they rode defiantly away from the council. Sherman increased the pressure. He directed General Phil Sheridan, his principal subordinate, to adopt whatever measures seemed necessary to bring the Sioux into compliance with the president's wishes. "Go ahead in your own way and I will back you with my whole authority," Sherman said.

If it results in the utter annihilation of these Indians, it is but the result of what they have been warned of again and again. . . . I will say nothing and do nothing to restrain our troops from doing what they deem proper on the spot, and will allow no mere vague general charges of cruelty and inhumanity to tie their hands, but will use all the powers confided to me to the end that these Indians, the enemies of our race and of our civilization, shall not again be able to begin and carry out their barbarous warfare on any kind of pretext they may choose to allege.[22]

Sheridan hardly needed the encouragement. The Union cavalry commander from the Civil War held all Indians in disdain; when a Comanche leader surrendered his force to Sheridan and identified himself as a "good Indian," Sheridan muttered, "The only good Indians I ever saw were dead Indians." Reported and repeated, Sheridan's characterization became a catchphrase of annihilation.[23]

As it happened, the extermination policy Sherman authorized wasn't implemented just yet. Red Cloud, recognizing that the Sioux couldn't hold out against the whites forever, led a delegation to Fort Laramie, where in November 1868 he signed a treaty accepting the reservation the Sherman commission had offered.[24]

Red Cloud's surrender won him a trip to Washington and New York, where he was applauded for his statesmanship by federal officials and for his foresight and sincerity by those Easterners who counted themselves friends of the Indians. "His earnest manner, his impassioned gestures, the eloquence of his hands, and the magnetism which he evidently exercises over an audience, produced a vast effect on the dense throng which listened to him yesterday," the *New York Times* observed after a rally in Red Cloud's honor in Manhattan.[25]

LIKE OTHER PLAINS tribes, the Sioux practiced a form of democracy that verged on anarchy. The various bands acknowledged no central authority, and the leader of one band held sway only so long as his arguments convinced the rest of the band. This feature of Indian governance consistently vexed Indian relations with federal authorities, for Washington might negotiate an agreement with one set of leaders only to have the agreement repudiated by other leaders and much of the Sioux nation.

The American government was hardly blameless in this. Federal nego-tiators regularly found compliant chiefs—often made deliberately drunk—who were willing to sign agreements the federals knew other members of the tribe would reject, and then treated those agreements as though they bound the whole tribe. When those other members did reject the agree-ments, Washington claimed willful violation and released itself to take what it wanted.

The Fort Laramie pact was an agreement that split the Sioux. Crazy Horse, Red Cloud's lieutenant, rejected the reservation the federals offered and determined to fight on. About the time Red Cloud was touring the East, Crazy Horse met a charismatic medicine man of the Hunkpapa Sioux named Sitting Bull. From youth Sitting Bull had been known for his visions, which frequently appeared to predict events that subsequently befell the Sioux. Of late he had gained a reputation for his vehement refusal to accept the reservation policy—"peace policy," it was called by its advocates in the U.S. government—embraced by Red Cloud. Crazy Horse similarly rejected what he considered Red Cloud's defeatism, and an affin-ity emerged between Crazy Horse and Sitting Bull, each determined that the Sioux should hold their territory against further white encroachment or die trying.[26]

They launched their defense of their homeland with a campaign against the construction crews of the Northern Pacific Railroad, then inching west from the Missouri River. During the summer of 1872 Crazy Horse and Sitting Bull sniped at surveyors and clashed more seriously with the mili-tary escorts sent to guard them. The Sioux resistance inspired Sherman to dispatch reinforcements, including the Seventh Cavalry, led by a long-haired hero of the Civil War battle of Richmond, George Armstrong Custer.

By the time Custer reached the Sioux country, construction on the Northern Pacific had been halted—not by Crazy Horse and Sitting Bull but by the Panic of 1873. Another development, however, no less linked to American capitalism, ensured that the struggle for the Plains would con-tinue and indeed intensify. Gold prospectors had skirted the Sioux region while less dangerous environs remained unexplored, but as they ran out of promising territory farther west, they were drawn to that easternmost island of Rocky Mountain topography, the Black Hills of Dakota. The Black Hills had long been holy to the Sioux, partly because their beetled ridges and dark canyons, contrasting so starkly with the open aspect of the plain that surrounds them, seemed an obvious home to spirits and other ethereal beings, but also because those canyons and their forests provided game in summer and shelter in winter.

The Sioux knew the Black Hills contained gold, but they wrapped their knowledge in a veil of enforced mystery. Decades earlier some Sioux had shown a Catholic missionary gold nuggets taken from the region; the missionary, warning them what the whites would do if they learned of the gold, advised them to bury the nuggets and suppress the knowledge. A Sioux council subsequently decreed death for anyone who told whites of the gold in the Black Hills.[27]

The mystery shrouding the area simply fired the imagination of the prospectors. With the possible exception of stock speculation, with which it shares many traits, no livelihood is more prone to rumor than gold prospecting. The slightest hint of gold in a new region can prompt a stampede to that place. This became the truer as the likely spots to look for gold dwindled. In the early 1870s reports of gold in the Black Hills surfaced periodically; by 1874 they had produced a groundswell of western demand that the Black Hills be opened to serious exploration. A Dakota editorialist spoke for many when he condemned the Fort Laramie treaty as an "abominable compact" that gave savages a veto over gold mining and other forms of economic development. "They will not dig the gold or let others do it," he wrote. "They are too lazy and too much like mere animals to cultivate the fertile soil, mine the coal, develop the salt mines, bore the petroleum wells, or wash the gold. Having all these things in their hands, they prefer to live as paupers, thieves and beggars; fighting, torturing, hunting, gorging, yelling and dancing all night to the beating of old tin kettles."[28]

As the depression in the East deepened, characterized by falling prices and other symptoms of shrinkage in the money supply, the Grant administration couldn't resist the opportunity to show it was taking steps to rectify the problem. It authorized an expedition to the Black Hills to determine whether the region was as rich as the rumors suggested.

George Custer headed the expedition, which included sufficient soldiers and armaments to discourage attack, a cadre of scientists to assay the

mineral resources of the region, a photographer to make a visual record of
the journey, and four newspapermen to publicize the fine work Colonel
Custer was doing for his country. The correspondents doubtless wished for
a scrape with the Indians to enliven their dispatches, but they had to make
do with Custer's confirmation of gold in the Black Hills. In a letter to the
War Department, Custer reported finding "40 or 50 small particles of pure
gold, in size averaging that of a small pin head, and most of it obtained
today from one panful of earth." The newsmen amplified Custer's words
for their lay readership. "Here, in Custer's Valley, rich gold and silver mines
have been discovered, both placer and quartz diggings," the reporter for
the *Bismarck Tribune* declared. "This immense section bids fair to become
the El Dorado of America." The *Yankton Press and Dakotan* headlined,
"Struck It at Last! Rich Mines of Gold and Silver Reported Found by
Custer. Prepare for Lively Times! . . . The National Debt to Be Repaid
When Custer Returns."[29]

The news set off a gold rush to the Black Hills, despite the Fort
Laramie treaty and despite initial efforts of the federal government, in
keeping with the "peace policy," to stop it. "You are hereby directed to use
the force at your command to burn the wagon trains, destroy the outfits,
and arrest the leaders," Phil Sheridan wired General Alfred Terry, the
commander of the Dakota district, regarding the gold rushers. But neither
Terry nor other officers in the field took more than rhetorical action
against the miners. Even these efforts were undercut by Grant's decision to
try to purchase the Black Hills from the Sioux. Red Cloud was ready to
deal, reckoning that what the whites wanted they sooner or later would get
and that the Indians ought at least to receive something in return. But
negotiations stuck on price (in part because a translator miscast the Indians' demand for $7 million as $70 million). And in any event, Crazy Horse
and Sitting Bull denied the authority of Red Cloud or anyone else to
barter away their sacred patrimony.[30]

Meanwhile the rush for gold continued. By the spring of 1876 some
fifteen thousand miners and camp followers had occupied the riverbanks
and gravel bars of the Black Hills. Their presence remained illegal, and in
public comments to persons critical of the government's unfair treatment
of the Indians, Grant reiterated that the region was off-limits to white settlement. Yet he made no effort to remove the intruders.

Instead he authorized a campaign to bring Crazy Horse, Sitting Bull, and the other holdouts—"non-treaty Indians"—to acknowledge the authority of the federal government. Their acknowledgment, Grant believed, would facilitate the negotiations with Red Cloud. Crazy Horse and the others were said to be in the valley of the Yellowstone; the president gave the order to pursue them there.

The planning for the campaign was complicated by the impeachment trial of War Secretary William Belknap, on charges of corruption. At a time when Custer should have been in Dakota preparing to march, he had to be in Washington testifying to Congress. Custer's military record, his theatrical good looks, and his willingness to court reporters made him a favorite of the press and, through the press, of the American people. With scandal swirling about the War Department and the Grant administration generally, the dashing colonel commanded the nation's attention.

The nation followed his progress from Washington, after his testimony, to Chicago, where he intended to catch another train, to Bismarck. But to his astonishment and that of the watching public, he was arrested at Chicago, on orders of the president. Grant hadn't appreciated Custer's revealing testimony before Congress, nor did he like the attention being lavished on the young officer. Custer, eager to rejoin his regiment, hadn't received proper authorization before departing Washington, and Grant took the opportunity to remind him who commanded the army.

Grant's critics, whose ranks were growing by the week amid the political scandals, employed the arrest to lambaste the administration yet again. Custer was lionized as the truth teller whom the administration sought to muzzle; the Democrats denounced the administration for playing politics with the security of the frontier and the lives of American soldiers.

The criticism forced Grant to release the colonel. Custer was allowed to continue west, although the War Department insisted that disciplinary action remained a possibility. When the Seventh Cavalry rode out of Fort Abraham Lincoln on the Missouri River below Bismarck in May 1876, Custer rode at their head, more famous than ever.

Custer reveled in his heightened celebrity. By one account, he told some Arikara and Crow scouts, enlisted for the campaign against their traditional Sioux enemies, that this would be his last western expedition. If they helped him defeat the Sioux, he would return to Washington and become the Great Father there. He added that he would remember his Indian friends. Whether Custer conjured a race for the presidency from thin air or was prompted by mischievous Democrats is unclear. But either way his mission against the Sioux acquired an importance a mere Indian fight would have lacked.[31]

"I WAS BORN in the Moon of the Popping Trees on the Little Powder River in the Winter When the Four Crows Were Killed," Black Elk remembered. Black Elk was an Oglala Sioux, the Moon of the Popping Trees was December, and the four Crows were killed in 1863. "I was three years old when my father's right leg was broken in the Battle of the Hundred Slain"—the ambush of Fetterman's column. "I had never seen a Wasichu"—a white man—"then, and did not know what one looked like, but everyone was saying that the Wasichus were coming and that they were going to take our country and rub us all out and that we should all have to die fighting." Black Elk was too young to fight, but he felt the presence of the invaders. "All this time I was not allowed to play very far away from our tepee, and my mother would say, 'If you are not good the Wasichus will get you.'" He also felt the hardship the white pressure caused. "We were going away from where the soldiers were, and I do not know where we went, but it was west. It was a hungry winter, for the deep snow made it hard to find the elk, and also many of the people went snowblind. We wandered a long time, and some of the bands got lost from each other."[32]

Black Elk's father was a medicine man, as were several of his uncles. The boy suspected he shared their gift and on occasion heard voices from beyond the mortal realm. But not till the summer when he was nine and fell ill with fever did he experience a full-blown vision. He felt himself being carried up and out of his body, high among the clouds. The clouds became snowy hills. "I looked and saw a bay horse standing there, and he began to speak." The bay horse told him to look to the west. "I looked, and there were twelve black horses yonder all abreast with necklaces of bison hoofs, and they were beautiful, but I was frightened because their manes were lightning and there was thunder in their nostrils." The bay horse guided him to a council of the Grandfathers of the North, East, South, and West. "Younger brother," said the Grandfather of the South, "with the powers of the four quarters you shall walk, a relative. Behold, the living center of a nation I shall give you, and with it many you shall save." The Grandfather of the South extended his arm.

He was holding in his hand a bright red stick that was alive, and as I looked it sprouted at the top and sent forth branches, and on the branches many leaves came out and murmured, and in the leaves the birds began to sing. And then for just a little while I thought I saw beneath it in the shade the circled villages of people and every living thing with roots or legs or wings, and all were happy. "It shall stand in the center of the nation's circle," said the Grandfather, "a cane to walk with and a people's heart, and by your powers you shall make it blossom."

The horses began to speak to Black Elk, explaining what the Grandfathers had done. "They have given you the sacred stick and your nation's hoop. . . . In the center of the hoop you shall set the stick and make it grow into a shielding tree, and bloom."

The horses carried Black Elk among the clouds again. They came to a village filled with the sounds of mourning. "When I looked around I saw that in nearly every tepee the women and the children and the men lay dying." Black Elk wanted to weep. But a voice told him to plant the stick and the hoop.

I took the bright red stick and at the center of the nation's hoop I thrust it in the earth. As it touched the earth it leaped mightily in my hand and was a waga chun, the rustling tree, very tall and full of leafy branches and of all birds singing. And beneath it all the animals were mingling with the people like relatives and making happy cries. The women raised their tremolo of joy, and the men shouted all together: "Here we shall raise our children and be as little chickens under the mother sheo's wing.". . . Then, when the many little voices ceased, the great Voice said: "Behold the circle of the nation's hoop, for it is holy, being endless, and thus all powers shall be one power in the people without end."[33]

Black Elk's vision of the nation's hoop became the theme of his life. Others respected his vision, though they reserved judgment of its significance till he grew older and proved its power. In the meantime they were more impressed with Crazy Horse, Black Elk's second cousin. Crazy Horse had a vision, too, one that convinced him that the real world existed behind the shadow world of everyday life. When Crazy Horse stepped into his real world, nothing in the shadow world could touch him. "It was this vision that gave him his great power," Black Elk said, "for when he went into a fight, he had only to think of that world to be in it again, so that he could go through anything and not be hurt." And in fact he never was hurt in battle.

Black Elk remembered Crazy Horse's strange charisma. "He was a small man among the Lakotas and he was slender and had a thin face and his eyes looked through things and he always seemed to be thinking hard about something." He would walk among the people of his village like a man in a trance. "In his own tepee he would joke, and when he was on the warpath with a small party he would joke to make his warriors feel good. But around the village he hardly ever noticed anybody, except little children. All the Lakotas like to dance and sing, but he never joined a dance, and they say nobody ever heard him sing." Yet he obviously cared for his people. "He never wanted to have many things for himself, and did not have many ponies like a chief. They say that when game was scarce and the people were hungry, he would not eat at all." His people loved and respected him. "They would do anything he wanted or go anywhere he said."[34]

DURING THE SPRING of 1876 Crazy Horse led his people to the Yellowstone country. They hunted and recovered their strength from the winter, and Crazy Horse and Sitting Bull gathered warriors for the fight against the Wasichus. Some of those who joined them were Cheyennes and Arapahos; others were Sioux who wintered on the reservation but now came north for what might be a last summer living the old, free life. Many were drawn by the reputation of Sitting Bull, who promised a Sun Dance for the month when the grass returned to the hillsides.

Perhaps Crazy Horse and Sitting Bull thought they could defeat the white soldiers. Unlike Red Cloud, who had been to the East and seen that the whites were a thousand times as many as the Sioux, neither Crazy Horse nor Sitting Bull had any clear idea what they were up against. Crazy Horse had his vision of the Wasichus as shadow soldiers, while Sitting Bull, after days of fasting, dancing, and self-mutilation (with the loss of considerable blood), reported a vision of his own, in which an army of white soldiers rode toward an Indian camp, but upside down, their horses' hooves clawing the sky and the soldiers' heads scraping the earth. This meant they would die, he said.[35]

The white soldiers had their own notions. During the first two weeks of June they hunted along the Yellowstone for Crazy Horse and the Indians. One column of troops, under General George Crook, made contact with a band of Sioux and Cheyennes on Rosebud Creek and fought a sharp battle there. But then they lost the trail. The officers argued among themselves as to how many warriors Crazy Horse had. Custer thought fifteen hundred; Crook said many fewer than that. In fact Crazy Horse had about three thousand. Custer meanwhile commanded about six hundred troops, while Crook had perhaps a thousand, as well as two or three hundred Crow and other Indian allies. But neither Custer nor Crook thought the numbers mattered much. The white soldiers were more powerfully armed than the enemy Indians, more stoutly mounted, and presumably more thoroughly disciplined. Custer in particular believed that if he could somehow corner Crazy Horse, he would certainly prevail.

In the last week of June, Custer's Crow scouts spotted Crazy Horse's camp on the west bank of the river the whites called the Little Big Horn and the Indians the Greasy Grass. The scouts warned Custer that the Sioux were far more numerous than he had guessed; Bloody Knife, the leader of the scouts, said Crazy Horse had more warriors than Custer's men had bullets. Custer dismissed the warning as counsel expected of a people terrorized for generations by the Sioux. His only concern was that the Sioux might escape, and to prevent this he pushed forward with all speed. He ordered Major Marcus Reno to attack the Sioux camp from the south while he looped north to cut off the Indians' escape. The trapped Indians would be forced to fight.[36]

BLACK ELK WAS thirteen now, and with several other boys he was tending horses along the Greasy Grass on the morning of June 25, 1876. His father had told him to be careful. "If anything happens," he said, "you must bring the horses back as fast as you can. . . . Keep your eyes on the camp." But nothing happened as the sun rose in the summer sky, and the boys grew hot and restless. They persuaded one of their number, a cousin of Black Elk, to mind the horses while they cooled off in the river. "I did not feel well," Black Elk remembered afterward. "I felt queer. It seemed that something terrible was going to happen. But I went in with the boys anyway." The river, running full with the snowmelt from the Bighorn Mountains, was bracingly cold, and Black Elk forgot his odd feeling. He and the others stayed in the water longer than they had planned; his cousin, impatient in their absence, brought the ponies down to the river's edge.

"Just then we heard the crier shouting in the Hunkpapa camp, which was not very far from us, 'The chargers are coming! They are charging! The chargers are coming!'" Black Elk remembered. The alarm spread to the other bands.

> The crier of the Oglalas shouted the same words, and we could hear the cry going from camp to camp northward clear to the Santees and Yanktonais. Everybody was running now to catch the horses. We were lucky to have ours right there just at that time. My older brother had a sorrel, and he rode away fast toward the Hunkpapas. I had a buckskin. My father came running and said: "Your brother has gone to the Hunkpapas without his gun. Catch him and give it to him. Then come right back to me." He had my six-shooter too, the one my aunt gave me. I took the guns, jumped on my pony and caught my brother. I could see a big dust rising just beyond the Hunkpapa camp and all the Hunkpapas were running around and yelling, and many were running wet from the river. Then out of the dust came the soldiers on their big horses. They looked big and strong and tall and they were all shooting.[37]

As the women and children of the Hunkpapa camp scrambled to escape the bullets of the white soldiers, Gall, also called Pizi, an orphan whom Sitting Bull had adopted as a younger brother, rallied the Hunkpapa warriors for a counterattack. Eight years earlier Gall had spoken for the Hunkpapas to the Sherman peace commission. "We were born naked and have been taught to hunt and live on the game," he said. "You tell us that we must learn to farm, live in one house, and take on your ways. Suppose the people living beyond the great sea should come and tell you that you must stop farming and kill your cattle, and take your houses and land. What would you do? Would you not fight them?" Gall's words, and his actions since then, had won him the following of most of the Hunkpapas, who respected him behind only Sitting Bull.[38]

Reno's attack killed several members of Gall's immediate family. "It made my heart bad," he explained later. "After that I killed all my enemies with the hatchet." Gall's example bolstered his comrades. "In the Hunkpapa camp a cry went up," Black Elk remembered. "'Take courage! Don't be a woman! The helpless are out of breath!'" For several moments confusion covered the battlefield. "It was all dust and cries and thunder," Black Elk said. "The women and children were running. . . . The warriors were coming on their ponies."

Gall's counterattack drove Reno's column into the trees along the river, where the federal soldiers dismounted to fight afoot. "The valley went darker with dust and smoke," Black Elk recalled.

> And there were only shadows and a big noise of many cries and hoofs and guns. On the left of where I was I could hear the shod hoofs of the soldiers' horses going back into the brush, and there was shooting everywhere. Then the hoofs came out of the brush, and I came out and was in among men and horses weaving in and out and going upstream, and everybody was yelling, "Hurry! Hurry!" The soldiers were running upstream and we were all mixed there in the twilight and the great noise. I did not see much, but once I saw a Lakota charge at a soldier who stayed behind and fought and was a very brave man. The Lakota took the soldier's horse by the bridle, but the soldier killed him with a six-shooter. I was small and could not crowd in to where the soldiers were, so I did not kill anybody. There were so many ahead of me, and it was all dark and mixed up.

During a lull in the fighting, Black Elk saw his people stripping dead and wounded white soldiers of their arms and uniforms. "There was a soldier on the ground and he was still kicking. A Lakota rode up and said to me, 'Boy, get off and scalp him.' I got off and started to do it. He had short hair and my knife was not very sharp. He ground his teeth. Then I shot him in the forehead and got his scalp."

Black Elk was old enough to mutilate an enemy but young enough to want his mother to be the first to know about it. He rode through the camp carrying the bloody prize till he found her on a hill overlooking the battlefield, where the women were singing encouragement to their husbands and sons. "My mother gave a big tremolo"—the song of celebration—"just for me when she saw my first scalp," he said.[39]

By now the center of the battle had shifted. Custer's column had appeared below the Indian camp, where the colonel expected to cut off the Indians he thought would be fleeing Reno's attack. But he discovered to his shock that Gall had broken Reno's attack and that Crazy Horse commanded twice the army he had guessed. The Sioux chief hurled his warriors against the federal cavalry, with himself in the lead. "Hokahey!"—Take courage!—he cried. "It is a good day to fight! It is a good day to die!" Others echoed the cry. "They were yelling 'Hokahey' like a big wind roaring, and making the tremolo, and you could hear eagle bone whistles screaming," Black Elk remembered.[40]

Custer found himself beset on all sides. He led his men to the highest point in the area, later called Custer Hill, where they dismounted and dug in. He might have thought his chances good, for though badly outnumbered he had better arms and the better position. And while Indians were known for their ambush and skirmishing abilities, they had shown little stomach for frontal assault. Custer knew that federal reinforcements were coming; if he and his men could hold out for several hours or overnight, they might escape.

Crazy Horse likewise knew there were other federals in the area. He also knew he would never have another such chance to strike a blow against the Wasichus. He probably couldn't have restrained his warriors anyway; they were as eager as he to avenge past wrongs and forestall future injuries.

The warriors charged before Custer's men were able to form a compact body. The Indian ponies slashed through the federal lines, such as they were. The bluecoats fell to bullets, arrows, lances, clubs, and hatchets. "The country was alive with Indians going in all directions, like swallows, yet the great body all the time moving down on Custer," an Oglala warrior remembered. An Arapaho recalled Crazy Horse that day as "the bravest man I ever saw. He rode closest to the soldiers, yelling to his warriors. All the soldiers were shooting at him, but he was never hit."[41]

The Indians knew Custer as "Long Hair," for his flowing reddish-blond locks. But he had cut them recently, and so he was hard to pick out from the other white soldiers. "We did not know till the fight was over that he was the white chief," one Indian warrior explained. All the bluecoats fought stubbornly. "They kept in order and fought like brave warriors as long as they had a man left," Crow King, one of the Sioux leaders, said.[42]

Custer's command survived for less than half an hour. He and 225 of his men died that afternoon above the Little Big Horn. Reno's column, pinned down in the woods by the river, survived an overnight siege till Crazy Horse, learning of the approach of federal relief, abandoned the siege and moved the camp.

"We could not see much of the battle for the big dust," Black Elk recalled of Custer's last moments. "But we knew there would be no soldiers left." The boy left his mother and the other women to scavenge the field with his peers.

> We rode across the Greasy Grass to the mouth of a gulch that led up through the bluff to where the fighting was. Before we got there, the Wasichus were all down, and most of them were dead, but some of them were still alive and kicking. Many other little boys had come up by this time, and we rode around shooting arrows into the Wasichus. There was one who was squirming around with arrows sticking in him, and I started to take his coat, but a man pushed me away and took the coat for himself. Then I saw something bright hanging on this soldier's belt, and I pulled it out. It was round and bright and yellow and very beautiful, and I put it on me for a necklace. At first it ticked inside, and then it did not any more. I wore it around my neck a long time before I found out what it was and how to make it tick again. . . .
>
> There was a soldier who was raising his arms and groaning. I shot an arrow into his forehead, and his arms and legs quivered.

Many Indians had been killed or badly wounded; the latter included one of Black Elk's cousins. "His father and my father were so angry over this that they went and butchered a Wasichu and cut him open. The Wasichu was fat, and his meat looked good to eat, but we did not eat any."

The celebration of the battle was postponed till the camp had moved safely beyond the reach of the new federal column. But the Sioux composed kill-songs as they traveled, and when they reached a resting place they feasted far into the night. Black Elk remembered some of the songs:

> Long Hair has never returned,
> So his woman is crying, crying,
> Looking over here, she cries. . . .

Long Hair, where he lies nobody knows.
Crying, they seek him.
He lies over here.[13]

CRAZY HORSE COULD defeat Custer, but he couldn't hold back the westering tide of capitalism. Conceivably the Sioux might have made peace with the presence of gold miners, but their way of living couldn't survive the activities of commercial buffalo hunters. During the centuries they had hunted afoot, the Sioux and other predatory Plains tribes had lived in rough equilibrium with their principal prey. The equilibrium could indeed be rough, not least since the buffalo themselves depended on resources—grasses, primarily—that in turn depended on resources—the various forms of precipitation—that fluctuated dramatically over the short and longer term. Drought was a recurrent feature of the climate of the Plains, and in periods of drought the grass withered and the buffalo dwindled. Tree-ring patterns and other forms of evidence indicate that drought afflicted the central Plains from 1761 to 1773, from 1798 to 1803, and from 1822 to 1832. Farther north the timing and duration of the droughts were different, with the worst patch being a fifteen-year shortfall in moisture from 1836 to 1851. During the driest spells, as much as 90 percent of the prairie grass died.[44]

Deaths among the buffalo were certainly not as great, as the buffalo possessed a mobility the grasses didn't. But the high reproductive rate of the buffalo—20 percent per year in optimal circumstances—suggests an evolutionary need to rebound from drastic mortality in bad times. Of course the increased buffalo mortality wasn't simply due to starvation. Wolves had evolved along with the buffalo, and though a strong adult buffalo could withstand a wolf attack, sick or malnourished buffaloes often couldn't. Nor could weakened adults defend their calves. The result was that during times of climatic stress the buffalo population could plunge. Neither were buffalo numbers guaranteed by adequate rainfall. Due to the potential for rapid population growth, during wet spells the herds could multiply exponentially and outstrip the ability of the range to support them. The resulting population crashes could be even more dramatic than those induced by drought.[45]

As long as the Plains tribes had remained pedestrian, they depended on the buffalo only in part. They hunted other game, gathered roots and berries, and planted beans and squashes. Though inadvertently, perhaps, they thereby insulated themselves from the worst effects of the buffalo crashes. But in acquiring horses they allowed themselves to become almost completely dependent on the buffalo, which in good times provided an easier living than their previous resource base but which in bad times forced them to share the buffalo's hardship. Meanwhile their horses (and the large herds of feral horses) competed with the buffalo for forage, intensifying the pressure on the range.

Like the buffalo, the Indians and their horses migrated during droughts away from the most severely stricken areas. The resulting contact with neighboring tribes and peoples often led to war. The Sioux raided the Pawnees, Hidatsas, and Arikaras to the east and the Crows and Blackfoots to the west. The Comanches, the dominant people of the southern Plains, thrust aside the Apaches and constantly threatened the Texas outposts of Mexico.

Had the Plains Indians exploited the buffalo for their own use alone, the pressure on the herds might have been sustainable. But a few decades after the equestrian revolution transformed life in the North American West, the capitalist revolution began transforming life in the North American East, and its influence could be felt even upon the Plains. Steamboats plied the Missouri by the 1820s, carrying traders of the American Fur Company and its rivals. Till then the fur trade had focused on beaver pelts, but changing tastes and the depletion of the resource caused the traders to seek a replacement. Although buffalo robes (for blankets and carriage throws) served a different fashion purpose than the beaver pelts (which had been made into hats), from the standpoint of company profits they were interchangeable. During the latter half of the 1820s, traders shipped nearly 800,000 buffalo robes through New Orleans. White hunters secured some of the robes, but the principal suppliers were the Plains tribes, who traded the robes (and sometimes the tongues of the buffalo) for guns, ammunition, blankets, steel knives, and liquor.[46]

Before long the hunting made noticeable inroads upon the herds. A traveler along the Missouri reported in 1849 that the buffalo—"the robes of which constitute by far the most important article of traffic" in the region—"are now not near as numerous as a few years since, and the number is every year diminishing."[47]

As it happened, the intensification of commercial hunting coincided with deepening drought in certain areas. It also overlapped the introduction of competing species and the pathogens they bore. Introduced disease wasn't a problem for the human species alone in North America; the animals the humans brought with them carried bacteria and viruses that sickened the native animal species. Anthrax was a particular scourge, and as the cattle herds of the settlers pushed up against the buffalo herds of the Indians, the anthrax bacterium jumped species. Because the buffalo had no inherited immunity to the disease, its progression could be devastating. "It destroys the bison in a kind of slow explosion," one authority later wrote. For reasons that remain unclear but doubtless involved climate, the effect was most acute on the far northern Plains, in Canada. But the impact rippled south into the United States.[48]

The disease and drought magnified the effect of the commercial hunting and accelerated the decline of the herds, threatening not merely the Indians' trade with the fur companies but the Indians' very existence. As early as 1855 the federal Indian agent at Fort Laramie declared, "The buffalo is becoming scarce and it is more difficult from year to year for the Indians to kill a sufficient number to supply them with food and clothing."[49]

The intrusion of the railroads onto the Plains sealed the doom of the buffalo culture. The construction gangs of the railroads required large quantities of meat, which buffalo hunters provided. Upon completion, the railroads dramatically reduced the transportation costs of buffalo products, including, for the first time, meat for Eastern markets. After tanners in Europe discovered the secret of curing buffalo hides, buffalo leather became a staple for the belts that spun the pulleys and flywheels of European and American factories. Chemical engineers learned to reduce buffalo bones to fertilizer and pigments. The railroads brought recreational hunters to the Plains, individuals who paid for the opportunity to kill the biggest game in North America.[50]

American arms makers designed special weapons for use against the buffalo. The most famous of the buffalo rifles was the Sharps "Big Fifty," which could drop the biggest bulls at long range. The use of the weapons required skill and experience; seasoned hunters knew, among other things, not to waste time on a head shot. "Against the frontal bone of the bison's skull, the lead falls harmless," declared an astonished hunter, who proceeded to explain:

I once approached a buffalo which stood wounded in a ravine. I took position upon the hillside, knowing that he could not readily charge up it, at a distance of only fifteen yards. I fired three shots from a Henry rifle full against the forehead, causing no other result than some angry head-shaking. I then took a Spencer carbine and fired twice with it. At each shot the bull sank partly to his knees, but immediately recovered again. I afterward examined the skull, and could detect no fracture.[51]

Yet once the hunters mastered their art, the killing proceeded with industrial efficiency. In the 1870s John and Wright Mooar roamed the Plains with a fleet of sixteen prairie schooners. On the outbound voyage the wagons carried ingots of lead and barrels of powder, besides the tools necessary to service the Mooars' arsenal of Sharps rifles. Inbound they replaced the lead and powder with buffalo hides, four to five thousand per season. Joe McCombs's outfit was even larger and more destructive; in 1877 his crew came home with nearly ten thousand hides.[52]

As with other resources of the West, the opportunity to profit from the buffalo engendered a gold-rush mentality. Because no one held legal title to the herds, no one had material incentive to preserve them. Rather, the incentives all pointed the other way: toward a frenzy of exploitation, lest others capture the prize first. The killing climaxed in the first years of the 1880s, when hundreds of thousands of buffalo were killed annually.[53]

Within a few years it was all over. The young Theodore Roosevelt traveled to western Dakota Territory in 1883 expressly to hunt buffalo, but where a decade earlier the herds had been immense, that September Roosevelt had to search for a week to find a single specimen—whose rarity didn't prevent his adding it to the slaughter's total.[54]

BY THEN the war for the Plains was over, too. Word of Custer's destruction on the Little Big Horn reached the East almost upon the hundredth anniversary of American independence. Some who heard the news sympathized with the Sioux in their desperate struggle to remain free, but more responded to the heroic myth that instantly sprang up about "Custer's Last Stand": how the valiant colonel and his men held out against overwhelming odds till the sheer weight of the savage attack brought them down. Not that it mattered much in the end, but the very magnitude of

Crazy Horse's victory probably cost him support among that minority of Americans disposed to treat the Indians leniently.

At the War Department, William Sherman was bombarded with demands to capture or kill Crazy Horse and his warriors. The governor of Montana Territory called on Congress to authorize a volunteer corps of Indian fighters. Sherman didn't relish dealing with volunteers, who would be beyond the discipline of the regular army, and anyway he thought the volunteer bill a boondoggle chiefly designed to provide work—at a rate far higher than Sherman could pay his own soldiers—for the flotsam of the frontier. He managed to deflect the volunteer corps but only by promising swift action by his own men.[55]

Sherman sent reinforcements to George Crook, who chased the Sioux around the upper Missouri during the summer of 1876. Crook's men burned Sioux villages and food stores, relying on hunger to succeed where direct force had failed. The Sioux occasionally counterattacked, but their lack of ammunition prevented them from inflicting serious damage on their pursuers. To the federals' surprise and perhaps their own, the Sioux held out through the winter of 1876–77, but by the following spring they could stand no more. Crook sent Red Cloud to offer Crazy Horse a reservation on the Powder River if he would stop running and fighting. Crazy Horse saw no alternative. His people were starving, those horses they hadn't eaten were barely able to stand, and his warriors lacked powder and bullets. He accepted the offer and led his people into what they all considered captivity.

But Crazy Horse wasn't meant for reservation life. The federals distrusted him, as did some of the reservation Sioux, who resented the way his long holdout had intensified the repression they lived under. When the federal government procrastinated on its promise of a Powder River reservation and some of the Sioux grew restive, Crazy Horse's Indian enemies spread stories that he intended to resume the fight. Crook ordered him arrested; as he was being transported to jail, he tried to break away. His guards mortally wounded him.[56]

Chapter 7

PROFITS ON THE HOOF

N ature may or may not abhor a vacuum, but empty ecological niches attract new species. The destruction of the buffalo left the grass-lands of the North American interior available for other grazers, animals whose innards contained the microbes necessary to break down the cellulose of the grass stems and leaves into a form the gastric juices of the grazers could handle. Horses had shown their ability to match the buffaloes' digestive feats, but horseflesh has never been honored in Euro-American cuisine. Beef was more to the taste of the newcomers, and so cattle became the replacement of (human) choice for the buffalo.

Yet the introduction of cattle to the Plains had to do less with anyone's desire to see that grass not die uneaten than with the growing appetite of American capitalism. From the beginning, cattle husbandry on the Plains was a business, one driven by the same imperatives that governed the oil business and the steel business. The cattle business required inputs of capital and labor, it called for a matching of supply and demand, and it rewarded economies of scale and the application of technology. No single cattleman became as wealthy as Andrew Carnegie or John D. Rockefeller, but a few built empires that would have given princes pause and that proved more durable than many of the corporate fiefdoms of the captains of non-animal industry.

CATTLE CROSSED THE Atlantic in the same Spanish ships that brought the horses, and they escaped into the wilds of the West about the same time the horses did. But they spread more slowly than the horses, largely because they didn't seem such an improvement on the aboriginal status quo. Horses gave their adopters new powers; cattle simply put something different on the dinner plate. And humans being culinary conservatives, the difference rarely worked in the cattle's favor. Until the middle of the nineteenth century, pork was the meat preferred by most Americans. Harriet Martineau, traveling across America in the 1830s, found pig flesh ubiquitous and inescapable. "In one house at Boston, where a numerous family lives in handsome style, and where I several times met large dinner parties, I never once saw an ounce of meat except ham," she wrote. Elsewhere the theme was the same, with minor variations. "Throughout the South the traveler meets little else than pork, under all manner of disguises, and fowls."[1]

Tastes shifted within decades. Most Americans who kept cattle did so for milk or draft, although the animals were often eventually eaten. But at the extreme southern edge of the Great Plains, where Texas meets Mexico, cattle were raised for beef and hides. For much of the century before the Civil War, feral cattle from northern Mexico roamed the broad valley of the Rio Grande. The mild winters and abundant grass allowed the herds to multiply almost unchecked. Mexican *rancheros* (ranchmen) and *vaqueros* (cowboys) learned to tend the cattle, rounding them up once or twice a year, branding them with the owners' marks, selling or slaughtering some for their beef and hides, and turning the rest loose to graze and multiply the more. The acquisition of Texas by the United States brought this cattle culture to Anglo-America, but it never lost its Latin flavor. The Anglos, mostly from the American East and South, knew cows as creatures kept in pens and small pastures, few in number and often treated as family pets; they had never seen anything like the giant herds of Texas longhorns. But the Anglo Texans were fast learners, adopting the tools and techniques of the cattle culture from the Mexican Texans, or *tejanos*. The Anglos adopted the terminology, too. *Rancho* anglicized to "ranch," *la riata* to "lariat," *vaquero* to "buckaroo."[2]

Not that the cattle noticed. They treated the Anglos with the same disdain they had always shown the Latinos. Keen of scent, wary of danger, rugged of constitution, the longhorns continued to thrive on the Rio Grande, and they spread up the coastal bend as the Americans and the Indians decimated the buffalo herds that had once dominated the Texas grasslands.

Before 1860 enterprising cattlemen occasionally attempted to transport Texas cattle to markets farther east. Small herds were driven to the Red River of Louisiana and shipped downstream to New Orleans. A few went by sea from Galveston to New Orleans, Mobile, and even Havana. One particularly ambitious individual gathered a herd of a thousand Texas steers and drove them all the way to Ohio. Some Texas cattle reached Chicago during the 1850s. Gold drew Texans to California in 1849 and after, and some trailed cattle there, only to discover that California, like Texas heir to the history and traditions of New Spain, had cattle enough for its own needs.

The impetus for the efforts to export cattle was the price difference between Texas and the various destinations. Cattle were almost free for the taking in Texas, the principal expense being the labor cost of rounding them up. In the East cattle commanded twenty to forty dollars per head. Simple arithmetic suggested that the man who could get a thousand head of Texas cattle to market in the East might nearly retire on the proceeds. One modest-sized herd transported to Chicago in 1856 was said to have netted its owners ten thousand dollars. The simultaneous continuing growth of the Texas herds and of the Eastern appetite for beef promised future profits greater still.[3]

The Civil War postponed the bounty. Secession cut Texas off from Northern markets, while the Union blockade and the capture of the Mississippi isolated Texas from Southern markets. With nowhere to go, the longhorns continued to multiply, till at war's end they numbered perhaps five million.

The Confederate surrender reopened Northern markets to Texas cattle. As the national economy readjusted to peace, the price of beef soared. The Department of Agriculture cited three-year-old steers selling for $86 in Massachusetts, $69 in New York, $40 in Illinois, and $38 in Kansas. Texans returning from military service read the price quotes and calculated how to cash in.[4]

The first step was catching the cattle. "We didn't call it round-up in those days," Lee Moore remembered. "We called it cow-hunts." Moore spoke for many in Texas drawn to the cattle business by the high Eastern prices. Some had grown cotton before the war, others corn. But with crop prices sagging, they turned to beef. At first they acted like the displaced farmers they were. "We had no wagon," Moore recalled, referring to a mess wagon. "Every man carried his grub in a wallet"—a cloth sack—"behind his saddle, and his bed under his saddle." They gathered the branded cattle and divided them among the owners, and they apportioned the unbranded cattle by various methods, including poker. "Yearlings at fifty cents a head and the top price for any class was $5 a head," Moore explained, "so if any-one run out of cattle and had a little money he could get back in the game. For $10, say, he could get a stack of yearlings." Moore was the youngster of the group and wasn't allowed to gamble. But he received twenty-five cents a night for tending the fires that furnished the light the others played by and was permitted to convert his cash into cattle.[5]

Summer had singed the prairies in 1865 before sufficient cattle were gathered to send to market, and so the first big drive awaited the following spring. Whether the same idea occurred to several dozen cattle owners independently or they compared notes is unclear, but in the spring of 1866 scores of herds set out from Texas for the railheads to the north and east. The most popular destination was Sedalia, Missouri, at that time the ter-minus of the Missouri Pacific Railroad. Some quarter million cattle began the journey and would have made their owners rich had they all arrived. But a series of misfortunes befell the cattle and the drovers who nudged them along. Creatures of the open plains, the cattle (and some of the drovers) became confused in the forests of the Ozarks. They wandered among the trees with no sense of direction. And even when the drovers regained their bearings, they discovered that their herding techniques—which in the open allowed a handful of men to control thousands of ani-mals—failed amid the trunks and bushes. The forests, moreover, provided little sustenance to the animals, which grew hungrier and more ornery the farther they penetrated into the woods.

The humans along the route posed even greater impediments. The drovers discovered during that first season that range cattle and farmers don't mix. The cornfields of the farmers struck the longhorns as the lush-est fodder they had ever seen or smelled; when the animals helped them-selves the farmers retaliated. Some shot the trespassers; others ran them off, provoking stampedes. The Missourians also worried that the Texas cattle brought Spanish, or Texas, fever, which would infect their own herds.

Lacking anything close to local sympathy, the drovers fell easy prey to larceny and personal violence. During the war Missouri had sheltered outlaws, deserters, and miscreants of other stripes; many remained there after the fighting ended. More than a few reckoned that the Texas herds must be worth something considerable if the drovers were risking all this trouble and effort, and they determined to claim a share of the portable prize. "A favorite scheme of the milder-mannered of these scoundrels to plunder the cattlemen was that of stampeding a herd at night," a veteran of the trail recalled. "This was easily done, and having been done the rogues next morning would collect as many of the scattered cattle as they could, secrete them in an out-of-the-way place—much of the country being hilly and timbered—and then hunt up the owner and offer to help him, for an acceptable money consideration per head, in recovering his lost property. If the drover agreed to pay a price high enough to satisfy the pirates, they next day would return with many, if not all, of the missing cattle; but if not, the hold-ups would keep them, and later take them to the market and pocket the entire proceeds."[6]

The 1866 drive proved a financial debacle and taught the Texans to keep clear of Missouri. But even though most of the pastoralist entrepreneurs lost money that season, the few cattle that did get to market commanded prices that convinced their owners and others to try again. The railroads continued to press west; by the spring of 1867 the Kansas Pacific had reached the plains of central Kansas. The herds that hit the trail that season were fewer and smaller than the previous year's, totaling no more than seventy-five thousand. But they had much better luck getting through. They had to cope with the tribes who inhabited the Indian Territory north of Texas, and though these bands were less formidable than the Comanches and Kiowas who still roamed free, they weren't uniformly above the same stampeding tricks the Missourians had employed the previous year. On the whole, however, the 1867 drive went well. The trail to Kansas kept to open country uninhabited as yet by farmers. Certain stretches compelled the cattle to go long periods without water, but here they showed the hardiness that made the cattlemen forgive their many faults.

ESSENTIAL TO THE success of the drive were the efforts of cattle buyers. Joseph McCoy traveled west from Illinois on the news the Texans were trying again. "The plan was to establish at some accessible point a depot or market to which a Texan drover could bring his stock unmolested," McCoy explained. "It was to establish a market whereat the Southern drover and Northern buyer would meet upon an equal footing and both be undisturbed by mobs or swindling thieves." McCoy rode the Kansas Pacific to Junction City, Kansas, and tried to purchase property from one of the town's leading businessmen for a stockyard and loading facility. "But an exorbitant price was asked," McCoy recalled. "In fact a flat refusal to sell at any price was the final answer of the wide-awake Junctionite. So by that one act of donkey stupidity and avarice Junction City drove from her a trade which soon developed to many millions." Solomon City, despite its name, was no wiser. "After one or two conferences with some of the leading citizens it became evident that they regarded such a thing as a cattle trade with stupid horror." Salina treated McCoy as a "monster threatening calamity and pestilence."

But Abilene possessed greater vision, largely because it possessed little else. "Abilene in 1867 was a very small, dead place, consisting of about one dozen log huts, low, small, rude affairs, four-fifths of which were covered with dirt for roofing," McCoy recalled. "The business of the burg was conducted in two small rooms, mere log huts." Yet Abilene's very lack of amenities made it ideal for McCoy's purposes. "The country was entirely unsettled, well watered, excellent grass. . . . It was the farthest point east at which a good depot for cattle business could have been made."

McCoy purchased a tract and set to work building fences, a barn, and an office. The wood had to be imported from Missouri, as did a scales for the cattle. Meanwhile he dispatched word to the Texans as to where to bring their cattle. "A man well versed in the geography of the country and accustomed to life on the prairie was sent into southern Kansas and the Indian Territory with instructions to hunt up every straggling drove possible (and every drove was straggling, for they had not where to go), and tell them of Abilene and what was being done there toward making a market and outlet for Texas cattle." The Texans greeted the news skeptically. "They were very suspicious that some trap was set, to be sprung on them. They were not ready to credit the proposition that the day of fair dealing had dawned for Texas drovers. Yet they turned their herds toward the point designated, and slowly and cautiously moved on northward, their minds constantly agitated with hope and fear alternately."

By the hundreds and then the thousands the longhorns arrived. They filled McCoy's stockyard and spilled beyond, until the Kansas Pacific built a special siding for the cattle cars. The first shipment, of twenty cars, headed east in early September, triggering a celebration in Abilene among the drovers and the gathered locals.

The partying was premature. Eastern consumers resisted the western meat as tough and stringy, and the first shipments from Abilene went begging. One cargo that couldn't find a buyer at Chicago was forwarded to Albany, where the nine hundred head were sold for less than the cost of their transport. Even so, almost one thousand cars of cattle made the journey that season, and both sellers and buyers were sufficiently encouraged to repeat the process the following season. The number of cattle shipped from Abilene grew from 35,000 in 1867 to 75,000 in 1868, before exploding to 350,000 in 1869 and 700,000 in 1871.[7]

By then Abilene had become the model of the western cow town. "Perhaps no point or village of its size ever had been so thoroughly advertised or had acquired such wide-spread fame," McCoy declared with self-satisfaction but no little accuracy. "One at a distance would suppose from the many reports that it was a large town or city of many thousand inhabitants, instead of a small village of a few hundred denizens. . . . No point in the West of five times its resident population did one-half the amount of business that was done at Abilene." The cattle commerce eventually totaled some three million dollars a year, which in turn supported the surrounding economy far beyond its ordinary means. Farmers in Dickinson County sold milk, eggs, fruit, vegetables, pork, and chicken to cowhands hungry for anything but beef. Cattle buyers and the less thrifty of the hands put up at the Drovers' Cottage, a hotel run by Mrs. Lou Gore, who won a reputation as the Florence Nightingale of the plains. "Many a sick and wearied drover has she nursed and tenderly cared for until health was restored, or in the event of death soothed their dying moments," McCoy explained. "Many western drovers, rough, uncouth men such as nature and the wild frontier produces, will ever hear the name of Mrs. Lou Gore mentioned only with emotions of the kindest respect and tenderest memory and feelings near akin to the holy passion that binds earth to heaven."

Occasionally Mrs. Gore had to summon qualities more akin to Wyatt

Earp's. Famous as Abilene was for its cattle, it was even more notorious for its debauchery and violence. The railroad divided the town into two quite distinct districts. "North side of the tracks you are in Kansas, and hear sober and profitable conversation on the subject of the weather, the price of the land, and the crops," a Topeka correspondent recorded. "When you cross to the south side you are in Texas, and talk about cattle. . . . Nine out of ten men you meet are directly or indirectly interested in the cattle trade; five at least out of every ten are Texans." The heart of the Texas district was Texas Street, crowded with saloons and dance halls. The "Alamo" held pride of place among these resorts. It served the best liquor in the greatest variety and quantity, and even exposed the cowboys to art. "Paintings, in remote but lascivious imitation of Titian, Tintoretto or Veronese, exhibiting nude women relaxed in beauty prostrate, seduced the Alamo's sporting life," a chronicler of the local culture related. Another observer described a typical evening at the Alamo:

> Here, in a well lighted room opening on the street, the "boys" gather in crowds round the tables, to play or to watch others; a bartender, with a countenance like a youthful divinity student, fabricates wonderful drinks, while the music of a piano and a violin from a raised recess enlivens the scene, and "soothes the savage breasts" of those who retire torn and lacerated from an unfortunate combat with the "tiger." The games most affected are faro and monte, the latter being greatly patronized by the Mexicans of Abilene, who sit with perfectly unmoved countenances and play for hours at a stretch.

Though the Mexicans took their losses with outward indifference, many of the Anglos did not. The booze brought out the touchiness in the average cowboy. "An affront or a slight, real or imaginary, is cause sufficient for him to unlimber one or more 'mountain howitzers' invariably strapped to his person, and proceed to deal out death in unbroken doses to such as may be in range of his pistols," Joseph McCoy explained. "Whether real friends or enemies, no matter—his anger and bad whisky urge him on to deeds of blood and death."[8]

McCoy didn't blame the cowboys. Abilene attracted low-lifes—card sharps, confidence men, pimps—who preyed on the cowboys' unsophistication and sudden cash. Moreover, after months on the trail, they were bored beyond bearing. "The time drags dull at camp or herd ground. There is nothing new or exciting occurring to break the monotony of daily routine events." Any diversion was welcome, the more exciting, even dangerous, the better.

Most of the cowboys survived their encounter with Abilene. "After a few days of frolic and debauchery, the cowboy is ready, in company with his comrades, to start back to Texas, often not having one dollar left of his summer's wages," McCoy said. And those who didn't live to leave perhaps didn't deserve to. "By far the larger portion killed are of that class that can be spared without detriment to the good morals and respectability of humanity."[9]

Some Kansans felt the same way about Abilene generally and weren't sorry when its moment of celebrity passed. The railroad continued to press west, making a rendezvous point even farther out on the plains possible. Such a more distant connection became necessary from the fact that farmers, following the railroad, filled in the territory south of Abilene and refused to let the Texas drovers cross their land. Though the cattlemen disliked to admit it, and many perhaps didn't even realize it, theirs was an intrinsically marginal existence, confined to the moving border between the empty range lands to the west and the populated farm districts to the east. As the farmers crept west, the cattlemen had no choice but to move on ahead of them.

The Texans rerouted their trails, meeting the railroad at Ellsworth and eventually at Dodge City. Abilene reverted to its previous subdued condition, like any number of other boom towns in the West. "Four fifths of her business houses became vacant," Joseph McCoy recalled sadly. "Rents fell to a trifle. Many of the leading hotels and business houses were either closed or taken down and moved to other points. Property became unsalable. The luxuriant sunflower sprang up thick and flourished in the main streets, while the inhabitants, such as could not get away, passed their time sadly contemplating their ruin."[10]

But the industry thrived. The best of the drovers made careers of their craft. Borrowing money for six or eight months, they purchased herds in Texas and trailed them north. To prevent losses they marked each of their steers with a trail brand, administered with a red-hot iron as the cattle crowded through a chute built for the purpose. The drovers hired trail hands, who supplied their own saddles and bedrolls but rode horses belonging to the drovers. A junior member of the outfit was designated the wrangler, with responsibility for the horses, collectively called the remuda. A hired cook completed the division of labor. The cowboys collected salaries, typically twenty-five to forty dollars a month, depending on experience, although the best hands could make as much as five dollars a day. The cook received a bit more than most of the hands; the trail boss—the supervisor of the whole outfit—earned well over a hundred dollars a month.[11]

After a few years of practice, the drovers knew what they were about. They spent the first several days of each drive breaking the cattle to the rhythm of the trail. They let the herd find its leaders and only slowly directed it north. (This practice wasn't universal. Some drovers, believing cattle were least manageable on their home range, pushed the herds hard at first to get them away from familiar territory.) Charles Goodnight remembered the first ten days of any drive as the critical period, as that was when a herd was most likely to stampede. "If we succeeded in holding the herd together for that length of time we seldom experienced trouble from stampedes farther along the trail," he said. But those ten days could be extremely trying.

> The men slept on the ground with the lariat wrapped around the wrist and with the horse so close he could be mounted at a bound. Sometimes the demands were so urgent that a man's boots would not be taken off his feet for an entire week. The nerves of the men usually became wrought up to such a tension that it was a standing rule that no man was to be touched by another when he was asleep until after he had been spoken to. The man who suddenly aroused a sleeper was liable to be shot, as all were thoroughly armed and understood the instant use of the revolver or the rifle.[12]

The men could do their work admirably only to have their efforts frustrated by a single steer spooked in the night.

> The herd of 2,500 or 3,000 cattle might be lying on the bed-ground in the most perfect peace and security, with everything as quiet as a graveyard, when, in a second and without the slightest warning to the

eye or ear of man, every animal would be on its feet, and the earth would tremble as the herd swept off through the darkness. The experience was one of the most thrilling a man could ever know. Every person in camp would be up and away. No one, not even the most experienced trailman, could, at the beginning of the stampede, guess the direction of the flight. The course appeared to be at random, for the cattle would plunge headlong against any obstacle and down any precipice that stood in their way.

The task of the men was to gain control of the herd and gradually turn the cattle until they were moving in a circle. Then, although they might break each other's horns off and crush one another badly, the great danger was past. A well-trained night-horse needed but little guidance, and knew that if the herd came his way, all that he had to do was to lead. The speed of the herd was terrific, but the position at the head of the stampede was just what the trailman desired, for there he was in a position to start the herd to turning. . . .

The heat developed by a large drove of cattle during a stampede was surprising. The faces of men riding on the leeward side of the herd would be almost blistered, as if they had been struck by a blast from a furnace; and the odor given off by the clashing horns and hoofs was nearly overpowering.[13]

Days on the trail began before dawn for the cook, who fed the nighthawks coming in and the rest of the crew heading out. The herd ambled north, grazing as it went. Gradually the cowboys prodded the animals, till all two or three thousand were striding along at about three miles an hour. Cattle and men broke at noon. The cattle grazed; the men dined on leftovers from the night before. All loafed for an hour or two. The march resumed by midafternoon and continued for a few hours till the herd again overtook the chuck wagon, which generally stopped by a stream. Goodnight recalled that clever drovers kept the cattle from water till evening. "The last half of the day's travel was accomplished much easier than the first half, for the cattle would be growing thirsty and becoming eager to get to water." The men ate in shifts, with those finished or not yet fed watering the cattle. Supper was typically beef, biscuits, and coffee. The cattle grazed before being bedded down for the night. The trail boss was happy if the herd had made fifteen miles since the last night's camp.[14]

The top hands rode "point," guiding the herd with the help of the lead animals, to whom they bonded almost as partners. Less senior or experienced cowboys rode "swing" and "flank," coaxing strays back into the main line of march. The newcomers rode "drag," coaxing the weary and reluctant and eating the dust of ten thousand hooves.

Periodically the herd encountered a river. The lay of the plains between Texas and Kansas is such that rivers run from west to east, requiring northbound travelers to find ways across. The herds that left early in the spring could expect the lushest grasses en route but also the highest water. The cattle could swim but had to be persuaded. Low water was no guarantee of hazardless crossing. Recurrent floods and droughts left the streambeds filled with unconsolidated sediment, which turned to quicksand as the first cattle trampled through. The terror that afflicted an animal caught by the sucking sand could spread among the other animals in seconds, triggering mass panic that mixed drownings with elements of a stampede.

Worse than the stretches where the crossings were too frequent were those where the crossings weren't frequent enough—where the herd had to travel for days between water. "Dry drives" tested the patience of the cattle and the mettle of the men. Andy Adams remembered the climax of an especially brutal march. Three days and two nights had passed since the last stream. "Holding the herd this third night required all hands. Only a few men at a time were allowed to go into camp and eat, for the herd refused even to lie down. What few cattle attempted to rest were prevented by the more restless ones. By spells they would mill, until riders were sent through the herd at a break-neck pace to break up the groups."

The men prayed for cooler weather, but dawn came still and sultry. By nine the air almost sizzled. The cattle grew more frantic till they couldn't be governed at all. "The lead cattle turned back several times, wandering aimlessly in any direction, and it was with considerable difficulty that the herd could be held on the trail," Adams said. "The rear overtook the lead, and the cattle gradually lost all semblance of a trail herd." With great effort the riders reconstructed the herd, stringing the animals out along the trail. But as soon as they relaxed, the confusion set in again.

The cattle congregated into a mass of unmanageable animals, milling and lowing in their fever and thirst. The milling only intensified their sufferings from the heat, and the outfit split and quartered them again and again, in the hope that this unfortunate outbreak might be checked. No sooner was the milling stopped than they would surge hither and yon, sometimes half a mile, as ungovernable as the waves of an ocean. . . . We threw our ropes in their faces, and when this failed, we resorted to shooting. But in defiance of the fusillade and the smoke they walked sullenly through the line of horsemen across their front. Six-shooters were discharged so close to the leaders' faces as to singe their hair. Yet, under a noonday sun, they disregarded this and every other device to turn them, and passed wholly out of our control. In a number of instances wild steers deliberately walked against our horses. And then, for the first time, a fact dawned on us that chilled the marrow in our bones—*the herd was going blind!*

The trail boss of Adams's outfit saw no alternative to going back to the latest water, despite the added mileage and time it would entail. "It's a good thing that they are strong," he said. "Five or six days without water will hardly kill any." Nor did it. But the experience brought to mind the remark of Phil Sheridan that if he owned hell and Texas, he'd rent out Texas and live in hell. "For if this isn't Billy hell," the boss said, "I'd like to know what you call it."[15]

ON HIS BUFFALO HUNT in western Dakota Territory, after days spent seeking the suddenly scarce beast among the broken plains and blocked valleys of the badlands, Theodore Roosevelt devoted evenings to discussions with resident Gregor Lang. Gregor's son Lincoln eavesdropped from the attic of the Lang cabin and recalled hearing Roosevelt congratulate his father, an immigrant from Scotland, on being one of fifteen children. "The first essential of human progress is the perpetuation of the human race, and I admire the men who are not afraid to propagate their kind as far as they may," Roosevelt said. Roosevelt was recently married but had no children yet; he assured Lang he intended to have several at least.

The two men spoke on other subjects. Politics fascinated both. Gregor had named Lincoln for the Great Emancipator; Roosevelt was taking time from his work as a New York assemblyman. He told Lang how he combated the forces of corruption in Albany and how good men must battle their ilk on the larger stage of national politics. He doubtless dropped that he had just published a book on the maritime aspects of the War of 1812 and that his historical research revealed a contemporary need for a stronger American navy.[16]

They spoke of Dakota and of how men made a living there. Roosevelt had come to this part of the frontier to experience the dying moment of a passing age, when a hunter might bag the largest animal in North America. But he had come, as well, to reconnoiter the dawn of a new age, when cattle were filling the niche vacated by the buffalo. For the past few years papers in the West and around the country had reported tremendous opportunities for investors in the cattle business. "Cotton was once crowned king," a livestock journal observed, "but grass is now. . . . If grass is King, the Rocky Mountain region is its throne and fortunate indeed are those who possess it." A U.S. army officer named James Brisbin, who spent the dozen years after the Civil War on service in various parts of the West, devoted an entire book to what he called *The Beef Bonanza*. "In the whole world there are but five great natural grazing areas," Brisbin wrote in 1881. Four were the steppe of Central Asia, the veldt of South Africa, the pampas of South America, and the outback of Australia. The fifth was "the boundless plains of the United States," comprising "1,650,000 square miles with over a billion acres." Americans had never appreciated the potential of this region, Brisbin said. They called it the Great American Desert. But it was no more a natural desert than the other four pastoral zones. "The day will come when the government will derive more taxes from the grazing country than the best agricultural regions. These arid plains, so long considered worthless, are the natural meat-producing lands of the nation, and in a few years 30,000,000 people will draw their beef from them."[17]

Potential investors received detailed advice on how their money would multiply. In a widely reprinted article entitled "How Cattlemen Grow Rich," the *Breeder's Gazette* explained:

> A good sized steer when it is fit for the butcher market will bring from $45 to $60. The same animal at birth was worth but $5.00. He has run on the plains and cropped the grass from the public domain for four or five years, and now, with scarcely any expense to his owner, is worth

forty dollars more than when he started on his pilgrimage. A thousand of these animals are kept nearly as cheaply as a single one, so with a thousand as a starter and with an investment of but $5,000 in the start, in four years the stock raiser has made from $40,000 to $45,000. Allow $5,000 for his current expenses which he has been going on and he still has $35,000 and even $45,000 for a net profit. That is all there is of the problem and that is why our cattlemen grow rich.[18]

The news spread across America and beyond the Atlantic. British newspapers sent correspondents to cover the cattle boom. The *Economist* of London in 1883 described the "remarkable success" of one cattle company organized in 1880, "which paid a dividend at the rate of 19½ per cent twelve months ago, and had recently declared a second, at nearly 28 per cent." Even Parliament got into the act, dispatching two members to America on a fact-finding tour. They reported with sober astonishment a typical return in the cattle industry of 33 percent per annum.[19]

Other Europeans entered the industry, as Roosevelt learned at first hand in Dakota. Across the Little Missouri River from the town of Little Missouri, the Northern Pacific rail stop where Roosevelt had alighted to commence his hunt, Antoine de Vallombrosa, the marquis de Morès and a relative of French kings, was building the headquarters of what he hoped would be an empire of beef. Stockyards had been constructed; an abattoir was going up. An entire town, named Medora for his wife (who nonetheless hadn't yet seen fit to join him in Dakota), was being laid out. De Morès intended to capitalize on recent innovations in rail technology, in particular the development of refrigerator cars. The cold cars allowed the decentralization of butchering and obviated sending whole steers east. The bones and entrails could stay in Dakota—along with the processor's profits, de Morès hoped.[20]

Roosevelt could see the de Morès empire abuilding. He heard from locals how the marquis anticipated sinking millions of dollars into the project. He had read the literature of the cattle boom with its testaments of doubled money in two or three years. His own wallet was heavy from an inheritance that had made him one of the wealthiest undergraduates at Harvard in the late 1870s and that still sought gainful employment. Politics was a pastime for Roosevelt, for now at least. A Republican reformer in a legislature dominated by Democrats and spoilsmen, he could tell that his future in Albany had limits. Besides, at twenty-four he wanted to strike out in a different direction from his urban upbringing. He had long read and reveled in the exploits of frontiersmen; as a sickly child he had dreamed of doing what they did: of riding horseback across the open West, sleeping under the stars, relying on courage and wit to win what the land had to give.

On the spot, with the same impulsiveness that was causing many others to take the plunge, Roosevelt determined to be a ranchman. He asked Gregor Lang to be his partner. "That is exceedingly kind of you, Mr. Roosevelt," Lang replied. "And I am more than sorry that I cannot see my way clear to accept. But Pender"—his current employer—"is depending on me to carry this undertaking through and I do not feel that I can disappoint him."

Roosevelt asked Lang if he could recommend anyone. Lang mentioned Sylvane Ferris and Bill Merrifield. Both were good men, he said. Roosevelt asked to meet them. They explained that they too were obligated. Roosevelt offered to buy out their current contracts and pay them more than they were now making. They said that they'd have to ride to Minnesota to clear the idea with their employer, but they liked it.

Roosevelt drafted a check for fourteen thousand dollars. This would purchase the small herd they were managing for the Minnesotan, allow them to buy a few hundred more cattle, and cover start-up expenses for the Roosevelt operation. They asked if he wanted a receipt. He said if he doubted their honesty he wouldn't have made them his partners. Years later Merrifield still marveled at the moment. "We were sitting on a log up at what we called Cannonball Creek," he said. "He handed us a check for fourteen thousand dollars, handed it right over to us on a verbal contract. He didn't have a scratch of a pen for it." Ferris added, "All the security he had for his money was our honesty."[21]

LIKE OTHER ASPECTS of American business, the cattle industry evolved continually during the decades after the Civil War. The drives from Texas to Kansas lasted about fifteen years, till the railroads arrived at the cattle regions of Texas. By then the business was shifting north. The longhorns flourished in south Texas, with its warm winters and twelve-month grass-growing season, but more than a few cattlemen wondered whether the longhorns might be able to survive winters on the northern Plains. In 1866 an adventurous soul drove six hundred longhorns from Dallas to Montana's Gallatin Valley. They thrived there, learning to paw through the typically light snow to the bunch grass blanched by the first frost. Like the buffalo they turned their tails to the arctic blasts of winter and slowly drifted downwind.

The news spread quickly. And even while the drives to Kansas continued, drives to Colorado, Wyoming, Dakota, and Montana grew larger and more numerous. The drives differed in certain respects. Those to the railheads—that is, to the dinner tables of the East—comprised chiefly steers, which fattened more readily and fought less frequently than uncastrated bulls. Those to the northern Plains—that is, to the ranches of prospective cattle barons—included mostly cows and bulls. (Drives from Texas to Indian reservations of the North, under contract with the War Department, constituted an exception to the latter rule, as the animals were for slaughter rather than propagation.)

Before long a rush mentality surrounded the northern drives, not unlike that which had characterized the gold rush to California. In both cases a piece of the public domain—gold in California, grass on the plains—was up for grabs. Early arrivals claimed the choicest locations and expected the highest profits. Unlike gold, grass was a renewable resource—but only up to a point. The scant rainfall on the plains limited the growth of grass and therefore the number of cattle any particular parcel could support. The person who got there first put his cattle on the range and preempted others.

But for a time there seemed enough for all. James Brisbin, the *Beef Bonanza* author, printed a letter he identified as having been written by a "gentleman of means" in the West to his brother in the East. Possibly Brisbin fabricated the letter—the practice was common in promotional literature of the era—but even so it conveyed the essentials of the cattle business as perceived by potential investors:

> *Dear Brother—I have bought a cattle ranch, and as you have long wished to engage in business out West, I do not know of a better thing you can do than raise cattle. As you have no knowledge or experience in breeding, I will tell you what I think, with proper care, we can make out of it. The ranch is twenty-two miles from a railroad, and contains 720 acres of land,*

600 acres of which is hay or grassland, and 120 acres good timber. The
meadow will cut annually 2½ tons of hay to the acre, and there is a living
stream on the land. The timber is heavy and will furnish logs for stables,
corrals, and fuel for many years to come. The hills in the vicinity afford the
best grazing, and we can have a range ten miles in extent.

The writer (perhaps Brisbin) reiterated the capitalist arithmetic of cattle procreation. "You can put in $2,500, and I will duplicate it and add $1,000 for bulls. For $5,000 we can get 400 head of Texas cows to start with, and I will add a sufficient number of Durham bulls to breed them. . . . At the end of one year the cows would have 400 calves, each worth $7.00. I count full yield, for in cross-breeding there is not one cow in a hundred barren. . . . Our first year's profit is 400 calves, $7.00 each, $2,800." From there the profits expanded exponentially. The second year would yield $4,800, the third year $6,800, the fourth $10,200, the fifth $14,600.[22]

In the face of such numbers, investors would have been fools not to take advantage of this unique and wasting opportunity. Or so concluded the many who poured money into cattle and made Cheyenne the reincarnation of San Francisco at the height of the gold rush or Virginia City in the salad days of the Comstock Lode. "Sixteenth Street is a young Wall Street," one observer wrote of Wyoming's territorial capital. "Millions are talked of as lightly as nickels, and all kinds of people are dabbling in steers. . . . Large transactions are made every day in which the buyer does not see a hoof of his purchase and very likely does not use more than one half of the purchase money in the trade before he has sold and made an enormous margin in the deal." Lawyers appeared to be particularly susceptible. "The chief justice of the Supreme Court has recently succumbed to the contagion and gone out to purchase a $40,000 herd. . . . A Cheyenne man who don't pretend to know a maverick from a mandamus has made a neat little margin of $15,000 this summer in small transactions and hasn't seen a cow yet that he has bought and sold."[23]

"HURRAH!" Theodore Roosevelt scrawled to his wife, Alice. "The luck has turned at last. I will bring you home the head of a great buffalo bull." This was supposed to be the good news. Alice may have interpreted it differently, as her tastes in interior decorating ran more to proper

Bostonian (she grew up in Chestnut Hill) than Dakota primitive. The announcement of their new wall decoration prefaced Roosevelt's announcement of his investment in cattle ranching. "The more I have looked into the matter—weighing and balancing everything, pro and con, as carefully as I knew how—the more convinced I became that there was a great chance to make a great deal of money, very safely, in the cattle business. Accordingly I have decided to go into it, very cautiously at first, and, if I come out well the first year, much more heavily as time goes on." He was less confident than this sentence made him sound. "Neither Uncle Jim nor, I am afraid, even Uncle Jimmie"—his financial advisers, after the death of his father—"will approve of the step I have taken," he conceded. But he was taking it anyway.[24]

Roosevelt's stake bought him a cattle ranch called the Chimney Butte, subsequently supplemented by a second place, the Elkhorn. But precisely what the two ranches included was problematic. Neither included any land to speak of. Roosevelt built a cabin on the Elkhorn place, on the bank of the Little Missouri. No one was likely to evict him, though he couldn't have shown a title to the plot on which it stood. But the land on which his cattle grazed was federal property, part of the public domain of the United States. When Roosevelt bought his two ranches he acquired cattle and the presumption of grazing rights. For the moment the presumption was reasonable, as western Dakota remained sparsely populated by people and cattle.

But the situation soon changed. Though Roosevelt didn't make any money his first year, neither did he lose much, and he decided to increase his play. In part his decision reflected personal circumstances. Roosevelt fell in love with the West at first exposure. The frontier life suited his temperament and made him feel like the man he had always wanted to be. He rode the range, shared grub with cowboys, tangled with outlaws. "I have been having a glorious time here," he wrote his sister Anna. "I feel as absolutely free as a man could feel." The personal element intensified when Alice suddenly and unexpectedly died in childbirth. Roosevelt was bereft, and in his grief he found solace in the loneliness of the great West. "One day I would canter hour after hour over the level green grass, or through miles of wild rose thickets, all in bloom," he told Anna. "On the next I would be amidst the savage desolation of the Bad Lands, with their dreary plateaus, fantastically shaped buttes, and deep, winding canyons."

Roosevelt's decision to extend his investment also reflected the economics of cattle ranching. The range of western Dakota began to fill up as newcomers—other Roosevelts, so to speak—moved in. Roosevelt's only claim to the range was priority, and if he didn't put cattle on all the land around the Elkhorn and Chimney Butte, someone else would. "I shall put on a thousand more cattle and shall make it my regular business," he informed Anna—who besides being his confidante was the acting mother of his and Alice's daughter, also named Alice.[25]

For a time Roosevelt did make ranching his regular business. "I have been three weeks on the roundup and have worked as hard as any of the cowboys," he wrote Henry Cabot Lodge, a recent acquaintance. "But I have enjoyed it greatly. Yesterday I was eighteen hours in the saddle—from 4 a.m. to 10 p.m.—having a half hour each for dinner and tea. I can now do cowboy work pretty well."[26]

Cowboy work on the roundup consisted of gathering all the cattle from a large portion of the range. Cowboys from several ranches took part; the cattle were sorted by brand, and calves were branded to match their mothers. At the autumn roundup, after a summer of fleshing out, those animals bound for slaughter were culled from the herd and shipped off. The rest were released to resume their feral ways.

Cowboy work also involved defending one's turf—that is, one's claim to the public turf. As Roosevelt expanded his herd his animals encroached on territory over which the marquis de Morès asserted control. Roosevelt thought the French aristocrat's claims excessive and said so. De Morès sent a gang of gunmen to Roosevelt's ranch. Roosevelt was gone, but the leader, a reputed killer named Paddock, told Roosevelt's foreman that his boss's cattle were trespassing on the marquis's territory. Roosevelt might purchase grazing rights from the marquis; if he chose not to, he'd better move his cattle.

Roosevelt refused to be intimidated. On his return (from a successful grizzly bear hunt), he rode directly to Paddock's place. He pounded on the door and demanded that Paddock come out. Paddock, observing Roosevelt's pistol and rifle and noting his determined air, declined to press his earlier threat. He said there had been a misunderstanding, he meant no harm.

Roosevelt's moral victory in this instance deepened his belief that forceful action in a righteous cause would carry the day. But it did nothing to solve the underlying problem of the range. In fact, by encouraging him to continue expanding his herd, it exacerbated the problem, which was that the carrying capacity of the range was limited but the ambitions and hopes of the cattlemen—collectively if not necessarily individually—were unlimited. Not owning the land, the cattlemen had little incentive to protect or improve it. On the contrary, they had every incentive to extract as much value from it as they could, lest others do so first.

Most of the ranchers recognized the problem; some sought to solve it. They formed livestock associations that wrote rules for the use and conservation of the range. Roosevelt organized one such group, the Little Missouri Stockmen's Association, whose members were so impressed by his political skills that they charged him to draft a constitution for the group. At an early meeting the members discussed measures for preventing disease, for branding strays, for foiling rustlers, for improving the herds by importing high-quality bulls. In the words of the *Bad Lands Cowboy*, the new local newspaper, "the utmost harmony and unanimity prevailed."[27]

But agreeable though the members might be among themselves, they couldn't bar outsiders elbowing onto the range. Some employed the intimidation de Morès attempted against Roosevelt, only more effectively. Others managed to have their actions confirmed in law, as when the Wyoming territorial legislature granted control of the range to the Wyoming Stock Growers' Association. Yet despite their efforts, the cattle population continued to swell.

The first sign of trouble was a drop in beef prices, which lost 50 percent between the spring of 1882 and the summer of 1886. Leveraged investors, who had hoped to profit on margin, now found their levers kicking them in the teeth. Roosevelt had sunk eighty thousand dollars into his cattle operation by the end of 1886 and had yet to turn a profit. Two partners he had recruited grew discouraged and pulled back.

Roosevelt might have retrenched, too, had he not been distracted. In the autumn of 1885 he encountered a childhood sweetheart whom he had thrown over for Alice. The flame rekindled and they engaged to be married. But because Roosevelt disapproved of second marriages, he insisted on a quiet ceremony—overseas. He and Edith Carow traveled to England in the autumn of 1886; they were married in London in December.

The newlyweds were honeymooning on the Continent when Roosevelt learned of the larger consequence of the overstocking. The summer and fall of 1886 had been dry on the northern Plains, and the cattle entered the winter thinner than usual. Ranchers with experience—a comparative term where even the longest-tenured cattlemen had operated less than a decade—expected snows and cold snaps before Christmas but nothing extended or severe till after New Year's Day. This year the first snows came in early November, and not as the tentative flakes of previous autumns but as a full-blown blizzard. Within hours the temperature fell to forty below zero. Humans were caught without their cold-weather stores; the cattle were still growing their winter coats. After several days the snow stopped falling and the wind diminished, but the warm Chinook wind that usually followed early storms never came. The snow kept the cattle from finding grass; already weak from the drought, they lost more weight and insulation. Further storms drove survivors into coulees and canyons, any places where they could escape the killing wind. But the quiet zones were precisely the spots where the snowdrifts accumulated, and the cattle were buried under four feet, six feet, twelve feet of icy powder.

So severe was the weather that the cowboys and other humans huddled indoors, happy to keep warm—and knowing, in any event, that there was nothing they could do. The range cattle business was premised on the ability of the cattle to fend for themselves during the winter. No one had built barns to shelter the animals from the cold; few harvested hay for winter feed.

Not till spring was the extent of the destruction known. With cruel irony, the same warm winds that finally lifted human hopes brought the bad news in a fashion that stunned even the hardiest spirits. "In the latter part of March came the Chinook wind, harbinger of spring, releasing for the first time the iron grip that had been upon us," Lincoln Lang remembered. "At last, it seemed, the wrath of Nature had been appeased." The melting proceeded, appallingly.

> A few days later such a grim freshet was pouring down the river valley as no man had ever seen before or ever would again. For days on end, tearing down with the grinding ice cakes, went Death's cattle roundup of the upper Little Missouri country. In countless valleys, gulches, washouts, and coulees, the animals had vainly sought shelter from the relentless "Northern Furies" on their trail. Now their carcasses were being spewed forth in untold thousands by the rushing waters, to be

carried away on the crest of the foaming, turgid flood rushing down the valley.

With them went our hopes. One had only to stand by the river bank for a few minutes and watch the grim procession ceaselessly going down, to realize the depth of the tragedy that had been enacted within the past few months.[28]

THE TERRIBLE WINTER of 1886–87 cured Roosevelt of his illusions about cattle ranching. "I am bluer than indigo," he wrote Anna, after returning to America and surveying the damage. "It is even worse than I feared. . . . I am planning how to get out."[29]

Many others had the same idea. As with most speculative bubbles, the same collective mania that had prompted thousands to buy simultaneously now prompted thousands to sell. Under different circumstances the massive die-off of cattle might have boosted beef prices, but with everyone rushing to get out they remained depressed. Roosevelt was rich enough to write off his eighty-thousand-dollar loss to a hard lesson in the school of capitalist experience, although he did have to scale back his living standard and begin looking for alternative employment. Many others were wholly ruined. Cattle companies failed by the score, bringing down banks in Wyoming and other ranching regions. The financial effects rippled across the country, and even to Britain and the European continent. The marquis de Morès fled to France.

Those who stuck it out changed their modus operandi. First to go—not surprisingly—was the idea that cattle could survive the winter unassisted. They needed shelter and especially hay. Growing hay required fencing the land (to keep the cattle out during the growing season). But fencing public land was frowned upon by both the land's official custodians and the neighbors, who saw no reason to allow one person to control what belonged to all. Early efforts to fence the public domain—using the cheap barbed wire recently developed by Joseph Glidden and others—triggered range wars that started with wire cutters and escalated to six-shooters and rifles. The biggest cattle barons could get away with the practice for a time; Charles Goodnight was reported to have run 250 miles of fence across the Texas Panhandle in 1884. In the more remote areas the illegal fencing persisted for decades. But eventually most ranchers came to the realization that in order to fence land permanently they had to purchase it.[30]

The need to purchase land altered the economics of ranching dramatically. No longer did the business appeal to the speculator interested in quick profits. Money could still be made in cattle; the growing population of the East had to be fed, and refrigeration was allowing American beef to be marketed abroad. But profits would be earned rather than conjured. The cost of land was only the start, for investment in land made other investments prudent. Ranchers with fenced land could segregate their herds from their neighbors', giving them incentive to improve those herds with imported bulls, which ought to be barned in winter and otherwise pampered, at least by comparison with run-of-the-range longhorns. The coddling extended to the offspring of the bulls, and it prompted a general devotion to details quite at odds with the carefree approach of the early days.

The transition didn't occur easily. Those closest to the work often had the greatest difficulty adjusting. "Cowboys don't have as soft a time as they did," one lamented.

> I remember when we sat around the fire the winter through and didn't do a lick of work for five or six months of the year, except to chop a little wood to build a fire to keep warm by. Now we go on the general roundup, then the calf roundup, then comes haying—something that the old-time cowboy never dreamed of—then the beef roundup and the fall calf roundup and gathering bulls and weak cows, and after all this, a winter of feeding hay. I tell you, times have changed.[31]

Chapter 8

TO MAKE THE DESERT BLOOM

W e are now ready to start on our way down the Great Unknown,"
John Wesley Powell wrote on August 13, 1869.

Our boats, tied to a common stake, are chafing each other, as they are
tossed by the fretful river. They ride high and buoyant, for their loads
are lighter than we could desire. We have but a month's rations
remaining. The flour has been resifted through the mosquito net sieve;
the spoiled bacon has been dried, and the worst of it boiled; the few
pounds of dried apples have been spread in the sun, and reshrunken to
their normal bulk; the sugar has all melted, and gone on its way down
the river; but we have a large sack of coffee. The lighting of the boats
has this advantage: they will ride the waves better, and we shall have
but little to carry when we make a portage.

We are three-quarters of a mile in the depths of the earth, and the
great river shrinks into insignificance as it dashes its angry waves
against the walls and cliffs that rise to the world above; they are but
puny ripples, and we but pigmies, running up and down the sands or
lost among the boulders.

We have an unknown distance yet to run; an unknown river yet
to explore. What falls there are, we know not; what rocks beset the

channel, we know not; what walls rise over the river, we know not. Ah, well! we may conjecture many things. The men talk as cheerfully as ever; jests are bandied about freely this morning, but to me the cheer is somber and the jests are ghastly.[1]

Powell's gloom might have intensified had he known that the world had given him and his small party up for dead. When the ten men and their four boats had put into the Green River at the town of Green River, Wyoming, where the just completed Union Pacific Railroad bridged the stream, amateur geographers and other followers of exploration anticipated a compelling story from the Powell party. Twenty-five years after emigrants to Oregon carved their trail to the Willamette Valley, twenty years after the forty-niners made a highway of the Humboldt River across Nevada, fifteen years after stage lines started rattling their passengers and mail across the northern and southern edges of the Great Basin, ten years after surveyors scouted the passes and river crossings that would enable the Pacific railroad to link Omaha to Sacramento, maps of the western United States contained a single blank region. The Colorado Plateau—the vast tableland bisected by the Colorado River—was almost as unknown to outsiders as when Coronado of Spain came through in the 1540s looking for the seven cities of Cíbola. By the 1860s geographers had inferred that the Green River and the Grand River, the former rising in Wyoming, the latter in Colorado, were actually branches of the Colorado River, which emptied into the Gulf of California. But no one had physically confirmed this inference by descending from the Green or Grand to the lower Colorado.

A few had tried. William Ashley and a party of fur trappers floated a stretch of the Green River in 1825. William Lewis Manly and a group of gold miners sought a shortcut to California and floated down the Green River for a hundred miles or so before encountering an Indian chief who through gestures and a few words they understood convinced them that to continue meant certain death.[2]

John Wesley Powell wasn't so easily dissuaded. Powell's strength of will became evident after the Civil War battle of Shiloh, in which a cannonball blasted his arm off at the elbow. Spurning a medical discharge, he transferred from engineers to artillery to get closer to the front and repay his injury in kind. He rose to command the field guns of the Seventeenth

Army Corps and at war's end boasted the rank of major, a striking black beard, and an irrefutable claim to have given his right arm for the Union.[3]

The combination made it impossible for the War Department to deny his request for support of a journey down the Colorado. Powell's interest in science antedated Sumter but blossomed only after Appomattox, when he landed a job in the geology department of Illinois State Normal University. The major-professor wanted to know what the rocks of the Rockies looked like up close, and he organized an expedition across Colorado. Nothing of particular value came of the journey except a larger appetite for adventure and a nagging curiosity as to where the Grand River went when it disappeared to the southwest. He traveled to Washington, where he asked the War Department for cash but settled for supplies drawn from army posts in the West. He might have pressed harder for money had he not guessed—correctly—that he would be able to convert some of his ration tickets to hard currency once he reached the frontier.

The interest of the War Department in an expedition to the Southwest began with the army's Indian troubles in that district, where Geronimo and the Apaches were vigorously disputing Washington's authority. But the interest also reflected a desire to please capitalist-minded members of Congress who had heard stories that the Colorado might be navigable. Powell's mission could open a whole new region to economic development, starting with the discovery of the gold and silver it was bound to contain.

Consequently, with enough War Department backing to get his expedition going but not so much that he couldn't ignore Washington's wishes when he chose, Powell returned to the West. He stopped in Chicago to pick up four boats crafted to his specifications. Keeled of oak and ribbed of pine, the boats ranged in length from sixteen to twenty-one feet. Their peculiarity consisted in watertight compartments fore and aft, which allowed them to float even when swamped or capsized. Powell pulled the boats off the Union Pacific at Green River, regathered the best men from his previous expedition, and at noon on May 24, 1869—two weeks after the golden-spike ceremony at Promontory, Utah, two hundred miles to the west—he and his hardy crew set off down the river.

The first fifty miles were uneventful. The men acquired the feel of the boats and learned to appreciate the power of the current, swollen by the late-spring runoff from the snowfields of the Wind River Mountains. But just at the border between Wyoming and Utah the south-flowing river bent abruptly to the west before circling back to the east. The cause of the river's confusion—already the men were anthropomorphizing the stream was the wall of the Uinta Mountains, one of the few ranges in North America with an axis that runs east and west rather than north and south. The river is older than the mountains, which thrust themselves athwart its path, forcing the waters to seek a way around. To the west the rocks were too hard and rising too fast, which compelled the river to turn east for an escape route. The battle between water and rock produced Flaming Gorge, so called by Powell and his men for the fiery-hued cliffs that soar a thousand feet above the river. "The rocks are broken and ragged," Powell wrote in his diary, "and the water fills the channel from cliff to cliff. Now the water turns abruptly around a point to the right, and the waters plunge swiftly down among great rocks; and here we have our first experience with cañon rapids." The current hurled the boats down between the cliffs and among the rocks. "We thread the narrow passage with exhilarating velocity, mounting the high waves, whose foaming crests dash over us, and plunging into the troughs, until we reach the quiet water below. . . . Then comes a feeling of great relief."[4]

The relief at danger survived enabled the men to appreciate the beauty of the park—an open space, in this case of some three hundred acres, amid the mountains—through which the river proceeded. "The river is broad, deep, and quiet, and its waters mirror towering rocks," Powell wrote. But the calm soon yielded to more rapids. "The river rolls down the cañon at a wonderful rate. . . . The water rushes into a narrow gorge; the rocks on the side roll it into the center in great waves, and the boats go leaping and bounding over these like things of life."

Again they passed the river's test and again congratulated themselves on their skill and luck. Yet as the rush of the last rapids diminished, a new sound displaced it. "A threatening roar is heard in the distance." Powell ordered a halt and walked along the bank till he could see the source of the noise: a waterfall over which the entire river plunged. The boats might weather the falls, he judged, but the men and cargo couldn't. Powell ordered the craft unloaded and their cargoes carried around the cataract. The boats were then lowered down the falls by ropes.

Just below the falls one of the party noticed writing on a rock face above the bank. "Ashley 18–5," it read. "The third figure is obscure," Powell remarked, "some of the party reading it 1835, some 1855." In fact it was 1825, which helped explain the confusion. Powell had heard of Ashley from an old mountain man, who thought he remembered that party had come to a bad end, with at least one man drowning. "The word 'Ashley' is a warning to us," Powell wrote, "and we resolve on great caution."

But not great enough. With each hazard overcome, the men gained self-assurance, till the rising curve of their confidence intersected the constantly falling curve of the river bed. The boats were maneuvering to shore above another falls when one of the boats passed the point of no return. The current grew too strong for the oars of the crewmen and the vessel was swept into the maelstrom. Powell on the shore watched in helpless dismay. "I pass around a great crag just in time to see the boat strike a rock and, rebounding from the shock, careen and fill the open compartment with water. Two of the men lose their oars; she swings around and is carried down at a rapid rate, broadside on, for a few yards, and strikes amidships on another rock with great force, is broken quite in two, and the men are thrown into the river." The men clung to the remnants of the boat and were carried into another set of rapids, where the boat parts were pulverized further.

Amazingly no one drowned, but the boat was lost, of course, along with most of the cargo. Powell had divided the provisions among the four boats so that the destruction of any one wouldn't doom the expedition. But for some reason he placed all the barometers—for measuring altitude—in a single boat, the one that crashed. To the great luck of the group, however, the portion of the boat containing the instruments snagged on a rock, and the next day the men were able to salvage them—along with a three-gallon keg of whiskey a few of the men had smuggled aboard when Powell wasn't looking. "Now I am glad they did," Powell wrote, "for they think it will do them good." While the men were building a fire to dry themselves and the salvaged instruments out, they discovered some old tin plates, a Dutch oven, and fragments of a boat. Powell concluded that this was where Ashley wrecked. "We adopt the name Disaster Falls for the scene of so much peril and loss."

The party proceeded more carefully. They portaged around a cataract they called Triplet Falls and a chute they labeled Hell's Half Mile. On the evening of June 16, while the others prepared supper, Powell and a companion explored a defile from which a brook emptied in the main canyon, in hope of gaining a vantage.

> We climb up to the left for half an hour, and are a thousand feet above the river, and six hundred above the brook. Just before us, the cañon divides, a little stream coming down on the right, and another on the left, and we can look away up either of these cañons, through an ascending vista, to cliffs and crags and towers, a mile back and two thousand feet overhead. To the right, a dozen gleaming cascades are seen. Pines and firs stand on the rocks, and aspens overhang the brooks. The rocks below are red and brown, set in deep shadows, but above they are buff and vermilion and stand in the sunshine. The light above, made more brilliant by the bright-tinted rocks, and the shadows below more gloomy by the somber hues of the brown walls, increase the apparent depths of the cañons, and it seems a long way up to the world of sunshine and open sky, and a long way down to the bottom of the cañon glooms. Never before have I received such an impression of the vast heights of these cañon walls.

Powell's ability to scramble up sheer walls and find his way across narrow ledges made the others wonder what he could have accomplished with two arms. But sometimes his reach exceeded his grasp. Powell spotted a cliff whose summit seemed a likely spot for measuring altitude. George Bradley accompanied him. Up they went, with Powell as usual in the lead. "We are nearly to the summit. Here, by making a spring, I gain a foothold in a little crevice and grasp an angle of rock overhead. I find I can get up no farther, and cannot step back, for I dare not let go with my hand and cannot reach foothold below without." Powell shouted to Bradley for assistance.

> He finds a way by which he can get to the top of the rock over my head, but cannot reach me. Then he looks around for some stick or limb of a tree, but finds none. Then he suggests that he had better help me with the barometer case, but I fear I cannot hold on to it. The moment is critical. Standing on my toes, my muscles begin to tremble. It is sixty or eighty feet to the foot of the precipice. If I lose my hold I

shall fall to the bottom, and then perhaps roll over the bench and tumble still farther down the cliff.

At this instant it occurs to Bradley to take off his drawers, which he does, and swings them down to me. I hug close to the rock, let go with my hand, seize the dangling legs, and, with his assistance, I am enabled to gain the top.

For seven weeks the party descended the river—running rapids, portaging falls, measuring cliffs, noting geology. In mid-July they reached the confluence of the Green River with the Grand. Powell had packed provisions for several months, but the loss of the one boat and various swampings and capsizings of the others ate into the supplies, leaving the men to live on musty flour, rancid bacon, redried apples, and black coffee. The canyon grew deeper than they had imagined a canyon could be—and then grew thousands of feet deeper still. "The walls now are more than a mile in height, a vertical distance difficult to appreciate," Powell wrote. "Stand on the south steps of the Treasury building in Washington and look down Pennsylvania Avenue to the Capitol Park, and measure this distance overhead, and imagine cliffs to extend to that altitude, and you will understand what I mean. Or stand at Canal street in New York and look up Broadway to Grace Church, and you have about that distance."

The forms and colors of the canyon walls stunned the men into silence. "The gorge is black and narrow below, red and gray and flaring above, with crags and angular projections on the walls, which, cut in many places by side canons, seem to be a vast wilderness of rocks. Down in these grand, gloomy depths we glide."

The river rumbled, often roared. The men came to recognize the different sounds and associate them with the degrees of danger they represented—but not always in time. One of the boats was sucked into a whirlpool and swamped; when the vortex released the vessel it wallowed amid the waves of the main stream. "Breaker after breaker rolls over her, and one capsizes her. The men are thrown out." The others watched helplessly, hoping for the men to surface amid the foam. They finally did, and clung to the overturned craft while the others attempted a rescue. It ultimately succeeded but not before the river claimed additional provisions.

By late August they had been on the river more than three months.

Powell's readings of altitude and latitude suggested that less distance remained than they had already traversed, but whether the route ahead would be more difficult than that behind neither he nor any of the others could say. Nor could he guarantee they wouldn't reach a point where the river became impassable and the cliffs unscalable. Then they would truly be trapped.

Three of the men decided to take their chances climbing the walls while they still could. As they, like all the others, had volunteered for the expedition, Powell couldn't order them to continue. He could only hope their example would not prove contagious. Some of the others did consider joining them but finally cast their lot with Powell and the river. "Two rifles and a shot gun are given to the men who are going out. I ask them to help themselves to the rations, and take what they think to be a fair share." They declined, saying they could shoot their dinner after they reached the canyon rim.

Later that day the others had reason to wish they'd left the canyon, too. A waterfall prompted Powell to order the boats lowered by ropes. Bradley took the helm of one of the boats, which got caught in a crosscurrent. Time and again the water smashed it against the sheer face of the canyon wall while the rope kept it from being washed free. Bradley determined to cut the rope before the boat shattered beneath him. But as he unsheathed his knife the stem post, to which the rope was fixed, tore away.

With perfect composure Bradley seizes the great scull oar, places it in the stern rowlock, and pulls with all his power (and he is an athlete) to turn the bow of the boat down stream, for he wishes to go bow down rather than to drift broadside on. One, two strokes he makes, and a third just as she goes over, and the boat is fairly turned, and she goes down almost beyond our sight, though we are more than a hundred feet above the river. Then she comes up again on a great wave, and down and up, then around behind some great rocks and is lost in the mad, white foam below. We stand frozen with fear, for we see no boat. Bradley is gone, so it seems.

But now, away below, we see something coming out of the waves. It is evidently a boat. A moment more, and we see Bradley standing on deck, swinging his hat to show that he is all right.

He signaled too soon. A whirlpool seized the boat, and without the stem post he couldn't fight the raging eddy. Powell and two other men leapt into their boat and followed Bradley over the falls. Now they became the victims of the river's strength and cunning. "A wave rolls over us, and our boat is unmanageable. Another great wave strikes us; the boat rolls over and tumbles and tosses." Powell perhaps hit a rock, for he lost consciousness. The next thing he remembered was being pulled from the water by Bradley, who somehow had escaped the whirlpool.

As fortune would have it, this closest brush with death was their last. The very next day the canyon walls suddenly receded, the current slackened, and they reached the lower part of the river, which Powell recognized from the accounts of Mormons who had settled near there. The men savored their release, but none more than Powell, who had particular memories of confinement. "When he who has been chained by wounds to a hospital cot, until his canvas tent seems like a dungeon cell . . . ," he wrote, "at last goes out into the open field, what a world he sees!" Powell suddenly saw that new world again. "How beautiful the sky; how bright the sunshine!"[5]

POWELL'S DESCENT OF the Colorado was the most dramatic of several postwar expeditions, but others drew scarcely less attention. Clarence King headed a survey of the West roughly along the 40th parallel, the object of which was "to examine and describe the geological structure, geographical condition and natural resources" of this central swath from Denver to Sacramento. King would assess railroad routes, assay mineral deposits, test soils, take temperatures, measure rainfall and stream flow, and, on return, publish his estimate of the uses to which the region might be put. The 40th parallel survey consumed several years starting in 1867 and concluded with King's debunking a bizarre hoax involving planted diamonds, dizzying share prices, the ruin of investors, the murder of one of the principal perpetrators, and the mysterious disappearance of the other.[6]

George Wheeler's survey of the Southwest concentrated on topography: on mapping the Colorado Plateau and the basin-and-range district to its west. Wheeler found desert far starker than anything previous explorers had encountered. The expedition traversed Death Valley on a forty-mile path of what Wheeler described as "light, white, drifting sand." (In fact this wasn't the worst of the valley, where the sand gave way to salt.) Wheeler had chosen the toughest wilderness men of the West for his trek, but this hellish place was too much for even some of them. "The stifling heat, great radiation, and constant glare from the sand were almost overpowering, and two of the command succumbed near nightfall." All counted themselves lucky to escape with their lives.[7]

Ferdinand V. Hayden's first survey, of western Nebraska, won him fame for its seeming confirmation of the theory promoted by a minority of scientists and a majority of western boosters that "rain follows the plow." The idea was that turning the soil and planting crops released moisture that subsequently returned to earth as rain. Pleased proponents of the theory sponsored additional surveys, for which Hayden had the insight to hire a photographer, who captured for public consumption the wonders of the upper Yellowstone basin and the beauties of the Colorado Rockies. One of William H. Jackson's prints, of the Mount of the Holy Cross (so named for the intersecting crevices near the summit, which caught snow in a cross-shaped pattern), allowed Americans of a mystically religious bent to see the hand of God in the work of the explorers. Hayden himself was moved to remark, "Never has my faith in the grand future that awaits the entire West been so strong as it is at the present."[8]

LIKE NEARLY ALL other emigrants to the Great Plains, Howard Ruede had heard of the Homestead Act of 1862 and its promise of free land to ordinary people. But like many of the others, he knew few details of the law's operation. Ruede arrived in western Kansas in the spring of 1877 from Bethlehem, Pennsylvania. He was twenty-two and single and for some years had eavesdropped on conversations of elders who complained that Pennsylvania's future wasn't what it once had seemed. The depression of the 1870s set many of them back, and the Molly Maguire violence alienated others. More than a few told young Howard that if they were his age they'd leave. So in March 1877 he withdrew his life savings of seventy-five dollars from a Bethlehem bank and boarded a train for the West.

Free land near the railroads had long since disappeared; the land for sale cost far more than Ruede could afford to pay. Besides, many of his fellow German Americans from Bethlehem had preceded him west to the vicinity of Osborne, fifty miles from the nearest railroad, and had established the "Pennsylvania Colony." Ruede reached Osborne on a Sunday; the next morning the son-in-law of the colony's founder appeared at Ruede's hotel and offered to show him available tracts of land. How much Ruede paid the agent for his services is unclear, but he could hardly do without such a guide. On the featureless prairie outside Osborne it was impossible for a newcomer to tell what land had been taken and what remained for claiming. The 1862 law required homesteaders to live on their claims for five years, but those who actually did so were a minority. Some evaded the condition by erecting a flimsy structure, summoning a witness who then swore to the federal land agent that an abode existed, and then dismantling the building for reuse elsewhere. Efficiency-minded finaglers put their structures on wheels. One imaginative homesteader acquired three empty wood crates in which apple trees had been shipped from the East. On end each could just accommodate a short man standing; on a crate laid horizontal the same small fellow could uncomfortably lie down. The homesteader got two friends to try each configuration; the trio then traveled to the land office, where the friends testified that the claimant had erected a house on his property tall enough to walk around in and roomy enough for three men to spend the night, each in his own bed. The claimant received his papers, and the crates went on to better things.[9]

Absentee homesteaders weren't the only problem confronting a newcomer looking for land. The Homestead Act lay in a series of laws dating to 1796 designed to facilitate the transfer of land from the public domain to private ownership. The motivation for the laws was at once ideological and fiscal: to spread the wealth of America to ordinary Americans and to fund the operations of the federal government. The most important of the pre-Homestead acts was the Preemption Act of 1841, which allowed small landowners (of not more than 320 acres in any state or territory) to purchase a quarter section (160 acres) from the public domain at a very modest price, in most instances $1.25 per acre. The principal constraint was that the land be held for use and not immediately resold. The Homestead Act differed primarily in that it eliminated the purchase price (although it allowed the homesteaded land to be purchased at the preemption price of $1.25 after six months' residence). Yet the Preemption Act remained in force, meaning that a person such as Howard Ruede could acquire a quarter section under the Homestead Act and another quarter section under the Preemption Act. A third land law, the Timber Culture Act of 1873, allowed a settler to claim an additional quarter section provided that forty acres of it were planted with trees. The three laws and their differences in conditions meant that many districts were patchworks of ownership impenetrable to outsiders. And, ownership aside, settlers weren't above simply lying, telling newcomers that land—perhaps surrounded by the settlers' claims—wasn't available in that neighborhood.[10]

Such bogus claims could be challenged, as Howard Ruede discovered. His agent led him and some potential partners to a pair of tracts not far from Osborne. "These two claims—one of 160 and one of 80 acres— would have to be contested before we could get hold of them," Ruede wrote home. "And it would cost us about $50. . . . As none of us could afford that, those claims will lie open awhile yet." The next day Ruede and his friends found available tracts farther from town. "My claim is the S.W. ¼ of section 4; Levin is next west, and Jim west of Levin, all on the same section line. . . . The land is of the intermediate grade, neither bluff nor bottom land, and is covered for the most part with buffalo grass, which Mr. S."—the agent—"says is a sure sign of its being good. This buffalo grass does not get more than 3 inches long, and about the middle of August turns into hay—cures on the ground, and if you pull up a bunch, you are sure to find green grass close to the roots." Ruede and the other two returned to Osborne and the next day filed their claims with the federal land agent there. Lacking the money to purchase the land by preemption, they applied for homestead status. "We must live on it five years. The first two years we live 'off and on'—that is, we must sleep on it once in a while and make some improvements on it within 6 months, or it will be forfeited. It is to be our home, but we can hire out by the day or month as we like."[11]

Had Ruede been a farmer, he would have begun plowing his quarter section at once. But like many other homesteaders he was a town boy and saw his land claim more as an investment—or even a speculation—than as a commitment to the farmer's life. He would "prove up" his claim (complete the requirements for a clear deed) and sell to a genuine son of the soil. Meanwhile he would find work where he could and make the minimal improvements on his property, starting with a house.

For the cash-strapped, the cheapest accommodation was a dugout. "We found a spot . . . where a patch of wild sunflowers had killed the grass," Ruede recorded. "Here we began to dig, and by noon had made some progress. We laid off the ground 10 x 14 feet, and we'll have to dig it about 6 feet deep." Ruede and Jim, his neighbor and coworker on the project, broke for dinner before resuming their labors. "We went back to the hole and in about two hours had dug about half of it to the depth of two feet." A spring shower compelled the diggers to quit, which was fine with them, as their hands were blistered and their backs sore. "Talk about hard work, will you? . . . The ground is packed just as hard as could be, and it is no fun to pick and shovel it." But already Ruede felt the pride of ownership. "My dugout is at the head of the prettiest draw on my claim, and if the clouds clear off we will have it finished by the middle of next week."

The pace of digging quickened when Levin joined them. The packed soil didn't loosen the deeper they got, but neither did it turn to anything harder. "We have not found a single stone as big as a marble yet," Ruede declared as they approached the five-foot mark. Late on the fourth day, a Saturday, the hole was completed, and after a break for Sunday—which happened to be Easter, celebrated in the German style—they started on the superstructure. Levin and Jim walked to Osborne for some lumber, which they paid for with a few days' work at the sawmill there. Ruede paid cash—$1.50—for a burr-oak ridgepole. More rain delayed construction further, but by the following Friday the hole in the prairie was beginning to look like a house, or what passed for a house in western Kansas. "We finished off the gable ends of the dugout and got the boards on the rafters, ready for the straw." Over the straw went sod, cut in 12 by 18 by 2½ inch bricks. "Covered the whole roof with a layer of sod, and then threw dirt on it, and the 'house' was finished." The three moved directly in, and the next day Ruede wrote, "We begin to feel right at home."[12]

FOR THREE MEN to share quarters (in this instance pending excavation and construction of dugouts for Levin and Jim) wasn't unusual on the Plains. Men greatly outnumbered women among the homesteaders, as they did among frontier folk generally. The aphorist wasn't wrong who declared that "plains travel and frontier life are peculiarly severe upon women and oxen." Yet if life on the Middle Border—as the Plains were often called—was hard on women, it could be rewarding as well. The Homestead Act drew no distinction between men and women, making it easier for women to acquire property in their own names in the West than in other parts of the country. Women, moreover, gained value from

allowing underage husbands to acquire homesteads. The 1862 act required
claimants to be twenty-one unless they were "the head of a family."
Howard Ruede learned of a nineteen-year-old who coveted a particular
quarter section. For several months the young man kept other claimants
away with the assertion that he was holding it for his brother-in-law, who
was coming from Iowa. But as more people arrived in that county, his ruse
wore thin. He was tempted to lie about his age and file a preemption claim.
But should his lie become known, his claim would be revoked and he
would lose the improvements he made to the property. He had a female
friend, however, the daughter of a neighbor, who agreed to a scam to help
him resolve his dilemma. "He saddled his pony and went over to Mary
Ann's home to confer with her," Ruede explained. "She looked favorably
on the project and consented to become his bride. . . . He continued his
journey to the county seat and got a license to wed. Next morning he was
over at Mary Ann's bright and early. She was busy with the week's washing,
but took her hands out of the suds, dried them, and went with Tommy to
the nearest justice of the peace, by whom they were made man and
wife. . . . Mary Ann returned to her wash tubs and Tommy hiked for Kir-
win where the land office was located. The officials were not overinquisi-
tive and Tommy got his homestead papers."[13]

More frequently the women followed the men to the Plains, often at
months' or years' remove. Husbands left wives and children with in-laws
farther east while they broke the sod, built the dugouts, and otherwise
smoothed the roughest edges of frontier life. Eventually the wives and little ones followed. Unattached men returned east after claiming and partly
improving their quarter section, hopeful that landownership made them
appealing to unattached women. Winter was courtship season; when the
snows and cold precluded outdoor work, a young man's fancy turned to
love. More than a few dugout doors rattled in the icy wind, secured by a
wire and a notice to claim jumpers: "Gone to get a wife."[14]

The strangeness of their new surroundings caused many women to
despair. One young mother held her emotions in check only to break down
when her young son, seeing nothing familiar or pleasing from horizon to
horizon, fell to the dirt floor and cried, "Mama, will we always have to live
here?" Her heart sank further when, upon being told that they would
indeed live there, the boy wailed, "And will we have to die here, too?"[15]

The prairie hid dangers of a sort those from the East didn't know.

Children—and adults—could be lost in blizzards only several feet from the doors of their houses. Rattlesnakes coiled in the tall grass. Indians remained a threat till the late 1870s. Distance itself became an enemy when business in town took the man of a house away for days at a time, leaving his wife and children to look out for the drifters that inhabit every frontier. Distance also magnified the ordinary trials of nineteenth-century life. Many women bore babies unattended by anyone except their husbands; complications could quickly become dire. The isolation of Plains life bred depression, which could be lethal to the depressed and, in extreme cases, to other members of the family.

HOWARD RUEDE HOPED to marry, but for the present the women he wanted to bring west were his mother and sister. His father would accompany them, and the family would be reunited. But he knew he couldn't ask the women to live in a dugout. "I don't want them to come till I get a decent house for them to live in, and that can be done in a couple of years," he explained. Meanwhile he scrimped on every expense imaginable. "I'll get Hoot to cut my hair; the barber here charges 25 cents, and that is a big sum for me now." His clothes wore out and weren't replaced. "Underclothes I don't wear. . . . Socks there are none." In summer he dispensed with shoes. Necessities in the East became luxuries on the Plains. "I never know what time it is when I get out of bed, because clocks are like angels' visits—few and far between. . . . Most people out here don't drink real coffee because it is too expensive. Green coffee berries sell at anywhere from 40 to 60 cents a pound." (By comparison, Ruede reckoned that his whole house, including lumber, a door and hinges, and a window, cost less than ten dollars to build.) "So rye coffee is used a great deal—parched brown or black according to whether the users like a strong or mild drink. . . . When rye is not used, wheat is sometimes used for coffee but is considered inferior."[16]

Hardships came in other forms. "The people who live in sod houses, and, in fact, all who live under a dirt roof, are pestered with swarms of bed bugs. . . . You don't have to keep a dog in order to have plenty of fleas, for they are natives, too, and do their best to drive out the intruding settlers. Just have a dirt floor and you have fleas, sure. They seem to spring from the dust of the earth." Fleas were the primary reason settlers got out of their dugouts and sod houses as soon as they could afford wooden ones. "People who have board floors are not bothered so much with these fleas." Smaller creatures caused the "Kansas itch"—"which attacks nearly everybody within a short time after arrival here. . . . There is only one way in which a sufferer can get relief: scratching. And that aggravates the itching and sometimes produces raw sore spots."

There were compensations. Itching aside, Ruede had never been healthier. He attributed his well-being to the massive doses of fresh air. "If I catch cold one day, the wind takes it away the next. I can stand more wet feet here than at home"—Pennsylvania—"and can sleep in an awful drafty room without taking cold." He ate well (except for the coffee). Much of his first season he devoted to acquiring capital to develop his claim, which was to say he hired himself out to neighbors; they paid cash and typically furnished bed and board. "For breakfast I ate about ½ lb. steak, a plateful of fried potatoes, 5 fried eggs, two rounds of bread, a slice of cake and two ginger cakes, and washed it all down with two cups of coffee." The food got better as the work grew heavier. "When you work for somebody in the harvest field, you may count on getting No. 1 board. They set a first-rate table then." Of one day in particular he wrote, "Had a staving good supper: fried rabbits"—flushed and killed in the process of the harvest—"bread and butter, onions, radishes, pie, and coffee ad libitum." Work continued after supper, but "when we got to the house we found Horace was making ice cream. After putting away the team and feeding them, I went back and had about a pint of the luxury."[17]

In March 1878 Ruede tallied his accounts for the previous month. He had been in Kansas a year and had spent most of that time hiring himself by the day and week to neighbors (meaning persons who lived within a fifty-mile radius of his homestead) who needed work done (nearly everyone) and who could pay cash for the labor (a much smaller group). He earned about five dollars a week, plus food and lodging. By the beginning of 1878 he had accumulated some hundred dollars, but he soon spent it all. "Total expenses for February were $105.01, divided as follows: oxen, yoke and chain, $61.25; wagon, $30; household goods and tools, $4.50; provisions, $4.30; oil"—to keep down the fleas—"30 cents; sundries, $4.41."[18]

During the first few years, most small Plains farms weren't expected to yield a profit. Homesteaders plowed money into the soil even as they turned the prairie sod. The money arrived in the homesteaders' pockets; it went to purchase provisions and the labor of the likes of Howard Ruede. In time, though, the new land had to return the favor: to produce sufficient profit to sustain those homesteaders who intended to make the Middle Border their home and to attract the second wave of immigrants who would buy out the speculators.

Profits, however, proved elusive. The farmers could control certain of their revenue and costs—by working long hours and weeks, by forgoing new shoes (or, as with Ruede, shoes at all), by subsisting in dugouts longer than they had intended. But they had no control over such central elements of the production process as the weather. Plains weather was notoriously fickle—or it would have been notorious had the homesteaders possessed any substantial knowledge of it. The remarkable fact was that whole tiers of the Middle Border were settled on the basis of wishful thinking about the climate of the region. Boosters so often told themselves that rain followed the plow that they came to believe it. But no one had any idea whether it was true, for rainfall records were either nonexistent or so short as to make extrapolation meaningless.

John Wesley Powell was sure it wasn't true. And he was equally certain that most of the American West would never yield agricultural profits, at least not by any honest accounting scheme. Powell's death-defying descent of the Colorado had made him a national celebrity, the Civil War hero who extended into peacetime his exploits on behalf of the American people. He didn't hurt his cause by befriending reporters, by recounting the adventure in evocative present-tense prose ("We are now ready to start on our way down the Great Unknown"), and by cultivating friendships in Washington. Congress funded further expeditions, which Powell parlayed into control of the scientific agenda for the public domain in the West.

At the top of Powell's agenda was disabusing the American people of the notion that settlement habits and patterns developed in the East might be readily translated to the West. In the same season when Howard Ruede was tallying his cash flow, Powell prepared a report on what he provocatively labeled the "Arid Region" of the United States. "The eastern portion of the United States is supplied with abundant rainfall for agricultural purposes, receiving the necessary amount from the evaporation of the Atlantic Ocean and the Gulf of Mexico," Powell wrote. "But westward the amount of aqueous precipitation diminishes in a general way until at last a region is reached where the climate is so arid that agriculture is not successful without irrigation. This Arid Region begins about midway in the Great Plains and extends across the Rocky Mountains to the Pacific Ocean."[19]

Powell took twenty inches of rain or its equivalent as the minimum to support unirrigated agriculture. The twenty-inch isohyet—the line connecting locations with the threshold amount of rainfall—ran roughly along the 100th meridian; from there to the Pacific, with the exception of the high mountains (which were unsuited to farming for other reasons) and a strip along the coast, the West was a great desert. Nor was the twenty-inch isohyet any guarantee of agricultural success. Rain along that line often fell irregularly. "Many droughts will occur; many seasons in a long series will be fruitless; and it may be doubted whether, on the whole, agriculture will prove remunerative." East of the isohyet was a band Powell called the "Sub-humid Region." Much of the region of the Plains settled to date lay in this region. Though the rainfall averaged as much as twenty-eight inches, Powell warned that even here agriculture was risky. "In the western portion disastrous droughts will be frequent; in the eastern portion infrequent."

Powell adopted the dispassionate tone of the scientist, but his purpose was explicitly political. He aimed to burst the bubbles of speculation that were populating the Plains with innocents whose fortunes would be lost and lives ruined by the land dealers, hucksters, railroad agents, and civic boosters who preached that rain followed the plow and other such nonsense. Beyond revealing the hucksters for what they were, Powell hoped to lay the foundation for the settlement of such portions of the West as could sustain populations over the long term.

Powell's West was divided into three parts. The "irrigable lands" were a small portion of the whole West, located on or near streams that could be dammed to focus the rainfall and snowmelt of an entire desert watershed upon a few fields, which could thereby thrive. The "timber lands" were the wooded mountain slopes and mesas. These lands could not be farmed but might be reserved for the production of lumber and firewood. The "pasturage lands" constituted the largest part of the West. Covered with native grass, these tracts could not sustain cultivation but, if carefully managed, might support livestock.

The key to developing the Arid Region was wise public stewardship. Land laws that had evolved in the wet East must be modified. The grid system of rectangular surveys, for example, made no sense where stream courses, rather than township and section lines, determined patterns of husbandry. "If the lands are surveyed in regular tracts as square miles or townships, all the water sufficient for a number of pasturage farms may fall entirely within one division. . . . For this reason divisional surveys should conform to the topography." The quarter section—the 160 acres hallowed in American tradition as the sustenance of the yeoman and his family—was similarly unsuited to the West. In those few places that could be irrigated, a quarter section was too large. A single family couldn't do all the work an irrigated farm required. Moreover, quarter section allotments were wasteful in the irrigated zones, which could support a denser population than the quarters allowed. In the region that ought to be reserved to pasturage, quarter sections were too small. "Pasturage farms, to be of any practicable value, must be of at least 2,560 acres, and in many districts they must be much larger."

Patterns of use needed to be as carefully regulated as patterns of ownership. Only the largest streams were worth damming, but to preserve their worth their tributaries had to be kept free of diversion—which often meant free of settlement. Fences should be banned from much of the pasture lands, as they prevented stock from finding shelter from storms and making the most of the available grasses. But common grazing required communal policies regarding the number of stock each farmer could place on the range.

Communalism informed Powell's vision from start to finish. Individualism had sufficed to develop the East, but individualism would fail in the West. Powell knew Congress—to which his report was addressed—well enough not to lecture the lawmakers explicitly on how this communalism ought to be accomplished. He pointed out that in Utah Territory the Mormon Church took the lead in developing and enforcing communal policies, especially with respect to irrigation. Yet, given the hostility most (Gentile) Americans held for the Mormons, Powell's example was really a caution and an implicit argument for action by secular government.[20]

POWELL SPOKE FOR a distant future, as things turned out. His views would inform the development of the Southwest during the twentieth century, when government did take the lead in making the desert habitable and profitable. For the rest of the nineteenth century, however, another vision—one better tuned to the times—shaped western development.

William Allen White was a Kansan, a child of Emporia who left his home to learn journalism but returned to purchase and edit the local paper, the *Emporia Gazette*. His vigorous style caught the attention of his colleagues in the fourth estate, who reprinted his editorials and appointed him pulse taker to the American people. The editors of *Scribner's Magazine,* as part of a series called "The Conduct of Great Businesses," commissioned White to assess the state of the agricultural industry. The assignment seconded certain notions White had reached while watching agriculture evolve on the Middle Border. "When one is cataloguing the callings of men, one says, 'the business man and the farmer,' never the 'the business man and farmer' or the 'business man engaged in farming,'" he wrote. "In daily speech modern men and women pay unconscious tribute to the ghost of the old order which seemed to decree that the farmer's existence depended upon brawn and not upon brain." The old order had vanished, White asserted, and with it the distinction between businessman and farmer. "The successful farmer of this generation must be a business man first, and a tiller of the soil afterward. . . . He must be a capitalist, cautious and crafty; he must be an operator of industrial affairs, daring and resourceful."

Nowhere was this truer than on the large farms of the West, where agriculture in the 1890s took a particular bent. In the Central Valley of California and on the volcanic plateaus of eastern Oregon and Washington, wheat growers plowed, planted, and harvested on vast tracts that dwarfed anything found in the East. But the most striking examples of the "bonanza farms," as the giant wheat operations were called, lay along the Red River in North Dakota. Accordingly, to the Red River Valley White traveled to observe the capitalist farmers at work.

The first thing that struck him upon entering the valley by train was the thoroughness of the cultivation. "There is not a barren acre. Wheat stretches away from the car window to the horizon, over a land flat as a floor. The monotonous exactness of the level makes one long for the undulating prairies of the middle west. Yet the very evenness of the plain has a commercial value, and makes the location here of the great wheat-farms possible. For in a rolling country there is waste land—here an 'eighty' on a hill top, there a 'forty' in a swamp. But in bonanza farming every foot of land must be productive with the expenditure of the least possible amount of human labor upon it."[21]

Providence and geology had combined to endow the Red River Valley with its flatness, which in turn produced the deep soil, nearly devoid of stones, that made the task of the plowman almost a pleasure. But it was capitalism that fostered the creation of the large tracts—of thousands and tens of thousands of acres—of the biggest bonanza farms. The Northern Pacific Railroad had reached the Red River in 1872, underwritten by the same sorts of land grants as the Union and Central Pacific railroads. The financial panic of the following year left the Northern (and many other railroads) starved for cash, which the Northern's directors partially obtained by unloading their land grants. Eastern and European investors shortly constructed some of the largest privately owned farms in North America.

The investors were betting on the future of the wheat industry, which during the late 1870s and 1880s indeed became an industry. Decades earlier millers had discovered the falls of the Mississippi and made Minneapolis a center of grain grinding. But after the Civil War they devised new methods for separating the coarse bran and oily germ of wheat from its starchy endosperm. Millstones gave way to steel rollers, which cracked the kernels and culled all but the fluffy white flour. This prized product yielded airy loaves and stayed fresh far longer than its whole-grain predecessors and so could be shipped across the country and across the sea. Not coincidentally—cause and effect being intimately entwined in economic and industrial development—the hard red wheat that grew best in the Red River hinterland of Minneapolis was ideally suited to the machining techniques of the milling industry. The investors envisioned their Red River farms feeding the world.[22]

But doing so required efficiency, for investors in other countries—Russia, Hungary, Argentina—had the same idea and access to the same markets and techniques. The farms of the Red River became outdoor factories, as mechanized in their own way as the refineries of John Rockefeller and the steelworks of Andrew Carnegie. "From the plough to the elevator," William White observed, "from the first operation in wheat farming to the last, one is forced to realize how the spirit of the age has made itself felt here." This was farming unlike anything previous generations had known. "The man who ploughs uses his muscle only incidentally in guiding the machine. The man who operates the harrow has half a dozen levers to lighten his labor. . . . The reaper needs a quick brain and a quick hand—but not necessarily a strong arm, nor a powerful back. . . . The threshers are merely assistants to a machine, and the men who heave wheat into the bins only press buttons." The farm laborer of the West became decreasingly distinguishable from the factory worker of the East. "Each is the tender of a machine."

The bonanza farms were to the yeoman's plot what Carnegie's works were to the corner blacksmith. "It is difficult to present the idea of the bigness of these farms to the person whose preconceived notion of a farm is a little checkerboard lying upon a hillside or in a valley," White said. Seven thousand acres constituted the average Red River farm. "Distances across fields are so great that horseback communication is impracticable. Crews of workmen living at one end of the farm and operating it may not see the crews in other corners from season's end to season's end." Most of the workers were full-time agriculturalists but part-time Red River men; they followed the spring from the southern Plains north, arriving in time to plow the warming ground. They worked in gangs, driving their horse-drawn harrows in echelon across the endless fields. Behind the harrows came the wheat drills, boring a bushel and a peck of the prime of last year's crop into each acre. After the seeding all but a skeleton crew of eight or ten workers were dismissed. Most of those let go circled back to the southern Plains, where crops were already beginning to ripen, and they harvested their way north. Few paid rail fare; the railroad corporations, as a service to their largest customers—the bonanza farms—ensured the arrival of the labor forces by letting them ride free.

The harvest was the frantic season in the valley. Beginning in late July, weather permitting, it continued till all the wheat was in the elevators or rain ruined the rest of the crop. The men worked hard and long. "They eat breakfast at five o'clock and supper at half-past seven," White wrote. They spent the intervening hours in the field. "It is found profitable to feed the hands in the fields rather than to allow them to trudge through the hot sun to the dining-halls for dinner." The shrewdest managers—the only ones who lasted in this competitive industry—took good care of their men. "In the old days, before the system of farming had been reduced to a business problem, no sleeping quarters were provided, and the men slept in the open and upon the straw. . . . But this plan brought sickness to the farms in the harvest season, and the farmers found that it was more expensive than housing and caring for the men in the best possible manner." Similar thinking inspired the menus. "The bonanza farmers—at least the better class of them—are as careful of the food set before the men as they are of the fodder that is put before their horses." A typical dinner consisted of "corned beef, boiled potatoes, salt pork, baked beans, stewed turnips, tea and coffee, milk, white sugar—and that is a point that has caused many a strike in the Mississippi Valley—syrup, hot and cold bread, cookies, doughnuts, pickles, two kinds of pie, and cheese." The foremen imposed a certain social discipline upon the crews. "On the best farms there is no drinking, and card-playing is strictly prohibited. The foremen say that cards keep men out of bed at night, and they have not their best strength to work during the day."

The hard work didn't end with the harvest. The wheat had to be threshed and the grain sorted. The field stubble had to be burned to kill pests and fertilize the soil with the ash. After the ground cooled the fields were plowed, again by gangs of machines staggered across the field, each turning a twin furrow. The plows averaged twenty linear miles a day and up to three hundred acres per season. When the plowing ended the men went home to Chicago or St. Louis or Milwaukee, to the embraces of their wives and the economic benefit of their communities. "They bring home probably a million dollars in wages." To White they seemed the salt of the earth. "They are steady, industrious men with no bad habits, and small ambitions."

The ambitions of their bosses were larger. White found fascinating the obsession of the farm managers with costs; John Rockefeller couldn't have been more ruthless in routing inefficiency. White laid out the operation as it appeared from the manager's office.

> This is his plant: First there is the land—about seven thousand acres of it. The raw land—if there were any raw land in this part of the world—would be worth about $175,000. The improvements are worth about $35,000. There are three divisions of the farm, each division having its division superintendent. . . . At each division house there are stables and implement barns. In each division stable are about one hundred head of horses. . . . In the machine-shed upon each division are ten four-horse ploughs, eight four-horse drills, half a dozen harrows, and seven binders. . . . There are three steam-motor threshing machines on the place, but except while they are in use they are kept at the division nearest the manager's house. . . . Two elevators, one with a capacity of 40,000 bushels and the other with a capacity of 60,000, are

located upon opposite corners of the farm by the railroad track which runs through the great field. A central office, wherein the bookkeeper and the manager conduct the business of the farm, is connected with the three division houses and with other important points on the farm by telephone. . . . A set of books, kept as carefully as the books of a bank are kept, and a telephone connecting the farm with a telegraph wire to the world's markets complete the list of articles which may properly be called the tools of the business.

The manager and the bookkeeper monitored every step of the productive process—that is, of the life cycle of the wheat. Planting the wheat, for example, cost seventy to ninety-five cents an acre, depending on weather (once the crews arrived at the farm they drew their weekly wage of nine to twelve dollars even if rain kept them in the dormitories for days at a time). Feeding the men cost thirty cents a day (a bit more at first, as the men bulked up after eating for months on their own accounts, a little less afterward). White noted that casual observers of modern farm life often blamed farmers for carelessness in leaving their equipment in the fields to rust over the winter. On the bonanza farms this wasn't carelessness but calculation. "The Dakota farmers, who buy machinery by the car-load, say that many times it does not pay to take a machine to the shed after a hard season's wear and tear. . . . More money is lost in time repairing and tinkering with an old implement than would pay for two new ones." On the bonanza farms, a piece of heavy equipment was not a capital investment but an item of consumption. If a harvester or a binder lasted a single season, the manager was satisfied, for he knew how much the equipment magnified the labor power of his men.

It was in the use of equipment that the big farms gained their greatest economies of scale. A farmer who planted a mere forty acres of wheat required a binder to tie it in sheaves. But the binder could easily tie the wheat from several times that acreage, leaving the small farmer to spread its cost over a much smaller harvest than the large farmer could. Likewise with harvesters and threshers. The small farmer might be tempted to share equipment with neighbors, and some did. But the wheat came ripe all at once, and the farmer who didn't have the equipment at his instant disposal could be ruined by an untimely rain.

The output of the bonanza farms was prodigious.

Averaging twenty bushels to the acre, as many farms will this year, the total number of bushels in a crop on a bonanza farm would be 140,000. Putting five hundred bushels of that crop in a freight car, and allowing forty feet to the car, the train which would haul the crop from the farm would be two miles long, and if it were to come charging down Fifth Avenue and Broadway in New York, the rear end brakeman would be craning his neck from the caboose to catch sight of the Vanderbilt mansion while the engineer and fireman were enjoying themselves bumping the cable car down by Union Square. . . . If this crop had to go to mill the old-fashioned way, in two bushel sacks on a mule, the procession would stretch more than halfway from Brooklyn to Buffalo.

Yet huge output was no guarantee of profit. The farm managers didn't open their books to White, and so he had to guess at some of the costs of production. Labor and equipment were relatively straightforward, as were the purchase cost and upkeep of livestock. Taxes were a matter of public record; interest and insurance premiums were not. Tallying it all up, White arrived at a cost of about eight dollars per acre to operate one of the big farms. In a good year this translated into a cost of about forty cents per bushel of wheat. The price of wheat the last several years had averaged more than fifty cents, leaving the bonanza farmers a tidy profit.

But not every year was a good year. When the rains came too soon or too late or not at all, the acre yield fell off dramatically, while the farmers' expenses did not. Over time the yields diminished even in good weather, as the wheat monoculture depleted the soil. And in even the best years, the Red River farmers were at the mercy of occurrences half a world away. Price tickers in managers' offices recorded fluctuations in the grain markets in Minneapolis and Duluth and Buffalo, which in turn responded to developments on the world market. "A rainfall in India or a hot wind in South America is felt upon the Dakota farm in a few hours. The nerves of trade thrill around the globe, and the wages of the harvester in the Red River Valley are fixed by conditions in the fields of Russia, or in Argentina, or in India. The distance between the fields has been lost. The world's wheat crop might as well lie in one great field, for the scattered acres are wired together in the markets, and those markets are brought to the farmer's door."[23]

Part Three

GOTHAM AND GOMORRAH

Chapter 9

THE TEEMING SHORE

T he capitalist revolution affected other countries besides America. Britain felt its influence first, as befitted the homeland of Adam Smith. The revolution then swept across the German states, causing Karl Marx to predict capitalism's ultimate self-destruction. It touched France and a dozen other countries of Europe. Most of Asia and Africa remained beyond its immediate reach, yet, like a tropical storm system roiling across one of the world's oceans, it sent ripples and eddies into regions far removed from its center. It created zones of high pressure and low pressure, so to speak, causing resources to flow from the former to the latter, often accompanied by the disruption turbulent weather entails. During the middle and late nineteenth century, for example, the American economy was a low-pressure zone for capital, sucking investment from Britain, a comparatively high-pressure zone.

The weather analogy applied equally, and more conspicuously, to human resources. The capitalist revolution in America created persistent low pressure that pulled immigrants out of Europe and Asia into North America. Not all parts of those people exporting continents responded equally to the pull. Microclimates within countries and regions caused Ireland to lose more sons and daughters to America than Scotland did, and Germany more than France. The microclimates shifted as the nineteenth century matured, with the center of European high pressure moving east and south. And the strength of the storm in America itself varied, over both space, as cities developed and the frontier shifted, and time, as the American economy surged and stalled.

The United States wasn't the only low-pressure zone. Empty land pulled immigrant farmers to the plains of Canada and Argentina, and expanding factories drew workers to the cities of England and Germany. But during the second half of the nineteenth century no country experienced such sustained and powerful low pressure as America. And the whirlwind that resulted transformed the face of American society.

THE IRISH RODE the leading edge of the storm. The capitalist revolution in England—in particular the introduction of steam-driven textile machinery—heightened demand for wool and prompted landlords in Ireland to convert their crop farms to sheep pastures. The enclosing of the fields crowded Irish peasants onto ever-smaller plots, where they became dependent on potatoes for their sustenance. A few Irish, those with the foresight to see where things were going and the means to act on their prescience, emigrated to America during the 1820s and 1830s, but most stayed home, praying the potatoes would hold out. The density of population increased and the potato monoculture deepened until in the 1840s the system became unsustainable. A fungus attacked the potato crop, and with entire districts devoted to the single species it ate through field after field, leaving nothing but blighted leaves and shriveled tubers.

As bad luck would have it, the onset of the potato blight in Ireland coincided with the triumph of free trade in Britain, Ireland's colonial master. London's free-traders, having devoted decades to making the principles of Adam Smith the law of the British empire, refused to jeopardize their capitalist experiment in order to save the Irish. Even as hundreds of thousands of peasants died of malnutrition, Irish landlords exported agricultural commodities by the boatload.[1]

Of those Irish who didn't die, some million and a half made their way to America. The newcomers weren't the poorest of the Irish poor, who, lacking the means or vision to emigrate, simply starved in place; but neither were they the entrepreneurs who had characterized the earlier emigration. They came with scant skills and scanter capital; though nearly all had been farmers, most stuck in the cities. Even after the Homestead Act made land available, few emigrated to the frontier, partly because they lacked the cash for travel, tools, and filing fees but also because American farm culture, with its solitary farm houses planted in the middle of large fields, sometimes miles from the nearest neighbors, contradicted the communal style and values of Ireland's peasant villages. Irish laborers built the Union Pacific and other railroads; Irish mine workers dug coal from the hills of Pennsylvania. But for most of the rest, the cities of the eastern seaboard became their home.

They took employment where they found it. They dug basements and ditches, drove piles and wagons, loaded railcars and barges. On the eve of the Civil War more than 80 percent of New York City's unskilled labor was Irish. Their employers appreciated their willingness to work for low wages—even as many of those employers despised the Irish as barely human. George Templeton Strong was building a house in New York and needed help. "Hibernia came to the rescue yesterday morning," he noted in his diary. "Twenty 'sons of toil' with prehensile paws supplied them by nature with evident preference to the handling of the spade and the wielding of the pickaxe and congenital hollows on the shoulder wonderfully adapted to make the carrying of the hod a luxury instead of a labor commenced the task yesterday morning." The Irish were loved even less by the workers they displaced, in particular African Americans. "Along the wharves where the colored man once done the whole business of shipping and unshipping, in stores where his services were once rendered, and in families where the chief places were filled by him, in all these situations there are substituted foreigners," a black newspaper complained. Frederick Douglass observed, "Every hour sees us elbowed out of some employment to make room for some newly arrived emigrant from the emerald isle, whose hunger and color entitle him to special favor." Yet Douglass himself realized that such preference as the Irish obtained didn't amount to much. "In assuming our avocation," he remarked, the Irish "also assumed our degradation."[2]

The competition at the bottom of the social and economic ladder burst shockingly into the open in the summer of 1863. Even as the Union army held fast at Gettysburg, the war came home to Manhattan. The new conscription law compelled young men to register for the draft; those who lacked the three hundred dollars for a replacement were subject to a lottery that determined which ones would actually serve. Many Irish asked why they should fight to free the slaves, whom they would then have to fight for jobs. They observed acidly that three hundred dollars would buy an Irish-man's life while a typical slave cost a thousand dollars. They wondered why blacks long resident in America should be exempt from the draft when the Irish were snatched straight off the boat. Many Irish took to the streets in protest of the draft, of the rich man's exemption, and of assorted other insults that grew more onerous in the stifling heat of the urban July. Pro-testers hurled rocks at targets identified with the Republican party, starting with shops and houses and escalating to persons, in particular African Americans. One band of rioters attacked the Colored Orphan Asylum, shouting "Burn the niggers' nest!" Patrick Merry, an Irish laborer, led another band down Broadway to a neighborhood inhabited by blacks, where the rioters spread out and began chasing those they found on the street. Blacks were dragged from streetcars and beaten. One black man was lynched and his body burned.

For three days the rioting raged. Blacks weren't merely victims of the violence; as they organized to defend themselves and their property they inflicted casualties on their attackers. The opposing sides armed and fired, till the riot looked alarmingly like urban warfare. Only the arrival of fed-eral troops, drawn in haste from the Pennsylvania front, restored order. By then more than a hundred persons had died, leaving blacks bitter, Irish aggrieved, and everyone wondering what would happen next.

The draft riots revealed a rift not simply between Irish and blacks but among the Irish themselves. Pre-famine immigrants had begun to assimi-late into the larger community; these "lace curtain Irish" took pride in pointing to the hundred thousand sons of Erin who fought on the side of the Union. But the arrival of the famine refugees—poorer, more ignorant, less accustomed to city life—threatened much of what their predecessors had attained. These "shanty Irish" rekindled the anti-Catholicism that for-ever lay close to the surface of American life, contributing, in the 1850s, to the surprising success of the nativist Know Nothing party. By then several good potato crops had reduced the pressure to leave Ireland, after which the Civil War—and the prospect of being drafted—diminished the attrac-tive power of the United States. But as the war ended the immigration resumed. The structural changes in the Irish economy continued, and if Irish peasants weren't dying as fast as before, neither were they thriving.

Modern Irish agriculture—like modern agriculture everywhere—required fewer and fewer farmers, and with little industry in Ireland, the displaced farmers had nowhere to go but abroad.

The same was true of their daughters, who formed a growing part of the Irish emigrant stream. In the post-famine years, in fact, women and girls outnumbered men and boys among those crossing the ocean to America. The female majority—quite unusual among immigrants—reflected at once the dismal prospects for women in Ireland and the comparatively bright outlook in America. Irish marriages traditionally required a dowry; with dowries harder to accumulate, marriages came later and later. For an increasing number of Irish women, marriage didn't come at all. By the latter part of the nineteenth century, a quarter of Irish women never married. In Irish society there were worse fates for a woman, but not many.

Those Irish women who went to America fared better. Traveling alone, they took jobs in the growing number of American households that could afford maids, in the hope of bringing brothers and mothers and fathers over after them. An Irishman—a priest, as it happened—who visited America after the Civil War described the arrangement:

> To better the circumstances of her family, the young Irish girl leaves her home for America. There she goes into service or engages in some kind of feminine employment. The object she has in view—the same for which she left her home and ventured to a strange country—protects her from all danger, especially to her character: that object, her dream by day and night, is the welfare of her family, whom she is determined, if possible, to again have with her as of old. From the first moment, she saves every cent she earns—that is, every cent she can spare from what is absolutely necessary to her decent appearance. . . . To keep her place or retain her employment, what will she not endure?—sneers at her nationality, mockery of her peculiarities, even ridicule of her faith, though the hot blood flushes her cheek with fierce indignation. At every hazard the place must be kept, the money earned, the deposit in savings-bank increased; and though many a night is passed in tears and prayers, her face is calm, and her eye bright, and her voice cheerful. One by one, the brave girl brings the members of her family about her.[3]

"Bridget"—as the Irish maids were stereotypically called—had to be brave. Her employers knew how much her wages mattered to her and her family, and they knew how a hint of dissatisfaction from one employer might make her unemployable forever. Under the best of circumstances it left her in no position to complain of long hours—from before dawn till long after dusk, in most cases—and meager pay. Under worse conditions it left her vulnerable to sexual predation, better off than female slaves in the antebellum South but not always by much. (The bitter antidraft observation about an Irish life being worth less than that of a slave was rooted in economic reality. Before the war a Southern planter told a visitor he had hired some Irishmen to drain a swamp for him. "It's dangerous work, and a negro's life is too valuable to be risked at it. If a negro dies, it's a considerable loss, you know.")

Some Irish women preferred work in factories to domestic service. "It's the freedom that we want when the day's work is done," said a woman who worked in a paper-box plant. "I know some nice girls . . . that make more money and dress better and everything for being in service. . . . But they're never sure of one minute that's their own when they're in the house. Our day is ten hours long, but when it's done it's done, and we can do what we like with the evenings. That's what I've heard from every nice girl that ever tried service. You're never sure that your soul's your own except when you are out of the house. . . . I couldn't stand that a day."[4]

Where to work was an important question, often the most pressing for immigrants. But another, deeper question for the Irish was how Irish to be. Because they arrived speaking English and sharing skin color with the dominant segments of American society, even first-generation Irish immigrants could consider assimilating. This course had obvious appeal: escape from the specific insults and undifferentiated prejudice visited upon the unassimilated, opportunity to climb the social and economic ladder.

Yet as the number of Irish continued to grow, an alternative strategy, of embracing Irishness, became increasingly viable. By 1870 the Irish composed more than a fifth of the populations of New York and Boston. In both cities they were the single largest identifiable group. If the Irish stuck together they could wield considerable power. If Irish employers hired Irish workers, and Irish customers patronized Irish merchants, the community would benefit economically; if Irish politicians catered to Irish voters, who returned the favor at the polls, the community would advance politically.[5]

In practice the Irish did a bit of both. Some of the better educated blended into the American mainstream; many of the poorer paraded their Irishness. The former were more successful as individuals; the latter exerted greater influence as a group. By the 1880s the Irish vote, to cite the most obvious manifestation of collective heft, could swing elections in New York City and State, in Boston and Massachusetts, and, in tight races, in the nation as a whole.

SINCE THE EIGHTEENTH century, Germans had composed the second-largest stream of immigration to America, after the English. They were eclipsed by the Irish during the potato famine and briefly after, but by the 1860s they again predominated—although until 1871 it could be hard to tell who was German and who wasn't. To the haphazard extent immigrants were enumerated, they were tallied by country of origin, and before Bismarck brought most of the German-speaking peoples into a single empire, the Saxons and Bavarians and Hessians and Prussians sometimes confused the tallymen.

No such collective trauma as the Irish famine drove Germans west. The failed revolution of 1848 sent a wavelet of liberals into exile, but their numbers never approached their symbolic value to Americans who flattered themselves as providing a haven for freedom fighters. Crop failures contributed to decisions by German farmers to leave, but because Germany never fell into such dependence on a single crop as Ireland did, the Germans were less susceptible to blight or rust or wilt.

German immigrants fought in the Civil War, in greater numbers and with greater enthusiasm than the Irish. Forty-eighter Carl Schurz, who rose to the rank of general in the Union army, was the most conspicuous of the 175,000 Germans who battled the secessionists. Some observers gave Missouri's Germans credit for saving that border state for the Union. Robert E. Lee himself had great respect for the Germans; the Confederate general was said to have declared, "Take the Dutch out of the Union army and we could whip the Yankees easily." The Germans weren't necessarily more devoted to abstract liberty than the Irish draft rioters; Henry Frank, a German living in Wisconsin, complained of the "miserable war" and declared, "I am no longer a friend of soldiers, and least of all do I wish to be shot to death for Lincoln and his Negroes." Many of those who fought did so because they were drafted and couldn't find substitutes; others simply backed a winner. (So did German investors who bought Jay Cooke's war bonds. As Carl Schurz sardonically remarked of his capitalist former countrymen, "During the Civil War, America was a friend in need whom her friends across the Atlantic did not abandon—and Germany was rewarded in gold for its idealism and trust in America to the tune of seven percent interest.")

In the immediate aftermath of the war, German farmers responded to the Homestead Act by emigrating in larger numbers than ever. Inheritance laws in the German states divided farms until they became uneconomic to operate, especially in the face of the increasing integration of world commodity markets. The existence of thriving German agricultural colonies in the American Midwest and in Texas drew new German immigrants to those districts, where they could expect to speak German, read German newspapers, attend German churches, and rear their children in German ways.

After about 1870 the German emigrant stream contained a growing number of displaced townsfolk. Industrialization destroyed the livelihoods of craftsmen, as did competition from immigrants *to* Germany from other countries. The consolidation of Bismarck's empire induced East Europeans to migrate to Germany, where they undercut the wages of native Germans, causing many of them to leave. Bismarck, for one, saw this free market in labor as a good thing. "The volume of emigration is a most exact index of our growing well-being," he declared. "The better it goes for us, the higher the volume of emigration. . . . There are two kinds of emigrants, . . . those who emigrate because they *still* have money enough . . . and those who emigrate because they *now* have money enough."[6]

JACOB RIIS KNEW Bismarck from a distance and hated him, as did every Dane of Riis's generation. The Iron Chancellor made Denmark a pawn in his imperial schemes, bullying the Danes and stealing their soil. Had Riis been a year or two older, he would have joined the army to fight the Germans. Instead he went to America.

His reasons for going were at once complicated and simple. His birthplace stuck in his memory as stubbornly as it stuck in the past.

To say that Ribe was an old town hardly describes it to readers at this day. A town might be old and yet have kept step with time. In my day

Ribe had not. It had never changed its step or its ways since whale-oil lanterns first hung in iron chains across its cobblestone-paved streets to light them at night. There they hung yet, every rusty link squeaking dolefully in the wind that never ceased blowing from the sea. Coal-oil, just come from America, was regarded as a dangerous innovation. I remember buying a bottle of "Pennsylvania oil" at the grocer's for eight skilling, as a doubtful domestic experiment. Steel pens had not crowded out the old-fashioned goose-quill, and pen-knives meant just what their name implies. Matches were yet of the future. We carried tinderboxes to strike fire with. People shook their heads at the tele-graph. The day of the stage-coach was not yet past. Steamboat and railroad had not come within forty miles of the town.

Ribe's one factory was a cotton mill employing half the town's work-force. Its owner had seen the American Civil War coming, stockpiled cotton, and grown rich after Sumter. He and the town took fright in 1863 when the German army approached, and though the city was spared, the specter of Prussian militarism never receded much below popular consciousness.

Jacob Riis was the next to youngest of the fourteen children of a schoolteacher in Ribe, who employed Latin ordinals to keep them straight. The sixth son was christened Sextus, the ninth Nonus, and so on. "How I escaped Tertius I don't know," Riis remarked. His father wished all the children to pursue professional careers but lacked the means to get them started. (The one who made it on his own, becoming a doctor, died just out of medical school.)

Young Jacob showed literary skills, which his father urged him to cul-tivate. But he also possessed a stubborn streak, and when school didn't suit him he announced he would become a carpenter. His father resignedly apprenticed him out. Jacob's master won a contract for work at the cotton mill, and the fifteen-year-old boy spent many days there.

On one of those days, crossing a bridge below the mill, he encountered the twelve-year-old daughter of the mill owner. He had known Elizabeth before, as a child in the town. But he saw her now with new eyes and was transfixed. "I fell head over heels in love," he wrote. The love was impossi-ble, he being a mere apprentice, she the daughter of the richest man in town. At the very least it must wait years. Yet he approached her, awk-wardly. She rebuffed him with the cruel laugh of the favored child.

Heartbroken, he pondered running off to join the army, which was again fighting the Germans. But he was underage, and so contented himself with flight to Copenhagen, where he lost himself in the larger city. For four years he worked, mastering the carpenter trade. Finally he came of age as a craftsman, winning admission to the Copenhagen carpenters' guild.

His new standing bolstered his confidence, and he returned to Ribe. Word quickly spread that he was back and intended to propose to Elizabeth—"which was annoying but true," Riis wrote. At her father's insistence she turned him down. Yet she did so in a way that made him love her the more. "She was not yet seventeen, and was easily persuaded that it was all wrong; she wept, and in the goodness of her gentle heart was truly sorry; and I kissed her hands and went out, my eyes brimming over with tears, feeling that there was nothing in all the wide world for me any more, and that the farther I went from her the better."

Copenhagen wasn't far enough; nowhere in Denmark put sufficient distance between the spurned lover and the object of his affection. For millennia Scandinavians had been wanderers, ranging the oceans from the Levant to North America. Recently many had gone to the United States, driven by the age-old difficulty of scratching a living from the lakes and fiords of their chilly homeland, drawn by the novel promise of free land and democracy.

Land meant nothing to Riis, a townsman born and bred. Democracy meant hardly more, as he was too young to have participated in politics of any kind. But others to whom land and democracy mattered had gone to America and written home. They said it was a place where a man might make a new start. Riis couldn't ask for more. "So it was settled that I should go to America."[7]

IF UNREQUITED LOVE drove Jacob Riis from Denmark, unrelieved hate sent Mary Antin from Russia. "Trouble begets trouble," she heard as a child in the Jewish Pale of settlement in the western part of the czar's domain, and the experience of her family appeared to confirm the dismal proverb. Her father fell ill and was sent by doctors from the family's home in Polotzk to another town for specialized treatment, leaving Mary's mother in charge of the family business. But the mother took sick and the father had to come home. He wasn't yet cured, and the strain of running the business and tending to his wife wore him down. The family had prospered well enough to afford servants, but as expenses rose and the business suffered they had to be dismissed. The burden of housework fell on Mary's sister, who herself became sick and was forced to bed. The baby grew colicky. "And by way of a climax," Mary remembered, "the old cow took it into her head to kick my grandmother, who was laid up for a week with a bruised leg."

To pay the bills Mary's father pawned the silver candlesticks, then some spare featherbeds. "There came a day when grandma, with eyes blinded by tears, groped in the big wardrobe for my mother's satin dress and velvet mantle; and after that it did not matter any more what was taken out of the house." Mary's mother lingered near death. "Her cheeks were red, red, but her hands were so white as they had never been before." Once energetic and hopeful, she now seemed to have lost the will to live. Mary's father, fretting over finances, grew old before her eyes.

A ten-year-old can't sustain sorrow forever, and after a time it seemed to Mary that things turned for the better. Her father found a job at a gristmill outside Polotzk. He would be superintendent, with use of a cottage. The house was small and bare, but Mary liked the way the sun shone in the windows, and she became friends with the freckle-faced children of the miller. They played together, exploring the country, hiding in the nooks of the mill, gathering wildflowers for bouquets. And Mary's mother improved in the fresh air and sunshine.

But the luck didn't last. The mill was sold and the new owner installed his own superintendent. Mary's family moved back to Polotzk. Her father searched for work; her mother's health declined again. Bills came due and couldn't be paid. Her father grew more and more worried. "Polotzk seemed to reject him, and no other place invited him."

Just when it appeared things couldn't get worse, they did. The Russian authorities recurrently bent the laws restricting Jews to the Pale; they did so because the Jews had skills the Russian economy required but also because Jews beyond the Pale were easy marks for extortion and ready scapegoats when things went wrong. Mary learned of the latest pogrom secondhand.

It was a little before Passover that the cry of the hunted thrilled the Jewish world with the familiar fear. The wholesale expulsion of Jews from Moscow and its surrounding district at cruelly short notice was the name of this latest disaster. Where would the doom strike next? The Jews who lived illegally without the Pale turned their possessions into cash and slept in their clothes, ready for immediate flight. Those who lived in the comparative security of the Pale trembled for their brothers and sisters without, and opened wide their doors to afford the fugitives refuge. And hundreds of fugitives, preceded by a wail of distress, flocked into the open district, bringing their trouble where trouble was never absent, mingling their tears with the tears that never dried.

The open cities becoming thus suddenly crowded, every man's chance of making a living was diminished in proportion to the number of additional competitors. Hardship, acute distress, ruin for many: thus spread the disaster, ring beyond ring, from the stone thrown by a despotic official into the ever-full river of Jewish persecution.

Passover was celebrated in tears that year. In the story of the Exodus we would have read a chapter of current history, only for us there was no deliverer and no promised land.

But what said some of us at the end of the long service? Not "May we be next year in Jerusalem," but "Next year—in America!"[8]

Had Mary's father not needed work so badly, he and they might have kept their heads down and ridden out this latest wave of persecution. Had there been no persecution, he and they might have waited and hoped for his job prospects to improve. But the combination of poverty and persecution made emigration irresistible.

He went first. He borrowed money from friends for a train ticket to Hamburg, where an emigrant aid society underwrote his passage to Boston.

In the short term his departure made the condition of the rest of the family worse. For months they heard nothing from him and received no money. Mary's mother tried to work, but her health wouldn't allow it. Mary's uncles had businesses and jobs and wanted to help, but they had large families and responsibilities of their own.

Mary and her mother and siblings waited anxiously for word from America. Finally it came. Her father said marvelous things about his new home.

In America, he wrote, it was no disgrace to work at a trade. Workmen and capitalists were equal. The employer addressed the employee as *you*, not, familiarly, as *thou*. The cobbler and the teacher had the same title, "Mister." And all the children, boys and girls, Jews and Gentiles, went to school! Education would be ours for the asking, and economic independence also, as soon as we were prepared.

Months more passed before he saved the money to send for them. But finally their summons came. Mary never forgot the feeling she had when her mother opened the letter that contained the steamship tickets. "At last I was going to America! Really, really going, at last! The boundaries burst. The arch of heaven soared. A million suns shone out of every star. The winds rushed in from outer space, roaring in my ears, 'America! America!'"

The news that the family was leaving spread rapidly through Polotzk.

Friends and foes, distant relatives and new acquaintances, young and old, wise and foolish, debtors and creditors, and mere neighbors—from every quarter of the city, from both sides of the Dvina, from over the Polota, from nowhere—a steady stream of them poured into our street, both day and night, till the hour of our departure. And my mother gave audience. Her faded kerchief halfway off her head, her black ringlets straying, her apron often at her eyes, she received her guests in a rainbow of smiles and tears. She was the heroine of Polotzk, and she conducted herself appropriately.

The guests gave warning for dealing with ticket agents and border guards; those with relatives in America pressed letters to their loved ones into her hand.

The day of departure dawned gray and wet. The train to the border was crowded, and the German guards at the frontier eyed the emigrants suspiciously. Mary's family held passports that were supposed to ensure easy transit, but a cholera outbreak in Russia had put the border patrol on notice to scrutinize travelers, especially the poorer sort. Yet one German officer took pity on the Antins. Herr Schidorsky was a Jew, and while he arranged with his brother, the chairman of a local emigrant-aid association, to secure their passage across Germany, he let Mary and the others stay in his home.

After several days the papers came through, and they crossed into Germany. Berlin was a daunting blur.

> Strange sights, splendid buildings, shops, people, and animals, all mingled in one great, confused mass of a disposition to continually move in a great hurry, wildly, with no other aim but to make one's head go round and round, in following its dreadful motions. Round and round went my head. It was nothing but trains, depots, crowds—crowds, depots, trains—again and again, with no beginning, no end, only a mad dance! Faster and faster we go, faster still, and the noise increases with the speed. Bells, whistles, hammers, locomotives shrieking madly, men's voices, peddlers' cries, horses' hoofs, dogs' barkings—all united in doing their best to drown every other sound but their own, and made such a deafening uproar in the attempt that nothing could keep it out.

Hamburg was more orderly—indeed, more orderly than anyone but the German authorities could have wanted. On arrival the emigrants were placed in quarantine, in carefully numbered rooms where they slept in neat rows, with roll call twice a day, morning and night. The quarantine was to protect the German populace from disease but also to safeguard the profits of German steamship lines. The borders of the United States were open to nearly everyone, but American authorities didn't hesitate to send disease-ridden ships back to Europe, leaving the companies to suffer the immediate loss and the longer-run damage to their reputations.

Finally the Antins' fortnight passed and their ship arrived. They filed aboard, grateful to have gotten this far but anxious as to what the ocean would bring. Seasickness came first: the North Sea pitched the vessel to and fro. The emigrants' distress was only amplified by the seasoned unconcern of the professionals aboard. "The captain and his officers ate their dinners, smoked their pipes and slept soundly in their turns, while we frightened emigrants turned our faces to the wall and awaited our watery graves."

By the time they reached the Atlantic, Mary had her sea legs. She explored the ship, befriended the crew, and stared in wonder at the vastness of the ocean—"the immeasurable distance from horizon to horizon; the huge billows forever changing their shapes, . . . the gray sky, with its mountains of gloomy clouds, flying, moving with the waves, . . . the deep, solemn groans of the sea, sounding as if all the voices of the world had been turned into sighs and then gathered into that one mournful sound." She scanned the western horizon constantly for her first glimpse of America. "We crept nearer and nearer to the coveted shore, until, on a glorious May morning, six weeks after our departure from Polotzk, our eyes beheld the Promised Land, and my father received us in his arms."[9]

THE ANTINS' JOURNEY to America was fairly typical for European emigrants after the Civil War, and it represented a decided improvement over what earlier generations had experienced. Some still walked from their home villages to the seaports that specialized in the emigrant trade— Liverpool, Le Havre, Hamburg, Bremen, Bergen, Naples, Trieste, and others—but more rode trains, like the Antins. Those who had to cross borders to reach their embarkation ports, again like the Antins, encountered increasing bureaucracy as the apparatus of empire and nation firmed up, but they were less likely to be victimized by highwaymen, confidence men, and related predators upon the transient. The emigrant trade grew more efficient; the bottlenecks at seaports diminished and, with them, the cost of waiting for a ship. Industrialization didn't always improve health conditions in those seaports—few other countries enforced public health laws with the German rigor the Antins experienced—but the shorter waiting times reduced the emigrants' exposure to disease.

The ships themselves were a distinct improvement over what had gone before. Steamships displaced sailing ships at the premium level first, conveying wealthy travelers west years before poorer emigrants saw their interiors. But the steamships bumped the better sailing ships down to the emigrant trade, then gradually joined them, until by the 1870s most emigrants traveled aboard the steam-driven craft.

The evolution of the emigrant fleet reflected technological innovation but also imperial competition. Industrialization compelled the European powers to seek both sources of raw materials and markets for exports; the seeking sometimes occurred peacefully but often by force or threat. Steel-hulled, steam-powered warships constituted the state of the art of power projection in the late nineteenth century, and a naval arms race began. The competing governments subsidized their shipbuilders, who honed their skills and kept their construction crews busy between naval orders by building merchant craft. During the 1880s a glut of ships caused ticket prices to fall till an emigrant could cross the Atlantic for the equivalent of ten or twelve American dollars.[10]

The crossing itself was likewise much improved from decades past. Passengers in steerage (the lowest class) were crowded together, with little privacy and few material comforts beyond those they brought along. In bad weather, with the hatches closed, the best ship could be a dark, lurching container that felt like the oversized coffin the worst of the afflicted almost wished it would be. But the size of the steamships—ten to twenty thousand tons—rendered them far more stable than their wind-powered forebears, and as uncomfortable as the crossing in them might be, it was mercifully brief—eight to twelve days, depending on the port of embarkation, compared with a month or two by sail.

Emigrant transport had always been a business, but in the late nineteenth century it became an industry. Steamship lines competed to carry the emigrants, advertising low fares, convenient schedules, good food, and healthy accommodations. Some lines boasted of labor agents in New York and other American cities who helped passengers from their ships find jobs on arrival. Needless to say, the service delivered didn't always match the service promised; caveat emptor remained the counsel of prudence. Yet the word got out as to which lines were honest and reliable and which not.

Something else—something almost unheard of in the pre-industrial age—enforced good performance as well. For the first time the ship companies could hope to attract substantial repeat patronage. More and more migrants weren't emigrants at all but "birds of passage" who spent a season or two in America before returning to their homes, and then did it again, and perhaps again and again. Among some nationalities the intent to return to the country of birth was almost universal. An Italian journalist in Chicago observed, "Italians do not come to America to find a home . . . but to repair the exhausted financial conditions in which they were living in Italy. . . . They leave the mother country with the firm intention of going back to it as soon as their *scarsellas* shall sound with plenty of *quibus*." In the event, about half the emigrants from Italy eventually returned. Emigrants from Greece returned in comparable proportions, as did certain

Central Europeans. Germans were more likely to remain in America, but not as likely as Russian and Polish Jews, many of whom, having fled religious persecution, had no desire to return to the ghettos and pogroms. The rates of return tended to rise with passing time, as the crossing continued to grow easier and cheaper. During particular periods of depression in America—in the 1870s and again in the 1890s—the returns to some European countries and districts outnumbered the emigrants.[11]

The return traffic, whether greater or less, helped the bottom line of the steamship companies and encouraged them to dedicate their vessels to the passenger trade rather than convert them to cargo on the eastbound voyage as they had formerly done. On cargo ships the emigrants felt like cargo, on passenger ships more like people. At the same time, the increasing return flow contributed to general knowledge of the transatlantic journey. For most emigrants the unknown was the hardest part of the decision to leave; whatever pierced the darkness made the decision easier.

THE STEAMSHIP COMPANIES weren't the only ones drumming for emigrants. In 1864 Congress, responding to pleas from industry that the Union army had stolen its best workers, approved the Act to Encourage Immigration. The measure enlisted federal officials and federal money in the search for industrial workers, created an Immigration Bureau within the State Department, and opened the federal courts to employers attempting to enforce labor contracts concluded on foreign soil. This was less than some supporters of industry wanted. Secretary of State William Seward had advocated using federal money to pay the passage of selected workers to America. But the endorsement the law gave to contract labor seemed a boon to business at a moment when the fighting had pinched the normal supply of workers.

Labor recruiters responded to the new law at once. The American Emigrant Company, proclaiming itself the "handmaid of the new Immigration Bureau," solicited orders for labor from American manufacturers and advertised for workers abroad. The company accepted compensation in two forms: fees paid directly by the manufacturers and commissions on rail and steamship tickets purchased by the emigrants.

The company's activities provoked immediate opposition. Organized labor in America, weak as it was during the 1860s, complained that the federal money and authority were being used to undermine native-born and previously landed workers. Foreign governments warned prospective emigrants that the American labor law was a ruse to fill the ranks of the Union army—that the workers would be drafted as soon as they reached American soil, just as Irish and other immigrants had already been drafted.

How the company's business model would have weathered the political attacks is hard to say; as things happened, the war ended before it had a fair test. The labor pinch eased as soldiers returned to the civilian work-force and prospective immigrants stopped worrying about the draft. Manufacturers refused to pay the company for what they could get free, and the company's revenues dwindled. Congress in 1868 put it out of its misery by acceding to the workers' complaints and repealing the immigration-encouragement act.[12]

The efforts by business to secure a labor supply continued, though. American manufacturers appreciated that inexpensive steam travel was creating an increasingly global market in labor; workers would go where their skills were best remunerated. Some American manufacturers looked to the tariff to maintain high prices and thereby allow the high wages that would ensure a steady supply of workers. "Let us keep up the walls about our continent," the chief lobbyist for the National Association of Wool Manufacturers declared, "so that there may be a sure refuge for the industries, or in other words, the capital and skill and labor which we will attract from Europe." In still other words, let American consumers pay to import the workers American industry required.[13]

When active recruiting was required, many companies preferred to do it themselves. They sought workers with specific skills the general stream of immigration failed to furnish in adequate amounts. At first their agents offered contracts in Europe to the targeted workers, but the companies discovered that such contracts were nearly impossible to enforce once the immigrants reached America. Workers simply walked away—to take employment elsewhere, often with rivals of the sponsoring firm, which was out the price of passage and suffered the additional blow of having strengthened the competition.

Despite the difficulties, the manufacturers kept trying. Before Andrew Carnegie and others shifted to the Bessemer process, steelmaking was as much an art as an industry, and experienced heaters and puddlers were worth the risk and expense of recruiting. American steel companies monitored the industrial workplace in Britain, and when labor disputes or other troubles angered skilled workers there, they swooped in to take advantage. Often utilizing American consuls, whose job description included promoting American business, they offered free passage to America and well-paying jobs on arrival. "Sober, industrious men can hardly fail of good employment, if well skilled in their work," one American publication promised.

The strategy triggered retaliation. British and German employers kept an eye on conditions in the United States; when unsuccessful strikes or business depressions put skilled American workers in a bad mood, their agents pounced. After the Panic of 1873 British cotton companies sent agents to New England with orders to find a thousand workers. How many they enticed east is unknown, but the return traffic to Britain rose sharply during this period. (Not all the British were unhelpful to American capitalists. British trade unionists occasionally collaborated with American labor recruiters, pointing out likely emigrants and otherwise doing what they could to fill the boats west—and thereby shrink the labor pool in Britain.)[14]

While the manufacturers focused their recruiting efforts on skilled workers, other American firms looked for other sorts of immigrants. Railroad companies, flush with land and chronically short of cash, sought farmers to purchase and populate their western domains. The purchasing would help the bottom line at once; the populating would produce traffic that would benefit the roads over time. The Northern Pacific, besides flogging its bonds in Europe, established an emigration office to entice Europeans to Jay Cooke's "Banana Belt." The company purchased newspapers in Germany and funded an elaborate exhibit at the Vienna Exposition of 1873. It went so far as to name what would become the capital of North Dakota for the famous chancellor of Germany. The town that arose near the place where the Northern Pacific crossed the Missouri River was originally called Edwinton, for one of the railroad's engineers. But someone in marketing got the idea of renaming it Bismarck in order to attract attention at the Vienna trade fair and throughout the German-speaking world. An invitation went out to Bismarck himself to visit the budding metropolis, but he declined. Other Germans responded more favorably, streaming to America's northern Plains, purchasing Northern Pacific land, and becoming the largest ethnic group in North Dakota after that half of the territory achieved independent statehood.[15]

The Southern Pacific, the holding company that subsumed Leland Stanford's Central Pacific after the latter ran into cash-flow problems, prospected for immigrants in much the way Stanford's California neighbors had prospected for gold. Some of its agents worked the home front, diverting already-arrived immigrants from the territories of the Northern Pacific and other railroads by meeting ships from Europe and passing out pamphlets and cut-rate tickets to the West Coast. Other Southern Pacific agents scoured Britain and the European continent for land buyers. The company established an emigration office in London, sponsored lecture tours by speakers touting California, and arranged transport to America for the most promising prospects. Its activities earned the applause of many Californians. "The complete and systematic plan of the Southern Pacific will doubtless bring thousands of the best kind of immigrants to this state each year, to the great benefit of the community at large, as well as to the immigrants themselves," the *San Francisco Call* asserted. The railroad's enemies—it was already being labeled the "Octopus" in California—cast a more jaundiced eye on its immigration schemes. "They lie and cheat," Ambrose Bierce said of the company and its agents. "Their dealings with settlers have been characterized by a multitude of rapacities. They skin their clients and sell them back the skins at an advance. They will settle the immigrants upon their lines and take the entire profit of their industry for carrying their crops to market. . . . In three years the people that they have tumbled from the frying pan into the fire will be fighting them on a crust of bread and a cold potato."[16]

The states got into the immigration business, too. Western states sought settlers: people to purchase state land, increase everyone's property values, and generally strengthen the state economies. Midwestern states sought settlers, as well, but also laborers. Michigan wanted miners; Minnesota and Wisconsin lumbermen; Illinois, Iowa, and several other states railroad workers. Southern states tried to counter their historic reputation for contempt of manual labor by advertising for plantation hands and domestic servants. The states seeking workers often collaborated with employers in the production and distribution of pamphlets and posters; Michigan mining companies paid to send state-printed flyers to Europe, while the Wisconsin State Immigration Commission shared agents with the Wisconsin Central Railroad.[17]

The effect of all the recruiting was hard to gauge. Some state officials

seem to have entered the immigration contest less from confidence that
their efforts would succeed than from fear that voters would blame them
for not trying. The beggar thy neighbor efforts of the railroads to divert
immigrants to their own domains did nothing directly to increase immigration but, by bidding up the overall rewards to immigrants, made America that much more appealing. The targeted campaigns by manufacturers
to lure skilled workers to America doubtless enticed some who wouldn't
have come on their own; how many is impossible to know.

BY EVERYONE'S ACCOUNT (including that of the recruiting agents),
the most effective form of marketing was the testimony of immigrants
themselves. Often this came in letters from America to friends and kin
in the old country. Jacob Riis had read such letters in Denmark; Mary
Antin's father sent them from Boston to Russia. Gustaf Jarlson, a Swedish
immigrant to Minnesota, wrote home every month to his brother Axel.
"This is a good country," he explained.

> It is like Sweden in some ways. The winter is long, and there are some
> cold days, but everything grows that we can grow in our country, and
> there is plenty. All about me are Swedes, who have taken farms and are
> getting rich. They eat white bread and plenty of meat. The people here
> do not work such long hours as in Sweden, but they work much
> harder, and they have a great deal of machinery, so that the crop one
> farmer gathers will fill two big barns. One farmer, a Swede, made more
> than 25,000 kroner on his crop last year.[18]

Even more compelling than letters were the actions of emigrants who
returned home. Lee Chew grew up on a farm near Canton during the
1860s. Some of the neighbors had left for California, but Lee Chew's
father wished to keep him home and so told him stories of what "foreign
devils" the Americans were. They were powerful, with great fire-belching
ships and a kind of sorcery that allowed them to light the darkest night and
communicate over long distances, but they lacked anything that passed for
civilization. Their language was barbaric, they practiced all manner of violence, and they disrespected their ancestors. No correct-thinking Chinese
should wish to go to America. Lee Chew had little reason to doubt his

father, and he resigned himself to life as a Chinese farmer—until new evidence surfaced.

> I was about sixteen years of age when a man of our tribe came back
> from America and took ground as large as four city blocks and made a
> paradise of it. He put a large stone wall around and led some streams
> through and built a palace and summer house and about twenty other
> structures, with beautiful bridges over the streams and walks and
> roads. Trees and flowers, singing birds, water fowl and curious animals
> were within the walls. . . . When his palace and grounds were com-
> pleted he gave a dinner to all the people, who assembled to be his
> guests. One hundred pigs roasted whole were served on the tables,
> with chickens, ducks, geese and such an abundance of dainties that our
> villagers even now lick their fingers when they think of it. He had the
> best actors from Hong Kong performing, and every musician for miles
> around was playing and singing. At night the blaze of lanterns could
> be seen for miles.

The lesson was lost on no one there, least of all Lee Chew.

> The man had gone away from our village a poor boy. Now he returned
> with unlimited wealth, which he had obtained in the country of the
> American wizards. . . . The wealth of this man filled my mind with
> the idea that I, too, would like to go to the country of the wizards and
> gain some of their wealth.[19]

EVERY IMMIGRANT HAD a story, and each was unique. But the
cumulative effect of the stories—the sum of the individual experiences—
was perhaps best conveyed by statistics that submerged the differences into
impersonal numbers. During the five years after Appomattox, 1.5 million
immigrants entered the United States. During the 1870s, 2.8 million more
arrived. During the 1880s, another 5.3 million landed, and during the
1890s, 3.7 million. The busiest single year for immigration was 1882,
when nearly 789,000 immigrants arrived; the preceding and succeeding
years ranked second and third, with 669,000 and 603,000, respectively.

The immigration boom of the 1880s, compared with the 1870s and

1890s, attested to the material motives of most of the immigrants. As the American economy expanded during the 1880s, jobs became plentiful and, to many potential immigrants, irresistible. The depressions of the 1870s and 1890s made the United States comparatively less attractive, and immigration declined. (During those decades, men and women who might have come to the United States either stayed home or went elsewhere. Brazil, for example, experienced a surge of immigration during the 1890s, just as immigration to the United States fell off.)

Measured against the existing resident population as well, the immigration of the 1880s was the era's largest. The 5.3 million persons who entered the country during that decade amounted to some 10.5 percent of the 50 million persons who lived in the United States in 1880. At the end of the 1880s, nearly 21 million residents were either immigrants or the children of immigrants; this total constituted nearly one-third of the American population in 1890. (The immigration increment of the 1880s was exceeded, as a percentage of the population, by only two decades in American history: the 1850s, when immigration equaled 12.1 percent of the 1850 population, and the 1900s, when immigration came to 10.8 of the 1900 population.)

The statistics also revealed the beginning of a trend that would become especially distinctive after the turn of the century. Till 1890 the great majority—substantially more than 80 percent—of immigrants hailed from northern and western Europe. Between 1820 (the year the federal government started collecting immigration statistics) and 1890, of a total of some 15 million immigrants to America, the German states sent nearly 4.5 million, Ireland 3.5 million, Britain 2.7 million, Scandinavia 1 million, and other western European countries 600,000. But starting in the 1890s (and accelerating in the following decade), the origins of immigration shifted east and south. By 1900 the shift was unmistakable. Russia sent four times as many immigrants to America that year as Germany did; Italy sent three times as many as Ireland. Immigration from eastern and southern Europe in 1900 nearly doubled that from northern and western Europe.

This shift said more about conditions in Europe than in the United States. (Other countries of the Americas experienced a similar shift.) Pogroms like those that drove the Antin family from Russia intensified. The continuing drop in the price of steamship tickets, which held out the possibility of regular returns home, made emigration more attractive to family- and village-oriented Italians and Greeks. Railroads reached farther into eastern and southern Europe, making the first stage of the journey to America more convenient. Meanwhile, the economic and social disruptions that had sent so many to America from Germany, Ireland, and Scandinavia diminished. The leading edge of the storm had moved on.[20]

The "new immigration," as it was called, evoked soul-searching among the native born. The newcomers from Russia and Poland were frequently Jews; how would they get along with the overwhelming Christian majority in America? The immigrants from Italy and Greece often had olive complexions; where would they fit among America's whites and blacks? Almost none of the new immigrants had experienced democracy in their homelands; would they adapt to it in America or undermine it?[21]

These and related questions would loom larger in the new century. For the time being they reinforced the ambivalence Americans had always felt toward immigration. Few disputed the beneficence of immigration in theory; many objected to certain aspects of immigration in practice.

A GENERATION HENCE, the objections would inspire the first broad-gauged restrictions on immigration, but in the late nineteenth century restrictions applied peculiarly to the Chinese. In 1882, after decades of agitation by native-born workers in California, who complained that Chinese immigrants drove pay rates down, Congress passed the Chinese Exclusion Act. The measure permitted businessmen, students, temporary visitors, and their spouses to continue to enter the country, but ordinary laborers were barred. More than a quarter million Chinese had emigrated since midcentury; they had dug the nation's gold and built the Pacific railroad. Suddenly, in 1882, nearly all immigration from Chinese stopped.[22]

Legal immigration, that is. The exclusion act created, at the stroke of Chester Arthur's pen, a phenomenon that was previously unknown in America but that would grow in size and complexity ever afterward: illegal immigration. Congress could modify the law of supply and demand, as it applied to labor, by raising the risks of entry to America for particular workers, but it couldn't repeal the law entirely. As long as those workers found it in their interest to hazard entry, they would do so. Employers, many of whom had opposed the ban, discovered merit—that is, profit—in the existence of a class of workers beyond the protection of the American legal system, who could be mistreated at will. The customers of those employers, sharing the wage savings, had little incentive to complain. Chinese continued to enter the United States, albeit in numbers impossible to measure accurately. Some came with forged documents declaring them to be merchants or students or tourists (or the wives of such authorized entrants). Some came with no documents, relying on stealth and bribery to get past immigration officials. They melted into the existing Chinese community and took jobs where they found them.

One part of the illegal immigration was more vulnerable and exploited than the rest. Chun Ho had been in America for five years when she came to the attention of the federal Immigration Commission. Her story was by no means unique, but it was particularly poignant. As the chairman of the commission questioned her, her answers were punctuated by sobs.

"How old are you?"

"Twenty-four."

"Where were you born?"

"At Ng Jow, in the province of Kwang Si."

"How did you happen to come to the United States?"

"When I was nineteen years old, the mistress Number Three of a noted procurer by the name of Gwan Lung, who lives in San Francisco, went back to Canton, where my mother happened to be living with me at that time, and gave me glowing accounts of life in California. She painted that life so beautifully that I was seized with an inclination to go there and try my fortune."

The woman paid Chun Ho's mother two hundred Mexican dollars and took the daughter away. With six other girls similarly acquired, Chun Ho boarded a steamer and arrived in San Francisco after a two-week voyage. "We all came on fraudulent certificates; the color of those certificates was reddish."

The girls were conducted to the house of a woman named May Sheen. "They always do that first," Chun Ho told the commission. "From time to time parties came to May Sheen's house to see me and to bargain with May Sheen as to what price I should be sold at." How much Chun Ho—or her mother—had known of the services she was expected to provide is unclear; the nature of these services grew obvious during her time with

May Sheen. "Two months after my arrival, a Chinaman by the name of Kwan Kay, a highbinder"—a member of a criminal gang, or "tong"—"and one who owned some of these houses"—of prostitution—"came with his woman, Shin Yee, and bought me for $1,950 gold. They gave me a written promise that in four years I should be free."[23]

Prostitution was a principal business of the tongs. It flourished on account of the enormous imbalance of the sexes among the Chinese in America, where men outnumbered women by as much as fifteen to one in the 1870s and 1880s. It battened as well on the poverty of Chinese in China and the practice of poor families there of selling daughters to be wives, concubines, and servants. Arbitragers unburdened by scruples could purchase a girl for as little as five dollars in China and sell her for a thousand dollars in the United States. American lawmakers tried to stop the traffic. The 1875 Page Act, named for California congressman Horace Page, banned the immigration of Chinese prostitutes (along with any other Chinese traveling involuntarily). But like most such prohibitions, the law simply raised the price of that which it forbade.[24]

Technically, the girls brought to America were contract workers, bound for a term of service in exchange for their passage east. The contracts could be quite explicit. "An agreement to assist a young girl named Loi Yau" declared:

> Because she became indebted to her mistress for passage, food, &c., and has nothing to pay, she makes her body over to the woman Sep Sam to serve as a prostitute to make out the sum of $503. The money shall draw no interest, and Loi Yau shall receive no wages. Loi Yau shall serve four and a half years. . . . When the time is out, Loi Yau may be her own master, and no man shall trouble her.

The contracts were rather less than they seemed, starting from the fact that the girls who were made to sign them typically couldn't read. Moreover, the pimps and mistresses devised various means to extend the contracts. The girls were docked for sickness; in Loi Yau's case, she had to repay one month for every fifteen days she was sick. Given their line of work, sickness was common, with the result that the girls found themselves falling farther and farther behind. (Some pimps and madams defined menstruation as a sickness, in that it kept the girls from working; these unfortunate souls were guaranteed an extended sentence.)[25]

Chun Ho learned the business the hard way. She received customers nearly every day, earning her masters almost three hundred dollars a month. She hoped that some of this might be credited to her account, but after two years they told her she was deeper in debt than when she started. For her—or anyone else—to purchase her freedom would now cost $2,100. Needless to say, she didn't have any money, and so she was sold to another tong man, who kept her working as hard as ever.

During this period she heard about groups devoted to rescuing sex slaves like herself, but her new owner warned her that if she tried to escape he'd kill her. The rescue societies staked out the brothels, to gather evidence against them and to encourage girls like Chun Ho to break for freedom, but the pimps took the girls to other houses, outside the city, to administer exemplary beatings where no one could hear their screams. "The instruments used were wooden clubs and sometimes anything they could lay their hands on," Chun Ho said. "One time I was threatened with a pistol held at me."

She survived and, by a stroke of fortune, eventually escaped, but she knew of many other girls who weren't so lucky. One was murdered by her pimp for not turning over money he said she owed him. "I saw her after she had been shot," Chun Ho said. At least three others Chun Ho knew met a similar fate. "Two of these were shot and one stabbed to death." The murderers were never brought to justice. "No one would dare to testify."[26]

Chapter 10

CITIES OF THE PLAIN

Nearly all the immigrants landed in cities of the American seaboard, especially New York, which during the last decades of the nineteenth century served as port of entry for four newcomers out of every five. Indeed, Ellis Island in New York harbor, where a federal immigration facility opened in 1892, became a symbol of all the immigration (approached in significance only, and then not closely, by Angel Island in San Francisco Bay and Galveston on the Texas Gulf Coast).

Many immigrants remained in the cities of their landing; many others proceeded to different cities. Some found their way to the frontier, but these grew comparatively less numerous as time passed. In 1890 immigrants and their children were three times as likely as the native born to live in cities. Industry was the engine of American growth, the eye of the capitalist storm, and industry centered on the cities. Immigrants might dream of homesteads, and some actually attained them. But the vortex was strong and hard to escape.[1]

By the early 1870s capitalism needed Chicago as much as Chicago needed capitalism. This hadn't always been so. A military outpost, Fort Dearborn, had been established in the early nineteenth century where the

Chicago River enters Lake Michigan, but the post was evacuated during the War of 1812, most of the evacuees were massacred by Indians friendly to Britain, and the stockade was destroyed. It was rebuilt after the war but never amounted to much and was abandoned for good in 1837.

The city, as distinct from the fort, got its start in 1830, after Illinois lawmakers decided to improve on nature and force the Illinois River to run uphill, or at least empty into the Mississippi River and the Gulf of Mexico rather than Lake Michigan and the Atlantic. The projected canal prompted the platting of a city at what amounted to the canal's lake entrance. The name, Chicago, derived from an Indian term for the wild garlic that grew there. (Town boosters long denied the link to an unpleasant odor, contending that the word simply meant "powerful.")

By the time the canal was completed, in 1848, the fat days of canalling had passed and railroads were stealing the waterways' traffic. This development actually benefited Chicago, for while the canal merely facilitated access to neighborhoods already served by boats and barges, railroads—the first of which reached Chicago almost coincident with the completion of the canal—opened entire new districts to efficient transport. Chicago became the queen city of the prairies, the gateway to the West.[2]

In the process it served as the model for a new generation of American cities. For a quarter millennium in America (and for longer in Europe, Asia, and Africa) cities had been sited on water, which afforded the only economic means of moving heavy cargoes. Boston, Newport, New York, Philadelphia, and Charleston were seaports; New Orleans, St. Louis, Cincinnati, and Pittsburgh were river towns. By putting bulk cargoes on wheels, railroads liberated cities from their transport dependence on water. The cities of the railroad age required water for drinking and bathing and industry, but large wells or small streams sufficed for these purposes. Navigation no longer mattered nearly so much. Chicago blossomed far beyond what the Illinois canal would have supported; Denver transcended the South Platte River, Dallas the Trinity, Minneapolis the upper Mississippi, Kansas City the Missouri, Atlanta the Chattahoochee.

Older cities felt the railroads' influence too. The center of city life had historically been the waterfront: the Long Wharf in Boston, the Battery and the East River in New York, the foot of Market Street in Philadelphia. The railroads pulled commerce away from the water to warehouses in cheaper districts. Dry land often became more valuable than harbor frontage. Boston filled in much of the surrounding waterways; New York did so to a lesser degree. Philadelphia had grown up looking east to the Delaware and the Atlantic; it settled into middle age looking west along the Main Line of the Pennsylvania Railroad. Newport disappeared as a commercial presence; the Rhode Island inlets that had made it a splendid port now made it a nightmare for railroad construction. New Orleans was similarly problematic, and if it didn't become as anachronistic as Newport, it surrendered much pride of Southern place to Atlanta, which simultaneously transformed Charleston nearly into a museum.

THE NEW CITIES faced new problems and some old ones. The latter included fire, which visited every city sooner or later. Philadelphia's eighteenth-century fires had prompted Benjamin Franklin to organize his famous fire department. New York burned during the American Revolution and recurrently thereafter. San Francisco went up half a dozen times during the first half decade of the Gold Rush, from bad luck, high winds, and the discovery by arsonists that gold mining was easier in the ashes of banks and hotels than in the streams of the Sierra.

Arson aside, the underlying cause of the fires was that Americans built for the moment rather than for the ages, and hence of wood more often than of brick or stone. Beyond this, American civic culture resisted the curbs on construction that might have restricted the use of wood in the most densely populated neighborhoods or guaranteed minimal separation between buildings. Americans begrudged spending money on fire departments (Franklin's firemen were volunteers). And until the late nineteenth century the most common source of light and heat was open flame. Candles tipped; kerosene spilled; creosote clogged chimneys till they burst into flame. Most such accidents had minor consequences, but when the stars were evilly aligned, devastation could result.

Chicago's star-crossed moment occurred in October 1871. That summer and early autumn had been dry; between July 3 and October 9 only two and a half inches of rain fell, one-fourth the average. A hot wind began blowing from the southwest in early October, drying the city still more and putting everyone on edge. A fire broke out on Saturday, October 7, in the western division of the city and destroyed nearly a million dollars' worth of property before the wind blew it into an undeveloped strip of land devoid of fuel and it died. Chicagoans sighed relief at the disaster escaped.[3]

But the wind kept blowing, and that night another fire began, in a West Side barn owned by Irish immigrants Patrick and Catherine O'Leary. Because cows were known to kick over lanterns, many Chicagoans assumed that one of the O'Leary cows started the fire. This theory was never proved, and Mrs. O'Leary denied it. The official report of the fire declined to specify a cause, although it did pinpoint the location as the O'Leary barn. However the flames originated, they were fanned by the wind and spread rapidly.[4]

"About two o'clock we were awakened by a very bright light and a great noise of carts and wagons," Mary Fales, a resident of the city's North Side, recalled. Because the Faleses' window faced north and the light seemed to be coming from that direction, Mary and her husband, David, concluded that a fire was burning to the north of them. He went outside to assess the situation. "David found that the fire was not at all on the North Side," Mary explained, "but was burning so furiously on the South Side that the whole sky was bright." Mary and David took comfort from the fact that the Chicago River separated their house from the South Side. "But it proved no obstacle, and the North Side was soon on fire, and Wells and La Salle streets were crowded with carts and people going north."

David told Mary to pack what she valued most and prepare to flee. Mary looked out her window at the clogged, smoky streets and decided packing would be a waste of time. If she loaded a trunk there would be no wagon to haul it. "Every vehicle demanded an enormous price and was engaged. Several livery stables were already burned." But David somehow found a loose horse and an abandoned buggy, and he and Mary threw their irreplaceables in a trunk and heaved the trunk in the buggy. They climbed aboard and set off.

"I cannot convey to you how the streets looked," Mary related to her mother the next day. "Everybody was out of their houses, without exception, and the sidewalks were covered with furniture and bundles of every description. The middle of the street was a jam of carts, carriages, wheelbarrows, and every sort of vehicle—many horses being led along, all excited and prancing, some running away. I scarcely looked right or left, as I kept my seat by holding tightly to the trunk. The horse would not be restrained, and I had to use all my powers to keep on. I was glad to go fast, for the fire behind us raged, and the whole earth, or all we saw of it, was a lurid yellowish red."

David dropped Mary and the trunk at the house of her aunt and returned for another load. "I saw him no more for seven hours," she said of the harrowing night. Her aunt's house became a refuge for many in similar straits. "One young lady, who was to have had a fine wedding tomorrow, came dragging along some of her wedding presents. One lady came with four servants, and one with six blankets of clothing. One lady came with nurse and baby, and, missing her little boy, went off to look for him; this was about daylight, and she did not come back at all." Most of the husbands, like David, were trying to salvage personal property ahead of the blaze; one and then another stopped by the house. "They only stayed long enough to say how far the fire advanced, and assured us of safety."

David eventually reappeared. He explained that he had buried his and Mary's china, some books, and even the piano on the grounds of a neighbor family. This family, the Hubbards, thought they were safe, as their lot was large and open and their house was brick. Mr. Hubbard followed the example of many others in hauling the carpets from his house, soaking them in water, and covering such wooden surfaces as the structure possessed. His efforts merely delayed the destruction. The heat grew so intense that it boiled the water from the carpets before bursting them into flame. Superheated air blasted through the windows and doors, and the house caught fire from inside as well as out.

Mary Fales learned from David that their house had been destroyed at the same time, but what she saw for herself was terrifying enough. "In the afternoon the wind blew more furiously"—by now the fire had become a storm itself and was creating its own weather—"the dust was blinding, the sky gray and leaden, and the atmosphere dense with smoke. We watched the swarms of wagons and people pass. All the men, and many of the women, were dragging trunks by cords tied in the handles; the children were carrying and pulling big bundles."

Mary's refuge—her aunt's house—had become a trap. Had she and the others left sooner, the streets would have been clearer and passage more ready. Most had come in by cart or buggy and could have continued rolling. But acquiring a vehicle now was nearly impossible. "Such confusion as there was! Everybody trying to get a cart, and not one to be had at any price." The husbands who had returned were frantically burying what they and their wives had brought. "Many of the ladies fairly lost their wits." The buggy David had acquired earlier had been lost, but he managed to locate a soot-blackened man with a run-down cart pulled by a jaded nag. David and Mary loaded their trunk and one of her aunt's in the cart and set off again.

"The West Side was safe, but to get there was the question," Mary recorded. Some of the bridges had burned; others were packed solid with refugees and their vehicles. Yet the cart driver thought he knew a way: a bridge more distant but still passable. "Our ride was an anxious one. The horse had been over-used, and when urged on would kick till the old cart bid fair to break in pieces. . . . Many times we were blocked, and it seemed as if the fire must reach the bridge before we did." Disabled carts and wagons littered the streets; people carried what the vehicles no longer could. Others dragged boxes and trunks; exhaustion and fear streaked the refugees' faces almost as grotesquely as the dust, smoke, and their sweat. As their strength failed and their fear continued to rise, they abandoned their possessions and staggered away, leaving these last of their belongings in the road.[5]

The story was the same across much of the city. Tens of thousands of men, women, and children fled for their lives as the wall of flame advanced. Lambert Tree was a Cook County judge; his first thought was to save his court records. He hurried to his South Side office, stuffed the most important papers into the pockets of his coat, and made his way back to the street. The buildings in this downtown district were built of masonry almost from bottom to top, which was why their owners hadn't worried much about previous fires. But this time the sparks and embers discovered each structure's most vulnerable spots. "When I got out of doors I found it literally raining fire," Tree recalled afterward. "Along Randolph and Clark streets canvas awnings in front of many of the stores, and in several instances the large wooden signs, also, were burning. Here and there where the sparks had found a lodgment small jets of flames were darting out from the wooden cornices on the tops of buildings, while the sparks and cinders which were constantly falling upon the streets were being whirled around in little eddies and scattered down the basement stairways." Not even the sidewalk beneath his feet was safe. "Along North State and Ohio streets, the dead leaves which the wind had from time to time caught up and deposited against and under the wooden sidewalks had been ignited in many places by the flying sparks, which had in turn set fire to the sidewalks, so that every few yards tongues of fire were starting up between the cracks in the boards."

Judge Tree's home lay north of the river, and, like the Faleses and many others, he thought the river would serve as a firebreak. He started to realize he might be wrong just as he was crossing the river and the bridge burst into flames, its wooden planks igniting from the sparks. Still he hoped to save his house. He climbed to the roof and with the help of his servants poured bucket after bucket of water upon the shingles, to cool them and douse any sparks that landed. He found himself under incendiary assault. "A burning mass, which was fully as large as an ordinary bed-pillow, passed over my head." He realized it was the remains of a hay bale sucked aloft and ignited by the raging updraft on the South Side. "There were also pieces of burning felt, some of which I should say were fully a foot square, flying through the air and dropping upon the roofs of the houses and barns." Tree himself might yet have stayed, but his servants valued their lives over his property and fled. He finally decided that if he and his family waited any longer they might be surrounded by the inferno. He and his wife buried their silver in a neighbor's yard, put their jewelry in a tin box small enough to carry, and, with the rest of the household, ventured into the street.

"We had scarcely got out of the door before we were assailed by a hurricane of smoke, sparks, and cinders, which nearly blinded and suffocated us. Fearing separation, I grasped my wife by one hand and my son by the other, and moved around to the west side of the house, intending to pass through one of the gates on Ohio Street. But we had no sooner got from under the protection which the north wall of the house afforded us, than we met the full force of this hurricane of smoke and fire. My wife's and sister's bonnets and my father's and son's hats were immediately blown from their heads, while the cinders were falling upon heads, hands, and faces and burning them." The shrubs in the yard burst into flames before their eyes. Judge Tree feared they would be trapped and either suffocated or burned alive. Salvation came, ironically, on the wings of the fire itself. As the heat and smoke drove them toward a corner of the yard from which Tree knew there was no escape, a large section of the fence suddenly collapsed, burned at the base by the flames and toppled by a sudden gust of the inferno. They ran through the gap to freedom.

But their danger hardly diminished on the street. The black sky continued to bombard them with burning missiles, which singed their skin and set their clothing alight. Coughing and running, they proceeded east on Ontario Street to the lake. There, on the shore, amid some fifty acres of open space, they felt reasonably safe.

Yet what they saw as they looked about was heartbreaking. "We found thousands of men, women, and children, and hundreds of horses and dogs, who had already fled there for refuge. The grounds were dotted all over at short intervals with piles of trunks, chairs, tables, beds, and household furniture of every description." Dawn remained hours distant, yet the light of the conflagration revealed the scene as starkly as day. "Whole families were huddled around their little piles of furniture, which was all they had left that morning of their yesterday's home. Here and there a mother sat upon the ground clinging to her infant, with one or more little ones, who, exhausted by the prolonged interruptions to their slumbers, were now sleeping, with their heads reclining on her lap, as peacefully as if nothing unusual was transpiring. Several invalids lay helplessly stretched upon mattresses, but still surrounded by relatives, who were endeavoring to soothe their fears. One young girl sat near me, with a cage containing a canary bird in her lap, whose life she was seeking to protect." Most bore up under the strain; others broke down. "Some men and women who had found liquor among the household stores there, and who sought to drown their present woes in the bottle, were now reeling about drunk." Tough-looking thugs broke into boxes and trunks, taking what they wanted while demoralized police officers and impotent judges—including Tree—looked on. A poor woman, seriously ill on arrival at the shore, died amid the crowd. "The fact seemed to be received with comparative indifference."

The eastern sky gradually brightened but none could take their eyes off the burning west. The flames moved closer and closer. A brewery and the city water works caught fire to the north, cutting off one potential avenue of escape. To the south the flames reached a planing mill and several lumber yards; their wood stocks fueled an especially intense blaze that prevented retreat in that direction. Fiery bombs fell among the refugees, igniting their furniture, their bedding, and in some cases their clothes. By tens and then hundreds they retreated toward the water.

"Then came the period of our greatest trial," Lambert Tree recalled. "Dense clouds of smoke and cinders rolled over and enveloped us, and it seemed almost impossible to breathe. Man and beast alike rushed to the water's edge, and into the water, to avoid suffocation. . . . Some persons drove their horses into the lake as far as the poor beasts could safely go, and men, women, and children waded out and clambered upon the wagons to which the horses were attached, while the lake was lined with people who were standing in the water at various depths, from their knees to their waists, all with their backs to the storm of fire which raged behind them." Everyone realized further retreat was impossible; if the fire continued to advance, the final choice of their lives would be to burn or drown.

For hours the fire pinned them to the lake's edge. Most had been up all night; the strain and the lack of sleep made them long for rest. Some on the wagons dozed; others lay down in shallow water. Tree's wife grew utterly exhausted and risked her fate by letting herself collapse on the shore, semiconscious. Tree was slightly more aware, enough to see her clothing catch fire and to beat out the flames with his bare hands. They both realized they had to stay on their feet if they hoped to live.

Ever so gradually the inferno weakened. The heat became less intense and the smoke diminished. Sometime after five o'clock—this was now Monday afternoon—a horse-drawn grocery wagon emerged from the smoke in the direction of Superior Street. Tree ran forward and offered the driver whatever he'd charge to rescue his family. The man might have demanded a thousand dollars but settled for ten. Tree and the others piled in. The driver turned the wagon back toward the smoke, and all aboard covered their heads and mouths as the dutiful horse plunged ahead. The worst of the fire had burned itself out, having consumed everything combustible in its path, but the ruins still smoldered profusely. "We saw enough to know that the North Side at least was destroyed," Tree wrote, "and that all that was left of the thousands of happy homes of the day before were a few chimney stacks and an occasional broken and cracked wall."[6]

The Tree family reached the safety of the West Side not far from where Mary and David Fales had finally crossed the river. Mary, too, remarked the entire devastation. "Every family I know on the North Side is burned out," she wrote her mother. "I can't enumerate them. It would be useless. It is sufficient to say every individual one." Though the fire had burned toward the east and the lake and had there run out of fuel, no one could say for certain that the worst was over. "Everyone felt nervous lest some change of wind might cause another conflagration on the West Side," Lambert Tree recalled. If it did, the city would be worse off than ever, for the fire had destroyed the water works, leaving firemen little with which to battle the flames. All Chicago spent an anxious evening and night until, about three in the morning, rain began to fall—first lightly, then more heavily. "I never felt so grateful in my life," Mary Fales recorded the next day, after the rain doused the last of the flames.[7]

SEVERAL QUESTIONS EMERGED in the wake of the fire. The first involved the extent of the damage. Journalists Elias Colbert and Everett Chamberlin conducted the most thorough survey and reported that the fire had burned 2,124 acres of urban real estate and destroyed, wholly or in large part, 17,450 buildings. More than 300 people died in the blaze; 100,000 lost their homes. The property damage exceeded $200 million.[8]

A second question had to do with public order. As Lambert Tree discovered on the shore of Lake Michigan even while the fire was raging, human greed took no time off for civil calamity. If anything, the fire provided opportunities for theft and looting that wouldn't recur till the next such disaster. (A similar observation had prompted Benjamin Franklin to specify that his Philadelphia firemen carry large leather bags to fire scenes, to preempt the theft of the valuables of those driven from their homes and offices.) Chicago's police could hardly keep up with crime under normal circumstances; in the extraordinary aftermath of the fire they needed help.

It arrived in Union blue. General Phil Sheridan was in Chicago when the fire broke out; at its height he employed a company of his men and some army gunpowder to blow up buildings in the fire's path, to deprive the blaze of fuel. The measure did little immediate good, but it reminded Chicago officials that federal help was at hand if necessary. As the flames died down, Sheridan suggested that the small federal force in Chicago could be supplemented by soldiers from forts farther west. Chicago mayor Roswell B. Mason accepted the offer and then some: he placed the city under martial law, with Sheridan in command. The condition lasted two weeks and provoked both opposition, chiefly from Illinois governor John Palmer, who alleged a power grab by Sheridan and contended that if soldiers were needed they should have been state militia, and applause, primarily from property owners. William Bross, a partner in the *Chicago Tribune*, recalled his reaction upon the arrival of the federal troops. "I saw Sheridan's boys, with knapsack and musket, march proudly by. *Never did deeper emotions of joy overcome me.*"[9]

The third question facing Chicago in the aftermath of the fire was the most challenging. Put simply, could the city be rebuilt? No major American city had ever been so completely destroyed as Chicago (only San Francisco, dealt the double blow of earthquake and fire in 1906, and New Orleans, hammered by hurricane and flood in 2005, have been since). Capitalism had built Chicago; could capitalism rebuild it?

In fact it did, and far more quickly than anyone expected. (So quickly that a popular joke told of an expatriate Chicagoan who rushed to buy a train ticket to his erstwhile home. The ticket agent asked if had lost a loved one in the fire. No, he said; he just wanted to see the ruins before a whole new city was built on top of them.) The first structures erected upon the ruins were not homes or hospitals but businesses. W. D. Kerfoot, a prominent real estate agent, returned to the site of his office at 89 Washington Street, between Dearborn and Clark, on the morning of October 10, with a load of lumber; discovering that the remains of the building were still too hot to allow entry, he built a shack in the street. A sign above the door proclaimed, "W. D. Kerfoot. Everything gone but wife, children, and energy."

Kerfoot rightly guessed that the fire had created opportunities for buying and selling land, which was about the only tangible thing the flames hadn't destroyed. Merchants were harder pressed, having lost their inventories along with their shops and warehouses. But people still needed what the merchants had sold—needed it now more than ever, in most cases—and this demand was sufficient collateral for the merchants' creditors. Alfred T. Andreas, a publisher, entrepreneur, and chronicler of Chicago's growth, destruction, and resurrection, told of merchants receiving telegrams from their creditors even before the extent of the destruction was known. "The general tenor of the dispatches was: 'We suppose you are burned out. Order what goods you need, and pay what you can. We want your trade.'"[10]

For centuries American Indians had burned the Great Plains to replenish the soil and ensure a fresh crop of grass for the buffalo; white farmers adapted the incendiary technique to their wheat fields. Chicagoans discovered that fire had a similar revivifying effect on a capitalist cityscape. Cities accrete old buildings and infrastructure, to which individuals and firms grow attached for emotional and pecuniary reasons. A fire can clear away the old stuff, making room for buildings that wouldn't have sprouted otherwise. Chicago sprang up from the ashes of the 1871 fire more vigorous than ever. Voters authorized the reconstruction of the major public buildings, including the post office, the custom house, and the court house. The work served the dual purpose of reasserting the city's identity and employing thousands of Chicagoans rendered jobless by the flames. Skilled workers did particularly well in the "great rebuilding," as their talents made them the object of increased demand and won them higher wages. Unskilled workers did less well, but after the Panic of 1873 the continuing construction in Chicago sheltered them from the worst of the depression.[11]

Chicago's entrepreneurs competed to hire the best architects, who, lured by the tabula rasa of the post-fire skyline, strove to imprint their particular visions of modern architecture upon the city. They might have built outward, onto the prairie that stretched away to the north, west, and south. But the burned-over district beckoned, and in any event Chicagoans had already defined their commercial area as bounded on the north and west by the Chicago River and on the south by the tangle of rail yards that connected Chicago to the outside world. For this reason, the *Chicago Tribune* explained, "Chicago must grow upward."[12]

It did so, more rapidly and spectacularly than any other city in the world. New York, Philadelphia, London, and Berlin built tall buildings, but they were scattered among existing shorter structures. Chicago's towers went up wall-to-wall, lining the major thoroughfares for blocks on end. Only the fire made this density possible, accomplishing in two days what deference to the prerogatives of private capital wouldn't have allowed in two decades. "That part of the burnt district north of Van Buren street and between La Salle street and the South Branch of the River," an investor recalled, "before the fire was covered with countless old rookeries and miserable shanties, occupied for the past twenty years as dens of infamy and low gambling dives, the resort and rendezvous of thieves, burglars, robbers, and murderers of all grades and colors, to the exclusion of all decency, or business purposes." Yet because those dens of infamy turned a profit, their landlords resisted their removal. The fire solved the problem.[13]

In place of the dives rose monuments of commerce. The Columbus Memorial Building soared sixteen stories above State Street; the Masonic Temple Building, at the corner of State and Randolph, became the world's tallest building (twenty-two stories and 302 feet) upon its completion in 1892. Chicago's architects and their clients made personal and civic statements with the buildings they erected. "From foundation to roof, every inch of the building bears the impress of superb workmanship," a contemporary remarked of the Chamber of Commerce Building. "There is not a trace of shoddyism about the structure. There is no veneering. There is no paint. Everything from the mosaic ceiling of the first floor to the Italian marble wainscoting of the thirteenth is real—not an imitation. No cheap substitutes have found their way into this work." The *Chicago Tribune* put the matter more succinctly in commenting on plans for the Columbus Memorial project: "A million dollars is a large sum to expend on a lot 100 x 90 feet, when a building costing from $650,000 to 750,000 would in all probability bring in the same rental."[14]

The new buildings married art to technology. Steel-frame construction took loads off the walls and allowed the inclusion of large windows, which transformed the interior aesthetics of the buildings. "With the owners, light has been a prime consideration," an architecture critic for the *Tribune* remarked. Skylights and multistoried foyers extended the feeling of openness deep into the heart of the structures and diminished the need for artificial lighting. "A perfect flood of light penetrates the central court, so that the interior of the building is almost as brightly illuminated as the exterior during the day," another critic said of the Chamber of Commerce Building. Elevators whisked visitors to the highest floors, in the highest style. The Hale Elevator Company, based in Chicago, produced a line of elevator cars that ranged in price from $200 to $2,000 and in design from the utilitarian to the baroque. Building lobbies served as portals to the interiors but also as gateways to distant lands and times. "Rising to the height of a story and a half, the walls of the outer vestibule are composed of Numidian, Alps, Green, and Siena marbles," a guidebook explained of the Unity Building. "Passing through the rotunda, the eye is dazzled by its surprisingly brilliant beauty, designed in the style of the Italian renaissance."[15]

The Chicago buildings set new standards for commercial offices. "Dark rooms will not rent, and it therefore does not pay to construct them," the *Tribune* explained. "The old practice was to cover the entire lot, and the consequence was dark rooms in a considerable proportion of the space." That old practice had become uneconomical. "Buildings constructed according to the latest ideas have readily taken tenants away." The directors of Chicago's First National Bank, justifying their decision to spare no expense in fitting out their building, described it as a market response to the "demand for perfect office quarters."[16]

Many architects left their signatures across Chicago's skyline, including Louis Sullivan, Dankmar Adler, Frederick Baumann, and William Le Baron Jenney. But the most distinctive autograph belonged to the firm of Burnham and Root. Daniel Burnham was the elder by three years and the face of the firm. "Daniel Hudson Burnham was one of the handsomest men I ever saw," remembered Paul Starrett, a Burnham and Root associate. "It was easy to see how he got commissions. His very bearing and looks were half the battle. He had only to assert the most commonplace thing and it sounded important and convincing." When proposing building designs, Burnham rarely asserted the commonplace. "Make no little plans; they have no magic to stir men's blood," he told his colleagues. (The message stuck with Starrett, who moved on from Burnham and Root to construct New York's Empire State Building.)

John Root was the better artist and designer, a man who could conjure whole buildings from thin air. "He would grow abstracted and silent," Burnham said of his partner. "A faraway look would come into his eyes, and the building was there before him—every stone of it." Together the two built several Chicago landmarks, among them the Montauk, which demanded a novel floating foundation and was the first structure to be called a "skyscraper" ("What Chartres was to the Gothic cathedral," a critic swooned, "the Montauk Block was to the high commercial building"); the Rookery, whose broad windows seemed to bring Lake Michigan indoors; and the Monadnock, which opened as the world's largest office building in 1893.[17]

BUILDINGS ARE THE bones of cities; streets and railways their arteries and veins. America's older cities suffered atherosclerosis as avenues built for smaller populations clogged with traffic never anticipated by the designers. New York had it worst, constrained as it was by geography and bursting with new arrivals. Writing at the end of the Civil War, a New York editor deplored the state of transit in his city. Horse-driven omnibuses, the primary mode of surface transport, were a formula for "modern martyrdom," he said. "The discomforts, inconveniences and annoyances of a trip in one of these vehicles are almost intolerable. From the beginning to the end of the journey a constant quarrel is progressing. The driver quarrels with the passengers, and the passengers quarrel with the driver. There are quarrels about getting out and quarrels about getting in. There are quarrels about change and quarrels about the ticket swindle. . . . Respectable clergymen in white chokers are obliged to listen to loud oaths. Ladies are disgusted, frightened and insulted. Children are alarmed and lift up their voices and weep." The principal alternative to the omnibuses, steam-driven city railway cars, were differently but comparably odious. "The cars are quieter than the omnibuses, but much more crowded. People are packed in them like sardines in a box, with perspiration for oil. The seats being more than filled, the passengers are placed in rows down the middle, where they hang on by the straps, like smoked hams in a corner grocery. To enter or exit is exceedingly difficult. Silks and broadcloths are ruined in the attempt. As in the omnibuses, pickpockets take advantage of the confusion to ply their vocation. . . . The foul, close, heated air is poisonous. A healthy person cannot ride a dozen blocks without a headache."[18]

This writer wasn't alone in believing New York would strangle—or New Yorkers strangle one another—if something wasn't done to alleviate the city's transit woes. The rectangular grid of avenues and cross streets was jammed from morning till night; pedestrians took their lives into their hands in simply crossing from one curb to the other. The only solution was to burrow beneath the surface or to rise above it.

Burrowing posed two challenges. The first was the trouble and expense of building a trolley line, railroad, or anything else underground. Costs soared the deeper one dug. The second was the difficulty of ventilating steam engines—the obvious power source—beneath the surface. Steam engines consumed oxygen and emitted carbon monoxide and other toxic gases; operating them underground without asphyxiating passengers tested the ingenuity of the era's best engineers. An underground railway had recently opened in London, and passengers complained of serious breathing distress.

Alfred Ely Beach proposed an ingenious solution to the ventilation problem. Compressed air, rather than the direct application of steam power, would drive his underground system. Passenger cars fitting snugly inside an iron tube would be whisked from station to station by jets of air pumped into the tube from above ground. Steam engines on the surface, vented to the atmosphere, would whirl the fans that produced the jets.

Beach believed his technology unassailable but reckoned that proponents of competing systems might try to scuttle his project. So he arranged—by methods unclear but apparently in conformance with the practices of Jay Gould, Cornelius Vanderbilt, and other transit magnates of the era—for authorization for his scheme to be slipped into an 1868 state transit bill. Then he surreptitiously commenced construction. His crews started in the basement of a clothing store and bored beneath Broadway, removing the dirt under cover of darkness. By early 1870 Beach's tube was ready for passengers. These were conducted down a stairway to a station lit with gas lamps and lined with frescoes; awaiting their turn the passengers lounged on upholstered sofas and listened to music performed on a grand piano. They entered a car that seated twenty-two in comparative luxury; when the door was closed the car shot silently and rapidly down the three-hundred-foot length of the tube. Nearly all professed delight at the experience and commended it to their friends. During the next several months some four hundred thousand persons paid twenty-five cents apiece for the "atmospheric ride."[19]

But there the experiment ended. Property owners complained that their foundations had been compromised; more tellingly, railroad owners, existing and prospective, mobilized to bar Beach from extending his line into something actually useful. Among those railroaders was a group that hoped to entice Cornelius Vanderbilt into financing a subway. The Commodore's conservatism had kept him out of surface railroads for years; now it prevented him from backing an underground version, which he considered unworkable. "I shall be underground a damned sight sooner than this thing," he said.[20]

He turned out to be right. Though various parties continued to press for underground railroads, the immediate future of mass transit in New York lay overhead. Since just after the Civil War, Charles T. Harvey had lobbied for permission to build an elevated railroad in lower Manhattan. In 1867 the legislature authorized an experimental line running north from Battery Place a half mile along Greenwich Street. The experiment was to determine how disruptive and dangerous an aerial railway was; critics forecast fires from embers that rained down on rooftops, fatal accidents of carriages and omnibuses whose horses were terrified by the mechanical thunder overhead, and the collapse of the towers supporting the tracks and trains. Less spectacular but more pervasive would be the plague of blackened laundry from the belching smokestacks lifted so high.

Harvey mollified some of the critics by employing cables rather than locomotives to propel his cars. The cables ran over pulleys from the cars to a central traction engine. This arrangement kept the sparks and noise to a minimum, but it also complicated the motion of the cars, which at first ran hardly faster than a man could walk. Harvey proclaimed the experiment a success in principle and began raising cash to improve the equipment and service. But his backers fell victim to the Gould-Fisk gold raid of 1869, and by the time the finances were reorganized Harvey no longer controlled the project.

Yet his idea was sound enough that others picked it up. In 1872 the New-York Elevated Railroad Company commenced service up Greenwich and Ninth Avenue to the Hudson River Railroad station on Thirtieth Street. The political future of elevated transit remained precarious, though, and the company felt obliged to circulate among passengers a petition to the state legislature asserting that "the trains have been regular, rapid and safe" and praying that "the road may be continued as a public convenience." The petition, and perhaps other considerations, had the desired effect. The elevated system survived the legislative scrutiny, and it expanded till it carried more than a million passengers a day.[21]

As EXCITING AS the sky trains could be—the new elevated dispensed with Harvey's cables in favor of regular locomotives, which did throw sparks, spook horses, and occasionally jump the rails—they had nothing on sky bridges. For generations the island character of Manhattan had defined the city of New York, which remained administratively separate from Brooklyn, itself one of the largest cities in America and rapidly growing. To reach New York directly from Brooklyn required taking a boat, catching some spray in the face, and feeling at least a bit of the thrill that inspired Walt Whitman's ode to the East River ferry:

> Flow on, river! flow with the flood-tide, and ebb with the ebb-tide!
> Frolic on, crested and scallop-edg'd waves!
> Gorgeous clouds of the sun-set! drench with your splendor me, or the
>   men and women generations after me;
> Cross from shore to shore, countless crowds of passengers![22]

But those crowds grew more countless each year, and the ferries became a bottleneck to the region's economic growth. Merchants on Manhattan clamored for faster deliveries; industrialists complained that the crowding on the island pushed their wage costs up. Yet it was Brooklyn that really drove the demand for change. Brooklyn's bakers and brewers wanted easier access to Manhattan's markets; Brooklyn's builders sought to house those Manhattan workers; Brooklyn's landowners lusted after Manhattan's money.

A bridge would solve everyone's problems and secure New York's future. In the half decade after the Civil War, the commerce of the world seemed up for grabs. The Suez Canal drew Atlantic traffic east; the Pacific railroad pulled American traffic west. New Yorkers hoped to command the junction of the two trade routes. "As the great flow of civilization has ever been from East towards the West," John Augustus Roebling wrote, "with the same certainty will the greatest commercial emporium be located on this continent, which links East to the West, and whose mission it is in the history of mankind to blend the most ancient civilization with the most modern. . . . Lines of steamers, such as the world never saw before, are now plowing the Atlantic in regular straight line furrows. The same means of communication will unite the western coast of this continent to the eastern coast of Asia. New York will remain the center where these lines meet."

Roebling was no idle philosopher of history—though he *had* studied under Hegel in Germany. Born in Saxony to a modestly successful tobacconist and his ambitious wife, young Johann enrolled in the engineering curriculum at the Polytechnic Institute of Berlin, where the great historical philosopher taught. Hegel pondered the trajectory of civilization and determined that America was next in the line of human progress. "It is a land of hope for all who are wearied of the historic armory of old Europe," he told Roebling and his other students. Roebling took the professor at his word and prepared to emigrate. The Prussian government made difficulties, not liking to lose a bright young man on whom it had lavished educational and technical resources. So Roebling proceeded by stealth, attaching himself to a group of farmers leaving to join their fellow Germans in the Pennsylvania countryside. Roebling lasted long enough behind the plow to watch his brother, another spurious agrarian, die of sunstroke in a wheat field; safely beyond Bismarck's border guards, he embraced engineering once more. He built canals and dams, then railroads and aqueducts and bridges. He developed a novel form of rope, fabricated of iron wire; his plant at Trenton churned out miles of the stuff and earned its inventor a fortune.

Roebling hoped to make still more money—not to mention a mark of which his philosophy professor would be proud—by building a bridge connecting Brooklyn to New York. Other engineers preferred a tunnel. *Scientific American*, lately cofounded by Alfred Beach, the pneumatic man, argued that going underground would save time and money. Roebling dismissed the moles with contempt. A soaring bridge would embody the soaring vision of America. "Let it illustrate the grandeur of our age; let it be the Mecca to which foreign peoples shall come. . . . Babylon had her hanging gardens, Nineveh her towers, and Rome her Coliseum. Let us have this great monument to progress."[23]

And such a bridge! The surging currents of the tidal East River, and the endless stream of ships and boats on its surface, required that any bridge leap the channel in a single span. Only a suspension bridge could accomplish the feat. But no suspension bridge of this size had ever been attempted. The towers to hold the main cables must be hundreds of feet high, to accommodate the sag in the cables and still give the tallest ships clearance. The cables themselves must be stronger than any cables ever spun, and the anchorages to hold the cable ends—to balance the immense weight of the cables and the bridge span—must be embedded deep into the living rock on either side of the bridge. Roebling's earlier bridges included suspension spans; these made his design for the East River Bridge plausible. But between the plausible and the actual yawned a gap that could swallow millions of dollars and hundreds of lives, perhaps to no ultimate avail. Who would shoulder the risk?

The City of Brooklyn, for one. In the spirit of the legislation that funded the Pacific railroad, the Brooklyn city government voted three million dollars toward Roebling's project. New York City pitched in a million and a half after several aldermen were bribed and Democratic boss William Tweed received a large ownership stake in the bridge construction company.[24]

Roebling now turned to making his vision real. But before the work began, a freak accident in the summer of 1869 crushed the toes of his right foot. He consented to amputation, lest his convalescence slow the project. He didn't move fast enough: tetanus set in, and in three weeks he was dead.

His son assumed the mantle. Washington Roebling lacked his father's sense of destiny, the Rensselaer Polytechnic Institute having had no Hegel on staff at the time Washington attended the college in Troy, New York. (Though he didn't correct people who assumed he had been named for the

Father of his Country, the younger Roebling's forename actually honored a friend of his own father.) Washington continued his training under his father, so that by the time of the elder man's death, Washington Roebling was the logical person to carry the construction forward.

The construction began with the caissons, the large, watertight, air-tight compartments set open-bottomed on the river bed that allowed the workers to excavate for the tower foundations. Cofferdams sufficed for other projects, but such comparatively flimsy structures couldn't withstand the depths, pressures, and currents of the East River. Caissons had been employed in France (as the name suggested), and James Eads used them in St. Louis, where he was building his bridge across the Mississippi. But they remained a temperamental technology, prone to spectacular failure. The key to the caissons was compressed air, supplied by powerful pumps, that held the water at bay and allowed the workers inside the caissons to carve into the river bed till they reached bedrock. Ingenious air locks enabled the workers to enter and exit the caissons without loss of air pressure; separate locks permitted the removal of the excavated material.

The work was hot, heavy, noisy, and exhausting. The workers—mostly Irish, German, and Italian immigrants—labored around the clock, in eight-hour shifts, six days a week. The excavation went slowly, at times only inches per week. In frustration Washington Roebling authorized the men to blast, and they, in equal frustration, agreed. The decision was fraught with danger; if the concussion didn't kill the men in the caissons or blow out their eardrums, it might upset the balance between the air pressure and the weight of the overlying water, allowing the water to pour under the sides of the caisson and drown everyone inside. Roebling experimented with a revolver before authorizing serious blasts; when the largest round his gun could fire produced a tolerable concussion, he stepped up to black powder. This spared the men's lives and hearing, but it filled the caissons with blinding smoke. Roebling solved this new problem by switching to smokeless rifle powder, and the excavation accelerated gratifyingly.

Another difficulty developed as the caissons and men descended into the river bed. The farther down they went, the greater the air pressure required to keep the water out. The men manifested strange symptoms on emerging at the ends of their shifts. They began to bleed from the nose and mouth and suffered inexplicable cramps, which gave rise to the name for their affliction: "the bends." Shortening the shifts afforded some relief, but not always enough. One man died, then another. The workers struck in protest, demanding still shorter shifts and higher pay: $3.00 for four hours. They held out for a few days, until the company threatened to fire them all and hire replacements. They accepted $2.75 and went back to work.

Meanwhile a doctor hired by the company to investigate the malady found nothing conclusive, and the company sought to suppress the truth about what was killing the workers. A number of decompression deaths were attributed to other causes, including spinal meningitis and "corpulence." Al Smith, the future mayor of New York, grew up on South Street during this period and recalled his mother's telling of the agonies of the workers dying from the bends during construction of the bridge. "Perhaps if they had known," she said, "they would never have built it." Those workers who exited slowly, returning to normal air pressure gradually, exhibited fewer symptoms, and the doctor recommended this for all the workers. But the company was anxious to finish the excavation, the workers were in a hurry to get home at the ends of their shifts, and his recommendation went largely unheeded. Workers continued to collapse and die.

Roebling, at a loss, finally called the digging to a halt. Though the excavation for the tower on the Brooklyn side had hit bedrock, the New York caisson still rested on sand, seventy-eight feet below high tide in the East River. Roebling decided to risk building the New York tower on the sand, relying on its enormous weight to hold the footing firm against the ebb and flow of the currents.

By contrast to the battle against the river bed and the bends, which took place largely out of sight, the building of the towers occurred in plain view. The Brooklyn tower broke the surface first, followed by the New York tower. Slowly the workers piled the masonry higher, stone upon stone. The Panic of 1873 retarded but didn't stop the work. In June 1875 the Brooklyn tower topped out, 276 feet above flood tide, and a year later the New York tower achieved the same final height. Cables—not the waist-thick main cables yet but smaller preliminaries—were floated across the river and hoisted into place. In August the first crossing was made by master mechanic Edwin Farrington in a bosun's chair hung from one of the cables. "The crowds below him held their breath in fearful suspense for a moment," a local correspondent related, "and then a wild shout went up, showing their appreciation at the boldness of the voyager. . . . He kissed his hand to the populace in response to their cheers."[25]

(ABOVE) Construction camp
on the Pacific railroad
*National Archives and Records
Administration*

(RIGHT) George Custer's
Black Hills expedition
*National Archives and Records
Administration*

(BELOW) Cattle roundup
in the West
*National Archives and Records
Administration*

A well-appointed sod house in Nebraska
Library of Congress, Prints & Photographs Division

Tenement inspectors taking note
National Archives and Records Administration

On top of the
(tenement) world
*National Archives and Records
Administration*

(RIGHT) A ragpicker in San
Francisco
*Library of Congress, Prints &
Photographs Division*

(BELOW) Walking the
Brooklyn Bridge
*National Archives and Records
Administration*

Urban transport, 1897
National Archives and Records Administration

New York's Fifth Avenue
on Easter morning
National Archives and Records Administration

Wall Street at work
*Library of Congress, Prints & Photographs
Division*

Cornelius Vanderbilt II's summer home, the Breakers
Library of Congress, Prints & Photographs Division

George Vanderbilt's Biltmore
Library of Congress, Prints & Photographs Division

Scenes from the railroad strike
of 1877

*Library of Congress, Prints &
Photographs Division*

Homestead, 1892

*Library of Congress, Prints & Photographs
Division*

THE MOB ASSAILING THE PINKERTON MEN ON THEIR WAY TO THE TEMPORARY PRISON.—DRAWN BY CHARLES MENTE AFTER A PHOTOGRAPH BY D.

(TOP) Ulysses Grant

(TOP RIGHT) Grover Cleveland

(ABOVE) William McKinley

(CENTER RIGHT) Booker T. Washington

(RIGHT) Jay Gould

All: Library of Congress, Prints & Photographs Division

Theodore Roosevelt and the Rough Riders
Library of Congress, Prints & Photographs Division

(LEFT) Andrew Carnegie
Library of Congress, Prints & Photographs Division

J. P. Morgan attacking a photographer
Library of Congress, Prints & Photographs Division

John D. Rockefeller with his son, John Jr.
Library of Congress, Prints & Photographs Division

Spinning the main cables, hanging the suspenders (the vertical lines connecting the main cables to the bridge span), and constructing the span itself took several more years. Not till May 1883 did the bridge open to traffic. When it did, it provoked celebrations like nothing since the end of the Civil War. Brooklyn congratulated itself on reaching the acme of civilization. A large banner paraphrased John Roebling: "Babylon had her hanging gardens, Egypt her Pyramids, Athens her Acropolis, Rome her Coliseum—so Brooklyn has her bridge. Over its broad roadway the teeming millions of the two cities may pass; under its spacious arch the commerce of the world may pass." Hundreds of thousands turned out from both Brooklyn and New York to commemorate the wonderful day; hundreds of politicians elbowed onto reviewing stands to capture the glory reflected from the cables and girders. Ferryboats and fireboats and lighters and yachts and smacks and scows filled the East River; special trains delivered guests from the suburbs. Nightfall brought "illuminations"—fireworks—that dazzled the multitude and might have ignited the woodwork of the bridge had the fireboats not hosed it down. "A grand line of fire shot up into the air and burst into a shower of golden rain and blue, red, and emerald stars, which dropped gently down into the river," a witness recorded. "The two towers of the bridge became ablaze with light. Fountains of gold and silver stars were set in motion on the towers, and from the western roadway Japanese shells were fired in rapid succession. These shells soared to a height of about 800 feet and then burst, scattering gold and silver rain, stars of gold, blue, emerald, and red, and writhing serpents which reached the water before their strength was spent." The grand finale to the show, which consumed fourteen tons of fireworks, was the simultaneous launch of five hundred "monster rockets" that exploded with a force that shook the bridge but, doing no damage, confirmed the consensus that this monument to American greatness would stand forever.[26]

As proud as urban achievements like the Brooklyn Bridge could make Americans, many viewed the emergence of big cities as a fall from grace. Cities were something Americans had long associated with vice and decay and Europe. "I view great cities as pestilential to the morals, the health and the liberties of man," Thomas Jefferson told Benjamin Rush. "True, they nourish some of the elegant arts, but the useful ones can thrive elsewhere, and less perfection in the others, with more health, virtue & freedom, would be my choice." Ralph Waldo Emerson, in an essay praising the pastoral life, declared, "Cities force growth and make men talkative and entertaining, but they make them artificial." Herman Melville decried the insidious effect of cities on the most personal relations. "In our cities families rise and burst like bubbles in a vat," he observed in *Pierre*. Horace Greeley famously told his young man to go west if he wished to flourish, not to venture into the great city at the New York editor's feet. Walt Whitman was the exception that proved the rule: Whitman extolled city life but in a poetry collection—*Leaves of Grass*—judged obscene by many contemporaries.[27]

When Americans did move to cities, they initially tried to make them look like villages. Until the middle of the nineteenth century the model residence for all who could afford it was the single-family home, sometimes attached to its neighbors in a row but often standing apart. In planned cities like Philadelphia (laid out at the end of the seventeenth century almost before anyone set foot on that part of the Delaware River shore) and New York (platted from Fourteenth Street to 155th in the second decade of the nineteenth century), houses stretched along streets and avenues as far as the eye could see or the foot walk. At the end of the Civil War the tallest structures in New York were the church steeples, with the spire of Trinity Church, at Broadway and Wall Street, overtopping the rest.

But gradually growth caught up with the cities. Empty lots filled in, driving real estate prices higher. Families of modest means strained to afford homes within the city limits. Some New York families crossed the East River to Brooklyn, consigning their breadwinners to daily ferry commutes (and prayers for a bridge). Others took refuge in a novel style of residence, imported from Europe.

New York's first apartment house was the Stuyvesant, designed by Richard Morris Hunt, completed in 1869, and named for the founder of New York by the builder, who happened to share Peter Stuyvesant's last name (although only by a quirk: Rutherfurd Stuyvesant had been Stuyvesant Rutherfurd until he transposed his names to satisfy a condition of the will under which he inherited the large Stuyvesant holdings of his mother's family). The Stuyvesant was located on East Eighteenth Street, in a neighborhood dominated by row houses. It didn't look much different from the buildings on either side and across the street, being five stories tall (many of the neighboring houses had that many floors) with a façade that betrayed the apartment building's true nature only by the fact of having a single exterior door where an equal frontage of the row houses had five or six.[28]

It was the idea of apartment living that required getting used to. George Templeton Strong, a conservative in most things, thought the Stuyvesant attractive in its modest way. He didn't want to move there but allowed that others might. "This substitute for householding seems to work well. . . . Rutherfurd is a public benefactor, especially to young people who want to marry on moderate means. Nothing could be brighter, more comfortable, or more refined-looking than these tiny, cosy drawing rooms." Other observers, however, warned that nothing good could come of "cohabitation," as they called apartment living. Unrelated people residing under the same roof suggested all manner of disturbing activities, starting with fornication and escalating unspeakably from there. Immigrants and the native poor shared accommodations, but they had no choice—and everyone knew, or at least suspected, what kind of immorality flourished on the Lower East Side. Farther up the island one expected better.[29]

Yet the economics of apartments were irrefutable. More units per lot meant lower prices for each. Within a year of the Stuyvesant's completion, two more apartment houses opened nearby. One was a renovation of a pair of adjoining houses; the other—the Stevens House—was purpose-built and towered eight stories, a feat made possible, or at least marketable, by the inclusion of an elevator. To mitigate concern that apartment living was déclassé, the eighteen suites in the new building contained quarters for servants, and the communal areas included a fine restaurant and frescoed walls. In fact, in striving for luxury it broke its business model; within a few years it was converted to a hotel.[30]

By then other apartment houses had sprung up. Generically called "French flats" after the residential buildings that graced the boulevards of Paris (where Richard Hunt had studied architecture, at the École des Beaux-Arts), they grew taller and broader and attracted an ever-expanding clientele. The upper class still snubbed them; one member proclaimed huffily, "Gentlemen will never consent to live on mere shelves under a common roof." Families with children preferred larger spaces, indoors and out, than the apartments afforded. But single men (single women usually lived with their parents) and couples without children came to consider them a perfectly acceptable solution to the problem of urban affordability.[31]

"IT HAS BEEN represented to me that America is not ready for the Fine Arts," Richard Hunt had written his mother from Paris as he was completing his studies. "But I think they are mistaken. There is no place in the world where they are more needed." They were still needed when Hunt turned from apartment houses to mansions for the wealthiest of the Gilded Age capitalists.[32]

Not long after he inherited the New York Central Railroad from his father, William Vanderbilt decided he required new digs. He commissioned Hunt to design a house for a lot on Fifth Avenue at Fifty-second Street. Hunt broke from the brownstone tradition of midcentury New York, which employed the Triassic sandstone of New Jersey and Connecticut that quarried easily and weathered to a rich chocolate color. He broke even more dramatically from the understated conventions of New York's burgher past, which dictated that money be reinvested in one's business rather than employed in conspicuous display. The house Hunt designed for Vanderbilt was modeled on a French château of the early Renaissance, and it employed silvery Indiana limestone that seemed to glow against the dark backdrop of its neighbors. The mansard roof sported spires and gables; carved stonework ornamented a three-story porch and numerous balconies. Like an American gargoyle, a statue of Hunt disguised as a stonemason stared down from the roof.

Neither New York nor anywhere else in America had seen the like of the Vanderbilt mansion, which the Vanderbilts celebrated with an 1883 ball that reminded some of the guests and more of those not invited that the centennial of the French Revolution was approaching. Hired dancers came dressed as horses and performed a "Hobby Horse Quadrille." William's wife, Alva, appeared as a Venetian princess. His sister-in-law wore a white satin gown trimmed with diamonds, and a diamond headdress, that made her, in her own characterization, "The Electric Light." A close friend dressed up as Queen Elizabeth. The ball put New York in a tizzy before and after. "It has been on every tongue and a fixed idea in every head," the *New York Times* reported. "It has disturbed the sleep and occupied the waking hours of social butterflies, both male and female, for over six weeks. . . . Amid the rush and excitement of business, men have found their minds haunted by uncontrollable thoughts as to whether they should appear as Robert Le Diable, Cardinal Richelieu, Otho the barbarian, or the Count of Monte Cristo, while the ladies have been driven to the verge of distraction in the effort to settle the comparative advantages of ancient, medieval, and modern costumes." Invitations were in high demand; the Vanderbilts finally settled on opening their doors to twelve hundred of their dearest friends. Hordes who didn't make the list crowded behind police lines to savor the event from afar.

On entry, the guests were transported to an urban Eden. "Throughout the hall and parlors on the first floor were distributed vases and gilded baskets filled with natural roses of extraordinary size," the *Times* reporter wrote. "Grouped around the clustered columns which ornament either side of the stately hall were tall palms overtopping a dense mass of ferns and ornamental grasses." The hall led to the gymnasium, a large apartment where a buffet dinner was served. "But it had not the appearance of an apartment last night; it was like a garden in a tropical forest. The walls were nowhere to be seen, but in their places an impenetrable thicket of fern above fern and palm above palm, while from the branches of the palms hung a profusion of lovely orchids. . . . Two beautiful fountains played in opposite corners of the apartment. The doors of the apartment, thrown back against the walls, were completely covered with roses and lilies of the valley."

Those who fought past the flora found an interior architecture more sumptuous than anything any had seen west of the Atlantic. A carved stairway of Caen stone rose fifty feet above the polished Echaillon stone floor. Italian tapestries lined the walls, topped by rich oak panels on the ceiling. Walnut replaced the oak elsewhere, and intricate paintings of scenes from classical mythology replaced the walnut. The furniture unselfconsciously recalled the ancien régime; a magnificent stained-glass window opposite the main doorway depicted the meeting of Henry VIII of England and Francis I of France on the Field of the Cloth of Gold.[33]

The night was accounted a stunning success. The Vanderbilts had planted their flag at the summit of New York society, where it would remain till someone built something grander.

THIS DIDN'T TAKE LONG. The Vanderbilt gala kicked off an orgy of conspicuous construction as the captains of industry converted their profits into assets more tangible—and visible. The move was partly strategic, for in an era of chronic financial turmoil, real estate promised a comparatively safe harbor. But it was also psychological, in that the clearest sign of material success was a home its master could be proud of. In every city and in many suburbs existing buildings were razed or empty lots developed to afford room for the mansions of the rich. Soon no mogul, actual or aspiring, felt comfortable without a large, gaudy residence. And each round of construction produced houses more opulent and expensive than those of the last; when the point of building was to make a statement, the buildings had to shout louder and louder to be heard.

The competition crossed generations and set members of families against one another. William Vanderbilt's son Cornelius II liked the ocean air of Newport, Rhode Island, where he built a summer place that dwarfed his father's Manhattan home. "The Breakers" comprised seventy rooms and put sixty-five thousand square feet under its Italian Renaissance roof. Construction required two years, including time to transport much of the wood and stone from Europe. The paneling in one of the smaller reception rooms came from a Paris house built for Marie Antoinette. The dining room featured two massive crystal chandeliers, twelve columns with gilded bronze capitals, and an oak table that seated thirty-four guests in elbow-swinging comfort. The billiard room had marble walls and alabaster arches; a weighing chair from England let the players determine their weight in stone. The ceiling of the grand salon riffed the Sistine Chapel, albeit with a secular twist; its figures symbolized Music, Harmony, Song, and Melody. The kitchen was bigger than most ordinary homes; the stables were roomier and cleaner than many urban apartments.

But this wasn't even the biggest house in the family. George Washington Vanderbilt, William's youngest son, preferred the Carolina piedmont to the New England shore; at Asheville he constructed a country home that could have swallowed his father's and brother's houses and several office buildings besides. Whether the name he gave the place—Biltmore—was intended to convey comparison was a matter of conjecture, but as a matter of fact no one ever built more home than George Vanderbilt. The 250 rooms and 175,000 square feet, in exaggerated imitation of the grandest French châteaux, made the house the symbol of Gilded Age excess; its

125,000 acres, replete with farms, village, church, and peasants, conjured alarming new images of France on the eve of the revolution.

By the time Biltmore was finished, the nation was mired in the depression of the 1890s. America's nouveaux riches weren't famous for their sensitivity to the feelings of lesser sorts, but even they realized there were limits to what one could do in a republic without inflaming public opinion unduly. As a result, when Mrs. Bradley Martin wanted to impress the neighbors she opted for something more ephemeral: a ball, after the fashion of the William Vanderbilts. And even then she defended her fun as being good for the economy of New York. The event took place at the Waldorf Hotel in the winter of 1897. "Mrs. Martin received the salutations of more than 600 men and women, one and all members of the society worlds of New York and other large American cities, and all in their gorgeous robes and garbs personating those kings and queens, nobles, knights, and courtiers whose names and personalities take up the pages of history," the society reporter for the *New York Times* recorded breathlessly. "The grand ballroom was quite a scene of splendor. The eye scarcely knew where to look or what to study, it was such a bewildering maze of gorgeous dames and gentlemen on the floor, such a flood of light from the ceiling, paneled in terra cotta and gold, and such an entrancing picture of garlands that hung everywhere in rich festoons." The guests danced past midnight, then dined on *filet de boeuf jardinière, terrapène désossée, poularde farcie aux truffes*, and other French delicacies.

The *Times* had been covering such events since the Vanderbilt ball, and it placed the Martin affair in historical context. "As the society of the metropolis has grown larger, and wealth, luxury, and the knowledge of the art of living have increased, these successive costume balls have in every instance surpassed in elegance of dress and in lavishness and perfection of appointment their predecessors," the paper declared. The event at the Waldorf "may truthfully be said to have been the climax in this form of entertainment thus far reached in the metropolis."[34]

Chapter 11

BELOW THE EL

After their joyful reunion at the Boston pier, Mary Antin's father led his family to the flat he had rented on Union Place. That this wasn't Polotzk became evident at once. "The first meal was an object lesson of much variety," Mary remembered.

> My father produced several kinds of food, ready to eat, without any cooking, from little tin cans that had printing all over them. He attempted to introduce us to a queer, slippery kind of fruit, which he called "banana," but had to give it up for the time being. After the meal, he had better luck with a curious piece of furniture on runners, which he called "rocking-chair." There were five of us newcomers, and we found five different ways of getting into the American machine of perpetual motion, and as many ways of getting out of it. One born and bred to the use of a rocking-chair cannot imagine how ludicrous people can make themselves when attempting to use it for the first time.

Novelties, like the bananas they encountered that first day, came in bunches. Public baths allowed even the poor to keep clean. At night no one needed to carry a lantern, for the city lit street lamps. "In America, then, everything was free, as we had heard in Russia," Mary marveled.

"Light was free; the streets were as bright as a synagogue on a holy day. Music was free; we had been serenaded, to our gaping delight, by a brass band of many pieces, soon after our installation on Union Place."

Mary's father insisted that they become American as quickly as possible. He taught them the word *greenhorn* and explained that it was what they didn't want to be. He had saved enough to buy them new clothes like the ones American children wore; they visited a department store—another novelty—and came out looking like the children of natives. Mary's mother needed help learning how to use the stove in their apartment; a neighbor lady—an "angel of deliverance," to Mary—stoked the first fire for them. The whole family grew accustomed to the idea that the policeman who walked their street was a friend and not a Cossack.

Much like Booker Washington and other emancipated slaves, many immigrants marked their new lives with new names. Yiddish names were simply too hard for Americans to understand or pronounce; these had to go, as Mary Antin explained.

A committee of our friends, several years ahead of us in American experience, put their heads together and concocted American names for us all. Those of our real names that had no pleasing American equivalents they ruthlessly discarded, content if they retained the initials. My mother, possessing a name that was not easily translatable, was punished with the undignified nickname of Annie. Fetchke, Joseph, and Deborah issued as Frieda, Joseph, and Dora, respectively. As for poor me, I was simply cheated. The name they gave me was hardly new. My Hebrew name being Maryashe in full, Mashke for short, Russianized into Marya *(Mar-ya)*, my friends said that it would hold good in English as *Mary;* which was very disappointing, as I longed to possess a strange-sounding American name like the others.

Mary's disappointment was mitigated by the American habit of employing surnames as a matter of course. "I found on my arrival that my father was 'Mr. Antin' on the slightest provocation and not, as in Polotzk, on state occasions alone. And so I was 'Mary Antin,' and I felt very important to answer to such a dignified title. It was just like America that even plain people should wear their surnames on week days."[1]

For Mary's father, the essence of America was the opportunity for his children to be educated in useful knowledge. He had imbibed from his parents a love of learning, but the learning he acquired in the old country did him little good in the new. Americans weren't interested in his knowledge of the Torah and the Talmud; they asked what he could *do*. Mary remembered his frustration. "'Give me bread!' he cried to America. 'What will you do to earn it?' the challenge came back." He stumbled over English, never acquiring facility, and his daily struggle left him scant time to read in any language. He felt what he once knew slipping away.

But his children would have what he lacked. "He could send his children to school, to learn all those things that he knew by fame to be desirable. The common school, at least, perhaps high school; for one or two, perhaps even college! His children should be students, should fill his house with books and intellectual company; and thus he would walk by proxy in the Elysian Fields of liberal learning. As for the children themselves, he knew no surer way to their advancement and happiness." The proudest day of his relatively young life—he was only thirty-five—was the day he walked them to school. "He would not have delegated that mission to the President of the United States," Mary said.

> The four of us stood around the teacher's desk; and my father, in his impossible English, gave us over in her charge, with some broken word of his hopes for us that his swelling heart could no longer contain. I venture to say that Miss Nixon was struck by something uncommon in the group we made, something outside of Semitic features and the abashed manner of the alien. My little sister was as pretty as a doll, with her clear pink-and-white face, short golden curls, and eyes like blue violets when you caught them looking up. My brother might have been a girl, too, with his cherubic contours of face, rich red color, glossy black hair, and fine eyebrows. Whatever secret fears were in his heart, remembering his former teachers, who had taught with the rod, he stood up straight and uncringing before the American teacher, his cap respectfully doffed. Next to him stood a starved-looking girl with eyes ready to pop out, and short dark curls that would not have made much of a wig for a Jewish bride.
>
> All three children carried themselves rather better than the common run of "green" pupils that were brought to Miss Nixon. But the figure that challenged attention to the group was the tall, straight

father, with his earnest face and fine forehead, nervous hands eloquent
in gesture, and a voice full of feeling. This foreigner, who brought his
children to school as if it were an act of consecration, who regarded the
teacher of the primer class with reverence, who spoke of visions, like a
man inspired, in a common schoolroom, was not like other aliens, who
brought their children in dull obedience to the law; was not like the
native fathers, who brought their unmanageable boys, glad to be
relieved of their care. I think Miss Nixon guessed what my father's best
English could not convey. I think she divined that by the simple act
of delivering our school certificates to her he took possession of
America.[2]

JACOB RIIS SETTLED less easily into American life, being alone and
still desperately in love. His ship docked at Castle Garden on the Hudson
River side of lower Manhattan on Whitsunday of 1870. "It was a beautiful
spring morning, and as I looked over the rail at the miles of straight streets,
the green heights of Brooklyn, and the stir of ferryboats and pleasure craft
on the river, my hopes rose high that somewhere in this teeming hive there
would be a place for me." What sort of place, he didn't know, and he
couldn't decide where to start looking. The obvious route for one of his
background was carpentry. New York needed builders, and trained tool-
men commanded good wages. But hammer and saw repelled him. "They
were indissolubly bound up with my dreams of Elizabeth that were now
gone to smash."

Riis's strongest impressions of America had been formed by conversation with a Danish veteran of the early, wild days of the California gold
rush; on the basis of this intelligence he purchased a large revolver, which
he strapped conspicuously outside his coat before setting off up Broadway,
"conscious that I was following the fashion of the country." A policeman
let him know he was off by twenty years and three thousand miles. Riis
took the hint and dispensed with the weapon gladly enough. "It was quite
heavy to carry around."[3]

He returned to Castle Garden, where a labor contractor enticed him
with the promise of a job at a steel mill near Pittsburgh. The contractor
bought railroad tickets for Riis and a score of other immigrants. Only Riis
and one other man reached the destination. "The rest calmly deserted in

Pittsburgh and went their own way." Riis took a lesson in American freedom. In Denmark workmen honored a contract almost unquestioningly;
in America apparently not. "Here they broke it as a matter of course the
minute it didn't suit them."

Riis labored for the steel company just long enough to repay his ticket
and then tried his hand at coal mining, which suited him no better. As he
was quitting the mine he learned that France had declared war on Prussia
and that Denmark would probably join France. Riis felt his patriotic
blood rising—the more so since a returning hero might win Elizabeth's
affection—and he headed for the Danish consulate in New York to enlist.
To his surprise, the consul wasn't interested. Neither was the French consul. Some Frenchmen he spoke to told him he was crazy to want to leave
America to fight in Europe's war. But he read an article in Charles Dana's
New York Sun describing a volunteer regiment that was forming to fight for
France. He visited the *Sun* office and demanded to see Dana. The editor,
intrigued by this pushy fellow, invited him into his office. Riis asked where
the regiment was. Dana asked what regiment he meant. The one in the
paper, Riis said. Dana confessed that editors didn't always know everything
that appeared in their papers.

> I turned to go, grievously disappointed, but he called me back. "Have
> you," he said, looking searchingly at me, "have you had your break-
> fast?"
>
> No, God knows that I had not; neither that day nor for many days
> before. That was one of the things I had at last learned to consider
> among the superfluities of an effete civilization. I suppose I had no
> need of telling it to him, for it was plain to read in my face. He put his
> hand in his pocket and pulled out a dollar.
>
> "There," he said, "go and get your breakfast; and better give up the
> war."
>
> Give up the war! and for a breakfast. I spurned the dollar hotly.
>
> "I came here to enlist, not to beg money for breakfast," I said, and
> strode out of the office, my head in the air but my stomach crying out
> miserably in rebellion against my pride.

Riis and Dana would meet again, the former recalling the New York
editor's generosity, the latter the immigrant's stubborn pride. For now Riis

required work. He signed on with a New Jersey brickyard for twenty-two dollars a month plus board. "That night, when I turned in after a square meal, in an old wagon I had begged for a bed, I felt like a capitalist." He slept in the wagon because the barracks of the brickyard was filled with Germans, who loudly celebrated the news of each Prussian victory.

Brickmaking—shaping raw clay into blocks to dry and fire—was a seasonal business in the 1870s, and with autumn's rains the workers were laid off. Riis returned to New York. As his money ran out he pawned what little he owned and sought whatever work offered. None did.

> The city was full of idle men. My last hope, a promise of employment in a human-hair factory, failed, and, homeless and penniless, I joined the great army of tramps, wandering about the streets in the daytime with the one aim of somehow stilling the hunger that gnawed at my vitals, and fighting at night with vagrant curs or outcasts as miserable as myself for the protection of some sheltering ash-bin or doorway. I was too proud in all my misery to beg. I do not believe I ever did. But I remember well a basement window at the downtown Delmonico's, the silent appearance of my ravenous face at which, at a certain hour in the evening, always evoked a generous supply of meat-bones and rolls from a white-capped cook.

In his desperation he made first acquaintance with the Five Points, the roughest neighborhood in New York. He slept in a doorway and wished he had never left Denmark. One rainy night he became thoroughly soaked and began shivering uncontrollably; all that saved him was a mongrel dog as miserable as he. Huddling close, each kept the other barely warm. After midnight Riis approached a police sergeant and asked for shelter in the Church Street station. The officer told him to leave the dog outside. "I pleaded for it in vain. There was no choice. To stay in the street was to perish." He fell into an exhausted stupor on the station floor, only to awaken hours later and discover that his one remaining treasure from Denmark— a gold locket he wore around his neck—had been stolen from under his shirt. When he complained to the sergeant, the officer growled that he must be a thief himself to have come by such a piece, and he told the doorman to throw him out. The doorman kicked him through the portal and down the stair. But on the stair waited Riis's canine friend, which, seeing his partner abused, bit the doorman. The doorman swore, angrily seized the dog by the hind legs, and battered its brains out upon the pavement.

Riis, already overwrought, nearly lost his mind. He hurled Danish curses and paving stones at the walls and windows of the station. The sergeant, apparently deciding that the doorman had overreacted and not wishing to provoke this lunatic further, instructed two patrolmen to escort him from the precinct. The officers marched him to the Hudson and put him on a ferry. Twenty minutes later he was in New Jersey, vowing never to return to New York.

He hoboed to upstate New York, where he had heard there was work in the woods for Scandinavians. He felled trees, harvested lake ice, and tried his hand at trapping. The following summer he joined an Irish construction crew on a railroad near Buffalo. "I had never done such work, and was not built for it. I did my best to keep up with the gang, but my chest heaved and my heart beat as though it would burst." Convinced that manual labor would kill him, he searched about for something else. Years earlier his father had edited a newspaper in Denmark, and he had occasionally helped. Now, despite a rudimentary grasp of English, he presented himself at the office of one of the Buffalo papers. The editor brusquely turned him away. He tried a second paper. The editor laughed scornfully and slammed the door in his face.

> For a moment I stood there stunned. His ascending steps on the stairs brought back my senses. I ran to the door, and flung it open. "You laugh!" I shouted, shaking my fist at him, standing halfway up the stairs, "you laugh now, but wait—" And then I got the grip of my temper and slammed the door in my turn. All the same, in that hour it was settled that I was to be a reporter. I knew it as I went out into the street.[4]

THE POOR NEIGHBORHOODS of New York were the ones the wealthy had left or hadn't yet reached. In the early nineteenth century, while money still clustered about Manhattan's foot, impecunious immigrants built cabins and shanties to the north of the developed district, along the Hudson in what would become Hell's Kitchen, on the East River near Fortieth Street, and in Harlem, then considered a distant village. As the older part of the city grew more crowded, as its inventory of buildings aged, and as the well-to-do migrated uptown, the poor filled in behind them. Land-lords converted single-family dwellings into apartments or boarding houses and filled garrets and basements and stables with renters besides. Factories and warehouses were likewise refitted; a brewery in the Five Points neighborhood became home to hundreds of Irish immigrants and African Americans.

Other buildings were constructed expressly for the new residents. Ten-ant houses, or tenements, were narrow and deep, to fit the lots, and three to six stories tall. The couple dozen apartments in a tenement each typically consisted of two rooms: a parlor with a window and a bedroom without. Designed for as many families as apartments, the tenements in practice usually held more, as the families themselves took in boarders or the land-lords simply rented floor space to individuals.[5]

The crowding in the tenements, the lack of ventilation and sanitation facilities (residents lined up to use outdoor privies and water pumps), and the general poverty of the residents contributed to recurrent outbreaks of disease. Until the mid-nineteenth century, infectious disease respected neither class nor income; yellow fever decimated Philadelphia in 1793, while an outbreak of cholera in 1832 prompted petitions to the White House for a national day of prayer (Andrew Jackson declined, judging it beyond his constitutional competence). But as cities improved their water supplies—New York's Croton aqueduct opened in 1842, to popular delirium—the worst of the water-borne epidemics diminished for those tied into the water systems.

For those not so blessed, high mortality rates persisted. An 1849 cholera outbreak prompted New York officials to commence a general cleanup. The many thousand pigs that rooted in the cellars and garbage of the poor neighborhoods were slaughtered or relocated. Cows were barred from the streets. Horses remained essential to transport, but contracts were let to clean their dung from the thoroughfares. Sewer pipes drained the effluent from various neighborhoods, starting with the wealthier ones. Garbage collection improved. Streets were paved.

The tenements were a harder problem. Repeated investigations publi-cized the crowded conditions in which the poor lived. An 1857 committee expressed shock at conditions in the Eleventh Ward. "It is astounding that everyone doesn't die of pestilence," the committee's report declared. An 1867 statute established minimum standards for tenements, requiring fire escapes, toilets (one per twenty residents), and better ventilation (via air shafts and more windows). During the following decade an architectural competition produced a model tenement, the "dumbbell," wide at the front and back, narrow in the middle to allow air and light to penetrate between adjacent buildings. The principles of the dumbbell informed an 1879 law that mandated a window for every tenement bedroom.[6]

"THE LAW HAS done what it could," Jacob Riis wrote a decade later. Riis had found his way back to New York as a journalist, a first of the breed of investigators derided, then respected, as "muckrakers." The label fit Riis particularly, for his investigations focused on the lives of those on the mudsill of society. Having dwelt there himself, he felt compelled to bring the plight of the lower classes to view. "Long ago it was said that 'one half of the world does not know how the other half lives,'" he wrote in 1890. "That was true then. It did not know because it did not care." It might not care still had the life of the lower half not intruded increasingly on that of the upper. Peasants in the Old World could starve invisibly, far from the manor; poverty in America elbowed wealth every day on the streets of New York and other cities.[7]

Yet wealth looked away and hurried by. Riis proposed to make it stop and look. With camera and pen he entered the slums of New York, and he invited readers and viewers to join him. "Down below Chatham Square, in the old Fourth Ward, where the cradle of the tenement stood, we shall find New York's Other Half at home," he wrote. "Leaving the Elevated Railroad where it dives under the Brooklyn Bridge at Franklin Square, scarce a dozen steps will take us where we wish to go. With its rush and roar echoing yet in our ears, we have turned the corner from prosperity to poverty. We stand upon the domain of the tenement." An arched gateway, a remnant of the neighborhood's better days, led to a dark alley. "The wolf knocks loudly at the gate in the troubled dreams that come to this alley, echoes of the day's cares. A horde of dirty children play about the dripping hydrant, the only thing in the alley that thinks enough of its chance to make the most of it: it is the best it can do. These are the children of the tenements, the growing generation of the slums; this is their home."

Riis guided the reader deeper. Blind Man's Alley got its name from a colony of blind beggars who had lived there as tenants of a blind landlord—

a capitalist who had made a fortune from his sightless tenants only to grow blind himself in old age. One of the tenement-reform laws had required a clean-up of the alley, resulting in the displacement of most of the blind beggars, who had dispersed to who knew where. Yet the clean-up was only relative, as Riis discovered. He was new at photography, and on one occasion, in one of the darker byways of a tenement in Blind Man's Alley, his clumsiness with the flash powder resulted in a minor explosion. As his eyes recovered from the dazzle, he realized he had set the walls on fire. He nearly panicked.

> There were six of us, five blind men and women who knew nothing of their danger, and myself, in an attic room with a dozen crooked, rickety stairs between us and the street, and as many households as helpless as the one whose guest I was all about us. The thought: how were they ever to be got out? made my blood run cold as I saw the flames creeping up the wall, and my first impulse was to bolt for the street and shout for help. The next was to smother the fire myself, and I did, with a vast deal of trouble. Afterward, when I came down to the street I told a friendly policeman of my trouble. For some reason he thought it rather a good joke, and laughed immoderately at my concern lest even then sparks should be burrowing in the rotten wall that might yet break out in flame and destroy the house with all that were in it. He told me why, when he found time to draw breath. "Why, don't you know," he said, "that house is the Dirty Spoon? It caught fire six times last winter, but it wouldn't burn. The dirt was so thick on the walls, it smothered the fire!"

Riis's tour led along another alley. "Be a little careful, please! The hall is dark and you might stumble over the children pitching pennies back there. Not that it would hurt them; kicks and cuffs are their daily diet. They have little else." The passageway snaked and dove down a flight of stairs. "You can feel your way, if you cannot see it." The air oppressed. "What would you have? All the fresh air that ever enters these stairs comes from the hall-door that is forever slamming, and from the windows of dark bedrooms that in turn receive from the stairs their sole supply of the elements God meant to be free, but man deals out with such niggardly hand." A woman passed with a pail, to be filled at the hydrant in the hall. "Hear the pump squeak! It is the lullaby of tenement-house babes. In summer, when a thousand thirsty throats pant for a cooling drink in this block, it is worked in vain. But the saloon, whose open door you passed in the hall, is always there. The smell of it has followed you up." Riis heard something. "Listen! That short hacking cough, that tiny, helpless wail—what do they mean? They mean that the soiled bow of white you saw on the door downstairs will have another story to tell—Oh! a sadly familiar story—before the day is at an end. The child is dying with measles. With half a chance it might have lived; but it had none. That dark bedroom killed it."

The Riis tour continued to "the Bend" of Mulberry Street, the most noisome of New York's slums. Here reformers had been at work for decades, trying to enforce the housing laws; here they had consistently discovered that the laws of supply and demand trumped the statutes of mere legislators. Landlords resisted the changes, claiming the right of property to a profit. Tenants resisted, for fear of displacement by the higher rents the changes would produce. Nature, it seemed, or at any rate capitalism, conspired to populate every nook and cranny of the Bend. "Incessant raids cannot keep down the crowds that make them their home. In the scores of back alleys, of stable lanes and hidden byways, of which the rent collector alone can keep track, they share such shelter as the ramshackle structures afford with every kind of abomination rifled from the dumps and ash-barrels of the city."

Capitalism had created the Bend, and it thrived within the Bend. Stalls and makeshift shops lined the alleys; a building called Bandit's Roost sheltered a veritable immigrants' exchange. The emporia were tiny—three feet by four, each scarcely large enough to hold the proprietor, with stock in a bucket or box or hanging from a board. One sold tobacco, another fish ("fish that never swam in American waters, or if they did, were never seen on an American fish-stand," Riis said), still another sausages of some sort ("what they are I never had the courage to ask"). The basic rule of American capitalism, of buyer beware, applied here no less than on Wall Street.

The men sit or stand in the streets, on trucks, or in the open doors of the saloons smoking black clay pipes, talking and gesticulating as if forever on the point of coming to blows. Near a particularly boisterous group, a really pretty girl with a string of amber beads twisted artlessly in the knot of her raven hair has been bargaining long and earnestly with an old granny, who presides over a wheel-barrow load of second-hand stockings and faded cotton yarn, industriously darning the biggest holes while she extols the virtues of her stock. One of the rude swains, with patched overalls tucked into his boots, to whom the girl's eyes have strayed more than once, steps up and gallantly offers to pick her out the handsomest pair, whereat she laughs and pushes him away with a gesture which he interprets as an invitation to stay; and he does, evidently to the satisfaction of the beldame, who forthwith raises her prices fifty per cent without being detected by the girl.[8]

IN NEW YORK and in every other American city, residents were sorted by various criteria. Wealth was an obvious one. The tenement districts Riis described on the Lower East Side were distinct from, and distinctly poorer than, the apartment-house neighborhoods uptown, which were themselves separate from, and markedly less luxurious than, the mansion enclave that grew up about the Vanderbilt palace. Boston's Beacon Hill and Back Bay housed the gentry of the old Puritan capital; Chicago's Gold Coast drew the merchants and industrialists of the inland entrepôt. In San Francisco the Stanfords and Huntingtons crowded Nob Hill, leaving the lowlands to the lesser classes.

This geographic segregation reflected, among other things, the state of transportation technology. When muscle power moved people, the wealthy tended to live within walking distance—measured by their own feet or their horses'—of their offices and mills. But as steam speeded traffic across the urban landscape, the wealthy typically preferred to separate work from residence, leaving the downtown districts to the tenements and their dwellers. In time many rich would move clear out of the cities, to the suburbs that sprang up along the train lines.

The urban sorting reflected other considerations as well. Immigrants clustered like with like. Every city developed ethnic neighborhoods: Irish-town, Kleindeutschland, Jewtown, Poletown, Little Italy, Chinatown. Much of this was voluntary: the mutual affinity of linguistic and cultural kin, the familial appeal of actual kin. Some was enforced: the refusal of landlords to rent to particular groups outside particular neighborhoods, violence perpetrated against group members who crossed understood boundaries.

Of the various immigrant neighborhoods, the Chinese districts were the most clearly—and rigidly—circumscribed. The formal effect of the Chinese Exclusion Act was to bar most new immigration from China, but its informal effect was to declare open season on Chinese already in America. Within months of the act's passage, what the Chinese called the "driving out" began. White hooligans waged racial war against Chinese across much of the West, killing twenty-eight in Rock Springs, Wyoming, thirty-one on the Snake River in eastern Washington, and smaller numbers elsewhere. Occasionally whites stuck up for their Chinese neighbors, if sometimes from selfish motives. A white gambler in Denver pulled six-guns on an anti-Chinese mob and told them to desist. "If you kill Wong, who in the hell will do my laundry?" he demanded. But in most places the mobs had their way. Rural communities of Chinese largely disappeared, their inhabitants driven off, their homes burned, their property seized by those doing the driving. Chinese in the cities were safer but not always safe: the entire Chinese community of Tacoma, Washington, was forcibly driven from that lumber port overnight. "They call it exclusion," one Chinese immigrant declared. "But it is not exclusion; it is extermination."[9]

Some of those who survived the violence returned to China, as their persecutors intended. Others went east, hoping for refuge in the cities there. Lee Chew, the boy who had discovered the promise of America at the feast his neighbor gave for his whole South China village, had emigrated to California, where he worked in mining and railroad construction before opening a laundry, a trade that attracted many Chinese on account of its minimal capital requirements and the comparative unimportance of fluency in English. Lee's business, based in a mining camp and shared with a partner, thrived until the anti-Chinese violence began. "All the miners came and broke up our laundry, chasing us out of town," he remembered. "They were going to hang us. We lost all our property and $365 in money, which members of the mob must have found." Lee had had the foresight to send most of his money to Chinese bankers in San Francisco; he now withdrew $500 and abandoned the West. He opened a laundry in Chicago, where he stayed for three years and increased his capital to $2,500. For reasons unclear he moved on to Detroit and then Buffalo. His laundry business eventually declined, the victim, ironically, of "American cheap labor," as he put it, and steam presses. So he moved again, to New York, and opened a shop in the Chinatown there.

He eventually returned to China, with thoughts of repatriating, but found he had grown too American to stay. He crossed the Pacific yet again. His emotions on approaching the Gold Mountain this time, though, were decidedly mixed. America afforded opportunity but withheld equality. Lee never got over his bitterness at the mistreatment he experienced in the wake of the Exclusion Act. "It was the jealousy of laboring men of other nationalities—especially the Irish—that raised all the outcry against the Chinese," he said. "No one would hire an Irishman, German, Englishman, or Italian when he could get a Chinese, because our countrymen are so much more honest, industrious, steady, sober and painstaking. . . . Irish fill the almshouses and prisons and orphan asylums; Italians are among the most dangerous of men; Jews are unclean and ignorant. Yet they are all let in, while Chinese, who are sober, or duly law abiding, clean, educated, and industrious, are shut out. There are few Chinamen in jails and none in the poor houses. There are no Chinese tramps or drunkards." Lee didn't blame all Americans, but he did blame their materialistic culture. "Americans make a mere practice of loving justice. They are all for money making, and they want to be on the strongest side always. They treat you as a friend while you are prosperous, but if you have a misfortune they don't know you."[10]

Of the urban refuges for the Chinese, San Francisco's Chinatown was the most prominent. Centered on Dupont Street (Grant Avenue after 1908) and running from California Street to Broadway, the seven-block district was home to between thirty and forty thousand Chinese in the 1880s. Few ghettos in Russia were more rigidly circumscribed. "In those days, the boundaries were from Kearny to Powell, and from California to Broadway," Wei Bat Liu, a longtime resident, recalled. "If you ever passed them and went out there, the white kids would throw stones at you. One time I remember going out and one boy started running after me, then a whole gang of others rushed out, too. We were afraid of them, and there were more of them than of us, so we would come right back." Living outside the district was nearly impossible. "I had trouble finding a good place in Chinatown," Wei Bat Liu continued. "It was so crowded; everyone was sleeping in double-decker beds and all that. So I went up just one block to Powell Street and asked in three places there. They told me no; no one had ever heard of Chinese living on Powell Street before. So we went back down to Chinatown, where all my cousins lived in one room. No bathroom, no kitchen."[11]

Not long after the Exclusion Act took effect, a special public school— the Oriental School—was established in Chinatown. By practice rather than by law, this became the required school for Chinese children (as well as Japanese and Korean). "I went there for two years," John Jeong remembered. "Then I wanted to change over to the American school on Geary Street, but after I was there for a week someone told me it was not for Chinese. We were only supposed to go to the Oriental School. So after that I just studied at home and worked in my brother's store."[12]

A 1790 federal law governing naturalization barred Asians—as not being "free white persons"—from eligibility for citizenship. Subsequent judicial decisions confirmed the ban, as did the 1868 Burlingame Treaty between the United States and China. California law and San Francisco practice largely excluded Chinese from participation in local politics. Consequently the Chinese developed a governance of their own. From the earliest days of the gold rush, Chinese immigrants had grouped themselves into clan and district associations. The associations afforded a measure of protection against the violence that characterized San Francisco's early days; they also provided social services to Chinese immigrants: job placement, medical care, language instruction. Allied together as the Chinese Six Companies (and eventually incorporated formally as the Chinese Consolidated Benevolent Association), the associations brought legal challenges against the various forms of anti-Chinese discrimination. The Six Companies arbitrated disputes among Chinese; the group was called the "supreme court of the Chinese in California." It even had a foreign policy: until the Chinese imperial government established a consulate in San Francisco in the late 1870s, the Six Companies filled the role.[13]

Operating beside the benevolent associations were the tongs. Modeled on the antigovernment secret societies that had taken root in China in the eighteenth century, the tongs emerged as working-class alternatives to the associations, which were dominated by the Chinese merchants. As challengers to the status quo, the tongs gravitated toward the less respectable kinds of business: gambling, prostitution, the sale of opium. The tongs had many white customers and so required the cooperation, or at least the acquiescence, of the white power structure; this they obtained by sharing their profits with police and elected officials. Crime being a business, the tongs struggled for market share. Sometimes the struggle involved competitive bribery, after the fashion of Cornelius Vanderbilt and Jay Gould. Sometimes it entailed efforts to take over the benevolent associations. The failure of the Six Companies to prevent passage of the 1882 Exclusion Act seriously diminished the prestige of that organization; in the wake of the failure the tongs seized control of the Six Companies. Often the competition gave rise to racketeering and extortion. Not infrequently it erupted in "tong wars" among the highbinders, or hatchet men, of the competing firms.[14]

The extent of the power of the tongs and the prevalence of vice in Chinatown were matters of constant dispute. Persons and parties antipathetic to the Chinese naturally emphasized the crime and violence, conflating the associations with the tongs and linking both to the infamous Triad gangs of China. Many Chinese themselves lamented the power of the tongs, although, for reasons of self-preservation, they rarely spoke out publicly.

Yet for Chinese struggling to get ahead the tongs serve a vital purpose. Lew Wah Get wasn't unbiased in the matter, having been an officer in one of the tongs. But he explained the basic operation:

> If you wanted to join a tong, you had to have a friend who was already a member sponsor you. He had to swear to your good character, and even then the tong would investigate your name for one month before they let you in. This was the rule for everybody. You could be a cook, a waiter, work in a gambling house or do any kind of work, but you had to have a friend to sponsor you. And once you were a member, you were on your honor to follow all the rules. If you did, then the tong would protect you. If anyone threatened you, or interfered with your business, the tong would help you out. Or if you couldn't find a job, the tong would send you someplace, or introduce you to someone who could give you work. This was why so many people wanted to join.

Lew Wah Get didn't deny that the tongs played rough. "Fighting was a very frequent issue. If members of our tong had been threatened or their businesses tampered with, naturally we had to take steps to protect them. Or suppose another party owed us money and refused to pay; we might decide to bear a grudge and force retribution." But the Chinese in America didn't have many alternatives. "Society at that time was very dangerous, you know."[15]

A PROVERB FROM medieval Europe held that "city air makes a man free." So it seemed to one group in particular in Gilded Age America.

Among the residents of New York's Lower East Side were an indeterminate number of individuals who did not fit easily into any of the communities recognized by respectable society. How these persons identified themselves varied from one to the next. Some called themselves "queers," others "fairies" or "faggots." The terms had different meanings, connoting both more and less than the later terms "homosexual" and "gay." But they all signified persons who refused to honor majority notions of proper gender behavior.[16]

Gay men found life in New York more tolerable than life in many other communities. The large number of effectively single men, including immigrants whose wives hadn't yet joined them in the new country, provided a population into which gay men might easily blend. And that large population of single men supported a sex and entertainment industry whose general transgression of moral norms afforded a cover to the particular transgressions of gay men. Dance halls and saloons catering to gay customers flourished among the many "resorts" in the Bowery district; Paresis Hall, at Fifth Street, was well known both to those who sought it out as a place where gay men might comfortably congregate and to those who wished to avoid it for the same reason. The police monitored the clubs and occasionally raided them, partly in response to pressure from such moral reformers as Charles Parkhurst, the Presbyterian minister who headed the City Vigilance League, but partly as a reminder to the club operators to keep up with the payments that normally kept the cops away.

For many gay persons the Bowery, the Tenderloin, the Rialto, and a few other neighborhoods served as essential gathering grounds. Wealthy men and women might find privacy in their homes or exclusive clubs, but the crowded conditions of working-class life forced the poor and even those of moderate means onto the street and into the dance halls. Public parks, too, served as places where gay men could meet other gay men. What a slightly later generation (of the 1920s) would call "cruising" could be done in relative anonymity, which was the closest many gay men could come to privacy. In some respects the situation of gay people wasn't much different from that of non-wealthy heterosexual couples, who likewise found privacy scarce in a crowded city. One vice squad agent said of Central Park, "We didn't see anything else but couples laying on grass, or sitting on benches, kissing and hugging each other . . . especially in the dark sections which are poorly lighted." Gay couples had to compete for the darkest corners and most sheltered alcoves. And they did so knowing that the price they would pay upon being discovered might be greater than that paid by heterosexuals, for whom illegally indecent behavior was defined more narrowly than it was for gay couples.[17]

Gay people came to New York for the same reasons straight people did, but for another reason as well. Not all knew before coming that the city offered an active, if partially covert, life for gay people, but most knew that the places they were leaving did not. Small towns in America were generally hostile to homosexual behavior; many foreign countries were equally so. A German gay man explained that he had been arrested in his homeland for sodomy. "I was condemned to imprisonment. My social position was totally destroyed, my family brought to sorrow and shame." Upon release he discerned no alternative to emigration. "In consequence of the disgrace which came upon me in my fatherland I am obliged to reside in America." And once in America he discovered that New York offered better refuge than almost anywhere else.[18]

Gay culture was considerably less well defined than the various ethnic cultures of New York, partly because the gay community crossed ethnic (and racial) lines but also because homosexual behavior connoted homosexual identity less clearly than it would at a later time. Even so, the gay experience mirrored the ethnic experience in certain ways. The gay neighborhoods, like the ethnic neighborhoods, were recognized as distinctive places, and they were treated with the same mixture of fascination and repugnance that often characterized attitudes of non-members toward the ethnic cultures. Straight men and women seeking an evening's thrill would visit the gay saloons and clubs to be shocked and titillated. And the gay community provided some of the same newcomer-assistance services for which the ethnic communities were famous. One German Jew, a gay man, didn't reach New York till the twentieth century, but his experience was certainly shared by earlier arrivals. He recalled not knowing anyone or having any idea how to get started in his new home. Someone told him that gay men gathered at the Soldiers and Sailors Monument on Riverside Drive. "I met a man there and we started talking. He was a Harvard man and taught ethical culture." The two commenced an affair, which lasted two years and introduced the new man to all aspects of American life. "That was the best contact I made."[19]

Part Four

THE FINEST GOVERNMENT
MONEY CAN BUY

Chapter 12

SCHOOL FOR SCANDAL

Before he became a Dakota rancher, Theodore Roosevelt took a step even more astonishing to his neighbors on New York's Upper East Side: he entered politics. "The men I knew best were the men in the clubs of social pretension and the men of cultivated taste and easy life," Roosevelt remembered.

> When I began to make inquiries as to the whereabouts of the local Republican Association and the means of joining it, these men—and the big business men and lawyers also—laughed at me and told me that politics were "low"; that I would find them run by saloon-keepers, horse-car conductors, and the like, and not by men with any of whom I would come in contact outside; and, moreover, they assured me that the men I met would be rough and brutal and unpleasant to deal with. I answered that if this were so it merely meant that the people I knew did not belong to the governing class, and that the other people did— and that I intended to be one of the governing class.[1]

Roosevelt chose the Republican party over the Democrats for two reasons. The first was that for a Northern Unionist whose childhood prayers during the Civil War had beseeched the Almighty to "grind the Southern troops to powder," the Democrats were preeminently the party of the rebellion. The second reason was that for a New York City boy who came of age in the decade after the Civil War, the Democrats were the party of Tammany Hall and Boss Tweed.[2]

There was irony in Roosevelt's damning the Democrats for disunion and Tammany together, for during the war the Tammany Hall Democrats (named for their traditional meeting place) were the loyal members of the party. Many New York Democrats harkened to Mayor Fernando Wood, who urged that the city secede from the state and the Union to form a political entity poised between North and South. Tammany, by contrast, stood firm for the Union. And none stood firmer than William Marcy Tweed, the man the Tammany Democrats made their chairman at the beginning of 1863.

Tweed was Scot by ancestry, his forebears having borrowed the name of the River Tweed before heading to America in the eighteenth century. Tweed's father crafted furniture in New York and sent young Bill to boarding school in New Jersey to study accounting. The boy learned quickly, and the father helped set him up in a business that made brushes. At twenty-one he married his childhood sweetheart; the newlyweds moved in with her father not far from the brush factory on Pearl Street.

Like most political parties at most times, the New York Democratic party was on the lookout for fresh talent, and Tweed seemed a likely prospect. His business allowed him freedom to campaign and serve not readily available to wage workers. And his physical presence—he was a tall, burly fellow, with bright blue eyes, a hearty laugh, and a confidence-inspiring handshake—was just what the party historically of the people required. Tammany's talent scouts invited him to run for city alderman; after hesitating he assented. His first race failed but his second succeeded, and in 1852 the Seventh Ward sent him to join the "forty thieves," as the aldermen were irreverently but not inaccurately called. Tweed didn't immediately recognize his own peculiar genius, and the following year he let himself be nominated and then elected to the United States Congress. Few eras in American political history have been more fraught for good and ill than the mid-1850s, with Congress overturning the Missouri Compromise and Kansas dissolving into civil war, but Tweed found Washington boring and he returned to New York after a single term. Thereafter he devoted himself to local politics, which proved to be his true calling. He won election to the school commission in 1856, the county board of super-visors in 1858, the street commission in 1861. In the process he discovered that the offices one held mattered less than the friends one cultivated. When those friends offered to nominate him for chairman of the Tam-many general committee, he happily accepted and handily won.

His first task was repairing the damage—literal and figurative—caused by the 1863 draft riots. New York governor Horatio Seymour urged the War Department to suspend the draft in New York, lest more riots erupt. Many New York City officials, heeding their Irish constituents, sec-onded the appeal. The War Department not surprisingly rejected the idea. Tweed brokered a compromise. Focusing on the part of the draft law that so provoked the rioters—the loophole exempting those men rich enough to pay the three-hundred-dollar commutation fee—he proposed a deal whereby the city would float a loan to pay the fee for anyone whose absence at the front would demonstrably burden his family, and it would pay the three hundred dollars directly to those men who chose to answer the call. Tweed and a fellow county supervisor, Republican Orison Blunt, gathered local support for the plan and took it to Washington. Secretary of War Stanton wasn't thrilled at this run around the federal law, but neither did he relish having to open a Manhattan front in the war, and he grudg-ingly agreed. Tweed and Tammany implemented the new policy with hardly a hitch.[3]

His role in the matter earned him a reputation as a man who could get things done, efficiently and honestly. "The Supervisors' Committee are now holding daily sessions, and are performing their duties with eminent satisfaction to all parties," the New York Times editorialized. "No money, no trust was ever more honestly administered than the loan of the Board of Supervisors."[4]

Tweed continued to get things done, albeit less efficiently and hon-estly, after the war ended. By then his hold on Tammany was complete, the product of his demonstrated patriotism and his deft use of patronage. As party boss he controlled hundreds of positions in the party organization; with these he expanded his influence to the city and county governments. Tammany's foot soldiers—"ward heelers," they were called, for the miles they put on their shoes—turned out the vote with verve and imagination. A Tammany loyalist afterward lamented how far things had fallen since the glory days of Tweed. "Elections nowadays are sissy affairs," he said.

"Nobody gets killed any more, and the ambulances and patrol wagons stay in their garages. . . . It was wonderful to see my men slug the opposition to preserve the sanctity of the ballot." Art complemented the strong arm. Another Tammany captain explained that the most valued voters grew beards before the balloting:

> When you've voted them with their whiskers on, you take them to a barber and scrape off the chin fringe. Then you vote them again with the side lilacs and a mustache. Then to a barber again, off comes the sides and you vote them a third time with the mustache. If that ain't enough and the box can stand a few more ballots, clean off the mustache and vote them plain face. That makes one of them good for four votes.

In fact this functionary was being modest; subsequent investigations revealed some voters casting as many as twenty ballots. And after the voting took place, Tammany operatives counted the votes to ensure the totals came out right. Tweed later declared candidly, "The ballots made no result; the counters made the result."[5]

As the grip of Tweed and his friends—the "Tweed ring," to its critics—on New York City tightened, some of their opponents retreated to Albany to mount a counterattack in the state legislature. Tweed riposted by getting himself elected to the state senate and establishing a branch office on the upper Hudson. "In Albany he had the finest quarters at the Delavan," journalist and reformer George W. Curtis remembered.

> And when he came into the great dining-room at dinner-time, and looked at all the tables thronged with members of the Legislature and the lobby, he had a benignant, paternal expression, as of a patriarch pleased to see his retainers happy. It was a magnificent rendering of Fagin and his pupils. You could imagine him trotting up and down in the character of an unsuspicious old gentleman with his handkerchief hanging out of his pocket, that his scholars might show their skill in prigging a wipe. He knew which of that cheerful company was the Artful Dodger and which Charley Bates. And he never doubted that he could buy every man in the room if he were willing to pay the price.[6]

To complement his legislative influence, Tweed purchased the services of several judges. George Barnard of the state supreme court became the most notorious of the Tweed jurists on account of his utter shamelessness and wry sense of humor. Barnard examined several attorneys seeking admission to the bar; these included a state senator. A contemporary recalled the conversation:

> "Senator, do you know there is such a thing as the State Constitution?"
>
> "Yes, sir."
>
> "If a proposed bill came up for consideration, which you knew was in violation of the Constitution, what would you do?"
>
> "I would move to suspend the Constitution, same as we sometimes suspend the rules of the Senate to pass a bill."
>
> "Stand aside," said the Judge with a smile. "You will make a profound lawyer."

Next candidate.

> "Now, sir, if you had a claim for a client of $50,000 against the City, what would be the first step you would take to recover it?"
>
> "I would go and see Bill Tweed."
>
> "You will make your mark as a Corporation lawyer."[7]

By the late 1860s the Tweed machine was running smoothly. Money greased the gears, collected from all who had to do business with the city. Railroads wishing to extend their lines or refurbish their stations applied for permission from the appropriate board and paid for the privilege; Tweed and his cronies split the bribe. Merchants bidding to provision the city included kickbacks to the ring in their bids. Lawyers trying cases before Tweed judges slipped gratuities to the bench, which passed a portion along. Bankers underwriting bonds for the city and county added a margin for the boss.

The money supported Tammany's electioneering. Some voters were simply bribed; others responded to the services Tammany provided. Immigrants, especially, needed help adjusting to life in the great city; Tammany guided the greenhorns to housing, jobs, medical care, and other essentials.

"I can always get a job for a deserving man," Tammany wheelhorse George Washington Plunkitt explained. "I know every big employer in the district—and in the whole city, for that matter—and they ain't in the habit of saying no to me when I ask them for a job." Emergency assistance was a Tammany specialty. "If there's a fire in Ninth, Tenth, or Eleventh Avenue, for example, any hour of the day or night, I'm usually there with some of my election district captains as soon as the fire engines," Plunkitt said. "If a family is burned out, I don't ask whether they are Republicans or Democrats, and I don't refer them to the Charity Organization Society, which would investigate their case in a month or two and decide they were worthy of help about the time they are dead from starvation. I just get quarters for them, buy clothes for them if their clothes were burned up, and fix them up until they get things running again." All Tammany asked in exchange for its generosity was loyalty on election day. It was rarely disappointed. "It's philanthropy, but it's politics too—mighty good politics," Plunkitt said. "The poor are the most grateful people in the world."[8]

Tweed and his cronies considered themselves agents of democracy, and some of them accounted their boodling nothing more than democracy's price. During the next century American democracy would formally incorporate into the emerging welfare state many of the services provided by Tammany (and similar machines in other cities). When it did, the sponsoring party, typically the Democrats, would be rewarded with much the same loyalty bestowed upon Tammany. But for now Tweed and company were happy to keep their arrangements informal. Plunkitt dismissed much of the peculation as "honest graft" hardly worth noting. "Let me explain by examples," he said.

My party's in power in the city, and it's going to undertake a lot of public improvements. Well, I'm tipped off, say, that they're going to lay out a new park at a certain place. I see my opportunity and I take it. I go to that place and I buy up all the land I can in the neighborhood. Then the board of this or that makes its plan public, and there is a rush to get my land, which nobody cared particular for before. Ain't it perfectly honest to charge a good price and make a profit on my investment and foresight? Of course it is. That's honest graft.[9]

Other graft was less honest, even by Tammany standards, and rather more spectacular. Tweed inherited plans to build a new county courthouse, which had been authorized before the Civil War at an estimated cost of $250,000. The war stalled construction, leaving Tweed and his partners to complete it. He persuaded the city to add another million to the authorization, on grounds that the building should embody the ambitions of America's greatest city. Construction recommenced, but the additional million didn't go far enough, and Tweed talked the city into another $800,000, and then another $300,000, and another $300,000, and another $500,000. The striking thing about all this was that there was little to show for the money spent. Civic-minded groups demanded an investigation. Tweed and company patiently explained that they, too, were wondering what had happened to the money and in fact had begun an investigation of their own. But in the interests of transparency they acceded to the second investigation.

Tweed's cooperativeness should have put the watchdogs on guard, for not only did the investigative committee clear the contractors and the officials involved, it submitted reimbursement requisitions that were shockingly irregular themselves. The total for twelve days' work came to more than $18,000, including $6,000 to have the committee's report printed by a publishing company controlled by Tweed. The reformers retreated in frustration lest they line the ring's pockets further.

Convinced they were untouchable, the ring engineered further appropriations from the city and some from the state. By 1871 some $13 million had been sunk into the courthouse, which still wasn't finished.

The details of the fraud were mind-boggling. A furniture maker received $180,000 for three tables and forty chairs (one for each thief). Carpet weavers and layers got $350,000. Plumbing and lighting fixtures totaled $1.5 million. Safes ate up $400,000. The windows of the courthouse cost $8,000 apiece. Brooms and assorted cleaning supplies ran to $41,000. Services were rewarded no less generously. A lithographer received $360,000 for one month's work. A plasterer got $500,000 for interior work, and then $1 million to repair what he had done. A carpenter made $800,000. Smaller payments went to lesser individuals, including a court clerk whose highest degree was from Sing Sing, an interpreter who couldn't read or write, and several dead men.

Needless to say, the recipients of this largesse didn't retain all their booty. The standard kickback was two for one: two dollars to the ring for every dollar the contractor kept. Tweed and his cronies pocketed millions, making them peers in profit of certain magnates of the private sector.[10]

BUT THE BARBECUE couldn't last forever. Tweed had long been pestered by Thomas Nast, an editorial cartoonist for *Harper's Weekly* who had honed his pen drawing pictures of heroic Union soldiers and dastardly Confederates. He celebrated Christmas in 1862 by showing Santa Claus visiting soldiers in their winter camps. The image attracted sufficient praise that Nast brought Santa back in subsequent years, giving him a round belly, a white beard, and the other characteristics by which the old elf became known. Yet there was always an edge to Nast's drawings. His first Santa held a dancing doll with a string attached not to its pate but to its neck; the effigy being lynched bore a striking resemblance to Jefferson Davis. At war's end Nast needed a new villain and hit upon Tweed, who, perhaps from a law of conservation of artistic energy, was drawn to look like an evil twin of Nast's Santa.

Nast's pictures formed an effective counterpoint to editorials by various daily and weekly newspapers, of which New York City then had dozens. In the summer of 1871, the *New York Times* began publishing specifics of the courthouse fraud, leaked to it by a member of the Tweed ring who thought he'd been shortchanged in the grafting. "The Secret Accounts—Proofs of Undoubted Frauds Brought to Light," the banner headline proclaimed. The publisher of the *Times*, George Jones, dribbled the information out over several weeks, partly so he could confirm details of the story but mostly to maintain the boost in circulation the story provided. The ring responded by offering Jones half a million dollars to stop. He rejected the offer both on principle and on a reckoning that the story was worth at least that much to his bottom line. Thomas Nast, lampooning Tweed and the ring more savagely than ever, likewise received an offer of a half million, in his case to study art in Europe for a year or so. Nast took a bit longer to say no—a refusal that dismayed Tweed more than Jones's had. "I don't care a straw for your newspaper articles," he explained. "My constituents don't know how to read, but they can't help seeing them damned pictures."[11]

The editorial campaign against Tweed mobilized various aspects of the electorate. Middle-class reformers took offense at the corruption per se, calling the ring a blight on democracy. Persons uneasy with surging immigration interpreted Tweed's rise as evidence of the pernicious effect of ignorant foreigners. The anti-Catholic crowd—which included the rabidly Rome-baiting Nast—resented the influence of Irish Americans in the Tammany coalition and hoped Tweed's fall would restore the Protestant Anglo-Saxonism of yore. Tweed's professional rivals anticipated his ouster as clearing a space for themselves at the trough. Particular politicians, including gubernatorial aspirant Samuel J. Tilden, hoped to leap from Tweed's back into office.

Tweed strove to appear above the furor. When an out-of-town reporter asked him if the allegations of corruption were true, he responded, "This is not a question one gentleman ought to put to another." Diarist George Templeton Strong marveled at the man's composure. "Tweed's impudent serenity is sublime," Strong wrote. "Were he not a supreme scoundrel, he would be a great man." But at least once the mask slipped. "The *Times* has been saying all the time I have no brains," Tweed told a correspondent for the rival *Sun*. "Well, I'll show Jones that I have brains. . . . I tell you, sir, if this man Jones had said the things he has said about me, twenty-five years ago, he wouldn't be alive now. But, you see, when a man has a wife and children, he can't do such a thing. I would have killed him."

The anti-Tammany forces rallied against the ring in 1871 state and city elections and landed some stinging blows, but they suffered a setback the following year when Tweed transported roughnecks to Rochester, where the state Democratic party was meeting. Tweed told the convention that the troubles in New York City were a local affair and that for the state party to intervene would simply invite trouble from which Republicans alone would benefit. His thugs nodded ominous assent. The convention backed Tweed's candidates.

The boss looked toward the 1872 elections with satisfaction, even smugness. Let scandal-seeking editors and dyspeptic reformers rail, he said. "I feel perfectly free to appeal to a higher tribunal, and have no fear of the result." As things turned out, fear would have been appropriate. The tribunal of the people rousted Tammany from office.[12]

The defeat left the ring suddenly vulnerable. "Tweed and his gang are doomed," Samuel Tilden promised. "Before many days pass it will be made so hot for the arch robber that New York will not hold him." Emboldened prosecutors brought criminal charges and civil suits against the ring, which now lacked the power to fend them off. Several of the conspirators fled to foreign soil; Tweed made his stand in court. He hired the best lawyers in New York, including young Elihu Root, who threw procedural hurdles in the prosecution's way for more than a year. A first trial ended in a hung jury, prompting rumors that Tweed had bribed one or more of the jurors. A second trial yielded guilty verdicts on over two hundred counts and a cumulative sentence of twelve years—a modest total that evinced the undeveloped contemporary attitude toward white-collar crime. Yet Tweed beat most of this rap, too, for an appeals court determined that the separate sentences shouldn't accumulate, and he was released after a year in prison.

By now Tilden was governor and aiming for the White House, and he wasn't about to let Tweed walk. Tilden's allies rearrested Tweed and brought a civil suit in the name of the people of the state of New York. Tweed made himself comfortable at the Ludlow Street jail, paying for first-class treatment and persuading the warden to let him take dinners at home with his wife and relatives while the jail guards waited outside. During one such dinner Tweed disappeared. A workman's wagon carried him to the shore of the Hudson, and a rowboat transported him across to New Jersey. He hid there under an assumed name, awaiting the outcome of his current trial. When the jury found him liable for six million dollars in damages to the state, he slipped out of New Jersey aboard a schooner to Florida. A fishing boat transported him to Cuba, still a colony of Spain, which lacked an extradition treaty with the United States. Tweed hoped to cross the Atlantic and disappear. "I should have lived in Spain my whole life," he said later. "I had designed to go into some quiet part, like Catalonia or somewhere living was inexpensive."

Unluckily for Tweed, Cuba was in rebellion against Spain, and the insurgents were being armed and reinforced from the United States. The Spanish government wanted the Grant administration to curtail the flow of weapons and filibusters, and to that end it cooperated with Washington whenever possible. Learning that Tweed had left Cuba for Spain, the Spanish government alerted its customs officials to watch for the American criminal. No one in Spain had a photograph of the fugitive, but a recent copy of *Harper's Weekly* carried a new cartoon by Nast, showing Tweed in prison stripes stealing New York's future, represented by two young boys he held by the scruff of their necks. A Spanish subscriber furnished the picture to the authorities, who passed it along to the customs men, who may or may not have believed they were on the lookout for an infamous kidnapper or child molester. In any case they caught Tweed and remanded him to America.[13]

The story soon ended. Tweed offered to testify against his cronies in exchange for leniency, but he couldn't generate much interest. Tilden had moved on to other battles, notably a tussle with Rutherford Hayes for the White House, and authorities in New York City were happy to blame Tweed for all the graft and corruption of the previous decade. No one wanted to bargain a plea with him. Anyway, the old boss was ailing. Flight, worry, diabetes, and finally pneumonia broke his once lusty constitution. He died in the Ludlow Street jail in April 1877 at the age of fifty-four.

HARDLY ANYONE NOTICED, for by that time the nation was awash in political scandal. Andrew Johnson had scandalized the country, or at least the North, by defying Congress over Reconstruction and especially over the Tenure of Office Act, a measure designed by its drafters to force a confrontation between the Democratic executive and the Republican legislature. The Republicans won the first round, impeaching Johnson in the House of Representatives. Johnson won, or rather survived, the second round, avoiding conviction in the Senate by a single vote. But the exercise served the purpose of the Radical Republicans in Congress, who seized control of Reconstruction from the emasculated Johnson and imposed their will on the occupied South. The state governments established under Radical Reconstruction promoted the welfare of the freedmen but in the process gained reputations for corruption, eventually tarnishing the whole enterprise with sufficient scandal that the former white ruling classes recaptured power—in a takeover proudly called "Redemption" by its participants and partisans—while the North stood aside.

By then Ulysses Grant was president. Grant made the ideal candidate for the first postwar election: a war hero with indistinct views on most political issues. His personal reputation was unsullied by scandal save what followed from the occasional bender. But Lincoln had absolved Grant of blame, reportedly saying that if he knew what kind of whiskey Grant drank he'd send a barrel to each of his other generals. Grant accepted the 1868 Republican nomination with the statement "Let us have peace." On that slogan—and that slogan alone, as he declined to campaign or even speak on his own behalf—he swept into the White House over Democrat Horatio Seymour.

For a time Grant avoided most taint of scandal. During his first term—with the exception of the Gould-Fisk gold conspiracy, which touched the Treasury and Grant's family but not the president himself— the greatest scandals involved members of Congress. Charles Dana at the *New York Sun* begrudged George Jones and the *New York Times* their Tweed scoop, and he set his hounds to sniff out something comparable. What they turned up delighted Dana and dismayed shareholders in the Union Pacific Railroad and taxpayers who had underwritten the construction of the transcontinental line. "The King of Frauds," ran the *Sun*'s main head on September 4, 1872. "How the Credit Mobilier Bought Its Way through Congress . . . Colossal Bribery . . . Congressmen Who Have Robbed the People and Who Now Support the National Robber . . . How Some Men Get Fortunes . . . Princely Gifts by the Chairmen of Committees in Congress." The article delineated the career of Crédit Mobilier, the construction company that did most of the road building for the Union Pacific and collected most of the profits. The existence of the company was neither unusual (other railroads and infrastructure contractors employed similar subcontractors) nor secret (the *Sun* story was based on public testimony more than a year old). And administration supporters detected a striking coincidence between the timing of the article and the approaching presidential election. Jones's pro-Grant *Times* airily dismissed the *Sun* report as "The Crédit Mobilier Slander."[14]

But the story had legs, and after the election Congress conducted an investigation. The charges, adjusted for partisanship, fell into two categories, the first alleging fraud against the public in the construction of the Union Pacific and the second bribery of members of Congress. The fraud charges contended that the railroad had taken the loans and land proffered by the government and converted these into liquid assets siphoned off by the shareholders in Crédit Mobilier. Although these charges would have the longest life, leading to a general impression that the Pacific railroad was a giant swindle, they turned out to be impossible to prove. No one, not even the directors of the Union Pacific, could account for all the resources and funds devoted to the road's construction. This inability reflected a certain amount of fraud, to be sure, but no evidence was adduced to show that the fraud was much greater than large projects typically produced. (It was incontrovertibly *less*, as a ratio of theft to expenditure, than the fraud perpetrated by the Tweed ring in New York.) To a large degree the failure to find all the money expended on the Union Pacific simply reflected the scale of the project and the fact that nothing like it had ever been attempted. Huge corporations were a recent and still evolving phenomenon; accounting practices capable of monitoring their activities lagged behind the institutions themselves.

In any event, the second set of allegations—involving bribery of members of Congress—was much juicier. The *Sun* article included a list of congressmen said to have received shares of Crédit Mobilier. The list included James G. Blaine, James Garfield, Schuyler Colfax, and Henry Wilson, and the number of shares linked to each individual ranged from 2,000 to 3,000. Knowledgeable readers immediately questioned the numbers, as the total said to have been distributed to the congressmen nearly equaled the entire issue of the company. But knowledgeable readers were a distinct minority, and even after the obvious correction was made—the figures represented the par value in dollars of the shares, not the number of shares—the bribery allegation titillated a public attuned by the Tweed scandal and the Gould-Fisk gold conspiracy to think the worst of public officials. Nor were these just any public officials: Blaine was the current speaker of the House, Colfax had been speaker at the time and was currently vice president, Wilson was the current Republican nominee for vice president, and Garfield was chair of the House appropriations committee.

Yet the list of names was riddled with errors, too. Oakes Ames, the Massachusetts congressman who had promoted the Pacific railroad, had compiled a list of congressmen who might be interested in purchasing shares of Crédit Mobilier. Blaine and some of the others on the list had rejected the offer, from propriety, perhaps, but also because it seemed a poor investment. Wilson had accepted the offer but subsequently sold his shares. The fact that the list included not a single Democrat added to the suspicions that the exposé was an election-season ploy.

But as the congressional investigation began, the public learned that there was fire behind at least some of the smoke. The star witness was Ames, no longer in Congress but still connected to the Union Pacific. "You could have heard a pin drop when Mr. Ames produced his red morocco covered memorandum book," a reporter observed. Ames's log of the Crédit Mobilier transactions exonerated Blaine; confirmed the involvement of Colfax, Garfield, and some others; and, while narrowing the scope of the scandal, lent it substance it had previously lacked.[15]

Questions remained, however, as to the degree of culpability of those involved. Ames himself professed to see nothing wrong in what he had done. "There is no law and no reason, legal or moral, why a member of Congress should not own stock in a road any more than why he should not own a sheep when the price of wool is to be affected by the tariff," he said. Former congressman Benjamin Boyer of Pennsylvania, one of Ames's investors, adopted a similar view. "I had no idea of wrong in the matter," he said. "Nor do I see how it concerns the public. . . . And as the investment turned out to be profitable, my only regret is that it was no larger in amount."[16]

Neither could anyone demonstrate, even of those who accepted Ames's offer, that it had purchased him votes he wouldn't have received anyway. Pennsylvania's William Kelley waxed indignant at the suggestion that his support could be purchased so cheaply (prompting speculation that it might be purchased more dearly). But most of the men on Ames's list were demonstrated friends of the railroad. The Crédit Mobilier shares might have been thanks for past favors rather than, or at least in addition to, enticement to future ones. Whether such thanks was illegal was unclear.

Yet something shady had happened; why else had Colfax, most conspicuously, at first denied involvement? "If Mr. Colfax's explanation is true, he is the victim of a train of circumstantial evidence almost unparalleled in judicial history," the *New York Tribune* jibed. The investigative committee, at a loss as to what to do, rendered its version of a Solomonic judgment. It concluded that Ames was guilty of having given bribes but that no one was guilty of receiving them. Declaring that Ames had brought the House into "contempt and disgrace" and had committed offenses of a "dangerous character," it nonetheless concluded that the other legislators neither were "aware of the object of Mr. Ames" nor "had any other purpose in taking this stock than to make a profitable investment."[17]

The reaction to the report mirrored its ambivalent content. Ames expressed outrage at being singled out. "I alone am to be offered up to appease a public clamor," he said. He added, "It's like the man in Massachusetts who committed adultery, and the jury brought in a verdict that he was guilty as the devil, but that the woman was as innocent as an angel." The *New York Herald* was upset that the others had got off. "Good government has received a deadly stab," it said. The previously skeptical *New York Times* was now even more skeptical of the whole business, but for the opposite reason. "To refuse to censure the holders of that stock is to say that the Congressional standard of morals is not high enough to condemn it."[18]

The scandal, however, wasn't without effect. Several politicians exited the affair badly wounded. Schuyler Colfax never recovered; James Blaine recovered but not fully. Oakes Ames dropped dead months later, from a combination of anger, embarrassment, and arterial blockage.

ALCOHOL AND EXCISE taxes had long been a problem for Americans, in part because liquor was (and is) so tempting to tax. The Sugar Act of 1764 helped trigger the American Revolution not because it jeopardized the colonists' candy but because it threatened their rum, into which the sugar—molasses—was distilled. The Whiskey Rebellion of 1794 provoked George Washington into reprising his role as horseback general, this time against tax-resisting Pennsylvania distillers.

Whiskey retained its popularity after the Civil War with both the drinking public and the taxing public officials. But now a new ingredient entered the cocktail, in the form of industrial capitalism. Distilling had become a big business, and distillers discovered a commensurately large interest in avoiding the taxes the government levied. A group of distillers in St. Louis might not have been more venal than distillers elsewhere, but they had better access to the Grant administration. General John McDonald was an old friend and wartime comrade of the president, and a favorite of Mrs. Grant's family besides. His connections accounted for his appointment as collector of internal revenue for the St. Louis district, which comprised seven midwestern states. McDonald had friends in St. Louis with allies in distilling; introductions were made and McDonald let out that he shared the whiskey men's view that their taxes were too high. He agreed to reduce the effective rate by undercounting the kegs; they demonstrated their appreciation monetarily. Doubtless both parties told themselves— accurately enough—that they weren't alone in their rebate arrangement.

But, like John Rockefeller and the railroads during this same period, they agreed that their deal should be kept quiet.

For a while it was. By the mid-1870s, however, the discrepancy between the number of barrels the distillers were shipping and the number they were paying tax on was so obvious as to elude only the willfully blind. In February 1875 the editor of the *St. Louis Democrat*, George Fishback, wrote to the secretary of the Treasury, Benjamin Bristow, that the tax evasion in Missouri had gotten out of control. "If the Secretary wants to break up the powerful ring which exists here," Fishback said, "I can give him the name of a man who, if he receives the necessary authority and is assured of absolute secrecy about the matter, will undertake to do it. . . . I will guarantee success."

Benjamin Bristow was a recent addition to Grant's cabinet. He had served in the Justice Department as solicitor general and had entertained hopes of becoming attorney general. But after Treasury secretary William Richardson came under fire for tax farming—for providing information on tax delinquents to bounty hunters, who then shook down the deadbeats in exchange for part of the payoff—Grant had to replace him. Bristow, with a reputation for belligerent incorruptibility, seemed just the person.

He accepted George Fishback's offer. Myron Colony, the man Fishback had referred to, was a tireless reporter who knew everyone with anything on the whiskey dodge. He compiled a huge dossier on McDonald, the distillers, and their many accomplices and delivered it to Bristow. The Treasury secretary summoned McDonald to Washington and showed him the evidence against him. McDonald confessed but apparently—testimony differed on this point—requested amnesty in exchange for a promise to collect and hand over all the unpaid taxes. To strengthen his request he warned that prosecution of himself and the distillers would gravely damage the Republican party and the president.

Bristow had no intention of letting McDonald cop a plea, and he proceeded with the investigation. At first he received the support of the president. "Let no guilty man escape," Grant declared, although adding the curious qualifier "if it can be avoided." But when the trail led to Orville Babcock, a Grant staffer from the war and currently a White House aide, the president's resolve flagged. A central part of the evidence was a series of telegrams to Babcock, including one that read:

WE HAVE OFFICIAL INFORMATION THAT THE ENEMY WEAKENS.
PUSH THINGS.

SYLPH

Bristow didn't know who "Sylph" was or what "enemy" was referred to, and neither did Attorney General Edwards Pierrepont, to whom he took the message. But they concurred that the matter required Grant's attention.

"We brought the telegrams to the President," Pierrepont afterward told congressional investigators. "The President called Babcock into the room before us and asked him what it meant." Babcock answered ambiguously. "The explanation gave me no light at all," Pierrepont said, "but it seemed to be a satisfactory explanation to the President." Grant's low threshold for satisfaction struck Pierrepont and Bristow as part of the problem. "The Secretary of the Treasury and I then both insisted that this was a matter so serious that if he"—Babcock—"could give an explanation which, as he said, was complete and perfect, and if he was perfectly innocent, as he said he was, he should go out there"—before the public—"and make an explanation. . . . We pressed it as a thing that he ought to do on the spot." Grant reluctantly agreed. Babcock, cornered, said he would give the explanation Pierrepont and Bristow demanded. But he left without doing so, and in fact never did.[19]

Instead he and the other conspirators threw up a smoke screen by suggesting that "Sylph" was a prostitute with whom Grant had conducted an adulterous liaison. To pursue the matter would subject the president and especially Mrs. Grant to public humiliation. Bristow and Pierrepont ignored the ruse, and the attorney general prepared to prosecute Babcock, who thereupon requested a military trial. Grant acceded, despite Pierrepont's express warning that a court-martial would not preclude civil prosecution. Grant packed the three-general tribunal with friends who understood that their job was to acquit Babcock and who did just that.

The case then went to the civil courts. A St. Louis grand jury indicted Babcock and McDonald, among hundreds of others. Grant let McDonald fend for himself but refused to abandon Babcock. Despite the overwhelming evidence against Babcock, the president determined to travel to St. Louis and testify to his innocence. Secretary of State Hamilton Fish and other senior members of the cabinet talked Grant out of the mission; the thought of America's chief executive under cross-examination made them shudder—for Grant and for the office. Grant contented himself with giving testimony at the White House. Chief Justice Morrison R. Waite presided over the session and signed Grant's deposition.

Grant's statement effectively stymied the prosecution. Despite the odor that had surrounded his administration since the gold conspiracy, not many Americans considered him personally dishonest. And those who knew him best were most convinced of his integrity. "I do not think it would have been possible for Grant to have told a lie, even if he had composed it and written it down," Hamilton Fish said. Largely as a result, Babcock was acquitted. Grant might have kept him on the White House staff, but Fish and others convinced the president he was badly damaged goods, and he was forced to resign. (He nonetheless landed appointment as inspector of lighthouses; he drowned on the job in Florida).

Yet many others, including McDonald, were convicted. "Sylph" became to the Grant administration what "Crédit Mobilier" was to Congress; popular opinions differed chiefly over which branch of government was the more venal.[20]

WILLIAM BELKNAP WEIGHED IN on the side of the executive, but not by choice. Belknap was a handsome man who married three beautiful and increasingly ambitious women. The first died before General Belknap—a veteran of Shiloh and Sherman's march to the sea—became Grant's secretary of war in 1869. The War Department post required special skills, not least the ability to get along with Sherman, who commanded both the army and the continuing adulation of many Republicans. The latter constantly tried to push him into politics. Sherman still resisted, to the relief of Grant and the several Republicans who hoped to succeed Grant in the White House. But one never knew with Sherman when his temper might explode and he decide he could run the country better than the fools who currently made a hash of it.

Belknap combined sufficient deference and avoidance to keep Sherman calm, for which Grant was grateful. But Belknap's second wife—the former Carrie Tomlinson—thought the president's gratitude ought to take more substantial form. Mrs. Belknap learned that a perquisite of her husband's office was the right to award concessions for army trading posts in the West. "She asked me one day in the course of a conversation why I did not apply for a post-tradership," Caleb Marsh, a Belknap acquaintance, subsequently informed a congressional committee. "I asked what they were, and was told that they were, many of them, very lucrative offices or posts in the gift of the Secretary of War, and that if I wanted one she would ask the Secretary for one for me." Marsh said he thought such favors went to people with important political connections. Carrie Belknap replied that other considerations sometimes tipped the balance. Marsh apparently caught her drift, although his memory wavered with the congressional committee. "I do not remember saying that if I had a valuable post of that kind that I would remember her, but I do remember her saying something like this: 'If I can prevail upon the Secretary of War to award you a post you must be careful to say nothing to him about presents, for a man once offered him $10,000 for a tradership of this kind, and he told him that if he did not leave the office he would kick him down stairs.'" Marsh kept these words in mind a few weeks later when Carrie Belknap informed him that the trading post at Fort Sill in Oklahoma Territory was vacant and that her husband was inclined to grant it to him. In fact the post wasn't vacant, and the current concessionaire, John S. Evans, wished to keep it. But Marsh didn't want to operate the post himself, merely to collect the profits, and so he cut a deal with Evans whereby Evans agreed to pay him $15,000 a year, in quarterly installments. This figure was later trimmed to $12,000 after the army decided to reduce the size of the garrison at Fort Sill. "When the first remittance came to me," Marsh said, "say probably in November 1870, I sent one-half thereof to Mrs. Belknap."[21]

The payments—a tidy complement to Belknap's eight-thousand-dollar annual salary—continued after Carrie Belknap suddenly died only a month later. Marsh comforted the grieving husband and the deceased's widowed sister, Amanda Tomlinson Bower, who took charge of the Belknaps' infant son. Marsh suggested that the payments could furnish a trust for the boy. Amanda Bower agreed to oversee the trust. But then the child, too, died, leaving no one to accept the payments but Belknap himself—and Amanda, who married Belknap in 1873.

Compared with the whiskey scandal, which involved hundreds of people and millions of dollars, the pay-for-trade conspiracy was puny. And had the Democrats, again in charge of the House of Representatives after the 1874 elections, not possessed other reasons to investigate the Grant administration, they probably never would have come across the War Department plot. Even then they might have missed the Belknap connection if Amanda Belknap hadn't insisted on entertaining in a fashion incommensurate with her husband's salary. But the Democrats did discover the trading post deal, which did directly involve a cabinet secretary. Belknap couldn't decide what to do—whether to brazen out the investigation or confess. He and Marsh agreed on a code. If Belknap telegraphed, "I hope your wife is well," Marsh should flee the country, preventing his examination by the committee. If Belknap wired, "I hope your wife is better," Marsh should meet with Belknap for further consultation.

The committee subpoenaed Marsh. Belknap, still not knowing whether to let Marsh talk, sent the second telegram, and Marsh came to the Belknap home. Amanda Belknap urged him to tell the committee that he and she had engaged in business over the years and that the payments were part of this business—"that all this money I had sent the Secretary was money that she had from time to time deposited with me as a kind of banker," Marsh later explained. Belknap himself credited the committee with more sense; the members would surely see through such a tale. Half his mind wanted Marsh to take the first ship to France; the other half realized Marsh's flight would be tantamount to a guilty plea by them both. "He was greatly excited," Marsh recalled. "He said if I went"—to Europe—"he would be ruined." Marsh replied that he wouldn't perjure himself to save Belknap. "I said I would ruin him if I went before the committee."

In the event, Marsh testified. The information he provided the committee persuaded the House to consider articles of impeachment against Belknap. Grant summoned Belknap to hear the secretary's side of the story; Belknap broke down and tearfully confessed to the bribery scheme. He implored Grant to accept his resignation, which the president did, hoping this would end the matter.

It ended the matter, but not at once. The Democrats in the House refused to be satisfied with Belknap's resignation and moved to impeach him. House Republicans, freed by Grant's acceptance of Belknap's resignation from having to defend the now-former secretary, joined in a voice vote endorsing the articles of impeachment. A desultory trial took place in the Senate, which failed to convict not because anyone doubted Belknap's culpability but because a score of senators thought their house lacked jurisdiction over someone no longer in the executive branch. "In this country, by the Constitution, private citizens are not impeachable," Roscoe Conkling of New York observed, explaining his acquittal vote.[22]

STILL THE SCANDALS didn't cease. Grant's minister to Britain was discovered to have employed his position to promote a mining scheme in which he had an ownership interest. The son of the secretary of the interior received favored treatment with respect to surveying contracts. And Grant's brother Orvil got paid for a surveying job in Wyoming Territory he didn't perform. "Did you ever know Orvil Grant to do any surveying in that territory?" the key material witness was asked. "No, sir," he replied. "I do not think he was ever *in* the territory."[23]

That the scandals climaxed in the summer of America's centennial struck many as evidence of how far the republic had fallen since the founding. Some observers cited a decline in the morality of public officials. The Reverend De Witt Talmage pointed to William Tweed as a caution against the pride that goeth before a fall. "Alas! Alas!" the minister declaimed from his Manhattan pulpit while Tweed coughed himself to death in the Ludlow Street jail. "Young men, look at the contrast—in an elegant compartment of a Wagner palace car, surrounded by wine, cards, and obsequious attendants, going to his Senatorial place at Albany; then look again at the plain box . . . behold the low-studded room, looking out upon a mean little dingy court where, a prisoner, exhausted, forsaken, miserable, betrayed, sick, William M. Tweed lies a-dying. From how high up to how low down!"[24]

Others blamed the competition among the newspapers—not for the misdeeds per se but for the scandal mongering that made the current generation appear especially culpable. Was the Crédit Mobilier affair really worse than the speculation in western land and Revolutionary War bonds that had inspired much of the support for the Constitution? Did Jay Gould and Jim Fisk, those first tempters of the Grant administration, do anything Robert Morris, the financier of the Revolution, hadn't dreamed of and gone to prison for? Tweed stole public money but didn't kill anyone or threaten the nation's security, unlike his Tammany Hall predecessor, Aaron Burr, who after shooting Alexander Hamilton tried to carve an empire for himself from the American Southwest.

Republicans blamed the Democrats for partisan exaggeration. Every administration had bad apples, the Republicans said. The surprise wasn't that there were so many in the Grant administration but that there were so few—so few, in fact, that the desperate Democrats had to resort, for their pièce de résistance, to impeaching a man who had already left office.

Yet for all the attempts to explain the scandals away, a feeling persisted that something was different this time. The scoundrels now operated on a scale surpassing anything imagined before the Civil War. The Tweed ring stole not thousands of dollars but millions. The whiskey ring involved hundreds of distillers and revenue agents, not the odd bootlegger and corrupt cop. The pall of Black Friday spread far beyond New York. Corporations were consolidating; criminals were, too.

Then there was the public reaction—or lack of public reaction. To many Americans, the really shocking thing about all the scandals was how *little* shock they generated. Voters ousted the Tweed ring, but Tammany Hall survived. The Grant administration spat out one crook after another, but the president won reelection in 1872 and voters might well have given him a third term if offered the chance.

Who could blame them? Weren't the bosses and the operators and the peculators simply employing in the public sector the same values for which Rockefeller, Carnegie, and Morgan were being so richly rewarded in the private sector? "Tweed was the most striking illustration of a very common faith," George Curtis wrote: "belief in the Almighty Dollar." Rockefeller and the other capitalists often professed motives of progress and efficiency, but at the end of the quarter and the year the undisputed measure of their success was the profit they amassed. Gould had deprived more people of more money than Tweed ever did, but Gould never went to jail. Rockefeller received more in kickbacks—from railroads—in a week than William Belknap got in his whole life, yet Belknap was ruined while Rockefeller grew richer and richer.[25]

There was a lesson in this, but the nature of the lesson was hard to discern. Did capitalism inevitably corrupt democracy? Was honesty, whether in business or government, simply outmoded? Buyers were warned to beware in the marketplace; should keepers of the public conscience declare *caveat civis* and leave it at that? Or should voters just throw the rascals out and start over?

Chapter 13

THE SPIRIT OF '76

———

Amid the growing and diversifying stream of immigration to America, the least noticed tributary was the one that had long been the largest and still flowed strong: from Britain. British immigrants assimilated easily into American life, arriving with the language and, for the most part, the Protestant religion of the American majority. At a time when the mass of immigrants seemed increasingly foreign to many of the native born, the British were gratifyingly familiar. Once judged the agents of perfidious Albion, the British were suddenly the model of what immigrants should be and do.

From the perspective of the British immigrants themselves, the adjustment to American life was indeed generally straightforward. They found work and homes; they settled in among their new neighbors more or less where they chose. Yet certain aspects of American culture required getting used to, even after some years in the States.

John Lewis had arrived from England before the Civil War. He took up residence in New York City and landed a job in a wholesale grocery. He applauded the Union victory although he didn't fight, and he broadly supported the principles of Republican Reconstruction although he wasn't especially active in politics. He was more interested in American folkways, which never failed to intrigue him, and in occasional letters to a brother back in England he described what he encountered.

"I went to Philadelphia on Xmas eve and stayed three days and was pressed to stay the week out," he explained at the beginning of 1876. "There was nothing special then but feasting—and I did feast, had to doctor myself when I came home." One aspect of the holiday celebration, besides the feasting, did merit special notice. "That is the Christmas trees, originally from Germany and I think first introduced into England by Prince Albert, but an old custom here. Usually the trees are decorated and loaded with sweets, toys &c, which are disposed of with great eclat (what's that, Willie?) and the matter ends." (Willie was Lewis's nephew.) "Not so in Philadelphia. There all the people seem to resolve themselves into children for the occasion." Philadelphians carried the decoration of Christmas trees to excess. Everyone who could afford it—and to Lewis's eye, nearly everyone could—devoted two whole rooms of their houses to Christmas trees and collateral decorations. "The usual arrangement in this country is to have two parlours—be it a large or small house—opening to each other by sliding doors, the front being for state occasions. As *large* and fine a tree as can be accommodated being procured and set up, it is covered with every conceivable shape into which coloured and gilt paper and card can be cut, and . . . little pictures, glass balls, chains, garlands &c, anything to make a gay and imposing display. . . . All the light possible is thrown upon it, often by reflectors, the lattice blinds thrown open, and it is open to inspection by passers by, which, as houses in Philadelphia are only a little above the street, is an easy matter." There was no limit, beyond the budget and imagination of the homeowners, to the extent of the decorations. "At one place I visited, an old doctor's, there was a very handsome river steamboat, perfect, three feet long with about fifty passengers (these last small pictures cut out) all of white, coloured and gilt card. Also a beautiful fire hose carriage."

After the trees were fully adorned, a procession began. "People go round with or without their children to see them, and frequently knock at the door to be admitted to a closer inspection, which is readily granted. I heard of one house where 75 were admitted in about two hours. Riding through the better class streets on the cars"—the horse-drawn trolleys— "the effect is novel and very fine." Lewis noted that though the decorations and ornaments often featured the names of the children of the households, the whole business was directed by the adults. "It appears to be got up more for the gratification of the older than the young ones." The youngsters preferred candy, to which the Americans were addicted. "The candy stores are among the gayest and most prosperous, and the consumption of their wares by women and children all the year round is enormous and is often spoken of by writers as a great national failing. If a woman goes out she must not forget a pound or at least half a pound of candy for baby—and herself."[1]

In an ordinary year the holiday season would have wound down after New Year's Day, but 1876 was no ordinary year, being the centennial of American independence. Philadelphia would lead the festivities, as the nation's birthplace and still its second-largest city. Lewis had to work in New York the week after Christmas, but on New Year's Eve he closed the shop and boarded an afternoon train back to Philadelphia. He met his son there, and together they went to a friend's house. The principal entertainment of the evening was an elaborate spoof on lawyers and judges. "The host in wig and gown (also specs) was mounted on a well constructed 'bench' and was engaged in trying a disreputable looking 'blaggard'"—blackguard— "Mr. Terence O'Sullivan (my son), for jilting a very prim old maid, and as nearly all the audience were called as witnesses the fun was uproarious. The prosecuting lawyer did not amount to much, but defendant's counsel John Moffitt, assistant clerk and a prospective relative, was a hit in his examining of the witnesses, especially when Mrs. Bridget O'Halloran, the widdy"— widow—"of a husband, was called as an expert in matrimonial matters. I never enjoyed anything so much before. The trial lasted nearly three hours, concluding with an elaborate address for the defense, counsel quoting from decisions in Buckwheat versus Muffins and other celebrated cases in support of his argument." After the prisoner was found guilty and the judge ordered "some ridiculous sentence which I forget," the entire court adjourned. "We then went down stairs to refresh on great moulds of ice cream of several flavours, jellies, cakes, and fruits of various kinds &c &c."

At the stroke of midnight the city erupted in what Lewis called "the most extraordinary noise ever heard. It had been arranged that at that hour every bell, whistle, or other instrument that would make a noise should be put into requisition. Philadelphia is a great railroad place and has many thousands of workshops—also churches." Everything heralded the centennial year. "The effect was wonderful, not loud, being scattered—rather melancholy, seeming as if some terrible disaster was occurring, such as the sacking of a great city, and the sound of a vast multitude wailing and shrieking at a distance."

The celebration continued for Lewis that night till half past three and resumed the following day for another banquet, featuring "two turkeys, at least twenty-pounders, with all the trimmings." The party segregated after dinner. "Gentlemen upstairs, ladies to the parlour. We smoked and played cards, but hearing a great row downstairs I left as soon as I could, went down, and found that I had missed part of the fun—charades and other games. After that we had nigger minstrelsy &c by my son, Moffitt, and another young man in black faces and appropriate costumes. Black Sal also appeared and danced a jig; she puzzled me, but I afterwards learnt that she was the doctor's wife next door, a romp—nearer fifty than any other age. . . . After that we had a variety of choruses and some good piano playing. Nobody waited to be asked to sing."[2]

THE NEXT DAY was Sunday and Lewis stayed over. But he had to return to New York to open the store on Monday. He didn't get back to Philadelphia till August, by which time the Centennial Exposition—commonly called "the Centennial"—had established itself as what Lewis called "the great event of the year if not of the Century." The grounds of the exposition at Fairmount Park were packed with the high and the humble; the former included, on Lewis's first day, the governors of several American states and Dom Pedro, the emperor of Brazil. The entrance fee was fifty cents; additional fees—"some of them pretty stiff"—were charged at exhibits inside the gates. The different sections of the country and diverse parts of the world were on display. "A great feature of the grounds were the 'state' houses. These were of various sizes, and some of them curiosities in style and ornament, but all built with the same object, to be a sort of headquarters to the people from the various states of the Union, mostly with handsome parlours, piano &c, and where they could register their names, meet friends or receive letters." The western states particularly strove to make a favorable impression. Kansas and Colorado joined forces to display "wonderful specimens of minerals and agricultural produce, corn twenty feet high, wheat and other grains of a wonderful growth. But the principal attraction was a collection of wild animals arranged on rocks, from the buffalo down to prairie dogs &c—all or nearly all the wild animals found in those states and all shot by a little woman, a Mrs. Maxwell who attended a photograph stand selling pictures of herself and animals."

As a native of England, Lewis took special interest in observing the customs of New England. "I may explain," he told his brother, "that by 'New England' is meant the present states of Vermont, New Hampshire, Maine, Massachusetts, Rhode Island and Connecticut, the real and only Yankee land, peopled from the colony of 'pilgrims' who landed in 1620." The centerpiece of the New England exhibit was "an old 'New England' log house with inmates to match—all old—and mostly historical furniture— veritable old spinning wheels at work and numberless old nic-nacs, real affair—also the cradle that Peregrine White was rocked in—the first white child born in 'New England.' . . . In the kitchen a crowd was feasting (at fifty cents a head) on real Yankee pork and beans (you ought to try them)."

Near the New England house stood "the Japanese bazaar, curiously built, and a little garden with Japanese plants . . . surrounded by a very neat bamboo fence, all very ingeniously made. There was also several of those dwarf trees that you may have read about—fifty or one hundred or more years old. Oaks and others, little, crooked, gnarled and yet all healthy, and mostly about eighteen to twenty-four inches each way. In the bazaar, natives in *our* clothes were busy selling all kinds of small wares at good prices. They have a residence on the ground—a large house of wood, all brought from Japan, and whilst it was being erected they were the centre of attraction, from their excellent work and curious tools."

The smaller Turkish pavilion also housed a bazaar, or souvenir shop. "But the pavilion is mostly used as a smoking saloon, and it was an amusing sight to see it full of fellows, mostly young, either smoking the long flexible tubed water pipes, or the long chiboucks, both fifteen cents, five feet long, and which they did not know how to handle, and trying to make believe that they were enjoying themselves, while Turkish waiters in costume were bringing eastern drinks (fifteen cents) and poking up the pipes." Next to the smoking saloon was another Ottoman curiosity: "a small Jerusalem tent, with olive wood work, all Catholic beads, crosses &c &c sold by sons of the prophet."

Though the American past had inspired the Centennial, the American future provided its theme. Machinery large and small revealed the power of industry to transform ordinary lives in extraordinary ways. Lewis was unimpressed by what was supposed to be the centerpiece of the industrial exhibits: a Corliss steam engine. "That's a fraud," he told his brother. "There are plenty of larger engines than that. It is imposing on account of its position and its having double beams and a large fly wheel. This last is certainly all that is said of it, being I think of 70 tons (our ton is 2000 lbs.)." Yet though the main attraction disappointed Lewis, the auxiliary exhibits delighted him. "If you can think of any kind of machine for any purpose, it was pretty sure to be there and numbers of them at work. I saw one *large* machine making paper, and another printing wall paper. Curious—just as easy to print in twenty colours as in one." Steam-driven fans like those employed in the mining industry to ventilate shafts made cyclones of the warm summer air. "The force of their wind was tremendous, and hats &c were in danger anywhere near them." While steam multiplied force, electricity conquered distance. "The 'London Graphic' was printed here, and so was the 'New York Times.' For the latter electrotype plates left *here*"—Lewis was writing from his home in New York—"at 4 a.m., and papers were ready when the doors opened at 8. An eight page paper." The importance of newspapers to Americans could not be overstated. A newspaper advertising agency—"This is a large business here"—had built a house where visitors could relax and catch up on the news. "In this house was a reading room, free, and any paper asked for was brought by attendants. There is probably 20,000 papers published in the U.S."

The fair included a "Women's Hall" displaying the products of women's work from America and around the world. "This is a failure," Lewis wrote, at least as it regarded America. "By far the most valuable and interesting of *women's work* is principally shown in Machinery Hall and in the Main Hall, for instance in watch-making, for which there are several large factories in this country, where every part, even the most delicate, are made by fine machines, mostly attended by girls, and turning out beautiful work."

American ingenuity had been applied to creature comforts as well. Lewis and other visitors appreciated ice water that gushed from a fountain and piqued his curiosity even as it quenched his thirst. "I could not make it out where it came from with so much force," Lewis said, "but next day I came there just as they were filling the tank with ice. In the ground, where the iron pipe from the water works came, there was sunk a giant iron tank which held several tons of ice (I saw five or six go in). The water pipe ran into this and from another side a pipe led to the fountain. The ice being all in, the *air tight* cover was put on, and the stopcock being turned, the full force of water passed through the ice to the fountain." In case his brother wondered why the Americans went to all that bother, Lewis added, "Ice water is a very important and necessary article during the hot weather, and was in fair supply in all parts of the grounds." Yet many visitors preferred other drinks. "The numerous soda water stands in all the buildings did a roaring trade, and so did the German 'lager bier' sellers. Lager bier is German, a pleasant refreshing real beer, but it is still an unsettled question whether or not it will intoxicate. Plenty of Germans can be found who would swear to drinking all the way up to 50 or 60 glasses a day—five cents a glass. Of late years, Americans are large consumers."

Power of another sort formed a conspicuous part of the display. The Krupp works of Germany had sent one of its great guns, an artillery piece with a long barrel—"mounted like a monster telescope, wrong end up," it seemed to Lewis—and a rifled bore. Less sophisticated but larger were the American weapons: "all sorts of guns of all sizes up to the twenty-inch 'Dahlgren' with a heap of its 1080 lb. shot. Also a monitor turret, with two fifteen-inch guns mounted, but I cannot conceive how they can work in so small a space." Inside the federal government's building was "every conceivable instrument for scientific murder: fire arms, old and new; shot and shell, whole and sawed in two to show the interior; edged weapons; pikes; torpedoes; models of vessels and other things; cordage; figures with all kinds of uniforms from 1800 to the present time." The signal corps contributed its latest lighthouse apparatus. "I had often wished to see a Fresnel lens and could never understand why they should be so complicated and expensive. But I can see it now. The lens is a great lantern (of course this goes inside the real lantern) which a man can—and has to—climb into, composed of a very great number of prisms of various sizes and curves of the finest glass and very heavy, and when the light is burning must multiply it many hundred times." The military exhibit also included "what I had hitherto thought a myth—the stump of a tree about five feet high and fifteen to eighteen inches thick that had been cut off by musket balls, at (I think) the battle of the Wilderness. This is authentic."[3]

THE CENTENNIAL YEAR was also a presidential election year, which added to the excitement. The election of 1868 had been a snooze, and that of 1872, when Ulysses Grant easily defeated Horace Greeley, still more somnolent. The Democratic victories in the congressional races in 1874 promised that 1876 would be the most competitive presidential contest since the war and challenged the Republicans to find a worthy candidate to succeed Grant.

Few initially suspected that the candidate would be Rutherford Hayes, and those few didn't include Hayes himself. "We are living happily—never more so," the Ohio governor wrote in his diary in March 1875. "Lucy is healthy, and as she grows older preserves her beauty. She is large but not unwieldy."[4]

Hayes had never expected to get as far in life as he had. His father died before he was born, and he entered the world so frail his mother braced for his early death. When he survived infancy, she clung to him tightly, the more so after his brother drowned ice-skating. She schooled him at home before sending him to a private academy; even after he attended college (Kenyon) and law school (Harvard), she kept close watch over him. With much of his generation he contracted the fever of Manifest Destiny and in 1847 attempted to enlist in the army that was invading Mexico. But his mother arranged for the local doctor to find that the young man's health couldn't stand the rigors of the campaign, and he was rejected.

In 1860 he was a lukewarm Unionist. "Let them go," he said of the seceding states. Yet the attack on Fort Sumter rekindled his patriotism, and he took a commission in Ohio's volunteers. He served with distinction, receiving four wounds and the grateful respect of his comrades and neighbors, who elected him to Congress and three times to the governorship of Ohio. The last time—in 1875—he won impressively enough that many Republicans looked to him to succeed that other Ohioan, Grant, in the White House.[5]

There was some question whether Grant *wanted* to be succeeded. No president had served three terms, although the Constitution didn't forbid it. After his thumping victory over Greeley in 1872, Grant thought he might be the one to break the tacit embargo. He and his wife, Julia, liked living in the White House, and he had no particular prospects after leaving office and no pension. Besides, he hated the thought of departing under the cloud of scandal. But precisely that cloud caused the Republican professionals to push him to the door.

The identity of his replacement evoked no such agreement. Benjamin Bristow believed the scandals favored the fearless sweeper of the Augean stables, namely him. But others argued that a Bristow nomination would play directly to the Democrats' strength: voters' distaste at what passed for politics as usual. Besides, Grant couldn't stand Bristow, and the president retained enough support among the party faithful to derail the Kentuckian's candidacy.

The mantle of favorite fell on James G. Blaine. Elected to Congress from Maine in 1862, Blaine had quickly earned a reputation for eloquence and charm. Some elder statesmen of the House compared him favorably with the young Henry Clay. Like Clay, he was elevated to speaker while still junior by years, and he deftly managed the affairs of the House. He spoke with a voice of moderate reason during Reconstruction and aided in efforts to bring the South back into the Union without excessive recrimination. Yet he drew the line where amnesty met amnesia. In January 1876, in the spirit of centennial reconciliation, House Democrats sponsored a bill to waive the civil disabilities imposed on Confederate office-holders by the Fourteenth Amendment; Blaine accepted the principle but offered a single amendment: that the waiver not include Jefferson Davis. Blaine's amendment itself spoiled the centennial spirit; his explanation drove the wedge deeper.

> I do not place his exclusion on the ground that Mr. Davis was, as he has been commonly called, the head and front of the Rebellion. . . . Mr. Davis was in that respect as guilty, no more so, no less so, than thousands of others who have already received the benefit and grace of amnesty. . . . It is not because of any particular and special damage that he above others did to the Union, or because he was personally or especially of consequence, that I except him. . . . I except him on this ground: that he was the author, knowingly, deliberately, guiltily, and willfully, of the gigantic murders and crimes at Andersonville.

Blaine recounted the horrors of the Confederate prison camp—of the Union soldiers starved, sickened, and beaten, and tracked and mauled by hounds when they tried to escape.

> It is often said that we shall lift Mr. Davis again into great consequence by refusing him amnesty. This is not for me to consider. I only see before me, when his name is presented, a man who, by a wave of his

hand, by a nod of his head, could have put an end to the atrocious cru-
elties at Andersonville. Some of us had kinsmen there, most of us had
friends there, all of us had countrymen there. In the name of those
kinsmen, friends, and countrymen, I here protest, and shall with my
vote protest, against calling back and crowning with the honors of full
American citizenship the man who organized that murder.

Blaine's amendment sparked an uproar in the House that lasted days.
The entire country followed the controversy and noted the man who
started it. As Blaine had hoped, the furor made him a leading candidate for
the Republican nomination.

But to gain the prize Blaine had to get past Roscoe Conkling, the formidable leader of New York's Republican delegation in Congress. "He was
of commanding, even magnificent presence," a contemporary wrote of
Conkling, "six feet three inches tall, with regular features, lofty forehead,
and piercing eyes—blond and gigantic as a viking." At a moment when the
scandals in the Grant administration provoked soul-searching among
some Republicans, Conkling was an unapologetic partisan. "I do not know
how to belong to a party a little," he said. From his seat in the Senate he
hurled imprecations at any who deserted the party in the name of reform.
"Who are these oracular censors so busy of late in brandishing the rod over
me and every other Republican?" he hissed. "Who are these men who, in
newspapers and elsewhere, are cracking their whips over Republicans and
playing schoolmaster to the Republican party and its conscience and convictions?" Answering his own question, he identified them as "the man
milliners"—the homosexuals—"the dilettanti and carpet knights of politics. . . . Their stock in trade is rancid, canting self-righteousness. They are
wolves in sheep's clothing. Their real object is office and plunder. When
Dr. Johnson defined patriotism as the last refuge of a scoundrel, he was
unconscious of the then undeveloped capabilities and uses of the word
'reform'!"[6]

Conkling didn't confine his hostility to reformers; he hated James
Blaine with an equal passion. The bad blood dated to a moment in the
House when Blaine was speaking on a measure Blaine supported and
Conkling opposed; Conkling conspicuously yawned and announced, "If
the member from Maine had the least idea how profoundly indifferent I
am to his opinion . . . I think he would hardly have troubled to rise here

and express his opinion." He then turned his back on Blaine and took up
some correspondence. Blaine answered in a diffident tone that grew more
assertive as its sarcasm became evident. "The contempt of that large-
minded gentleman is so wilting, his haughty disdain, his grandiloquent
swell, his majestic, super-eminent, turkey-gobbler strut has been so crushing to myself and all the members of the House, that I know it was an act
of greatest temerity for me to venture upon a controversy with him." Citing an article in one of the New York newspapers likening Conkling to
another dandy, Blaine declared that Conkling had taken the comparison
seriously. "It has given his strut additional pomposity. The resemblance is
great. It is striking. Hyperion to a satyr, Thersites to Hercules, mud to
marble, dunghill to diamond, a singed cat to a Bengal tiger, a whining
puppy to a roaring lion."7

Conkling never forgave the insult, and no sooner had Blaine's star
begun to rise over the Capitol on its way toward the 1876 nomination than
Conkling engineered an intercept. His allies reiterated Blaine's role in
the Crédit Mobilier scandal, and they related new tales of impropriety.
Blaine was said to have received a loan of $64,000 from the Union Pacific
that he never repaid, to have been given bonds by the Little Rock & Fort
Smith Railroad in exchange for political favors, and to have traded influence for cash with the Northern Pacific.

Blaine responded with righteous indignation to the charges. He
denied them point by point, to the satisfaction of many impartial auditors.
A congressional committee summoned to investigate the general question
of influence peddling declined to include Blaine on its list of targets. But
then a man named James Mulligan stepped forward with some letters by
Blaine regarding the Little Rock & Fort Smith. Blaine was attending the
hearing; as soon as he heard Mulligan mention the letters he signaled to an
ally on the committee to move an adjournment. The ally announced that
he was sick and requested to have the session suspended; the chairman
granted the request.

That afternoon Blaine went to Mulligan's hotel. According to Mulligan, Blaine begged for the letters. "He prayed, almost went on his knees—
I would say on his knees—and implored me to think of his six children and
his wife, that if the committee should get hold of this communication, it
would sink him immediately and ruin him forever." When this appeal to
sympathy failed, Blaine tried cupidity. He "asked me if I would not like a

consulship," Mulligan said. This too failed, but Mulligan consented to let Blaine examine the letters on his promise to return them.

Blaine contested Mulligan's account of their meeting, starting with the lament about being ruined, continuing with the offer of a consulship, and concluding with the promise to return the letters. Nor did he, in fact, return them. Instead he rose before the full House and dramatically drew the letters from the breast pocket of his coat. "I am not afraid to show the letters," he declaimed. "Thank God Almighty! I am not afraid to show them. There they are. There is the very original package." He proceeded to read the letters, although not every one completely, as they were too many and too long. The theatricality of the performance was obvious to all, but this hardly diminished its effect.

Blaine had the galleries hanging on his words when he threw a surprise at the Democratic chairman of the committee. An informant had told him that the chairman had received a telegram, from a person well placed to know, that Blaine was innocent of the charges against him. The chairman hadn't revealed the telegram; he said later that he first wanted to authenticate it. But Blaine forced him to admit that he was holding exculpatory evidence. "You got a dispatch last Thursday morning . . . completely and absolutely exonerating me from this charge, and you have suppressed it!"

The galleries erupted and the members began shouting. The House speaker gaveled for order and threatened to toss the visitors out. The members ignored the gavel and the sergeants said they lacked the muscle to remove the guests. Blaine accepted the handshakes and backslaps of his colleagues.

But the bravura performance merely reinforced the belief among Blaine skeptics that he was too clever and smooth to be completely honest. As the spell he had conjured in the House diminished and members asked to see the letters for themselves, they discovered how artfully he had excerpted them. No single phrase did Blaine more damage than an underlined postscript to one of the messages: "*Burn this letter.*"[8]

Blaine and his supporters struggled to regain momentum. At the Republican convention in the summer of 1876, Robert Ingersoll placed Blaine's name before the gathering with a speech that supplied a label to its subject. "Like an armed warrior, like a plumed knight," Ingersoll said, recalling Blaine's speech against Jefferson Davis, "James G. Blaine marched down the halls of the American Congress and threw his shining lance full and fair against the brazen forehead of every traitor to his country."[9]

Blaine's backers roared approval; briefly it appeared the "Plumed Knight" would carry the convention by storm. But the Conkling faction chanted, "Burn this letter," and the delirium dissipated. No alternative candidate emerged through several ballots, till someone suggested Rutherford Hayes as a compromise all could get behind. A few did so with enthusiasm, others with the attitude archly expressed by Henry Adams, who called Hayes "a third-rate nonentity, whose only recommendation is that he is obnoxious to no one." Yet under the circumstances, this was no mean recommendation, and as the convention prepared to ballot for a seventh time, on Friday, June 16, Hayes was hopeful. "Friday has been a lucky day for me before!" he wrote. When his hopes proved out, the experience was more than he had anticipated. "It for a few moments quite unmanned me."[10]

SAMUEL TILDEN RECEIVED the Democratic nomination with greater composure. Having parlayed his prosecution of William Tweed into election as New York governor, Tilden soon became a contender for the presidency. The Republican scandals provided an opening for a Democrat with clean hands, and none were conspicuously cleaner than Tilden's.

Tilden's immaculacy reflected his eschewing not simply the sins of ordinary people but most ordinary people themselves. "He is the supreme illustration in American political history of sheer intellect unrelieved by any of those human qualities which win men's love," New Yorker Harry Peck observed. Tilden's father had run the post office in New Lebanon, New York, where the local philosophers debated the issues of the day. Tilden, a sickly child, listened and came to identify more closely with adults than with his peers. His aloofness served him well during the Civil War, when he kept his distance from both Union Republicans and antiwar Democrats, and afterward, when as a corporate lawyer he earned a reputation as "the Great Forecloser." He was cold to his clerks; to one who inquired about vacation he responded, "Your vacation will begin at once and continue indefinitely." Many of his contemporaries underestimated him. Tweed called him the hero of "the cheese press and hay loft democracy" of upstate New York. Yet Harry Peck saw shrewdness in Tilden's quiet method. "Both in law and politics he brought to bear all the resources of a cold, calculating nature, unmoved by passion or by prejudice, able to bide its time, to temporize, to dissemble, and to scheme, not merely for the present but for the distant future." He made a fortune in law and lived in silent elegance.[11]

And when the Democrats needed a candidate in 1876 they looked his way. Tilden efficiently mounted a publicity campaign in the months before the Democratic convention, reminding voters in critical states of his success snaring Tweed and of his eagerness to do likewise to the scandal-plagued, Republican-appointed federal workforce. His organization hosted distinguished Democrats from around the country, courting Southerners especially. "Never a leading Southern man came to town who was not seen," Henry Watterson, the editor of the *Louisville Courier-Journal*, recalled. "If of enough importance he was taken to No. 15 Gramercy Park"—Tilden's house. "Mr. Tilden measured to the Southern standard of the gentleman in politics."

At the convention Tilden's nominator struck the keynote of the campaign. "The great issue upon which this election will be lost or won is the question of needed administrative reform," Senator Francis Kernan of New York asserted. "If we have a man who has laid his hand on dishonest officials, rooted out abuses, lowered taxes, and inaugurated reforms, and if we are wise enough to select him as our leader, we will sweep the Union." In their wisdom the delegates chose Tilden, on the second ballot.[12]

THE GENERAL CAMPAIGN reflected the subdued personalities of the candidates. Republican voters were urged to "vote as they shot"; Democrats called for the kind of reform only a change of party in the White House could accomplish. But the Republican entreaties lacked the fire of years past, and the Democratic demands were widely interpreted as being synonymous with "our turn." Journalists lamented that there was little to cover. "A flat and tame campaign," the *New York Herald* called it.[13]

The central question of the campaign was not what the candidates stood for but who would count the votes. Charges of theft and fraud weren't uncommon in the history of American presidential elections; nearly every close contest had elicited complaints from the losers. But manipulation of the vote was particularly tempting in 1876 on account of continuing disputes regarding governance in the three states of South Carolina, Louisiana, and Florida. The Democrats expected to carry the Southern states where their party had regained local control; they might well win fairly, so despised were the Republicans by nearly all whites, but they would certainly win unfairly, by suppressing the African American vote. The Republicans reckoned that memories of the war would work in Hayes's favor in most Northern states, although they couldn't count on New York, Tilden's home. By both sides' estimate, the race would be close, and the three Southern states where Republicans still held control in the waning days of Reconstruction could easily provide the winning margin.

This was just how the election played out. The turnout was huge; eight and a half million voters trooped to the polls, two million more than in 1872. Tilden led in the popular vote and, in the North alone, carried New York, New Jersey, Indiana, and Connecticut. If he held all or nearly all the South, as both sides expected, he would triumph comfortably. He and Hayes both went to bed on election night thinking Tilden had won.

Most newspapers thought so, too. "Tilden Is Elected," Charles Dana's Democratic *New York Sun* declared happily on the Wednesday after the election. The Republican *Chicago Tribune* lamented, "Lost. The Country Given Over to Democratic Greed and Plunder."

Yet the vote wasn't quite final. Tilden's electoral total stood at 184, one shy of the 185 needed for victory. Hayes had 166. The nineteen votes unaccounted for belonged to the three anomalous Southern states. (A separate, technical dispute arose over one electoral vote from Oregon; this was resolved in Hayes's favor.) Although Hayes was ready to concede—as late as the following Saturday he wrote in his diary, "The election has resulted in the defeat of the Republicans"—his managers were not. They sent urgent telegrams to Republicans in South Carolina, Louisiana, and Florida: "Hold your state." Meanwhile the chairman of the Republican national committee, Senator Zachariah Chandler of Michigan, brazenly claimed the nineteen votes for his man. "Hayes has 185 electoral votes and is elected," Chandler told the press.

As the Republicans dug in their heels, Tilden's momentum toward the White House diminished and then disappeared. Democrats in the three states swore that Tilden had received solid majorities of the votes cast, which was probably true. Republicans in those states countered that the

Democrats had prevented thousands of black Republicans from voting, which was also true. "They have killed colored men in every precinct," a black South Carolinian explained.[14]

With the contradictory confidence of their mutually exclusive convictions, the two sides pushed the fight forward. The Republicans and the Democrats each sent teams of lawyers and politicians to assess matters on the disputed ground; predictably the teams returned conflicting reports. The Twelfth Amendment empowered Congress (somewhat confusingly) to count the electoral votes, but because Congress was split, with the Democrats controlling the House and the Republicans the Senate, the issue was left unresolved. The best the lawmakers could manage was to appoint a special commission, comprising five Republican legislators, five Democratic legislators, and five members of the Supreme Court. The judges were presumed to be less partisan than the elected politicians, but just in case they weren't, they too were apportioned by party, with two being Republicans, two Democrats, and the fifth to be chosen by the other four. By understanding, the fifth judge would be Associate Justice David Davis of Illinois, who belonged to neither party (having been appointed by Abraham Lincoln in 1862 on precisely that account). But Davis, in a career move, accepted election to the Senate by the Illinois legislature and vacated his seat on the electoral commission. The other Supreme Court justices all had party affiliations, but lest the election never be decided, the Democrats acquiesced to the appointment of Republican justice Joseph P. Bradley.

Some Democrats soon regretted their complaisance. The electoral commission ruled on point after point of the dispute and in a series of eight-to-seven decisions awarded the contested electors to Hayes. According to the commission, Hayes won by a single vote, 185 to 184.

Yet the commission's finding was only advisory; Congress had to accept or reject it. The Republican Senate naturally accepted; the Democratic House stalled. Most Democrats recognized they couldn't keep Hayes from the White House forever without risking an ugly backlash, but they hoped to get something in exchange for letting him in. "I could appoint a Southern Democrat to the Cabinet," Hayes mused in his diary, and perhaps let the musing slip. More to the point, he made clear his desire for sectional reconciliation. The war was over; the South should be allowed to manage its own affairs. Individuals purporting to speak for Hayes promised he would withdraw the last of the federal troops from the political affairs of the South—meaning, at this juncture, South Carolina and Louisiana—and the candidate didn't contradict them.

The House convened on Thursday, March 1, only seventy-two hours before the scheduled inauguration, to decide the election at last. The session ran past midnight, but by dawn Hayes was indubitably the winner.

Some Democrats remained unreconciled. "Today is Friday," Joseph Blackburn of Kentucky observed. "Upon that day, the savior of the world suffered crucifixion between two thieves. On this Friday constitutional government, justice, honesty, fair dealing, manhood, and decency suffer crucifixion amid a number of thieves." Yet others, weighing the risks of a continued contest, deemed the bargain acceptable. "I prefer four years of Hayes' administration to four years of civil war," said Abram Hewitt, chairman of the Democratic national committee.

Tilden himself was philosophical about what came to be called the Compromise of 1877. "I can retire to private life," he said, "with the consciousness that I shall receive from posterity the credit of having been elected to the highest position in the gift of the people without any of the cares and responsibilities of the office."[15]

Chapter 14

LIVES OF THE PARTIES

James Bryce would have been called Scotch Irish had his family emigrated to America from Ulster. Instead, amid the potato famine of the 1840s they moved back to Scotland, to Glasgow, where James's father taught school. The boy excelled at his studies and won a chance for a scholarship to Trinity College at Oxford. But Trinity students were required to subscribe to the Thirty-nine Articles of Anglican orthodoxy, and James, with the double determination of the Scot and the Presbyterian, refused. His case became a test, and his persistence resulted in a partial victory for religious and intellectual tolerance: though refused a master's degree, he was allowed to take a bachelor's. His brilliance eventually broke down the remaining barriers, and in 1870 he became the Regius Professor of Civil Law at Oxford.

That same year he visited the United States, consorting in Boston with Emerson, Longfellow, Lowell, and Holmes *père et fils*. He conceived an enthusiasm for America as both a field of study and a portent of civilization's future, and after returning to England he published a series of articles that established his reputation as Britain's expert on the American republic. He traveled again to the United States in 1881 for an extended tour, and once more in 1883 to conduct a seminar at Johns Hopkins, the new research university in Baltimore, where the class included John

Dewey, John Franklin Jameson, and Woodrow Wilson. The text for the course was Alexis de Tocqueville's *Democracy in America*, which Bryce considered "a model of art and a storehouse of ethical maxims" but woefully deficient as an interpretation of its nominal subject. Some of Tocqueville's arguments were out of date, Bryce asserted; others had always been wrong. "That is to say, some were true of America, but not of democracy in general, while others were true of democracy in general but not true of America."[1]

Bryce thought he could do better, and in 1888 he published *The American Commonwealth*, in three volumes. A century after the founding of the federal republic, Bryce—and others—could detect a pattern in American politics. Americans initially organized into parties based on causes, but as the causes lost their power to motivate, the parties remained. The fight over the Constitution had produced America's first party system, of Federalists and Republicans. The struggle for democracy had spawned the second party system, of Democrats and Whigs. The sectional crisis had generated the third party system, of Republicans and Democrats. This third system had manifested the greatest power to motivate: witness the inordinate passions of the 1850s, the monumental carnage of the Civil War, the violence and vindictiveness of Reconstruction and Redemption. But a decade after Redemption, the fire had gone out of the parties (as the fire had previously gone out of their forerunners). Their members still spoke the language of their causes; the Republicans claimed equality and opportunity, and the Democrats defended states' rights. But mostly they squabbled for office and the spoils it brought. The best men—those with the most conspicuous talent and ambition—looked elsewhere than politics for their challenges and rewards.

Recruitment was a particular problem during the declining phase of each party system, but Bryce perceived it as a chronic issue for Americans. And it was most striking at the top of the American political pyramid: the presidency. Considering the powers of the chief executive and the relative openness of American society, Bryce wrote, the naïve observer of American politics should have expected the presidency to attract the most brilliant and gifted men.

> But since the heroes of the Revolution died out with Jefferson and
> Adams and Madison some sixty years ago, no person except General
> Grant has reached the chair whose name would have been remembered

had he not been President, and no President except Abraham Lincoln has displayed rare or striking qualities in the chair. Who now knows or cares to know anything about the personality of James K. Polk or Franklin Pierce? The only thing remarkable about them is that being so commonplace they should have climbed so high.

Bryce adduced various reasons for this talent dearth in the White House. "One is that the proportion of first-rate ability drawn into politics is smaller in America than in most European countries." In France, in Britain, and in Germany, politics was the most exciting field of human endeavor, but in America, politics competed with a peculiarly dynamic brand of capitalism—"the business of developing the material resources of the country," Bryce called it—and often lost out.

A second reason was that American political life offered few opportunities for individual distinction. Congress operated by committees and compromises; the states, the other major source of presidential candidates, were many and diffuse. National reputations were hard to come by, which explained the frequent success of generals, whose gifts lay in the martial rather than the political line.

A third reason had to do with the interaction of democracy and human nature.

Eminent men make more enemies, and give those enemies more assailable points, than obscure men do. They are therefore in so far less desirable candidates. It is true that the eminent man has also made more friends, that his name is more widely known, and may be greeted with louder cheers. Other things being equal, the famous man is preferable. But other things never are equal. The famous man has probably attacked some leaders in his own party, has supplanted others, has expressed his dislike to the crotchet of some active section, has perhaps committed errors which are capable of being magnified into offences. No man stands long before the public and bears a part in great affairs without giving openings to censorious criticism. Fiercer far than the light which beats upon a throne is the light which beats upon a presidential candidate, searching out all the recesses of his past life. Hence, when the choice lies between a brilliant man and a safe man, the safe man is preferred. Party feeling, strong enough to carry in on its back a man without conspicuous positive merits, is not always strong enough to procure forgiveness for a man with positive faults.[2]

FROM BIRTH THE Republican party had really been two parties: one stressing social issues, starting with antislavery and extrapolating to Radical Reconstruction; the other emphasizing economics, in particular aid to business. The war had welded the two wings together, and the bond persisted, albeit weakened, during the decade after the war. But under Rutherford Hayes, who terminated Reconstruction by removing the last federal troops from the South, and thereby delivered the South to the Democrats for the foreseeable future, the two wings abandoned all pretense of comity. Each now treated the other as more dangerous than the Democrats.

Roscoe Conkling led one faction, the Stalwarts, so called (at first by themselves, later by others) for their devotion to the great causes of Lincoln and Grant. The Grant they preferred was the brave general, but when pressed they were willing to settle for the scandal-prone president, who, whatever his faults, had kept the party in power for eight years. Realists among the Stalwarts recognized that the Civil War was over, and Reconstruction too, but they—and the unrealists as well—hoped to squeeze a few more victories out of the bloody shirt.

James Blaine led the other faction, the Half-Breeds, so called at first by their enemies but eventually by themselves. The Half-Breeds believed the party must move on to the new issues raised by industrialization. With each year that passed, the Civil War meant ever less, particularly to the millions of immigrants who had arrived since Appomattox. To harp on the old themes risked conceding the newcomers to the Democrats.

The politics of post-Reconstruction America put the Republicans in a particular bind. The Democrats' reconquest of the South gave them a lock on the electoral votes of the old Confederacy. Even modest inroads into the North or West could hand them the White House. To be sure, they had to choose their candidates carefully; Southerners were essentially disqualified. But a Northern Democrat with pull in one of the large Northern states became almost an odds-on favorite for president. The formula would have worked for New York's Tilden in 1876 had the votes been counted fairly; it might well work the next time around.

Or the time after that. In the 1880 election Republican James Garfield squeezed one more victory out of the old formula, beating Democrat (and Union war hero) Winfield Scott Hancock by less than 40,000 votes out of 9 million cast. "Your real troubles will begin now," fellow Republican Carl Schurz told Garfield in lieu of congratulations, referring to the continuing fight within their own party. Garfield did his best, trying to balance appointments of Stalwarts against those of Half-Breeds. But the task proved impossible, for every Republican acted as though he had a claim on the president's patronage. "The fountains of the population seemed to have overflowed and Washington is inundated," Garfield lamented. More than once he asked himself whether the presidency was worth the headaches. "My God!" he said. "What is there in this place that a man should ever want to get into it?"[3]

His troubles ended unexpectedly. In July 1881, before the appointments were completed and long before the country learned what kind of president the former congressman would make, Garfield decided he needed a vacation. Walking to catch a train at Washington's Union Station, he was confronted by Charles Guiteau, an unsuccessful applicant for a consulship. Guiteau raised a pistol and fired two shots. "I am a Stalwart and Arthur will be president!" he was heard to say. Garfield survived the shooting but not the consequent care. He lingered for several weeks while doctors probed for the bullets, to Garfield's excruciating pain. By September he seemed sufficiently out of danger that the doctors let him take his delayed vacation, to the New Jersey shore. But complications, including pneumonia, set in, and on September 19 he collapsed and died.[4]

THEODORE ROOSEVELT HAD a grudge against Chester Arthur that antedated Arthur's succeeding to the presidency upon Garfield's death. In 1877, when Roosevelt was in college and Arthur was customs collector in New York, President Hayes nominated Roosevelt's father, also called Theodore, to replace Arthur. The nomination angered Roscoe Conkling, Arthur's mentor, and the Stalwart leader marshaled his troops to block the nomination. Conkling's campaign started with parliamentary maneuvers—he claimed a breach of the senatorial courtesy allowing members to veto home-state appointments—but quickly escalated to nasty rumors about the elder Roosevelt and his failure to serve in the Union army during the Civil War. Theodore Sr. was a tyro at party politics, and the stress of the nomination fight strained a physical constitution already wracked, as it turned out, by colon cancer. He died just weeks after the Senate rejected his nomination. Arthur retained the customs post.[5]

The younger Theodore Roosevelt had spent a childhood sheltered by wealth and sickness; his father was at once his role model and closest friend. The Stalwart campaign against Theodore Sr., culminating in his death, made his son a bitter enemy of all Stalwarts, including Arthur. Roosevelt's hostility to the spoilsmen helped motivate his entry into politics, and upon his election to the New York assembly it inspired an early campaign against the party machine. About the time Roosevelt went to Albany, Jay Gould seized control of the Manhattan Elevated Railway. The takeover involved Gould's typical finagling, including some questionable rulings by Judge Theodore Westbrook. Roosevelt indignantly demanded an investigation of the affair. Isaac Hunt, who became a Roosevelt ally, remembered the twenty-three-year-old lawmaker as "a society man and a dude," with tailored coat, silk hat, gold fob, eyeglasses, and hair parted down the middle. The sight of the college boy taking on the Mephistopheles of Wall Street tickled Hunt's imagination and that of reporters and editors across the state. "Mr. Roosevelt has a most refreshing habit of calling men and things by their right names," the *New York Times* asserted, "and in these days of judicial, ecclesiastical, and journalistic subservience to the barons of the Street"—Wall Street—"it needs some little courage in any public man to characterize them and their acts in fitting terms." George Curtis's *Harper's Weekly* applauded the young assemblyman who "does not know the meaning of fear and to whom the bluster and bravado of party and political bullies are as absolutely indifferent as the blowing of the wind."[6]

Roosevelt got his investigation but nothing more than a reprimand of the judge, who almost certainly was guilty of unethical, if perhaps not illegal, conduct. He also got a lesson in real-world politics. Roosevelt had married Alice, but like most legislators he left his wife at home when he went to Albany. Gould's agents trailed him to discover whether he, like more than a few lawmakers, strayed from fidelity among the fleshpots of the state capital. When the private dicks found nothing, they tried to lure him into sin and scandal. An attractive young woman fainted on the sidewalk as he was passing by. He helped her up and hailed a cab to take her home. She asked him to accompany her. This aroused his suspicion and he refused, but as he put her in the cab and paid the driver, he noted the address she gave the man. He sent a detective of his own to the place; the investigator reported criminal-looking characters loitering about.

New York assemblymen served single-year terms, and Roosevelt had to defend his seat in November 1882. The elevation of Arthur to the presidency, at a time when Conkling's influence was waning, cast New York's Republicans into confusion; compounding their difficulties was the surprising emergence of Buffalo mayor Grover Cleveland, whose popular nomination for governor topped a strong Democratic ticket. Cleveland led the Democrats to a landslide victory in the state races; Roosevelt was one of the few Republican survivors.

Roosevelt took the debacle as an opportunity to move up in the party. With most of his seniors gone, he sought and won the Republican nomination for speaker of the assembly. It was an honor without substance, as the Democratic majority guaranteed a Democratic speaker, but Roosevelt made the most of it, casting himself—at twenty-four—as the putative leader of his party in the assembly.[7]

HIS STANDING WAS his ticket to the Republican national convention in 1884. By the time the GOP (as Republican headline writers had taken to calling the "Grand Old Party") gathered in Chicago, Roosevelt's personal situation had changed dramatically. His wife had died, leaving him stricken with grief and wondering whether he could carry on as before. He was of two minds about politics when he reached Chicago, and the circumstances of the convention only increased his ambivalence.

Chester Arthur's performance as president, while less dismal than most students of politics expected, had done nothing to endear him to the Blaine wing of the Republicans. "I do not desire or expect the nomination," Blaine said honestly but unconvincingly, before adding, quite believably: "But I don't intend that man in the White House shall have it." Arthur might have struggled harder for election in his own right had he not been secretly sick, of the kidney failure then called Bright's disease. Yet he felt obliged, for the sake of honor and the Stalwart cause, to make a run. And those many persons who owed their offices to Arthur felt obliged, for his sake and theirs, to support him.[8]

More than a few Republicans sought to draft William Sherman, who might be positioned as Grant without the corruption. Blaine led the Sherman movement, writing the general a letter a week before the convention offering to choreograph the nomination. "Your historical record, full as it is, would be rendered still more glorious by such an administration as you would be able to give the country," Blaine told Sherman. The general need simply keep quiet. "Do not say a word in advance of the convention, no matter who may ask you. . . . Do not answer this."

But Sherman did answer it, with characteristic bluntness. He said he would be "a fool and a madman and an ass to embark anew, at sixty-five years of age, in a career that may at any moment become tempest-tossed by the perfidy, the defalcation, the dishonesty or neglect of any one of a hundred thousand subordinates." Soldiers did not make good presidents. "I remember well the experience of Generals Jackson, Harrison, Taylor, Grant, Hayes, and Garfield, all elected because of their military services, and am warned, not encouraged, by their sad experiences. No, count me out. . . . Leave us old soldiers the peace we fought for and think we earned."[9]

Blaine saw no alternative to running himself. Eight years earlier he had sought the nomination eagerly; four years ago he would have accepted it gladly. Now he wasn't so sure the prize outweighed the cost. He wanted to be president and thought he'd make a good one, but he knew a national campaign would revive all the old allegations and doubtless invent new ones. He sincerely wanted Sherman to run, in part because he hoped to become the general-president's right-hand man. When Sherman refused, Blaine decided that honor and country required him to step forward. Anything was better than Arthur.

THE UNSAVORY CHOICE between Blaine and Arthur initially drove Theodore Roosevelt to Senator George Edmunds, a quiet reformer from Vermont. In the days before primary elections, much of the battle for a presidential nomination took place at state party conventions, where delegates committed to the competing candidates slugged it out for slots in the state delegations to the national convention. New York's Republicans met in April 1884 in Utica, and Roosevelt argued that neither Arthur nor Blaine stood a chance in the general election. Only a candidate unsullied by scandal, with a record for reform, could hope to rally Republicans to the polls and stave off a Democratic victory. Few of the party regulars at Utica were convinced, with most lining up behind either Arthur or Blaine. But the balance between the two was close enough that they were willing to send four uncommitted delegates to Chicago. Roosevelt was one.

Roosevelt spent the weeks before the national convention trying to carve space for Edmunds between Arthur and Blaine by blasting the prospects of both. Blaine was a "most dangerous man," he declared, while Arthur "would be beaten out of sight." Roosevelt corresponded with others of independent mind, including Henry Cabot Lodge, the acquaintance from Boston who was becoming a friend and ally. "For Heaven's sake," Roosevelt wrote Lodge, "don't let the Massachusetts delegation commit any such act of suicidal folly as (from panic merely) supporting Arthur would be."[10]

Edmunds's supporters acknowledged his blandness, but their regard for themselves made up for the deficiencies in their candidate. In Chicago, Roosevelt thrilled to be associated with the Edmunds bloc. "It included all the men of the broadest culture and highest character that there were in the convention, all those who were prominent in the professions or eminent as private citizens," he told his sister afterward. "And it included almost all the 'plain people,' the farmers and others, who were above average, who were possessed of a keen sense of personal and official honesty, and who were accustomed to think for themselves." The nominating speech for Edmunds, by Massachusetts governor John Long, was "the most masterly and scholarly effort I have ever listened to."

But even Roosevelt had to admit it lacked something Blaine inspired in his followers.

> Blaine was nominated by Judge [William] West, the blind orator of Ohio. It was a most impressive scene. The speaker, a feeble old man of shrunk but gigantic frame, stood looking with sightless eyes towards the vast throng that filled the huge hall. As he became excited his voice rang like a trumpet, and the audience became worked up to a condition of absolutely uncontrollable excitement and enthusiasm. For a quarter of an hour at a time they cheered and shouted so that the brass

bands could not be heard at all, and we were nearly deafened by the noise.

Roosevelt couldn't gainsay the enthusiasm for Blaine, but he did question the character of those who shouted so loudly.

Their ranks included many scoundrels, adroit and clever, who intend to further their own ends by supporting the popular candidate, or who know Mr. Blaine so well that they expect under him to be able to develop their schemes to the fullest extent; but for the most part these Republicans were good, ordinary men, who do not do very much thinking, who are pretty honest themselves, but who are callous to any but very flagrant wrongdoing in others, unless it is brought home to them most forcibly, who "don't think Blaine any worse than the rest of them," and who are captivated by the man's force, originality, and brilliant demagoguery.

When Blaine won the nomination, on the fourth ballot, Roosevelt had to wonder about the future of Republicanism, and of the republic. "It may be that 'the voice of the people is the voice of God' in fifty-one cases out of a hundred; but in the remaining forty-nine it is quite as likely to be the voice of the devil, or, what is still worse, the voice of a fool."[11]

DEVIL OR FOOL, it was a voice Roosevelt ignored only at his peril. The Blaine nomination provoked many who thought like Roosevelt to bolt the party. The defectors called themselves independents; their critics called them "Mugwumps," a word supposedly derived from an Indian language and meaning "big chief." (A more sardonic etymology suggested that the persons so described had their "mugs" on one side of the fence and their "wumps" on the other.) The revolt began in Boston, where Republican respectables of the Massachusetts Reform Club pledged to prevent Blaine from dishonoring New England and disgracing the party of Lincoln by getting himself elected. "All was excitement and everybody was on fire," wrote a participant at an early meeting. "Not a man in the room wished to support Blaine." Charles Francis Adams couldn't attend but sent best wishes; cousin Josiah Quincy opened his law office to a follow-up gathering. From Boston the movement spread to New York. *New York Evening Post* editor E. L. Godkin's plague-on-both-your-houses temperament made him a natural Mugwump. The more genteel George Curtis came aboard. Carl Schurz signed on. Henry Ward Beecher expostulated, "Put me down against Blaine one hundred times in letters two feet long."[12]

The party regulars derided the Mugwumps as feckless do-gooders. Such men had never elected a candidate, they said, and never would. And if somehow their man did achieve office, he wouldn't know what to do with it. Blaine himself swatted the Mugwumps as "noisy but not numerous, pharisaical but not practical, ambitious but not wise, pretentious but not powerful."

Theodore Roosevelt couldn't dismiss them so easily. They included men whose opinion he valued, persons like those he had grown up with and still lived among. Yet Roosevelt had experienced enough of politics in Albany to understand that parties mattered. For better or worse, American democracy operated through parties, and if he intended to continue his political career, abandoning his party was a reckless way to proceed.

He tried for a time to avoid a decision. When the Chicago convention broke up and the rest of the New York delegation headed east for home, Roosevelt turned the other way, toward Dakota. He dodged reporters and disappeared into the Badlands, where he rode the range from morning till night, chasing cattle and dreaming of the ranch he was constructing. "I have just come in from spending *thirteen* hours in the saddle," he boasted to his sister, "for every day I have been here I have had my hands full." He contemplated staying out on the range, and out of the political crossfire, till after the November election.[13]

But as the campaign developed he reconsidered. The Democrats, after a quarter century in exile, were desperate to regain the White House. Though several states put forward favorite sons at the Democratic convention in Chicago, the vote counters in the party determined—again—that New York held the key to success. Grover Cleveland had been governor of the Empire State for little over a year, which meant that he hadn't made many enemies. Tammany Hall didn't like him, but its animus served the party's larger purpose of contrasting the "ugly honest" Cleveland to the scandal-tainted Blaine. Various state delegations gradually fell in line behind Cleveland, who led on the first ballot and won on the second.

Even after the Cleveland nomination, Roosevelt might have kept mum but for a report linking him to the Mugwumps. A newspaper published a hearsay account from Chicago asserting that Roosevelt, in his anger at Blaine's victory, had said that honest Republicans ought to support any credible Democratic nominee over Blaine. Roosevelt vehemently denied the report but then discredited his denial by saying that if he had said such a thing, he had done so in the heat of passion. "At midnight, two hours after the convention had adjourned, when I was savagely indignant at our defeat, and heated and excited with the sharpness of the struggle, I certainly felt bitterly angry at the result, and so expressed myself in private conversation."

To set the record straight, Roosevelt explained that he would vote for Blaine in the fall. "A man cannot act both without and within the party; he can do either, but he cannot possibly do both. . . . I did my best and got beaten, and I propose to stand by the result. . . . I am by inheritance and education a Republican; whatever good I have been able to accomplish in public life has been accomplished through the Republican party. I have acted with it in the past, and wish to act with it in the future."[14]

THE GENERAL ELECTION campaign of 1884 was the most entertaining in decades and the least edifying. The Democrats didn't discover much new to throw against Blaine, but they merrily recycled the old charges. At Cleveland rallies the Democratic barkers led audiences in chants of "Burn this letter" and, when that grew tiresome, the slightly more complex "Blaine, Blaine, James G. Blaine, continental liar from the state of Maine." Democratic leaders kept a healthy distance from the Mugwump Republicans, accepting their votes for Cleveland but fully realizing that the genteel likes of *Harper's* editor Curtis and Harvard president Charles Eliot wouldn't win them many votes outside the silk-stocking districts.

The Republicans had to work harder to find material to use against Cleveland, but their detectives struck dirt by midsummer. The obvious lead was Cleveland's unmarried state, which was presumed to mean one of two things, both salacious. The truth lay on the less salacious side: his predilection was for women, in particular one Maria Halpin, a widow with whom Cleveland had been involved several years before. The affair produced a child, or so the evidence suggested. Mrs. Halpin admitted to having entertained other men during the period in question; possibly one of them was the father. But Cleveland accepted responsibility for the child—a boy—and paid for his support. The tale grew a bit more complicated when Mrs. Halpin suffered a nervous breakdown, partly brought on by alcohol, and had to be institutionalized. Cleveland paid for her care and arranged a foster home for the boy.

The story hit a Republican paper in Buffalo under the headline "A Terrible Tale." The author was the Reverend George H. Ball, who subsequently elaborated his account into a saga of seduction and abandonment. Mrs. Halpin wasn't the only victim of Cleveland's animal appetites, the Baptist preacher said; Cleveland kept a "harem" of women. Lest anyone miss the conclusion to be drawn from the sordid business, Ball explained that the difference between Cleveland and Blaine was that "between the brothel and the family, between indecency and decency, between lust and law."

The revelation threatened a serious blow to the image of "Grover the Good." Cleveland's spokesmen stammered in embarrassment till the candidate telegraphed them a terse order: "Tell the truth." This proved a brilliant stroke, especially after Cleveland's advisers showed the telegram to the press. Their man had stumbled but accepted responsibility for his mistake. Some of Cleveland's supporters, citing the confusion in the paternity, suggested that he had gone beyond the call of duty, saving the reputation of the real father, a married man. More than a few were relieved to be able to say that Cleveland's single flaw was excessive masculinity. Henry Ward Beecher jokingly asserted that if every New Yorker who violated the Seventh Commandment voted for Cleveland, he'd carry the state in a landslide. The overall effect was just what the Cleveland side wanted: to emphasize the difference in integrity between their candidate and Blaine. It also gave Democrats ammunition to fire back at the Republicans. When Republican hecklers interrupted Democratic rallies with taunts of "Ma, ma, where's my pa?" the Democrats rejoined: "Going to the White House, ha, ha, ha!"

So they could say, and so they certainly hoped. But in the days before anything like scientific polling, no one knew what the voters would actually do. This ignorance didn't prevent all sorts of people from professing intelligence. "A very singular thing happened on a horse-car recently," a journalist wryly reported.

A gentleman thought to canvass the occupants as to their presidential preferences. He had taken the votes of two old ladies, and then inquired of the only male rider besides himself, "Whom are you going to vote for, my friend?" when the unsympathetic individual replied, "Go to thunder." It is clear from this incident that Mr. Blaine's majority in Massachusetts cannot be less than seventy thousand. A hard-workingman fell down on a banana skin last week, and has since been unable to do any labor, which proves conclusively that the votes of the workingmen will all be thrown for Blaine. An earnest Cleveland man, so his son informs us, will not vote in the coming election. He died last Wednesday. The Democratic candidate, it is believed, will lose many more votes in the same way . . . "Blaine" is a word of one syllable, while "Cleveland" has two syllables. This will give the former an increased advantage among the younger class of voters.[15]

Had more of substance separated the candidates, the auguries would have been easier to interpret. On a few issues the Republicans and the Democrats did draw apart. Blaine and the Republicans favored a protective tariff; Cleveland and the Democrats didn't. Most Republicans wanted dearer money, preferably gold, than most Democrats. The Democrats demanded restraints on anticompetitive business practices; the Republicans were generally willing to let capitalists be capitalists.

But the issues had trouble rising above the personal attacks, not least since both sides believed their opponents' weaknesses were more potent than their own strengths. For all his ability to play to the galleries, Blaine could point to little of constructive legislation in his record. Cleveland might be honest, but what had he actually accomplished in his brief career in office?

Turnout promised—or threatened—to decide the race. The major parties in the 1880s might have lost their zeal, but their organizational capacity remained impressive. Every campaign featured rallies, parades, and barbecues, with placards, speeches, songs, and drink. As the elections neared, the city machines turned out the vote by the methods Tammany made notorious; in the countryside the promise of spoils—in particular postmasterships, of which some forty thousand remained at the disposal of the president, despite the inroads of the 1883 Pendleton Civil Service Reform Act—inspired office-holders and their would-be replacements, and the relatives and friends of each group, to vote early and as often as they thought they could get away with. Public voting was the norm, with each party supplying its own ballots, distinctively sized, colored, and shaped, and with the party's candidates already marked. Voters cast their ballots in full view of neighbors, employers, and party hacks. Christopher Buckley, the Democratic "Blind Boss" of San Francisco, was renowned for haunting the polls in a large overcoat with deep pockets from which, at the whisperings of sighted spotters, he distributed gold quarter eagles ($2.50 coins) to those who upheld the California Democracy. (Apparently he didn't think to emulate Tammany's "Big Tim" Sullivan, who perfumed his ballots in order that loyal Democrats might be identified by scent as well as sight.) For just such reasons, the Australian ballot—nonpartisan and cast in secret, so named for having been introduced Down Under in the 1850s—was gaining support, but the parties stoutly and for the most part successfully resisted it. Voting continued to be a public act.[16]

Whatever the influence of the party activities on the fairness of elections, a conspicuous result was that Americans in the Gilded Age—indeed throughout the latter two-thirds of the nineteenth century—went to the polls in numbers that would shame their great-grandchildren. From the 1840s to the 1890s, percentage turnout in presidential races consistently ran in the high seventies to low eighties. The highest participation in American history occurred in 1876, when nearly 82 percent of eligible voters cast ballots, but each of the next five presidential elections came within several points of that figure. (By comparison, turnouts in the 1990s and early 2000s ranged from the high forties to midfifties.)[17]

WITH TURNOUT THE KEY, each side in the 1884 race looked frantically for anything that would inspire its marginal supporters—those few faithhearts who couldn't automatically be counted on to brave rain, muddy roads, or other discouragements—to get to the polls. Blaine attended a rally in New York City on October 29, the Wednesday before the election. Several Protestant clergymen were on the agenda; Blaine distractedly prepared his own remarks. One of the ministers, a Presbyterian named Samuel Burchard, warmed up the crowd for the candidate. "We are your friends, Mr. Blaine," Burchard declared, eliciting cheers. "And notwithstanding all the calumnies that have been urged in the papers against you, we stand by your side." From various parts of the audience arose shouts of "Amen!" "We expect to vote for you next Tuesday." More cheers and shouts. "We are Republicans, and don't propose to leave our party and identify with the party of rum, Romanism, and rebellion. We are loyal to our flag. We are loyal to you." Still more cheers.

Blaine wasn't the next speaker; more ministers intervened. Blaine continued to work on his comments. When he did get up, he concentrated on the tariff and the way it embodied the principles of Christian charity. He went home and thought nothing more of the affair. One of the reporters, however, who had actually listened to the speeches and jotted down Burchard's alliteration of "rum, Romanism, and rebellion," asked Cleveland's managers if they cared to comment. They kept quiet for the moment, but that Sunday handbills at thousands of Catholic churches across the state and the nation repeated the Republican identification of Catholics with drunkenness and treason. The strictly honest among the Democratic propagandists explained that the statement had been made in Blaine's presence and gone unrebutted; the less scrupulous put the words in Blaine's own mouth.[18]

Blaine had almost no time to respond, and what he said seemed weak and defensive. How many Catholic votes he lost by the blunder is impossible to say. But every one hurt, as soon became apparent. Cleveland carried New York state by a mere eleven hundred votes in the popular balloting. And New York's thirty-six electoral votes made the difference in the election, as both sides had guessed they might. The South went solidly for Cleveland and was joined by Indiana, New Jersey, Connecticut, and Delaware, in addition to New York. Cleveland totaled 219 electoral votes to Blaine's 182. In a national turnout of 77.5 percent, Cleveland received 4,880,000 popular votes to Blaine's 4,850,000.

Chapter 15

CAPITAL IMPROVEMENTS

———

The sound and fury of popular politics during the Gilded Age couldn't conceal an underlying but undeniable truth: that after almost a century during which the tide of democracy had risen ever higher, an ebb was setting in. The Fourteenth and Fifteenth amendments nominally extended the rights of citizenship and voting to the freedmen, but those rights were being gutted in much of the South as the old elites reconstituted themselves and reconsolidated their power. In the North and West, the faith in democracy that had sustained the Union during the Civil War weakened with the scandals of the postwar era. If democracy produced the Tweed ring, the gold ring, the whiskey ring, and Crédit Mobilier, perhaps it required rethinking. Citizens—white male citizens, that is; women still couldn't vote in most places—might be voting in record numbers, but given the dismal performance of the officials they elected, the high turnout seemed to skeptics merely another reason to doubt democracy.

For this reason subscribers to the *Atlantic Monthly*, the Boston journal edited by William Dean Howells and consulted by the most serious thinkers in America, were intrigued to read an account of an unidentified country by a recent visitor there. "As soon as I had learned to speak the language a little, I became greatly interested in the people and the system of government," the visitor related.

> I found that the nation had at first tried universal suffrage pure and simple, but had thrown that form aside because the result was not satisfactory. It had seemed to deliver all power into the hands of the ignorant and non-taxpaying classes; and of a necessity the responsible offices were filled from these classes also.
>
> A remedy was sought. The people believed they had found it, not in the destruction of universal suffrage, but in the enlargement of it. It was an odd idea, and ingenious. You must understand, the constitution gave every man a vote; therefore that vote was a vested right and could not be taken away. But the constitution did not say that certain individuals might not be given two votes, or ten! So an amendatory clause was inserted in a quiet way, a clause which authorized the enlargement of the franchise in certain cases to be specified by statute.

The amendment declared that an elementary school education entitled a person to a second vote, beyond the first he possessed by virtue of being a citizen. A high school diploma added two more votes, for four total. The holder of a university degree got nine votes altogether. Wealth, too, translated into extra votes, but less readily than education. Only the wealthiest few had more votes than the college graduates.

This novel system was not without critics. Many newspapers had opposed it from the start, saying it would destroy the liberties of the people. But the critics had failed to prevent its approval, and after its implementation more than a few had been obliged to admit their mistake. The new system evoked a beneficent striving unlike any the country had witnessed.

> Whereas formerly a man was honored only according to the amount of money he possessed, his grandeur was measured now by the number of votes he wielded. A man with only one vote was conspicuously respectful to his neighbor who possessed three. And if he was a man above the commonplace, he was as conspicuously energetic in his determination to acquire three for himself. This spirit of emulation

invaded all ranks. Votes based upon capital were commonly called "mortal" votes, because they could be lost; those based upon learning were called "immortal," because they were permanent.

On account of their permanency, the immortal votes were esteemed above the mortal votes, and their possessors were commonly called "immortals." The visitor accompanied a resident down a street of one of the main cities. The resident nodded lightly to a pedestrian, then explained to the visitor that this was a one-vote nod, as the man to whom he had nodded possessed one vote. A second pedestrian approached; the resident bowed. A four-vote bow, he said. Anticipating the traveler's question, he said that nothing compelled his acknowledgments; these were simply a matter of custom and respect. Another pedestrian approached; the resident bent at the waist and doffed his hat.

"What grandee is that?" the traveler inquired.

"That is our most illustrious astronomer. He hasn't any money, but is fearfully learned. Nine immortals is *his* political weight! He would swing a hundred and fifty votes if our system were perfect."

"Is there any altitude of mere moneyed grandeur that you take off your hat to?"

"No. Nine immortal votes is the only power we uncover for."

The spirit of emulation suffused the whole people, including women, who earned votes the same way the men did.

It was common to hear people admiringly mention men who had begun life on the lower levels and in time achieved great voting-power. It was also common to hear youths planning a future of ever so many votes for themselves. I heard shrewd mammas speak of certain young men as good "catches" because they possessed such-and-such a number of votes. I knew of more than one case where an heiress was married to a youngster who had but one vote, the argument being that he was gifted with such excellent parts that in time he would acquire a good voting strength, and perhaps in the long run be able to outvote his wife, if he had luck.

The visitor naturally wondered what kind of government this system produced. An inspection revealed the answer. "Ignorance and incompetence had no place in the government," he reported. "Brains and property managed the state." A common man—or woman—might aspire to office, but only if he or she possessed intelligence or acquired property. Public office was as well compensated as the most distinguished professions, and more highly respected. For this reason graft had disappeared. Justice was impartially and wisely administered, as the judges earned their offices by education, experience, and talent and held them for life. Schools and colleges were amply funded, as befit the avenues to immortality, and were free to all.

The traveler inquired whether school attendance was compulsory, as in many countries. His host smiled tolerantly at the unthinking character of the question. "When a man's child is able to make himself honored according to the amount of education he acquires," the resident said, "don't you suppose that that parent will apply the compulsion himself? Our free schools and free colleges require no law to fill them."[1]

MARK TWAIN WAS still a journalist, and still Sam Clemens to most of those who knew him, when he set sail in 1866 from San Francisco for Hawaii. The *Sacramento Union* had assigned him to tour the Sandwich Islands, as they were called by Americans and other outsiders, and report their sights, customs, and prospects back to the *Union*'s readers. The success of the venture—in terms of Twain's discovered affinity for overseas travel and the marketability of what he wrote about it—prompted further journeys. In 1867 he embarked from New York for Europe aboard the side-wheel steamer *Quaker City*. "I am going on this trip for fun only," Twain fibbed to a friend; in fact he was on assignment for the *Alta California* of San Francisco, which expected a series of humorous letters home. Twain toured Europe and the Mediterranean, finally reaching what Christians called the Holy Land, which inspired the book he eventually expanded his letters into: *The Innocents Abroad; or, The New Pilgrims' Progress*.

The book was Twain's first best seller, and its success steeled his nerve to propose marriage to Olivia Langdon. "I want a good wife—I want a couple of them if they are particularly good," he had told a friend, but he hadn't seen how he could afford one on a journalist's salary. "I can't turn an inkstand into Aladdin's lamp." The Langdons, one of the wealthiest families in Elmira, New York, hadn't seen much hope for a journalist, either, but a well-published author was another matter, and as the sales of Twain's *Innocents* soared, Livy's parents blessed the union.[2]

The couple settled in Hartford, Connecticut, where the neighbors included Harriet Beecher Stowe. Henry Ward Beecher dropped by for visits and impressed Twain as a solid fellow. "Puritans are mighty straitlaced," Twain told his mother, "and they won't let me smoke in the parlor, but the Almighty don't make any better people." Twain particularly appreciated that Henry didn't let religion intrude on his enjoyment of life. When Twain suggested that wine ought to be served with meals, Beecher agreed. "But it wouldn't do to say it loud," Beecher added. Twain concluded, "Henry Ward is a brick."

Family business took Twain to Washington in 1870, when Congress was considering a bill to reconstruct the Tennessee judiciary. A company in Memphis owed half a million dollars to one of Livy's father's firms, and Twain lobbied the Connecticut delegation to facilitate payment. His influence on the legislation was minimal, but the influence of the legislative process on Twain was substantial. To date the objects of his satire had been foreigners and persons at the margins of society; Washington opened an entirely new literary front. He discovered "material enough for a whole book," he said. "This a perfect gold mine."[3]

Production began shortly after his return to Hartford. Other neighbors were Susan and Charles Dudley Warner; Charles edited the *Hartford Courant*, and over dinner he and Twain made light of the novels their wives enjoyed reading. The women challenged the men to do better. Neither Twain nor Warner had ever written a novel, but they accepted the challenge and decided to collaborate. Twain wrote the first section, establishing the premises of the book and introducing its major character; after that the two men alternated chapters. The title apparently was Twain's.

The Gilded Age: A Tale of Today was published in 1873 to strong sales and weak reviews. The plot didn't hold together, the critics said, but betrayed the dual hands that wrote it. The satire was clumsily broad, overstating the corruption in American political and economic life. Twain couldn't deny the first criticism (which he and Warner implicitly acknowledged by claiming separate copyright control of the characters in their own chapters). He defended himself against the second charge, of exaggeration, with uncharacteristic meekness. "In America, nearly every man has his

dream, his pet scheme, whereby he is to advance himself socially or pecu-
niarily," he explained in the preface to the British edition. "It is this all-
pervading speculativeness which we have tried to illustrate in *The Gilded
Age*. It is a characteristic which is both bad and good, for both the individual and the nation. . . . But I have a great strong faith in a noble
future for my country. A vast majority of the people are straightforward
and honest."[4]

Straightforward and honest, perhaps, but dangerously ignorant. With
more than a few of his contemporaries, Twain despaired of democracy's
ability to deliver good government. The scandals of the Gilded Age—the
title caught on though the book itself soon faded from view—suggested
that the greed to which capitalism appealed was more than most people
could put aside when they turned to politics. The commercial success of
The Gilded Age convinced Twain he might have a future as a novelist—he
set to work on what would become *Tom Sawyer*—but he didn't abandon
political criticism. In October 1875 he published the anonymous account
of the mythical republic where education and wealth augmented the voting power of men and women, making "immortals" of the best educated
and yielding higher-minded, more responsible government than existed in
the United States. The positive response to the article caused *Atlantic* editor Howells to urge Twain to file more dispatches from the model republic.
But though Twain had no difficulty generating the indignation of the
satirist, he lacked the patience of the reformer. And in any event the work
he produced under his own name—even if assumed—was too lucrative for
him to abandon.[5]

OTHERS TOOK UP the cudgels against democracy, at least as currently
practiced in the United States. Henry Adams devoted an entire 1880
novel, straightforwardly called *Democracy*, to lampooning the habits of
Americans in the political arena. Adams's politicians were venal and vulgar,
his voters silly, stupid, or self-interested. Like Twain, Adams thought dis-
cretion the better part of critical valor and declined to put his name on his
work; the secret of his authorship held for decades. John Hay, former personal secretary to Abraham Lincoln and future secretary of state to
William McKinley and Theodore Roosevelt, was no less critical of American democracy in his 1884 novel, *The Breadwinners*. But he was even more

cautious, refusing till death to acknowledge writing such a scathing attack on the practice, if not the principle, of popular government.

Francis Parkman frankly avowed his anti-democratic opinions. Writing under his own name in the *North American Review* in 1878, the historian (and botanist: his Harvard appointment was in horticulture) described what he morosely called "the failure of universal suffrage." Susan B. Anthony and other feminists would have disputed Parkman's premise that universal suffrage existed in America, as would the growing number of disfranchised African Americans in the South, but Parkman thought the franchise had spread quite far enough already. "The transfer of sovereignty to the people, and the whole people, is proclaimed the panacea of political and social ills," he said, "and we are but rarely reminded that popular sovereignty had evils of its own, against which patriotism may exercise itself to better purpose. Here and there one hears a whisper that perhaps the masses have not learned to use their power; but the whisper is greeted with obloquy." Americans had dethroned King George only to enthrone a new monarch, King Demos, who had begun as "a reasonable and sensible monarch who had a notion of good government, and ruled himself and his realm with wisdom and moderation," but who had degenerated till "he begins to lose his wits and forget his kingcraft."

More than Twain and some other critics of democracy, Parkman faulted not democracy per se but democracy's perversion by capitalism. Democracy had suited the New England villages that constituted its American birthplace. That birthplace, however, no longer existed. "The village has grown into a populous city, with its factories and workshops, its acres of tenement-houses, and thousands and ten thousands of restless workmen, foreigners for the most part, to whom liberty means license and politics means plunder." The effects of capitalism spread insidiously across the land.

> Population increased, wealth grew apace; men became rabid in making money, and women frivolous in spending it. . . . A vast industrial development, an immense prosperity rested safely for a while on the old national traditions, love of country, respect for law, and the habit of self-government. Then began the inevitable strain. Crowded cities, where the irresponsible and ignorant were numerically equal, or more than equal, to the rest, and where the weakest and most worthless was

a match, by his vote, for the wisest and best; bloated wealth and envi-
ous poverty; a tinseled civilization above, and a discontented prole-
tariat beneath—all these have broken rudely upon the dreams of equal
brotherhood once cherished by those who made their wish the father
of their thought, and fancied that this favored land formed an exception to the universal laws of human nature.

Among these laws was the one dictating that some people were more
gifted than others. "Vaguely and half unconsciously, but every day more
and more, the masses hug the flattering illusion that one man is essentially
about as good as another. They will not deny that there is great difference
in the quality of horses or dogs, but they refuse to see it in their own genus.
A jockey may be a democrat in the street, but he is sure to be an aristocrat
in the stable. And yet the essential difference between man and man is
incomparably greater than that between horse and horse, or dog and dog."

Advocates of democracy argued that education was the answer to
democracy's ills. Parkman thought the problem wasn't simply intellectual.
"It consists also in the want of feeling that his own interests are connected
with those of the community, and in the weakness or absence of the sense
of moral and political duty." Immigrants lacked this feeling on arrival, and
little in their experience caused it to grow. "It may be doubted, as a general
rule, whether the young Irish-American is a better or safer citizen than his
parent from Cork. He can read, but he reads nothing but sensation stories
and scandalous picture-papers, which fill him with preposterous notions
and would enfeeble a stronger brain than his and debauch a sounder conscience. He is generally less industrious than his sire, and equally careless
of the public good."

Parkman had no easy answer to the problem he described. In fact he
had no real answer at all. Democracy was too entrenched as an ideology,
and capitalism too powerful as a practice. He advocated reforming higher
education. "What we need most is a broad and masculine education, bearing on questions of society and government; not repelling from active life,
but preparing for it and impelling toward it. The discipline of the university should be a training for the arena." He cited the Civil War in evidence
of the principle that patriotism could elevate politics above the grasping
and mundane, if only briefly; the challenge was to preserve that patriotism
during peacetime. He called on idealistic young people to put country

before self and oust those who did the opposite. Yet though he professed optimism he hardly engendered it. "The strife is strangely unequal," he acknowledged, "for on one side are ranged all the forces of self-interest, and on the other only duty and patriotism." In a political economy that celebrated the former, the latter labored at a severe disadvantage. "Universal suffrage is applicable only to those peoples, if such there are, who by character and training are prepared for it." Masses of Americans lacked the preparation, rendering the failure of universal suffrage inescapable.[6]

HERMAN MELVILLE HAD gone to sea and come home to write *Moby-Dick*. Henry George went to sea and returned to write *Progress and Poverty*. The difference doubtless revealed divergent sensibilities in Melville and George; no Ahab so haunted the dreams of George as of Melville. But it also reflected the changing times. Melville shipped out in 1839, when America remained largely rural; his most popular book during his lifetime, the 1846 *Typee*, addressed an audience attuned to the rhythms and needs of an agrarian age. Henry George, by contrast, plowed the Pacific in the wake of the California gold rush; when he turned to writing, industrialization was in full roar, oil came from the stony deep rather than the briny deep, and the cannibalism that sent frissons through readers occurred mostly in the marketplace. Henry George's white whale was no symbolic cetacean but rather American capitalism.

George was the second of ten children of a Philadelphia customhouse clerk and his wife; at thirteen he left school and sought a job to help support his siblings. Philadelphia was still a major seaport, and its merchant marine required a regular infusion of cabin boys. Henry signed on with the *Hindoo*, bound for the East Indies. In Australia, though, the crew contracted gold fever and threatened to desert for the mines back of Melbourne. The captain locked them up till the symptoms passed. On the vessel's return to Philadelphia, George worked as a typesetter before shipping out again, on a coastal schooner ferrying coal from Pennsylvania to New England. But the Panic of 1857 curtailed the demand for coal and terminated George's job. He headed west: to California, British Columbia, and California again. He eventually landed a job in San Francisco, setting type again. In 1861, as the eastern half of the country went to war, he pooled meager resources with four partners to found the San Francisco

Daily Evening Journal. George threw himself into the venture. "I worked until my clothes were in rags and the toes of my shoes were out," he said later. "I slept in the office and did the best I could to economize." But readers weren't buying what he and the others were writing, and the paper folded.

He married, despite his poverty and lack of prospects, to an Australian-born orphan who had found her way to California. Her uncle opposed the match, prompting the eighteen-year-old girl and her twenty-one-year-old suitor to elope. They lived on love for several years, as the feckless Henry couldn't find the rungs of the ladder of success. His spirits plumbed murderous depths. His wife was about to give birth to their second child; the cupboard was empty and so was George's wallet. "I walked along the street and made up my mind to get money from the first man whose appearance might indicate that he had it to give," he later wrote. "I stopped a man—a stranger—and told him I wanted five dollars. He asked me what I wanted it for. I told him that my wife was confined and that I had nothing to give her to eat. He gave me the money. If he had not, I think I was desperate enough to have killed him."[7]

Through all this, Henry George puzzled over why he did so poorly. He didn't lack energy or intelligence, or at least he didn't think so. But circumstances seemed to conspire against him—even as circumstances made it possible for others to become very rich. On many days pounding the sidewalks of San Francisco seeking work, he passed the Nob Hill mansions of Leland Stanford and his cronies and wondered what their secret was.

He pondered the matter further as his fortunes began to improve. Another typesetting job led to a reporting assignment to cover the local mourning for Abraham Lincoln; this segued into a stint writing editorials. As the Pacific railroad neared completion, he asked "What the Railroad Will Bring Us" and concluded that its benefits would be less than its boosters promised. Merchants and manufacturers might profit, but workers would face increased competition from goods produced elsewhere, and they would pay higher rents as land values rose. Towns along the rail line would prosper, but others would wither and die. The political consequences would be hardly less significant.

In the growth of large corporations and other special interests is an element of great danger. Of these great corporations and interests we shall have many. Look, for instance, at the Central Pacific Railroad Company, as it will be, with a line running to Salt Lake, controlling more capital and employing more men than any of the great eastern railroads who manage legislatures as they manage their workshops, and name governors, senators and judges almost as they name their own engineers and clerks.

California's experience after the driving of the golden spike confirmed George's predictions. The rich got richer, corporations grew more powerful, and workers struggled as never before. George covered the great railroad strike of 1877 as it spread to California, and in its aftermath he commenced work on what would become his magnum opus.

By his later testimony, the insight that inspired *Progress and Poverty* hit George on a horseback ride along the route of the recently completed Central Pacific.

> Absorbed in my own thoughts, I had driven the horse into the hills until he panted. Stopping for breath, I asked a passing teamster, for want of something better to say, what land was worth there. He pointed to some cows grazing off so far that they looked like mice and said: "I don't know exactly, but there is a man over there who will sell some land for a thousand dollars an acre." Like a flash it came upon me that there was the reason of advancing poverty with advancing wealth. With the growth of population, land grows in value, and the men who work it must pay more for the privilege.[8]

Turning this idea into a manuscript required most of a decade, turning the manuscript into a book another two years. Several publishing houses rejected the manuscript as unlikely to cover costs; only after he set the type himself and paid for plates did a publisher agree to produce a small edition, offered to the public in 1879.

The book began by noting that for generations scientific progress had held forth the promise of lightening humanity's burdens—of ending hunger, diminishing disease, eradicating ignorance. At no time had science progressed more rapidly than of late. And some in society benefited immensely, as anyone who visited the wealthy neighborhoods of American cities readily observed. But for millions of others, the promise of progress went unfulfilled. "Disappointment has followed disappointment. . . . Discovery upon discovery and invention after invention have neither lessened the toil of those who most need respite nor brought plenty to the poor." If anything, poverty had grown deeper and more punishing. In good times workers struggled from day to day and week to week, slaving long hours under harsh conditions. In bad times workers lost their jobs and homes and watched their children sicken and die.

This association of poverty with progress was "the great enigma of our times," George said.

> It is the central fact from which spring industrial, social, and political difficulties that perplex the world, and with which statesmanship and philanthropy and education grapple in vain. From it come the clouds that overhang the future of the most progressive and self-reliant nations. It is the riddle that the Sphinx of Fate puts to our civilization and which not to answer is to be destroyed. So long as all the increased wealth which modern progress brings goes but to build up great fortunes, to increase luxury and make sharper the contrast between the House of Have and the House of Want, progress is not real and cannot be permanent.

To deliver the promise of progress to those trapped in poverty was the challenge of American democracy, George said. He devoted chapters of his book to assessing the problem from different angles, but in the end he proposed a simple solution—one so simple it had eluded the most brilliant thinkers on political economy. George illustrated with an example from San Francisco. In 1848 property there had been essentially worthless; the finest lot in that sleepy village sold for a pittance. Five years later the same lot sold for tens of thousands of dollars. What had happened? Gold had been discovered, hundreds of thousands of people had rushed to California, and those who settled in San Francisco bid up the price of that lot. The owner became a rich man. Did he deserve his riches? Had he done anything to earn them? No; the increase in the value of the lot was the result of the development of California's economy as a whole, which in turn embodied the efforts of thousands upon thousands of ordinary people, who received no share in the lot owner's windfall.

This was wrong, George declared. It was inefficient. It mustn't continue. He proposed that since society as a whole generated the increase in value of the property, society should capture that gain. He advocated a tax on the appreciation of land values; the rate of the tax might start low but it should eventually rise until society claimed the entire appreciation. At this point the tax would produce sufficient revenues to replace all other taxes—taxes on capital, taxes on labor, taxes on consumption. The single tax on land appreciation would fund measures to alleviate poverty, but, more to the point, it would change the entire dynamic of the American political economy. "Land, no matter in whose name it stood or in what parcels it was held, would be really common property, and every member of the community would participate in the advantages of its ownership." George admitted the radical nature of his recommendation, and he understood that even those classes that would benefit most might blanch at its implications. "It is difficult for workingmen to get over the idea that there is a real antagonism between capital and labor. It is difficult for small farmers and homestead owners to get over the idea that to put all taxes on the value of land would be to tax them unduly. It is difficult for both classes to get over the idea that to exempt capital from taxation would be to make the rich richer, and the poor poorer." Such resistance simply revealed how thoroughly the values of the capitalist class permeated social thought. "Behind ignorance and prejudice there is a powerful interest, which has hitherto dominated literature, education, and opinion. A great wrong always dies hard, and the great wrong which in every civilized country condemns the masses of men to poverty and want will not die without a bitter struggle."

But once workers and farmers got past their mistaken prejudices, a brilliant future would open up to them and all of American society.

Give labor a free field and its full earnings; take for the benefit of the whole community that fund which the growth of the community creates, and want and the fear of want would be gone. The springs of production would be set free and the enormous increase of wealth would give the poorest ample comfort. Men would no more worry about finding employment than they worry about finding air to breathe; they need have no more care about physical necessities than do the lilies of the field. The progress of science, the march of invention, the diffusion of knowledge, would bring their benefits to all. With this abolition of want and the fear of want, the admiration of riches would decay and men would seek the respect and approbation of their fellows in other modes than by the acquisition and display of wealth. In this way there would be brought to the management of public affairs, and the administration of common funds the skill, the attention, the fidelity and the integrity that can now be secured only for private interests.[9]

EDWARD BELLAMY'S ANCESTORS included pirates and preachers. The preachers were more numerous but the pirates, naturally, more intriguing. Samuel Bellamy raided along America's Atlantic coast from a base in New England in the early eighteenth century; according to the compiler of a pirates' who's who, Captain Bellamy possessed "considerable gifts for public speaking"—perhaps deriving from the same sources as the preachers' fluency—and a progressive social conscience. "His views were distinctly socialistic."[10]

Edward Bellamy's immediate antecedents were more conventional but still distinctive. His mother was the straightest-laced woman in Chicopee, Massachusetts. "My grandmother was orthodox about everything, even to sewing a seam," Bellamy's daughter remembered. Idleness was not permitted her children. " 'Get a book' was Mother's never failing suggestion," Bellamy's brother recalled. Bellamy's father was the family libertine, although given his wife's Calvinist views and the conventions of mid-nineteenth-century Massachusetts, he confined his indulgences to the dinner table. "That he will in the end kill himself with his knife and fork there is not the slightest doubt," Edward wrote. "But I hope we may, by constant endeavors, persuade him to postpone his suicide for a few years." A few years was all they managed: the elder Bellamy died young, of obesity-aggravated causes.[11]

After a year at Union College in Schenectady, New York, Edward Bellamy toured Europe with a cousin. Conditions in the English countryside appalled him. Farm laborers lived in tiny huts with sodden floors, generations jumbled all together. "It is very common indeed for the father and mother of a family with their grown up sons and daughters, together with men lodgers, to be compelled to share between them one small bedroom," he wrote. "The immorality is shocking, and crimes of the most abominable descriptions are exceedingly frequent." Conditions were better in Germany, in part because German workers were better organized, in the German Workers' Party, in part because the German state was stronger, under Chancellor Bismarck.[12]

Bellamy studied law but never practiced, choosing a literary career instead. He wrote editorials for the *Springfield Union* of Massachusetts, occasional pieces for the *New York Evening Post*, and freelance articles for assorted periodicals. At thirty, in 1880, he started a paper, the *Springfield Daily News*, with his brother. The paper suffered its share of birthing problems; Bellamy searched for readers even as he struggled to find his voice. The plight of labor—and the problems labor's plight caused the rest of society—furnished an early theme. "Don't make it a point to say that the workmen are in the wrong when there is a strike," a letter writer who sounded suspiciously like Bellamy himself requested of the editor. "Don't fill your paper with lies about how terribly easy it is for a poor man to live on $1.00 a day. Remember it isn't so very much easier than it would be for you, and don't forget either that there are a hundred poor fellows for one even decently well off. I shall keep my eye on you, and a good many of my sort beside."[13]

The demands of the paper didn't monopolize Bellamy's time, nor its columns exhaust his store of ideas. The strikes of the 1870s and 1880s seemed to Bellamy signs that democracy couldn't stand the strains of capitalism; the Haymarket affair of 1886, in which a bomb at a Chicago rally on behalf of striking workers, and gunfire that followed, killed several policemen and civilians and wounded many others, suggested that a crisis was imminent. In the months after Haymarket, Bellamy raced to commit his thoughts to paper; the result was published in 1888.

Looking Backward, 2000–1887, was a socialist tract wrapped in science fiction romance. Bellamy put his Boston protagonist, Julian West, to bed in 1887 and kept him slumbering till 2000, when he awakens to find his home city transformed into an urban paradise. His hosts in the future, the insightful Dr. Leete and his charming daughter, Edith, master their surprise at seeing this Yankee Rip Van Winkle and query him regarding the world whence he has come. They have read of the labor troubles and other capitalist strife of the nineteenth century, but they want to hear the grim story from a survivor.

"I cannot do better than to compare society as it then was to a prodigious coach which the masses of humanity were harnessed to and dragged toilsomely along a very hilly and sandy road," Julian explains, in an image and a passage that became famous among Bellamy's many enthusiasts.

> The driver was hunger, and permitted no lagging, though the pace was necessarily very slow. Despite the difficulty of drawing the coach at all along so hard a road, the top was covered with passengers who never got down, even at the steepest ascents. These seats on top were very breezy and comfortable. Well up out of the dust, their occupants could enjoy the scenery at their leisure, or critically discuss the merits of the straining team. Naturally such places were in great demand and the competition for them was keen, every one seeking as the first end in life to secure a seat on the coach for himself and to leave it to his child after him. By the rule of the coach a man could leave his seat to whom he wished, but on the other hand there were many accidents by which it might at any time be wholly lost. For all that they were so easy, the seats were very insecure, and at every sudden jolt of the coach persons were slipping out of them and falling to the ground, where they were instantly compelled to take hold of the rope and help to drag the coach on which they had before ridden so pleasantly. It was naturally regarded as a terrible misfortune to lose one's seat, and the apprehension that this might happen to them or their friends was a constant cloud upon the happiness of those who rode.
>
> But did they think only of themselves? you ask. Was not their very luxury rendered intolerable to them by comparison with the lot of their brothers and sisters in the harness, and the knowledge that their own weight added to their toil? Had they no compassion for fellow beings from whom fortune only distinguished them? Oh, yes; commiseration was frequently expressed by those who rode for those who had to pull the coach, especially when the vehicle came to a bad place in the road, as it was constantly doing, or to a particularly steep hill. At such times, the desperate straining of the team, their agonized leaping and plunging under the pitiless lashing of hunger, the many who fainted at the rope and were trampled in the mire, made a very distressing spectacle, which often called forth highly creditable displays of feeling on the top of the coach. At such times the passengers would call down encouragingly to the toilers of the rope, exhorting them to patience, and holding out hopes of possible compensation in another

world for the hardness of their lot, while others contributed to buy salves and liniments for the crippled and injured. It was agreed that it was a great pity that the coach should be so hard to pull, and there was a sense of general relief when the specially bad piece of road was gotten over.

The worst pieces of Bellamy's road were the strikes and violence that resulted when workers attempted to diminish the gap between themselves and the riders of the carriage they pulled. Julian's first question, upon observing the wealth and splendor of the new Boston, is how America has solved the labor problem. "It was the Sphinx's riddle of the nineteenth century," he says, "and when I dropped out the Sphinx was threatening to devour society."

"I suppose we may claim to have solved it," Dr. Leete replies. "Society would indeed have fully deserved being devoured if it had failed to answer a riddle so entirely simple. In fact, to speak by the book, it was not necessary for society to solve the riddle at all. It may be said to have solved itself. The solution came as the result of a process of industrial evolution which could not have terminated otherwise. All that society had to do was to recognize and cooperate with that evolution, when its tendency had become unmistakable."

Julian is mystified. The keenest minds of his age wrestled with the labor problem only to make it worse; now Dr. Leete says the problem has vanished of its own.

The doctor traces its demise. "What should you name as the most prominent feature of the labor troubles of your day?" he asks Julian.

"Why, the strikes, of course."

"Exactly. But what made the strikes so formidable?"

"The great labor organizations."

"And what was the motive of these great organizations?"

"The workmen claimed they had to organize to get their rights from the big corporations."

"That is just it. The organization of labor and the strikes were an effect, merely, of the concentration of capital in greater masses than had ever been known before. Before this concentration began . . . the individual workman was relatively important and independent in his relations with the employer. Moreover, when a little capital or a new idea was enough to start a man in business for himself, workingmen were constantly becoming employers, and there was no hard and fast line between the two classes. Labor unions were needless then, and general strikes were out of the question." Things changed as capitalism matured and large corporations supplanted and subsumed the small. The individual laborer lost autonomy and bargaining power. "Self-defense drove him to union with his fellows." Strikes and violence were the inevitable result.

But equally inevitable was continuing consolidation in the capitalist sphere. "Small businesses, as far as they still remained, were reduced to the condition of rats and mice, living in holes and corners, and counting on evading notice for the enjoyment of existence. The railroads had gone on combining till a few great syndicates controlled every rail in the land. In manufactories, every important staple was controlled by a syndicate. These syndicates, pools, trusts, or whatever their name, fixed prices and crushed all competition except when combinations as vast as themselves arose."

Workers and others decried the consolidation and demanded its undoing. But they were shouting into the wind, for the trend was irresistible. "Early in the last century"—the twentieth—"the evolution was completed by the final consolidation of the entire capital of the nation. . . . The epoch of trusts had ended in The Great Trust." But because the Great Trust controlled the entire productive capacity of the nation, the people recognized that it was nothing other than the nation itself. Capitalism no longer commanded the nation, for capitalism was no longer distinct from the nation.

"In a word, the people of the United States concluded to assume the conduct of their own business, just as one hundred-odd years before they had assumed the conduct of their own government, organizing now for industrial purposes on precisely those same grounds that they had organized for political purposes. At last, strangely late in the world's history, the obvious fact was perceived that no business is so essentially the public's business as the industry and commerce on which the people's livelihood depends, and that to entrust it to private persons to be managed for private profit is a folly similar in kind, though vastly different in magnitude, to that of surrendering the functions of political government to kings and nobles to be conducted for their personal glorification."

Julian, having listened in astonishment, remarks that the final step—the nationalization of industry and commerce—must have entailed terrible convulsions.

"On the contrary," Dr. Leete replies. "There was absolutely no violence. The change had been long foreseen. Public opinion had become fully ripe for it, and the whole mass of people was behind it." And capitalism itself had been the agent of the people's education.

> "They had seen for many years syndicates handling revenues greater than those of states, and directing the labors of hundreds of thousands of men with an efficiency and economy unattainable in smaller operations. It had come to be recognized as an axiom that the larger the business the simpler the principles that can be applied to it. . . . Thus it came about that, thanks to the corporations themselves, when it was proposed that the nation should assume their functions, the suggestion implied nothing which seemed impracticable even to the timid."[14]

BELLAMY'S BOOK INCLUDED a great deal more: of elaboration on how democracy's takeover of capitalism occurred, of detail regarding daily life under the new socialist order, of insight into relations between the sexes in the twenty-first century (including the inevitable love affair between Julian West and Edith Leete). Many reviewers and perhaps a comparable portion of readers found the narrative framework flimsy, but the glories of postmodern science and technology appealed to the same American audience that for decades had been snatching up translations of the works of Jules Verne.

Yet it was the promise of an end to strife, of the peaceful resolution of the problems that appeared so insoluble to Americans in the late 1880s, that caused Bellamy's book to create a political sensation. *Looking Backward* sold 200,000 copies in its first year; meanwhile it inspired the establishment of "Nationalist Clubs" all across the country, comprising doctors and lawyers, journalists and professors and clergymen. William Dean Howells of the *Atlantic Monthly* urged Bellamy to head up a Nationalist political party embodying the principles of the book. Some Boston Bellamyites started a newspaper called the *Nationalist* and drafted a declaration of principles embracing brotherhood as "one of the eternal truths," decrying competition as "the application of the brutal law of the survival of the strongest and most cunning," and echoing Bellamy in calling for democracy to seize control of capitalism and "have all industries operated in the interest of all by the nation."[15]

The Bellamyites thrilled as the Nationalist idea caught on. "The intelligent and educated are joining," one exulted. "Men and women of wealth, brains, and of heart are interested. . . . This movement has reached out and is beginning to unite the farmers with the toilers of the city. It has inspired and is inspiring countless books, magazine articles, editorials and articles in the daily press. We have fifty or more papers unreservedly advocating Nationalism." When skeptics and defenders of the capitalist status quo attacked Bellamy's ideas, the Nationalists mobilized in defense. "Professor Harris remarks sententiously: 'Real human beings have other needs than food, clothing, and shelter,'" the *Nationalist* declared of one critic. "He seems to forget, however, that these wants must be satisfied *before* any other needs can be considered. Would the professor try to feed the hungry on a lecture entitled 'The Higher Aims of the Concord Philosophy'? . . . Man must have bread before Browning." The professor and his ilk had better beware. "Two strong currents of thought are converging toward Nationalism—one running through the hearts of the wage-slaves, the other through the minds and hearts and consciences of clear-headed, men-loving men and women. Does Prof. Harris stand so firm that neither current may sweep him off his feet?"[16]

Part Five

THE DECADE OF THE CENTURY

Chapter 16

MEET JIM CROW

———

In December 1890 Booker Washington received a letter from a woman he had heard of but hadn't met.

> *Prof. B. T. Washington:*
>
> *I am so impressed with the reply to your critics in the current issue of the* Plaindealer *that I at last do what I have been intending ever since I read your manly criticism of our corrupt and ignorant ministry— write to one who is a stranger to me in every respect save that of reputation.*
>
> *I have long since seen that some one of the name and standing of yourself,* among ourselves, *must call a halt and be the Martin Luther of our times in condemning the practices of our ministers, and I know no one more fitted for the task than yourself. . . .*
>
> *To a man whose conscience is his guide, words of encouragement and sustenance are not necessary, yet I cannot refrain from adding my mite to the approbation your utterances and work have received from the rank and file of our people.*
>
> *Respectfully,*
> *Ida B. Wells*[1]

Ida Wells was a few years younger than Washington. Like Washington, she had been born a slave, in her case in Mississippi. Her mother was a cook and her father a carpenter who became active in Republican politics during Reconstruction. "My earliest recollections are of reading the newspaper to my father and an admiring group of his friends," Ida wrote later. But her father had encountered the violence of the Ku Klux Klan, the purpose of which was precisely to discourage freedmen like him from participating in politics. "I heard the words Ku Klux Klan long before I knew what they meant," she recounted. "I knew dimly that it meant something fearful, by the anxious way my mother walked the floor at night when my father was out to a political meeting." Her father survived the Klan and Redemption—although his political career, like the political careers and indeed participation of nearly all Southern blacks, did not—only to succumb, with her mother and youngest brother, to an 1878 yellow fever epidemic. Ida had attended a Freedmen's Bureau school and the Methodist Rust College, and on the strength of this education and a boldness born of desperation she made herself up to look older than her sixteen years and attempted the state examination to certify teachers. She passed and became the breadwinner to her five surviving siblings.[2]

In time an aunt invited her to Memphis. Ida found foster families for the elder children and took the younger ones with her. She taught school in Memphis and contributed a regular column to a local black newspaper. "I wrote in a plain, common-sense way on the things which concerned our people," she explained. "Knowing that their education was limited, I never used a word of two syllables where one would serve the purpose." The column, which was reprinted by other papers, bolstered her confidence and gave her a feeling of responsibility for the black community; when a railroad conductor on the Chesapeake, Ohio & Southwestern one day told her to move from the first-class car to the smoking car, she refused. He tried to move her bodily, and she physically resisted. Finally he stopped the train. This time she did leave, only to march to the courthouse and file suit against the road for assault and illegal discrimination. The trial judge dismissed the assault charge but awarded Wells five hundred dollars in damages on grounds that the railroad had failed to comply with a Tennessee law mandating that railcars set aside for blacks be comparable to those reserved for whites. The victory astonished Memphis. "A Darky Damsel

Obtains a Verdict for Damages," a local paper headlined. "What It Cost to Put a Colored School Teacher in a Smoking Car."[3]

The Tennessee supreme court, however, reversed the judgment, accepting the railroad's argument that the smoking car *was* comparable to the first-class car (it wasn't even very smoky, the railroad's lawyers contended) and that Wells was a chronic troublemaker. Not only did Wells lose the five hundred dollars but she was assessed two hundred dollars in court costs.

The penalty strained her budget, and the notoriety endangered her teaching job, from which she was ultimately fired. But the experience heightened her stature in the African American community. The black press ran stories she wrote of her clash with the railroad and carried her critique of other aspects of life in the South. She didn't hesitate to challenge black leaders when she thought they fell shy of their obligations to the race; her own criticism of members of the black clergy was what disposed her to congratulate Booker Washington for his efforts in that regard. The owners of a Memphis paper, the *Free Speech and Headlight*, offered her a regular writing position; she countered with the condition that they accept her as co-owner and equal partner. When they agreed, she became a still greater force in journalism and in African American affairs generally. She attended national conventions of journalists and won election as an officer of the National Colored Press Association. By the early 1890s no black women in America and few black men were better known than Ida Wells.

WASHINGTON WAS HAPPY for Wells's praise but didn't know what to make of the rest of her letter. It suggested that she labored under a misconception as to his aims and approach. He was no Martin Luther, and he intended no reformation.

In 1890 Washington headed the Tuskegee Institute, a teacher's college and industrial school in central Alabama's cotton belt. He had landed the job nine years earlier on the strength of a recommendation from the Hampton Institute's General Armstrong, who described Washington to the Tuskegee trustees as "a very competent capable mulatto, clear headed, modest, sensible, polite and a thorough teacher and superior man; the best man we ever had here." Washington spent the 1880s building

Tuskegee from a struggling, unnoticed school for black teachers to a bustling showpiece of African American self-help. To support the school and train the students, he borrowed money, bought a farm, and put the students to work planting and hoeing. To expand the school, he directed the students to build new classrooms and dormitories. "I told those who doubted the wisdom of the plan," he later explained regarding his construction strategy, "that I knew that our first buildings would not be so comfortable or so complete in their finish as buildings erected by experienced workmen, but that in the teaching of civilization, self-help, and self-reliance, the erection of the buildings by the students themselves would more than compensate for any lack of comfort or fine finish."

Self-reliance became the Tuskegee motto. In the course of the building campaign Washington decided his students should even make the bricks for their structures. He knew no more about brick-making than they; he tried one recipe, then another and another, all of which failed. Only the fourth try, funded by the pawn of his watch, yielded a passable product. The multiple results of the effort—cheap bricks for the buildings, on-the-job training for the students, a surplus of bricks to sell for cash—exemplified the Washington method. An additional outcome was no less important. "The making of these bricks caused many of the white residents of the neighborhood to begin to feel that the education of the Negro was not making him worthless, but that in educating our students we were adding something to the wealth and comfort of the community."[4]

Yet self-reliance had its limits, some of which Washington transcended by ceaseless fund-raising. On numerous trips to the North he became an enthusiast of American capitalism. He called on capitalists and their children to support Tuskegee and his vision of black progress. Many were initially skeptical, but Washington often brought them around. "The first time I ever saw the late Collis P. Huntington, the great railroad man," Washington remembered, "he gave me two dollars for our school." Washington interpreted the miserly contribution as a challenge. "I did not blame him for not giving me more, but made up my mind that I was going to convince him by tangible results that we were worthy of larger gifts." Washington's persistence paid. "The last time I saw him, which was a few months before his death, he gave me fifty thousand dollars." Andrew Carnegie was a similar long-term project. "The first time I saw him, ten years ago," Washington wrote in 1901, "he seemed to take but little interest in our school, but I was determined to show him that we were worthy of his help." The decade's effort netted a twenty-thousand-dollar donation.

Washington's years of asking and receiving inspired him to defend the likes of Huntington and Carnegie against their radical detractors.

> My experience in getting money for Tuskegee has taught me to have no patience with those people who are always condemning the rich because they are rich, and because they do not give more to objects of charity. In the first place, those who are guilty of such sweeping state- ments do not know how many people would be made poor, and how much suffering would result, if wealthy people were to part all at once with any large proportion of their wealth in a way to disorganize and cripple great business enterprises. Then very few persons have any idea of the large number of applications for help that rich people are con- stantly being flooded with. I know wealthy people who receive as many as twenty calls a day for help. More than once, when I have gone into the offices of rich men, I have found half a dozen persons waiting to see them, and all come for the same purpose, that of securing money.[5]

That Washington often succeeded where the half dozen didn't testi- fied to his persuasiveness, but also to his personal conservatism. Washing- ton's deference to the status quo suited one who constantly solicited the help of the rich and powerful, but it also reflected his deeply held belief that change came best when it came incrementally. He had lived through the dramatic changes of Reconstruction and had watched them provoke the backlash of Redemption. And though the largesse of North- ern capitalists underwrote much of what happened at Tuskegee, Washing- ton judged that Southern capitalists were more dependable allies in the long run. Conscience might motivate Huntington and Carnegie for a while, but conscience was fickle. In the spirit of Adam Smith, Washington looked not to the beneficence of whites for Tuskegee's daily bread but to their self-interest. He would align the self-interest of Southern whites with the success of Tuskegee. The bricks were but the start.

DEMOCRACY WAS EVEN less reliable than conscience. Better than most of his contemporaries, Washington understood that democracy

sooner or later expressed the will of the majority, whatever courts or constitutional amendments might declare. Democracy hadn't prevented
Redemption, which in fact had been accomplished in the name of democracy. Blacks were a minority in America and always would be; for them to
demand what the majority wasn't ready to give was to spit into the wind.

Washington had seen the democratic rights of blacks unravel in the
wake of Reconstruction. The Ku Klux Klan delivered the heavy first blows,
driving black voters from the polls by terror. But the brutal tactics of the
Klan—the many hundreds of murders and the countless beatings and
threats—compelled the Grant administration to take ameliorative measures, which broke up the Klan. Subsequent methods of disfranchisement,
in most cases more subtle, worked better over time. The simplest was
fraud: not counting black votes. This could be done by itself or, more easily, in conjunction with the secret ballot, which was catching on across the
country as an ostensible step toward greater democracy. Slightly more
complicated were various schemes for suppressing registration by blacks.
Literacy tests, which required prospective voters to read and interpret constitutional passages to the satisfaction of white registrars, disqualified
many African Americans. Extended residency requirements discriminated
against those ambitious blacks who moved around trying to better their
economic condition. Poll taxes made poor blacks think twice about casting
their votes. Racial gerrymandering—dividing the black vote among several
districts, in none of which blacks formed a majority—suggested that even
if blacks did vote, their votes would be wasted. Grandfather clauses, which
exempted potential voters from literacy or other tests if they or their forebears had voted prior to Reconstruction, ensured that the constraints operated upon blacks but not upon whites.

Such tactics, though less egregious than the actions of the Klan, didn't
go unnoticed in the North. Some Republicans bridled at the affront to
egalitarianism; others merely chafed at the Democrats' renewed dominance of the Southern states. Henry Cabot Lodge, Theodore Roosevelt's
ally and a Massachusetts congressman, in 1890 proposed a measure to prevent such political discrimination. Lodge's federal elections bill would
place congressional elections under federal supervision; should federal
monitors detect fraud, intimidation, or discrimination and the Southern
states fail to provide remedies, the president would be authorized to employ
the army to guarantee fair elections. "The Government which made the

black man a citizen is bound to protect him in his rights as a citizen of the United States," Lodge declared, "and it is a cowardly Government if it does not do it. No people can afford to write anything into their Constitution and not sustain it. A failure to do what is right brings its own punishment to nations as to men."[6]

Democrats naturally opposed the Lodge bill—the Lodge "force bill," they called it—on partisan grounds but also as federal coercion of the kind voters had rejected in terminating Reconstruction. Republicans of the GOP's capitalist wing were lukewarm at best about the bill, fearing that restarting the old battles was a sure formula for losing elections. Some Western Republicans sided with Southern Democrats against the bill, in part to protest the dominance of the Northeast in the GOP, in part as payback for Southern support on silver, and in part from hope for Southern endorsement of an extension of Chinese exclusion. Lodge and his elections bill found allies among the democratic wing of the Republican party, the heirs of the conscience Radicals, but also among fretful, cynical conservatives who hoped to undermine the interracial alliance that was building among populist-minded Southerners.[7]

The Lodge bill passed the House in time for the 1890 elections, which the Republicans lost disastrously (for reasons besides the elections bill, in particular the tariff). Senate Democrats took heart and filibustered the bill for thirty-three days during the lame-duck session, till the Republicans conceded defeat and the measure died. Meaningful federal interest in civil rights died with it, not to be resurrected till the second half of the twentieth century. The capitalist wing of the Republicans solidified its grip on the party of Lincoln; the democratic wing declined still further. Race as an issue all but disappeared from national politics.

The Democrats chortled in triumph, and Southern Democrats declared open season on black voting rights. Heretofore diffident Southern states adopted discriminatory measures that had proven effective elsewhere; others enshrined in law practices that had evolved informally. Some states wrote new constitutions. "I told the people of my county before they sent me here," a delegate to Virginia's 1901 constitutional convention declared, "that I intended . . . to disfranchise every negro that I could disfranchise under the Constitution of the United States, and as few white people as possible." When the Supreme Court nodded acceptance of the new regime in the South—asserting, for example, in 1898 that a Mississippi literacy test was not unconstitutional, because its language was race neutral—there was little to deter the disfranchisers, who worked quickly and efficiently. In Mississippi in the mid-1890s, fewer than 10,000 blacks were registered out of a black voting-age population of nearly 150,000. In Louisiana, black registration plummeted from 130,000 in 1896 to fewer than 2,000 eight years later. In Georgia, barely one black voter out of a potential twenty-five was registered. (In Texas, discriminatory laws targeted Mexican Americans as well as blacks, with similar effect.)[8]

The erosion of black political rights took place over a generation, but observers far less acute than Booker Washington could see where things were headed. And even one as congenitally optimistic as Washington could be forgiven for despairing of democracy as the path to black improvement. Battered by the Civil War and Reconstruction, discredited by the scandals at various levels of government, democracy had slipped into reverse gear; the train that had carried America toward ever greater political participation during the first two-thirds of the nineteenth century was now rolling backward, at least on the Southern portions of the line. And there seemed little Washington or any other African Americans could do about it.

THE BIG STORY from Memphis in the spring of 1892 was supposed to be the opening of the new Mississippi Bridge. Memphis commerce had declined from the glory days of the Mississippi steamboats; even barge traffic had fallen off since railroads started moving goods and people more directly and less expensively than the waterways of the heartland. Memphis, the northern outpost of what inhabitants of the region called the Mississippi Delta, hoped to recapture some of that lost traffic when the new railroad and roadway bridge opened. It was the first bridge across the Mississippi below the Ohio, and it promised to make Memphis once more the business center it had been. Because the federal government had underwritten construction, a delegation from Washington was expected; the War Department, which had oversight of the project on account of the army's expertise in construction and its interest in moving troops about the country, would send the secretary of war or a top assistant. Memphians liked to point out that their city stood where De Soto had first laid eyes on the mighty river and that in 1845 John Calhoun had predicted that a transcontinental highway would pass through Memphis; the city fathers hoped the new bridge would fulfill Calhoun's predictions and recapture the primacy of the days of De Soto.[9]

But two months before the ribbon cutting, another story spoiled the affair. This story also involved commerce, yet of a more local variety. W. H. Barrett, a white man, had long operated a grocery store in a neighborhood called the "Curve" for a bend in the streetcar track at the corner of Walker Avenue and Mississippi Boulevard. The neighborhood was integrated, as was much of Memphis at this time. "We lived in patches," one black resident of the city said later. "There was no big black belt, no solid black belt anywhere in this city." Barrett for years had the only grocery store in the neighborhood, and he liked it that way.[10]

Unsurprisingly he grew upset when competition arrived in 1889. The People's Grocery Company was a cooperative venture of some black businessmen who thought Barrett's monopoly ought to be broken. Yet they appealed to more than their customers' desire for lower prices; they called on Memphis blacks to show racial solidarity by patronizing the store. Barrett would have resented any rival; he resented this one particularly for playing race against him.

For a time he muttered quietly. But in early March 1892 a scuffle broke out among some boys in the neighborhood. A mixed group of youngsters had been shooting marbles, perhaps for money; a dispute led to curses and then to blows. The parents became involved; one white father, Cornelius Hurst, apparently whipped one of the black boys. Several angry black fathers congregated in front of Hurst's house, which stood near the People's Grocery. Someone notified the police that a riot was brewing in the Curve, but by the time officers arrived the crowd had dispersed.

Yet the matter wasn't settled. Accounts differed as to what happened next, but Barrett apparently entered the People's Grocery looking for the black men who had disappeared. Or he may simply have been looking for trouble. A black clerk at the store, Calvin McDowell, said Barrett brandished a pistol and then hit him with it. McDowell said he was defending himself. "Being the stronger, I got the better of that scrimmage," McDowell explained. Barrett alleged that McDowell had jumped him. Whichever way it happened, Barrett wound up with a bloody face and a further grievance against his competitor. He persuaded a (white) county judge to issue an arrest warrant for McDowell, and a (white) grand jury to indict the owners of People's Grocery for operating a public nuisance.

Black residents of the neighborhood called a meeting to protest what seemed the patent misuse of the legal system. Some at the meeting denounced Barrett as "white trash"; by at least one report dynamite was mentioned as a solution to the Barrett problem. Whether or not the threat was intended seriously, Barrett took it so when he heard of it. He went back to the judge and complained that a conspiracy against him existed; the judge issued more arrest warrants.

By now the dispute between Barrett and the People's Grocery had thoroughly engaged the racial loyalties of the neighborhood. A band of armed white men accompanied the (white) deputies to serve the arrest warrants; a band of armed black men prepared to defend the People's Grocery and its employees and patrons. By malevolent design or bureaucratic ineptitude, the confrontation took place on a Saturday night, when visibility was poor and liquor had been flowing; the result was a shootout in which three deputies were wounded and perhaps some civilians, though the latter fled without filing injury reports. The deputies called for reinforcements, who rounded up some dozen black men, including Calvin McDowell and a co-owner of the store named Will Stewart. Thomas Moss, the president of the People's Grocery, was subsequently arrested.

The Memphis papers next day described the "bloody riot" and characterized the People's Grocery as a "nest of turbulent and unruly negroes." Whites responded by looting the store while freshly deputized white men ransacked a hundred black homes in the process of arresting dozens more black men on charges of conspiracy.

The black community of Memphis knew what to expect next, and an African American state militia unit called the Tennessee Rifles ringed the jail to prevent the prisoners from being kidnapped from custody and executed. But the same judge who had handed down all the arrest warrants now ordered the militia—and the rest of the black citizenry—disarmed. The Tennessee Rifles protested but didn't forcibly resist.

This development may have averted a bloodbath in Memphis, but it left the prisoners defenseless when whites indeed stormed the jail and seized Calvin McDowell, Thomas Moss, and Will Stewart. Conspicuously, of all the prisoners none had cleaner police records than these; Moss was both a federal employee and a Sunday school teacher. The one thing that distinguished them from the others was their connection to the People's Grocery.

The kidnapping occurred at three in the morning; the prisoners were transported in the dark to a field a mile north of Memphis. The three were shot dead, and McDowell's eyes were gouged out. The bodies were left in the field.[11]

The lynching embarrassed the respectable part of the white community even as it outraged the blacks. "The bad effect of the lynching on the reputation of Memphis is recognized and deplored by every decent citizen," a local reporter writing for the *New York Times* asserted. The city fathers had hoped to draw attention to Memphis for the new bridge and the bright future it promised; now the only thing the nation heard from Memphis was a sordid tale of vigilante violence. The attorney general vowed to find the perpetrators and prosecute them to the full extent of the law. A grand jury was impaneled to weigh evidence and hear testimony.[12]

But days passed, and then weeks. A wall of silence descended on the white community, and the witnesses summoned by the grand jury professed to be unable to identify any of the perpetrators. The panel returned no indictments, and no one was ever tried for the murders.

The anger of the black community turned to dismay. Memphis had suffered lynchings before, but these latest murders targeted men whose sole offense was to challenge the monopoly of a white merchant. If they could be killed with impunity—as the failure of the grand jury to indict anyone made clear they could—no black person in Memphis was safe. "I was born and raised in Memphis," Cash Mosby, a black man who had built a business guiding railroad tours up and down the Mississippi, told a reporter. "But I cannot live here any longer." Mosby said he had sent his family north to Cincinnati and intended to follow them as soon as he could liquidate his holdings. "My house here cost me $3,200. The lot has a fifty-foot front. Anybody can have the whole business for $2,500." Another black man, with a Main Street property for which he had been offered $15,000, said he'd take $9,000 to get out. A lawyer who doubled as a landlord offered a rental house, which yielded $360 annually, for $500. About the time the grand jury was discharged, a news article from Memphis stated, "Negroes are leaving this locality in large numbers for Oklahoma and other points, and a general exodus is apprehended."[13]

THE EXODUS INCLUDED Ida Wells. She knew Tom Moss and the murdered man's widow, whom she called "the best friends I had in town." Their daughter was her godchild. The personal loss she felt informed an angry editorial in the *Free Press*. "The city of Memphis has demonstrated that neither character nor standing avails the Negro if he dares to protect himself against the white man or become his rival," she declared. "There is nothing we can do about the lynching now, as we are out-numbered and without arms. The white mob could help itself to ammunition without pay, but the order was rigidly enforced against the selling of guns to Negroes. There is therefore only one thing left that we can do: save our money and leave a town which will neither protect our lives and property nor give us a fair trial in the courts, but takes us out and murders us in cold blood when accused by white persons." Wells noted that many blacks had likened Memphis to hell; she thought they slandered hell. "Hell proper is a place of punishment for the wicked; Memphis is a place of punishment for the good, brave and enterprising." She blamed the whites of Memphis for their racism and violence, but she also blamed the leaders of black Memphis for failing to defend the African American community. "Where are our 'leaders' when the race is being burnt, shot, and hanged? Holding good fat offices and saying not a word. . . . However much the Negro is abused and outraged, our 'leaders' make no demands on the country to protect us, nor come forward with any practical plan for changing the condition of affairs."[14]

The Memphis murders caused Wells to examine the lynching phenomenon more generally. "Like many another person who had read of lynching in the South," she wrote later, "I had accepted the idea meant to be conveyed: that although lynching was irregular and contrary to law and order, unreasoning anger over the terrible crime of rape led to the lynching—that perhaps the brute deserved death anyhow and the mob was justified in taking his life." But Tom Moss, Calvin McDowell, and Will Stewart hadn't been accused of rape or any other crime against white women, and they had been murdered brutally anyway. "This is what opened my eyes to what lynching really was: an excuse to get rid of Negroes who were acquiring wealth and property and thus keep the race terrorized and 'keep the nigger down.'"[15]

Wells commenced her public campaign against lynching with an editorial that might have gotten her lynched had she been in Memphis when it appeared. In the May 21, 1892, issue of the *Free Speech* she reported several recent murders and drew an incendiary inference.

> Eight negroes lynched since last issue of the *Free Speech*: one at Little Rock, Ark., last Saturday morning where the citizens broke (?) into the penitentiary and got their man; three near Anniston, Ala.; one near New Orleans; and three at Clarksville, Ga., the last three for killing a white man, and five on the same old racket—the new alarm about raping white women. The same program of hanging, then shooting bullets into the lifeless bodies was carried out to the letter.
>
> Nobody in this section of the country believes the old threadbare lie that Negro men rape white women. If Southern white men are not careful, they will over-reach themselves and public sentiment will have a reaction; a conclusion will then be reached which will be very damaging to the moral reputation of their women.[16]

Whites responded with outrage to Wells's suggestion that white women were having consensual relations with black men. "There are some things the Southern white man will not tolerate," one white Memphis paper spluttered, "and the obscene intimations of the foregoing have brought the writer to the outermost limit of public patience." Another paper, assuming that the editorial writer was Wells's male partner, J. L. Fleming, was more direct: "If the negroes themselves do not apply the remedy without delay it will be the duty of those whom he has attacked to tie the wretch who utters these calumnies to a stake at the intersection of Main and Madison Sts., brand him in the forehead with a hot iron and perform upon him a surgical operation with a pair of tailor's shears."

Wells was in New York at the time, but Fleming was in Memphis. When a white mob gathered at the Merchants Exchange and worked itself into a frenzy reviling the *Free Speech*, Fleming decided to flee the city. Wells briefly thought she might return to Memphis, as even an angry mob would hesitate to attack a woman. But inquiries to friends on the scene convinced her that her life would be in jeopardy should she appear in the city, and she stayed in New York. The *Free Speech* fell silent.[17]

But Wells didn't. Exile simply amplified her voice. "We cannot see what the 'good' citizens of Memphis gained by suppressing the *Free Speech*," a Minnesota paper remarked. "They stopped the papers of a few hundred subscribers and drove Miss Ida B. Wells to New York, and now she is telling the story to hundreds of thousands of readers." The story she told was that of the noose—and the whip and the pistol and the other instruments of violence against blacks. The more she researched the subject of lynching, the more convinced she became that it had little to do with rape but much to do with sex. "The question must be asked," she wrote in a widely distributed pamphlet entitled *A Red Record: Lynchings in the United States*, "what the white man means when he charges the black man with rape. Does he mean the crime which the statutes of the civilized states describe as such? Not by any means. With the Southern white man, any misalliance existing between a white woman and a colored man is a sufficient foundation for the charge of rape. The Southern white man says that it is impossible for a voluntary alliance to exist between a white woman and a colored man, and therefore the fact of an alliance is a proof of force." In this pamphlet and a second, *Southern Horrors: Lynch Law in All Its Phases*, Wells furnished examples of alleged rapes that proved to be consensual. Mrs. J. S. Underwood, the wife of an Ohio minister, charged a black man, William Offett, with rape. He escaped lynching but not the penitentiary, to which he was sentenced for fifteen years. Yet the woman's conscience got the better of her, and she told the true story, which Wells repeated:

> I met Offett at the Post Office. It was raining. He was polite to me, and as I had several bundles in my arms he offered to carry them home for me, which he did. He had a strange fascination for me, and I invited him to call on me. He called, bringing chestnuts and candy for the children. By this means we got them to leave us alone in the room. Then I sat on his lap. He made a proposal to me, and I readily consented. Why I did so, I do not know, but that I did is true. He visited me several times after that, and each time I was indiscreet. I did not care after the first time. In fact I could not have resisted, and had no desire to resist.

Questioned why she had charged Offett with rape, Mrs. Underwood said she had various reasons. "I was afraid I had contracted a loathsome disease. . . . I feared I might give birth to a Negro baby. . . . I hoped to save my reputation." Upon her confession, Offett was released and her husband secured a divorce.[18]

Wells multiplied these stories. A Natchez woman of the white upper class gave birth to a child "whose color was remarked but traced to some brunette ancestor." The woman carried on as before, continuing, among other habits, long rides with her black coachman. Another child was born. "It was unmistakably dark. All were alarmed, and 'rush of blood, strangulation' were the conjectures. But the doctor, when asked the cause, grimly told them it was a Negro child." The coachman fled west before the vengeance of the family could reach him. The woman was sent away in disgrace. The husband died—of mortification, apparently, as much as anything else—within the year.

"Hundreds of such cases might be cited," Wells wrote. "But enough have been given to prove the assertion that there are white women in the South who love the Afro-American's company even as there are white men notorious for their preference for Afro-American women."

Wells could hardly have written anything more provocative—but she came close. In the process of cataloging 241 persons lynched in 1892 (and hundreds more during the following two years), she included stomach-turning details of gratuitous torture, victims being burned alive, and mobs acting like insatiable beasts. Line drawings and photographs illustrated the text. Her purpose was to shame the whites who read her pamphlets—and to stiffen the spines of blacks. Under the heading "Self Help," she urged African Americans to take matters into their own hands. "Of the many inhuman outrages of this present year, the only cases where the proposed lynching did *not* occur was where the men armed themselves in Jacksonville, Fla., and Paducah, Ky., and prevented it," she wrote.

> The only times an Afro-American who was assaulted got away have been when he had a gun and used it in self-defense. The lesson this teaches, and which every Afro-American should ponder well, is that a Winchester rifle should have a place of honor in every black home, and it should be used for that protection which the law refuses to give. When the white man who is always the aggressor knows he runs as great risk of biting the dust every time his Afro-American victim does, he will have greater respect for Afro-American life. The more the Afro-American yields and cringes and begs, the more he has to do so, the more he is insulted, outraged, and lynched.

Beyond self-defense, Wells preached economic direct action. "The white man's dollar is his god. . . . The appeal to the white man's pocket has ever been more effectual than all the appeals ever made to his conscience." Black consumers should boycott white businesses, and black workers strike against white employers. The latter technique would have particular effect. "To Northern capital and Afro-American labor the South owes its rehabil-itation. If labor is withdrawn, capital will not remain." Temporary strikes and boycotts should be attempted first; if these failed, the effect could be made permanent by wholesale black emigration from the South. The emi-gration from Memphis in the wake of the lynchings there had caused "great stagnation in every branch of business." Repeated across the South, the strategy could make capitalism shudder. Then the white leadership would take action to stamp out lynch law, "that last relic of barbarism and slavery."[19]

ATLANTA FANCIED ITSELF a world apart from Memphis. In many ways it was. Where Memphis was a child of the Mississippi, a belle of the old South, Atlanta emerged with the railroad, the midwife of the New South. Starting during Reconstruction but continuing afterward, railroad companies expanded feverishly across the South, laying track faster in that region than in any other part of the country. As elsewhere, the construction of railroads reflected collaboration between the private and public sectors, with states, counties, and cities vying for the railroads' favor and putting money and other resources at the corporations' disposal. Land grants were a common device, as in the West. Texas by itself granted thirty-two million acres to railroads, a transfer from the democratic realm to the capitalist of an empire the size of Indiana.[20]

Those districts that won the contest for the railroads congratulated themselves on their brilliant futures. "Harrison is a Railroad Town at Last," the local paper of that Ozark community in Arkansas boasted. "The Con-struction Train Laid Yesterday the Steel Which Puts Us in Touch with the World." The railroads introduced thousands, eventually millions, of Southerners to the more frenetic pace of urban life. "All that they said was true, and much more," a young son of the soil reported after his first encounter with the "Big Terminal" in Atlanta. "People were crowded and seemed to be excited. Hundreds of people, many of them hurrying, were pushing against each other, pages were yelling names, a big Negro was calling stations for departing trains; train bells ringing, steam escaping with strange and frightening sounds."[21]

As they had in the North, the railroads refashioned the economy of the South. Railroads knitted the South together as it had never been before and wove the Southern economy into the national—and world— economy. Cotton culture penetrated new districts with the railroads, as cotton producers sought cheaper land with which to combat low-cost production in foreign countries. Lumber production increased exponentially as railroads gave the loggers economic access to markets they hadn't been able to reach previously. The mining of coal and iron and phosphate expanded greatly. The railroads spawned the Southern steel industry, particularly in the city of Birmingham, which became the Pittsburgh of the South (prompting no less an authority than Andrew Carnegie to declare, after a visit: "The South is Pennsylvania's most formidable industrial enemy"). The railroads allowed the Southern textile industry to spread along the Piedmont, and the Southern furniture and tobacco industries to reach their customers more efficiently than before. The railroads enabled merchants in cities like Atlanta to extend their operations far into the hinterland.[22]

As elsewhere, the railroad-induced integration yielded winners and losers. The expansion of the cotton culture provided jobs and other opportunities where they hadn't existed, but it undercut existing producers; and though the rise in land values that accompanied cotton's expansion benefited landowners, it raised rents for tenants. That the landowners were often Northern or foreign speculators limited the local gains even from the rise in land prices. Moreover, although the railroads afforded Southern cotton producers readier access to the world market, it rendered those producers, and all who depended on them, more susceptible to the vagaries of that market. The lumber industry likewise brought jobs to previously stagnant districts, but it stripped huge swaths of the South of their trees, leaving little but stumps and naked red clay behind. Here again, external ownership, as by the London-based North American Land and Timber Company, meant that profits were often expatriated. The mining and steel industries provided work to many thousands of Southerners, but because Southern mine and mill operators were even more successful than their Northern counterparts at resisting unionization, the work was especially difficult, dangerous, and poorly paid. And, as with commercial agriculture,

Southern industry was vulnerable to events far away and utterly beyond Southern control. Financial panics hit the South harder than ever; industrial depressions laid Southern mines and mill towns low. Southern consumers benefited from the reduced rates on shipping from department stores and mail-order houses in the cities, but small-town merchants watched their businesses wither. Eventually even Southern cities felt the pressure of direct Northern competition.[23]

In other words, what was new about the New South, in economic terms, was that it looked increasingly like the rest of the country. The South had joined capitalist America. Southern living standards rose, though they remained far below those outside the region; as late as 1900 the average per capita income in the South was scarcely more than half that of the rest of the country. Success in the South, as elsewhere, went to the ambitious, clever, and strong, who tended to get stronger, if not necessarily more clever and ambitious, leaving the weaker, duller, and less driven at a deepening disadvantage.[24]

BOOKER WASHINGTON UNDERSTOOD the dynamics of modern capitalism and shaped his message accordingly. Washington's travels in the North had brought him to the attention of Thomas Bicknell, the president of the National Educational Association, who took an interest in Tuskegee and invited Washington to address the association's 1884 meeting in Madison, Wisconsin. Washington accepted the invitation as an opportunity to speak not simply of Tuskegee but of relations between the races.

The audience of four thousand was the largest he had ever encountered. He chose his words carefully. Speaking to teachers, he stressed the primacy of education—for whites as much as for blacks. "Any movement for the elevation of the Southern Negro, in order to be successful, must have to a certain extent the cooperation of the Southern whites," Washington said. "They control government and own the property." Blacks and whites must rise together, if either were to rise at all. "Whatever benefits the black man benefits the white man. The proper education of all the whites will benefit the Negro as much as the education of the Negro will benefit the whites." For blacks, the right to advancement by education mattered more at present than the right to vote. "Brains, property, and character for the Negro will settle the question of civil rights. . . . Good school teachers and plenty of money to pay them will be more potent in settling the race question than many civil rights bills and investigating committees." Blacks who could contribute to the betterment of their communities would be sought out, not shunned, by whites. "Let there be in a community a Negro who by virtue of his superior knowledge of the chemistry of the soil, his acquaintance with the most improved tools and best breeds of stock, can raise fifty bushels of corn to the acre while his white neighbor only raises thirty, and the white man will come to the black man to learn." Washington had seen such things happen at Tuskegee. "In Tuskegee a Negro mechanic manufactures the best tinware, the best harness, the best boots and shoes, and it is common to see his store crowded with white customers from all over the county. His word or note goes as far as that of the whitest man."[25]

Washington's message of salvation through individual enterprise rather than politics pleased the emerging capitalist class in the South, which during the late 1880s and early 1890s promoted him as a spokesman for the black race. Washington spared no effort to exploit his opportunity. He received an invitation to address a large group of whites in Atlanta in 1893. He had already committed to be in Boston just before and after the proposed engagement. "Still, after looking over my list of dates and places carefully," he recalled, "I found that I could take a train from Boston that would get me into Atlanta about thirty minutes before my address was to be delivered, and that I could remain in that city about sixty minutes before taking another train for Boston." As he had been asked to speak for only five minutes, he decided to make the trip and pray the trains would run on time.[26]

They did, and the audience responded well. The Atlanta papers lauded his moderation and good sense, and newspapers around the country picked up the story. The following year a delegation of Atlanta capitalists asked him to join them in Washington to lobby Congress to fund the upcoming Cotton States and International Exposition, to be held in Atlanta in 1895. House Speaker Charles F. Crisp of Georgia ensured that the group received a respectful hearing from the commerce committee, despite the long-windedness of several of the Atlantans. The committee members didn't know Booker Washington, and they may have been surprised at his articulateness. But they listened intently as he described his philosophy of race relations. "I tried to impress upon the committee, with all the earnestness and plainness of language that I could command, that if Congress wanted to do something which would assist in ridding the South of the race question and making friends between the two races, it should, in every proper way, encourage the material and intellectual growth of both races," he remembered. "I tried to emphasize the fact that while the Negro should not be deprived by unfair means of the franchise, political agitation alone would not save him, and that back of the ballot he must have property, industry, skill, economy, intelligence, and character, and that no race without these elements could permanently succeed."

Washington had been allotted seven minutes, but the entranced committee let him run twice that long. Here was a man white Southerners could do business with—precisely because business, not politics, was what he wanted to do. When he concluded, the Georgia delegation leaped up as one to shake his hand, and the other committee members joined in. The committee unanimously endorsed the appropriation for the Atlanta exposition, which the full Congress approved a few days later. The organizers of the exposition decided Booker Washington must speak on opening day.[27]

Washington didn't daunt easily, but as he reflected on what was expected of him, he was taken aback. "I remembered that I had been a slave; that my early years had been spent in the depths of poverty and ignorance; and that I had had little opportunity to prepare me for such a responsibility as this. It was only a few years before that time that any white man in the audience might have claimed me as his slave; and it was easily possible that some of my former owners might be present to hear me speak." Never before had a black man been given such a stage in the South. "I was asked now to speak to an audience composed of the wealth and culture of the white South, the representatives of my former masters." Northerners would be there, also, as well as many African Americans. Some who could not be present conveyed congratulations and encouragement, which only intensified the pressure Washington felt. "Surely, what hath God wrought?" exclaimed T. McCants Stewart, a black lawyer in New York. The *Colored American* of Washington, D.C., declared, "Every colored woman, man, and child who can possibly get there ought to go, if for no other reason than to hold up the hands of Prof. Washington, as the children of Israel held up the arms of Moses while he fought the battles of the Lord."[28]

"I felt a good deal as I suppose a man feels when he is on his way to the gallows," Washington wrote of his departure from Tuskegee for Atlanta the day before the exposition opened. "In passing through the town of Tuskegee I met a white farmer who lived some distance out in the country. In a jesting manner this man said: 'Washington, you have spoken before the Northern white people, the Negroes in the South, and to us country white people in the South; but in Atlanta tomorrow you will have before you the Northern whites, the Southern whites, and the Negroes all together. I am afraid that you have got yourself into a tight place.'" Washington couldn't disagree. "But his frank words did not add anything to my comfort," he remembered.

On the train to Atlanta, everyone seemed to know who he was, where he was going, and why. Some wished him well; others simply stared. Washington quoted an elderly black man who saw him at the Atlanta station: "Dat's de man of my race what's gwine to make a speech at de Exposition tomorrow. I'se sho' gwine to hear him."

Washington slept poorly that night and woke before dawn. He reviewed what he intended to say, and whispered a prayer for guidance and strength. After breakfast a delegation from the exposition committee arrived to take him to his place in the parade that would march about Atlanta en route to the fair grounds. The day was hot and the procession long. "When we reached the grounds," Washington recalled, "the heat, together with my nervous anxiety, made me feel as if I were about ready to collapse."

The auditorium was packed from floor to rafter. Whites had the best seats; blacks crowded the galleries. Thousands more, mostly blacks, milled outside. Washington heard and felt the encouragement of the blacks; he sensed the skepticism, indeed hostility, of many of the whites. A visitor described the entrance of the speakers: "A door behind the platform opened and the guests as they came in were welcomed with enthusiasm. But when amongst them a colored man appeared, there was an instant cessation of the applause, and a sudden chill fell upon the whole assemblage. One after another asked angrily, 'What's that nigger doing on the stage?'" Washington himself remarked, "I had been told, while I had been in Atlanta, that while many white people were going to be present to hear me speak, simply out of curiosity, and that others who would be present would be in full sympathy with me, there was a still larger element of the audience which would consist of those who were going to be present for the purpose of hearing me make a fool of myself."

Rufus Bullock, a former Georgia governor who had left politics for business, hosted the afternoon's festivities. He introduced one speaker after another; all extolled the virtues of private enterprise and the future of Atlanta and the South. A band played the "Star-Spangled Banner," which elicited polite applause, and "Dixie," which evoked a more heartfelt reaction. Governor Bullock thanked the musicians and then introduced the next speaker. "We shall now be favored with an address by a great Southern educator," he said. Clapping ensued—until Washington rose and everyone in the audience realized who the Southern educator was. The hall fell silent. Bullock proceeded unfazed. "We have with us today a representative of Negro enterprise and Negro civilization." Some of the whites applauded perfunctorily; the blacks cheered loudly.

The afternoon sun streamed in a window, falling full on Washington's face as he reached the lectern. He always tried, when speaking, to talk directly to his audience, looking his listeners in the eye to narrow the gap between himself and them. Now he discovered he couldn't see any of them, from the blinding sun. But the light cast him into unexpected relief. A New York reporter described him as "a remarkable figure, tall, bony, straight as a Sioux chief, high forehead, straight nose, heavy jaws and strong, determined mouth, with big white teeth, piercing eyes and a commanding manner." The light, apparently, was playing tricks; Washington was neither tall nor bony. But the tricks favored him. "The sinews stood out on his bronzed neck, and his muscular right arm swung high in the air with a lead pencil grasped in his clenched brown fist. His big feet were planted squarely, with the heels together and the toes turned out."[29]

Washington liked to say that what he knew of public speaking he learned from General Armstrong, who told him: "Give them an idea for every word." Washington briefly thanked the organizers of the exposition for including him in the program and then launched directly into his theme: the inescapable connection between the races in the South. "One-third of the population of the South is of the Negro race," he said. "No enterprise seeking the material, civil, or moral welfare of this section can disregard this element of our population and reach the highest success." It was fitting, he continued, that he should be speaking at an exposition celebrating business enterprise, for therein lay the future of both races in the South. Blacks had sometimes lost sight of this fact. "Ignorant and inexperienced, it is not strange that in the first years of our new life we began at the top instead of at the bottom; that a seat in Congress or the state legislature was more sought than real estate or industrial skill; that the political convention or stump speaking had more attractions than starting a dairy farm or truck garden." But blacks had learned, and they now were putting first things first.

Like the lay preacher he was, Washington wrapped his message in a story.

> A ship lost at sea for many days suddenly sighted a friendly vessel. From the mast of the unfortunate vessel was seen a signal, "Water, water; we die of thirst!" The answer from the friendly vessel at once came back, "Cast down your bucket where you are." A second time the signal, "Water, water; send us water!" ran up from the distressed vessel, and was answered, "Cast down your bucket where you are." And a third and a fourth signal for water was answered, "Cast down your bucket where you are." The captain of the distressed vessel, at last heeding the injunction, cast down his bucket, and it came up full of fresh, sparkling water from the mouth of the Amazon River.

The story had a moral for both the races. Some blacks, despairing of improvement in the South, were leaving the region for the North and West and even other countries; others sought to create a wholly separate sphere for blacks within the South. To them Washington said, "Cast down your bucket where you are—cast it down in making friends in every manly way of the people of all races by whom we are surrounded. Cast it down in agriculture, mechanics, in commerce, in domestic service, and in the professions." Those who did so would discover a secret of the South: "Whatever other sins the South may be called to bear, when it comes to business pure and simple, it is in the South that the Negro is given a man's chance in the commercial world." The current exposition, which showcased the accomplishments of blacks as well as whites, attested to this truth. Yet it bore repeating. "Our greatest danger is that in the great leap from slavery to freedom we may overlook the fact that the masses of us are to live by the productions of our hands, and fail to keep in mind that we shall prosper in proportion as we learn to dignify and glorify common labor, and put brains and skill into the common occupations of life; shall prosper in proportion as we learn to draw the line between the superficial and the substantial, the ornamental gewgaws of life and the useful. No race can prosper till it learns that there is as much dignity in tilling a field as in writing a poem."

The moral for whites was similar. Some white employers were looking to foreign immigrants to fill the mines and mills of the South. "Were I permitted, I would repeat what I say to my own race," Washington declared. "Cast down your bucket where you are. Cast it down among the eight millions of Negroes whose habits you know, whose fidelity and love you have tested in days when to have proved treacherous meant the ruin of your firesides. Cast down your bucket among these people who have, without strikes and labor wars, tilled your fields, cleared your forests, builded your railroads and cities, and brought forth treasures from the bowels of the earth." Whites would never regret such a vote of confidence in blacks. "You and your families will be surrounded by the most patient, faithful, lawabiding, and unresentful people that the world has seen. As we have proved our loyalty to you in the past, in nursing your children, watching by the sick-bed of your mothers and fathers, and often following them with tear-dimmed eyes to their graves, so in the future, in our humble way, we shall stand by you with a devotion that no foreigner can approach, interlacing our industrial, commercial, civil, and religious life with yours in a way that shall make the interests of both races one." At this point Washington raised his hand high, with fingers outstretched, then drew it dramatically toward him as he clutched his fingers together. "In all things that are purely social we can be as separate as the fingers, yet one as the hand in all things essential to mutual progress."

This was the image and the message that stuck in the minds of everyone present. Yet Washington wasn't quite finished. He had been allotted ten minutes and he meant to use them. He stressed again the shared fate of blacks and whites in the South. "Nearly sixteen millions of hands will aid you in pulling the load upward, or they will pull against you the load downward," he told his white listeners. "We shall constitute one-third and more of the ignorance and crime of the South, or one-third its intelligence and progress; we shall contribute one-third to the business and industrial prosperity of the South, or we shall prove a veritable body of death, stagnating, depressing, retarding every effort to advance the body politic."

To the whites, but equally to the blacks, he declared, "The wisest among my race understand that the agitation of questions of social equality is the extremest folly, and that progress in the enjoyment of all the privileges that will come to us must be the result of severe and constant struggle rather than of artificial forcing." Again affirming his faith in the redemptive power of capitalism, Washington asserted, "No race that has anything to contribute to the markets of the world is long in any degree ostracized. It is important and right that all privileges of the law be ours, but it is vastly more important that we be prepared for the exercise of these privileges. The opportunity to earn a dollar in a factory just now is worth infinitely more than the opportunity to spend a dollar in an opera-house." Washington spoke of capitalism as akin to religion. "Here bending, as it were, over the altar that represents the results of the struggles of your race and mine . . . ," he said of the exposition, "I pledge that in your effort to work out the great and intricate problem which God has laid at the doors of the South, you shall have at all times the patient, sympathetic help of my race." With God's blessing, the white race and the black race, working together, would bring to the South "a new heaven and a new earth."[30]

JOHN MARSHALL HARLAN had his own views about race and capitalism, and they were rather surprising for one of his background. Harlan's father had named him John Marshall for the great chief justice, whose Southern origins and nationalist sentiments the elder Harlan shared. Harlan senior was a Kentucky contemporary and close friend of Henry Clay, with whom he served in Congress; like Clay he owned slaves but never became an apologist for the peculiar institution (at a time when John Calhoun and others were extolling slavery as a boon to both the white and the black races). The younger Harlan owned slaves briefly but was even less enamored than his father of the institution. After studying law at Transylvania College in Lexington, John Marshall Harlan joined his father's law practice and might have followed him into the Whig party, but the Whigs fell apart amid the sectional troubles of the early 1850s, prompting Harlan (and his father) to seek refuge in the American, or Know-Nothing, party. Harlan won his first elective office, a county judgeship, as a Know-Nothing. Yet that party, too, dissolved, and Harlan migrated to the Constitutional Unionists and eventually the Republicans. During the Civil War he served as an officer in the Union army and became a friend of fellow Kentuckian Benjamin Bristow, Grant's treasury secretary. Harlan was a delegate to the 1876 Republican national convention, at which his well-timed shift to Rutherford Hayes helped the Ohioan win the nomination. Hayes returned the favor by appointing Harlan to the Supreme Court seat vacated in the postelection maneuvering. As a Southerner, Harlan suited Hayes's policy of reconciliation, but as a Republican he didn't alienate the rest of the GOP.

Harlan's thinking on race shifted with the changing times. During the war's early going he argued that Kentucky should secede if Lincoln imposed emancipation on the state. He called the Emancipation Proclamation unconstitutional and initially condemned the Reconstruction amendments as "a complete revolution in our republican government." Blacks, he said, were inferior to whites and should be kept in a subordinate position. But by the time he ran for Kentucky governor in 1871 on the Republican ticket he was disavowing his previous positions. "There is no man on this continent . . . ," he said, "who rejoices more than I do at the extinction of slavery."[31]

He lost this race (and another in 1875) but didn't abandon his new convictions, and after he joined the Supreme Court he gained a reputation as the regular odd man out—to the point that his fellow justices teased him for his chronic "dissent-ery." He stood alone against the other eight in the *Civil Rights Cases* of 1883, which struck down the Civil Rights Act of 1875. The majority held that Congress had overstepped by barring private discrimination (albeit in public conveyances and accommodations); the Fourteenth Amendment, the majority said, forbade only state discrimination. "It does not authorize Congress to create a code of municipal law for the regulation of private rights," Associate Justice Joseph Bradley wrote. Harlan dismissed this reasoning as sophistry. The point of Reconstruction, he said, and in particular of the Thirteenth Amendment, had been not simply to end slavery but to remove the "burdens and disabilities which constitute badges of slavery and servitude." The drafters of the Thirteenth Amendment had recognized that African Americans, given their history as slaves, might require special protection. "Congress, therefore, under its express power to enforce that amendment by appropriate legislation, may enact laws to protect that people against the deprivation, on account of their race, of any civil rights enjoyed by other freemen. . . . Such legislation may be of a direct and primary character."[32]

The 1883 decision encouraged Southern states to experiment with new forms of discrimination—to write, among other laws and regulations, the municipal codes Justice Bradley denied to Congress. Much of daily intercourse between the races was governed by custom and followed patterns decades in place. Whites generally associated with whites and blacks with blacks. In those areas where interaction was unavoidable—in commerce, for example—contact was often brief and clearly a matter of business. Black customers might patronize white department stores, and white customers black barbers, and no one feel threatened or unusually demeaned. In certain public places and events, the races could associate quite freely. Charles Dudley Warner, Mark Twain's friend and collaborator, traveled to New Orleans for a business exposition in 1885 and remarked the easy interaction between the races. "On 'Louisiana Day' in the Exposition, the colored citizens took their full share of the parade and the honors," Warner wrote. "Their societies marched with the others, and the races mingled on the grounds in unconscious equality of privileges." Even observers attuned to discrimination could be hard pressed to find it. T. McCants Stewart, the African American lawyer, had been born in South Carolina but was living in Boston when he decided, in 1885, to return to his native state as part of a larger tour of the South. "On leaving Washington, D.C., I put a chip on my shoulder and inwardly dared any man to knock it off," he wrote. His railcar filled up; passengers had to sit on their luggage. "I fairly foamed at the mouth, imagining that the conductor would order me into a seat occupied by a colored lady so as to make room for a white passenger." But the conductor said nothing, and the black and white passengers crowded elbow to knee. Stewart continued to Columbia, South Carolina, where the tolerant atmosphere astonished him. "I feel about as safe here as in Providence, R.I.," he wrote. "I can ride in first class cars on the railroads and in the streets. I can go into saloons and get refreshments even as in New York. I can stop in and drink a glass of soda and be more politely waited upon than in some parts of New England." In other Southern cities the situation was much the same. No one harassed him; whites struck up conversations with him apparently oblivious to his color. "I think the whites of the South," he concluded, "are really less afraid to have contact with colored people than the whites of the North."[33]

Yet the situation changed, for several reasons. The political campaign to disfranchise black voters fostered, indeed almost required, an increasingly rigid ideology of white superiority. The Fourteenth and Fifteenth amendments might be nullified in Southern practice, but not without emotional effort. Meanwhile the emergence of Southern industry, at a time of labor strife nationally, disposed white employers toward any measures that would weaken the bargaining power of their black workers. Marginalizing the black race as a whole served the capitalists' purpose well. Similarly, the development of an agrarian protest movement gave opponents of the protesters an incentive to try to split the movement along racial lines, as some attempted with the Lodge elections bill. Finally, at the level of mere logistics, the spread of railroads across the South put blacks and whites in closer contact for longer periods of time than most had ever experienced.

As it happened, the railroads were where much of the new discrimination—the Jim Crow system, named for a black caricature—was first formalized. In 1890 Louisiana adopted a law "to promote the comfort of passengers on railway trains"; the crucial clause mandated "equal but separate accommodations for the white and colored races." Like nearly all such legislation, this measure was race-neutral on its face; whites could no more sit in black cars than blacks could sit in white cars. And there were exceptions: black nurses attending white children might ride in the white cars (and, theoretically, vice versa). But the intent of the law was as plain as that of the other laws curtailing African American rights. And it was emphasized by the cinders and ash that blew into the black cars, which were placed in the least desirable spot in the trains, just behind the locomotives.[34]

Louisiana wasn't the first state to pass a segregationist railroad law. Florida had done so in 1887, Mississippi in 1888, and Texas in 1889. Other states were poised to follow. But Louisiana's circumstances were unusual. As Charles Warner had noted just five years earlier, the races in Louisiana mingled more freely than in many other Southern states (and, indeed, than in several Northern states). The descendants of the *gens de couleur libres*—the free blacks of French heritage and culture—were accorded respect denied to most African Americans elsewhere. If legally enforced segregation took root in Louisiana, it could spring up anywhere.[35]

For this reason advocates of racial equality determined to challenge the Louisiana law. "We'll make a case, a test case, and bring it before the federal courts," wrote Louis Martinet, the editor of the leading black paper in Louisiana, the *New Orleans Crusader*. A committee of prominent Louisiana African Americans was formed, and funds were solicited. Northern civil rights advocates offered to help. Albion Tourgée, a New

York lawyer who had carpetbagged in North Carolina during Reconstruction, winning a seat on the state's superior court, wrote Martinet volunteering his services. Tourgée suggested having a woman, nearly white in appearance but black by Louisiana law, sit in a white coach. She would make a sympathetic defendant, he reasoned.[36]

Martinet replied that things were more complicated in Louisiana than Tourgée realized. "It would be quite difficult to have a lady *too* nearly white refused admission to a 'white' car," Martinet said. "There are the strangest white people you ever saw here. Walking up and down our principal thoroughfare—Canal Street—you would be surprised to have persons pointed out to you, some as white and others as colored, and if you were not informed you would be sure to pick out the white for colored and the colored for white. Besides, people of tolerably fair complexion, even if unmistakably colored, enjoy here a large degree of immunity from the accursed prejudice." If Martinet and the committee were to have their test case, they might have to announce the presence of the intruder in the white car and insist on his or her black identity.[37]

Things came to that, but not at once. Even while debating the skin tone of their test subject, Martinet and the committee had trouble finding a railroad that enforced the separate-car law. The railroad corporations were agnostic on the morality of segregation but didn't like its impact on their bottom lines. The separate cars were expensive to operate, and the law alienated black passengers, some of whom threatened a boycott. In time the committee found a company willing to enforce the law, in the hope—of the company no less than the committee—of having the law overturned. Daniel Desdunes, the son of a member of the committee, boarded a train at New Orleans bound for Mobile. He sat in the white car, was told to relocate, refused, and was arrested. Tourgée came from New York to direct the case, which ascended through the lower Louisiana courts to the state supreme court, where it intersected another case, brought by the Pullman Palace Car Company and alleging that the Louisiana law infringed the commerce clause of the Constitution. The Louisiana high court agreed, voiding the law as it applied to interstate travel. Because Desdunes was bound for Alabama, the charge against him was dismissed.[38]

On their next try the New Orleans committee made sure the test passenger bought an intrastate ticket. Homer Plessy later described himself as seven-eighths Caucasian and one-eighth African; he commonly passed for white in New Orleans. In June 1892 he purchased a ticket from New Orleans to Covington, Louisiana, on the East Louisiana Railroad. Either at the time of purchase or when he sat down in the white car, Plessy identified himself as a black man. By agreement, the conductor asked him to move; he refused and was arrested.

The case came before Judge John H. Ferguson of the state district criminal court. Ferguson found for the prosecution, causing Tourgée, on Plessy's behalf, to appeal to the Louisiana supreme court. As most observers expected, the Louisiana high court upheld the decision, although the court's reasoning occasioned some surprise. "The sole question involved in this case . . . ," Associate Justice Charles Fenner asserted for the court, "is whether a statute requiring railroads to furnish separate, but equal, accommodations for the two races . . . violates the Fourteenth Amendment." In ruling that it did not, Fenner cited precedents not from Southern or federal courts but from state courts of the North, in particular from two states historically identified with abolitionism. The supreme court of Massachusetts had ruled as early as 1849 that segregated schools were constitutional. That court, answering the claim that segregation perpetuated race prejudice, had declared, "This prejudice, if it exists, is not created by law and cannot be changed by law." The supreme court of Pennsylvania, in a case quite similar to the present one, involving a law mandating separate railcars for the two races, had decreed, "To assert separateness is not to declare inferiority. . . . It is simply to say that following the order of Divine Providence, human authority ought not to compel these widely separated races to intermix." Fenner, speaking in the voice of the Louisiana court, said that the law in question applied to the races with "perfect fairness and equality" and noted "if the fact charged be proved, the penalty would be the same whether the accused were white or colored." Fenner expressed a certain puzzlement as to why the case had come up at all. "Even were it true that the statute is prompted by a prejudice on the part of one race to be thrown in such contact with the other, one would suppose that to be a sufficient reason why the pride and self-respect of the other race should equally prompt it to avoid such contact, if it could be done without the sacrifice of equal accommodations." Plessy's appeal was denied.[39]

That left the United States Supreme Court as the sole hope for overturning the Louisiana law. Martinet and the Louisianans wished to press forward at once. Tourgée and some other civil rights advocates from outside the state hesitated. If the national court reversed the Louisiana decision, well and good. But if the high court affirmed the Louisiana decision, it would legitimize segregation not simply in Louisiana but in every state. The result could be devastating to the cause of racial equality.

Tourgée had a second reason for proceeding slowly. Of the justices currently on the Supreme Court, only John Marshall Harlan could be counted on to oppose the Louisiana law. The other justices engendered no such confidence. "One is inclined to be with us legally, but his political bias is the other way," Tourgée told Martinet. "There are two who may be brought over by the argument. There are five who are against us. Of these one may be reached, I think, if he 'hears from the country' soon enough. The others will probably stay where they are until Gabriel blows his horn." Tourgée hoped time would change either the makeup of the court or the minds of some of the justices.[40]

Tourgée put off the appeal as long as he could, but eventually he had to bring it forward or accept defeat by default. The Supreme Court heard the case of *Plessy* v. *Ferguson* in the autumn of 1895. Tourgée attacked the Louisiana law at several points. He adopted Justice Harlan's phrase and logic in saying it branded blacks with a "badge of servitude" and thereby defied the spirit of the Thirteenth Amendment. The law also denied blacks the equal protection promised them by the Fourteenth Amendment, Tourgée said. It failed to define race, leaving this determination to railroad company officials and thereby depriving blacks of due process. It willfully ignored that separate accommodations for blacks would not remain equal accommodations for long in Louisiana (or anywhere in America, for that matter). "When the law distinguishes between the civil rights or privileges of two classes, it always is and always must be to the detriment of the weaker class or race." The provision allowing black nurses to ride in white cars demonstrated the true purpose of the law, for only so long as blacks were in positions subservient to whites could their presence be endured; otherwise it was insufferable. Governments were established to promote the *general* welfare and happiness; the Louisiana act, by design, did no such thing. It was "plainly and evidently intended to promote the happiness of one class by asserting its supremacy and the inferiority of another class." In a sentence that summarized his case and the entire argument against the Jim Crow law, Tourgée declared: "Justice is pictured blind, and her daughter, the Law, ought at least to be color-blind."[41]

THE SUPREME COURT rendered its decision in May 1896. By a vote of 7 to 1, the court upheld the Louisiana law. Associate Justice Henry Billings Brown, writing for the majority, dismissed the contention that the law in any way violated the Thirteenth Amendment. Quoting the majority opinion in the *Civil Rights Cases*, Brown declared, "It would be running the slavery question into the ground to make it apply to every act of discrimination which a person may see fit to make as to the guests he will entertain, or as to the people he will take into his coach or cab or car, or admit to his concert or theater, or deal with in other matters of intercourse or business." As to the Fourteenth Amendment, it was indeed written to enforce political equality between the races. "But, in the nature of things, it could not have been intended to abolish distinctions based upon color, or to enforce social, as distinguished from political, equality, or a commingling of the two races upon terms unsatisfactory to either. Laws permitting, and even requiring, their separation, in places where they are liable to be brought into contact, do not necessarily imply the inferiority of either race to the other, and have been generally, if not universally, recognized as within the competency of the state legislatures in the exercise of their police power." Brown cited the Boston case upholding segregated schools as an example. But the essential weakness—"the underlying fallacy"—of the plaintiff's argument lay in the contention that enforced separation of the races implied the inferiority of blacks. "If this be so, it is not by reason of anything found in the act, but solely because the colored race chooses to put that construction upon it." Brown asserted that during Reconstruction blacks had held the dominant position in the Louisiana legislature without causing whites to acknowledge their own inferiority. He added, "The argument also assumes that social prejudices may be overcome by legislation, and that equal rights cannot be secured to the negro except by an enforced commingling of the two races. We cannot accept this proposition. If the two races are to meet upon terms of social equality, it must be the result of natural affinities, a mutual appreciation of each other's merits, and a voluntary consent of individuals." To think otherwise was to ignore history and human nature. "Legislation is powerless to eradicate racial instincts or to abolish distinctions based upon physical differences, and the attempt to do so can only result in accentuating the difficulties of the present situation. If the civil and political rights of both races be equal, one cannot be inferior to the other civilly or politically. If one race be inferior to the other socially, the Constitution of the United States cannot put them upon the same plane."[12]

John Marshall Harlan's years of isolation on the court had only deepened his conviction that American jurisprudence was failing American democracy. Harlan was no social leveler. "The white race deems itself to be the dominant race in this country," he wrote in his solitary dissent. "And so it is, in prestige, in achievements, in education, in wealth, and in power. So, I doubt not, it will continue to be for all time, if it remains true to its great heritage, and holds fast to the principles of constitutional liberty." But part of that heritage and the essence of those principles was equality before the law. "In view of the Constitution, in the eye of the law, there is in this country no superior, dominant, ruling class of citizens. There is no caste here. Our Constitution is color-blind, and neither knows nor tolerates classes among citizens. In respect of civil rights, all citizens are equal before the law. The humblest is the peer of the most powerful. The law regards man as man, and takes no account of his surroundings or of his color when his civil rights as guaranteed by the supreme law of the land are involved."

Harlan returned to his argument from the *Civil Rights Cases*, referenced by the counsel for Plessy, that the Thirteenth Amendment barred the imposition of any "badge of servitude," and he judged that the Louisiana law imposed just such a badge on blacks. But he now placed greater weight on the equal protection and due process clauses of the Fourteenth Amendment. For the state of Louisiana to assert, and the majority of the Supreme Court to accept, that the segregation law was race-neutral was fatuous or deceitful. "Every one knows that the statute in question had its origin in the purpose, not so much to exclude white persons from railroad cars occupied by blacks, as to exclude colored people from coaches occupied by or assigned to white persons. . . . No one would be so wanting in candor as to assert the contrary." Moreover, the Louisiana law deprived members of both races of individual freedom. "If a white man and a black man choose to occupy the same public conveyance on a public highway, it is their right to do so; and no government, proceeding alone on grounds of race, can prevent it without infringing the personal liberty of each."

Should the principle of racial discrimination once be accepted, there might be no end to its applications.

> If a state can prescribe, as a rule of civil conduct, that whites and blacks shall not travel as passengers in the same railroad coach, why may it not so regulate the use of the streets of its cities and towns as to compel white citizens to keep on one side of a street, and black citizens to keep on the other? Why may it not, upon like grounds, punish whites and blacks who ride together in street cars or in open vehicles on a public road or street? Why may it not require sheriffs to assign whites to one side of a court room, and blacks to the other? And why may it not also prohibit the commingling of the two races in the galleries of legislative halls or in public assemblages convened for the consideration of the political questions of the day?

The present decision recalled one of the worst moments in the history of the court. "The judgment this day rendered will, in time, prove to be quite as pernicious as the decision made by this tribunal in the Dred Scott Case."

Harlan intended the analogy very seriously. The Dred Scott case had closed the door of democracy to blacks as a people and unleashed the demons of divisiveness in the nation as a whole; the current judgment could have consequences no less dire.

> The present decision, it may well be apprehended, will not only stimulate aggressions, more or less brutal and irritating, upon the admitted rights of colored citizens, but will encourage the belief that it is possible, by means of state enactments, to defeat the beneficent purposes which the people of the United States had in view when they adopted the recent amendments of the constitution. . . . Sixty millions of whites are in no danger from the presence here of eight millions of blacks. The destinies of the two races, in this country, are indissolubly linked together, and the interests of both require that the common government of all shall not permit the seeds of race hate to be planted under the sanction of law. What can more certainly arouse race hate, what more certainly create and perpetuate a feeling of distrust between these races, than state enactments which, in fact, proceed on the ground that colored citizens are so inferior and degraded that they cannot be allowed to sit in public coaches occupied by white citizens? That, as all will admit, is the real meaning of such legislation as was enacted in Louisiana.

Harlan couldn't know how truly he spoke. The resounding decision of the court in the *Plessy* case drove the final nail in the coffin of racial egalitarianism. The executive branch of the federal government had abandoned blacks in the Compromise of 1877; the legislature deserted them definitively when the Senate rejected the Lodge elections bill in 1891. Now the judiciary turned its back on African Americans who simply wished to exercise rights they had won at such great cost thirty years before. During the Civil War it was possible—for Northerners, at any rate—to conceive of freedom and democracy as marching together toward victory; Lincoln's Emancipation Proclamation had been followed just months later by his Gettysburg Address, with its stunningly eloquent definition of democracy as government "of the people, by the people, for the people." But at war's end the alliance between freedom and democracy began to splinter, as wartime alliances often do. Freedom for blacks—including the freedom to participate in politics and public life—required curtailing democracy for whites; the Fourteenth and Fifteenth amendments were essentially restraints on white majorities disposed to deny political rights to blacks.

The problem of minority rights within majority rule wasn't unique to Gilded Age America; it is inherent in democracy. But it became acute and undeniable in the United States during the decades after the Civil War, for although the constitutional restraints on the white legislative and practical majorities held for a while, they couldn't withstand the relentless pressure of personal prejudice and political partisanship. In other respects, Gilded Age democracy was under siege from capitalism; in the matter of race relations, democracy besieged itself.

John Marshall Harlan understood this, and he articulated his frustration in the bitter coda to his *Plessy* dissent. "We boast of the freedom enjoyed by our people above all other peoples," he declared. "But it is difficult to reconcile that boast with a state of the law which, practically, puts the brand of servitude and degradation upon a large class of our fellow citizens, our equals before the law. The thin disguise of 'equal' accommodations for passengers in railroad coaches will not mislead any one, nor atone for the wrong this day done."[43]

Chapter 17

AFFAIRS OF THE HEARTLAND

═══

During the early 1890s, a problem even older in American history than the race question, and equally intractable, if that were possible, came to a dismal resolution. For centuries the native peoples of North America had turned to prophets when the pressure from whites became irresistible; the most successful—though ultimately futile—campaign of Indian resistance, led by Tecumseh during the War of 1812, had been inspired by Tecumseh's brother, known as the Prophet, who preached that the bullets of the white soldiers couldn't penetrate the faith of his followers.

Black Elk remembered the first stirrings of a similar dispensation in 1889. "Strange news had come from the West," the Sioux seer recalled. "It was hard to believe, and when I first heard of it, I thought it was only foolish talk that somebody had started somewhere. This news said that out yonder in the West at a place near where the great mountains"—the Sierra Nevada—"stand before you come to the big water"—the Pacific—"there was a sacred man among the Paiutes who had talked to the Great Spirit in a vision, and the Great Spirit had told him how to save the Indian peoples and make the Wasichus disappear and bring back all the bison and the people who were dead and how there would be a new earth." The report prompted some Sioux to travel west to see the holy man for themselves. He had lived among whites long enough to acquire the name Jack Wilson and a basic knowledge of Christianity, but now he employed his Paiute name, Wovoka, and called himself the Messiah. A new world was coming, he said, in which all the dead Indians and dead animals would be restored to life and from which all the living would be excluded, except for those Indians who performed a dance he taught them.

The Sioux returned to Dakota with the news, and all that winter Black Elk's neighbors could speak of nothing else. In the summer of 1890 several other Sioux made the pilgrimage to Nevada's Walker Lake, where Wovoka resided. Either the revelation had changed over the winter or it was transmitted more clearly now, for it appeared that Wovoka was the son of the Great Spirit and that he had come to earth long ago and been killed by the Wasichus, who had rejected his teaching. This time he came to the Indians. And the new world would arrive the next spring.

In the autumn of 1890 Wovoka's dance—the Ghost Dance—caught on among Indians throughout the West. Black Elk had lost his vision lately, having spent, by his reckoning, too much time among the whites. But the Ghost Dance brought it back. "I remembered how the spirits had taken me to the center of the earth and shown me the good things, and how my people should prosper. I remembered how the Six Grandfathers had told me that through their power I should make my people live and the holy tree should bloom. I believed my vision was coming true at last, and happiness overcame me."[1]

Other Ghost Dancers interpreted their visions differently, and the whites who observed the Ghost Dance from the outside differently still. The federal agents and soldiers posted to the Pine Ridge reservation grew nervous as the cult took hold, not least since some dancers claimed that the special "ghost shirts" they wore rendered them impervious to the white men's bullets. Among the Sioux, with their record of resistance, battle magic appeared particularly ominous.

General Nelson Miles, commanding U.S. army forces in the West, ordered reinforcements to the Pine Ridge reservation. The troop deployment increased the tension and drew criticism from some of the older hands in the region. Valentine McGillycuddy, a former Indian agent, thought Miles was overreacting. "I should let the dance continue," McGillycuddy said. "If the Seventh Day Adventists prepare their ascension robes for the second coming of the Savior, the United States Army is not put in motion to prevent them. Why should not the Indians have the same privilege? If the troops remain, trouble is sure to come." But Miles ignored the advice, preferring to take still stronger action. Sitting Bull lived at Pine Ridge and even yet commanded a following. Lest he become a nucleus of armed resistance, Miles ordered him arrested.

On December 15, a large force of Indian police surrounded Sitting Bull's cabin on the Grand River. They seized Sitting Bull, only to discover that they were surrounded in turn by a much larger group of Ghost Dancers. The Indian police tried to bluster their way past the Ghost Dancers, but one of the latter opened fire. By accident or design, the return fire of the police struck Sitting Bull, killing him instantly. At this point, according to eyewitnesses, something very strange happened. Sitting Bull had received a gift horse from Buffalo Bill Cody, a pony that had performed tricks in Cody's Wild West show. One of the cues was a pistol shot, and when the animal now heard the gunfire, it started its routine of raising its hooves and shaking its head. The Ghost Dancers interpreted this as a version of the Ghost Dance and held their fire to watch. By the time the pony trotted away, a cavalry company had arrived to rescue the Indian police.[2]

This chance event simply deferred the reckoning, and perhaps made it worse. Fearing retaliation from the soldiers, the Sioux scattered; a band led by a chief named Big Foot started for the Pine Ridge agency, where they hoped to find protection with Red Cloud, the most faithful of the Sioux allies of the whites. Big Foot's band was mostly women and children, but it contained enough warriors to worry the local army commander, who diverted the band to a camp on the banks of Wounded Knee Creek. Big Foot acquiesced, though the exposed campsite put his ill-equipped people at risk of death from exposure. He himself had caught pneumonia and could barely ride.

In the last week of December, Colonel James Forsyth, George Custer's successor as commander of the Seventh Cavalry, received orders to disarm Big Foot's band. Black Elk happened to be at the Pine Ridge agency as the cavalry moved out. "When I saw them starting, I felt that something terrible was going to happen," he recalled. "That night I could hardly sleep at all. I walked around most of the night."[3]

The next morning—December 29—Forsyth distributed rations of hardtack to Big Foot's hungry band. Then he demanded that they turn over their weapons. Some did; others resisted, although whether from defiance or confusion as to what qualified as weapons was unclear. Someone—

perhaps an Indian, perhaps a soldier—fired a shot, triggering a general melee of gunfire and desperate hand-to-hand fighting. Several Indians and soldiers fell on the spot; other Indians broke away, only to be mowed down by the Hotchkiss machine guns the cavalry had mounted above the camp. The fire from the guns raked the camp, ripping through tepees and cutting down men, women, and children indiscriminately.

Black Elk heard the big guns from a distance. "I knew from the sound that it must be wagon guns"—the Hotchkiss guns—"going off. The sounds went right through my body." He donned his sacred shirt (not a Ghost Shirt but one of his own), painted his face red, put an eagle feather in his hair, mounted his buckskin, and galloped in the direction of Wounded Knee Creek. He carried no gun, only a sacred bow that he had seen in his great vision and crafted later. On the road he joined up with several other Sioux, till they numbered about twenty. In time they mounted a rise that looked down upon Big Foot's camp. "Wagon guns were still going off," he remembered. "There was much shooting. . . . There were many cries, and we could see cavalrymen scattered over the hills ahead of us. Cavalrymen were riding along the gulch and shooting into it, where women and children were running away and trying to hide in the gullies and the stunted pines."

Black Elk spotted a group of women and children huddled under the bank of the gulch. Several soldiers had rifles trained on them. Black Elk shouted over the din to his comrades: "Take courage! These are our relatives. We will try to get them back." As they prepared to charge, they shouted to one another: "Take courage! It is time to fight!" They galloped headlong toward the gulch. The soldiers fired at them. "I had no gun, and when we were charging I just held the sacred bow out in front of me with my right hand," Black Elk said. "The bullets did not hit us at all." Black Elk found a baby lying on the ground crying for her mother. He stopped long enough to wrap her tightly in the shawl that had fallen loose around her. Then he set her down, out of the line of fire. "It was a safe place, and I had other work to do."

By this time many more Sioux had raced up from Pine Ridge to join the fight. "We all charged on the soldiers. They ran eastward toward where the trouble began." The soldiers retreated to the creek and there dug themselves in. The Indians couldn't dislodge them. Eventually the soldiers marched away up the creek.

The carnage was all too evident by then. Black Elk rode slowly along the dry gulch. "Dead and wounded women and children and little babies were scattered all along there where they had been trying to run away. The soldiers had followed along the gulch, as they ran, and murdered them in there. Sometimes they were in heaps because they had huddled together, and some were scattered all along. Sometimes bunches of them had been killed and torn to pieces where the wagon guns hit them. I saw a little baby trying to suck its mother, but she was bloody and dead."

The official statistics registered 146 Indians dead, including 44 women and 18 children, and 51 wounded. The Indian death toll almost certainly was higher, perhaps much higher, as many uncounted wounded ran or crawled away to die unmolested further by the soldiers. The soldiers suffered 25 dead and 39 wounded. Several, perhaps many, of the casualties among the soldiers were inflicted by their own fire.

"It was a good winter day when all this happened," Black Elk remembered. "The sun was shining. But after the soldiers marched away from their dirty work, a heavy snow began to fall. The wind came up in the night. There was a big blizzard, and it grew very cold. The snow drifted deep in the crooked gulch, and it was one long grave of butchered women and children and babies, who had never done any harm and were only trying to run away."[4]

WOUNDED KNEE, as matters proved, marked the end of an era, the last armed resistance to white control of the territory claimed by the government of the United States. For three hundred years Indians had fought the Anglo-Americans; the struggle had stained every state and nearly every county with the Indians' blood or the whites'. Now the struggle was finally over. The Indians could no longer resist; the invaders had won.

A less sanguinary sign of the white victory was being registered even as the Seventh Cavalry rolled its Hotchkiss guns away from Wounded Knee. During 1890 the federal government conducted its constitutionally mandated decennial census; the tally—the first census to employ mechanical tabulating machines—revealed a population of 63 million living in the forty-two states. This aggregate population represented an increase of 25 percent over 1880, resulting from both heavy immigration and healthy natural increase. Nine million of those 63 million were foreign born. Most

Americans, 64 percent, still lived in rural districts, although the cities were growing rapidly. The largest cities were New York, with 1.5 million inhabitants; Chicago, with 1.1 million; Philadelphia, 1 million; and Brooklyn (still separate from New York), 800,000.

The most intriguing part of the report was a statement inserted near the end of the summary on the population and its distribution:

> Up to and including 1880 the country had a frontier of settlement, but at present the unsettled area has been so broken into by isolated bodies of settlement that there can hardly be said to be a frontier line. In the discussion of its extent and its western movement it can not, therefore, any longer have a place in the census reports.[5]

Politicians read the census report for guidance on redrawing legislative districts; merchants studied its tables in search of business opportunities; speculators scanned the maps for clues to future movements of population. Frederick Jackson Turner read it for insight into America's past. A young historian at the University of Wisconsin, Turner judged existing interpretations of American history inadequate. The graybeards of the history profession, preeminently Herbert Baxter Adams at Johns Hopkins, had adapted the evolutionary thinking of Charles Darwin to the study of history and concluded that American institutions had evolved from English precursors, which in turn reflected Germanic practices. The roots of American history lay in Europe; to understand America, one must examine Europe.

Turner had studied with Adams and mastered the conventional wisdom sufficiently to earn his doctorate in 1890. But he thought Adams and the Teutonists fundamentally wrong. No doubt the germ of American democracy could be discovered in Europe, but its distinctiveness reflected the New World soil in which the seed had sprouted and blossomed. Turner didn't reject Darwin, but he was a Lamarckian at heart, believing acquired characteristics could be passed from one generation to the next.

He was also a Westerner. Born in Portage, Wisconsin, at a time when Indians still roamed the forests among the lakes, Turner believed the West—in particular, the moving frontier of settlement—had made America what it became. Turner deemed history inseparable from geography, as he explained to the annual meeting of the American Historical Association held in Chicago in 1893. "The United States lies like a huge page in the history of society," he said.

> Line by line as we read this continental page from West to East we find the record of social evolution. It begins with the Indian and the hunter; it goes on to tell of the disintegration of savagery by the entrance of the trader, the pathfinder of civilization; we read the annals of the pastoral stage in ranch life; the exploitation of the soil by the raising of unrotated crops of corn and wheat in sparsely settled farming communities; the intensive culture of the denser farm settlement; and finally the manufacturing organization with city and factory system.

In his thirty-two years Turner had observed the frontier passing across Wisconsin; now he asked his audience to imagine its motion in their mind's eye.

> Stand at Cumberland Gap and watch the procession of civilization, marching single file—the buffalo following the trail to the salt springs, the Indian, the fur-trader and hunter, the cattle-raiser, the pioneer farmer—and the frontier has passed by. Stand at South Pass in the Rockies a century later and see the same procession with wider intervals between. The unequal rate of advance compels us to distinguish the frontier into the trader's frontier, the rancher's frontier, or the miner's frontier, and the farmer's frontier. When the mines and the cow pens were still near the fall line the traders' pack trains were tinkling across the Alleghenies, and the French on the Great Lakes were fortifying their posts, alarmed by the British trader's birch canoe. When the trappers scaled the Rockies, the farmer was still near the mouth of the Missouri.

The moving frontier had shaped American history in distinctive ways. It attracted the disparate nationalities that differentiated the United States from the European countries. The Atlantic Coast was predominantly English, but Germans and Scotch Irish quickly filled in behind the coast. The frontier diminished the dependence of the Americans on Europe; the individual self-reliance evoked by the frontier extrapolated into a national self-reliance that led to separation from Britain. The frontier promoted egalitarianism; the gentry didn't leave the coast, and those persons who did leave were judged on their accomplishments, not on their breeding. Most important, the frontier fostered democracy. Those independent Westerners wouldn't tolerate the restrictions on the franchise practiced in the East; as the numbers of Westerners increased and their influence in national politics grew—manifested most clearly by their election of Andrew Jackson as president—the Easterners had to lower their restrictions out of self-defense.

All this mattered to historians, but not to historians alone. The statement by the census director that the frontier had disappeared suggested that American society had reached a turning point in its evolution.

Since the days when the fleet of Columbus sailed into the waters of the New World, America has been another name for opportunity, and the people of the United States have taken their tone from the incessant expansion which has not only been open but has even been forced upon them. He would be a rash prophet who should assert that the expansive character of American life has now entirely ceased. Movement has been its dominant fact, and, unless this training has no effect upon a people, the American energy will continually demand a wider field for its exercise.

But never again will such gifts of free land offer themselves. For a moment, at the frontier, the bonds of custom are broken and unrestraint is triumphant. There is not *tabula rasa*. The stubborn American environment is there with its imperious summons to accept its conditions; the inherited ways of doing things are also there; and yet, in spite of environment, and in spite of custom, each frontier did indeed furnish a new field of opportunity, a gate of escape from the bondage of the past; and freshness, and confidence, and scorn of older society, impatience of its restraints and its ideas, and indifference to its lessons, have accompanied the frontier.

What the Mediterranean Sea was to the Greeks, breaking the bond of custom, offering new experiences, calling out new institutions and activities, that, and more, the ever retreating frontier has been to the United States directly, and to the nations of Europe more remotely. And now, four centuries from the discovery of America, at the end of a hundred years of life under the Constitution, the frontier has gone, and with its going has closed the first period of American history.[6]

AMERICAN FARMERS READ the 1890 census, too, and it confirmed a decades-old belief that history was tilting against them. As America industrialized, as corporate capitalism became the dominant mode of economic enterprise, farmers felt their autonomy diminish, and, against the inclinations of many of them, they grew increasingly radical. Industrial workers squeezed by wage cuts might complain about particular capitalists—their bosses, most obviously—without rejecting capitalism per se. And in fact this was what most American workers did. But farmers, typically being their own bosses, could hardly damn falling crop prices and rising interest rates without condemning capitalism as a whole. In the 1890s farmers were still the largest occupational group in America, although they no longer constituted an absolute majority of workers; and they still considered themselves the repository of the nation's core values. But their numbers continued to slip compared with industrial workers and with the emerging white-collar class of office personnel, and their incomes eroded relative to workers and big capitalists both. Like other petty capitalists—the victims of John Rockefeller's conquest of oil, the merchants left stranded by J. P. Morgan's reorganization of railroads—the farmers could easily believe that capitalism was failing them. Or perhaps they were failing capitalism. Either way, capitalism had to be radically transformed. The obvious means was democracy.

Farmers didn't reach this conclusion all together or all at once. Many, viewing their problems as chiefly economic, at first sought to tackle them by economic means. With capitalists consolidating into trusts, and workers into trade unions, many farmers sought to consolidate into organizations of their own. In 1867 Minnesota's Oliver Kelley founded the Patrons of Husbandry, commonly called the Grange. An erstwhile employee of the federal Department of Agriculture, Kelley worked the contacts he had made among farmers to advocate a brotherhood (and sisterhood: the Grange admitted women) of children of the soil. His program emphasized cooperation in purchasing supplies and marketing crops, and a united front against railroads and other shippers. Kelley's concept caught on; the Grange grew to nineteen thousand chapters and 750,000 members by 1875.[7]

The Grange self-consciously eschewed politics and avoided endorsing candidates. Yet members gravitated to politics nonetheless. The Panic of 1873 revealed the limits of private-sector activism; though Grange cooperatives increased farmers' leverage with suppliers and customers, they couldn't cope with the general destabilization of American finance. Farmers took to the hustings in the mid-1870s, running independent candidates who promised to curb the railroads and pressure the federal government to loosen the money supply or backing Republicans and Democrats who promised the same thing. In several midwestern states they won approval of "Granger laws" regulating railroad and warehouse rates. The railroads and their allies challenged the laws in court, contending that they violated the commerce clause of the Constitution and the due process clause of the Fourteenth Amendment. At this point in American constitutional history, however, the concept of "substantive" due process remained undeveloped, and the Supreme Court, in the 1877 case of *Munn v. Illinois*, upheld the Granger laws. Chief Justice Morrison Waite, writing for the 7-to-2 majority, asserted that the popular prerogatives of democracy trumped the property rights of capitalism, at least in the area of commerce. "For protection against abuses by legislatures the people must resort to the polls, not to the courts," he said. Yet Associate Justice Stephen J. Field sounded a warning in dissent: "If this be sound law, if there be no protection, either in the principles upon which our republican government is founded, or in the prohibitions of the Constitution against such invasion of private rights, all property and all business in the State are held at the mercy of a majority of its legislature."[8]

The Granger laws didn't address the currency issue, which began to emerge as the crucial one for farmers. In the industrial era farmers typically carried a heavy load of debt: for land, equipment, seed, fertilizer, and living expenses till their crops were sold. Falling crop prices in the decades after the Civil War increased the real cost of repayment—a thousand-dollar loan incurred when wheat fetched a dollar a bushel represented a thousand bushels; when wheat fell to fifty cents, two thousand. Had farmers been able to organize among themselves and reduce their output (in much the way the trusts restrained *their* output, and labor unions attempted to reduce the supply of labor), they might have boosted prices through the marketplace. But the farmers faced two daunting handicaps. In the first place, there were millions of farmers, in contrast to the scores, perhaps, or fewer of corporations potentially competing in a given industry. Organizing all those farmers, and enforcing any agreement, was nearly impossible within the confines of the private sector. (Workers faced similar problems, which was a principal reason the larger unions—conspicuously the Knights of Labor—didn't last.) Second, even if American farmers organized, they would still face foreign competition. Basic farm commodities were fungible: wheat was wheat, whether grown in North Dakota or the northern Ukraine, and cotton was cotton, whether from the vicinity of Alexandria, Louisiana, or Alexandria, Egypt.

For such reasons farmers looked beyond the marketplace to solve their price problem. During the 1870s and early 1880s many joined the Greenback party, which agitated to extend the life of the paper currency introduced during the Civil War. Since the war's end the Republican-controlled Treasury had gradually retired greenbacks in favor of gold, steadily shrinking the supply of currency, which fell from thirty dollars per capita in 1865 to less than twenty dollars in 1880. The Greenbackers loudly resisted this trend, not illogically equating more money with higher prices. Yet paper currency wasn't the whole of the Greenback financial platform. Party theorists fully understood that currency constituted but part of the money question; increasingly money consisted of bank deposits and the checks drawn on them. For this reason the Greenbackers included strict regulation of banks among their political demands. Democracy must rescue what capitalism threatened. "Corporate control of the volume of money has been the means of dividing society into hostile classes, of the unjust distribution of the products of labor, and of building up monopolies of associated capital," the party's 1880 platform asserted. "It has kept money scarce, and scarcity of money enforces debt. . . . The right to make and issue money is a sovereign power to be maintained by the people for the common benefit. The delegation of this right to corporations is a surrender of the central attribute of sovereignty."[9]

But the message didn't catch on. After failing to prevent passage of the 1875 Specie Resumption Act, which accelerated the return to a hard-money standard, the Greenbackers fared dismally in the 1876 presidential election, in which candidate Peter Cooper polled but 80,000 votes nationwide. The labor troubles of 1877 gave the Greenbackers a momentary boost by attracting urban workers to the movement, and in 1878 they elected more than a dozen candidates to Congress and many more to state offices. But the farmer-labor coalition proved unstable, and with the return of prosperity the two groups gradually parted. James B. Weaver, the Greenback nominee for president in 1880, improved on Cooper's dismal showing by mounting the first nationwide personal campaign. But the modest results didn't repay the heroic effort, and the party disintegrated.

Many of the farmers took refuge in the Farmers' Alliance. The roots of the alliance ran in various directions. In 1877 small farmers and ranchers in Texas gathered at Lampasas, northwest of Austin, to complain of the high cost of credit and transport, the low price of corn and beef, and the arrogance of corporate speculators and big cattlemen. They devised measures for catching rustlers, branding strays, and purchasing barbed wire and other necessities. And they agreed they'd have better luck if more like-minded people joined them. They talked up their program and persuaded their neighbors, till by 1885 the Texas alliance claimed fifty thousand members, enough to start thinking of itself as a political movement. Farmers in neighboring states, and then across the South, signed on; in 1890 the Southern alliance numbered a million.

During the same period, on the prairies west of Chicago, farmers mobilized similarly. The moving spirit of what became the Northern (or Northwestern) alliance was a Chicago editor named Milton George, who calculated that whatever else a farmers' organization might accomplish, it ought to boost circulation of his paper, the *Western Rural*. George and the *Rural* got the alliance started and held it together through the good times of the early 1880s, which were bad for this protest movement, as good times are generally bad for protests. Brutal weather in 1886 and 1887—summer drought followed by winter blizzards—punished the Plains, killing crops by the section and livestock by the herd. The suffering farmers might not have blamed the political system but for a veto by President Cleveland of a bill to buy seed for destitute Texas wheat growers. Cleveland sympathized with the Texans but contended that the ten-thousand-dollar appropriation would promote an enervating dependency. "Though the people support the Government," Cleveland asserted, "the Government should not support the people."[10]

Cleveland's words summarized the thinking of many, perhaps most, Americans in the 1880s, and in fact his pithy formulation would be quoted by small-government conservatives down to Herbert Hoover and beyond. Yet a countervailing philosophy—the one motivating the congressional supporters of the Texas-seed bill—contended that government *should* support the people, at any rate during emergencies. Abraham Lincoln went so far as to say that "the legitimate object of government is to do for a community of people whatever they need to have done but can not do at all or can not so well do for themselves." Yet Lincoln added, "In all that the people can individually do as well for themselves, government ought not to interfere."[11]

The trick was knowing where to draw the line. Cleveland and the conservatives drew it tightly around the Constitution and the prerogatives of capital; the farmers who joined the Southern and Northern alliances sketched a more generous role for government, at any rate regarding themselves and their troubles. The Texas-seed appropriation was small even by the modest standards of government in that era, but the bill became a symbol of what the farmers felt they were up against. Cleveland's veto, combined with newly falling prices, reenergized the alliance movement. A Minneapolis convention in 1887 wrote a constitution for the Northern group, elected officers, and forecast a bright future for the organization, not least on account of the clouds over the farm economy. State after state and county after county in the upper Mississippi Valley sprouted alliance chapters like spring wheat after April rains. By 1890 the Northern alliance listed 130,000 members in Kansas and only somewhat fewer in the Dakotas, Minnesota, and Nebraska. The secretary's office reported new members enrolling at the rate of a thousand per week.[12]

"THIS SEASON IS without a parallel in this part of the country," a farmer wrote to the editor of a Nebraska farm journal in 1891.

> The hot winds burned up the entire crop, leaving thousands of families wholly destitute, many of whom might have been able to run through the crisis had it not been for the galling yoke put upon them by the money loaners and sharks—not by charging 7 per cent per annum, which is the lawful rate of interest, or even 10 per cent, but the unlawful and inhuman country-destroying rate of 3 per cent a month, some going still farther and charging 50 per cent per annum. We are cursed, many of us financially beyond redemption, not by the hot winds so much as by the swindling games of the bankers and money loaners,

who have taken the money and now are after the property, leaving the farmer moneyless and homeless.

This writer explained farm finance from the perspective of the debtor.

> I have borrowed, for example, $1,000. I pay $25 to the commission man. I give my note and second mortgage of 3 per cent of the $1,000, which is $30 more. Then I pay 7 per cent on the $1,000 to the actual loaner. Then besides all this I pay for appraising the land, abstract, recording, etc., so when I have secured my loan I am out the first year $150. . . . This is on the farm, but now comes the chattel loan. I must have $50 to save myself. I get the money; my note is made payable in thirty or sixty days for $35, secured by chattel of two horses, harness and wagon, about five times the value of the note. The time comes to pay. I ask for a few days. No, I can't wait; must have the money [says the lender]. If I can't get the money, I have the extreme pleasure of seeing my property taken.[13]

The editor of the Nebraska journal, receiving many such letters, responded with a grim summary of the average farmer's plight. "Take a man, for instance, who labors hard from fourteen to sixteen hours a day to obtain the bare necessaries of life. He eats his bacon and potatoes in a place which might rather be called a den than a home; and then, worn out, lies down and sleeps. He is brutalized both morally and physically." The horizons of this man were incomparably narrower than the horizons of the land on which he struggled. "He has no ideas, only propensities. He has no beliefs, only instincts. He does not, often cannot, read. His contact with other people is only the relation of servant to master, of a machine to its director. . . . This man's name is Million. He is all about us." And he would shake the world, or at least the capitalist system, with the editor's full approval. "The tendency of the competitive system is to antagonize and disassociate men. The survival of the fittest is a satanic creed. . . . Deny it if you can; competition is only another name for war. It means slavery to millions; it means the sale of virtue for bread; it means for thousands upon thousands starvation, misery, and death. After four thousand years of life, is this the best that we can achieve? If so, who cares how soon the end may come?"[14]

A North Carolina editor, after reading the laments of farmers in his own state, indicted the status quo in a voice that was less apocalyptic but more poignant.

> There is something radically wrong in our industrial system. There is a screw loose. The wheels have dropped out of balance. The railroads have never been so prosperous, and yet agriculture languishes. The banks have never done a better or more profitable business, and yet agriculture languishes. Manufacturing enterprises never made more money or were in a more flourishing condition, and yet agriculture languishes. Towns and cities flourish and "boom" and grow and "boom," and yet agriculture languishes. Salaries and fees were never so temptingly high and desirable, and yet agriculture languishes.[15]

The most obvious manifestation of the languishing was what it had been for two decades: the inexorable decline in the prices farmers received for their produce. From 1870 to the mid-1890s corn prices slumped by a third, wheat by more than half, cotton by two-thirds. Most farmers initially responded to the falling prices by working harder. But they didn't take long to realize they were digging their hole deeper. "We were told two years ago to go to work and raise a big crop; that was all we needed," one farmer bitterly declared. "We went to work and plowed and planted; the rains fell, the sun shone, nature smiled, and we raised the big crop that they told us to; and what came of it? Eight cent corn, ten cent oats, two cent beef, and no price at all for butter and eggs—that's what came of it. Then the politicians said that we suffered from over-production."[16]

The politicians were partly right. Overproduction was one cause of the farmers' distress. But overproduction wasn't simply an American problem. Farmers in Canada and Argentina and Egypt and India responded to the low prices much as the American farmers did; the resulting glut in the major commodities wasn't simply regional or national but global. Even if American farmers could solve their own overproduction problem, they'd still have to deal with the foreigners.

Closer to home but no more susceptible to the farmers' control were the prices they had to pay to sustain their operations—prices that were rising either absolutely or relative to the prices farmers received for their crops. Cotton farmers, even in the best Black Belt districts, had to fertilize their fields or watch their harvests decline; the Southerners paid up to a third of the value of their crop for guano and other fertilizers. Wheat farmers had to mechanize loot their labor costs kill them; the machinery cut through profits faster than it cut through the standing wheat.

More painful than the costs for fertilizer and equipment were the charges the farmers paid to transport their crops to market. Nearly every farmer fell hostage to the railroads at harvest time—in particular, to the single railroad that typically held a local monopoly in the farmer's district. By the 1880s barely a bushel of wheat or corn or a bale of cotton moved to market without riding the rails, and the railroads exploited their strategic advantage. This wasn't to say they didn't provide an essential service at an unprecedentedly low price. "What would it cost for a man to carry a ton of wheat one mile?" the president of the Union Pacific asked. "What would it cost for a horse to do the same? The railway does it at a cost of less than a cent." Nor did the railroads rake in profits so egregiously as their critics alleged. Viewed nationally, the railroad industry was quite competitive, which was why roads kept sliding into receivership and why they cut wages even at the risk of crippling strikes.[17]

But what they lost on their trunk lines, where they faced direct competition, the railroads tried to recoup on the routes they monopolized. Farmers continually complained that it cost more to ship a bushel of wheat a hundred miles across Dakota than it did to ship the same bushel the seven hundred miles from Chicago to New York. Railroad operators acknowledged the differential and shrugged; this was simply how capitalism worked. Farmers responded that however capitalism worked for the railroads, it didn't work for *them*. Northern farmers noted that rail rates rose in the winter, when lakes and rivers froze and barge traffic ceased; the railroaders shrugged again, citing the basic rule of pricing: whatever the traffic would bear. And when the farmers attacked the railroads for failing to serve the public, the more forthright of the railroad men quoted their colleague William Vanderbilt: "The public be damned."

FINALLY THE FARMERS became overtly political. Against the money power of the capitalists they proposed to array their voting power. But to maximize their voting power they needed to organize more effectively than ever. An initial attempt to merge the Northern and Southern alliances took place in St. Louis in late 1889, when the two groups held simultaneous conventions. A general coincidence of views was obvious, but certain policies and practices caused friction. The Southern alliance admitted women but not blacks (the ostensible reason for excluding the blacks was to preserve the virtue of the white women); Southern black farmers had established a separate Colored Farmers' Alliance (which suited many of its members, who distrusted their white neighbors). The Northern alliance included black members (albeit not many, as there were few black farmers in the North). The Southern alliance shrouded some of its activities in secrecy, which put off the Northerners. Personal considerations also inhibited a merger. The opposite sides included veterans of the Civil War whose wounds still smarted; even after twenty-five years Johnny Reb and Billy Yank found cause for anger. And at least some of the Northern alliance men felt intimidated by their Southern counterparts, who outnumbered them considerably and came to St. Louis more experienced and better organized.

The differences between the Northerners and Southerners trumped their desire for unity, and the proposed merger failed. Yet the two groups agreed to work together, and they endorsed similar platforms, which included demands for government ownership of the railroads, expansion of the currency, and preference for small farmers over corporations and speculators in the distribution of land.[18]

Each group went home eager to elect friendly candidates in the 1890 elections. Southern alliance members worked within the two-party system—which meant, in their case, within the Democratic party. Northerners often created or joined independent parties, which varied in name and composition by state. The overall success of the movement amazed even the most optimistic members. More than forty alliance-sponsored candidates were elected to the U.S. House of Representatives, where they dominated the delegations of Georgia and the Carolinas; several alliance candidates were elected to the Senate. Alliance members and allies controlled legislatures in seven Southern states and the lower house of the Kansas legislature.[19]

The strong showing confirmed the democratic faith of many alliancemen, who hoped to sustain the momentum. At the December 1890 convention of the Southern alliance, a substantial faction agitated for the creation of a new political party. Some alliance leaders demurred, in part for fear of losing control of such a party, in part from hope of capturing the

Democratic party. The Northern alliance met a short while later and expressed greater enthusiasm for a third party, pulling many of the Southerners along. A preliminary meeting for the new party took place in the spring of 1891 and laid the groundwork for a major convention at Omaha in July 1892.

A thousand farmers traveled to Omaha, where they were joined by hundreds of other reforming types: workers, temperance advocates, Bellamyite socialists, Henry Georgian single-taxers. The talk was earnest and the optimism palpable. The world needed changing and they would do it. "We meet in the midst of a nation brought to the verge of moral, political, and material ruin," the preamble to the charter platform of the People's party declared. "Corruption dominates the ballot-box, the Legislatures, the Congress, and touches even the ermine of the bench. . . . The fruits of the toil of millions are boldly stolen to build up colossal fortunes for a few, unprecedented in the history of mankind; and the possessors of these, in turn, despise the republic and endanger liberty. From the same prolific womb of governmental injustice we breed the two great classes—tramps and millionaires." The existing parties had entrenched themselves but failed the people; hence the need for a new party "to restore the government of the Republic to the hands of 'the plain people.'"

The representatives of these plain people declared, therefore:

> First: That the union of the labor forces of the United States this day consummated shall be permanent and perpetual; may its spirit enter all hearts for the salvation of the republic and the uplifting of mankind.
>
> Second: Wealth belongs to him who creates it, and every dollar taken from industry without an equivalent is robbery. "If any will not work, neither shall he eat." The interests of rural and civic labor are identical; their enemies are identical.
>
> Third: We believe that the time has come when the railroad corporations will either own the people or the people must own the railroads. . . . The government should own and operate the railroads in the interest of the people.

Other platform planks and supporting resolutions called for a national currency "safe, sound, and flexible, issued by the government only" and

restored to its earlier magnitude by the "free and unlimited coinage of silver and gold at the present legal ratio of 16 to 1"; a federal "subtreasury
plan" allowing farmers to borrow against crops stored in government warehouses, thus releasing them from dependence on banks and adding flexibility to the money supply; a graduated income tax; public ownership of
telephone and telegraph companies; confiscation by the government of
land held by railroads and other corporations "in excess of their actual
needs," which land would be made available to "actual settlers"; shorter
hours of labor for industrial workers; abolition of the "large standing army
of mercenaries known as the Pinkerton system"; a single term for the president and vice president; the secret ballot; popular election of senators; and
such techniques of direct democracy as the initiative and referendum. The
platform went on to condemn the current policy of essentially unlimited
immigration, "which opens our ports to the pauper and criminal classes of
the world," and to demand the rigid enforcement of the existing eight-
hour law for government labor.[20]

To carry the message to the country and make the fight on the people's
behalf, the convention nominated James Weaver, the erstwhile Iowa
Greenbacker. "Serene while others are in tumult; clear while others are
confused; secure in his orbit while others are erratic—these characteristics
make him a man of value second to none in a great epoch like the present,"
one of Weaver's supporters said of the nominee. "A person of such sym-
metrical, harmonious development that each excellent trait is balanced by
all others." But just to balance the ticket further, the convention nominated
former Confederate general James G. Field of Virginia for vice president.[21]

SERENITY AND BALANCE at the top of the ticket appealed to the
Populists—as the members of the new party were christened by one
who remembered his Latin—not least because serenity and sometimes
balance were wanting among others who spoke for the movement. Mary
Elizabeth Lease was the daughter of Irish refugees from the great famine;
her parents settled in Pennsylvania, and her father and brother died in the
Civil War. The circumstances of her father's death—at the prison camp at
Andersonville—made her, like James Blaine, an inveterate foe of Democrats. After the war she moved to Kansas and married a pharmacist, whose

practice failed in the depression of the 1870s. The family relocated to Texas, where two children died in infancy. As the other children (including the youngest, Ben Hur Lease, named for the protagonist of the best-selling novel of the same name by Lew Wallace) matured, Mary grew active in the woman suffrage and prohibition movements. After a return to Kansas she studied law, was admitted to the bar, and joined the labor wing of the Farmers' Alliance. When the alliance spawned the People's party, she became a charter member.

Her passion for popular democracy, against the plutocracy of big capital, made her a Populist favorite. "Wall Street owns the country," she declared.

> It is no longer a government of the people, by the people, and for the people, but a government of Wall Street, by Wall Street, and for Wall Street. The great common people of this country are slaves, and monopoly is the master. The West and South are prostrate before the manufacturing East. Money rules. . . . Our laws are the output of a system which clothes rascals in robes and honesty in rags. The parties lie to us and the political speakers mislead us. . . . There are thirty men in the United States whose aggregate wealth is over one and one-half billion dollars; there are half a million looking for work. . . .
>
> We want money, land, and transportation. We want the abolition of national banks, and we want the power to make loans direct from the government. We want the accursed foreclosure system wiped out. Land equal to a tract thirty miles wide and ninety miles long has been foreclosed and bought in by loan companies of Kansas in a year. We will stand by our homes and stay by our firesides by force if necessary, and we will not pay our debts to the loan-shark companies until the government pays its debts to us. The people are at bay; let the blood-hounds of money who have dogged us thus far beware.

Her opponents called her shrill and corrupted her middle name to Ellen, so they could dub her "Mary Yellin'." She may never actually have said "What you farmers need to do is to raise less corn and more hell," but she didn't disavow it when it was attributed to her.[22]

Jeremiah Simpson was another Easterner radicalized by hard times in Kansas. A New Brunswick, Canada, native, Simpson moved to upstate

New York with his parents as a child. He became a Great Lakes sailor and eventually a lake boat captain, and then a partner in a Chicago sawmill. After the Panic of 1873 he moved to Kansas to raise cattle, with scant success. He blamed railroads, banks, and speculators in land and commodities. "Man must have access to the land, or he is a slave," he said. "The man who owns the earth owns the people, for they must buy the privilege of living on his earth." Government must guarantee access to land, and it must protect those who worked the land from those who gambled on the product of the farmers' labor. "If the government had protected the farmer as it protects the gambler, this would not have happened," he said after one speculative raid that left his Kansas neighbors empty-handed while the brokers grew rich. In an 1890 race for Congress, Simpson branded his Republican opponent, James Hallowell, "Prince Hal" and accused him of wearing silk stockings. A Simpson opponent stabbed back, saying that Simpson wore no stockings at all. Simpson became "Sockless Jerry," an image he played to full political effect. "Jerry Simpson was not a sockless clown," fellow Kansan William Allen White later observed. "He accepted the portrait which the Republicans made of him as an ignorant fool because it helped him to talk to the crowds. . . . The real Jerry Simpson profited by his own effigy."[23]

Ignatius Donnelly profited by an alter ego, too. Irish like Mary Lease and likewise from Pennsylvania, Donnelly traveled northwest to Minnesota before the Civil War and became, in sequence, a Republican, a Liberal Republican, a Granger, a Greenbacker, and a Union Laborite. A Minnesota reform meeting without Donnelly, Charles Dana's *New York Sun* remarked, would have been "like catfish without waffles in Philadelphia." Donnelly held audiences rapt by his oratory, but his fame spread far beyond his voice on account of the novels and essays he wrote. Some of the essays were abstruse and literary; he devoted two volumes to demonstrating that Shakespeare was really Francis Bacon. His novels were filled with blood and polemic. The most popular, the dystopian *Caesar's Column*, grimly recounted a despotism that emerged upon the ruins of democracy (the column of the title was a giant tomb containing the bones of a quarter million of the victims). Readers presumably recognized the literary license Donnelly employed in telling his dark tale; more directly applicable to the politics of the present were certain images he conjured of current government policies. "Take a child a few years old; let a blacksmith weld around his waist an iron band," Donnelly wrote, with reference to the hard-money policies of Benjamin Harrison's administration.

> At first it causes him little inconvenience. He plays. As he grows older it becomes tighter; it causes him pain; he scarcely knows what ails him. He still grows. All his internal organs are cramped and displaced. He grows still larger; he has the head, shoulders and limbs of a man and the waist of a child. He is a monstrosity. He dies. This is a picture of the world of to-day, bound in the silly superstition of some prehistoric nation. But this is not all. Every decrease in the quantity, actual or relative, of gold and silver increases the purchasing power of the dollars made out of them; and the dollar becomes the equivalent for a larger amount of the labor of man and his productions. This makes the rich man richer and the poor man poorer. The iron band is displacing the organs of life. As the dollar rises in value, man sinks. Hence the decrease in wages; the increase in the power of wealth; the luxury of the few; the misery of the many.

Donnelly drafted the preamble to the Omaha platform of the People's party and won the support of some of the delegates for the party's presidential nomination. But a skeptic pricked the balloon by circulating a likely epitaph for Populism should the idiosyncratic author become the party's standard-bearer:

> Forbear, good friend, to touch these bones,
> For underneath these piled stones
> Lies party third, ne'er to awaken,
> Killed by Ignatius Donnelly Bacon.[24]

Tom Watson would become more controversial than any of the other Populists, largely because he outlived nearly all of them and much of what they—and he—had stood for. But as he campaigned for the party in Georgia and across the South in the early 1890s, he drew attention chiefly for his belief that poor whites and poor blacks should make common cause against the capitalists and gentry who oppressed them. This view wasn't unheard of in the South, even in the wake of Redemption, but it was sufficiently unusual that Watson took pains to justify it. Watson contended that the wealthy and well placed in the South had for years employed the race issue to keep the lower classes divided. "Both the old parties have done this thing until they have constructed as perfect a 'slot machine' as the world ever saw," he said.

> Drop the old, worn nickel of the "party slogan" into the slot, and the machine does the rest. You might beseech a Southern white tenant to listen to you upon questions of finance, taxation, and transportation; you might demonstrate with mathematical precision that herein lay his way out of poverty into comfort; you might have him almost persuaded to the truth. But if the merchant who furnished his farm supplies (at tremendous usury) or the town politician (who never spoke to him except at election times) came along and cried "Negro rule!" the entire fabric of reason and common sense which you had patiently constructed would fall, and the poor tenant would joyously hug the chains of an actual wretchedness rather than do any experimenting on a question of mere sentiment.

Watson didn't rely on the generosity of whites, or for that matter of blacks; instead he appealed to their self-interest. "Suppose two tenants on my farm; one of them white, the other black. They cultivate their crops under precisely the same conditions. Their labors, discouragements, burdens, grievances, are the same." The white tenant decided the Democratic party was ignoring him and decided to join the People's party. Why? Because its principles and policies seemed more likely to remedy the ills that afflicted him. "Now go back to the colored tenant. His surroundings being the same and his interest the same, why is it impossible for him to reach the same conclusions?" In fact it was not impossible, Watson said, or even remarkable. It just took some getting used to. "Cannot these two men act together in peace when the ballot of one is a vital benefit to the other? Will not political friendship be born of the necessity and the hope which is common to both? Will not race bitterness disappear before this common suffering and this mutual desire to escape it?"[25]

THE ISSUES the Populists pushed ran the gamut of comprehensibility from the transparent to the mystical. Government ownership of the railroads was self-explanatory, if socialistic. A graduated income tax meant the wealthy would pay at a higher rate than the poor (who ideally wouldn't pay at all). Popular, or direct, election of senators would take control of the upper house of Congress away from the state legislatures and confer it upon the people.

The Populists' so-called subtreasury plan was more complicated, not least because it attempted to achieve multiple goals. Farmers hated having to borrow operating funds when interest rates were highest—that is, when everyone else was borrowing—and having to sell their crops when prices were lowest, when everyone else was selling. Moreover, they despised the bankers from whom they had to borrow and the brokers to whom they had to sell. The subtreasury scheme would allow them at once to circumvent the bankers and the brokers and get lower rates on loans and higher prices for crops. The farmers would store their crops in government warehouses and receive Treasury notes for up to 80 percent of the current market value of the crops. The farmers would decide individually when to sell their stored crops, based on their needs and their expectations regarding prices. In this way the gluts that accompanied each harvest and depressed farmers' incomes would be diminished. Meanwhile the Treasury notes would circulate essentially as money, freeing farmers further from the grip of the banks.

If the subtreasury scheme took paragraphs to explain—the practical details added layers of complexity—the Populists' currency program required chapters. "Free coinage of silver at 16 to 1" was the standard shorthand; often this reduced to "free silver." The words meant both more and less than they appeared to, and they required some history to comprehend. From the establishment of the federal government in 1789 the United States government had attempted to operate a bimetallic money standard of gold and silver. A single metal, preferably gold, would have been more manageable, but there wasn't enough gold in the United States to keep the gears of commerce from seizing up. In fact there wasn't enough gold and silver together, which was why various forms of paper—bank notes, letters of credit, and, during and after the Civil War, greenbacks—were summoned into service. But gold and silver were the currency of choice for those to whom money was owed, precisely because they were scarce (and therefore valuable). The difficulty of bimetallism, aside from the collective shortage of the two metals, was that the ratio of gold to silver varied over time, depending on discoveries of new mines and of new uses for the two metals. From the 1790s until the 1830s silver was comparatively plentiful and accordingly cheap, prompting debtors to hoard gold and pay their debts with silver. During much of this period ordinary people never saw gold; in effect the United States operated on a silver standard. The discovery of gold in California in 1848 and elsewhere during the following decades flooded the economy with gold, driving silver into hiding. The country shifted, in effect, to a gold standard (supplemented by the Civil War greenbacks). In 1873, as part of an effort to tidy up the currency, Congress passed a Coinage Act that dropped the silver dollar from the list of coins the U.S. mint would produce. At the time the measure seemed little more than prudent financial hygiene, an acknowledgment of an existing state of affairs.

Subsequent events cast a different light on the subject. The American money supply had always been part of the global money supply (until 1848 the United States was utterly dependent on foreign countries for its gold and silver), and the same influences that drove silver from circulation in America did so elsewhere. As a result, several European countries dropped silver from their currencies at about the same time the United States did, in favor of a formal or informal gold standard. Unwanted silver sloshed across the Atlantic, dismaying silver producers in the American West, who watched the demand for their favorite metal fall, and arousing the suspicion of American farmers, who suffered from slumping crop prices and reasoned, accurately enough, that if silver were still being minted their prices would recover. These strange bedfellows—the silver capitalists and the farmers—looked back and detected conspiracy in the Coinage Act, which they dubbed the "Crime of '73." They demanded the fell deed be undone and silver restored to the currency.

They succeeded partially. The Bland-Allison Act of 1878, passed over Rutherford Hayes's veto, mandated the minting of between $2 million and $4 million of silver monthly. This amount was considerably less than the ardent silverites wanted but more than suited the goldbugs. In practice the measure did little to stem the long-term slide in prices that underlay the demands of the farmers, whose complaints continued through the 1880s. The silver chorus added voices at the end of the decade with the admission of the new states of North and South Dakota, Montana, Wyoming, Idaho, and Washington, all of which produced silver or angry farmers or both. "I wish this free coinage of senators would stop," President Benjamin Harrison lamented. Under the influence of the enlarged silver caucus, Congress approved the Sherman Silver Purchase Act of 1890, which roughly doubled the amount of silver the federal government committed to purchase and coin.[26]

The silverites cheered but the goldbugs shuddered. "He that loveth silver shall not be satisfied with silver," Treasury secretary William Windom warned the New York Board of Trade, and collapsed on the spot of a fatal heart attack. The omen spooked the financial markets and inspired Republicans to seek an early opportunity to repeal the Sherman Act. Not even John Sherman himself stood by it. The Ohio senator and former Treasury secretary explained that the measure had been a prophylactic against full-blown silver mania. "I voted for it, but the day it became law I was ready to repeal it, if repeal could be had without substituting in its place absolute free coinage." The opportunity appeared in 1893, when a new financial panic seized international markets and caused a massive loss of confidence in the dollar. Amid a political panic of their own, American legislators repealed the Sherman Act, thereby terminating Treasury purchases of silver.[27]

SUCH WAS THE situation when William Harvey broke a story that astonished the millions who read it in the months after its 1894 publication. Harvey, a self-trained economist of Populist persuasion, recounted a series of speeches—lectures, actually—given by a mere slip of a man in the auditorium of the Art Institute of Chicago during May of that year. The young fellow—he seemed scarcely more than a boy—went by the single name of Coin, which suited his topic well enough. "My object," he told his audience in the first lecture, "will be to teach you the A, B, C of the questions about money that are now a matter of everyday conversation." Coin's background was blurry, but his command of the subject soon quieted most doubts regarding his expertise. He traced the history of American currency to the early years of the republic—"the days of Washington and Jefferson and our revolutionary forefathers, who had a hatred of England and an intimate knowledge of her designs on this country," he said significantly. He reminded his listeners that in 1792 Congress had defined the dollar as consisting of 371¼ grains of pure silver. Silver, he stressed, not gold, had been the basis for the dollar. Silver, he said, had remained the basis of the dollar, and hence of the American currency, until 1873. During that time the people had come to embrace silver as the money of the common man. The rich dealt in gold, the rest in silver.

In a city like Chicago, with its large population of capitalists and creditors, Coin's audience inevitably included individuals who favored gold. One such person, a novice reporter for the financial press, interrupted the speaker with a question evidently designed to throw him off balance. Coin answered it easily. William Harvey remarked, "The young journalist turned red in the face and hung his head." A second challenger rose, putting to Coin a more esoteric question requiring specific mastery of the laws relating to the currency. This man was sure he had caught Coin out. "He sat down looking as proud as a cannoneer who has just fired a shot that has had deadly effect in the enemy's ranks," Harvey wrote. But Coin stood his ground. Reciting the statutes as though the law books lay open to his mind's eye, he rebuffed the challenge masterfully. The questioner slunk away.

Coin returned to the Coinage Act of 1873. Though "purporting to be a revision of the coinage laws," he said, the new law soon proved to be far more. It accomplished a revolution in the American money system, overthrowing silver and replacing it with gold. Quoting a senator who had been present, Coin said the revision had slipped through Congress with "the silent tread of a cat." Coin conceded that most of the lawmakers didn't know what they were doing; confusion was precisely the aim of the sponsors, who *did* know what the law was about. "An army of a half million of men invading our shores, the warships of the world bombarding our coasts, could not have made us surrender the money of the people and substitute in its place the money of the rich," Coin declared. "A few words embraced in fifteen pages of statutes put through Congress in the rush of bills did it. The pen was mightier than the sword."

A new challenger leaped up. The act of 1873, he said, had simply formalized an existing state of affairs. Silver had long been out of circulation. No conspiracy was required to remove it.

Coin rejected this assertion as precisely what the conspirators wanted people to believe. Such arguments were "all the bastard children of the crime of 1873," he said. The cabal against silver was undeniable. "It was demonetized secretly, and since then a powerful money trust has used deception and misrepresentations that have led tens of thousands of honest minds astray."

This exchange concluded the initial lecture, which piqued the interest and affronted the interests of Chicago's bankers and other big capitalists, who crowded the next day's session. William Harvey suspected a plot to embarrass the wunderkind. "Knotty questions would be hurled at him—perplexing queries and abstruse propositions," Harvey wrote. "They would harass him, worry him, and tangle him, laugh at his dilemma and then say: 'We told you so.' This was the programme."

The leader of the plot, Lyman Gage, the chairman of Chicago's First National Bank, commenced the assault almost as soon as Coin began speaking. "All eyes were on him," Harvey said. "He had been watching for an opening, and now he thought he had it, where he could deliver a telling, and follow it up with a knock-out, blow." Gage went right to the heart of the issue of bimetallism; noting the vagaries of supply and demand, he queried how the government could maintain a fixed ratio of value between gold and silver.

Coin nodded knowingly. This *was* the question, he granted. And for ordinary commodities, supply and demand could create imbalances. But gold and silver were not simply commodities: they were money, the measure of commodities. And because the government was—or should be—the purchaser of last resort for gold and silver, a condition of essentially unlimited demand developed.

Coin illustrated with pictures. On a blackboard he drew a board suspended by two ropes. One rope represented gold, the other silver. So long as both ropes held steady, the board—signifying the national economy—remained in balance. But should one rope be severed, as the silver rope had been severed in 1873, the economy must swing dangerously awry, as the economy had swung awry since then. Coin drew another picture, this time of two tanks of water. The two tanks were connected by a pipe beneath them, and separate spigots poured water into the top of each tank. So long as the connecting pipe remained open and unclogged, the water levels in the two tanks remained the same, regardless of the inflows into the separate tanks. But should the connection be broken—as the connection between gold and silver had been broken in 1873—one tank might overflow while the other drained to empty.

"A pin could almost have been heard to drop at any moment," Harvey related. Coin had answered the hardest question the big capitalists could hurl at him—had answered the fundamental question of money—in a way that made sense to the simplest man or woman. "They had listened critically, expecting to detect errors in his facts or reasoning," Harvey said of the capitalists in the crowd. "There were none. They were amazed."

In subsequent sessions Coin continued to amaze. He illustrated the confining effects of gold as single specie by having assistants measure off on the floor and walls of the auditorium an imaginary cube twenty-two feet in length, width, and height. This cube, he said, could encompass all the gold ever dug from the ground and made available as money. The audience murmured in disbelief. Coin compared a one-metal currency to a one-legged man or a one-winged bird. The man could walk, but only with difficulty; the bird couldn't fly at all. So the economy hobbled and crashed. He depicted the earnings and savings of ordinary Americans as a maiden about to be ravished by big capital in the form of a banker wearing a silk hat labeled "England." Employing a favorite image of the Populists, he showed the American economy as a giant cow straddling the Appalachians. Hardworking Western farmers fed the cow; parasitic Eastern bankers milked the cow. Another Populist image appeared as a monster octopus with tentacles that reached from London across the oceans and continents. The octopus was named "Rothschild," and the caption declared, "The English Octopus: It Feeds on Nothing but Gold!"

Coin created a sensation in Chicago with his financial school. By the end of the week the city could speak of nothing else. Erstwhile skeptics converted to silver by the thousands. But something troubled even the most devoted of the silverites. The American economy existed as a part of the world economy. The capitalists of the other great trading powers had embraced gold and shunned silver; how could the United States resist their power? How could America remonetize silver unilaterally?

Coin reserved this final, implementation question till the last day of the seminar. He reminded his audience what was at stake. "In the midst of plenty, we are in want," he said. "Helpless children and the best womanhood and manhood in America appeal to us for release from a bondage that is destructive of life and liberty." Nor were ordinary Americans alone in their distress. "All the nations of the Western Hemisphere turn to their great sister republic for assistance in the emancipation of the people of at least one-half the world. The Orient, with its teeming millions of people, and France, the cradle of science and liberty, look to the United States to lead in the struggle to roll back the accumulated disasters of the last twenty-one years." Humanity cried for relief. "What shall our answer be?"

The audience strained to hear.

"If it is claimed we must adopt for our money the metal England selects, and can have no choice in the matter," Coin declared in a rising voice, "let us make the test and find out if it is true. It is not American to give up without trying." What if England resisted? "Let us attach England to the United States and blot her name out among the nations of the earth!"

The audience burst into patriotic hurrahs.

"A war with England would be the most popular war ever waged on the face of the earth!"

The audience cheered louder.

"If it is true that she can dictate the money of the world and thereby create world-wide misery, it would be the most just war ever waged by man!"

The blood lust of the audience was up, and Coin let them roar their defiance at perfidious Albion.

"Fortunately, this is not necessary," he said, now calm again. Britain might be the banker to the world, but America was the breadbasket and the workshop. London might stick with gold, but if America added silver to its money supply, the resulting surge of economic growth would leave England far behind. "The bimetallic standard will make the United States the most prosperous nation on earth." England would crawl to America, willing to do whatever was necessary to obtain America's business.

This bounteous future would be lost if Americans preemptively surrendered. The independence Americans had won from England in the eighteenth century by arms might be lost at the end of the nineteenth century by gold. And just as the Tories, those minions of King George, had tried to sap Americans' will to fight in the war for American political independence, so today's Tories, the big capitalists and their allies, strove to undermine the American spirit in the war for economic independence. "The business men of New York City passed strong resolutions against the Declaration of Independence in 1776, and they are passing strong resolutions against an American policy now," Coin said. American liberty was in peril; Americans must spring to action.

> The integrity of the government has been violated. A Financial Trust has control of your money, and with it, is robbing you of your property. Vampires feed upon your commercial blood. . . . This is a struggle for humanity. For our homes and firesides. For the purity and integrity of our government. . . . Go among the people and awake them to the situation of peril in which they are placed. Awake them as you would with startling cries at the coming of flood and fires. Arouse them as did Paul Revere as he rode through the streets shouting: "The British are on our shores!"

Coin's audience stamped their feet and yelled themselves hoarse. Those near the front surged onto the stage to clap the young man on the back. Even one banker, well known about the city for his strong support for gold, was swept up in the enthusiasm. "Three cheers for Coin!" he shouted. The audience shouted back, "Hip! Hip! Hurrah!" and poured into Michigan Avenue.

"Thus ended the school," William Harvey wrote. "Chicago has had its lesson on bimetallism." Harvey was one of those cheering for Coin, and he hoped silver would triumph. But he understood that truth and virtue were no guarantee of success. "In the struggle of might against right, the former has generally triumphed. Will it win in the United States?"[28]

DURING THE MID-1890S William Harvey's account of the Coin Financial School, as the lecture series was called, was the best-selling, most influential book in America. A million copies were sold between its 1894 publication and the elections of 1896, and the average copy certainly found multiple readers. Doubtless a large portion of those millions caught on that Coin wasn't real and that the Chicago seminar never took place. But many others believed—or certainly *wanted* to believe—that the boy genius actually existed and that he had truly bearded the lions of capitalism in their lakefront den.

Harvey's book, which made the author wealthy, inspired imitations. Ignatius Donnelly wrote a tale of a banker and a farmer thrown together on a long train ride. The banker tries to instruct the farmer regarding the intricacies of the currency question and the multiple advantages of the gold standard, but the farmer, with the naïve wisdom of the earth, refutes every argument and converts the banker to silver.[29]

Harvey's book spawned an even larger counterliterature. *The Mistakes of Coin, Coin's Financial Fool, Coin's Financial School Exposed and Closed*, and similar titles rebutted the lessons of Coin. The gold authors attacked Harvey on the law (the 1792 coinage act had defined only the dollar *coin* exclusively in terms of silver; the dollar as a unit of money had been defined in both silver and gold), on history (the currency system had operated far less smoothly before 1873 than Coin suggested; the pipe connecting his two tanks was constantly getting clogged), and on the feasibility of a unilateral American adoption of silver (the American economy, whether the silverites liked it or not, was fully enmeshed in the world economy; those most damaged by a loss of international faith in the dollar, which remonetization of silver was bound to provoke, would be the poor).

Yet the critics missed much of the point. *Coin's Financial School* was about the money question, but it was also about the relationship of ordinary people to the wealthy and powerful—that is, about the relationship of democracy to capitalism. Readers might or might not have followed Coin's—Harvey's—reasoning, and they might or might not have been persuaded by his analogies. But most of those millions of readers presumably endorsed Coin's claims that the money power had gutted America's traditional values. When the silverites called silver the "dollar of our daddies," they summoned an entire constellation of values, real and imagined. For obvious reasons they avoided the phrase "golden age" in referring to the time when everything had been better, but that was what they meant.

To explain the demise of that blessed era, in a country nominally democratic, Harvey and the Populists turned to conspiracy theories. The demonetization of silver in 1873 couldn't have been an accident, for that would have indicted democracy. Instead it must have been the work of self-conscious, self-interested elites—and hence a "crime." Every reform movement requires enemies, the more specific and identifiable the better. Many Populists realized that the farmers' predicament involved industrialization and related trends over which they had no control, but industrialization didn't make a satisfactory villain. Industrial*ists*, on the other hand, and especially their collaborators in finance, made perfect villains. Railroad magnates and bankers really *did* pursue policies inimical to farmers. And their foreign connection—the specter of London's Lombard Street—made the bankers especially tempting targets. That some of the most prominent foreign bankers, notably the Rothschilds, were Jews lent an implicit—and occasionally explicit—anti-Semitism to the Populist conspiracy theories. Harvey and other Populists could cast their movement as an exercise in patriotism and traditional values, a revival of the American Revolution, and hope for a patriotic and traditionalist response. The Populists were probably no more xenophobic or anti-Semitic than most other Americans of their day, but they couldn't resist an opportunity to march into political battle under the flag of all things dear to the historic heart of the American people.[30]

WILLIAM ALLEN WHITE had a different bone to pick with the Populists. The Emporia editor considered them whiners who couldn't get ahead and were determined to see that others didn't either. "What's the Matter with Kansas?" he demanded in an editorial that became one of the most reprinted pieces in the history of American journalism. White noted a report from the Kansas Department of Agriculture that the population of the state was stagnating. The country overall was growing rapidly, but Kansas was barely holding its own. "In five years ten million people have been added to the national population, yet instead of gaining a share of this—say, half a million—Kansas has apparently been a plague spot and, in the very garden of the world, has lost population by ten thousands every year." To make matters worse, the leavers were just the ones Kansas couldn't spare. "Every moneyed man in the state who could get out without loss has gone. Every month in every community sees someone who has a little money pack up and leave the state. This has been going on for eight years. Money has been drained out all the time. In towns where ten years ago there were three or four or half a dozen money-lending concerns, stimulating industry by furnishing capital, there is now none, or one or two that are looking after the interests and principal already outstanding." Any Kansan could describe the result. "What community knows over one or two men who have moved in with more than $5,000 in the past three years? And what community cannot count half a score of men in that time who have left, taking all the money they could scrape together?"

It wasn't simply the hardship of life at midcontinent. White noted that Missouri to the east had gained two million in population; Nebraska to the north and Colorado to the west were likewise growing. (The Indian Territory—Oklahoma—to the south was growing, too, but White didn't mention it.) "What's the matter with Kansas?" he demanded again.

The matter was the politics of the state, he said. In particular, the matter was the Populists, who preached against progress and railed at success.

> We have an old mossback Jacksonian who snorts and howls because there is a bathtub in the State House; we are running that old jay for Governor. We have another shabby, wild-eyed, rattle-brained fanatic who has said openly in a dozen speeches that "the rights of the user are paramount to the rights of the owner"; we are running him for Chief Justice. . . . Then, for fear some hint that the state had become respectable might percolate through the civilized portions of the nation, we have decided to send three or four harpies out lecturing, telling the people that Kansas is raising hell and letting the corn go to weed.

White gave his sarcasm free rein.

> Oh, this is a state to be proud of! We are a people who can hold up our heads! What we need is not more money, but less capital, fewer white shirts and brains, fewer men with business judgment, and more of those fellows who boast that they are "just ordinary clodhoppers but they know more in a minute about finance than John Sherman." . . . We don't need population, we don't need wealth, we don't need well-dressed men on the streets, we don't need standing in the nation, we don't need cities on the fertile prairies; you bet we don't! What we are after is the money power. Because we have become poorer and ornerier and meaner than a spavined, distempered mule, we, the people of Kansas, propose to kick; we don't care to build up, we wish to tear down.

The Populists and their allies had declared class war against the rich. They hobbled the successful in the belief, as one of their spokesmen put it, "that if you legislate to make the masses prosperous, their prosperity will find its way up through every class which rests upon them." White couldn't contain himself:

> Oh, yes, Kansas is a great state. Here are people fleeing from it by the score every day, capital going out of the state by the hundreds of dollars; and every industry but farming paralyzed, and that crippled, because its products have to go across the ocean before they can find a laboring man at work who can afford to buy them. Let's don't stop this year. Let's drive all the decent, self-respecting men out of the state. Let's keep the old clodhoppers who know it all. . . .
>
> What's the matter with Kansas? Nothing under the shining sun. She is losing wealth, population and standing. She has got her statesmen, and the money power is afraid of her. Kansas is all right. She has started in to raise hell, as Mrs. Lease advised, and she seems to have an over-production. But that doesn't matter. Kansas never did believe in diversified crops.[31]

Chapter 18

THE WAGES OF CAPITALISM

B y the 1890s Chicago had fully recovered from the fire of 1871, and the city fathers were eager to debut their darling child to the world. The 1889 Exposition Universelle, a world's fair in Paris that featured a thousand-foot iron tower designed by Alexandre Gustave Eiffel, inspired American politicians and business leaders to ponder how they might outdo the French and assert commercial and technical preeminence for the United States. The approaching quadricentennial of Columbus's landing in the New World provided the occasion, and the principal cities of the country vied for the honor. New York, Washington, and St. Louis made serious proposals, but when Congress—which would underwrite the fair—finally voted, Chicago won out.

The architectural firm of Burnham and Root took charge of the planning, but before it got far John Root suddenly died. Daniel Burnham paid his partner the appropriate respects in public, yet privately he fumed. "I have worked," he said. "I have schemed and dreamed to make us the greatest architects in the world. I have made him see it and kept him at it. And now he dies. Damn! Damn! Damn!" Burnham pressed on, enlisting Frederick Law Olmsted, the designer of New York's Central Park and most recently of the California university Leland Stanford dedicated to the memory of his deceased son, to carve a fairgrounds from swampland along

Lake Michigan south of the Loop. Louis Sullivan, Burnham's Chicago rival, lately feted for the new Chicago Auditorium, would design the centerpiece structure: the transportation building. Frank Lloyd Wright, Sullivan's young assistant, would help. George Ferris volunteered to make the world forget Eiffel and his tower by engineering something more impressive: a giant structure of iron that would *rotate*, lofting visitors high and sending them soaring above the fairgrounds and the city. George Westinghouse, the inventor of the railroad air brake, which was saving hundreds of lives each year, and recently the developer of electrical dynamos, or generators, won the contract to power the fair. Thomas Edison, Westinghouse's foe in the "battle of the currents"—alternating current (Westinghouse) or direct current (Edison)—lost the power contract but won the consolation prize of lighting the fairgrounds with tens of thousands of his incandescent bulbs.

Burnham envisioned a "white city" of gleaming neoclassical structures set among lagoons and greenswards. Sullivan grumbled that Greece and Rome were no model for a progressive country; besides, he detested decoration and insisted on letting function dictate form. He ignored Burnham's directions and built what turned out to be the sensation of the fair. But the other architects conformed to Burnham's blueprint, albeit more slowly than he wished. As opening day approached, Burnham had to figure out how to get the buildings painted white in time. A New York painting contractor, Francis Millet, was brought in. Millet and his crews devised a novel method of applying the mixture of white lead and oil—through hoses and nozzles from tanks pressurized by air. The "whitewash gang," Burnham called them, and their spray equipment, even while launching a revolution in the painting industry, finished the Chicago job with just hours to spare.

The World's Columbian Exposition, as it was formally styled, opened on May 1, 1893. (Burnham could never have made a deadline of the actual four-hundredth anniversary, in October 1892; but anyway no one wanted to hold a fair during Chicago's winter.) Half a million people crammed the grounds that first day. President Cleveland came from Washington; the Infanta Eulalia arrived from Spain. The organizers found two direct descendants of Columbus. Governor John Peter Altgeld greeted the guests on behalf of the state of Illinois.

The throng gawked at a telescope donated by Chicago railroad magnate Charles Yerkes to the University of Chicago. They ogled the latest weapons technology from Germany's Krupp works. Edison displayed his phonograph and the Kinetoscope, a forerunner of the motion picture projector. The exhibit of the American Bell Telephone Company enabled fairgoers to communicate by long-distance telephone with friends in New York. Many visitors got their first direct appreciation of standard time zones (adopted by American railroads during the 1880s) by observing the fair clocks, which were connected electrically to the Naval Observatory in Washington, an hour ahead of Chicago. George Ferris's giant wheel wasn't finished when the fair began, but its size and shape drew gasps nonetheless.

The fair brought out reformers of every stripe and cause: prohibitionists, who found themselves swimming upstream against the river of liquor that flowed through Chicago for the fair; consumer safety advocates, who protested the shocking conditions in the slaughterhouses of the city; bicyclists, who agitated for better roads on which to ride their two-wheeled vehicles; labor unionists, who hoped to promote solidarity; silverites, who plumped the white metal; feminists, who demanded the vote for women. Exotic dancer Little Egypt made a feminist statement of a different sort, against conventional notions of a woman's role; the size of the crowds at her performances suggested substantial agreement, at least among those many who stayed for the encores.

A touching scene unfolded after Susan B. Anthony crashed a meeting of managers discussing whether to keep the fair open on Sundays. Anthony, despite having no voice in the decision, volunteered that it should stay open. A sarcastic male inquired whether she'd prefer having a son of hers— if she had had any—attend the Wild West show Buffalo Bill Cody was putting on at the fair or go to church. She opted for Cody's show. "He would learn far more," she said. When Cody heard of her sacrilege, he sent her tickets. She sat in the best box in the house, and at the beginning of the show he galloped up and saluted her. She stood—"as enthusiastic as a girl," a friend remarked—and waved her handkerchief in reply.[1]

LIKE MOST SUCH expositions, the Chicago fair cost a great deal of money to stage, and the fair organizers and sponsors were counting on heavy attendance to recoup their investment. The enormous opening day crowd boded well for the bottom line. But before the week was out, the fair was blindsided by an event that seemed to have no connection whatsoever to the exposition—unless one assumed that all things capitalistic were connected, one to the other. Since the passage of the Sherman Silver Purchase Act in 1890 the world financial markets had looked askance at the United States, wondering whether the Treasury would or could fulfill its promise to redeem the dollar for gold. The emergence of the Populist party increased the worries; should the agrarian radicals have their silver way, the dollar would plunge in value, leaving dollar holders drastically short. During the early months of 1893 the Treasury received an unusual quantity of dollars for redemption, till the government's gold reserve approached the $100 million minimum generally thought necessary to maintain investor confidence. On April 22, just nine days before the fair opened, the gold reserve briefly touched the threshold, causing throats to catch on both sides of the Atlantic.[2]

The stock market shared the nervousness, as it always did. Railroads were especially vulnerable. Jay Gould had died of consumption, or tuberculosis, the previous December, and though editors and other keepers of the public conscience bade the arch-speculator good riddance—Joseph Pulitzer's *New York World* called Gould "one of the most sinister figures that ever flitted bat-like across the vision of the American people"—many investors had come to perceive him as a stabilizing force in the railroad industry. Two months later the Philadelphia & Reading Railroad closed its doors. The Reading wasn't the nation's largest railroad, but it was one of the oldest, and its failure made brokers and investors wonder who or what was next.[3]

They got their answer the week the Chicago fair opened. It wasn't a railroad that went down but the National Cordage Company—the "rope trust." National Cordage was arguably less central to the country's economy than the Reading Railroad, although it did command four-fifths of the market for rope and related binders. But the already skittish markets took the failure as cause for panic. Banks folded by the scores. In June the British government of India, one of the last large consumers of silver, declared that it would no longer purchase the metal, sending silver stocks, which had risen after the Sherman silver law and upon the emergence of Populism, into a death spiral. In July the New York, Lake Erie & Western Railroad (the successor to Jay Gould's Erie) failed. This drove the financial system off a cliff, despite the swift repeal of the Sherman law. Now banks by the hundreds—more than six hundred in all—closed their doors, leav-

ing depositors pounding helplessly outside. Persons solvent just weeks
before found themselves bereft and disoriented. Henry Adams awoke one
day to discover that his inherited savings had all but vanished. "As a starting point for a new education at fifty-five years old," he later wrote with an
equanimity he didn't feel in the moment, "the shock of finding oneself suspended, for several months, over the edge of bankruptcy, without knowing
how one got there, or how to get away, is to be strongly recommended."
Though a student of other people's money, Adams had never much worried about his own. Suddenly he had to, but to little avail. "The more he
saw of it," he wrote of the panic, "the less he understood it. He was quite
sure that nobody understood it much better. Blindly some very powerful
energy was at work, doing something that nobody wanted done." Yet the
effects of this imponderable, implacable force were inescapable. "Men died
like flies under the strain, and Boston grew suddenly old, haggard, and
thin."[4]

By this point in America's economic development, bank drafts and
checks played a larger role in the day-to-day money supply than currency,
and the collapse of the banking system caused a strangling shrinkage of the
money supply. Interest rates soared, capital investment clanked to a halt,
inventories clogged warehouses, new orders vanished, businesses failed by
the thousands, and workers lost jobs by the millions. Twenty years further
into the industrial age than at the last such panic, twenty years further
from the comparative safety net of the farm, the American economy suffered that much more. Evictions followed layoffs, and hunger followed
both. The tide of immigration slowed, and even reversed for some countries, but unemployment continued to rise.

THE DEPRESSION INTENSIFIED the strain between labor and management. After the Haymarket riot of 1886, organized labor had retrenched. Smaller, focused unions of skilled workers emerged from the
remnants of larger groups; among the most successful skilled unions was
the Amalgamated Association of Iron and Steel Workers, with some
twenty-five thousand members, concentrated in the mills around Pittsburgh. The state of the art in steel production was Andrew Carnegie's
Homestead works, seven miles east of Pittsburgh on the bank of the
Monongahela River, where Carnegie had installed open-hearth furnaces

and other equipment that dramatically improved efficiency. Yet these very improvements threatened the wages and even the jobs of members of the Amalgamated union, as the innovations allowed Carnegie to employ unskilled, nonunion workers in place of the Amalgamated men. Carnegie and the union first collided in 1889, when he proposed a 25 percent wage reduction. The Amalgamated leadership rejected the proposal but was forced to accept a three-year deal pegging wages to steel prices. If prices rose, the workers would share the gain; if prices fell, they'd suffer the loss, albeit only till prices hit a floor of $25 per ton of steel billets. The company would swallow any loss beyond that.[5]

As the contract approached its end in the summer of 1892, the price of billets had fallen substantially, and the company proposed to lower both the sliding scale and the minimum. Carnegie fancied himself an enlightened employer. "For twenty-six years I had been actively in charge of the relations between ourselves and our men," he wrote, "and it was the pride of my life to think how delightfully satisfactory these had been." Doubtless sensing that his record might soon be spoiled, he delegated authority to Henry Clay Frick and departed for a holiday in Scotland. Frick had no such unsullied record as Carnegie and few compunctions about utilizing whatever leverage he had over the workers and their union. Frick made clear that the company's offer was nonnegotiable; the workers could accept it or seek work elsewhere. His demeanor and overall approach indicated he'd be just as happy if the union rejected his proposal, as he could then replace the union workers with non-union men. This interpretation gained credence when company workmen constructed a twelve-foot-high fence about the Homestead works, with steel gates, barbed wire, and rifle slits. What the workers didn't know was that Frick had meanwhile contracted with Robert Pinkerton, the son and successor of Allan Pinkerton, to provide a private security force to the Homestead plant.[6]

The June 30 deadline arrived without agreement. Frick informed the workers that the plant would close till July 6; any who wished to return could apply for jobs then, but as individuals rather than union members. The Amalgamated union had laid in supplies and saved what cash its members could spare; it organized a strike committee to assist members in need and maintain solidarity. Union members, in round-the-clock shifts, kept watch over the plant lest Frick try to slip scabs onto the premises.

On July 5 union sympathizers at Bellevue, Pennsylvania, not far from

Homestead, reported the arrival by train of the Pinkerton men, who boarded two barges for the final approach to Homestead. Before the barges came within sight of the plant, the workers had spread the alarm. An informal militia of workers raced to the waterfront below the plant, and as the barges, propelled by a tug, drew near, the workers opened fire.

How much the Pinkertons knew of the details of the dispute between the company and the union is hard to tell; their surprise at the violence their arrival provoked suggests that Robert Pinkerton hadn't informed them of the depth of the workers' determination. When Pinkerton's lieutenants began handing out rifles, some of the agents declined, preferring not to fight it out with the workers. Yet others accepted the weapons and returned the workers' fire.

After the captain of the tugboat grounded the barges on the bank of the Monongahela, several of the Pinkertons tried to get off. The leader of the squad, Frederick Heinde, boldly declared that he and his men had been hired by the steel company to secure the steelworks, and they intended to do precisely that. The workers, he warned, had better step aside. The workers refused, and when Heinde attempted to force his way past, one of the workers shot him in the thigh. Several more shots followed, one hitting Heinde in the shoulder, another hitting a Pinkerton standing beside Heinde and killing him instantly. Four more Pinkertons were wounded. Their fellows returned the fire, killing two workers and wounding about twenty others before the agents returned to the barges and the workers retreated up the bank.

An ugly standoff ensued. The Pinkertons suffered from the summer heat and the close quarters of the barges, and the thought of what the angry workers might do to them. Some of the workers tossed sticks of dynamite at the barges; these effected little damage to the steel craft but seriously dented the Pinkertons' morale. Another group of workers pumped hundreds of gallons of oil into the river upstream from the barges and attempted to set it alight as it drifted down. But the fuel wouldn't catch. Still another group improved on the incendiary idea, commandeering a raft, filling it with oily refuse, setting it ablaze, and pushing it downstream toward the barges. This variant came close to succeeding, but the current redirected the fiery vessel at the last moment and spared the Pinkertons from roasting.

Gradually the leaders of the workers recognized that further bloodshed, even if justified as retaliation for those killed, would jeopardize popular sympathy for the workers' cause. As the afternoon waned, this view caught hold among the rank and file. When the Pinkertons expressed a desire to have done with private policing, the union leaders offered to let them leave the barges and get out of town. The Pinkertons accepted. But they had hardly set foot on the bank when the union leaders lost control of the workers, who fell upon the Pinkertons quite brutally. Most of the agents were cuffed and kicked; some were beaten unconscious. Two died. Those who remained on their feet took refuge in the town theater, where the union leaders posted guards to protect them from further abuse. Finally a special train sent by Henry Frick from Pittsburgh fetched them and carried them off.[7]

THE UNION LEADERS were right to be concerned about a loss of popular sympathy. Diehard unionists praised the Homestead workers for standing up to arrogant capital, but neutral observers—and of course apologists for management—tended to think the workers had gone too far. This feeling intensified two weeks later when a man posing as an employment agent from New York entered Frick's office and fired at the steel executive twice from close range. The first bullet clipped Frick's ear before penetrating his neck; the second just missed his spinal column below the skull. Frick's assistant knocked the gunman's hand awry as he fired a third shot, which missed. The intruder thereupon pulled a knife and stabbed Frick three times—in the hip, in the leg, and just over the kidney. Finally Frick, bleeding profusely, and the assistant wrestled the intruder down.[8]

Investigation revealed the man to be a Russian-born anarchist named Alexander Berkman. He had no connection to the strike beyond reading about it in the papers, which gave him the idea that he might begin dismantling the capitalist order by killing Frick. In fact he could not have done Frick a greater favor. Frick didn't have to equate the Amalgamated union with anarchy; the workers' own actions against the Pinkertons and now this assassination attempt did the job for him. When his newborn son, Henry Jr., coincidentally died just days later, the image of the brave, beleaguered man of business—"man of steel" was the favored phrase— crowded out the specifics of the dispute with the Amalgamated union. The governor of Pennsylvania sent the state militia to prevent additional violence, and under the guns of the guard Frick hired replacements for the union men. By the time the union conceded defeat, in November, it had become irrelevant to the operations of Carnegie Steel. "We had to teach our employees a lesson," Frick wrote Carnegie. "And we have taught them one that they will never forget."[9]

THE LESSON—that capital would protect its prerogatives, by force if necessary—was amplified two years later. Workers at the Pullman Palace Car Company in Pullman, Illinois, just south of Chicago, lived in one of the finest company towns in America. Modeled after Saltaire in England, where Titus Salt had built a community for his woolen workers, and similar projects in Essen, Germany, and Guise, France, the town of Pullman boasted neat brick houses with gas, water, sewer connections, and basements. Fenced yards contained tidy lawns and flower beds; a larger commons included a lake, an artificial waterfall, a concert stage, and athletic fields. Although more densely populated than parts of many cities, the town had a mortality rate far below the urban norm. Epidemics—of cholera, yellow fever, typhoid—that still scourged American cities bypassed Pullman. It employed but a third of the national average of physicians per capita and scarcely produced enough illness to support those.[10]

But there was something about Pullman that bothered the inhabitants. Visitors noticed it right away. "The corporation is everything and everywhere," a journalist from Pittsburgh recorded. "The corporation trims your lawn and attends to your trees; the corporation sweeps your street, and sends a man around to pick up every cigar stump, every bit of paper, every straw or leaf; the corporation puts two barrels in your back yard, one for ashes and one for refuse of the kitchen; the corporation has the ashes and refuse hauled away. . . . The corporation does practically everything but sweep your room and make your bed, and the corporation expects you to enjoy it and hold your tongue."[11]

In flush times the residents of Pullman—the workers in the company shops and their dependents—accepted the trade-off. For a decade after its founding in the early 1880s the town thrived. But the Panic of 1893 and the ensuing depression punished the Pullman company severely. The company sold luxury items—the sleeping and parlor cars favored by first-class passengers—and when traffic slumped, the roads postponed new purchases.

George Pullman was a paternalist, but before that he was a capitalist, and when orders ceased he slashed his workforce by three thousand men and women and cut piecework pay rates by as much as half. Had he trimmed rents in the company town and prices at the company stores, the workers might have tolerated the wage cuts, but he didn't, treating his landlord role as separate from his role as employer. The workers suffered for several months before deciding to strike. On May 11, 1894, they walked out of the company shops.

For a month the strike proceeded uneventfully. Pullman might have evicted striking workers—for arrears of rent, if nothing else—but he didn't. Skeptics said he feared a public backlash; cynics contended he wanted the arrears to mount so he could squeeze the workers even further. The town remained calm, if tense.

Things changed when the American Railway Union entered the dispute. The ARU wasn't a year old, having been founded just the previous summer in Chicago. Less ambitious than the Knights of Labor, which had aimed to organize the entire working class, but more ambitious than the Amalgamated Association of Iron and Steel Workers, which focused on skilled labor within a single industry, the ARU proposed to organize the railroad industry as a whole. From engineers to porters (except for black porters: African Americans weren't accepted as members) and brakemen to boilermakers (the union included not simply persons who operated railroad equipment but also those who built the locomotives and cars, which was how it became interested in the Pullman strike), the ARU hoped to weld the rail workers into an organization powerful enough to meet the railroad owners as their equal. In his dreams, ARU president Eugene V. Debs envisioned the rail union as the first step toward something broader. "The forces of labor must unite," he told the second annual meeting of the ARU in June 1894. "The dividing lines must grow dimmer day by day until they become imperceptible, and then labor's hosts, marshaled under one conquering banner, shall march together, vote together, and fight together, until working men shall receive and enjoy all the fruits of their toil. Then will our country be truly and grandly free, and its institutions as secure and enduring as the eternal mountains."[12]

But the millennium had to start somewhere, and Pullman appeared as good a place as any. At the June 1894 meeting, as the Pullman strike entered its second month, the ARU voted to refuse to handle Pullman cars.

This raised the stakes dramatically, for it brought most of the American railroad network into play. Debs and the union hoped to pressure railroad management into leaving the Pullman cars on the sidings; if the railroads did so, Pullman must cave in before long. But if the managers defended Pullman, then a relatively minor contest in a Chicago suburb would become a major test of strength over the nation's transportation lifelines.

In fact the railroads, represented by the General Managers' Association, were itching for just such a test of strength. The ARU had won a surprising victory in a smaller strike against James J. Hill's Great Northern, and the other owners, while cursing Hill as a class traitor, determined to crush the union before the idea of industry-wide solidarity caught on. The ARU, by backing the Pullman strikers so explicitly, played into the managers' hands.

The nature of the contest was no secret. "While the boycott is ostensibly declared as a demonstration of sympathy in behalf of the strikers in the Pullman shops," the *New York Times* remarked, "it in reality will be a struggle between the greatest and most powerful railroad labor organization and the entire railroad capital."[13]

Yet it was an egregiously unequal fight. The railroads enjoyed the advantage not merely of their much greater financial resources but of a friendly federal government. Richard Olney had made a lawyer's fortune representing railroads before becoming Grover Cleveland's attorney general—an appointment he accepted only after being assured by Cleveland that he could continue his private practice and receive his customary retainers from the railroads. Olney had advised his rail clients on breaking strikes in the past, with singular success. Indeed, one such broken strike, against the Chicago, Burlington & Quincy, helped convince Debs of the futility of the brotherhood model of organizing rail workers, driving him to the industrial approach embodied by the ARU. In the Pullman strike, Olney and Debs squared off again.[14]

Olney very quickly decided that the ARU's boycott was illegal. The railroads refused to uncouple the Pullman cars, and ARU members refused to handle the trains, many of which included cars carrying mail. Olney might have determined that the railroads were at fault and arranged an order for them to shunt the Pullman cars from trains transporting the mail, but, true to form, he took the opposite tack. He blamed the union and persuaded a judge to issue an injunction against the ARU boycott.

The basis for the boycott was an imaginative reading of the Sherman Antitrust Act of 1890. Congress had passed the Sherman law after years of agitation by victims and other opponents of Rockefeller's Standard Oil and its monopoly-minded mimics. The law barred "every contract, combination in the form of trust or otherwise, or conspiracy, in restraint of trade or commerce among the several states, or with foreign nations." During discussion of the bill, spokesmen for labor worried that it might be applied against unions. John Sherman asserted that such was not the intent at all. "Combinations of workingmen to promote their interests, promote their welfare, and increase their pay if you please, to get their fair share in the division of production, are not affected in the slightest degree, nor can they be included in the words or intent of the bill," he said.[15]

This may have been Sherman's view, and it was probably the view of most of those voting in favor. But it didn't take corporate lawyers long to craft an interpretation that persuaded courts to include unions under the act's proscription. "A strike is essentially a conspiracy to extort by violence," a federal judge in Milwaukee declared the month before the Pullman strike began. "Whatever other doctrine may be asserted by reckless agitators, it must ever be the duty of the courts, in the protection of society, and in the execution of the laws of the land, to condemn, prevent, and punish all such unlawful conspiracies and combinations." The Chicago court to which Olney applied for an injunction in the Pullman case agreed in principle if not in detail, and the ARU was ordered to move the mail.[16]

Although the strike put the whole national rail network at risk, both sides—the railroad managers and the ARU—reckoned that Chicago was where the contest would be won or lost. Twenty-six rail lines converged on Chicago, making it the choke point of the nation's transport system. Not by accident had the General Managers' Association and the ARU alike chosen the city for their headquarters. Olney believed that the strike must be defeated at Chicago, where the ARU and sympathizers were already well mobilized, lest it mushroom out of control. "It has seemed to me that if the rights of the United States were vigorously asserted in Chicago, the origin and center of the demonstration," he wrote to the Chicago federal attorney's special counsel (who was also chief counsel to the Chicago, Milwaukee & St. Paul Railroad), "the result would be to make it a failure everywhere else and to prevent its spread over the entire country."[17]

To enforce the injunction against the strikers, who besides halting trains committed vandalism against rolling stock and fixed facilities, President Cleveland directed Nelson Miles, still the commander of the Western army, to deploy federal troops against the strikers. Cleveland took no chances; speaking through chief of staff General John Schofield, the president ordered "the entire garrison at Fort Sheridan—infantry, cavalry, and artillery—to the lake front in the city of Chicago."[18]

The troop deployment made the tense situation explosive. General Miles was as determined to crush this labor rebellion as he had been to crush the Ghost Dancers. "Men must take sides either for anarchy, secret conclaves, unwritten law, mob violence, and universal chaos under the red or white flag of socialism on the one hand, or on the side of established government," he declared. Eugene Debs feared that the government action made much larger violence almost inevitable. "The first shot fired by the regular soldiers at the mobs here will be the signal for a civil war," Debs warned. "I believe this as firmly as I believe in the ultimate success of our course. Bloodshed will follow, and ninety percent of the people of the United States will be arrayed against the other ten percent."[19]

For a time it appeared matters would come to that. Strikers, sympathizers, and elements of Chicago's floating population—their numbers swollen by the depression—surged through the streets of the city on the evening of July 4. The crowd tipped over railcars and hurled bricks through windows. The excitement brought out many more people; the next day the mob, by now utterly beyond the control of Debs and the ARU, numbered perhaps ten thousand. The rioters wrecked and burned more cars and swarmed across the Union Stock Yards, where they challenged the federal troops, who responded with bayonet and cavalry charges. Arsonists set a fire that was whipped by the infamous Chicago winds into a blaze that consumed part of the fairgrounds left over from the Columbian Exposition and conjured terrifying memories of the 1871 conflagration.

The next evening the arson expanded. A security guard shot two rioters, enraging the crowd, which marched as a body on the Panhandle yards below Fiftieth Street in South Chicago. A reporter for the *Chicago Inter Ocean* watched in amazement.

> From this moving mass of shouting rioters squads of a dozen or two departed, running toward the yards with fire brands in their hands. They looked in the gloaming like specters, their lighted torches bobbing

about like will-o'-the-wisps. Soon from all parts of the yard flames shot up and billows of fire rolled over the cars, covering them with the red glow of destruction. . . . It was pandemonium let loose, the fire leaping along for miles and the men and women dancing with frenzy. It was a mad scene where riot became wanton and men and women became drunk on their excesses.[20]

As satisfying as the destruction may have been to the primal urges of the mob—and as profitable as the associated looting may have been to those rioters who took care to empty the cars of marketable items before setting them afire—the violence proved a public-relations disaster for the ARU. The Chicago riots triggered outbreaks in several other cities across the Midwest and West, and although many of those persons smashing, burning, and looting had no connection with the ARU, anxious observers could easily fear that what the rail workers had started might turn into a revolution. Cleveland received requests for federal troops from half a dozen governors; the president responded by sending a total of sixteen thousand soldiers into the riot zones. The federal troops in Chicago were supplemented by Illinois militia ordered out by Governor Altgeld, who resisted the introduction of the federal troops but nonetheless felt obliged to take action. The soldiers in Chicago engaged the rioters with bayonets and gunfire; ultimately more than a dozen people were killed and more than fifty wounded. Fighting in the other states between rioters and federal and state troops produced forty additional deaths and many more injuries.[21]

Public comment almost universally condemned the rioters and demanded that the president take even stronger action. *Harper's Weekly* called the strike and boycott "blackmail on the largest scale" and said the country was "fighting for its own existence just as truly as in suppressing the great rebellion." The *Washington Post* ran an article under the banner "Fired by the Mob, Chicago at the Mercy of the Incendiary's Torch." The *Chicago Tribune* denounced the "riotous emissaries of dictator Debs," while the *Chicago Inter Ocean* asserted, "This is not a fight of labor against capital. It is a criminally injudicious attack of certain forces of organized labor upon every other kind of labor and upon all popular interests in common." Chicagoans and citizens of other afflicted cities deluged the White House with appeals for sternness. "I write for the interest of my wife and babies," a Chicago man wrote, "and pray God to guide you and show you the terrible volcano on which we stand."[22]

Cleveland responded with an executive proclamation that stopped just short of placing Chicago under martial law. All persons involved in the riots would be considered "public enemies"; all other persons had better stay home or risk being mistaken for rioters. "Troops employed against such a riotous mob will act with all the moderation and forbearance consistent with the accomplishment of the desired end," the president said, "but the stern necessities that confront them will not with certainty permit discrimination between guilty participants and those who are mingling with them from curiosity and without criminal intent."[23]

THE SHOW OF military force suppressed the violence, but what broke the back of the strike was the arrest of Debs and other ARU leaders. Debs was charged with conspiracy in inciting the riots; he was also charged with contempt of court for violating Olney's injunction. The conspiracy charge was potentially the more serious but also the more pedestrian; union leaders had been charged with conspiracy for years. Debs beat the conspiracy charge, although not without difficulty. His attorneys, Stephen Gregory and Clarence Darrow, mounted a defense that seemed to be persuading the jury that if anyone had been conspiring, it was the railroad managers. But shortly before the scheduled closing arguments, one of the jurors became mysteriously ill. Debs and the lawyers moved to replace the juror, but the judge refused. He suspended the trial, only to have the prosecution, after some face-saving delays, drop the charges.

The contempt charge was the more ominous, for it turned on the legality of the injunction in the first place. Injunctions were relatively new in labor actions, and the scope of the injunction in the Pullman case was unprecedented. Debs and his colleagues were barred from engaging in any action that even indirectly obstructed the mails—which was to say they were forbidden from engaging in ordinary strike activities.

Debs lost in the lower courts and appealed to the Supreme Court, which took the case in light of the obvious importance of the principle at issue. Stephen Gregory denounced injunctions in labor cases as a subordination of democracy to capital. A judge, unelected and irresponsible, could frustrate the will of legislatures; he could circumvent grand and petty juries. "No more tyrannous and arbitrary government can be devised than the administration of criminal law by a single judge by means of injunction and proceedings in contempt," Gregory asserted. "To extend this power generally to criminal cases would be absolutely destructive to liberty and intolerable to a free people. It would be worse than ex post facto legislation. No man would be safe; no limits could be prescribed to the acts which might be forbidden nor the punishment to be inflicted." Clarence Darrow, junior to Gregory and hardly the celebrity he would become, appealed to the justices' humanity and patriotism.

> When a body of 100,000 men lay down their implements of labor, not because their rights have been invaded, but because the bread has been taken from the mouths of their fellows, we have no right to say they are criminals. It is difficult for us to place ourselves in the position of others, but this Court should endeavor to do so and should realize that the petitioners in this case are representatives of the great laboring element of this country, upon which this country must so largely depend for its safety, prosperity, and progress.[24]

The justices were unmoved. All nine found for the government in favor of injunctions. Associate Justice David Brewer, writing for the court, cited the commerce clause as granting the federal government jurisdiction over rail transport, and he asserted that to deny the federal courts the authority to issue injunctions would impair this jurisdiction. Should the government be required to wait until criminal obstruction of commerce had been committed before taking action, the interests of the entire nation would be at the mercy of small groups. "There is no such impotency in the national government," Brewer declared. "The entire strength of the nation may be used to enforce in any part of the land the full and free exercise of all national powers and the security of all rights intrusted by the constitution to its care. The strong arm of the national government may be put forth to brush away all obstructions to the freedom of interstate commerce or the transportation of the mails. If the emergency arises, the army of the nation, and all its militia, are at the service of the nation, to compel obedience to its laws."[25]

This carte blanche to federal strike-breaking sealed the doom of the

Pullman strike, and indeed of the ARU. From jail and the various court-rooms, Debs found it impossible to coordinate the activities of the strikers, who were already overmatched by the federal and state troops. The boycott of the Pullman cars disintegrated, and the trains began running again. The workers at Pullman, deprived of the leverage the ARU boycott had provided, had no choice but to capitulate. The railroad managers' victory became complete when the ARU, having staked its credibility on the Pullman strike, disintegrated in the wake of the strike's failure. Not for two more generations would the industrial principle of labor organization take hold in the United States. In the interim the injunction would be used again and again to handcuff labor leaders as the courts continued to side with capital.

Yet Debs refused to be discouraged. The failure of the Pullman strike simply made him more radical; he entered jail a moderate unionist and emerged a socialist. The courts had been corrupted by capital, he declared after serving six months on the contempt charge. "If not this, I challenge the world to assign a reason why a judge, under the solemn obligation of an oath to obey the Constitution, should, in a temple dedicated to justice, stab the Magna Carta of American liberty to death in the interest of corporations, that labor might be disrobed of its inalienable rights and those who advocated its claim to justice imprisoned as if they were felons." But the support of the many ordinary people who had expressed their confidence in him—including the hundred thousand who cheered his release from jail—gave him hope, for it suggested that change was coming. "It means that American lovers of liberty are setting in operation forces to rescue their constitutional liberties from the grasp of monopoly and its mercenary hirelings. It means that the people are aroused in view of impending perils and that agitation, organization, and unification are to be the future battle cries of men who will not part with their birthrights."[26]

IT WAS DOUBTLESS small comfort to the defeated rail workers, as they straggled back to their jobs, to know that others were worse off than they. Millions of Americans had no jobs at all during the depression of the 1890s, and until the economy revived they had little hope of finding any. Government officials lamented the high unemployment but lacked the knowledge of economic theory and the tools of monetary policy to do much about it. The Populists thought *they* had the answer, in the form of free silver. They may have been right; eventually the government would learn to loosen the money supply to prevent recessions from deepening into depressions. But theirs was a minority view for the time being; conventional wisdom dictated that the economy would have to find its own way to recovery.

If Jacob Coxey had known either more or less about economics he might have agreed. Coxey had operated businesses in Pennsylvania and Ohio; a quarry in the latter state earned him a modest fortune. In 1893 he traveled to Chicago for the Columbian Exposition, where he marveled at the sights and especially the sound of the voice of a Californian named Carl Browne, an accomplished huckster and agitator who currently flogged free silver and reincarnation, not necessarily in that order. Coxey's material success had failed to fill his soul. "I felt within a craving and a longing on the subject of religion which the churches seemed entirely unable to satisfy," Coxey recalled. "There were many undefined beliefs in my mind which I was unable to concentrate into any concrete form, and when Carl Browne explained to me his theories of reincarnation, I knew in a flash that it was what I had been searching for."[27]

Browne's promise of future lives didn't prevent Coxey from focusing on his current existence and a pet enthusiasm of his own. His travels across the Ohio Valley had convinced him that the nation desperately needed better roads. Railroads sufficed for big cargoes and long journeys, but for the farm-to-market coming and going that occupied the daily and weekly lives of most Americans, the dirt surfaces they traveled on were an anachronistic disgrace. In spring the roads' mud swallowed wagons to the hubs and horses to the flanks; in summer their dust made hacking, gasping ghosts of travelers; in winter their icy ruts broke axles and bones. Coxey had long believed the country couldn't prosper without better roads, and the depression of the 1890s reinforced this conviction. Viewed properly, the depression was a godsend, for—by Coxey's thinking, publicized in *Bulletin Number 1* of his Good Roads Association—it provided just the excuse the government needed to get to work on the roads. Among the millions of able-bodied unemployed were men who would eagerly take shovel and mule team to the nation's roads. All that was required was for Congress to appropriate $500 million.

Carl Browne's contribution to the scheme was the idea of a march to Washington. The lawmakers could ignore petitions and circulars; they'd be harder pressed to ignore a caravan of voters. Coxey's *Bulletin Number 3* announced a starting date of Easter Sunday, March 25, 1894, and the starting point of Massillon, Ohio, Coxey's home. The marchers would arrive at Washington by May 1. The movement needed a name; Browne supplied the "Commonweal of Christ." It needed a banner; he commissioned an oil painting of the Savior, for which he personally sat.

The gloom of the depression had been darker than ever that winter, and Massillon's merchants were eager for anything that would bring business to town. The local paper set a young reporter on the Coxey-Browne story; his dispatches went out over the Associated Press wires and provided light relief from the prevailing misery. Browne made good copy, and Coxey chimed in with extravagant promises. "The success of my undertaking is assured," he said. "I shall camp on the Capitol steps at Washington with 500,000 men." Letters brought promises of reinforcement. Pittsburgh pledged 1,500 recruits to what the papers began calling "Coxey's Army," to the chagrin of Browne. Wabash, Indiana, volunteered 1,000. One H. B. Clark of Illinois offered to field 150 baseball players, who would scrimmage townsfolk along the way to raise money. A convicted murderer in Chicago said he wanted to come but unfortunately had a date with the hangman.[28]

On the morning of departure the army numbered somewhat more than a hundred, including undercover agents sent by the nervous chief of Pittsburgh's police to reconnoiter the radical column headed his way. The press corps was smaller, but only by about half; editors throughout the region decided the Coxey story was the best one going. Carl Browne kept the reporters entertained. He gave interviews by the dozen, revealing such secrets as that he was a partial reincarnation (whatever that meant) of Jesus Christ. He lectured on the currency question, in favor of silver. And he introduced, so to speak, the journalists to "the Great Unknown," a mysterious fellow who appeared one day preaching class warfare of the poor against the rich. The reporters naturally inquired into his background. He silenced them with a ferocious glower. "I am the Great Unknown," he said, "and the Great Unknown I must remain."[29]

All the coverage of Coxey's army inspired imitators. In San Francisco jobless men gathered by the hundreds, pledging to join Coxey in Washington if they could find rail passage. By the time their number topped a thousand, local elected officials and police were pleading with the Southern Pacific to carry the men east, simply to get them out of town. The company tried to charge full fares; when the men refused to pay, it knocked the price down and the journey began. All went smoothly to Utah, where the Southern Pacific lines linked up with those of the Union Pacific. The latter company hadn't been consulted about the discount for the protesters and declined to match it. The men insisted, the railroad resisted, and now the Utah authorities began to sweat. The depression was punishing the mining industry; the last thing the state needed was another thousand angry drifters. The men started walking toward Wyoming before the official pressure and the bad publicity prompted the Union Pacific management to hitch some empty boxcars to an eastbound train and let the men climb aboard.

A similar problem developed at Council Bluffs, Iowa, where the Union Pacific tracks terminated. The plight of the California Coxeyites attracted the interest of some locals who didn't like the railroad and determined to help out by hijacking a train and offering it to the travelers. Some of the protesters would have happily accepted the favor, but others, preferring not to lend credence to allegations that they were bums and hooligans, declined for the group.

A separate western wing of the Coxey movement suffered no such scruples. Two hundred unemployed Montana miners asked the Northern Pacific for cheap passage to Washington; when the company refused, the miners and some sympathetic railmen simply stole a train and headed east. The company found a federal marshal and deputies and dispatched a second train in pursuit. Across the mountains and plains of Montana the Coxeyites flew, with the law on their tail. A rockslide had closed a tunnel near Bozeman; the runaway train stopped, and the men got out to move the debris aside. But the chase train was closing in, and to thwart capture the engineer of the Coxey train called the diggers back on board, summoned a full head of steam, and crashed into the blockage. Rocks flew, sparks shot into the air, metal shrieked, but the train got through and continued east. The Northern Pacific management arranged another roadblock, this one deliberately contrived by dynamite. But the artificial landslide only partly crossed the track, and it scarcely slowed the fugitives. The company, which had the signal advantage of controlling the telegraph lines, then ordered its station managers to drain the water tanks all the way to Dakota. Without water, the fugitive train would quite literally run out of steam.

Yet the company didn't count on the sympathy for the hijackers among the Montana populace. The Northern Pacific was as hated as many railroads in that era, and townsmen along the route offered assistance to the Coxeyites. At Billings they threw a feast for the hungry miners; when the chase train rolled into town and the deputies tried to seize the fugitives—shooting several, one fatally—the townsfolk rallied to the Coxeyites' defense. They threw rocks, swung sticks and metal pipes, and gave every appearance of wanting to massacre the Pinkertons, as they called the deputies. The Coxeyites, their stomachs full and their ranks now swollen to five hundred, tore off east again.

By this time the chase had made headlines across the country. "Blood Flows from Coxeyism," the *New York Times* blared. "Battle between Law and Anarchy." Grover Cleveland and Richard Olney grew alarmed. The attorney general persuaded the president to mobilize federal troops; the Northern Pacific obliged by sending a special train to fetch them. The troop train intercepted the miners at Forsyth, Montana, where they had to stop for spare parts. In the dark the troops surrounded them with leveled bayonets; the Coxeyites had no choice but to yield.[30]

The dramatic escapades in the West made the progress of the main column of Coxey's army appear mundane by comparison. Coxey and Browne led their men through the mud of Pennsylvania's spring, reminding themselves of the need for better roads. They crossed into Maryland wet, footsore, and famished; Browne and the Great Unknown began bickering. The animosity grew until the Unknown attempted a mutiny. Coxey called for a vote of the marchers; they sided with the Unknown by 158 to 4, whereupon Coxey declared, "I cast 154 votes for Brother Browne." While the rank and file puzzled over how Coxey rated so many votes, the Unknown conceded defeat and left, almost as mysteriously as he had arrived. (Reporters eventually revealed that they had discovered the Unknown's identity—he was one A. P. B. Bozarro, a purveyor of patent medicine whom Browne had met at the Columbian Exposition—but had kept his secret to improve their stories.)[31]

The army trailed into Washington at the end of April, just hours before Coxey's May Day deadline. The capital police turned out in force, augmented by federal soldiers from the Washington Barracks and Fort Myer. The police refused Coxey's request for a parade permit and threatened to arrest him if he proceeded. He answered that he and his men had marched four hundred miles and didn't intend to be stopped four miles short of their goal. The police hovered but didn't descend upon the column as it proceeded down Fourteenth Street and then turned up Pennsylvania Avenue toward Capitol Hill. Curious crowds thronged the sidewalks, wondering whether there would be a riot.

The column halted at the east entrance to the Capitol grounds. Coxey and Browne conferred, then approached the Capitol steps. A policeman on horseback blocked the way and told them to turn back. Coxey, now within just yards of his goal, refused. He darted past the officer, hurdled a stone wall, and ran through the crowd toward the building. Browne, apparently by plan, tore off in another direction. The police gave chase.

They caught Browne, who resisted with surprising vigor. Dozens of onlookers joined him, making a melee of the affair. Batons cracked heads and broke arms till Browne was manhandled into a police wagon.

The diversion allowed Coxey to reach the Capitol steps. He began to speak but was cut short by two policemen who dragged him away and threw him bodily back into his carriage. The crowd started chanting his name and seemed ready for a set-to. Had Coxey been a little more belligerent, a full-scale riot might have erupted. But he merely acknowledged the crowd, said a few words no one could hear above the shouting, and led his army back down Capitol Hill to a campsite a short distance away.

The protest fizzled to an end in the following days. Coxey was arrested the next morning and charged, along with Browne, with breaking an 1882 law governing the use of the Capitol grounds. The trial and the guilty verdict elicited derision among persons with any sympathy for Coxey's cause. "Every detail of the proceedings was stamped with the effort on the part of the prosecutor to make a mountain out of a mole hill," the *Omaha World-Herald* hooted. "The crime: Carrying banners on the Capitol grounds! Trespassing on the grass! Great Caesar! If the several kinds of fools who are managing the anti-Coxey crusade at the national capital were in the employ of Coxey, they could not do him better service than they are doing today."[32]

Coxey spent twenty days in jail. The army dissolved; those who had homes to return to headed there; those who didn't simply wandered off.

The Western Coxeyites never got anywhere near Washington. The Californians stranded without rail transport in Iowa eventually took to the Des Moines River in homemade boats. They drifted down to the Mississippi, where friendly tugboat captains pushed them upstream into the Ohio. They reached Cincinnati before fatigue, boredom, and the knowledge that they had long missed Coxey and the main branch of the army caused them to give up the quest. The Montana contingent sat in jail in Helena till the citizens of that state decided they didn't want to feed and house the miners any longer. The city funded a flotilla of riverboats and sent the Coxeyites down the spring-swollen Missouri. They got as far as St. Louis before their enthusiasm gave out, almost three months after Coxey's arrest in Washington.[33]

Chapter 19

TARIFF BILL AND DOLLAR MARK

———

T he workings of democracy during the 1890s were less bloody than those of capitalism but hardly more genteel. The inauguration of Grover Cleveland in 1885 had broken the Republican stranglehold on the White House but not materially deflected the course of American politics. Cleveland delivered his inaugural address from memory—the only president to attempt the feat—yet in other respects he proved a disappointment. Democrats hungered for the spoils of office after their decades in the wilderness, but the fastidious Cleveland insisted on honesty and efficiency in administration. "Why, Mr. President, I should like to see you move more expeditiously in advancing the principles of the Democracy," a party loyalist admonished; Cleveland replied sourly, "I suppose you mean that I should appoint two horse thieves a day instead of one." A Nebraska Democrat complained of the president, "We are New Yorked to disgrace and death, and mugwumped to a state of idiocy." Although the Democrats held a majority in the House, the Republicans controlled the Senate and largely stifled Cleveland's efforts at positive action. He was left to wield his veto—against the Texas seed bill and, most controversially, against measures to expand pension payments to Civil War veterans and their dependents. Pensions had become a major expense of the federal government, and while Cleveland was willing to support veterans crippled by war injuries, he rejected the use of pensions for simple income replacement or—heaven forbid!—political purposes. Veterans and their kin naturally found him less than irresistible. When, in addition, Cleveland in 1887 responded unthinkingly and affirmatively to a request to return captured Confederate battle flags to their Southern regiments, the Republicans waved the bloody shirt one last time. They nominated Benjamin Harrison, a Civil War general and the grandson of William Henry Harrison, and sent him to battle Cleveland on the pensions, on the honor of the Union, and on the protective tariff, which they endorsed and Cleveland opposed. Cleveland carried the 1888 popular vote by 100,000 (of 11 million votes cast) but lost in the Electoral College by 233 to 168.[1]

Harrison's split decision summarized the state of national politics as the 1880s ended. Since 1876 the major parties had been as evenly balanced as they ever had been or would be in American history. Though Republicans won the presidency in three of the four elections from 1876 to 1888, the Democratic candidates actually polled more popular votes (19.1 million total to 18.8 million for the Republicans). Republicans controlled the Senate for ten of the twelve years after 1876; Democrats controlled the House for ten of the twelve years. Each party controlled the two houses simultaneously for just two years; during the other eight years Congress was divided.

The balance seemed a feature of American geography. The Democrats were entrenched in the South, and they became ever more entrenched as the politics of the region grew ever whiter. The Republicans retained their advantage in the Northeast and Ohio Valley. Smart money might have forecast a continuation of the balance, with the Republicans and the Democrats trading control of Congress and of the presidency for the indefinite future.

Yet smarter money—including money the Republicans were pouring into political campaigns in increasing quantities—suggested a different future. The "New South" wasn't as new as its publicists liked to boast, and compared with the dynamically growing, industrializing, immigrant-attracting North, it was a veritable backwater. The party that dominated the nation's manufacturing districts—which was to say, the Republican party—had a potentially decisive edge in national elections. The West was a wild card; its farmers, ranchers, and miners were as unpredictable as the region's notorious weather. But if the Republicans could convince urban workers that their interests aligned with those of their employers, and if they could prevent the Populists from making effective common cause with the Democrats, there might be no end to the victories the GOP could win.

BALDING, JOWLY, AND generous of girth, Thomas Reed could have been the model of the Gilded Age politician if not for his mordant sense of humor. Maine's Republicans (and some of its rare Democrats) had been electing Reed to the House of Representatives since 1876; they probably would have promoted him to the Senate had he not considered it too staid—"a place where good Representatives went when they died," he remarked. So he remained in the House, where he delighted in skewering his opponents and occasionally himself. He refused to reveal his weight, estimated by others at three hundred pounds. "No gentleman ever weighed over two hundred pounds," Reed said. At a time when Republican office seekers often inflated their Civil War records, Reed dismissed his service as a navy paymaster. "Tell them I kept a grocery on a gunboat down in Louisiana," he replied to a supporter eager to spread the word of his exploits. He acknowledged his own inconsistencies. "I do not promise the members of this House whenever they listen to me to give them wisdom of adamant. I do not promise them I shall not change my mind when I see good reason for doing it. I only promise that I will give them honestly what my opinion is at the time. They must take their chances about it being for eternity." He deprecated his entire class by coining the phrase about a statesman's being a dead politician. When a eulogist inquired as to what he should say about a recently deceased colleague, Reed answered, "Anything but the truth." He understood the rules of the political game; after doing something honorable he told a friend, "I do not expect, by acting thus strictly, to escape public slander. I only expect not to deserve it." On another occasion he declared, "One, with God, is always a majority, but many a martyr has been burned at the stake while the votes were being counted."

Reed was an unabashed partisan and consequently reserved his sharpest stabs for the Democrats. "We live in a world of sin and sorrow," he said. "Otherwise there would not be any Democratic party." He declared of certain Democrats that they never opened their mouths without subtracting from the sum of human knowledge. He told a gathering of Democrats that members of their party could always be counted on to do some "mean, low-lived, and contemptible thing." When the audience hissed and hooted, he said, "There, I told you so." Harley Kilgore, a Democratic congressman from Texas particularly irked Reed. Kilgore boasted of a boldness that put his seat in jeopardy; Reed responded, "The gentleman from Texas is safe. His district is Democratic, naturally. The common-school system does not prevail there." Interrupted by a Democratic heckler during a speech, Reed promptly silenced the challenger with a wicked retort. He then declared, in the nasal drawl of his native state, "Having embedded that fly in the liquid amber of my remarks, I will proceed."[2]

Reed headed the Republican majority in the House in 1890, having been nominated for speaker over William McKinley of Ohio and Joseph Cannon of Illinois (and elected by virtue of that GOP majority). He outraged the Democrats by orchestrating a rule change that prevented members of the minority from declaring themselves absent when they were physically present, thereby blocking a quorum. For his pains he earned the title "czar," which he wore thereafter with pride.

The rule change helped the Republicans have their way in the Fifty-first Congress. At the top of their agenda was tariff reform, on which Republicans had long campaigned. Like other sorts of political reform, tariff reform meant more or less whatever the person using the term intended, but for the Republicans in 1890—in particular for William McKinley, who as chairman of the Ways and Means Committee directed tariff considerations—it meant a continuation and perhaps elaboration of the protection American industry had enjoyed since the Civil War. Until the war the tariff had been designed chiefly for revenue, with rates set low enough not to discourage imports excessively (and thereby eliminate the revenue they were counted on to produce). During the war the reigning philosophy changed. The new income and excise taxes cut sharply into net profits of businesses; to soften the blow Congress allowed the tariff rates to rise to a level that afforded protection to American industry. "If we bleed manufacturers," Republican congressman Justin Morrill of Vermont explained, "we must see to it that the proper tonic is administered at the same time." American manufacturers grew accustomed to the protection, and even though the wartime taxes were discontinued after Appomattox, the tariff rates stayed high. In time this caused a problem, in the form of a large and growing federal surplus, which the Democrats demanded be reduced by lowering the tariff. The Republicans sought other solutions. They expanded the Civil War pension program, thereby securing the loyalty of additional Union veterans and dependents and allowing James Tanner, the pension commissioner, to boast persuasively: "I will drive a six-mule team through the Treasury. . . . God help the surplus!" Other spending, on public works, a bigger navy, and the Columbian Exposition, boosted federal outlays to record levels by 1890. The "billion dollar Congress," critics called the Fifty-first, prompting Reed to reply, "This is a billion dollar country."[3]

The tariff McKinley devised added to the complaints. It raised existing rates and added many items to the protected list. While the additions spread the wealth on the producers' side, they meant that consumers suddenly found themselves paying more for an entire range of products (and they led to headlong races across the Atlantic by ships carrying newly dutied goods, to arrive just before the law took effect; one steamer, the *Etruria*, reached New York with minutes to spare, saving its cargo's owners a reported million dollars in duties). Lest the revision appear a total loss to consumers, McKinley arranged for sugar to be placed on the free list. Yet even this victory was ambiguous, for the big gainer was the sugar trust, whose control of the market allowed it to pocket the savings rather than pass them on to consumers. At the urging of James Blaine, again secretary of state, McKinley permitted the addition of a reciprocity clause to the new tariff: if other countries lowered their tariffs on American goods, the United States would reciprocate.[4]

The tariff was a triumph for the capitalist class but a disaster for the Republican party. It played into populist perceptions of the GOP as the lackey of big business, causing even some Republicans to object. "About two thousand millionaires run the policies of the Republican party and make its tariffs," muttered Joseph Medill of the *Chicago Tribune*. "Whatever duties protect the two thousand plutocrats is protection to American industries. Whatever don't is free trade." The Democrats made the most of their opportunity, blaming the McKinley tariff for every price increase on every item in every store. Tom Reed thought the effect was particularly pronounced among women, who, while not voting in most states, influenced their men, who did. "It is the women who do the shopping," Reed observed, "who keep the run of prices, who have the keenest scent for increased cost. They heard in every store the clerks behind the counters explain how this article or that could not be sold hereafter at the former price because of the McKinley Bill; they went home and told their husbands and fathers."[5]

Those husbands and fathers handed the Republicans a monumental defeat in the 1890 elections. Democrats and Farmers' Alliance candidates obliterated the Republican majority in the House, leaving the GOP outnumbered there by 3 to 1. McKinley went down with the ship, as did Joseph Cannon. McKinley, a chronic optimist, suggested that things had worked out for the best. He would now be able to practice law, make some money, and spend time with his family. Cannon sagely puffed his cigar. "That's what I tell all the boys," he said. "But, Mack, don't let's lie to one another."[6]

PRESIDENTS ARE MADE by good luck as often as by great talent, and sometimes the good luck first looks bad. The Republican debacle of 1890 opened the way for the Democrats to reclaim the White House in 1892, which Grover Cleveland did by beating Benjamin Harrison in a rematch of the 1888 contest. But Cleveland hardly had time to savor his revenge before the Panic of 1893 hit, and as the economy spiraled downward, so did the Democrats' chances of retaining office. The repeal of the Sherman Silver Purchase Act did little for either the economy or the Democrats' prospects, and their other significant response to the crisis, an 1894 tariff bill named for Congressman William Wilson of West Virginia and Senator Arthur Gorman of Maryland, simply made matters worse. Its rate reductions didn't noticeably ease the plight of consumers, but they eroded the profits of already weakened manufacturers and hence the job tenure of their workers. The income tax the measure included, in part to offset the tariff reductions, in part to preempt the anti-capitalist demands of the Populists, guaranteed an adverse reaction from the wealthy and powerful. "The Democrats are in favor of an income tax for the reason that Democrats, as a rule, have no incomes to tax," the *Los Angeles Times* declared acidly but not wholly inaccurately. Joseph Choate called the tax "communistic in its purpose and tendencies" in argument before the Supreme Court in the 1895 test case of *Pollock* v. *Farmers' Loan & Trust Company*. The income tax signaled renewal of class warfare and struck a blow at "the very keystone of the arch upon which all civilized government rests," Choate said. The court agreed in principle, albeit most disagreeably (John Marshall Harlan wrote confidentially that Associate Justice Stephen Field behaved like a "madman" during deliberations). By 5 to 4 the court struck down the income tax.[7]

By then the Democrats had been driven from Congress. Tom Reed had anticipated the 1894 elections with glee, predicting, "The Democratic mortality will be so great next fall that their dead will be buried in trenches and marked 'unknown.'" He subsequently added: "Until the supply of trenches gives out." Voters made Reed a prophet, prompting Democrat Champ Clark, one of the casualties, to call the election the greatest slaughter of innocents since Herod.[8]

William McKinley observed the massacre from the relative calm of Columbus, Ohio. After his ouster from Congress, McKinley had retreated to his home state, where he was taken in hand by Mark Hanna, a Cleveland businessman who increasingly found politics more interesting than the iron mines and coal barges that earned him his fortune. Hanna had long backed John Sherman for president, but his eye fell upon McKinley at the 1888 Republican convention when McKinley, having pledged to Sherman, refused to countenance a boomlet in his own direction. "I would not respect myself if I could find it in my heart to do so," he told the convention. Hanna, watching from the wings, afterward asserted that McKinley's statement "destined him as a marked man for President."[9]

Hanna's attachment to McKinley was opportunistic—the capitalist to the candidate, the kingmaker to the king-to-be—but it was also emotional. Hanna was the senior of the two, the wealthier and more experienced, and casual observers often assumed Hanna directed the relationship. Yet those who watched closely saw something different. William Allen White recalled that Hanna was "just a shade obsequious" around McKinley. Chicago editor Herman Kohlsaat spent a lot of time with the two together, and said of Hanna, regarding McKinley: "His attitude was always that of a big, bashful boy toward a girl he loves."[10]

For love or money, Hanna began grooming McKinley for the presidency. He mined his own bank account when McKinley ran for Ohio governor, and he dunned other businessmen on McKinley's behalf. After McKinley won, Hanna paid him visits in Columbus and hosted the governor at the Hanna home in Cleveland. Any Republican governor of Ohio was, by virtue of that office and the state's electoral votes, a contender for the party's presidential nomination ("Some are born great," a chestnut of the era explained, "some achieve greatness, and some simply come from Ohio"), and Hanna busied himself prepping McKinley for 1896. The two held late-night policy sessions, and Hanna arranged for McKinley to appear in public as often as possible. "He has advertised McKinley as if he were a patent medicine," groused Theodore Roosevelt, who preferred Tom Reed. After the depression left McKinley responsible for some notes he had cosigned for a friend, he looked to Hanna for help. "I have kept clear of entanglements all my life," he was heard to lament. "Oh, that this should come to me now! . . . I wish Mark was here." Hanna soon arrived. "I have no heart for any other work until McKinley is relieved from this awful strain," he said. Hanna gathered a small group of capitalists who nominated themselves trustees for McKinley and took control of his finances. They kept creditors at arm's length while they urged other capitalists to join the McKinley bailout. Henry Frick gave $2,000, George Pullman and Philip Armour, founder of Chicago's giant meatpacking firm, $5,000 each. Hanna appreciated the potential for criticism in the course he was following, and so kept the campaign quiet. "We are doing this in a semi-confidential way and will not receive any money from persons except those who give from *proper motives*," he declared. Apparently some donations were returned after the donors hinted too openly at what McKinley might do for them. But when the crisis finally passed, McKinley couldn't help concluding that America's capitalists were a good bunch and worthy of whatever assistance, within reason and decorum, he could provide them.[11]

As 1896 approached, the Republican nomination for president loomed as the great prize in American politics. The economic depression, the labor troubles, and the disarray of the Democrats made the Republican nominee a nearly prohibitive favorite to take the White House. Hanna redoubled his efforts on behalf of McKinley. He purchased publicity promoting McKinley as the "advance agent of prosperity," and he sent the governor on tour around the country. McKinley spoke to Republican leaders and the rank and file, praising the tariff, condemning the Democrats, and dodging the money question. Hanna worked the South assiduously, fully aware that while the Southern states meant little to Republicans in the general election, due to the disfranchisement of blacks and the marginalization of the few white Republicans, they meant much at the Republican national convention. Hanna's mastery of the political process allowed McKinley himself to shun anything that smacked of deal making. In a fit of fatigue Hanna one day suggested that the nomination would be McKinley's if he would merely offer guarantees to certain key party bosses: Matthew Quay of Pennsylvania, Nelson Aldrich of Rhode Island, Thomas Platt of New York. McKinley responded soberly, "Mark, some things come too high. If I were to accept the nomination on those terms, the place would be worth nothing to me and less to the people. If those are the terms, I am out of it." Hanna caught himself, saying he had merely identified the easy way to the nomination. They could win without the deals, only it would take longer. By all evidence, Hanna loved McKinley the more for his refusal.[12]

Hanna spent at least $100,000 of his own money and an undetermined amount of others' money on the McKinley campaign and succeeded in overwhelming the GOP competition. Tom Reed, McKinley's most plausible rival, all but conceded defeat. As the delegates traveled to St. Louis, a friend supportively declared Reed the party's obvious choice. Reed knew better. "The convention could do worse," he said, "and probably will."[13]

By then the only drama surrounded the writing of the platform. Hanna and the party professionals wished to be as vague as possible, relying on the depression to defeat the Democrats. Activists advocated specificity, the more clearly to commit the party to their favorite causes. The money question brought the platform drafters nearly to blows. Goldbugs argued for the yellow stuff, demanding that it be mentioned by name. The party pros argued against it with equal vehemence. Whitelaw Reid, no pro but the editor of the *New York Tribune*, had just returned from Arizona, and he told McKinley, "If a gold plank is adopted, we will not carry a state west of the Mississippi River." Hanna agreed. When Henry Cabot Lodge pushed his way into a meeting of the McKinley men at Hanna's St. Louis hotel room and said, "Mr. Hanna, I insist on a positive declaration for a gold-standard plank in the platform," Hanna glared at the intruder and demanded, "Who in hell are you?" "Senator Henry Cabot Lodge, of Massachusetts," Lodge replied. "Well, Senator Henry Cabot Lodge, of Massachusetts, you can go plumb to hell. You have nothing to say about it." "All right, sir," Lodge rejoined, "I will make my fight on the floor of the convention." "I don't care a damn where you make your fight," Hanna said.[14]

In the end, though, the platform spoke the pregnant word. "The existing gold standard must be maintained," the currency plank asserted. McKinley accepted the statement as the will of the convention, Hanna as the cost of solidifying the party behind his man.[15]

THOSE FATEFUL FOUR letters gave William Jennings Bryan the opening he needed. Sooner than some of his Democratic colleagues, the Nebraska congressman had seen the tsunami of Republicanism rising in 1894, and he declined to defend his House seat that year. Whether the Republicans or the Cleveland Democrats were the happier to see him go was a fair question; Bryan excoriated the president on the money issue more consistently and vehemently than he ever assailed the Republicans. He made himself the spokesman of silver and the tribune of the ordinary people of the American heartland, arriving at the former position by virtue of his ambition for the latter. "I don't know anything about free silver," he said as late as 1892. "The people of Nebraska are for free silver, and I am for free silver. I will look up the arguments later." But once converted and informed, he spoke ceaselessly on behalf of silver as the people's money. "You may make fun of the West and South if you like. You may say that their people are not financiers," he told the Eastern members of the House. "But these people have just as much right to express their ideas and to guard their interests as you have to guard yours, and their ideas are as much entitled to consideration as yours."[16]

Bryan retired to Omaha to edit the *World-Herald*, which provided a forum for his silverite views without demanding much of his energy. For the next eighteen months he traveled the lecture circuit, thumping for populist—and occasionally Populist—candidates, reiterating the virtues of easy money in hard times, and castigating the capitalists for subverting democracy. As the 1896 Democratic convention neared, the gold men and the silverites prepared to battle for the soul of the party. Cleveland stood for gold, but no one stood with Cleveland. "Any man with even the smallest knowledge of the conditions which surrounded my second administration knows that I could not have commanded the support of half a dozen delegates in the whole country," he admitted afterward. Yet on good days he still hoped to influence the choice of his successor. He would have been happy with Richard Olney or John Carlisle, the Treasury secretary, or even

William Whitney, the former navy secretary whose ties to the Rockefeller trust prompted jokes that he would "pour Standard Oil upon the troubled waters."[17]

By the time the Democrats gathered in Chicago, three weeks after the Republicans nominated McKinley on the gold platform, the conservatives were deeply discouraged. David Bennett Hill of New York would deliver the keynote but could hardly mount the dais. "Senator Hill, why don't you ever smile and look pleasant?" a reporter inquired. "I never smile and look pleasant at a funeral," Hill replied. Critics of the administration raged from the start. "We of the South have burned our bridges behind us so far as the Eastern Democrats are concerned," Ben Tillman of South Carolina declared. "We denounce the administration of President Cleveland as undemocratic and tyrannical!" The silverites seized control of the platform committee, whose handiwork lashed Cleveland for clinging to gold, for siding with the capitalists in the Pullman strike, and for acting in general more like a Republican than the Republicans themselves.

Most portentously, the draft platform called for silver. "We are unalterably opposed to monometallism, which has locked fast the prosperity of an industrial people in the paralysis of hard times," the money plank asserted. "We demand the free and unlimited coinage of both silver and gold at the present legal ratio of 16 to 1, without waiting for the aid or consent of any other nation."

The conservatives tried half-heartedly to arrest the runaway train. "I speak more in sorrow than in anger," David Hill said. "You know what this platform means to the East." Summoning the spirits of the party's founders, Hill declared, "We want the principles of Jefferson and Jackson."[18]

So did the silverites, who interpreted those principles rather differently. As the whole convention considered whether to adopt the platform committee's draft, Bryan stepped forward. Just thirty-six years old, Bryan was a boy beside the veterans of the party. His youth showed as he sprang from his seat among the delegates and ascended the stage two steps at a time. He acknowledged his callowness in his opening words. "I would be presumptuous indeed to present myself against the distinguished gentlemen to whom you have listened if this were a mere measuring of abilities," he said. "But this is not a contest between persons. The humblest citizen in all the land, when clad in the armor of a righteous cause, is stronger than all the hosts of error. I come to speak to you in defense of a cause as holy as the cause of liberty—the cause of humanity."

The delegates cheered, catching Bryan's mood. He let the cheering swell and then subside before he continued. The advocates of gold contended that silver would disturb the business interests of the country, he said. This misrepresented the business of America. "You have made the definition of a business man too limited in its application. The man who is employed for wages is as much a business man as his employer; the attorney in a country town is as much a business man as the corporation counsel in a great metropolis; the merchant at the cross-roads store is as much a business man as the merchant of New York." The farmers who grew the nation's grain were businessmen as fully as the brokers who sold it. The miners who dug precious metals from the earth were in business beside the financiers who gambled on the rise and fall of those metals. "We come to speak for this broader class of business men," Bryan said.

Their foes branded them as belligerent. Yet if belligerence marked their tone, it did so with cause. "We are fighting in the defense of our homes, our families, and posterity. We have petitioned, and our petitions have been scorned. We have entreated, and our entreaties have been disregarded. We have begged, and they have mocked when our calamity came. We beg no longer; we entreat no more; we petition no more. We defy them!"

The gold men decried silver as a sectional issue. "You come to us and tell us that the great cities are in favor of the gold standard. We reply that the great cities rest upon our broad and fertile prairies. Burn down your cities and leave our farms, and your cities will spring up again as if by magic. But destroy our farms, and the grass will grow in the streets of every city in the country."

The gold men said silver couldn't be adopted without the consent of Britain and the other great powers. Bryan refused to believe it. "It is the issue of 1776 all over again. Our ancestors, when but three millions in number, had the courage to declare their political independence of every other nation. Shall we, their descendants, when we have grown to seventy millions, declare that we are less independent than our forefathers? . . . That will never be the verdict of our people."

The gold men—the bankers and all the big capitalists—had thrown down the gauntlet. The people would take it up.

If they dare to come out in the open field and defend the gold standard as a good thing, we will fight them to the uttermost. Having behind us the producing masses of this nation and the world, supported by the commercial interests, the laboring interests, and the toilers everywhere, we will answer their demand for a gold standard by saying to them: You shall not press down upon the brow of labor this crown of thorns! You shall not crucify mankind upon a cross of gold![19]

For a long moment the delegates stood silent, raptly viewing Bryan, his head bowed and arms outstretched, the image in silhouette of the crucified Christ. Then, as they realized he'd reached the end, they roared their approval, sending wave after wave of bedlam crashing about the coliseum. John Peter Altgeld, who would have contended for the nomination but for his foreign birth, declared, "That is the greatest speech I ever listened to." The convention might have nominated Bryan on the spot, but Bryan insisted that protocol be observed. "If my boom won't last overnight," he said, "it won't last until November."

The convention proceeded to adopt the silver plank and, the next day, to nominate Bryan. The silverites were delirious, the gold men morose. "Lunacy having dictated the platform," Joseph Pulitzer's *World* grumbled, "it was perhaps natural that hysteria should evolve the candidate."[20]

AFTER THE HYSTERIA of the Democrats, if such it was, came the puzzlement of the Populists. Since the elections of 1894 their most potent issue had been silver, and now Bryan and the Democrats had stolen it. Where that left the Populists was what the party had to decide as it gathered in St. Louis. To nominate a candidate other than Bryan might preserve the party's identity, but it would split the silver vote and diminish the chances of seeing silver soon cross the counters of banks and stores and fill the pockets of farmers and laborers. To back Bryan could have the opposite effects: boosting silver's prospects but dooming the Populists.

Jerry Simpson of Kansas judged the issue more important than the party. "I care not for party names," he said. "It is the substance we are after, and we have it in William J. Bryan." James Weaver agreed, as did many others from the Midwest.

But Tom Watson couldn't have disagreed more. The Georgia Populist warned his fellows to "avoid fusion as they would the devil." Henry Demarest Lloyd summarized the Populists' dilemma: "If we fuse, we are sunk; if we don't fuse, all the silver men will leave us for the more powerful Democrats."

In the end the Populists tried to have it both ways. They nominated Bryan for president, but in place of Arthur Sewall, the Democratic nominee for vice president, they forwarded the anti-fusionist Watson, who accepted the nomination under the duress of believing that his candidacy alone could prevent a fatal fracture in the party.

The result satisfied no one but Bryan's foes. "Wall Street bankers and McKinley managers wild with delight over convention's action," a reporter wired from New York. "They felt crushed at prospect of silver forces being combined. Today they bet 10 to 1 on McKinley and gold."[21]

"MR. BRYAN IS an optimist," a journalist who observed the candidate in action explained. "He believes the world is getting better all the time, and it is impossible to be around him a great deal without sharing his hopeful view of things."[22]

Given the power and wealth of the forces arrayed against him, Bryan had scant alternative to optimism. The economic depression disposed voters to punish the incumbent Democrats, and the predominantly Republican press portrayed Bryan as irresponsible, even fanatic. Mark Hanna's campaign machine facilitated such portrayals by writing news articles and editorials for distribution to papers all around the country. Some papers simply got the text, sufficient to fill more than three columns per week. Others received prints ready for circulation, still others the plates to print their own. The Republican national committee, which Hanna headed, commissioned cartoons, posters, and buttons. Hundreds of millions of pamphlets and flyers blanketed the country, courtesy of the committee, which also mobilized an army of some fourteen hundred campaign speakers whose trips were scheduled and expenses paid by the committee.

The Republicans lavished more money on the 1896 campaign than had ever been spent in American political history, and supplying that money required novel methods of fund-raising. Hanna had ties to industry, but not especially to finance, and so required help from people with

Wall Street links. Railroader James J. Hill personally introduced Hanna around the banking community. Hanna impressed the bankers with the efficiency of his organization; they impressed him with the amount of cash they had on hand. Quickly warming to his audience, Hanna harped on the threat Bryan and silver posed to the capitalist class, and he proceeded to assess each bank a campaign tax, so to speak, of one-quarter percent of its capital. Some of the bankers complained but most paid up. Other corporations contributed in similar proportion to their size. Rockefeller's Standard Oil donated a quarter million dollars. Estimates of the total raised ran as high as $12 million; a postelection audit, which certainly missed much, put the figure at $3.5 million.[23]

Whatever the precise figure, it was far more than Bryan and the Democrats commanded. Against the Hanna money machine, Bryan threw himself and his personal charisma. He toured the Ohio and Mississippi valleys by train, making scores of stops and giving hundreds of speeches. People turned out by the many thousands to see and hear him: 10,000 in Springfield, 30,000 in Toledo, 50,000 in Columbus, 70,000 in Louisville. They applauded him; they shouted his name; they pumped his hand. They sang his praises, literally:

> Tramp, tramp, tramp, the boys are marching,
> Marching on to victory.
> And we'll vote for Billy Bryan
> And we'll show the British lion
> That they'd better keep their goldbugs o'er the sea.

He maintained his murderous pace by force of will, lack of sleep, and enormous quantities of food. The farm boy's appetite hadn't diminished after the boy became a man and left the farm; he ate six times a day during the campaign, each meal sufficient to plow five acres or speak ten thousand words. (Even so, he lost weight.) His marvelous voice grew husky by the end of the campaign, but still it reached the back of the largest crowds without appearing to strain. Though he didn't drink, neither did he forswear alcohol entirely; he freshened himself between whistle stops by stripping off his shirt and rubbing himself with gin.

Everywhere he preached the gospel of the people against the plutocrats, of democracy against big capital. His opponents accused him of fomenting class warfare; he turned the charge against them. "They have tried to array the money loaner against the man who borrows money; they have tried to array the financiers against the rest of the people. . . . There is not a class to which they have not appealed." Yet on occasion he did resort to the language of combat. "We ask no quarter; we give no quarter. We shall prosecute our warfare until there is not an American citizen who dares to advocate the gold standard."

Bryan's campaign concluded with a massive parade and demonstration in Chicago. Hundreds of thousands of supporters and onlookers filled the streets of the city. Bryan rode in an open carriage; he stood, acknowledged the adulation, and in a weary voice urged his people to carry the fight to the bitter end. Some responded by beating up Republican hecklers and torching McKinley posters.[24]

BRYAN'S BRAVURA PERFORMANCE alarmed Hanna. "Things are going against us, William," he told McKinley. "You've got to stump or we'll be defeated." The candidate knew better. "I will not try to compete with Bryan," he said. "I am going to stay here"—in Canton, Ohio, his hometown—"and do what campaigning there is to be done. If I took a whole train, Bryan would take a sleeper; if I took a sleeper, Bryan would take a chair car; if I took a chair car, he would ride a freight train. I can't outdo him, and I am not going to try."[25]

Hanna, as usual, bent to McKinley's will. But he determined that if Canton wouldn't go to the country, the country must come to Canton. McKinley's famous "front porch" campaign featured an endless stream of visitors to his home. They arrived by horse and wagon, in buggies and early automobile, but especially by train. Hanna persuaded the railroads that their future profits depended on a McKinley victory and therefore that they should offer discount fares to eastern Ohio. Many did, till visiting Canton became "cheaper than staying at home," as the *Cleveland Plain Dealer* remarked. The pilgrims were ushered, delegation by delegation, to the front yard of the candidate, who on cue would step forth. The spokesmen of the delegations would read scripted speeches avowing the enthusiasm of their counties and business sectors for McKinley and sound money. McKinley would reply with equal unspontaneity. The visitors would return to their trains, happy for this brush with celebrity, and be headed home by supper. Even happier were the reporters who covered the McKinley campaign. Unlike their brethren chasing Bryan, the McKinley contingent kept regular hours, slept in the same beds each night, learned which restaurants to patronize and which to avoid.[26]

While McKinley manned the front porch, Hanna took the back stairs. He sent agents to shadow Bryan and memorize his speeches; these operatives would then beat Bryan to the next stop and give his speech for him. When Bryan himself arrived, his jokes fell flat and his applause lines elicited blank stares. Hanna reportedly encouraged merchants to place conditional orders with vendors—if McKinley won, the goods would be shipped; if Bryan won, the orders would be canceled—and factory owners to tell their employees not to bother to report for work in the event of a Bryan victory. The reports were doubtless exaggerated; the merchants and factory owners already believed that a Bryan victory would be bad for business, and the workers didn't need Hanna to inform them that what was bad for business endangered their jobs.[27]

As the election neared the race seemed close. The underdog Democrats were hopeful; the Republican favorites were worried. "Most of my friends think Bryan will be elected," John Hay told Henry Adams. "And we shall be hanged to the lampions of Euclid Avenue."[28]

Hanna took no chances. The Saturday before the election he staged an enormous parade in New York, essentially commanding clerks, brokers, bankers, and directors to march for McKinley. On election day itself he mobilized tens of thousands of Republican precinct chairmen and foot soldiers to get friendly voters to the polls by any means necessary. Republican employers gave workers time off to vote—and to ponder those termination warnings trailing Bryan.

The dueling campaigns elicited a record turnout. Bryan's popular total topped that of every previous candidate in American history. But McKinley's total topped Bryan's: 7.1 million to 6.5 million. The electoral vote favored McKinley by 271 to 176. The result was strongly sectional. McKinley carried the Northeast, the Ohio Valley, and the Great Lakes; Bryan swept the South, the Plains but for North Dakota, and the West except California and Oregon.

For those who knew how to interpret the results, their significance could hardly have been greater. Coming after the Republican congressional landslide of 1894—an outcome confirmed if not entirely reproduced in the 1896 legislative races—McKinley's triumph indicated that the Republicans had secured control of America's industrial base. Urban workers, confronted with a choice between job security and class solidarity, crossed class lines to vote with their employers rather than with the farmers of the South and West. Though none could know it in 1896, they would continue to do so for decades; McKinley's election inaugurated an era of Republican dominance of the federal government that lasted till the Great Depression of the 1930s.

"God's in his heaven; all's right with the world," Hanna wired McKinley as the returns came in.

"Oh, God, keep him humble," McKinley's mother prayed.[29]

Chapter 20

IMPERIAL DREAMS

―――

W hen Frederick Jackson Turner and the U.S. census director couldn't find a frontier in the West, they cited the growth and spread of the American population as the cause. Another reason, no less significant, was the abrupt halt of American territorial expansion. The American population didn't grow much faster in the 1870s and 1880s than it had during most of the previous century, but for the first time the region available for settlement had stopped growing. The American domain effectively doubled in 1783, when Britain handed over the eastern half of the Mississippi Valley; it doubled again in 1803 when Jefferson acquired the western half of the valley from France in the Louisiana Purchase; it added another 50 percent in the 1840s upon the annexation of Texas, the conquest of California, New Mexico, and Utah, and the negotiated transfer of greater Oregon. William Seward bought Alaska from Russia in 1867.

And there the expansion stopped, to the surprise of much of the world, including many Americans. There were sufficient reasons for the halting, though they weren't apparent all at once. In fact three decades would pass before the full meaning of American expansion would become clear, amid a bitter debate over whether it ought to resume and what it had to do with the continuing capitalist revolution.

OMENS OF THAT debate informed the purchase of Alaska. Nearly all Americans found that frigid region less attractive than William Seward did. It was large but obviously unsuited to extensive settlement; the handful of non-indigenes—Russian fur traders, chiefly—clung to the shore at Sitka and a few other villages, dependent on provisions shipped in from outside. The precariousness of their existence was what compelled czars Nicholas I and then Alexander II to broach unloading Alaska to the Americans. Furs had drawn the Russians to Alaska, but the furs were playing out and the Russian treasury couldn't stand the continued drain. The czars might have offered Alaska to Britain, but Britain was an enemy, or had been in the recent Crimean War. To strengthen an enemy would be foolish. Better to bequeath Alaska to the Americans, who were so convulsed by their internal problems as to threaten neither Russia nor anyone else.

William Seward understood Russia's reasons for dumping Alaska; he had his own reasons for accepting it, starting with the bounty Alaska offered to American capitalists. Alaska's furs might be thinning, but its fish—salmon that weighed a hundred pounds apiece, herring that schooled by the millions—would last forever. Timber—giant cedars and spruces, larger than anything Americans had seen outside the redwood belt of California—crowded to the ocean's edge. Coal creased the mountains; iron deposits made compasses forget which way was north. Gold doubtless awaited only the discovering. Alaska's harbors afforded shelter for ships plying the North Pacific, especially to Japan—lately opened to American trade—and China.

As obvious as Alaska's charms were to Seward, the secretary of state understood that others in Washington were less discerning. "This negotiation must be conducted in the greatest secrecy," he told the Russian minister, Edouard de Stoeckl, once the discussions grew serious in early 1867. "Let us see first if we can agree. It will be time then to consult Congress." Seward offered $5 million for Alaska. Coincidentally or otherwise, Stoeckl's instructions were to consider nothing less than $5 million. But he declined to commit, and a few days later Seward raised the offer to $7 million. Stoeckl accepted in principle, yet while Seward's lawyers were formalizing the offer, one suggested stipulating that the transfer be unencumbered by any existing licenses or franchises. To compensate the Russian government for extinguishing such claims, an additional $200,000 was added to the purchase price. Stoeckl relayed the offer to St. Petersburg and received a favorable reply on Friday evening, March 29. He visited Seward's home that night to tell him. The secretary was playing whist with family and friends; Stoeckl supposed that closing the deal could await the next day or the following Monday. Seward would hear nothing of the sort. Dropping his cards, he asked Stoeckl to meet him at the State Department in an hour. The American secretary and the Russian minister, flanked by their lawyers, initialed, engrossed, signed, and sealed the treaty for presentation to their respective governments.[1]

Seward hoped by his swiftness to present the Senate with a fait accompli, a bargain so tempting none but the willfully perverse could reject it. The pennies-per-acre price conjured parallels to the Louisiana Purchase, another impulsive acquisition, which had worked out splendidly. Yet opposition immediately arose. The *New York Herald* called Alaska an "ice house" and a "worthless desert"; the *New York World* declared the deal "one of the very neatest operations of Russian diplomacy."

The treaty nonetheless cleared the Senate, largely on the strength of a marathon speech by Charles Sumner, chairman of the foreign relations committee, dilating upon the history, resources, and prospects of Alaska and summoning the spirit, lately silent, of Manifest Destiny. "The republic is something more than a local policy," Sumner said. "It is a general principle, not to be forgotten at any time, especially when the opportunity is presented of bringing an immense region within its influence."[2]

The House, which had to appropriate the money to underwrite the deal, put up greater resistance. "Seven million dollars in gold!" Hiram Price of Iowa expostulated. "How many hearts would this lift from the verge of despondency? How many orphans' tears would it wipe away?"[3]

Yet Seward got the votes he needed. Some, in the spirit of Gilded Age politics, were purchased. "Do you wish to know how that treaty was consummated?" Seward asked editor and diplomat John Bigelow afterward. Bigelow said he did. "Then I must put you under oath," Seward continued. "Before that money could be voted"—by the House—"twenty thousand had to be given to R. J. Walker"—formerly senator from Mississippi and secretary of the Treasury, lately legal adviser to Stoeckl and the Russian government—"ten thousand to his partner F. K. Stanton, ten thousand to ten members of Congress, and twenty thousand to Forney"—John W. Forney, friend of Walker and newspaper publisher of many pro-purchase articles "Ten thousand more were to be given to poor Thad Stevens, but no one would undertake to give that to him, so I undertook it myself. The poor fellow died, and I have it now."

Bigelow recorded this conversation in a diary that wasn't made public for many years. Long before then the House approved the Alaska appropriation—by a margin of 113 to 43, which suggests either that Seward bought votes he didn't need or that he didn't tell Bigelow of all the votes he bought. The money evidently came from the $7.2 million purchase price, meaning that those congressmen who received payment were in the enviable position of voting their own bribes.[4]

WILLIAM GRAHAM SUMNER wasn't related to Charles Sumner, and he didn't share the latter's penchant for politics, instead devoting himself to science, history, and philosophy. He early imbibed the thinking of Charles Darwin, and that of Herbert Spencer when a bit older, and he followed Spencer in believing that Darwin's theories explained the rise of civilization. Some people were better at the contest of life than others, Spencer and Sumner said; the good ones climbed out of the jungle of savagery and passed their talents to their offspring, who climbed still higher. The sorting took place both among nations, with the industrial powers of Europe and North America having made the greatest progress so far, and within nations, as certain individuals and families accomplished and attained more than the rest.

Such, to William Sumner, seemed as obvious as the inflamed nose on J. P. Morgan's face, and as undeniable as death. Nor were these views especially controversial in America among the kinds of people who encountered Sumner's essays in the leading journals of the 1880s and 1890s. Religious conservatives—who tended *not* to read the *Forum*, the *North American Review*, *Harper's*, and similar fare—disputed anything to do with Darwin, but among the intelligentsia the description provided by Sumner and the other Social Darwinists didn't elicit inordinate objection.

Sumner's *pre*scriptions were another matter. Sumner argued that attempts to overrule evolution—as by alleviating the plight of the poor— were both immoral and imprudent. "Those whom humanitarians and philanthropists call the weak are the ones through whom the productive and conservative forces of society are wasted," he declared. "They constantly neutralize and destroy the finest efforts of the wise and industrious, and are a dead-weight on the society in all its struggles to realize any better things." The do-gooders had made a cottage industry of weeping for the weak.

> They see wealth and poverty side by side. They note great inequality of social position and social chances. They eagerly set about the attempt to account for what they see, and to devise schemes for remedying what they do not like. In their eagerness to recommend the less fortunate classes to pity and consideration, they forget all about the rights of other classes, they gloss over the faults of the classes in question, and they exaggerate their misfortunes and their virtues. They invent new theories of property, distorting rights and perpetuating injustice, as anyone is sure to do who sets about the readjustment of social relations with the interests of one group distinctly before his mind, and the interests of all other groups thrown into the background. When I have read certain of these discussions, I have thought that it must be quite disreputable to be respectable, quite dishonest to own property, quite unjust to go one's own way and earn one's own living, and that the only really admirable person was the good-for-nothing.

The reformers, Sumner said, were constantly hatching plans to employ the power of government on behalf of their favored victims. "Their schemes, therefore, may always be reduced to this type—that A and B decide what C shall do for D." A and B were the reformers; they derived power and self-satisfaction from this arrangement. D, the object of their concern, received material benefits. C, whom Sumner called the "Forgotten Man," unwillingly supported the others. "We should get a new maxim of judicious living," Sumner said sarcastically: "Poverty is the best policy. If you get wealth, you will have to support other people; if you do not get wealth, it will be the duty of other people to support you."[5]

The immorality of freeloading aside, Sumner held that tampering with the social mechanism reduced total welfare. "If any one will look over his dinner table the next time he sits down to dinner, he can see the proofs that thousands of producers, transporters, merchants, bankers, policemen, and mechanics, through the whole organization of society and all over the globe, have been at work for the last year or more to put that dinner within his reach." All this happened not by accident but by an interlocking set of agreements and expectations evolved over time. Reformers thought they could improve the operation of the social mechanism by bending this lever or adjusting that flywheel; instead they threw the whole thing out of order.[6]

Rejecting reform, Sumner put his faith in laissez faire. "Let us translate it into blunt English," he said of the French phrase. "It will read: Mind your own business. It is nothing but the doctrine of liberty. Let every man be happy in his own way." Sumner didn't promise paradise. "We never supposed that *laissez faire* would give us perfect happiness. We have left perfect happiness entirely out of our account." He would settle for imperfection not made worse by reformers. "If the social doctors will mind their own business, we shall have no troubles but what belong to Nature. Those we will endure or combat as we can. What we desire is that the friends of humanity should cease to add to them."[7]

Sumner's philosophy supported domestic capitalism in obvious ways and was often cited to that effect; but it had implications for foreign policy as well. The struggle among humans took sharpest form in war, with the fit inheriting the earth and the meek finding early graves. This had been so from time out of mind, and the onset of industrialization hadn't changed anything essential. "War has always existed and always will," Sumner wrote. "It is in the conditions of human existence." Tribes and nations competed for the resources of the earth, starting with land but extending, in the modern age, to vital minerals, markets for exports, and opportunities for investment. The deft and strong advanced, the rest retreated, and each tear devoted to the losers was water wasted. "The inevitable doom of those who cannot or will not come into the new world system is that they must perish. Philanthropy may delay their fate, and it certainly can prevent any wanton and cruel hastening of it; but it cannot avert it, because it is brought on by forces which carry us all along like dust upon a whirlwind."

Yet Sumner refused to celebrate war, any more than he celebrated famine, pestilence, or other winnowers of the human race. "Shall any statesman . . . ever dare to say that it would be well, at a given moment, to have a war, lest the nation fall into the vices of industrialism and the evils of peace? The answer is plainly: No! . . . No war which can be avoided is just to the people who have to carry it on, to say nothing of the enemy. . . . A statesman who proposes war as an instrumentality admits his incompetency."[8]

Even so, wars would come whether humans willed them or not. And like the other riders of the apocalypse they left improvement in their wake. "While men were fighting for glory and greed, for revenge and superstition, they were building human society. They were acquiring discipline and cohesion; they were learning cooperation, perseverance, fortitude and patience. . . . War forms larger social units and produces states. . . . The great conquests have destroyed what was effete and opened the way for what was viable."[9]

Not all the Social Darwinists were as gloomy as Sumner. John Fiske, by comparison, was positively sunny. The struggle of nations, Fiske asserted in a widely reprinted essay bearing the historically resonant title "Manifest Destiny," was the struggle against barbarism; as the barbarians succumbed, civilized society emerged. And with its emergence the temptation to war diminished. "Men become less inclined to destroy life or to inflict pain. Or, to use the popular terminology, which happens to coincide precisely with that of the doctrine of evolution, they become less brutal and more humane."

Yet Fiske conceded that it might be centuries before humanity evolved to where war was obsolete. "For a very long time," he said, "the possibility of peace can be guaranteed only through war." And the surest guarantee was that the most pacific nations possess the most potent weapons.

Fiske nominated the United States for avenging angel of peace. The Civil War had shown Americans' willingness to die—and kill—for principle. It also revealed the astonishing effects of industrialization on human conflict. "Never did any war so thoroughly illustrate how military power may be wielded by a people that has passed entirely from the military into the industrial stage of civilization."

Most significantly, the war confirmed the redemptive power of American democracy. Fiske followed Lincoln in declaring the crux of the conflict to be not whether people could own others but whether they could govern themselves. As important as emancipation proved to be, the deeper issue was whether democracy "should be overthrown by the first deep-seated social difficulty it had to encounter, or should stand as an example of priceless value to other ages and to other lands." Democracy had stood its test, and it now gleamed its light across the whole planet.

Yet Fiske wasn't content for America merely to set an example. Americans must spread their values, institutions, and even their offspring as vigorously as their ancestors had done. The momentum of history was on their side; to turn from the task was to ignore the logic of evolution. "The work which the English race began when it colonized North America is destined to go on until every land on the earth's surface that is not already the seat of an old civilization shall become English in its language, in its religion, in its political habits and traditions, and to a predominant extent in the blood of its people. The day is at hand when four-fifths of the human race will trace its pedigree to English forefathers, as four-fifths of the white people in the United States trace their pedigree today." The world was America's for the taking. "There is really no reason, in the nature of things, why the whole of mankind should not constitute politically one federation. . . . The time will come when such a state of things will exist upon the earth, when it will be possible . . . to speak of the United States as stretching from pole to pole."[10]

Josiah Strong thought like Fiske—so much so that he felt compelled to say he had been preaching assertive Anglo-Saxonism "three years before the appearance of Prof. John Fiske's 'Manifest Destiny.'" Strong was the general secretary of the American Evangelical Alliance, and he gave God due credit for America's astonishing rise. Democracy was but half of America's secret; the other was "pure *spiritual* Christianity," by which Strong meant Northern European Protestantism, untainted by Romish superstition.

Strong's God had no difficulty with Darwin. Under the aegis of heaven, the Anglo-Saxons had evolved into the dominant race on the planet, and nowhere more convincingly than in America. Strong quoted Darwin: "There is apparently much truth in the belief that the wonderful progress of the United States, as well as the character of the people, are the results of natural selection; for the more energetic, restless, and courageous men from all parts of Europe have emigrated during the last ten or twelve generations to that great country, and have there succeeded best." Statistics showed clearly that the Anglo-Saxons were thriving. "In 1700 this race numbered less than 6,000,000 souls. In 1800 Anglo-Saxons (I use the term somewhat broadly to include all English-speaking peoples) had increased to about 20,500,000, and now, in 1890, they number more than 120,000,000." America had witnessed the greatest explosion in Anglo-Saxon numbers: a 250-fold increase in two centuries, by Strong's count. But the race spread even as it multiplied, colonizing the Indies, the Antipodes, and parts of Africa. "This mighty Anglo-Saxon race, though comprising only one-thirteenth part of mankind, now rules more than one-third of the earth's surface, and more than one-fourth of its people."

Strong credited Anglo-Saxon military prowess for much of the historic advancement of the race, but he suggested that this talent was being superseded by others. "The world is making progress. We are leaving behind the barbarism of war. As civilization advances, it will learn less of war and concern itself more with the arts of peace." In this new world the Anglo-Saxon would continue to dominate. He possessed a "genius for colonizing," among his other gifts. "His unequaled energy, his indomitable perseverance, and his personal independence make him a pioneer. He excels all others in pushing his way into new countries." He was especially suited to the competition of the capitalist age. "Among the most striking features of the Anglo-Saxon is his money-making power—a power of increasing importance in the widening commerce of the world's future." With money, there was little the Anglo-Saxons couldn't accomplish. "Money is power in the concrete. It commands learning, skill, experience, wisdom, talent, influence, numbers."

Fiske called Anglo-Saxons, but especially Americans, to embrace their destiny. "I believe it is fully in the hands of the Christians of the United States, during the next ten or fifteen years, to hasten or retard the coming of Christ's kingdom in the world by hundreds, and perhaps thousands, of years," he said. "We of this generation and nation occupy the Gibraltar of the ages which commands the world's future."[11]

"MY DEAR CAPTAIN Mahan," Theodore Roosevelt wrote in May 1890, "During the last two days I have spent half my time, busy as I am, in reading your book, and that I have found it interesting is shown by that fact that having taken it up I have gone straight through and finished it. I can say with perfect sincerity that I think it very much the clearest and most instructive general work of the kind with which I am acquainted. . . . I am greatly in error if it does not become a naval classic."[12]

The book that disrupted Roosevelt's busy schedule—by day he was a member of the federal Civil Service Commission, charged with implementing the Pendleton Act; by evenings and weekends he was a gentleman scholar, writing a monumental history of the early American West—was Alfred Thayer Mahan's *The Influence of Sea Power upon History*. Mahan worked at the recently established Naval War College in Newport, Rhode Island; his book, written with the encouragement of the college administration and the navy brass, helped justify the existence of the college and the navy more broadly by contending that naval power had long tipped the balance in the conflict of nations. Though this first book dealt with the fairly distant past—it covered the seventeenth and eighteenth centuries—Mahan followed it up with books and essays carrying the story to the present. The lesson persisted throughout: who owned the waves won the wars.

For those left cold by the laissez faire determinism of William Sumner or put off by the ethnocentric religiosity of the Manifest Destinarians, Mahan provided a bracingly rationalistic and secular alternative justification for American expansion. There was nothing preordained, by either nature or heaven, Mahan said, about the prowess of certain countries. Their ascendancy reflected conscious choices made by their governments and people to purchase the ships and infrastructure necessary to naval success. Modern navies of steel and steam were expensive and slow to build. Their support systems were even costlier and slower to construct and required a revolution in attitudes toward international affairs. In the naval age of wood and wind, the foreign needs of a navy were modest, hardly more than what its pursers could buy from grocers in foreign ports and its carpenters hew from the forests of distant shores. The shift to steam freed fleets from the vagaries of wind but chained them to the vicissitudes of the market for coal; to safeguard against fuel famine, prudent nations acquired coaling stations strategically located around the world's oceans. A steamship, besides, was infinitely more complicated than a sailing vessel and far more prone to mechanical mishap; naval bases abroad, for maintenance and repair, were almost as essential as coaling stations.

Mahan's histories revealed the costs of failure to prepare. The French lost the battle of Trafalgar long before that fateful October day; the dismal performance of the United States in the early phase of the War of 1812 reflected the "deeply mortifying condition" of the U.S. navy at the conflict's start. The future would be different, but only for those who seized it. Americans, Mahan asserted, must adopt a "Twentieth-Century outlook," one anchored in the best navy the country could afford and the stations and bases to support it.[13]

WHETHER THE AMERICAN capitalists who toppled the Hawaiian government of Queen Liliuokalani in 1893 had read anything by Fiske, Strong, or Mahan is unclear. But they did read the sugar clause of the McKinley tariff, which evoked a sudden longing for their homeland. American vessels had called at Hawaii since the eighteenth century; America missionaries arrived in the early nineteenth. The missionaries wrote of the rich volcanic soil and the luscious climate, attracting American entrepreneurs who planted sugar cane and discovered it grew quite well. The sugar men had allies in Washington who in 1875 finagled a deal allowing Hawaiian sugar to enter the American market duty-free. This triggered a boom in Hawaiian production, in land speculation, in Chinese and Japanese immigration to the cane fields, and in Hawaiian sugar imports to America. The surging imports annoyed domestic American sugar interests, who even while tolerating elimination of the tariff on foreign sugar, as part of the McKinley package, slipped in a bounty on domestic production. The Hawaiian producers, having lost their edge over other foreigners and their level field with the Americans, quickly concluded that their fields must become American.

This conclusion gained credence from the reaction of the Hawaiian government to the Americans' outsized influence in the country. In the early 1890s Hawaii's population comprised perhaps 40,000 Hawaiians, 30,000 Asians, and 2,000 Americans, in addition to several thousand Europeans and other Pacific islanders. But the Americans wielded most of the economic power, which they were converting into political power. They had sponsored a constitution, which limited the power of the Hawaiian monarchy, and they controlled the legislature. But when Queen Liliuokalani inherited the throne from her brother in 1891, she moved to curtail the Americans' power. She abrogated the constitution and replaced it with one far more favorable to herself and the native Hawaiians.

At this the Americans, led by sugar baron Sanford Dole, staged a coup. In January 1893 they seized government offices and announced the establishment of a provisional government, whose primary objective would be the annexation of Hawaii to the United States. They had reason to expect a favorable response from Washington, for President Harrison, eyeing Pearl Harbor from the navalist perspective of Mahan, had already indicated strong interest in part or all of the islands. Harrison's representative in Hawaii, American minister John Stevens, was an ardent annexationist, and he immediately recognized the provisional government and ordered U.S. marines from the cruiser *Boston* to surround the Iolani Palace and forestall a countercoup. No submarine cable had yet reached Hawaii, leaving Stevens to formulate policy unperturbed by instructions from Washington; he proceeded to declare an American protectorate over Hawaii.

Stevens's stroke was a bit much even for the Harrison administration, which disavowed the protectorate. But the administration accepted the credentials of commissioners sent by the revolutionary regime, and it negotiated a treaty of annexation. With time running out on his presidency, Harrison forwarded the treaty to the Senate in mid-February 1893, stressing the need for swift ratification.

The Senate, however, balked long enough to let Grover Cleveland be inaugurated, and the new president promptly withdrew the treaty. Cleveland claimed a need to investigate the matter more fully, to determine whether Stevens or any other American officials had acted improperly. His claim was sincere enough, but he also wanted to let opposition to the treaty build. With most of his party, Cleveland doubted the wisdom and, especially in this case, the virtue of territorial expansion. It favored particular groups in the United States—the sugar trust, as Cleveland discovered, had cut a deal with the Hawaiian producers to the effect that in exchange for the trust's support of annexation, the producers would split their share of the sugar bounty with the trust—and it arrogated to the American government authority that properly rested with the people of the territories involved. The provisional government in Hawaii had little popular support, it refused to submit the question of annexation to a referendum, and those few Hawaiians who had signed petitions in favor of annexation seem to have acted under the duress of their American employers.

Cleveland's investigation consumed four months, and it confirmed the president's belief that annexation would be unwise and immoral. Secretary of State Walter Gresham agreed and in fact contended that the United States must undo the mischief done in its name, by restoring Lilioukalani to her throne. Attorney General Olney responded that this would be carrying an admirable principle to an impractical extreme. To oust Dole and the new rulers would require the active use of military force, for which there was no support in the United States. When Lilioukalani promised to behead the plotters in the event of her restoration, this course grew still less attractive. Cleveland dithered till year's end, when he threw the Hawaii matter to Congress, urging the legislators to be guided by "honor, integrity, and morality." The Democratic majority interpreted these virtues as Cleveland knew they would, and annexation expired, for the time being.[14]

LEONARD WOOD KNEW Theodore Roosevelt through mutual friends in Washington. Both enjoyed exercise, and one day in February 1898 they arranged to go for a hike along Rock Creek, not far from Wood's house. Wood watched through his window while waiting for Roosevelt, and examined the trees in his yard for the first buds of spring.

> Suddenly I saw him trotting around the court from Connecticut Avenue to my house at 2000 R Street, with a broad smile on his face. As I met him at the door he said, "Well, I have had my chance, Leonard, and I have taken advantage of it. Yesterday afternoon the Secretary of the Navy left me as acting secretary. He has gone to take a short and much-needed rest, and I have done what I thought needed to be done. I have placed various ships in commission with orders to be ready for sea at once. I have given large orders for the purchase and shipment of coal. I have assembled supplies and forwarded munitions. In other words, I have done everything I can to get the navy ready. . . . I may not be supported, but I have done what I know to be right. Some day they will understand."

Wood understood at once, and he supported Roosevelt's efforts on behalf of war. Wood was an army surgeon, and when he wasn't hiking with Roosevelt he served as McKinley's personal physician. He visited his patient regularly, and after one White House examination McKinley joked, "Have you and Theodore declared war yet?" Wood replied, "No, Mr. President, we have not. But I think you will, sir."[15]

The war Wood and Roosevelt wanted was against Spain, and by the late winter of 1898 they were hardly alone. For years Roosevelt and others of his generation, men too young to have fought in the Civil War, had grown tired, and at the same time jealous, of the war stories of their elders. Roosevelt's combat envy was perhaps extreme; two uncles had covered themselves in glory during the war, albeit on the Southern side, while his own father had failed to serve. Roosevelt's sister suggested that her brother's obsession with war reflected an unspoken desire to make up for their father's failing. But many others of Roosevelt's cohort exhibited a comparable desire to prove their valor.

Most would have been happy for any war; the one on offer was against Spain. Decades after nearly all the rest of Spanish America had broken free from the mother country, Cuba remained the "ever faithful isle." But modernity tested the faith of the Cuban people, and during the latter part of the nineteenth century insurgents raised the banner of Cuban independence. One ten years' war for independence ended in failure in 1878, but a generation later a new crop of insurgents joined some of the old ones, and in 1895 another war of liberation began. The nationalists' grievances included corruption, lack of political participation for the masses, racism on the part of the Spanish-descended criollos against the blacks who constituted the largest part of the Cuban population, and a devastating depression in the sugar industry brought on by the 1894 Wilson-Gorman tariff of the United States, which laid fresh duties on Cuban sugar.

Because the insurgents lacked the numbers of troops and quantities of arms to challenge Spanish rule directly, they resorted to guerrilla warfare: sabotage, ambushes, sporadic raids, destruction of private property. The Spanish army responded by imposing harsh policies on the populace at large in regions affected by the insurgency; of these policies the most notorious was *reconcentrado*, which forced peasants into armed camps, the better to monitor their comings and goings. The mere fact of relocation entailed hardship; the appalling conditions in the camps magnified the suffering immensely. Thousands—mostly women and children—sickened and died. Before long the situation in Cuba assumed the proportions of a humanitarian disaster.

The nightmare would have made headlines in American newspapers on its own, but it received crucial help. The insurgents established a junta, or propaganda bureau, in New York, which fed stories to the American press. These naturally cast the insurgents in the most flattering light and the Spanish government in the most lurid. The aims of the junta dovetailed with the interests of certain American newspapers, especially the "penny press" of New York, where Joseph Pulitzer's *Journal* battled William Randolph Hearst's *World*. At substantial expense Pulitzer and Hearst had installed new printing equipment that allowed them to produce papers for the masses; now, to attract those masses, they required stories with an emotional immediacy ordinary news often lacked. Atrocity tales from Cuba—whether reported honestly, embellished, or fabricated—served perfectly.[16]

American politicians had reason to get into the act as well. American investors in Cuba—in the sugar industry, most conspicuously—lobbied Congress for protection for their assets. More broadly, the depression in the United States caused incumbents to welcome distraction. While Cleveland remained president, the Republicans who controlled Congress could excoriate the administration for not taking stronger measures on behalf of the suffering Cubans, and hope voters wouldn't notice how little they were doing for suffering Americans. After the 1896 election gave the Republicans control of the White House as well as Congress, the party's strategists saw Cuba as an antidote to the issues that continued to divide the country at home. "If we should have war," Henry Cabot Lodge explained, "we will not hear much of the currency question in the elections."[17]

Yet even if American leaders had wanted to stay out of the Cuban affair, they would have had difficulty doing so. The junta in New York was simply the most visible insurgent presence in the United States; rebels based in Florida and other Atlantic and Gulf states launched numerous raids and supply operations against Cuba from American shores. The U.S. navy interdicted many such ventures as violations of American neutrality laws, but others got through, prompting complaints from Spain that the United States was already intervening in the Cuban war.

By the time McKinley inherited the problem it was nearing full boil. The Republican platform of 1896 had endorsed independence for Cuba without committing McKinley to any means toward that end. He initially resisted intervention. The economy was finally pulling out of the depression, and war might spook investors and abort the recovery. McKinley's own experiences in the Civil War still haunted him. "I shall never get into a war until I am sure that God and man approve," he told Leonard Wood. "I have been through one war; I have seen the dead piled up; and I do not want to see another." Yet the advocates of war grew stronger every day. Hearst and Pulitzer brayed loudly for intervention. Whitelaw Reid of the soberer *New York Tribune* implored the president to act. Leonard Wood and Theodore Roosevelt hissed warlike thoughts in McKinley's ear. Senators of both parties argued vehemently and at length for Cuban freedom. Members of the House would have done the same had Tom Reed let them. But Reed opposed intervention and suppressed debate. "Mr. Reed has the members of that body bottled up so tight they cannot breathe without his consent," one congressman declared. Yet neither Reed nor McKinley expected to hold the line forever. Mark Hanna thought the slightest accident could make Congress uncontrollable. "A spark might drop in there at any time and precipitate action," he said. The French ambassador declared in wonder, "A sort of bellicose fury has seized the American nation."[18]

McKinley stood against the fury as long as he could. He bought time with a fact-finding mission to Cuba. William Calhoun, an Illinois friend, spent a month on the island in the spring of 1897 but on his return filed a report that gave McKinley no comfort, characterizing the country as "wrapped in the stillness of death and the silence of desolation." McKinley dispatched a protest to the Spanish government declaring that the United States had "a right to demand that a war, conducted almost within sight of our shores and grievously affecting American citizens and their interests throughout the length and breadth of the land, shall at least be conducted according to the military codes of civilization."[19]

The American protest simply provoked the Spanish government. Cuba had become a test of Spanish will, and resistance to American meddling the proof of Spanish pride. When McKinley floated an idea that the United States might purchase the island as a way to resolve the conflict, the Spanish prime minister, Antonio Cánovas del Castillo, retorted publicly: "Spain is not a nation of merchants capable of selling its honor."

Some American war hawks asserted that what Spain wouldn't sell, the United States might seize. But McKinley rejected that thought. Forcible annexation, he said, would be "criminal aggression."[20]

With each passing month the president's options narrowed. To do nothing would be to countenance the continued destruction of the island. To push the Spanish harder, as by recognizing the insurgents' provisional government, would risk war. The assassination of Cánovas in August 1897 gave McKinley some breathing space as he awaited the formation of a new government, which turned out to be headed by Cánovas's opponents, the Liberals. And in fact the Liberals announced a series of reforms, including home rule for Cuba under a Spanish protectorate. McKinley interpreted the measures as a positive sign, declaring hopefully in his December annual message that the Spanish government had embarked on a course of amelioration "from which recession with honor is impossible." He added, however, in words chosen as much to appease American war hawks as to encourage the Spanish, that if a satisfactory settlement in Cuba was not soon reached, "the exigency of further and other action by the United States will remain to be taken."[21]

Now it was the Spanish government that was trapped. Loyalists in Cuba rioted against the autonomy plan, reasonably fearing the loss of their political and economic power. To protect American nationals and their property on the island, the McKinley administration requested permission to dispatch an American naval vessel. The Spanish government, hoping to demonstrate that the Americans had nothing to fear, approved the request. On January 25, 1898, the *Maine* steamed into Havana harbor and dropped anchor.

The momentary calm that followed was shattered by two explosions. The first was diplomatic: the publication of a confidential letter purloined by the Cuban junta from the Spanish minister in Washington, Enrique Dupuy de Lôme. In the letter Dupuy de Lôme sneered at McKinley as "weak and a bidder for the admiration of the crowd, besides being a would-be politician who tries to leave a door open behind himself while keeping on good terms with the jingoes of his party." The junta handed the letter to Pulitzer's *Journal*, which printed a facsimile under the banner headline "Worst Insult to the United States in Its History."[22]

A week later a second explosion occurred, in Havana harbor. On the evening of February 15 a tremendous ball of fire engulfed the *Maine*, killing 266 and wounding many more. The American press seized at once on Spanish perfidy as the cause, ignoring the captain of the *Maine*, who judged it an accident. McKinley called for an investigation, uncertain what it would yield beyond time to consider his next move. Meanwhile, to placate the growing war party in Congress, he requested an appropriation of $50 million for national defense. Congress approved the measure almost at once. The war hawks were pleased; the Spanish were awed. "To appropriate fifty millions out of money in the Treasury, without borrowing a cent, demonstrates wealth and power," McKinley's minister to Spain wrote home. "The Ministry and press are simply stunned."

The *Maine* report reached the president in late March. The examiners concluded that an external explosion, probably a mine, had sunk the ship. The board wouldn't say who planted the mine, but the American press and public weren't so diffident. "Nine out of ten American citizens doubtless believe that the explosion which destroyed the *Maine* was the result of the cowardly Spanish conspiracy," the *Cleveland Leader* asserted, probably accurately. Hearst's *World*, having got out front of the story by declaring, "Remember the Maine and to Hell with Spain!" considered its judgment confirmed.[23]

It was while the explosion was being investigated that Roosevelt seized control of the Navy Department. He had campaigned hard for McKinley in 1896 and been rewarded with the second slot at the Navy Department. His chief was John Long, whose uncertain health often kept him out of the office. During one such absence, on a Friday afternoon in February 1898, Roosevelt exploited his opportunity as acting secretary to prepare the navy for the war with Spain he hoped to provoke. He dashed off orders on scraps of paper, handing them to clerks who coded and cabled them to American commanders around the globe. He repositioned the Atlantic and Pacific fleets. He requisitioned coal and ammunition. He placed docked ships on alert to get up steam at the first hint of war. And he sent a portentous cable to George Dewey, the commander of America's Asiatic squadron:

SECRET AND CONFIDENTIAL. ORDER THE SQUADRON EXCEPT *MONOCACY* TO HONGKONG. KEEP FULL OF COAL. IN THE EVENT OF

DECLARATION OF WAR WITH SPAIN, YOUR DUTY WILL BE TO SEE
THAT THE SPANISH SQUADRON DOES NOT LEAVE THE ASIATIC
COAST, AND THEN OFFENSIVE OPERATIONS IN THE PHILIPPINE
ISLANDS.[24]

Roosevelt's cable became operative when the findings of the *Maine*
commission forced McKinley's hand. The war hawks in Congress screamed
louder than ever. "By God!" one apoplectic senator thundered on a visit to
the State Department. "Don't your president know where the war-
declaring power is lodged? Well, tell him, by God, that if he don't do something Congress will exercise the power and declare war in spite of him!
He'll get run over and the party with him!" Roosevelt attended the annual
Gridiron Dinner in Washington and waved his fist in the face of Mark
Hanna. "We'll have this war for the freedom of Cuba in spite of the timid-
ity of the commercial interests!" he vowed.[25]

Yet McKinley still hesitated. He sent a note to Spain demanding an
end to hostilities in Cuba, a definitive reversal of reconcentration, relief for
the Cuban people, and American arbitration toward full independence.
When the Spanish government balked, McKinley's time ran out. "If the
President of the United States wants two days, or if he wants two hours, to
continue negotiations with the butchers of Spain, we are not ready to give
him one moment longer for that purpose," Democratic congressman
Joseph Bailey of Texas warned. One of the lingering congressional holdouts asked Tom Reed to dissuade the war hawks. "Dissuade them!" Reed
told a reporter. "He might as well ask me to stand out in the middle of
Kansas and dissuade a cyclone."[26]

McKinley prepared a war message, convinced he had no choice. Not
even an eleventh-hour suspension of hostilities, announced by Spain in the
second week of April, could avert the inevitable. "It comes too late,"
Republican senator Stephen Elkins of West Virginia, one of the last doves,
declared. "Had it come a few days ago, I think we could have averted war."
But no longer.[27]

Yet the war message was hardly a clarion of righteous wrath. In fact,
McKinley didn't even ask for a war declaration. He simply requested
authority to secure an end to hostilities in Cuba, to establish a stable government there, and to "use the military and naval forces of the United
States as may be necessary for these purposes."[28]

The war hawks had expected more, and they made their disappointment plain. "It is the weakest and most inconclusive speech sent out by any president," Bailey of Texas asserted. Senate Republican Joseph Foraker of Ohio told a reporter, "I have no patience with the message, and you may say so." Democrat Joseph Rawlins of Utah called the message "weak, impotent, imbecile, and disgraceful."

But it did the job. Congress granted the president the authority he requested, adding demands for Spanish withdrawal and recognition of Cuban independence. Senator Henry Teller of Colorado appended a clause forswearing annexation by the United States, and the war hawks had no choice but to accept it. Spain broke diplomatic ties with the United States and, after American ships began blockading Cuba, declared war. Congress reciprocated, backdating its war declaration to the day Spain cut ties.[29]

THE ONSET OF WAR inspired Roosevelt to one of the most impetuous and least responsible acts of his thirty-nine years of life. He abruptly resigned his post at the Navy Department, where he might have had significant influence on the outcome of the war he had helped precipitate, to join a regiment of volunteers, in which he would have next to none. Roosevelt's friends and allies, including his political sponsor, Henry Cabot Lodge, urged him to remain in Washington. His family noted that his wife, Edith, was incompletely recovered from complications attending the birth of their fifth child. Who would tend the children if he left home? How would she and they cope if he were killed? But Roosevelt closed his ears, his mind, and his heart to all influences save the martial. "I suppose, at bottom, I was merely following my instinct instead of my reason," he acknowledged afterward. "It was my one chance to do something for my country and for my family and my one chance to cut my little notch on the stick that stands as a measuring rod in every family. I know now that I would have turned from my wife's deathbed to answer that call."[30]

America mustered for the Spanish war the way it had mustered for all of its wars till then. To the small core of the regular army it added a much larger force of volunteers raised in the states and territories and led by a combination of career and newly commissioned officers. Roosevelt's regiment was peculiar but not unique. When Congress authorized the raising of special cavalry units from the West consisting of cowboys, Indians, hunters, and frontier scouts, Roosevelt lobbied friends at the War Department for a commission with one such regiment. The secretary of war, Russell Alger, granted Roosevelt's request and more, offering him command of the regiment. Roosevelt, for once in his life, judged himself inadequate to a task, and he demurred on grounds of utter lack of pertinent experience. He suggested Leonard Wood for command, with himself as second. Alger accepted.

Between the announcement and the muster, the War Department discovered funds to increase the regiment from 780 saddles to 1,000. Consequently, in addition to the Westerners the First Volunteer Cavalry included two hundred soldiers who learned their horse craft not on the plains of Colorado or the deserts of Arizona but on the polo fields of Long Island and the steeplechase courses of Newport. "You would be amused to see three Knickerbocker club men cooking and washing dishes for one of the New Mexico companies," Roosevelt wrote Lodge from camp at San Antonio. Roosevelt, an awkward child whose athletic endeavors had been limited by myopia and characterized by enthusiasm rather than grace, gushed over the athletes who joined the regiment. One was "perhaps the best quarterback who played on a Harvard eleven," he wrote; another was a former national tennis champion. A Yale high jumper and the captain of the Columbia crew team were almost as impressive. Yet the cowboys, whom Roosevelt revered even more than he did the athletes, were the heart and soul of the outfit. "They were a splendid set of men, these southwesterners," he wrote afterward: "tall and sinewy, with resolute, weather-beaten faces, and eyes that looked a man straight in the face without flinching."[31]

Long before Roosevelt's Rough Riders—as an editorial alliteralist labeled them—shipped out for Cuba, Roosevelt landed the first blow against Spain, albeit vicariously. On May 1 George Dewey and the American Asiatic squadron, following Roosevelt's order from the Navy Department, steamed into Manila Bay and in a six-hour battle sank three Spanish ships and burned seven others. Hundreds of Spanish seamen were killed or wounded. Dewey lost no ships, and only seven of his men were wounded, none seriously.

The news required several days to reach America, as Dewey had cut the submarine cable on the way in, but when it did arrive it made Dewey a national hero and the envy of all those, like Roosevelt, who dreamed of covering themselves in comparable glory. Roosevelt's special worry was that the Spanish would surrender before he bloodied his lance. "Do not make peace until we get Porto Rico," he urged Lodge, presumptively exploiting a loophole in the Teller amendment, which said nothing about Spain's other Caribbean colony. When it became apparent that the War Department had raised far more troops than it could transport to Cuba, Roosevelt grew nearly frantic. He hustled his men from San Antonio to Tampa, the port of embarkation for the invasion across the Florida Strait, and he fought, almost physically, for a place for his regiment aboard one of the transports. He couldn't, however, find space for most of their horses, and the Rough Riders prepared to become weary walkers.[32]

They landed at Daiquirí, on Cuba's south coast, not far from Santiago. The landing was uncontested but nearly disastrous, as almost none of those involved had any experience putting troops ashore on an open beach. Massive confusion resulted in the drowning of many horses and mules but, miraculously, only two men, troopers of the African American Tenth Cavalry.

Santiago was the objective of the invasion, chosen because the city's harbor protected the Spanish Cuban fleet, which American strategists hoped to drive out to sea, where American warships waited. Protecting Santiago were San Juan Hill and the smaller Kettle Hill, so called by the American troops for the large iron vessel, used for boiling sugar cane, they found on top. The Americans assaulted the heights on July 1. Roosevelt led the Rough Riders up Kettle Hill in the face of daunting fire from the Spanish troops' German Mauser rifles, which outclassed the Civil War–era Springfield rifles most of the Americans carried. "The Mauser bullets drove in sheets through the trees and the tall jungle grass, making a peculiar whirring or rustling sound," Roosevelt wrote. "Some of the bullets seemed to pop in the air, so that we thought they were explosive; and, indeed, many of those which were coated with brass did explode, in the sense that the brass coat was ripped off, making a thin plate of hard metal with a jagged edge, which inflicted a ghastly wound."[33]

The Rough Riders took Kettle Hill before joining other American units in the assault on San Juan Hill. The Spanish fought bravely but were badly outnumbered and forced to retreat, leaving the Americans in command of the heights before Santiago, from which their guns could bombard the city and the ships in the harbor. Admiral Pascual Cervera thereupon decided to hazard the open sea. His fleet steamed out into the

Caribbean, only to be crushed by the American ships there. The war might have ended at this point had Lodge and others in Washington not heeded Roosevelt's advice that Puerto Rico must be captured first. Seizing the second island required modest effort and a few more weeks, but on August 12 Spain's representatives in Washington capitulated.

JOHN HAY CALLED IT ironically a "splendid little war," yet that was before the full cost of the conflict became evident. The American war effort wasn't egregiously inefficient by historical military standards, but because the battles went so well, the losses beyond the battlefield loomed large by comparison. American soldiers' experience of the tropics had been limited to the Mexican War, and most of what had been learned at Vera Cruz had been forgotten in the intervening fifty years. Hygiene was abysmal in some of the American camps, reflecting the still rudimentary state of epidemiological knowledge. Malaria, typhoid, yellow fever, and dysentery claimed about twenty-five hundred lives, or ten times the number lost in battle. Refrigerated railcars and ships brought fresh beef almost to the front, but unscrupulous jobbers passed tainted meat—beef injected with chemicals to mask its putridity—off on the troops. The soldiers' complaints eventually produced a public outcry and an investigation of the "embalmed beef" scandal. The commissary general of the army was court-martialed and convicted, although for insulting a fellow officer—Nelson Miles—rather than for poisoning the rank and file.

Theodore Roosevelt led a mutiny against the hazardous conditions in which his men were compelled to live in Cuba. Promoted to colonel of the regiment after Leonard Wood was reassigned, Roosevelt fought as hard against the War Department to obtain proper provisions, clothing, and shelter for his men as he had fought against the Spanish to gain the San Juan Heights. He jumped the chain of command to write Lodge in Washington imploring that the regiment be removed from Cuba as soon as possible, now that the fighting was over, lest more take ill and die. "It is simply infamous to keep us here during the sickly months that are now on and which will last until October," he told Lodge. "If there was need of our holding a town against any foe, I would care not one jot more for yellow fever than for Spanish bullets and would not mind sacrificing the lives of my entire command. But to sacrifice them pointlessly from mere stupidity and inefficiency is cruel." Roosevelt gathered signatures of division and brigade commanders in Cuba on a round-robin letter to the commanding general in Cuba, William Shafter, warning that the army faced destruction from disease. "The army must be moved at once, or perish," Roosevelt and the others wrote. In a separate letter Roosevelt suggested Maine as a suitable landing spot; the men might recuperate there in quarantine till the danger of transmission to the American population passed.[34]

Roosevelt's outspokenness didn't endear him to the careerists at the War Department, who vetoed his nomination for a Medal of Honor. (It was awarded posthumously a century later.) But unlike some of the other signers, Roosevelt didn't intend to remain in the army, and anyway he had nearly all the rewards he could want. From the moment the Rough Riders mustered at San Antonio, reporters followed them like boys behind a circus parade. Richard Harding Davis took a special shine to Roosevelt, featuring him in numerous dispatches home. "Roosevelt, mounted high on horseback, and charging the rifle-pits at a gallop and quite alone, made you feel that you would like to cheer," Davis wrote of the fight for San Juan Hill. "He wore on his sombrero a blue polka-dot handkerchief, à la Havelock, which, as he advanced, floated out straight behind his head like a guidon." Not to be outdone, Roosevelt told his own story in a memoir first serialized in *Scribner's* and then published in book form, bound in khaki, as *The Rough Riders*. The book swelled to bursting with Roosevelt's pride in himself and his men. "Is it any wonder I loved my regiment?" he asked after recounting one gallant deed of many. Reviewers poked fun at Roosevelt's egotism. Rumor claimed that the publisher had run out of the uppercase letter *I* in setting the type. Finley Peter Dunne's Mr. Dooley characterized the book as "Th' Biography iv a Hero be Wan who Knows." Dooley didn't begrudge Roosevelt his turn in the limelight. "If Tiddy done it all he ought to say so an' relieve th' suspinse." But he suggested a new title: "Alone in Cubia."[35]

THE HUMOR SOON wore thin. Dewey's victory at Manila, and a follow-on landing of marines there, gave American forces possession of the Philippine capital but not much else of the archipelago. Filipino nationalists who had fought against the Spanish before the arrival of the Americans protested the new foreign presence and began to challenge it militarily. Nonetheless American and Spanish negotiators signed a treaty in December 1898 transferring title of the Philippines (and Puerto Rico) from Spain to the United States.

McKinley appreciated that annexation of the Philippines might cause trouble, but he couldn't discover a preferable alternative. To withdraw from the islands would leave them at the mercy of Germany, Japan, or some other imperialist power at a time when those countries were making short work of the independence of dozens of poorly defended peoples of Asia and Africa. McKinley was no enthusiast of empire. "If old Dewey had just sailed away when he smashed that Spanish fleet," the president told Herman Kohlsaat, "what a lot of trouble he would have saved us." (When the war began, McKinley had hardly known what ocean the Philippines were in. "I could not have told where those darned islands were within 2,000 miles," he told Kohlsaat.) But after long and careful consideration, he concluded that since Dewey had stayed, so must the United States. "I walked the floor of the White House night after night until midnight," he explained to a visiting group of ministers and missionaries (according to their later recounting).

> And I am not ashamed to tell you, gentlemen, that I went down on my knees and prayed Almighty God for light and guidance more than one night. And one night late it came to me this way—I don't know how it was, but it came: (1) That we could not give them back to Spain—that would be cowardly and dishonorable; (2) that we could not turn them over to France or Germany—our commercial rivals in the Orient— that would be bad business and discreditable; (3) that we could not leave them to themselves—they were unfit for self-government, and they would soon have anarchy and misrule over there worse than Spain's was; and (4) that there was nothing left for us to do but take them all, and to educate the Filipinos, and uplift them and civilize and Christianize them, and by God's grace do the very best we could by them, as our fellow-men for whom Christ also died. And then I went to bed, and went to sleep, and soundly, and the next morning I sent for the chief engineer of the War Department (our map-maker), and I told him to put the Philippines on the map of the United States, and there they are, and there they will stay while I am president![36]

The Spanish treaty provoked a vigorous debate when the Senate considered it for ratification. All the senators and the myriad pundits understood that taking the Philippines would make an empire of the American republic. E. L. Godkin, the editor of the *Nation* and the *New York Evening Post*, thought his countrymen had troubles enough of their own. "We do not want any more states until we can civilize Kansas," he said. He listed the evils attendant to annexation:

> The sudden departure from our traditions; the absence from our system of any machinery for governing dependencies; the admission of alien, inferior, and mongrel races to our nationality; the opening of fresh fields for carpetbaggers, speculators, and corruptionists; the un-Americanism of governing a large body of people against their will, and by persons not responsible to them; the entrance on a policy of conquest and annexation while our own continent was still unreclaimed, our population unassimilated, and many of our most serious political problems still unsolved; and finally the danger of the endorsement of a gross fraud for the first time by a Christian nation.

Empire would be the end of America as Americans knew it, Godkin said. "This triumph over Spain seals the fate of the American republic."[37]

Carl Schurz deplored the embrace of empire as only a refugee from imperial Europe could. "The character and future of the Republic and the welfare of its people now living and yet to be born are in unprecedented jeopardy," Schurz asserted. Americans didn't know what they were getting themselves into. "The Filipinos fought against Spain for their freedom and independence. . . . They will fight against us."

Andrew Carnegie hadn't yet retired from steel-making, but after the bloody battle at Homestead he spent less time at the mill and more in politics and philanthropy. He worried aloud that annexing the Philippines would produce collisions between the United States and the other imperial powers. The first wreck would occur in Asia. "It is in that region the thunderbolt is expected," Carnegie wrote. "It is there the storm is to burst." McKinley boasted of the uplifting influence American civilization would have upon the Filipinos; Carnegie gravely doubted any such effect. "Has the influence of the superior race upon the inferior ever proved beneficial to either? I know of no case in which it has been or is. . . . Soldiers in foreign camps, so far from being missionaries for good, require missionaries themselves more than the natives."

The debate on Capitol Hill revealed similar convictions and prejudices. Lest the United States be accused of stealing the Philippines, the treaty with Spain specified a cash payment to the Spanish government; for this reason the House held hearings on the treaty and let its members weigh in on annexation. Democrat Jehu Baker of Illinois contended that annexation would sully American virtue irretrievably. "The attempt to suddenly sweep us into a colonial policy similar to that of Britain—so suddenly that we scarce have time to note where the leap will carry us—is, in my opinion, the most audacious and reckless performance of jingoism that this or any other country has ever witnessed," Baker said. Jerry Simpson, the bare-ankled Kansas Populist, detected aggrandizement of the most shocking sort in McKinley's imperialism. Annexation would furnish an excuse for the creation of a large army, which would be deployed against the ordinary people of America just as federal troops had been deployed to crush the labor strikes of the previous decade. "This is what they want it for," Simpson asserted, "along with a scheme for colonial empire, and to place on the throne in this country William McKinley, President of the United States, Emperor of the West Indian Islands and of the Philippines."

Other opponents leveled more prosaic complaints against annexation. Henry Johnson of Indiana predicted that the products of the Philippines would enter America tariff-free, doing "immense injury to the American farmer and laborer." Hernando Money of Mississippi took the trade issue in another direction. The key to American prosperity, Money declared, was not colonies but markets. "Are conquests and subjugation necessary to the spread of American products?" he asked. Not at all, he answered. "The commerce of the United States, fortunately for this great Republic, has been founded more wisely upon the skill of its artisans. . . . That which carries American commerce abroad is not the protection of this Government; it is not that the flag of the fighting Navy of the United States is found on every sea and in every port; it is the skill of the American workingman."

Still other objectors took the low road of racism. John Daniel of Virginia asked the Senate if its members understood the intimate consequences of annexation. "Today we are the United States of America. Tomorrow, if a treaty now pending in the Senate is ratified, we will be the United States of America and Asia." This would be no mere political union. "It is a marriage of nations. This twain will become one flesh. They become bone of our bone and flesh of our flesh."

The annexationists countered certain of the objections, ignored others, and generally portrayed the taking of the Philippines as the logical, even inevitable, extension of venerable American traditions. Theodore Roosevelt contended that the United States had won the Philippines as fairly as it had won northern Mexico a half century earlier. "We have hoisted our flag," he said, "and it is not fashioned of the stuff which can be quickly hauled down." Henry Cabot Lodge, who seemed to some the evil genius behind Roosevelt—"Lodge is the Mephistopheles whispering poison into his ear," anti-imperialist Edward Atkinson said—proclaimed that to relinquish the Philippines would be an "act of infamy."[38]

But the most impassioned articulation of the argument for empire came from Albert Beveridge. The Indiana Republican amalgamated Mahanism, Social Darwinism, Manifest Destinarianism, and rampant capitalism in a Senate speech extolling annexation and everything it stood for and promised. "This island empire is the last land left in all the oceans," Beveridge asserted of the Philippines. Its ports and harbors held the key to the "illimitable markets" of China. In that direction lay America's future.

> Our largest trade henceforth must be with Asia. The Pacific is our ocean. More and more Europe will manufacture the most it needs, secure from its colonies the most it consumes. Where shall we turn for consumers of our surplus? Geography answers the question. China is our natural customer. She is nearer to us than to England, Germany, or Russia, the commercial powers of the present and the future. . . . The Philippines gives us a base at the door of all the East. . . . The Philippines command the commercial situation of the entire East.

Beveridge, one of the rare Americans who had actually visited the Philippines, extolled the natural bounty of the islands. "I have cruised more than 2,000 miles through the archipelago, every moment a surprise at its loveliness and wealth. I have ridden hundreds of miles on the islands, every foot of the way a revelation of vegetable and mineral riches." Rice, coffee, sugar, coconuts, hemp, tobacco, and a dozen other commercial crops grew like weeds in the rich soil of Luzon. Hardwood forests cloaked the mountains, which in turn contained coal enough to fuel all the ships of the world. Precious minerals abounded. "I have a nugget of pure gold picked up in its present form on the banks of a Philippine creek. I have gold dust washed out by crude processes of careless natives from the sands of a Philippine stream."

But material considerations were only part of what called America to the Philippines. "It is elemental," Beveridge said. "It is racial. God has not been preparing the English-speaking and Teutonic peoples for a thousand years for nothing but vain and idle self-contemplation and self-admiration. . . . He has made us the master organizers of the world to establish system where chaos reigns. He has given us the spirit of progress to overwhelm the forces of reaction throughout the earth." To take the Philippines, to embrace empire, was to seize America's destiny. "It holds for us all the profit, all the glory, all the happiness possible to man."[39]

THE SENATE AND the House agreed, in substance if not in every detail. In February 1899 the Senate ratified the treaty in a close vote, and the House approved the money by a more comfortable margin. The Philippines and Puerto Rico became American colonies and the United States an empire.

But it was an empire unlike any the world had known. America's capitalist economy comported well enough with imperialism; already England's John A. Hobson was formulating a capitalist explanation of modern imperialism in which he would cite the United States as a prime example. Theodore Roosevelt and his fellow martial enthusiasts might be the public face of American imperialism, Hobson asserted, but they were hardly its driving force. That role went to the big capitalists. "It is Messrs. Rockefeller, Pierpont Morgan, Hanna, Schwab, and their associates who need Imperialism and who are fastening it upon the shoulders of the great Republic of the West. They need Imperialism because they desire to use the public resources of their country to find profitable employment for the capital which otherwise would be superfluous." In Russia, V. I. Lenin would follow Hobson's lead and declare imperialism the "highest stage of capitalism."[40]

One didn't have to be a Hobsonite or a Leninist to note the expansive spirit of American capitalism. Amid the excitement surrounding the war with Spain, Congress in July 1898 approved the annexation of Hawaii (by joint resolution rather than treaty), to the delight of investors in the plantations there (and to the dismay of Grover Cleveland. "Hawaii is ours," the former president wrote Richard Olney. "As I look back upon the first steps in this miserable business, I am ashamed of the whole affair"). In 1899 and 1900, McKinley's secretary of state, John Hay, circulated a pair of notes calling for an "open door" in China, by which Hay meant that Americans' imperialist competitors must neither partition China nor bar American merchants and investors from equal access to the markets of that country.[41]

Yet for all its consonance with capitalism, empire accorded ill with American democracy. The premise of democracy is that people ought to govern themselves; the essence of imperialism is that some of them—those in the colonies—don't. In asserting imperial control over the Philippines and Puerto Rico, Americans denied democracy to Filipinos and Puerto Ricans. The opponents of the Spanish treaty considered this contradiction decisive, but they lost the argument, and the contradiction became embedded in American foreign policy.

To those already inclined to view the American political economy as a battleground between capitalism and democracy, the decision for empire seemed simply one more illustration of capitalism's currently dominant position. This may have overread the result. As the debate over the Spanish treaty demonstrated, capitalists were hardly of one mind regarding empire. Albert Beveridge spoke for those who coveted the resources of the Philippines and the markets of China, yet Andrew Carnegie, whose capitalist credentials none could gainsay, adamantly opposed the imperialist project as productive of future conflict. Capitalism required markets, Carnegie and his like-thinkers acknowledged, but markets might be had without acquiring colonies. Meanwhile some democrats, conspicuously Theodore Roosevelt, were no less enthusiastic for empire than the most imperially ardent investors and market-struck merchants.

Even so, the doubts regarding empire came mostly from the democratic side of the American public mind. If empire could be shown to pay, the capitalists would swallow such qualms as some of them had and pocket their profits. Empire, however, would always nag at the democractic conscience.[42]

Chapter 21

THE APOTHEOSIS OF PIERPONT MORGAN

⸻

For all the attention devoted to empire, the American market remained the preoccupation of the vast majority of American entrepreneurs, especially as the economy revived from the depression of the mid-1890s. Ironically, the McKinley revival revealed that there was something to be said for the monetary theories of the Populists and the Bryan Democrats. The campaign for silver had been, at bottom, a call for a weaker dollar. The dollar did weaken under McKinley, although silver remained unmonetized. New gold strikes in South Africa, Australia, and the Yukon expanded gold production dramatically, as did innovations in refining, particularly the employment of cyanide to separate the precious metal from its base matrix. As the world supply of gold expanded, much of the increment found its way to the United States via trade and investment, allowing the American money supply to grow without resort to silver. By the end of the century the currency question had become almost academic. Not quite four years after the Republicans had hesitated even to mention gold in their party platform, Congress enshrined the yellow metal by means of the Gold Standard Act of 1900, and the country yawned—while the economy boomed.

If the triumph of gold reflected fortunate geology and clever chemistry (albeit chemistry that wreaked environmental havoc on the gold districts), other developments of the period, no less happy for capital, were rooted in the more familiar soil of political economy. The return of prosperity predictably corroded agrarian and labor radicalism. The Populists disappeared, with most being reabsorbed into the Democrats, and labor strikes diminished in frequency and extent. Complaints against the railroads and the trusts didn't end, but with corporate America again manufacturing profits, the capitalists' need to squeeze the workers and small farmers diminished.

The court system, moreover, proved friendlier to capital than at any time since John Marshall in the century's first quarter had sanctified contracts and blessed the Bank of the United States. The bellwether commercial case of the era involved an effort to punish the sugar trust for anticompetitive practices. American sugar refiners had lobbied hard for the McKinley tariff of 1890 and its freeing of imported sugar; their success encouraged them to think bigger, in terms of a monopoly. In 1892 the American Sugar Refining Company, the market leader, acquired four Pennsylvania firms, with the result being a combination that refined 98 percent of America's sugar. Henry Havemeyer, the president of the trust, frankly credited the McKinley tariff with giving him and his collaborators the courage to combine. "Without the tariff I doubt if we should have dared to take the risk of forming the trust," Havemeyer said. "It could have been done, but I certainly should not have risked all I had, which was embarked in the sugar business, in a trust unless the business had been protected as it was by the tariff."[1]

Had the Republicans remained in power, the sugar trust might have continued to receive the undivided protection of government. But after the election of Grover Cleveland, the Justice Department brought suit against the refiners under the Sherman Antitrust Act. The government's case appeared irrefutable; not even John Rockefeller's Standard Oil wielded the market power the sugar trust's 98 percent share afforded it. But the Supreme Court determined in *United States* v. *E. C. Knight Co.* that a monopoly of manufacturing, which it conceded the sugar trust possessed, did not constitute a monopoly of commerce as defined by the Sherman Act and the Constitution. Chief Justice Melville W. Fuller, writing for the eight-man majority, explained:

> Contracts, combinations, or conspiracies to control domestic enterprise in manufacture, agriculture, mining, production in all its forms, or to raise or lower prices or wages, might unquestionably tend to

restrain external as well as domestic trade, but the restraint would be an indirect result, however inevitable, and whatever its extent, and such result would not necessarily determine the object of the contract, combination, or conspiracy.

If the states wanted to restrain such combinations in production, Fuller said, they might do so. But they had not, and therefore the merger could stand.

John Marshall Harlan, unsurprisingly, was the sole dissenter. Harlan thought the majority was splitting hairs on an issue that had already been settled, by no less an authority than the justice for whom he was named. "Commerce, undoubtedly, is traffic, but it is something more; it is intercourse," Harlan quoted John Marshall. And if such intercourse wasn't jeopardized by the sugar trust's stranglehold on manufacturing, Harlan didn't know when it would be. The majority's reading of the Sherman Act rendered antitrust a nullity. "This view of the scope of the act leaves the public, so far as national power is concerned, entirely at the mercy of combinations which arbitrarily control the prices of articles purchased to be transported from one state to another state." Harlan thought democracy deserved better. "In my judgment, the general government is not placed by the Constitution in such a condition of helplessness that it must fold its arms and remain inactive while capital combines, under the name of a corporation, to destroy competition, not in one state only, but throughout the entire country."[2]

THE *KNIGHT* DECISION effectively offered carte blanche to capitalists contemplating additional mergers and acquisitions. During the next several years some two hundred trusts—the term had lost its original, specific meaning and now referred to just about any giant corporation that dominated its market sector—arose in industries as diverse as leather and lead, copper and coal, insurance and machine tools. Some trusts (sugar, oil, leather, coal, insurance) touched individual consumers directly; others (lead, machine tools, farm equipment, transport) pinched producers, who then passed the monopoly prices along.

The trusts didn't always raise prices in absolute terms. In fact consumer prices on average held steady during the second half of the 1890s (after falling by a third since 1870). But prices were almost certainly higher than they would have been in competitive markets. Capitalism wasn't philanthropy; the point of the integration was profit—and power. The integrators aimed to fatten their bottom lines, but they also intended to shelter themselves from the vicissitudes of competition. Having—in many but not all cases—bested their capitalist competitors, the trust makers now sought to rest on their victories, protected by their size and strength from the essential anarchy of the capitalist marketplace.[3]

Of all the mergers of the era, one stood out for its size and for the power it conferred upon its creators. Perhaps predictably, this behemoth of behemoths combined the resources of the grand triumvirate of Gilded Age capitalism: Carnegie, Rockefeller, and Morgan.

Carnegie was still repenting from Homestead. The Pennsylvania town had become synonymous with capitalist oppression, drawing visitors to the site of the 1892 battle. The hard times of the depression punished the place further, leading author Hamlin Garland, for one, to see Homestead as where organized labor went to die. "The town, infamously historic already, sprawled over the irregular hillside, circled by the cold gray river," Garland wrote in 1894.

> On the flats close to the water's edge there were masses of great sheds, out of which grim smoke-stacks rose with a desolate effect, like the black stumps of a burned forest of great trees. Above them dense clouds of sticky smoke rolled heavily away. Higher up the tenement-houses stood in dingy rows, alternating with vacant lots. . . . Everywhere the yellow mud of the street lay kneaded into a sticky mass, through which groups of pale, lean men slouched in faded garments, grimy with the soot and grease of the mills. The town was as squalid and unlovely as could well be imagined, and the people were mainly of the discouraged and sullen type to be found everywhere where labor passes into the brutalizing stage of severity.[4]

Carnegie's steel business suffered, too, during the depression, but not as much as his competitors', and his position in the industry simply grew stronger. He had a scare when Rockefeller, flush with profits so large he couldn't reinvest them all in petroleum, diversified into iron ore. For a time it appeared that the giants of steel and oil would engage in mortal combat. But Rockefeller's heart wasn't in the new venture, and when Carnegie offered to lease Rockefeller's mines and transport the ore via Rockefeller's steamship and rail lines, Rockefeller withdrew. Carnegie congratulated himself, perhaps excessively: "It does my heart good to think I got ahead of John D. Rockefeller on a bargain." Yet *Iron Age*, the industry journal, concurred that Carnegie had made a good deal. "It gives the Carnegie Company a position unequaled by any steel producer in the world," the paper proclaimed.[5]

Rockefeller's position in petroleum was no less dominant. In 1892, responding to an antitrust finding of Ohio's state courts, Rockefeller and his partners had dissolved the Standard Oil trust. But to the dismay of Standard's many critics, the trust simply reorganized under a New Jersey law allowing a corporation to own shares in other corporations. The directors of the companies that had composed the trust became directors of a holding company called Standard Oil (New Jersey), exchanging their shares of the former for shares of the latter. Operations proceeded as before, directed, as ever, by John D. Rockefeller.

Yet the industry was changing, even if its dominant firm was not really. New oil strikes in Southern California shifted the industry's center of gravity west, although the biggest find of the era—the Spindletop gusher southeast of Houston, which blew in at the beginning of 1901—kept it from moving beyond East Texas. Less dramatic though ultimately more revolutionary were the changes on the demand side. Since the early 1880s German engineers Gottlieb Daimler and Karl Benz had been experimenting with gasoline-powered engines mounted on wheeled vehicles of various sorts. By the 1890s the concept had crossed the Atlantic to America, where Henry Ford and others elaborated and improved it. Ford's first motorcar—the "quadricycle," he called it—rolled out of his shop in Detroit in 1896. The car was a sensation with all who saw and rode in it, and Ford returned to the shop to produce more and better machines. In 1899 he offered a two-passenger model that made America's millions of bicyclists reconsider their devotion to exercise.

YET AS FULLY AS Carnegie dominated steel and Rockefeller oil, neither shaped the broader economy as decisively as Morgan, who at times during the 1890s might have been the most powerful person in the country, not excluding the president.

Morgan's power became evident in early 1895 when the Treasury's gold reserve again dipped toward the witching mark of $100 million—and then crashed into the nether region beyond. By the end of January the reserve had shrunk to $50 million; in another week it was down to $40 million, with daily withdrawals running at $2 million and more. Grover Cleveland felt trapped. The president had no choice but to borrow gold if he wished to maintain the credit of the government. But under the circumstances such borrowing would be on terms dictated by the big bankers and would enrage large numbers of Democrats. "Outside the hotbeds of goldbuggery and Shylockism," the Atlanta *Constitution* fulminated, "the people of this country do not care how soon gold payments are suspended." Many Americans, indeed, would have been happy for the government to be forced off gold, as this would compel the acceptance of silver. Cleveland requested new authorization to purchase gold, but the Democratic lame-duck Congress—after the Democrats' 1894 debacle—threw the request back in his face.[6]

Cleveland might have waited for the Republicans to arrive, but the financial markets didn't allow him time. The gold reserve in the Treasury's New York vaults—that part of the government's supply immediately available for redemption—plunged below $10 million. A single large draft could wipe it out, and with it the government's financial credibility.

J. P. Morgan didn't propose to let this happen. Morgan considered himself as much an American patriot as any man, but he believed capitalism a surer guide to the national interest than democracy. Capitalism was predictable; the pursuit of profit enforced reason on men and sifted the able from the incompetent. Democracy was unpredictable; politicians appealed to passion and were rarely held accountable for their mistakes. National interest aside, Morgan's self-interest dictated an effort to rescue the Treasury. He had made his fortune on the rise of the American economy; should that economy implode, he would be one of the big losers.

Accordingly Morgan in early February attached his private railcar to the Congressional Limited and traveled through a snowstorm from New York to Washington. Cleveland learned he was coming and sent Daniel Lamont, his secretary of war and closest adviser, to Union Station to meet him. Cleveland was desperate, but not so desperate as to risk giving Morgan a personal interview, which the Populists and silver Democrats would seize on as a sellout to big capital. Lamont thanked Morgan for coming to Washington but told him he couldn't speak directly to the president. Morgan refused to be put off. "I have come down to Washington to see the president," he said, "and I am going to stay here until I see him."[7]

Within hours Cleveland relented, informing Morgan that he might come to the White House next morning. Morgan telephoned New York for the latest reports before hiking across Lafayette Square to the mansion. He was shown to the president's office, where Cleveland, Treasury secretary John Carlisle, and Attorney General Olney soon joined him. Cleveland initially seemed evasive, not wishing to take the fateful step of asking Morgan for help. He mumbled about a public bond issue that might yet save the Treasury.

Morgan brought him up short. Morgan knew that the subtreasury at New York possessed only $9 million in gold. He had just learned that the subtreasury was about to be served with a draft for $10 million. "If that $10 million draft is presented," Morgan told Cleveland, "you can't meet it. It will be all over before three o'clock."

Cleveland, his mind focused by the desperate news, asked what Morgan suggested.

Morgan proposed that the Treasury sell bonds to a private syndicate he would organize. This syndicate would pay gold for the bonds. The double effect of the deal would be to reverse the outflow of gold from the Treasury and to restore investor confidence in the United States government.

Cleveland was skeptical. Congress had refused to grant him new bonding authority, he reminded Morgan.

Morgan replied that he didn't need new authority. A Civil War law— "section four thousand and something," he said—allowed the Treasury secretary to sell bonds for gold whenever the national interest required. Morgan said he didn't think the law had ever been repealed.

Cleveland turned to the attorney general. "Is that so, Mr. Olney?" he inquired. Olney said he didn't know but would find out at once. He left the room, and returned carrying a volume of the Revised Statutes. Morgan had the number wrong—it was section 3700—but the gist was right. Olney handed the open volume to Cleveland, who examined it carefully and then passed it to Carlisle, who read the pertinent sentence aloud: "The Secretary of the Treasury may purchase coin with any of the bonds or notes of the United States, authorized by law, at such rates and upon such terms as he may deem most advantageous to the public interest." Looking at Morgan and then at Cleveland, Carlisle remarked, "That seems to fit the situation exactly."

Morgan suggested $100 million as a suitable amount for the transaction, but Cleveland refused to go higher than the amount required to restore the Treasury's reserve to the $100 million mark. As the reserve was now a little below $40 million, the banker and the president agreed that Morgan's syndicate would supply the government with 3.5 million ounces of gold, worth $65 million at the current world price, in exchange for thirty-year bonds with a face value of $62 million and paying 4 percent. The syndicate would recoup the $3 million premium by reselling the bonds.

Before they closed the deal, Cleveland asked Morgan a crucial question. "Mr. Morgan," he said, "what guarantee have we that if we adopt this plan, gold will not continue to be shipped abroad, and while we are getting it in, it will go out, so that we will not reach our goal? Will you guarantee that this will not happen?"

Cleveland was asking more than he and the whole federal government had been able to accomplish, and probably more than anyone besides Morgan could credibly promise: to halt the run on the Treasury's gold and restore confidence in the dollar.

Morgan didn't hesitate. "Yes, sir," he told the president. "I will guarantee it during the life of the syndicate. . . . That means until the contract has been concluded and the goal has been reached."[8]

Of course Morgan's guarantee was no stronger than his word. If he failed, Cleveland couldn't well sue him. But in fact Morgan's word was the strongest guarantee Cleveland could have hoped for in the economy's present parlous state. Morgan was marshaling the power of capitalism, which would supply what democracy currently couldn't.

Morgan proved as good as his word. News of the bargain brought immediate relief. Morgan's syndicate included European bankers, who now returned to the Treasury vaults much of the gold they had been withdrawing during the previous months. More important was the psychological support the government drew from its association with Morgan. The word of Cleveland and Carlisle meant nothing to investors at this stage; the word of Morgan meant everything.

The deal received immediate praise from the capitalist classes and their sympathizers. Columbia University president Seth Low lauded Cleveland for holding the line against devaluation. "History will accord to you a place in the struggle as significant as that of General Grant when he vetoed the inflation bill [of 1874]," Low said. Henry Adams declared, with less irony than usual: "I support Pierpont Morgan for President on a distinct monometallic platform."[9]

Yet debtors and Democrats took a different view. When Morgan and his partners resold the bonds, which they had purchased at the equivalent of 104.5, for 112.25, the critics cried theft. William Jennings Bryan branded the deal a sacrifice of the people upon the altar of wealth. Joseph Pulitzer's *World* called it an "excellent arrangement for the bankers." The *World* added, "For the nation it means a scandalous surrender of credit and a shameful waste of substance."

Morgan didn't improve the popular mood by his testimony before a Senate committee summoned to investigate the deal. "What profit did you make on this investment?" Democrat George Vest of Missouri demanded.

"I decline to answer," Morgan responded. He said he would reveal "every detail" of the transaction up to the point where the bonds were paid for by his syndicate. But further he would not go. "What I did with my own property subsequent to that purchase I decline to state."

Nor did he ever tell what he made on the deal. Contemporary and historical estimates ranged from $250,000 to $16 million, conflating all manner of costs and payouts, germane and otherwise, including the expense of marketing the bonds and the shares of Morgan's partners. Whatever he earned directly, it was far less than the indirect benefit he derived from rescuing the dollar. Of course, that was a benefit he shared with the rest of the country—or at least the portion of the country that valued a strong dollar. For the others he accepted no responsibility.[10]

THE TREASURY RESCUE confirmed Morgan's preeminence among the money men, but it was his creation of the U.S. Steel trust that cemented his title as grand master capitalist. Morgan later claimed that entering the steel business wasn't his idea. The plan, he said, grew out of an attack by John Gates, a maker of steel wire, and others on Carnegie's dominant position. "Bet-a-Million" Gates had a reputation for risk; he reportedly once bet a thousand dollars on a raindrop race—on which of two drops rolling down a window would reach the sill first—and won his nickname wagering seven figures on a single horse race. Gates took a gamble that Carnegie's grip on steel could be broken, and he lined up allies, including Elbert Gary, a former judge and the head lawyer for Illinois Steel. The two men approached Morgan for financing. Morgan always asserted that character counted for more with him than collateral. "The first thing is character," he told a congressional committee investigating his lending habits. "Before money or property?" his dubious questioner asked. Yes indeed, Morgan replied. "A man I do not trust could not get money from me on all the bonds in Christendom." Morgan didn't trust the gambling Gates, but he liked Judge Gary, and he consented to back the anti-Carnegie campaign.[11]

Experienced Wall Streeters battened the hatches. The *New York Commercial* declared the Morgan-Gary agreement "the beginning of one of the greatest contests for supremacy that the world has ever seen. It is a fight between a new concern and the Carnegie interests, both backed by almost unlimited capital." But Morgan kept quiet, shunning publicity as he always did. Nor did Carnegie publicly profess to worry. He relied on the company he had built over decades, he said, to defeat the firm Morgan was cobbling together in a fortnight. "Mr. Morgan buys his partners," Carnegie said. "I grow my own." Carnegie was somewhat less sanguine in private. "The situation is grave and interesting," he wrote one of his own-grown partners, company president Charles Schwab. "A struggle is inevitable, and it is a question of the survival of the fittest."[12]

Schwab didn't doubt the Carnegie Company's fitness, but he wasn't sure Darwin provided the appropriate model for the steel industry. Schwab hosted a large dinner for friends and associates at the University Club on Manhattan's Fifty-fourth Street in December 1900, and he invited Morgan to sit beside him at the head table. Carnegie didn't attend, and in his absence Schwab sketched a future for the steel industry based on cooperation rather than competition. The big firms should join forces in the pursuit of maximum efficiency and profits. Schwab's vision appealed to Morgan, as Schwab supposed it would. (Schwab's personal lifestyle held less appeal for Morgan. Schwab shared John Gates's favorite vice, and after a particularly riotous weekend at the gambling tables of Monte Carlo, Schwab jokingly apologized to his by-then partner Morgan: "At least I didn't do it behind closed doors." Morgan rejoined: "That's what closed doors are for.")[13]

Morgan pursued Schwab's suggestion, and during the following weeks the two men imagined what a merged steel company might look like. Their final meeting took place in Morgan's mahogany-paneled library at 219 Madison Avenue, and it included Gates and Robert Bacon, a Harvard classmate of Theodore Roosevelt's, besides Morgan and Schwab. The four men smoked cigars and talked all night; by morning they had reduced the merger impediments to one: Carnegie.

All understood that Carnegie would have to be bought out. The shrewd Scot had never been other than boss since entering the steel business, and his ego could hardly submit to orders, or even suggestions, from Morgan or anyone else. Schwab had reason to think a buyout was possible. Carnegie was spending ever more time on his non-business causes, and his wife, Louise, was entreating him to retire. She told him they had more than enough money and he had nothing left to prove; why not celebrate the new century by letting others break their backs in the corporate trenches?

Louise Carnegie conspired with Schwab against her husband. Shortly after Schwab informed her of the merger scheme, she telephoned to say that Carnegie would be playing golf the next morning at the St. Andrews club in Westchester. He was always more cooperative after winning at the Scottish national sport, she suggested. Schwab took the hint, whiffed a few for the cause, and broached the subject of selling. Carnegie didn't reject the plan outright, which Schwab took to be a good sign. Carnegie said he'd think it over.

The next morning he gave Schwab his answer. In the stubby pencil he habitually carried, he outlined his terms: $480 million for the Carnegie Company and all its holdings.

Schwab took Carnegie's offer straight to Morgan. The banker prided himself on never dickering; when he saw something he wanted—a piece of real estate, a work of art, a corporation—he asked the owner to name a price. If Morgan deemed the price fair, he paid it. If not, he walked away. Morgan glanced at the paper Schwab carried and accepted Carnegie's price at once.

Several days later Morgan visited Carnegie to close the deal personally. The banker and the steel man had never been friendly, and they weren't now. But as Morgan shook Carnegie's hand, he said, "Mr. Carnegie, I want to congratulate you on being the richest man in the world."[14]

JOHN ROCKEFELLER MIGHT have disputed Morgan's characterization—his net worth was close to Carnegie's, if less liquid—and he might have spoiled Morgan's merger. Rockefeller still held iron mines independent of Carnegie's, and while he had no present plans to expand downstream into refining or production, the profits that kept pouring in from Standard Oil made it possible for him to do so on short notice. Elbert Gary warned Morgan that Rockefeller had to be neutralized if the new steel combine were to be secure.

Morgan at first refused. "We have got all we can attend to," he told Gary. But Gary reiterated that Rockefeller was too dangerous to leave out. The new firm must have Rockefeller's iron mines.

"How are we going to get them?" Morgan inquired unenthusiastically.

"You are going to talk to Mr. Rockefeller," Gary said.

"I would not think of it."

"Why?"

"I don't like him."

Morgan's dislike for Rockefeller was well known, as was the fact that Rockefeller reciprocated. The two men had first met at the home of William Rockefeller, John's brother. "We had a few pleasant words," Rockefeller remembered. "But I could see that Mr. Morgan was very much— well, like Mr. Morgan: very haughty, very much inclined to look down on other men." Morgan thought Rockefeller a desiccated prig, too devout and too devoted to business at the cost of the finer things in life. He doubtless also begrudged Rockefeller's success in financing the growth of Standard Oil without recourse to banks or bondsmen.

Gary appreciated Morgan's animus toward Rockefeller, though he didn't share it. And now he refused to allow it to intrude on the matter at hand. "Mr. Morgan," he said, "when a business proposition of so great importance to the Steel Corporation is involved, would you let a personal prejudice interfere with your success?"

"I don't know," Morgan replied.

Eventually Morgan came around. He asked Rockefeller if he might drop by his office. Rockefeller, fully aware of how much Morgan needed him, told Morgan he was retired and didn't go to the office. Morgan could come to Rockefeller's home. When Morgan did so, they made awkward small talk till Morgan thrust to the point: How much did Rockefeller want for his mines?

Rockefeller put Morgan off. He said again that he was retired; Morgan would have to talk to his son, John Jr. Morgan, miffed, muttered that the boy could come to his Wall Street office.

He did so near the end of February 1901. Morgan made him wait while he completed some inconsequential business. Finally he looked up and growled, "What's your price?"

He was taken aback when Junior affected surprise. "Mr. Morgan," he said, "I think there must be some mistake. I did not come here to sell. I understood you wished to buy." Junior's boldness with Morgan surprised his father, when the old man heard of it. He hadn't thought the boy had it in him. "Great Caesar," he chortled to his wife. "John is a trump!" Yet Junior's diffidence accurately reflected the elder Rockefeller's honest attitude toward the incipient steel trust. After further jousting Junior and Morgan agreed to appoint Henry Frick as arbitrator, to establish a price for the Rockefeller mines. "As my son told Mr. Morgan," Rockefeller explained to Frick, "I am not anxious to sell my own properties. But as you surmise, I never wish to stand in the way of a worthy enterprise."

Frick was an unlikely choice for arbitrator, being famously blunt and opinionated. He and Carnegie were partners for a decade but never friends, and after Carnegie spent the latter 1890s hanging Homestead on him, they parted acrimoniously. Even years later Frick held a grudge. The aging Carnegie sent a messenger to Frick suggesting a reconciliation; Frick responded, "Tell Mr. Carnegie I'll meet him in hell." But Frick and the Rockefellers got along well, perhaps because they all disliked Carnegie. Frick proposed a generous price for the Rockefeller mines. Rockefeller probably would have accepted the proposal on its own merits, but he received encouragement from new, secret evidence suggesting the existence of large iron deposits outside the region he controlled.

The result was the deal Morgan had sought. Rockefeller sold the iron mines for $80 million and his fleet of ore boats for another $8.5 million. With this last piece in place, Morgan in March 1901 announced the creation of the United States Steel Corporation. Capitalized at $1.4 billion, the steel trust surpassed Rockefeller's Standard Oil to become the largest corporation in the world. With its armies of workers, fleets of ships and barges, thousands of railcars, tens of thousands of acres of coal and iron properties, and hundreds of millions of dollars of plant and equipment, it dominated the most basic industry in modern America.

"Pierpont Morgan is apparently trying to swallow the sun," Henry Adams remarked.[15]

THE DEMOCRATIC COUNTERREVOLUTION

A nd the moon too, as it turned out. Not long after closing the deal with Carnegie and Rockefeller, Morgan sailed for France on his annual vacation and art-hunting expedition. He bagged a Raphael altarpiece, the *Colonna Madonna*, and some smaller game in Paris before retiring to Aix-les-Bains. There, in early May, he received a cable from New York explaining that unknown raiders had mounted an assault on the Northern Pacific Railroad.

Morgan's tie to the Northern Pacific dated from the 1880s, when he had rescued it from collapse and reorganized its finances. The revival of the road attracted the unfavorable attention of James J. Hill, whose Great Northern competed with the Northern Pacific for traffic between Chicago and the Pacific Northwest. Hill knocked heads with Morgan for a time, till the two arranged a truce. Hill purchased 10 percent of the Northern Pacific, which, with the larger portion Morgan commanded, gave the Morgan-Hill alliance effective control of the line.

Or so Morgan thought until May 1901, when the raid on the Northern Pacific that disrupted his vacation began. Morgan's spies soon discovered the identity of the raider: Edward H. Harriman, who had swooped down to grab the Union Pacific after the Panic of 1893 and followed this coup by snatching the Southern Pacific from the successors of Leland

Stanford. Harriman's ambition appeared boundless; he sought nothing less than a continental empire of rails. Already he controlled the southwestern quarter of the country; with the Northern Pacific he could reach the Canadian border.

Harriman's challenge to Morgan and Hill triggered a frenzy in rail stocks. Day after day the market set records for volume as share prices soared and plunged. "Titans Fight for Control of Big Road," a typical headline blared. As the nature of the contest grew clear, outside speculators placed their bets on the contenders, raising the stakes still more. Northern Pacific shares doubled in price in three days, then doubled again and again, topping 1,000 before plummeting 400 points in mere seconds. "Brokers acted like insane men," the *New York Times* reported. "Big men lightly threw little men aside, and the little men, fairly crying with indignation, jumped anew into the fray, using hands, arms, elbows, feet—anything to gain their point. And, all the while, there was such yelling and shouting as had not been heard even on the recent wildest days in the Street. . . . It was something incomprehensible, almost demonic—this struggle, this Babel of voices, these wild-eyed, excited brokers, selling and buying, buying and selling."[1]

The battle left Wall Street strewn with the wreckage of speculation, and in the end only Morgan and Hill, on one side, and Harriman, on the other, remained standing. As the dust settled they discovered they owned, between them, $79 million of the $80 million of Northern Pacific common stock. They also discovered a shared interest in averting another such contest. Morgan returned from Europe to organize a holding company called Northern Securities, subsuming his and Hill's Northern Pacific shares, Hill's Great Northern shares, and Harriman's stake in Northern Pacific. Its $400 million market capitalization made it second in size only to Morgan's other recent creation, U.S. Steel.[2]

THE CAPITALIST REVOLUTION was in many ways the best thing ever to befall the ordinary people of America. The country's population grew from 40 million in 1870 to 76 million in 1900, with the two-thirds of that growth derived from natural increase reflecting the healthful, hopeful conditions among those already in America, and the one-third from immigration the belief of the newcomers that they might share the natives' health and hope. Infant mortality declined by a third; life expectancy increased by a seventh (to nearly fifty years for whites; blacks died about a decade sooner). The nation's total output tripled in real terms; average per capita income nearly doubled. The portion of the workforce engaged in agriculture fell by almost half (till scarcely one worker out of three toiled on a farm), but that smaller group, employing machinery like the equipment showcased on the bonanza farms of North Dakota, outproduced their forebears by a substantial margin. Productivity gains among the nonfarm workforce were even more dramatic, as electricity gradually supplanted steam power, freeing tools from their tethering to central plants and allowing a closer fit between workers and their tasks.[3]

Electricity transformed life beyond the workplace as well. Edison's electric bulbs, energized by Westinghouse's dynamos, displaced Rockefeller's kerosene from the lamp stands of America. Telephones were common, though hardly universal. Phonographs played scratchy but recognizable music. Movies were migrating from the small screen of the kinetoscope to the large screen of the movie theater. Electric fans cooled public buildings and some private homes during the summer. Willis Carrier was working on his first air conditioner; an alternative design, installed in 1902, lowered temperatures and tempers on the New York Stock Exchange.

Loss of the lighting market for kerosene might have worried Rockefeller if not for the prospect of a new, much larger market for another petroleum product. The automobiles of Henry Ford and others were just beginning to pour from shops and factories in Detroit and elsewhere; besides affording Americans unprecedented freedom of movement, the gasoline-powered cars guaranteed huge and lasting growth in the demand for oil. Another new market was merely a gleam in the eyes of Orville and Wilbur Wright, who bolted a gasoline engine onto an ungainly machine that nonetheless flew at Kitty Hawk, North Carolina, in 1903. The airplane industry would be much slower lifting off than the car business, but in time the planes too would guzzle large quantities of petroleum derivatives (in particular, oddly enough, kerosene). Railroads stuck to proven steam technology (diesel-electric engines wouldn't catch on for another two decades), but their networks continued to ramify across the country until hardly a hamlet couldn't be reached by rail. The trains traveled underground in Boston, where America's first subway opened in 1897, and would do so soon in New York, where construction crews started digging for the Interborough Rapid Transit system in 1900.

Besides passengers, the trains carried freight, including much of the food that allowed Americans to eat better than almost anyone else on earth. Refrigerated cars brought fresh meat to tables far from slaughterhouses and fruits and vegetables from the winter gardens of Florida, Texas, Arizona, and California to the pantries of the snow belt. Other cars carried wheat to Minneapolis, where it was ground into flour of a fineness the mothers and grandmothers of turn-of-the-century homemakers would have given their favorite pie pans for. When Americans wearied of traditional fare, they could partake of cuisines imported by immigrants from China, Italy, Greece, Poland, Russia, and a dozen other countries.

Housing continued to improve, albeit more rapidly in some cities and neighborhoods than in others. Apartments still attracted the young and single, but families increasingly caught on to the savings and convenience of vertical integration in living quarters. In 1901 New York passed another tenement law, mandating more space, light, and air. This law was more effectively enforced than some earlier versions; the most dramatic result was a steep decline in the New York City death rate, which fell by a third during the next decade and a half.

Americans at the turn of the century traveled more than they ever had before. They traveled on business but increasingly for pleasure. Faster and more comfortable trains made domestic journeys more attractive; falling ticket prices made them more widely available. Yet the most rapid growth was in foreign travel. In 1900 nearly 125,000 American tourists ventured across the oceans, mostly to Europe. Although this was less than 1 percent of the population, it was four times the number of overseas tourists in 1870. Americans traveled to Canada and Mexico as well; although no one kept track of the number of such tourists, their expenditures nearly quintupled between 1870 and 1900, suggesting a surge comparable to that in transoceanic travel.[4]

Education became more widely available during the final decades of the nineteenth century. In Chicago, seats in public schools multiplied eight-fold between 1870 and 1900, to accommodate the waves of immigrants from overseas and in-migrants from the countryside and to allow students to stay in school longer. Other cities and towns expanded school facilities commensurately. By 1900 nearly eight out of ten young people of school age (five years old to seventeen) attended school, and the proportion of high school graduates was three times what it had been in 1870 (with girls greatly outnumbering boys, who frequently left school early for jobs). Illiteracy had fallen by half, to 10 percent of the juvenile and adult population (although nearly 45 percent of blacks remained illiterate).[5]

Post-secondary education blossomed. The number of colleges and universities increased dramatically (to nearly a thousand), with many of the largest new schools being public universities established under the terms of the Morrill Act of 1862. Private colleges funded by the great capitalists (including Vanderbilt University, Stanford University, and the University of Chicago, by John D. Rockefeller) challenged the older private colleges for preeminence. In 1900 nearly 240,000 young people attended college; although this figure was less than 5 percent of the population between eighteen and twenty-four years of age, it was twice the percentage of thirty years earlier. Many of the new colleges admitted women as well as men; some (such as Vassar, Wellesley, Smith, Bryn Mawr) admitted only women. African Americans joined whites at many of the new and certain of the old schools; they also attended colleges (Howard, Morehouse, and Spelman, among others) dedicated specifically to teaching young blacks.[6]

YET FOR ALL the advances in American material and cultural life, there remained a feeling that things had gone wrong, that—as the North Carolina farm editor had said—a screw had come loose and the wheels fallen out of balance. Prosperity was precarious, as the recent depression had revealed. Inequality—the distance between the segment of society headed by the Vanderbilts in their gaudy mansion and Jacob Riis's other half in the alleys around the corner—was more obvious than ever. The capitalists controlled the government: the legislative branch, which protected their profits with tariffs and their assets with a gold standard; the executive branch, which dispatched troops to crush the capitalists' working-class opponents; and the judicial branch, which defined dissent as conspiracy and monopoly as accepted practice. The trusts grew more numerous and more powerful by the month. In the contest between capitalism and democracy, capitalism had never enjoyed such a formidable advantage.

But the contest wasn't over, and as the new century began, democracy showed fresh signs of life. A first stirring—a strong kick, in fact—followed the bursting of Theodore Roosevelt upon the national consciousness. Roosevelt parlayed his celebrity from the Spanish war into the Republican nomination for governor of New York in 1898, when Tom Platt, the New York Republican boss, required a clean candidate to replace his soiled incumbent. Roosevelt campaigned with an entourage of Rough Riders, who blew the bugle and testified to the valor of their colonel. Roosevelt won, although not by much, and Platt assumed he'd follow orders the way the boss's other placemen did. But Roosevelt revealed an independent streak that persuaded Platt to find another governor at first opportunity. He contrived to foist Roosevelt upon the national party at the convention of 1900, which nominated Roosevelt for vice president to replace the deceased Garret Hobart. Most delegates thought little about the matter, knowing that the vice presidency, by long custom, conferred nothing but terminal anonymity on nearly all those who held the office. Mark Hanna, however, assumed the worst. "Don't any of you realize that there's only one life between that madman and the presidency?" he thundered.[7]

Hanna's nightmare materialized in September 1901. Leon Czolgosz, an anarchist of Polish descent and unstable mind, determined to commence the overthrow of the capitalist system by murdering McKinley. On September 6 at the Pan American Exposition in Buffalo, he shot the president twice at short range. McKinley survived the shooting but not the infection. He died on September 14.[8]

Roosevelt received the news atop Mt. Marcy in the Adirondacks. He raced to Buffalo to pay his respects and take the oath as McKinley's successor. "It is a dreadful thing to come into the presidency this way," he wrote Henry Cabot Lodge. "But it would be a far worse thing to be morbid about it. Here is the task, and I have got to do it to the best of my ability; and that is all there is about it."[9]

Roosevelt initially pledged to carry out the policies of his predecessor. One wit who knew Roosevelt suggested that he would indeed carry out McKinley's policies—much as people carry out their garbage. Roosevelt's actions soon made the joke seem true. In his first annual message, in December 1901, he acknowledged America's debt to capitalism and its leaders. "The captains of industry who have driven the railway systems across this continent, who have built up our commerce, who have developed our manufactures, have on the whole done great good to our people," he declared. Moreover, capitalism functioned best when unburdened by excessive regulation. "The mechanism of modern business is so delicate that extreme care must be taken not to interfere with it in a spirit of rashness or ignorance." Yet the capitalists needed to understand and acknowledge the debt they owed to democracy. "Great corporations exist only because they are created and safeguarded by our institutions; and it is therefore our right and our duty to see that they work in harmony with these institutions."[10]

Roosevelt moved rapidly from warning the capitalists to attacking them. In February 1902 he directed the Justice Department to bring an antitrust suit against Northern Securities, the Morgan railroad combine.

Morgan received the news badly. Having several times rescued, as he saw it, the American railroad system from self-inflicted disaster and the financial markets from full-blown panic, he thought he deserved gratitude, not sanction, from the government. At the very least he expected the kind of consideration other presidents, in particular Grover Cleveland, had accorded him. He once again made the journey from Wall Street to Washington. Roosevelt, unlike Cleveland, had no compunctions about a face-to-face meeting. Morgan cut straight to the point. "If we have done something wrong," he said, regarding the railroad trust, "send your man to my man and they can fix it up."

"That can't be done," Roosevelt replied. The president turned to Philander Knox, his attorney general (and a railroad lawyer by profession), who added, "We don't want to fix it up. We want to stop it."

"Are you going to attack my other interests?" Morgan demanded. "The steel trust and the others?"

"Certainly not," Roosevelt said, "unless we find out that in any case they have done something that we regard as wrong."

Morgan left angry, whereupon Roosevelt remarked to Knox, "That is a most illuminating illustration of the Wall Street point of view. Mr. Morgan could not help regarding me as a big rival operator who either intended to ruin all his interests or else could be induced to come to an agreement to ruin none."[11]

Roosevelt proceeded to prove he wasn't an operator but the chief executive of a democratic government. He pushed the Northern Securities prosecution forward and won a signal victory in 1904 when the Supreme Court, which included four justices new since the *Knight* decision, ordered the dismantling of the railroad trust. John Marshall Harlan, the veteran dissenter, wrote the opinion for the 5 to 4 majority.

This breakthrough for democratic oversight of corporate capitalism gave rise to other antitrust prosecutions. Ida Tarbell had nursed her father's grudge against John Rockefeller for decades; starting in November 1902 she published a nineteen-part exposé of Standard Oil in *McClure's Magazine*. Tarbell's indictment spurred the newly created federal Bureau of Corporations to conduct its own investigation and Roosevelt's Justice Department in 1906 to file an antitrust suit. Other legal actions followed, including prosecution for accepting banned rebates. One such case yielded the largest fine in American history till then: $29 million. Rockefeller learned of the decision amid a round of golf; unruffled, he kept playing and shot one of his best scores ever. (Mark Twain's reaction was more newsworthy. He quoted a bride on the morning after: "I expected it, but didn't suppose it would be so big.") The coup de grâce came four years later when the Supreme Court ordered Standard Oil dissolved. This time Harlan had more company; the decision was unanimous.[12]

WHILE ROOSEVELT ASSAULTED the citadel of capitalism by design, he affronted the racial mores of the South by accident. Just weeks after entering the White House he brought Booker Washington to dinner. Washington remained the most prominent African American in the country, although his position didn't go unchallenged. Six years after his Atlanta exposition speech—by now commonly called his "Atlanta Compromise" speech—and five years after the Supreme Court's *Plessy* decision, the rights of African Americans were under increasing attack. John Marshall Harlan's prediction that segregated railcars would lead to segregated streetcars and courtrooms and public halls was coming true. Ever more were Southern blacks treated as a caste apart, with predictable effects on blacks in the rest of the country.

Rival voices to Washington's protested the trend; of these W. E. B. Du Bois's carried the farthest. Massachusetts-born and Harvard-educated, Du Bois was as different from Booker Washington as a black man in America could be, and his comparatively privileged background informed his rejection of Washington's accommodationist philosophy. In 1901 he was teaching at Atlanta University and writing his first book, *The Souls of Black Folks*, which devoted a whole chapter to Booker Washington and drew invidious comparisons between the schoolmaster of Tuskegee and the black rebels Denmark Vesey and Nat Turner. Washington placed too much emphasis on economics, Du Bois said, till his program became "a gospel of Work and Money." And Washington put entirely too much faith in capitalists. "Through the pressure of the money-makers, the Negro is in danger of being reduced to semi-slavery, especially in the country districts." Du Bois didn't deny that Washington's vision encompassed certain positive traits. "So far as Mr. Washington preaches Thrift, Patience, and Industrial Training for the masses, we must hold up his hands and strive with him, rejoicing in his honors and glorying in the strength of this Joshua called of God and of man to lead the headless host." But his subordination of black democratic rights to the imperatives of the capitalist marketplace made his preaching ultimately pernicious.

> So far as Mr. Washington apologizes for injustice, North or South, does not rightly value the privilege and duty of voting, belittles the emasculating effects of caste distinctions, and opposes the higher training and ambition of our brighter minds—so far as he, the South, or the Nation, does this—we must unceasingly and firmly oppose them. By every civilized and peaceful method we must strive for the rights which the world accords to men, clinging unwaveringly to those great words which the sons of the Fathers would fain forget: "We hold these truths to be self-evident: That all men are created equal; that they are endowed by their Creator with certain unalienable rights; that among these are life, liberty, and the pursuit of happiness."[13]

Yet even though Washington was losing the "talented tenth," as Du Bois called the educated elite of African Americans, he remained a leading figure of Southern Republican politics, and for this reason his opinions mattered to politicians like Roosevelt. The then–vice president had planned a visit to Tuskegee for September 1901, but the shooting of McKinley canceled it. Roosevelt nonetheless still wanted to talk to Washington—about Republican patronage in the South and the election in 1904—and after becoming president he invited him to the White House for dinner.

The meal was objectively innocuous. Roosevelt's wife and four of their children joined the president, Washington, and longtime Roosevelt friend and hunting partner Philip Stewart of Colorado. The table topics included politics and the affairs of the South generally. At evening's end Roosevelt bade the guests good night, went to bed, and slept the sound Roosevelt sleep of moral self-assurance and physical exhaustion.

He awoke the next morning to the self-righteous rage of the white South. That the president had dined with a Negro insulted almost every man, child, and especially woman on the white side of Jim Crow's color line. "White men of the South, how do you like it?" spluttered the *New Orleans Times-Democrat*. "White women of the South, how do YOU like it?" The *Richmond Times* extrapolated from the dining room to the bedroom in interpreting Washington's visit: "It means that the President is willing that negroes shall mingle freely with whites in the social circle— that white women may receive attentions from negro men; it means that there is no racial reason in his opinion why whites and blacks may not marry and intermarry, why the Anglo-Saxon may not mix negro blood with his blood." The *Raleigh Post* put its outrage to rhyme:

> Booker Washington holds the boards—
> The President dines a nigger.
> Precedents are cast aside—
> Put aside with vigor.
> Black and white sit side by side,
> As Roosevelt dines a nigger.[14]

Roosevelt hadn't intended to spark a firestorm in Dixie. "No one could possibly be as astonished as I was," he wrote a British friend. The very Southerners who were now excoriating him for breaking bread with Washington were the ones who had held Washington up as a model of racial common sense. Though Roosevelt's mother was a Georgian, he had never spent much time in the South; but even if he had, the experience might not have prepared him for the current explosion. Southern attitudes were changing rapidly. As the color line carved more deeply into the Southern psyche, the consequences of crossing it grew more pronounced. Not even the president could avoid them. Roosevelt indignantly denounced his critics and pledged to ignore them. "The idiot or vicious Bourbon element of the South is crazy because I have had Booker T. Washington to dine," he said. "I shall have him to dine just as often as I please."[15]

In practice, however, it pleased Roosevelt not to have Washington to dine again. The president didn't know Washington personally; his interest in Washington was purely political. And when Washington proved a polit-ical liability, Roosevelt let him drop.

Washington apparently understood. Politics was politics, and racial politics in America at the beginning of the twentieth century was as strange as politics got. Anyway, making it to the White House even once for dinner was quite an accomplishment for the slave boy from Virginia.

As the Booker Washington flap faded, other troubles remained for Roosevelt. The most vexing involved the project of which Roosevelt had been most hopeful: imperialism. Almost coincident with the Senate ratification of the Philippine treaty with Spain, Filipino nationalists raised the flag of revolt against American rule. The nationalists had fought against the Spanish before the arrival of Dewey; they now directed their fire against the new imperialists. For several months the fighting pro-ceeded more or less conventionally, with the nationalists, under Emilio Aguinaldo, challenging the Americans in pitched battles. But as more American troops arrived in the islands, the nationalists shifted to a guerrilla strategy. Aguinaldo dispersed his troops, who ambushed and otherwise harassed the Americans. Before long the Americans found themselves in much the same position the Spanish had occupied in Cuba, and they resorted to a chillingly similar strategy. Filipino peasants were herded into camps, where they fell victim to deprivation and disease. American soldiers and their Filipino collaborators, especially the notorious Macabebe Scouts, employed torture against captured nationalists. The most feared technique was the "water cure," involving gallons of water forced down the throats of prisoners till their bellies burst or they talked. Yet the insurgency contin-ued. General Jacob Smith—"Hell-roarin' Jake"—grew exasperated at the ability of the insurgents to blend into the populace and ordered his men to make a "howling wilderness" of their sector. "I want no prisoners," Smith said. "I wish you to kill and burn. The more you kill and burn the better you will please me. I want all persons killed who are capable of bearing arms in actual hostilities against the United States." One of Smith's subordinates asked if there was any lower age limit for this order. "Ten years," Smith replied.[16]

The American atrocities may or may not have contributed to the eventual defeat of the insurgents. Internal squabbling played a role as well. Roosevelt, by now president, declared victory on July 4, 1902. But the Philippine war had exacted a heavy toll. More than four thousand Americans died and thousands more were wounded—a substantially higher cost than the American war against Spain had entailed. The Filipino casualties were many times greater than the American.

A different sort of casualty was Americans' enthusiasm for empire. The reports of the atrocities stabbed the American democratic conscience, making unmistakable the contradiction between the self-government Americans demanded for themselves and the colonialism they were imposing upon the Filipinos. At the same time, the unexpected costs of the Philippine war persuasively rebutted the bottom-line arguments for empire that had appealed to the capitalist spirit in America. The result was a reversal of American attitudes that was almost as swift and stunning as the turn toward empire had been. The United States didn't relinquish the Philippines for four more decades; as often happens in imperial relationships, getting out proved much more complicated than getting in. But never again would formal empire seriously tempt Americans; never again would they endorse a venture so blatantly at odds with the ideals of democracy.

Roosevelt rarely admitted to second thoughts in himself, and he didn't admit to any regarding the Philippines. Yet he reflected others' rethinking when he said, "In the excitement of the Spanish War people wanted to take the islands. They had an idea they would be a valuable possession. Now they think they are of no value." In fact they were of less than no value. Possession of the Philippines drew the United States into the imperial coils of Asia, prompting Roosevelt to lament, "The Philippines form our heel of Achilles."[17]

J. P. MORGAN died in 1913, and his friends thought they knew what did him in. Morgan had rescued the country once more in 1907, when another financial panic had threatened to recapitulate the destruction of

1873 and 1893. This time Roosevelt didn't wait for Morgan to come to Washington; as soon as the Knickerbocker Trust Company—the 1907 equivalent of Jay Cooke & Company in 1873—failed, the president rushed his Treasury secretary to New York. Roosevelt still distrusted Morgan's motives, but he couldn't deny Morgan's power, and he authorized George Cortelyou to give Morgan whatever he needed to keep the financial panic from engulfing the whole economy. Morgan added this democratic vote of confidence to the influence he already wielded among the capitalists and by promises, threats, and liquid cash held the situation together.

His performance earned him no more gratitude than his comparable action in 1895 had. The political heights were increasingly occupied by progressives—democratic skeptics of capitalism—who took Morgan's latest success as additional evidence of his irresponsible power. In 1912 Congress conducted investigations into what the progressives called the "money trust." Democrat Arsène Pujo of Louisiana led the probe, which uncovered the tangle of interlocking directorates that provided J. P. Morgan & Company the financial intelligence that had long been the secret of Morgan's power. Morgan himself took the witness stand, but despite a rigorous interrogation by the counsel for the investigative committee, he admitted to nothing improper.

Yet the experience told on his health. Early the next year, on a Mediterranean holiday, he suddenly fell ill and died. (It was shortly after this that Andrew Carnegie commiserated with the heirs on Morgan's comparative penury.)

With Morgan gone the progressives moved to prevent anyone from taking his place. Roosevelt had departed the White House in 1909 to hunt big game in Africa ("Let every lion do its duty," Morgan was supposed to have said). Roosevelt left the presidency in what he thought were the reliably progressive hands of William Howard Taft. But Taft lacked the political flamboyance of Roosevelt, and such victories as he won for democracy over capitalism—including the final judgment against Rockefeller's Standard Oil—failed to satisfy Roosevelt and most other progressives. Roosevelt challenged Taft for the 1912 Republican nomination; when he lost that, he bolted the GOP for the Progressive, or Bull Moose, party. Many Republicans followed him. The defection afforded the Democrats their first good chance to capture the White House since 1892, and Woodrow Wilson exploited the opportunity by pledging to dismantle the money trust. "The control of the system of banking and of issue"—of money—"which our new laws are to set up must be public, not private, must be vested in the Government itself, so that the banks may be the instruments, not the masters, of business and of individual enterprise and initiative," Wilson declared.[18]

As president Wilson delivered what he'd promised. The Federal Reserve Act of 1913 took effective control of the nation's money supply away from capitalists like Morgan and bestowed it upon the presidentially nominated and senatorially approved Federal Reserve Board. No single reform ever shifted the balance between American capitalism and democracy more decisively. For the first time in its history, the United States had a central bank answerable to the country's democratic institutions. The linkage was deliberately loose: once appointed, the Federal Reserve governors were essentially beyond recall. This freedom prudently insulated them from political pressure. Yet their responsibility was not to the shareholders of the member Reserve banks but to the people of the United States.

Wilson complemented his de-Morganization of American monetary policy with a de-McKinleyfication of the tariff. Like other progressives—and citing no less an authority than sugar truster Henry Havemeyer—Wilson contended that "the tariff made the trusts." To weaken the trusts he proposed to revise the tariff. The objects of his attack—the producers of nearly every protected item on the list of thousands—screamed in pain, predicted the ruin of the economy, and vowed revenge at the ballot box. But Wilson and the Democrats plunged ahead, effecting the first serious reduction of the tariff in twenty years.

As a third prong of his anti-capitalist offensive, Wilson rewrote the rules of antitrust policy. For all the symbolism of the breakup of Standard Oil, other monopolies—with lower profiles or better lawyers—continued to conduct business more or less as usual. Some progressive antitrusters demanded broad legislation outlawing restrictive trade practices; others preferred the flexibility of a federal commission empowered to tailor rules to particular industries. Wilson, on the counsel of Louis Brandeis, his economics tutor, ultimately opted for the commission, which likewise suited a majority of Congress. In 1914 Wilson signed the measure that created the Federal Trade Commission. Yet those progressives who called for a broad law weren't left empty-handed. The Clayton Act of 1914, while less rigorous than Senator Henry Clayton of Alabama had intended, marked a substantial advance—or setback, as laissez faire capitalists viewed it—from the Sherman Act of 1890.

Wilson might have done still more on behalf of democracy against capitalism, but the troubles in Europe that exploded into war in 1914 distracted him, then preoccupied him, and finally shattered his presidency (and his health). The Republican reaction of the 1920s reversed democracy's advance, with Calvin Coolidge declaring that "the business of America is business" and most Americans apparently agreeing. But capitalism undid itself in the Great Crash of 1929 and the Great Depression that followed, leaving Franklin Roosevelt to sweep into office on a mandate to employ the tools of democracy to remedy the failures of capitalism. During the Hundred Days of the early New Deal he and the Democratic majority in Congress raced to do just that—their hurry reflecting, in some, a fear that the democratic momentum would diminish before capitalism was fully reformed and restrained, and, in others, a concern that capitalism would collapse before democracy could shore it up.

BY THEN NEARLY all the heroes—or villains—of the capitalist revolution were gone. Jay Gould had died in 1892, unmourned by any save his family. "He was an incarnation of cupidity and sordidness—nothing nobler, nothing more," the *New York World* observed. Andrew Carnegie lived nearly two decades after selling his steel company to Morgan. He never quite washed away the bloodstains from the Homestead debacle, although the $350 million he gave to literacy, world peace, and numerous other worthy causes bought him as much earthly forgiveness as a man could ask. He died in 1919—just four months before Henry Frick, who may have hastened to meet the infernal appointment he had forecast for himself and his Homestead accomplice.[19]

John D. Rockefeller survived the longest, well into the age of the second Roosevelt. Many years earlier he had handed control of his business interests to his son, who darkened the family name by brutally mishandling a coal strike at Ludlow, Colorado, during the spring of 1914. Militiamen in the pay of the Rockefellers assaulted miners and their families with machine guns and torches, killing twenty, including a dozen women and children. The Ludlow massacre became to the Rockefellers what Homestead had been to Carnegie, a symbol of ruthless capitalism crushing the ordinary people of America.[20]

Like Carnegie, Rockefeller sought absolution by lavish philanthropy. At his death in 1937 he had outdone Carnegie, spending some half-billion dollars on the University of Chicago, the Rockefeller Institute for Medical Research, the Great Smoky Mountains National Park, and other projects. A minuscule part of his giving, however, afforded him the greatest personal pleasure; he habitually handed shiny new dimes to whomever he met. The older he got, the more devout he grew. In his days of building the Standard Oil monopoly his Baptist beliefs had inspired charges of hypocrisy; now they simply appeared the understandable response of one sliding toward death.

Yet Henry Ford remembered the old days and would have none of Rockefeller's religiosity. As the automaker left an interview with the oil man, Rockefeller said, "Good-bye, I'll see you in heaven."

"You will if you get in," Ford muttered.[21]

ACKNOWLEDGMENTS

The author would like to thank the many people who made this book possible. David M. Kennedy suggested the project and provided valuable critiques of various drafts, although the project ultimately took a turn neither of us expected. Eric Foner and Richard White likewise read early drafts and offered insightful comments. My colleagues and students at Texas A&M University and the University of Texas at Austin have let me test my thinking on them for years, and have happily informed me when my evidence or logic has fallen short. Roger Scholl, Bill Thomas, and Kristine Puopolo at Doubleday and James D. Hornfischer of Hornfischer Literary Management have been consummate professionals throughout. Roslyn Schloss remains the queen of copy editors.

NOTES

PROLOGUE: THE CAPITALIST REVOLUTION

1. H. W. Brands, *Masters of Enterprise: Giants of American Business from John Jacob Astor and J. P. Morgan to Bill Gates and Oprah Winfrey* (New York: Free Press, 1999), 40, 55, 66; Ron Chernow, *The House of Morgan: An American Banking Dynasty and the Rise of Modern Finance* (New York: Simon & Schuster, 1990), 21–22.
2. Chernow, *House of Morgan*, 159.
3. Matthew Josephson, *The Robber Barons* (1934; San Diego: Harcourt, 1995), 15.

CHAPTER I: SPECULATION AS MARTIAL ART

1. H. W. Brands, *Masters of Enterprise: Giants of American Business from John Jacob Astor and J. P. Morgan to Bill Gates and Oprah Winfrey* (New York: Free Press, 1999), 11.
2. H. W. Brands, *The Age of Gold: The California Gold Rush and the New American Dream* (New York: Doubleday, 2002), 471.
3. James M. McPherson, *Battle Cry of Freedom: The Civil War Era* (New York: Oxford University Press, 1988), 442–50, 593–94; Paul Studenski and Herman E. Kroos, *Financial History of the United States* (New York: McGraw-Hill, 1963), chs. 13–14; Bray Hammond, *Sovereignty and an Empty Purse: Banks and Politics in the Civil War* (Princeton: Princeton University Press, 1970), 211–28, 263–82, 321–51.
4. The best history of Wall Street is Charles R. Geisst, *Wall Street: A History* (New York: Oxford University Press, 1997). See also John Steele Gordon, *The Great Game: The Emergence of Wall Street as a World Power, 1653–2000* (New York: Scribner, 1999).

Steven Fraser, *Every Man a Speculator: A History of Wall Street in American Life* (New York: HarperCollins, 2005), shows how Wall Street eventually wended through every city and state in America.

5. John Steele Gordon, *A Thread across the Ocean: The Heroic Story of the Atlantic Cable* (New York: Walker & Co., 2002), recounts the birth of transatlantic telegraphy. David Paull Nickles, *Under the Wire: How the Telegraph Changed Diplomacy* (Cambridge: Harvard University Press, 2003), examines the international impact.

6. William Worthington Fowler, *Ten Years in Wall Street; or, Revelations of Inside Life and Experience on 'Change* (Hartford: Worthington, Dustin & Co., 1870), 19–20.

7. Ibid., 24–25, 33–35.

8. Ibid., 33–37, 40–42.

9. Edwin G. Burrows and Mike Wallace, *Gotham: A History of New York City to 1898* (New York: Oxford University Press, 1999), 475; John Steele Gordon, *The Scarlet Woman of Wall Street: Jay Gould, Jim Fisk, Cornelius Vanderbilt, the Erie Railway Wars, and the Birth of Wall Street* (New York: Weidenfeld & Nicolson, 1988), 18–19.

10. Burrows and Wallace, *Gotham*, 658.

11. James K. Medbery, *Men and Mysteries of Wall Street* (Boston: Fields, Osgood & Co., 1870), 169.

12. Harold Evans, with Gail Buckland and David Lefer, *They Made America: From the Steam Engine to the Search Engine; Two Centuries of Innovators* (New York: Little, Brown, 2004), 26–35. Evans notes the debt of Fulton to John Fitch, whose Delaware River steamboat didn't catch on. On *Gibbons* v. *Ogden*, a concise summary is Kermit L. Hall, ed., *The Oxford Companion to the Supreme Court of the United States* (New York: Oxford University Press, 1992), 337–38. On Vanderbilt, see Arthur D. Howden Smith, *Commodore Vanderbilt: An Epic of American Achievement* (New York: R. M. McBride, 1927); Wheaton J. Lane, *Commodore Vanderbilt: An Epic of the Steam Age* (New York: Knopf, 1942); and the gossipy Meade Minnigerode, *Certain Rich Men: Stephen Girard, John Jacob Astor, Jay Cooke, Daniel Drew, Cornelius Vanderbilt, Jay Gould, Jim Fisk* (New York: G. P. Putnam's Sons, 1927).

13. Matthew Josephson, *The Robber Barons* (1934; San Diego: Harcourt, 1995), 15. This is the classic skeptical study of nineteenth-century American capitalism.

14. A succinct history of American railroads is John F. Stover, *American Railroads* (Chicago: University of Chicago Press, 1997). Stewart Hall Holbrook, *The Story of American Railroads* (New York: Crown, 1947), is more capacious, while Albro Martin, *Railroads Triumphant: The Growth, Rejection, and Rebirth of a Vital American Force* (New York: Oxford University Press, 1992), is more celebratory. William D. Middleton, *Landmarks on the Iron Road: Two Centuries of North American Railroad Engineering* (Bloomington: Indiana University Press, 1999), covers the technology of construction. Sarah H. Gordon, *Passage to Union: How the Railroads Transformed American Life, 1829–1929* (Chicago: Ivan R. Dee, 1996), traces the social and cultural significance. Thomas C. Cochran and William Miller, *The Age of Enterprise: A Social History of Industrial America* (New York: Harper & Row, 1961), writes the social history of railroads into the social history of industrialization.

15. *American Railroad Journal*, Sept. 2, 1854, in Alfred D. Chandler Jr., *The Visible Hand: The Managerial Revolution in American Business* (Cambridge: Belknap Press of Harvard University Press, 1977), 104. Chandler, ed., *Railroads: The Nation's First Big Busi-*

ness (New York: Harcourt, Brace & World, 1965), provides contemporary perspective and revealing statistics, besides Chandler's own insights.

16. Chandler, *Visible Hand*, 92; Geisst, *Wall Street*, ch. 2.
17. Josephson, *Robber Barons*, 70; Brands, *Masters of Enterprise*, 20–25.
18. Ibid., 22.
19. Josephson, *Robber Barons*, 66.
20. Fowler, *Ten Years in Wall Street*, 480–82.
21. Brands, *Masters of Enterprise*, 38–39.
22. Ibid., 40; Maury Klein, *The Life and Legend of Jay Gould* (Baltimore: Johns Hopkins University Press, 1986), 66.
23. Fowler, *Ten Years in Wall Street*, 495–96.
24. Brands, *Masters of Enterprise*, 24.
25. Fowler, *Ten Years in Wall Street*, 502.
26. Brands, *Masters of Enterprise*, 24; Charles Francis Adams Jr., "A Chapter of Erie," in Charles Francis Adams Jr. and Henry Adams, *Chapters of Erie* (Ithaca: Cornell University Press, 1956), 52–55.
27. Gordon, *Scarlet Woman of Wall Street*, 189–93.
28. Henry Adams, *The Education of Henry Adams* (1907; Boston: Houghton Mifflin, 1961), 211.
29. Ibid., 224.
30. Ibid., 238.
31. Henry Adams, "The New York Gold Conspiracy," in Adams and Adams, *Chapters of Erie*, 114.
32. Report of the Majority of the Committee on Banking and Currency, *Investigation into the Causes of the Gold Panic*, 41st Cong., 2d sess., 1870, HR Rep. 31, 152–53.
33. Ibid., 153.
34. Ibid., 6–7.
35. Ibid., 174, 232, 444.
36. Ibid., 252.
37. Ibid., 256.
38. *New York Times*, Sept. 24, 1869.
39. *Investigation into the Causes of the Gold Panic*, 141.
40. Klein, *Jay Gould*, 111–12; Gordon, *Scarlet Woman of Wall Street*, 272.
41. Gordon, *Scarlet Woman of Wall Street*, 275; *Investigation*, 16; Brands, *Masters of Enterprise*, 46–47.
42. Brands, *Masters of Enterprise*, 47.
43. *Investigation*, 176.
44. Ibid., 7, 19–20.
45. Adams, *Education*, 282–83.
46. Adams, "New York Gold Conspiracy," 130–31, 135–36.

CHAPTER 2: ONE NATION UNDER RAILS

1. David Haward Bain, *Empire Express: Building the First Transcontinental Railroad* (New York: Viking, 1999), 16–17.

2. James M. McPherson, *Battle Cry of Freedom: The Civil War Era* (New York: Oxford University Press, 1988), 122.

3. H. W. Brands, *The Age of Gold: The California Gold Rush and the New American Dream* (New York: Doubleday, 2002), 394–400.

4. George T. Clark, *Leland Stanford: War Governor of California, Railroad Builder, and Founder of Stanford University* (Stanford: Stanford University Press, 1931), is the most complete biography. In Oscar Lewis, *The Big Four: The Story of Huntington, Stanford, Hopkins, and Crocker and the Building of the Central Pacific* (New York: Knopf, 1938), Stanford shares space with his partners.

5. Clark, *Leland Stanford*, 73–78.

6. Bain, *Empire Express*, 109.

7. Ibid., 112.

8. Stuart Daggett, *Chapters on the History of the Southern Pacific* (New York: Ronald Press, 1922), 23–24.

9. Clark, *Leland Stanford*, 208.

10. Brands, *Age of Gold*, 422.

11. *Congressional Globe*, 38th Cong., 1st sess., June 21, 1864, 3150–52.

12. Ibid., 3154.

13. Bain, *Empire Express*, 137.

14. Liping Zhu, *A Chinaman's Chance: The Chinese on the Rocky Mountain Frontier* (Niwot: University Press of Colorado, 1997), 21.

15. Benson Tong, *The Chinese Americans* (Westport: Greenwood Press, 2000), 21.

16. Brands, *Age of Gold*, 63.

17. Ibid., 479; Huping Ling, *Surviving on the Gold Mountain: A History of Chinese American Women and Their Lives* (Albany: State University of New York Press, 1998), 21; Mark Twain, *Roughing It* (Hartford: American Publishing Co., 1872), 391.

18. Andrew Gyory, *Closing the Gate: Race, Politics, and the Chinese Exclusion Act* (Chapel Hill: University of North Carolina Press, 1998), 17; Robert Louis Stevenson, "Across the Plains" (1892), in Stevenson, *From Scotland to Silverado*, ed. James D. Hart (Cambridge: Belknap Press of Harvard University Press, 1966), 138–39.

19. Gyory, *Closing the Gate*, 19–20.

20. Clark, *Leland Stanford*, 78–79, 126–27.

21. Bain, *Empire Express*, 208, 221.

22. Stephen E. Ambrose, *Nothing Like It in the World: The Men Who Built the Transcontinental Railroad, 1863–1869* (New York: Simon & Schuster, 2000), 156–57.

23. Bain, *Empire Express*, 220.

24. Ibid., 360–62.

25. Maury Klein, *Union Pacific: Birth of a Railroad, 1862–93* (Garden City: Doubleday, 1987), 66–67. Grenville M. Dodge, *How We Built the Union Pacific Railway, and Other Railway Papers and Addresses* (1910; Ann Arbor: University Microfilms, 1966), includes the superintendent's own version. Robert G. Angevine, *The Railroad and the State: War, Politics, and Technology in Nineteenth-Century America* (Stanford: Stanford University Press, 2004), situates Dodge, a Civil War general, among the many military officers and military-minded civilians who contributed to railroad construction.

26. Klein, *Union Pacific*, 216.

27. The war for the Plains is discussed in detail in ch. 6.

28. Bain, *Empire Express*, 351.

29. Ambrose, *Nothing Like It in the World*, 200–01, 235–36.

30. Brands, *Age of Gold*, 432.

31. Clark, *Leland Stanford*, 244.

32. Bain, *Empire Express*, 447; Klein, *Union Pacific*, 193–94.

33. Klein, *Union Pacific*, 220.

34. Ibid., 220–27; Bret Harte, "Opening of the Pacific Railroad"; Walt Whitman, "Passage to India"; Ambrose, *Nothing Like It in the World*, 366; Brands, *Age of Gold*, 437.

CHAPTER 3: THE FIRST TRIUMVIRATE

1. H. W. Brands, *Masters of Enterprise: Giants of American Business from John Jacob Astor and J. P. Morgan to Bill Gates and Oprah Winfrey* (New York: Free Press, 1999), 64.

2. Ron Chernow, *The House of Morgan: An American Banking Dynasty and the Rise of Modern Finance* (New York: Simon & Schuster, 1990), 87.

3. Jean Strouse, *Morgan: American Financier* (New York: Random House, 1999), 65. This is the best recent biography. Herbert L. Satterlee, *J. Pierpont Morgan: An Intimate Portrait* (New York: Macmillan, 1939), is the authorized biography (Satterlee was Morgan's son-in-law) but very useful nonetheless.

4. Chernow, *House of Morgan*, 24–25; Byron, "Don Juan: Canto the Twelfth."

5. Ron Chernow, *Titan: The Life of John D. Rockefeller, Sr.* (New York: Random House, 1998), xxii, 8–9, 31. Allan Nevins, *Study in Power: John D. Rockefeller, Industrialist and Philanthropist*, 2 vols. (New York: Scribner, 1953), is still valuable. John T. Flynn, *God's Gold: The Story of Rockefeller and His Times* (New York: Harcourt, Brace, 1932), reveals the strengths and weaknesses of the journalistic approach.

6. Chernow, *Titan*, 20–22, 38.

7. Matthew Josephson, *The Robber Barons* (1934; San Diego: Harcourt, 1995), 46.

8. Ibid., 33–35, 39–41.

9. Daniel Yergin, *The Prize: The Epic Quest for Oil, Money, and Power* (New York: Simon & Schuster, 1991), 26–28.

10. Ibid., 28–29.

11. Chernow, *Titan*, 79, 100.

12. Ibid., 79–80; Nevins, *Study in Power*, 1:33; Ida M. Tarbell, *The History of the Standard Oil Company*, 2 vols. (1904; New York: Peter Smith, 1950), 1:43. Tarbell's is the original exposé of Rockefeller's business practices and still the starting point on Standard.

13. John D. Rockefeller, *Random Reminiscences of Men and Events* (New York: Doubleday, Doran, 1937), 81.

14. Chernow, *Titan*, 106–10. Flagler, who would gain greater fame for making Florida a tourist destination, is the subject of David Leon Chandler, *Flagler: The Astonishing Life and Times of the Visionary Robber Baron Who Founded Florida* (New York: Macmillan, 1986), and the somewhat more restrained Edward N. Akin, *Flagler: Rockefeller Partner and Florida Baron* (Kent: Kent State University Press, 1988).

15. Rockefeller, *Random Reminiscences*, 81; Brands, *Masters of Enterprise*, 85–86.

16. Joseph Frazier Wall, *Andrew Carnegie* (New York: Oxford University Press, 1970), 65. A more recent biography is Peter Krass, *Carnegie* (New York: John Wiley, 2002). Burton J. Hendrick, *The Life of Andrew Carnegie*, 2 vols. (Garden City: Doubleday, Doran, 1932), remains valuable. Harold C. Livesay, *Andrew Carnegie and the Rise of Big Business* (Boston: Little, Brown, 1975), and Louis M. Hacker, *The World of Andrew Carnegie: 1865–1901* (Philadelphia: Lippincott, 1968), sketch his world and significance.

17. Wall, *Andrew Carnegie*, 67–71.

18. Andrew Carnegie, *Autobiography of Andrew Carnegie* (1920; Boston: Houghton Mifflin, 1948), 33.

19. Ibid., 67–69.

20. Wall, *Andrew Carnegie*, 138.

21. Ibid., 189; Hendrick, *Life of Andrew Carnegie*, 1:123–24.

22. Carnegie, *Autobiography*, 136–37.

23. Ibid., 170–71; Wall, *Andrew Carnegie*, 197.

24. Henrietta M. Larson, *Jay Cooke: Private Banker* (New York: Greenwood Press, 1968), 177. A brief account of Cooke's Civil War career is H. W. Brands, *The Money Men* (New York: Norton/Atlas, 2006), ch. 3.

25. Josephson, *Robber Barons*, 94–98.

26. Ellis Paxson Oberholzer, *Jay Cooke: Financier of the Civil War*, 2 vols. (Philadelphia, 1907), 2:421–22.

27. Edwin F. Burrows and Mike Wallace, *Gotham: A History of New York City to 1898* (New York: Oxford University Press, 1999), 1020–21. An insightful and engaging account of the causes and manifestations of the Panic of 1873 is Robert Sobel, *Panic on Wall Street* (New York: E. P. Dutton, 1988), ch. 5. Other Sobel chapters detail other panics.

28. Josephson, *Robber Barons*, 187.

29. Chernow, *House of Morgan*, 43–44; Strouse, *Morgan*, 197–99.

30. Ibid., 248–49; Brands, *Masters of Enterprise*, 68–69.

31. Ibid., 69–70; George Wheeler, *Pierpont Morgan and Friends: The Anatomy of a Myth* (Englewood Cliffs: Prentice-Hall, 1973), 178; *New York Times*, Jan. 11, 1889.

32. Nevins, *Study in Power*, 1:93–94; Chernow, *Titan*, 117.

33. Chernow, *Titan*, 132.

34. Brands, *Masters of Enterprise*, 84–85.

35. Nevins, *Study in Power*, 1:104.

36. Flynn, *God's Gold*, 401; Chernow, *Titan*, xxi–xxii; Nevins, *Study in Power*, 1:141.

37. Yergin, *The Prize*, 52.

38. Chernow, *Titan*, 153.

39. Ibid., 226–27; Nevins, *Study in Power*, 1:385–402.

40. Chernow, *Titan*, 228–29.

41. Nevins, *Study in Power*, 2:101; Yergin, *The Prize*, 51–54.

42. Carnegie, *Autobiography*, 167.

43. Ibid., 129–30.

44. Hendrick, *Life of Andrew Carnegie*, 1:211–13; Wall, *Andrew Carnegie*, 331–32.

45. Brands, *Masters of Enterprise*, 58–59.

46. Ibid., 59; Wall, *Andrew Carnegie*, 337.

47. Hendrick, *Life of Andrew Carnegie*, 1:202–03

48. Brands, *Masters of Enterprise*, 63.

CHAPTER 4: TOIL AND TROUBLE

1. Kevin Kenny, *Making Sense of the Molly Maguires* (New York: Oxford University Press, 1998), 181–82.

2. Ibid., 57–60; *The Story of Anthracite* (New York: Hudson Coal Company, 1932), ch. 7.

3. *Story of Anthracite*, 168; Kenny, *Making Sense of the Molly Maguires*, 126–27; Priscilla Long, *Where the Sun Never Shines: A History of America's Bloody Coal Industry* (New York: Paragon House, 1989), 31–32; Andrew Roy, *A History of the Coal Miners of the United States* (Columbus: J. L. Trauger Printing Company, 1906), 81–85.

4. Marvin W. Schlegel, *Ruler of the Reading: The Life of Franklin B. Gowen, 1836–1889* (Harrisburg: Archives Publishing Company of Pennsylvania, 1947), is the only biography of Gowen.

5. Kenny, *Making Sense of the Molly Maguires*, 61–62; Long, *Where the Sun Never Shines*, 105–06.

6. Perry K. Blatz, *Democratic Miners: Work and Labor Relations in the Anthracite Coal Industry, 1875–1925* (Albany: State University Press of New York, 1994), 18–20; Kenny, *Making Sense of the Molly Maguires*, 127.

7. Kenny, *Making Sense of the Molly Maguires*, 176; Roy, *History of the Coal Miners*, 95–96; Long, *Where the Sun Never Shines*, 108–09.

8. Allan Pinkerton, *The Mollie Maguires and the Detectives* (New York: G. W. Dillingham, 18870), 16–17.

9. Wayne E. Broehl Jr., *Molly Maguires* (Cambridge: Harvard University Press, 1964), 152–55, 202–03, 225–26, 235; Kenny, *Making Sense of the Molly Maguires*, 155–56.

10. Kenny, *Making Sense of the Molly Maguires*, 269–74.

11. Ibid., 290–94; Edward Winslow Martin, *The History of the Great Riots . . . Together with a Full History of the Mollie Maguires* (Philadelphia: National Publishing Company, 1877), 511–12.

12. Broehl, *Molly Maguires*, 299–300.

13. Kenny, *Making Sense of the Molly Maguires*, 219–20; *New York Times*, May 14, 1876.

14. Broehl, *Molly Maguires*, 337–39; Kenny, *Making Sense of the Molly Maguires*, 250–56; Anthony Bimba, *The Molly Maguires* (New York: International Publishers, 1932), 116–21.

15. Long, *Where the Sun Never Shines*, 109.

16. Robert V. Bruce, *1877: Year of Violence* (Indianapolis: Bobbs-Merrill, 1959), 40.

17 Ibid., 39–42; *New York Times*, April 9, 1877.

18. H. W. Brands, *Masters of Enterprise: Giants of American Business from John Jacob Astor and J. P. Morgan to Bill Gates and Oprah Winfrey* (New York: Free Press, 1999), 88; Allan Nevins, *Study in Power: John D. Rockefeller, Industrialist and Philanthropist*, 2 vols. (New York: Scribner, 1953), 1:237. George H. Burgess and Miles C. Kennedy, *Centennial History of the Pennsylvania Railroad Company* (Philadelphia: Pennsylvania

Railroad Company, 1949), gives the company's view. James A. Ward, "Power and Accountability on the Pennsylvania Railroad, 1846–1878," *Business History Review* 49 (1975): 37–59, focuses on top corporate leadership of the Penn, including Tom Scott.

19. Bruce, *1877*, 50–52.

20. Ibid., 57–62.

21. Ibid., 76–85; Samuel Yellen, *American Labor Struggles* (New York: Harcourt, Brace, 1936), 9–11; Edward Winslow Martin, *The History of the Great Riots, Being a Full and Authentic Account of the Strikes and Riots on the Various Railroads* (Philadelphia: National Publishing Company, 1877), 17–49.

22. Barton C. Hacker, "The United States Army as a National Police Force: The Federal Policing of Labor Disputes, 1877–1898," *Military Affairs* 33 (1969): 255–64, shows how Hayes's decision became a precedent. Jerry M. Cooper, *The Army and Civil Disorder: Federal Military Intervention in Labor Disputes, 1877–1900* (Westport: Greenwood Press, 1980), covers the same ground in much greater detail.

23. Bruce, *1877*, 90–114; Yellen, *American Labor Struggles*, 12; Martin, *History of the Great Riots*, 50–75.

24. Bruce, *1877*, 118–36.

25. Ibid., 141–57; Yellen, *American Labor Struggles*, 15–18; Martin, *History of the Great Riots*, 76–124.

26. Bruce, *1877*, 159–64.

27. Ibid., 135–36, 226; *New York Times*, July 21 and 25, 1877.

28. Bruce, *1877*, 188–201; Martin, *History of the Great Riots*, 125–88.

29. Bruce, *1877*, 128, 203–08, 239–70; Martin, *History of the Great Riots*, 369–430; Philip Taft, *Organized Labor in American History* (New York: Harper & Row, 1964), 76–83.

30. Bruce, *1877*, 279; Ari Hoogenboom, *The Presidency of Rutherford B. Hayes* (Lawrence: University Press of Kansas, 1988), 79–92.

31. Walter Nelles, "A Strike and Its Legal Consequences: An Examination of the Receivership Precedent for the Labor Injunction," *Yale Law Journal* 40 (1931): 507–54. For context and consequences, see Gerald G. Eggert, *Railroad Labor Disputes: The Beginnings of Federal Strike Policy* (Ann Arbor: University of Michigan Press, 1967).

32. *Diary and Letters of Rutherford Burchard Hayes*, ed. Charles Richard Williams, 5 vols. (Columbus: Ohio State Archaeological and Historical Society, 1922–26), 3:440–41.

CHAPTER 5: THE CONQUEST OF THE SOUTH

1. Booker T. Washington, *Up from Slavery: An Autobiography* (1901; New York: Dover, 1995), 9–10. For context and a check on Washington's memory, see Louis R. Harlan, *Booker T. Washington: The Making of a Black Leader, 1856–1901* (New York: Oxford University Press, 1972), ch. 1. John W. Blassingame, ed., *Slave Testimony: Two Centuries of Letters, Speeches, Interviews, and Autobiographies* (Baton Rouge: Louisiana State University Press, 1977), sec. 5, contains recollections of other former slaves of their moments of emancipation.

2. William Tecumseh Sherman and John Sherman, *The Sherman Letters: Correspondence between General and Senator Sherman from 1837 to 1891*, ed. Rachel Sherman Thorndike (New York: C. Scribner's Sons, 1894), 55; John E. Marszalek, *Sherman: A*

Soldier's Passion for Order (New York: Vintage Civil War Library, 1994), 109; Lloyd Lewis, *Sherman: Fighting Prophet* (New York: Harcourt, Brace & Co., 1932), 119.

3. William Tecumseh Sherman, *Memoirs of General W. T. Sherman* (New York: Library of America, 1990), 727–28.

4. Ibid., 725–27.

5. Ira Berlin et al., eds., *The Wartime Genesis of Free Labor: The Lower South* (New York: Cambridge University Press, 1990), 338–40. This volume is part of the series *Freedom: A Documentary History of Emancipation, 1861–67*, based on documents from the National Archives.

6. Ella Gertrude Clanton Thomas, *The Secret Eye: The Journal of Ella Gertrude Clanton Thomas*, ed. Virginia Ingraham Burr (Chapel Hill: University of North Carolina Press, 1990), 253–54. Clarence L. Mohr, *On the Threshold of Freedom: Masters and Slaves in Civil War Georgia* (Athens: University of Georgia Press, 1986), provides the background for Thomas's story. James L. Roark, *Masters without Slaves: Southern Planters in the Civil War and Reconstruction* (New York: Norton, 1977), depicts the travails of the class to which the Thomas family belonged.

7. Thomas, *Secret Eye*, 257–58.

8. Ibid., 261–65.

9. W. E. Burghardt Du Bois, *Black Reconstruction in America* (New York: Russell & Russell, 1935), 601–04.

10. Claude F. Oubre, *Forty Acres and a Mule: The Freedmen's Bureau and Black Land Ownership* (Baton Rouge: Louisiana State University Press, 1978), 52–54; Steven Hahn, *A Nation under Our Feet: Black Political Struggles in the Rural South from Slavery to the Great Migration* (Cambridge: Harvard University Press, 2003), 143–44.

11. Thomas, *Secret Eye*, 267–72.

12. J. T. Trowbridge, *A Picture of the Desolated States; and the Work of Restoration* (Hartford: L. Stebbins, 1868), 454.

13. Ibid., 361. George R. Bentley, *A History of the Freedmen's Bureau* (New York: Octagon Books, 1970), offers a concise account of the work of the bureau.

14. Trowbridge, *Desolated States*, 363–65.

15. Ibid., 423–24, 442–44.

16. Leon F. Litwack, *Been in the Storm So Long: The Aftermath of Slavery* (New York: Knopf, 1979), 333–35.

17. U.S. Congress, Senate Executive Document 6, 39th Cong., 2nd sess., 1867, 193–95, 208–09.

18. Ibid., 218–19. Theodore Brantner Wilson, *The Black Codes of the South* (University: University of Alabama Press, 1965), characterizes the origins, essence, and effects of the black codes.

19. U.S. Congress, Senate Executive Document 6, 39th Cong., 2nd sess., 1867, 194, 211.

20. Litwack, *Been in the Storm So Long*, 366; Robert W. Johannsen, ed, *Reconstruction, 1865–1877* (New York: Free Press, 1970), 41.

21. Litwack, *Been in the Storm So Long*, 369.

22. Heather Cox Richardson, *The Death of Reconstruction: Race, Labor, and Politics in the Post–Civil War North, 1865–1901* (Cambridge: Harvard University Press, 2001), 17.

23. Washington, *Up from Slavery*, 19.

24. Ibid., 20–23.

25. Ibid., 23–25.
26. Ibid., 28–29, 35. Washington's Hampton years are covered in Harlan, *Booker T. Washington*, 52–77.
27. Henry Lee Swint, *The Northern Teacher in the South, 1862–1870* (Nashville: Vanderbilt University Press, 1941), 89.
28. Trowbridge, *Desolated States,* 427–28.
29. Litwack, *Been in the Storm So Long,* 387.
30. Ibid., 416, 437; Whitelaw Reid, *After the War: A Southern Tour* (Cincinnati: Moore, Wilstach & Baldwin, 1866), 447.
31. Reid, *After the War,* 561.
32. Litwack, *Been in the Storm So Long,* 390.
33. John Richard Dennett, *The South as It Is: 1865–1866,* ed. Henry M. Christman (New York: Viking, 1965), 53.
34. Trowbridge, *Desolated States,* 386.
35. Crop-lien laws, and the emergence of sharecropping in general, are discussed in Charles S. Aiken, *The Cotton Plantation South since the Civil War* (Baltimore: Johns Hopkins Press, 1998), chs. 1 and 2.

CHAPTER 6: LAKOTA'S LAST STAND

1. H. W. Brands, *The First American: The Life and Times of Benjamin Franklin* (New York: Doubleday, 2000), 598; Jon Kukla, *A Wilderness So Immense: The Louisiana Purchase and the Destiny of America* (New York: Knopf, 2003), 231; H. W. Brands, *Andrew Jackson: His Life and Times* (New York: Doubleday, 2005), 217–70; James M. McPherson, *Battle Cry of Freedom: The Civil War Era* (New York: Oxford University Press, 1988), 638.
2. Henry G. Waltmann, "Sioux Indians" (revised by Kathryn Abbott), in Howard R. Lamar, ed., *The New Encyclopedia of the American West* (New Haven: Yale University Press, 1998), 1051–54. See Richard White, *The Middle Ground: Indians, Empires, and Republics in the Great Lakes Region, 1650–1815* (New York: Cambridge University Press, 1991), for details and context.
3. Andrew C. Isenberg, *The Destruction of the Bison: An Environmental History, 1750–1920* (New York: Cambridge University Press, 2000), 41; Richard White, "The Winning of the West: The Expansion of the Western Sioux in the Eighteenth and Nineteenth Centuries," *Journal of American History* 65 (1978): 323. White expands on this theme and others in *It's Your Misfortune and None of My Own: A History of the American West* (Norman: University of Oklahoma Press, 1991).
4. White, "Winning of the West," 322.
5. George Catlin, *Letters and Notes on the Manners, Customs, and Conditions of the North American Indians* (1844; New York: Dover, 1973), 256.
6. White, "Winning of the West," 321.
7. Ibid., 325, 329–30; White, *It's Your Misfortune,* 25–26. Jared M. Diamond, *Guns, Germs, and Steel: The Fates of Human Societies* (New York: Norton, 1997), has much to say on this subject and related ones.
8. White, "Winning of the West," 337.

9. Ibid., 337–41; Remi A. Nadeau, *Fort Laramie and the Sioux Indians* (Englewood Cliffs: Prentice-Hall, 1967), 66–82.

10. Dee Brown, *Bury My Heart at Wounded Knee: An Indian History of the American West* (New York: Holt, Rinehart & Winston, 1970), 79, 83, 90.

11. Ibid., 89–90; Stan Hoig, *The Sand Creek Massacre* (Norman: University of Oklahoma Press, 1961), 145–62, 177–92; Elliot West, *The Contested Plains: Indians, Goldseekers, and the Rush to Colorado* (Lawrence: University Press of Kansas, 1998), 299–307.

12. Hoig, *Sand Creek Massacre*, 162–76.

13. Brown, *Bury My Heart at Wounded Knee*, 95–96.

14. Ibid., 97, 130. Perhaps needless to say, this is a translation into English of Red Cloud's actual words. Brown's book is based largely on such translations, which vary in faithfulness and eloquence according to the translators.

15. Mike Sajna, *Crazy Horse: The Life behind the Legend* (New York: John Wiley, 2000), 196.

16. Ibid., 200–02; Stephen E. Ambrose, *Crazy Horse and Custer: The Parallel Lives of Two American Warriors* (Garden City: Doubleday, 1975), 222–25.

17. Lloyd Lewis, *Sherman: Fighting Prophet* (New York: Harcourt, Brace, 1932), 575, 585.

18. Ibid., 577–78; H. W. Brands, *The Age of Gold: The California Gold Rush and the New American Dream* (New York: Doubleday, 2002), 409–10.

19. Lewis, *Sherman*, 596; Brands, *Age of Gold*, 429.

20. Lewis, *Sherman*, 597; David Haward Bain, *Empire Express: Building the First Transcontinental Railroad* (New York: Viking, 1999), 312.

21. Sherman, *Memoirs*, 926; Lewis, *Sherman*, 598; Brands, *Age of Gold*, 431–32.

22. Ambrose, *Crazy Horse and Custer*, 281.

23. Dee Brown, *Bury My Heart at Wounded Knee*, 170–72.

24. Sajna, *Crazy Horse*, 217–19.

25. Ibid., 223–24.

26. Robert M. Utley, *The Lance and the Shield: The Life and Times of Sitting Bull* (New York: Ballantine Books, 1993), 88–92.

27. Ambrose, *Crazy Horse and Custer*, 346.

28. Sajna, *Crazy Horse*, 251.

29. Ibid., 253–54; Ambrose, *Crazy Horse and Custer*, 350; Donald Jackson, *Custer's Gold: The United States Cavalry Expedition of 1874* (New Haven: Yale University Press, 1966), 87–89.

30. Ambrose, *Crazy Horse and Custer*, 363–64; Sajna, *Crazy Horse*, 255.

31. Ambrose, *Crazy Horse and Custer*, 372–74.

32. Black Elk, *Black Elk Speaks*, as told through John G. Neihardt (1932; New York: Pocket Books, 1972), 6–12. This most celebrated Sioux memoir has troubled scholars and other readers for decades, on account of their inability to tease out how much of the tale, and especially the language, is Black Elk's and how much John Neihardt's. Yet the issue is hardly peculiar to Indian memoirs, characterizing countless "as told to" recollections by famous persons of various ethnicities and backgrounds. And whatever questions the text raises, the work remains a classic. The fullest consideration of the Black Elk–John Neihardt collaboration can be found in *The Sixth Grandfather: Black Elk's Teachings Given to John G. Neihardt*, ed. Raymond J. DeMallie (Lincoln: University of Nebraska Press, 1984).

33. *Black Elk Speaks*, 18–29.

34. Ibid., 70–72.
35. Ambrose, *Crazy Horse and Custer*, 384; Sajna, *Crazy Horse*, 277–78.
36. Ambrose, *Crazy Horse and Custer*, 384–96.
37. *Black Elk Speaks*, 91–92.
38. Brown, *Bury My Heart at Wounded Knee*, 293.
39. Ibid., 294; *Black Elk Speaks*, 92–95.
40. Ambrose, *Crazy Horse and Custer*, 405; *Black Elk Speaks*, 93.
41. Ambrose, *Crazy Horse and Custer*, 405–08; Sajna, *Crazy Horse*, 282–89. These accounts differ somewhat, as battle accounts generally do. Sajna's is the more measured, Ambrose's the more dramatic. John S. Gray, *Custer's Last Campaign: Mitch Boyer and the Little Bighorn Reconstructed* (Lincoln: University of Nebraska Press, 1991), painstakingly reconstructs the battle and the larger campaign. Gregory F. Michno, *Lakota Noon: The Indian Narrative of Custer's Defeat* (Missoula: Mountain Press Publishing Co., 1997), tells the story of the battle from the side of the winners.
42. Brown, *Bury My Heart at Wounded Knee*, 296. On this same page, Brown includes a comment by Red Horse, a Sioux council chief, that some of the surrounded whites begged to be taken prisoner. This sounds unlikely, given what the whites knew of Indian treatment of prisoners.
43. *Black Elk Speaks*, 104–08.
44. Isenberg, *Destruction of the Bison*, 27; Dan Flores, "Bison Ecology and Bison Diplomacy: The Southern Plains from 1800 to 1850," *Journal of American History* 78 (1991): 469–70.
45. Isenberg, *Destruction of the Bison*, 27–28; Flores, "Bison Ecology," 476; Dale F. Lott, *American Bison: A Natural History* (Berkeley: University of California Press, 2002), 74–75.
46. Isenberg, *Destruction of the Bison*, 103–06.
47. Ibid., 108.
48. Ibid., 110; Lott, *American Bison*, 114–15; Flores, "Bison Ecology," 481.
49. Isenberg, *Destruction of the Bison*, 112.
50. Tom McHugh, with the assistance of Victoria Hobson, *The Time of the Buffalo* (New York: Knopf, 1972), 267; Lott, *American Bison*, 176.
51. McHugh, *Time of the Buffalo*, 265–66.
52. Lott, *American Bison*, 177–79.
53. David A. Dary, *The Buffalo Book: The Full Saga of the American Animal* (Athens: Ohio University Press, 1989), 118–20.
54. H. W. Brands, *TR: The Last Romantic* (New York: Basic Books, 1997), 157–58.
55. Robert G. Athearn, *William Tecumseh Sherman and the Settlement of the West* (Norman: University of Oklahoma Press, 1956), 310–13.
56. Larry McMurtry, *Crazy Horse* (New York: Lipper/Viking, 1999), 125–31.

CHAPTER 7: PROFITS ON THE HOOF

1. Harriet Martineau, *Society in America*, vol. 2 (London: Saunders and Otley, 1837), 203. Pork remained Americans' favorite meat till the early twentieth century, when, as a result of the events described below, it was overtaken by beef. See Waverly Root and

Richard de Rochemont, *Eating in America: A History* (New York: William Morrow, 1976), 192–93.

2. David Dary, *Cowboy Culture: A Saga of Five Centuries* (New York: Knopf, 1981), 3–104.

3. Edward Everett Dale, *The Range Cattle Industry* (Norman: University of Oklahoma Press, 1930), 21–26.

4. Ibid., 31.

5. Ernest Staples Osgood, *The Day of the Cattleman* (Chicago: University of Chicago Press, 1929), 29.

6. *Prose and Poetry of the Live Stock Industry of the United States*, Prepared by the Authority of the National Live Stock Association (1904; New York: Antiquarian Press, 1959), 433.

7. Joseph G. McCoy, *Historic Sketches of the Cattle Trade of the West and Southwest* (1874; Columbus: Long's College Book Co., 1951), 40–53; Walter Prescott Webb, *The Great Plains* (Boston: Ginn & Co., 1931), 223.

8. Dary, *Cowboy Culture*, 211–12; McCoy, *Historic Sketches*, 138.

9. McCoy, *Historic Sketches*, 120–21, 134–41, 202–04. Robert R. Dykstra, *The Cattle Towns* (New York: Knopf, 1968), places Abilene and Joseph McCoy in context.

10. Dary, *Cowboy Culture*, 231.

11. Dale, *Range Cattle Industry*, 65; Charles Goodnight's recollection in *Prose and Poetry of the Live Stock Industry*, 532–33.

12. Goodnight in *Prose and Poetry*, 533.

13. Ibid., 534.

14. Ibid., 535.

15. Andy Adams, *The Log of a Cowboy: A Narrative of the Old Trail Days* (1903; Boston: Houghton Mifflin, 1931), 62–64.

16. H. W. Brands, *TR: The Last Romantic* (New York: Basic Books, 1997), 151–55.

17. James S. Brisbin, *The Beef Bonanza; or, How to Get Rich on the Plains* (1881; Norman: University of Oklahoma Press, 1959), 13.

18. Osgood, *Day of the Cattleman*, 85–86.

19. Ibid., 100; Dale, *Range Cattle Industry*, 94.

20. D. Jerome Tweton, *The Marquis de Mores: Dakota Capitalist, French Nationalist* (Fargo: North Dakota Institute for Regional Studies, 1972), has the full story of the eccentric count.

21. Lincoln A. Lang, *Ranching with Roosevelt, by a Companion Rancher* (Philadelphia: J. B. Lippincott, 1926), 116; Hermann Hagedorn, *Roosevelt in the Bad Lands* (Boston: Houghton Mifflin, 1930), 43–45; Brands, *TR*, 156–57.

22. Brisbin, *Beef Bonanza*, 51–55.

23. Osgood, *Day of the Cattleman*, 96.

24. Brands, *TR*, 158.

25. Ibid., 172–73.

26. Ibid., 189.

27. Ibid., 186.

28. Ibid., 206–08; Harold E. Briggs, "The Development and Decline of Open Range Ranching in the Northwest," *Mississippi Valley Historical Review* 20 (March 1934): 533–35.

29. Brands, *TR*, 209.

30. Osgood, *Day of the Cattleman*, 190–93; Briggs, "Development and Decline of Open Range Ranching," 535–36.

31. Osgood, *Day of the Cattleman*, 229; Dale, *Range Cattle Industry*, 111–12.

CHAPTER 8: TO MAKE THE DESERT BLOOM

1. John Wesley Powell, *The Exploration of the Colorado River* (1875; Garden City: Doubleday, 1961), 103–04.

2. Manly tells his own story in *Death Valley in '49* (1894; Chicago: R. R. Donnelly & Sons, 1927).

3. The best biography of Powell is Wallace Stegner, *Beyond the Hundredth Meridian: John Wesley Powell and the Second Opening of the West* (Boston: Houghton Mifflin, 1954).

4. Powell, *Exploration of the Colorado*, 18.

5. Ibid., 19–23, 32–38, 43, 107, 110, 127–32.

6. William H. Goetzmann, *Exploration and Empire: The Explorer and the Scientist in the Winning of the American West* (Austin: Texas State Historical Association, 1993), 437–57.

7. Ibid., 473.

8. Ibid., 498–501.

9. Everett Dick, *The Sod-House Frontier, 1854–1890: A Social History of the Northern Plains from the Creation of Kansas and Nebraska to the Admission of the Dakotas* (1937; Lincoln: University of Nebraska Press, 1979), 129.

10. The most thorough treatment of the various land laws is Benjamin Horace Hibbard, *A History of the Public Land Policies* (New York: Macmillan, 1924).

11. Howard Ruede, *Sod-House Days: Letters from a Kansas Homesteader, 1877–78*, ed. John Ise (1937; Lawrence: University Press of Kansas, 1983), 12–19.

12. Ibid., 30–41.

13. Ibid., 21; Dick, *Sod-House Frontier*, 232.

14. Dick, *Sod-House Frontier*, 232.

15. Ibid., 234–35.

16. Ruede, *Sod-House Days*, 43, 76–77, 85, 99–100.

17. Ibid., 70, 75–76, 91–92, 110–11.

18. Ibid., 219.

19. John Wesley Powell, *Report on the Lands of the Arid Region of the United States*, ed. Wallace Stegner (1878; Cambridge: Belknap Press of Harvard University Press, 1962), 11.

20. Ibid., 13–36; Donald Worster, *Rivers of Empire: Water, Aridity, and the Growth of the American West* (New York: Pantheon Books, 1985), 131–43.

21. William Allen White, "The Business of a Wheat Farm," *Scribner's Magazine*, Nov. 1897, 531–32.

22. Hiram M. Drache, *The Day of the Bonanza: A History of Bonanza Farming in the Red River Valley of the North* (Fargo: North Dakota Institute for Regional Studies, 1964), 3–30.

23. White, "Business of a Wheat Farm," 532–48.

CHAPTER 9: THE TEEMING SHORE

1. Lawrence J. McCaffrey, *The Irish Diaspora in America* (Bloomington: Indiana University Press, 1976), 56–58; Roger Daniels, *Coming to America: A History of Immigration and Ethnicity in American Life* (New York: HarperCollins, 1990), 133–34; Ronald Takaki, *A Different Mirror: A History of Multicultural America* (Boston: Little, Brown, 1993), 144.

2. George Templeton Strong, *The Diary of George Templeton Strong*, ed. Allan Nevins and Milton Halsey Thomas, abridg. Thomas J. Pressly (Seattle: University of Washington Press, 1988), 52; Takaki, *Different Mirror*, 153–54; Edwin G. Burrows and Mike Wallace, *Gotham: A History of New York City to 1898* (New York: Oxford University Press, 1999), 744.

3. John Francis Maguire, *The Irish in America* (New York: D. & J. Sadlier & Co., 1868), 319.

4. Takaki, *Different Mirror*, 151, 158.

5. Leonard Dinnerstein and David M. Reimers, *Ethnic Americans: A History of Immigration and Assimilation* (New York: New York University Press, 1977), 29.

6. La Vern J. Rippley, *The German-Americans* (Boston: Twayne, 1976), 62–83.

7. Jacob A. Riis, *The Making of an American* (1901; New York: Macmillan, 1937), 7–19; Louise Ware, *Jacob A. Riis: Police Reporter, Reformer, Useful Citizen* (New York: D. Appleton-Century Co., 1938), 1–16.

8. Mary Antin, *The Promised Land* (Boston: Houghton Mifflin, 1912), 137–41. L. M. Rubinow, *Economic Condition of the Jews in Russia* (Washington: United States Department of Commerce and Labor, 1908), provides background.

9. Antin, *Promised Land*, 148, 162–79.

10. Oscar Handlin, *The Uprooted* (1951; Boston: Little, Brown, 1990), 48–49.

11. Thomas A. Guglielmo, *White on Arrival: Italians, Race, Color, and Power in Chicago, 1890–1945* (New York: Oxford University Press, 2003), 16; John Bodnar, *The Transplanted: A History of Immigrants in Urban America* (Bloomington: Indiana University Press, 1985), 53; Thomas J. Archdeacon, *Becoming American: An Ethnic History* (New York: Free Press, 1983), 137–40. The statistics on returns are at best guesses, as various discrepancies between Bodnar and Archdeacon demonstrate.

12. Charlotte Erickson, *American Industry and the European Immigrant, 1860–1885* (Cambridge: Harvard University Press, 1957), 13–29.

13. Ibid., 33.

14. Ibid., 18, 41–49.

15. Rippley, *German-Americans*, 93–94.

16. Richard J. Orsi, *Sunset Limited: The Southern Pacific Railroad and the Development of the American West, 1850–1930* (Berkeley: University of California Press, 2005), 148–54.

17. Erickson, *American Industry and the European Immigrant*, 72–76.

18. "A Swedish Emigrant's Story," in Wayne Moquin, ed., *Makers of America: Natives and Aliens, 1891–1903* (Chicago: Encyclopedia Britannica, 1971), 264.

19. Lee Chew, "The Life Story of a Chinaman," in Hamilton Holt, ed., *The Life Stories of Undistinguished Americans, as Told by Themselves* (1906; New York: Routledge, 1990), 178–79.

20. *Historical Statistics of the United States: Colonial Times to 1970* (Washington: Bureau of the Census, 1976), 1:105–08; Archdeacon, *Becoming American*, 37–38, 55, 114–15.
21. On the "new immigration" and its impact on American thought, see John Higham, *Strangers in the Land: Patterns of American Nativism, 1860–1925* (New Brunswick: Rutgers University Press, 2002).
22. *Historical Statistics*, 1:108.
23. "A Rescued Chinese Slave Girl," in Moquin, *Makers of America*, 115–20.
24. Lisa See, *On Gold Mountain* (New York: St. Martin's Press, 1995), 17.
25. George Anthony Peffer, *If They Don't Bring Their Women Here: Chinese Female Immigration before Exclusion* (Urbana: University of Illinois Press, 1999), 117.
26. "A Rescued Chinese Slave Girl," 115–20.

CHAPTER 10: CITIES OF THE PLAIN

1. Thomas J. Archdeacon, *Becoming American: An Ethnic History* (New York: Free Press, 1983), 95, 145–46.
2. This is the theme of William Cronon's *Nature's Metropolis: Chicago and the Great West* (New York: Norton, 1991).
3. Elias Colbert and Everett Chamberlin, *Chicago and the Great Conflagration* (1871; New York: Viking Press, 1971), 196–205.
4. Karen Sawislak, *Smoldering City: Chicagoans and the Great Fire, 1871–1874* (Chicago: University of Chicago Press, 1995), 43–44.
5. *Reminiscences of Chicago during the Great Fire*, introd. Mabel McIlvane (Chicago: R. R. Donnelly & Sons, 1915), 120–24.
6. Ibid., 92–106.
7. Ibid., 106–07, 124–25.
8. Colbert and Chamberlin, *Chicago and the Great Conflagration*, 8–10.
9. Ibid., 252; Sawislak, *Smoldering City*, 49–59.
10. A. T. Andreas, *History of Chicago: From the Earliest Period to the Present Time*, 3 vols. (Chicago: A. T. Andreas Company, 1886), 2:61–62.
11. Sawislak, *Smoldering City*, 183.
12. Daniel Bluestone, *Constructing Chicago* (New Haven: Yale University Press, 1991), 109.
13. Ibid., 112–14.
14. Ibid., 123, 128.
15. Ibid., 119.
16. Ibid., 133–35.
17. Erik Larson, *The Devil in the White City: Murder, Magic, and Madness at the Fair That Changed America* (New York: Crown, 2003), 18–28; Donald L. Miller, *City of the Century: The Epic of Chicago and the Making of America* (New York: Simon & Schuster, 1996), 314–19.
18. James Blaine Walker, *Fifty Years of Rapid Transit, 1864–1914* (1918; New York: Arno Press, 1970), 7–8.
19. Ibid., 88–91; Edwin G. Burrows and Mike Wallace, *Gotham: A History of New York City to 1898* (New York: Oxford University Press, 1999), 932.
20. Walker, *Fifty Years of Rapid Transit*, 99.

21. Ibid., 70–85; *New York Times*, Feb. 3, 1872.
22. Walt Whitman, "Crossing Brooklyn Ferry."
23. David McCullough, *The Great Bridge* (New York: Simon & Schuster, 1972), 26–27, 42, 90.
24. Burrows and Wallace, *Gotham*, 935.
25. McCullough, *Great Bridge*, 313–17; *New York Times*, Aug. 26, 1876.
26. *New York Times*, May 25, 1883.
27. Thomas Jefferson to Benjamin Rush, Sept. 23, 1800, Jefferson Papers, Library of Congress (online); Ralph Waldo Emerson, "Farming," *The Complete Works of Ralph Waldo Emerson* (Boston: Houghton Mifflin, 1903–04), 7:154; Herman Melville, *Pierre; or, the Ambiguities* (1852; Evanston: Northwestern University Press and the Newberry Library, 1971), 9; Elizabeth Hawes, *New York, New York: How the Apartment House Transformed the Life of the City (1869–1930)* (New York: Henry Holt, 1993), 13.
28. Hawes, *New York, New York*, 5–9.
29. *The Diary of George Templeton Strong: Postwar Years, 1865–1875*, ed. Allan Nevins and Milton Halsey Thomas (New York: Macmillan, 1952), 339.
30. Hawes, *New York, New York*, 35–36.
31. Burrows and Wallace, *Gotham*, 970.
32. Hawes, *New York, New York*, 15.
33. *New York Times*, May 27, 1883.
34. *New York Times*, Feb. 11, 1897; Sven Beckert, *The Monied Metropolis: New York City and the Consolidation of the American Bourgeoisie, 1850–1896* (New York: Cambridge University Press, 2001), 1–2.

CHAPTER II: BELOW THE EL

1. Mary Antin, *The Promised Land* (Boston: Houghton Mifflin, 1912), 185–88.
2. Ibid., 202–05.
3. Jacob A. Riis, *The Making of an American* (1901; New York: Macmillan, 1937), 21–23.
4. Ibid., 24–63.
5. Edwin G. Burrows and Mike Wallace, *Gotham: A History of New York City to 1898* (New York: Oxford University Press, 1999), 746–47.
6. Ibid., 789, 1173. Ford Herbert MacGregor, *Tenement House Legislation, State and Local* (Madison: Wisconsin Library Commission, 1909), describes other tenement laws. Roy Lubove, *The Progressives and the Slums: Tenement House Reform in New York City, 1890–1917* (Pittsburgh: University of Pittsburgh Press, 1963), assesses what the New York legislation led to.
7. Jacob A. Riis, *How the Other Half Lives: Studies among the Tenements of New York*, ed. David Leviatin (1890; Boston: Bedford/St. Martin's, 1996), 59, 236.
8. Ibid., 77–91, 96–98.
9. Lisa See, *On Gold Mountain* (New York: St. Martin's Press, 1995), 45; Victor G. Nee and Brett de Bary Nee, *Longtime Californ': A Documentary Study of an American Chinatown* (New York: Pantheon, 1973), 55.
10. Lee Chew, "The Life Story of a Chinaman," in Hamilton Holt, ed., *The Life Stories of*

Undistinguished Americans, as Told by Themselves (1906; New York: Routledge, 1990), 181–85.

11. Nee and Nee, *Longtime Californ'*, 60–61.

12. Ibid., 73.

13. Thomas W. Chinn, H. Mark Lai, and Philip P. Choy, eds., *A History of the Chinese in California* (San Francisco: Chinese Historical Society of America, 1969), 64–69.

14. Ibid.; Gunther Barth, *Bitter Strength: A History of the Chinese in the United States* (Cambridge: Harvard University Press, 1964), 102–03; Nee and Nee, *Longtime Californ'*, 67–68.

15. Nee and Nee, *Longtime Californ'*, 80–82.

16. George Chauncey, *Gay New York: Gender, Urban Culture, and the Making of the Gay Male World, 1890–1940* (New York: Basic Books, 1994), 12–23.

17. Ibid., 196. An overview of laws regarding homosexual activity in the late nineteenth century can be found in Vern L. Bullough, *Homosexuality: A History* (New York: New American Library, 1979), 43–45.

18. Jonathan Katz, ed., *Gay American History: Lesbians and Gay Men in the U.S.A.: A Documentary* (New York: Thomas Y. Crowell, 1976), 38–39.

19. Chauncey, *Gay New York*, 181.

CHAPTER 12: SCHOOL FOR SCANDAL

1. Theodore Roosevelt, *An Autobiography*, in Louis Auchincloss, ed., *Theodore Roosevelt* (New York: Library of America, 2004), 2:310.

2. H. W. Brands, *TR: The Last Romantic* (New York: Basic Books, 1997), 17.

3. Kenneth D. Ackerman, *Boss Tweed: The Rise and Fall of the Corrupt Pol Who Conceived the Soul of Modern New York* (New York: Carroll & Graf, 2005), 11–29; Leo Hershkowitz, *Tweed's New York: Another Look* (Garden City: Anchor/Doubleday, 1977), 90–93.

4. *New York Times*, Sept. 11, 1863.

5. Alexander B. Callow Jr., *The Tweed Ring* (New York: Oxford University Press, 1966), 209–13.

6. George William Curtis, *Other Essays from the Easy Chair* (New York: Harper & Brothers, 1893), 49.

7. Matthew P. Breen, *Thirty Years of New York Politics Up-to-Date* (New York: published by the author, 1899), 159. Breen was writing from memory; the impression was doubtless accurate even if the language was reconstructed.

8. William L. Riordon, *Plunkitt of Tammany Hall: A Series of Very Plain Talks on Very Practical Politics*, ed. Terence J. McDonald (1905; Boston: Bedford Books, 1994), 27–28.

9. Ibid., 49.

10. Callow, *Tweed Ring*, 199–206; Hershkowitz, *Tweed's New York*, 112–18.

11. *New York Times*, July 22, 1871; Callow, *Tweed Ring*, 254.

12. Callow, *Tweed Ring*, 268–74; *The Diary of George Templeton Strong: Postwar Years, 1865–1875*, ed. Allan Nevins and Milton Halsey Thomas (New York: Macmillan, 1952), 394.

13. Ackerman, *Boss Tweed*, 261, 298–309.

14. Maury Klein, *Union Pacific: Birth of a Railroad, 1862–93* (Garden City: Doubleday, 1987), 291; David Haward Bain, *Empire Express: Building the First Transcontinental Railroad* (New York: Viking, 1999), 679.

15. Bain, *Empire Express*, 696. The findings of the commission were published as *Report of the Select Committee to Investigate the Alleged Credit Mobilier Bribery* (Washington: Government Printing Office, 1873).

16. Klein, *Union Pacific*, 296.

17. Ibid., 296–97; Bain, *Empire Express*, 700.

18. Klein, *Union Pacific*, 298; Bain, *Empire Express*, 700–03.

19. *Whisky Frauds*, 44th Cong., 1st sess., 1876, HR Miscellaneous Document 186 (Serial Set Document 1706), 3.

20. William S. McFeely, *Grant: A Biography* (New York: Norton, 1981), 405–14; Jean Edward Smith, *Grant* (New York: Simon & Schuster, 2001), 584–93.

21. *Malfeasance of W. W. Belknap, Late Secretary of War*, 44th Cong., 1st sess., 1876, HR Rep. 186, (Serial Set Document 186), 3.

22. Ibid., 5–6; McFeely, *Grant*, 427–36; Smith, *Grant*, 593–95.

23. McFeely, *Grant*, 430.

24. Callow, *Tweed Ring*, 297–98.

25. Curtis, *Other Essays from the Easy Chair*, 47.

CHAPTER 13: THE SPIRIT OF '76

1. "John Lewis Reports the Centennial," *Pennsylvania Magazine of History and Biography* 79 (1955): 364–66.

2. Ibid., 366–67.

3. Ibid., 368–74.

4. *Hayes: The Diary of a President, 1875–1881*, ed. T. Harry Williams (New York: David McKay, 1964), 1–2.

5. Ari Hoogenboom, *The Presidency of Rutherford B. Hayes* (Lawrence: University Press of Kansas, 1988), 8–11.

6. De Alva Standwood Alexander, *A Political History of the State of New York* (New York: Henry Holt, 1906–23), 3:32; Matthew Josephson, *The Politicos, 1865–1896* (New York: Harcourt, Brace & World, 1938), 245–47.

7. David Saville Muzzey, *James G. Blaine: A Political Idol of Other Days* (New York: Dodd, Mead, 1934), 60–61.

8. Ibid., 23–28; Muzzey, *Blaine*, 82–97.

9. Harry Thurston Peck, *Twenty Years of the Republic, 1885–1905* (New York: Dodd, Mead, 1917), 17–20.

10. Josephson, *Politicos*, 216; *Hayes Diary*, 26–27.

11. Peck, *Twenty Years*, 115–16; II. Wayne Morgan, *From Hayes to McKinley: National Party Politics, 1877–1896* (Syracuse: Syracuse University Press, 1969), 74–76.

12. Roy Morris Jr., *Fraud of the Century: Rutherford B. Hayes, Samuel Tilden, and the Stolen Election of 1876* (New York: Simon & Schuster, 2003), 107–15.

13. Ibid., 136.

14. Ibid., 164; *Hayes Diary*, 47; Lewis L. Gould, *Grand Old Party: A History of the Repub-*

licans (New York: Random House, 2003), 74–75; Eric Foner, *Reconstruction: America's Unfinished Revolution, 1863–1877* (New York: Harper & Row, 1988), 574; Keith Ian Polakoff, *The Politics of Inertia: The Election of 1876 and the End of Reconstruction* (Baton Rouge: Louisiana State University Press, 1973), 199–231.

15. *Hayes Diary*, 74; Hoogenboom, *Presidency of Rutherford B. Hayes*, 48–49; Morris, *Fraud of the Century*, 237–38, 253; Alexander Clarence Flick, *Samuel Jones Tilden: A Study in Political Sagacity* (New York: Dodd, Mead, 1939) 401–02, 410.

CHAPTER 14: LIVES OF THE PARTIES

1. James Bryce, *Studies in History and Jurisprudence* (Oxford: Clarendon Press, 1901), 1:382.
2. James Bryce, *The American Commonwealth* (London: Macmillan, 1888), 1:100–02.
3. Ibid., 117–28.
4. Kenneth D. Ackerman, *Dark Horse: The Surprise Election and Political Murder of President James A. Garfield* (New York: Carroll & Graf, 2003), 379–427.
5. H. W. Brands, *TR: The Last Romantic* (New York: Basic Books, 1997), 77–80.
6. Ibid., 130–49.
7. Ibid.; Edmund Morris, *The Rise of Theodore Roosevelt* (New York: Ballantine Books, 1979), 227–45; Paul Grondahl, *I Rose Like a Rocket: The Political Education of Theodore Roosevelt* (New York: Free Press, 2004), 68–98.
8. Mark Wahlgren Summers, *Rum, Romanism, and Rebellion: The Making of a President, 1884* (Chapel Hill: University of North Carolina Press, 2000), 124–25.
9. David Saville Muzzey, *James G. Blaine: A Political Idol of Other Days* (New York: Dodd, Mead, 1934), 274–75.
10. Brands, *TR*, 167–71.
11. *The Selected Letters of Theodore Roosevelt*, ed. H. W. Brands (New York: Cooper Square Press, 2001), 33–35.
12. Summers, *Rum, Romanism, and Rebellion*, 198.
13. Harry Thurston Peck, *Twenty Years of the Republic, 1885–1905* (New York: Dodd, Mead, 1917), 32; *Selected Letters of Theodore Roosevelt*, 35.
14. Brands, *TR*, 176–78.
15. Summers, *Rum, Romanism, and Rebellion*, 162.
16. Morton Keller, *Affairs of State: Public Life in Late Nineteenth-Century America* (Cambridge: Belknap Press of Harvard University Press, 1977), 310–11, 522–23.
17. *Historical Statistics of the United States: Colonial Times to 1970* (Washington: Bureau of the Census, 1976), 2:1071–72.
18. Muzzey, *Blaine*, 316–19.

CHAPTER 15: CAPITAL IMPROVEMENTS

1. "The Curious Republic of Gondour," *Atlantic Monthly*, Oct. 1875.
2. Fred Kaplan, *The Singular Mark Twain* (New York: Doubleday, 2003), 218.

3. Ibid., 220–21, 260.

4. Ibid., 306–07; *Mark Twain's Letters*, vol. 5, ed. Lin Salamo and Harriet Elinor Smith (Berkeley: University of California Press, 1997), 613–14.

5. Albert Bigelow Paine, *Mark Twain: A Biography* (New York: Harper & Brothers, 1912), 1:554–55.

6. Francis Parkman, "The Failure of Universal Suffrage," *North American Review*, July–Aug. 1878, 1–20.

7. Charles Albro Barker, *Henry George* (New York: Oxford University Press, 1955), 3–64; Jacob Oser, *Henry George* (New York: Twayne, 1974), 17–23; John L. Thomas, *Alternative America: Henry George, Edward Bellamy, Henry Demarest Lloyd, and the Adversary Tradition* (Cambridge: Belknap Press of Harvard University Press, 1983), 6–16.

8. Barker, *Henry George*, 102–37; Oser, *Henry George*, 25–28.

9. Henry George, *Progress and Poverty: An Inquiry into the Cause of Industrial Depressions and of Increase of Want with Increase of Wealth: The Remedy* (1879; New York: Robert Schalkenbach Foundation, 1966), 5–10, 406–07, 461–62.

10. Arthur E. Morgan, *Edward Bellamy* (New York: Columbia University Press, 1944), 9.

11. Ibid., 20–25.

12. Ibid., 45–49.

13. Ibid., 127–29.

14. Edward Bellamy, *Looking Backward, 2000–1887* (1888; New York: Signet, 2000), 7–9, 32–38.

15. Morgan, *Edward Bellamy*, 250–62.

16. John Hope Franklin, "Edward Bellamy and the Nationalist Movement," *New England Quarterly* 11 (Dec. 1938): 754–57.

CHAPTER 16: MEET JIM CROW

1. *The Booker T. Washington Papers*, ed. Louis R. Harlan, Stuart B. Kaufman, and Raymond W. Smock (Urbana: University of Illinois Press, 1972–), 3:108.

2. *Crusade for Justice: The Autobiography of Ida B. Wells*, ed. Alfreda M. Duster (Chicago: University of Chicago Press, 1970), 7–10; Linda O. McMurry, *To Keep the Waters Troubled: The Life of Ida B. Wells* (New York: Oxford University Press, 1998), 3–15.

3. *Crusade for Justice*, 23–24, McMurry, *To Keep the Waters Troubled*, 26–28.

4. Louis R. Harlan, *Booker T. Washington*, vol. 1: *The Making of a Black Leader, 1856–1901* (New York: Oxford University Press, 1972), 110; Booker T. Washington, *Up from Slavery* (1901; New York: Dover, 1995), 71–75.

5. Washington, *Up from Slavery*, 88–93.

6. Alexander Keyssar, *The Right to Vote: The Contested History of Democracy in the United States* (New York: Basic Books, 2000), 107–09.

7. The most thorough (and recent) account of the Lodge bill controversy is Thomas Adams Upchurch, *Legislating Racism: The Billion Dollar Congress and the Birth of Jim Crow* (Lexington: University Press of Kentucky, 2004), chs. 4–8.

8. Keyssar, *Right to Vote*, 113–15. For the case of Mexican Americans in Texas, see David

Montejano, *Anglos and Mexicans in the Making of Texas, 1836–1986* (Austin: University of Texas Press, 1987), 143–47.

9. *New York Times*, April 5 and 26, 1892.
10. McMurry, *To Keep the Waters Troubled*, 357n1.
11. Ibid., 131–33.
12. *New York Times*, March 11, 1892.
13. Ibid., March 11 and 24, 1892.
14. *Crusade for Justice*, 47–52; McMurry, *To Keep the Waters Troubled*, 139–41.
15. *Crusade for Justice*, 64.
16. *Southern Horrors and Other Writings: The Anti-Lynching Campaign of Ida B. Wells, 1892–1900*, ed. Jacqueline Jones Royster (Boston: Bedford Books, 1997), 51–52.
17. Ibid., 52; McMurry, *To Keep the Waters Troubled*, 147–49.
18. McMurray, *To Keep the Waters Troubled*, 150; *Southern Horrors*, 54–55, 78.
19. *Southern Horrors*, 57–58, 68–72, 82–87. Other students of lynching have disagreed with Wells (and with one another) on the number of persons lynched during this period. Current estimates for the 1890s range from about 1,000 to about 1,500. The most careful enumeration is Stewart E. Tolnay and E. M. Beck, *A Festival of Violence: An Analysis of Southern Lynchings, 1882–1930* (Urbana: University of Illinois Press, 1995). But see also Michael J. Pfeifer, *Rough Justice: Lynching and American Society, 1874–1947* (Urbana: University of Illinois Press, 2004).
20. C. Vann Woodward, *Origins of the New South, 1877–1913* (Baton Rouge: Louisiana State University Press, 1971), 117–18.
21. Edward L. Ayers, *The Promise of the New South: Life after Reconstruction* (New York: Oxford University Press, 1992), 10–11.
22. Woodward, *Origins of the New South*, 127.
23. Ibid., ch. 5; Ayers, *Promise of the New South*, chs. 3–5.
24. Woodward, *Origins of the New South*, 318–19.
25. *Selected Speeches of Booker T. Washington*, ed. E. Davidson Washington (Garden City: Doubleday, Doran, 1932), 2–4.
26. Washington, *Up from Slavery*, 99–100.
27. Ibid., 100–01; "An Account of Testimony before the House Committee on Appropriations," *Booker T. Washington Papers*, 5:422–23.
28. Washington, *Up from Slavery*, 102; Harlan, *Booker T. Washington*, 1:210; *Booker T. Washington Papers*, 5:572.
29. Washington, *Up from Slavery*, 103–05; Harlan, *Booker T. Washington*, 1:213–17.
30. *Booker T. Washington Papers*, 5:583–87.
31. G. Edward White, "John Marshall Harlan I: The Precursor," *American Journal of Legal History* 19 (1975): 6–7. More recent, fuller accounts of Harlan's career and jurisprudence are Loren P. Beth, *John Marshall Harlan: The Last Whig Justice* (Lexington: University Press of Kentucky, 1992); Tinsley E. Yarbrough, *Judicial Enigma: The First Justice Harlan* (New York: Oxford University Press, 1995); and Linda Przybyszewski, *The Republic according to John Marshall Harlan* (Chapel Hill: University of North Carolina Press, 1999).
32. *Civil Rights Cases*, 109 U.S. 3 (1883).
33. Otto H. Olsen, ed., *The Thin Disguise: Plessy v. Ferguson: A Documentary Presentation*

(1864–1896) (New York: Humanities Press, 1967), 43; C. Vann Woodward, *The Strange Career of Jim Crow* (New York: Oxford University Press, 1974), 38–40.

34. Olsen, *Thin Disguise*, 54.

35. Charles A. Lofgren, *The Plessy Case: A Legal-Historical Interpretation* (New York: Oxford University Press, 1987), 21–22.

36. Tourgée's remarkable career is the subject of Otto H. Olsen, *Carpetbagger's Crusade: The Life of Albion Winegar Tourgée* (Baltimore: Johns Hopkins University Press, 1965).

37. Olsen, *Thin Disguise*, 55–57.

38. Lofgren, *Plessy Case*, 39–40.

39. Olsen, *Thin Disguise*, 71–74.

40. Ibid., 78.

41. Ibid., 80–103.

42. *Plessy v. Ferguson*, 163 U.S. 537 (1896).

43. Ibid.

CHAPTER 17: AFFAIRS OF THE HEARTLAND

1. Black Elk, *Black Elk Speaks*, as told through John G. Neihardt (1932; New York: Pocket Books, 1972), 196–202.

2. Dee Brown, *Bury My Heart at Wounded Knee: An Indian History of the American West* (New York: Holt, Rinehart & Winston, 1970), 431–38.

3. *Black Elk Speaks*, 217.

4. Ibid., 217–23; Brown, *Bury My Heart at Wounded Knee*, 439–45; Robert M. Utley, *The Last Days of the Sioux Nation* (New Haven: Yale University Press, 1963), 200–30.

5. *Eleventh Census: 1890*, Report on Population, part I, xxxiv.

6. Frederick Jackson Turner, "The Significance of Frontier in American History," in *The Frontier in American History* (1920; New York: Holt, Rinehart & Winston, 1947), 11–12, 37–38.

7. Elizabeth Sanders, *Roots of Reform: Farmers, Workers, and the American State, 1877–1917* (Chicago: University of Chicago Press, 1999), 105–06.

8. *Munn v. Illinois*, 94 U.S. 113 (1877).

9. Sanders, *Roots of Reform*, 109–16; *National Party Platforms, 1840–1968*, comp. Kirk H. Porter and Donald Bruce Johnson (Urbana: University of Illinois Press, 1970), 57.

10. Richard E. Welch Jr., *The Presidencies of Grover Cleveland* (Lawrence: University Press of Kansas, 1988), 80; Allan Nevins, *Grover Cleveland: A Study in Courage* (New York: Dodd, Mead, 1964), 331–32.

11. *Of the People, By the People, For the People . . . and Other Quotations by Abraham Lincoln*, ed. Gabor S. Boritt et al. (New York: Columbia University Press, 1996), 60.

12. John D. Hicks, *The Populist Revolt: A History of the Farmers' Alliance and the People's Party* (Lincoln: University of Nebraska Press, 1961), 96–113; Fred A. Shannon, *The Farmer's Last Frontier: Agriculture, 1860–1897* (New York: Farrar & Rinehart, 1945), 309–17.

13. Norman Pollack, ed., *The Populist Mind* (Indianapolis: Bobbs-Merrill, 1967), 34–35.

14. Ibid., 3–4.

15. Hicks, *Populist Revolt*, 54.

16. Ibid., 57; *Historical Statistics of the United States: Colonial Times to 1970* (Washington: Bureau of the Census, 1976), 1:208.

17. Hicks, *Populist Revolt*, 62.

18. Ibid., 119–27; Robert C. McMath Jr., *Populist Vanguard: A History of the Southern Farmers' Alliance* (Chapel Hill: University of North Carolina Press, 1975), 87–88; Lawrence Goodwyn, *Democratic Promise: The Populist Moment in America* (New York: Oxford University Press, 1976), 162–66.

19. Sanders, *Roots of Reform*, 127.

20. *National Party Platforms*, 89–91; Pollack, *Populist Mind*, 60–66.

21. Hicks, *Populist Revolt*, 165; Fred Emory Haynes, *James Baird Weaver* (Iowa City: State Historical Society of Iowa, 1919), 310–43.

22. Hicks, *Populist Revolt*, 159–60.

23. Ibid., 162–63; Karek Denis Bicha, "Jerry Simpson: Populist without Principle," *Journal of American History* 54 (1967): 291–306.

24. Hicks, *Populist Revolt*, 162–64, 235; Martin Ridge, *Ignatius Donnelly: The Portrait of a Politician* (Chicago: University of Chicago Press, 1962), 279–309; Ignatius Donnelly, *Caesar's Column: A Story of the Twentieth Century* (1890; New York: AMS Press, 1981), 123–24.

25. Pollack, *Populist Mind*, 363–70; C. Vann Woodward, *Tom Watson: Agrarian Rebel* (New York: Macmillan, 1938), 186–209.

26. H. Wayne Morgan, *From Hayes to McKinley: National Party Politics, 1877–1896* (Syracuse: Syracuse University Press, 1969), 343.

27. Ibid., 451–52.

28. William H. Harvey, *Coin's Financial School* (1894), ed. Richard Hofstadter (Cambridge: Belknap Press of Harvard University Press, 1963), 95–110, 114–19, 126–30, 140, 183, 191–93, 215, 220–39.

29. Ignatius Donnelly, *The American People's Money* (Chicago: Laird & Lee, 1895).

30. The conspiratorial aspect of Populist rhetoric has inspired considerable controversy among historians. Richard Hofstadter, in *The Age of Reform: From Bryan to F.D.R.* (New York: Vintage, 1955), argued that the rhetoric captured the reality of the Populists' thinking and that their movement was fundamentally irrational. From irrationality, xenophobia and anti-Semitism followed naturally. Populism's defenders responded with angry reviews of Hofstadter's book and with books and articles of their own. Norman Pollack landed several blows, including "Hofstadter on Populism: A Critique of *The Age of Reform*," *Journal of Southern History* 26 (Nov. 1960): 478–500; "The Myth of Populist Anti-Semitism," *American Historical Review* 68 (Oct. 1962): 76–80; and *The Populist Response to Industrial America: Midwestern Populist Thought* (Cambridge: Harvard University Press, 1962). For accounts of the controversy, see Lawrence Goodwyn, *Democratic Promise: The Populist Moment in America* (New York: Oxford University Press, 1976), 600–14 (which discusses the literature on Populism generally), and Robert M. Collins, "The Originality Trap: Richard Hofstadter on Populism," *Journal of American History* 76 (June 1989): 150–67.

31. William Allen White, "What's the Matter with Kansas?" in *The Autobiography of William Allen White* (New York: Macmillan, 1946), 280–83.

CHAPTER 18: THE WAGES OF CAPITALISM

1. Erik Larson, *The Devil in the White City: Murder, Magic, and Madness at the Fair That Changed America* (New York: Crown, 2003), 107, 175, 286; Robert Muccigrosso, *Celebrating the New World: Chicago's Columbian Exposition of 1893* (Chicago: I. R. Dee, 1993).

2. Mark Carlson, "Causes of Bank Suspensions in the Panic of 1893," Federal Reserve Board Finance and Economics Discussion Series, 2002; Paul Studenski and Herman E. Krooss, *Financial History of the United States* (New York: McGraw-Hill, 1963), 218–19.

3. H. W. Brands, *Masters of Enterprise: Giants of American Business from John Jacob Astor and J. P. Morgan to Bill Gates and Oprah Winfrey* (New York: Free Press, 1999), 38.

4. Robert Sobel, *Panic on Wall Street* (New York: E. P. Dutton, 1988), 251–58; Henry Adams, *The Education of Henry Adams* (1907; Boston: Houghton Mifflin, 1961), 338–39.

5. Arthur G. Burgoyne, *Homestead* (Pittsburgh: Rawsthorne Engraving and Printing Co., 1893), 16–19.

6. *Autobiography of Andrew Carnegie* (1920; Boston: Houghton Mifflin, 1948), 219.

7. Paul Krause, *The Battle for Homestead, 1880–1892: Politics, Culture, and Steel* (Pittsburgh: University of Pittsburgh Press, 1992), 12–43; Burgoyne, *Homestead*, 52–88.

8. Les Standiford, *Meet You in Hell: Andrew Carnegie, Henry Clay Frick, and the Bitter Partnership That Transformed America* (New York: Crown, 2005), 208–11. Standiford notes the slight differences among observers in the details of the attack.

9. H. W. Brands, *The Reckless Decade: America in the 1890s* (Chicago: University of Chicago Press, 2002), 140–44.

10. Almont Lindsey, *The Pullman Strike: The Story of a Unique Experiment and of a Great Labor Upheaval* (Chicago: University of Chicago Press, 1942), 38–49.

11. William H. Carwardine, *The Pullman Strike* (1894; New York: Arno Press, 1969), 24.

12. Lindsey, *Pullman Strike*, 127.

13. *New York Times*, June 27, 1894.

14. David Ray Papke, *The Pullman Case: The Clash of Labor and Capital in Industrial America* (Lawrence: University Press of Kansas, 1999), 29–31.

15. Hans B. Thorelli, *The Federal Antitrust Policy: Origination of an American Tradition* (Baltimore: Johns Hopkins Press, 1955), 164–232; Sherman quoted on 190.

16. Lindsey, *Pullman Strike*, 157–61. On the use of injunctions in labor disputes, see Felix Frankfurter and Nathan Greene, *The Labor Injunction* (New York: Macmillan, 1930).

17. Allan Nevins, *Grover Cleveland: A Study in Courage* (1932; New York: Dodd, Mead, 1964), 616–17.

18. Grover Cleveland, *The Government in the Chicago Strike of 1894* (Princeton: Princeton University Press, 1913), reprinted in Leon Stein, ed., *The Pullman Strike* (New York: Arno, 1869), 22.

19. Lindsey, *Pullman Strike*, 174–75.

20. Ibid., 208.

21. Papke, *Pullman Case*, 34–35.

22. Ibid.; Lindsey, *Pullman Strike*, 211.

23. Lindsey, *Pullman Strike*, 211; Cleveland, *Government in the Chicago Strike*, 34–36.

24. Papke, *Pullman Case*, 64–73.

25. *In re Debs*, 158 U.S. 564 (1895).

26. Brands, *Reckless Decade*, 160; Ray Ginger, *The Bending Cross: A Biography of Eugene Victor Debs* (New Brunswick: Rutgers University Press, 1949), 168–83.

27. Carlos A. Schwantes, *Coxey's Army: An American Odyssey* (Lincoln: University of Nebraska Press, 1985), 36.

28. Ibid., 41.

29. Ibid., 43–46.

30. *New York Times*, April 26, 1894.

31. Schwantes, *Coxey's Army*, 69; Brands, *Reckless Decade*, 167.

32. Schwantes, *Coxey's Army*, 183.

33. Ibid., 186–221.

CHAPTER 19: TARIFF BILL AND DOLLAR MARK

1. Richard E. Welch Jr., *The Presidencies of Grover Cleveland* (Lawrence: University Press of Kansas, 1988), 47–65; H. Wayne Morgan, *From Hayes to McKinley: National Party Politics, 1877–1896* (Syracuse: Syracuse University Press, 1969), 252–58.

2. Morgan, *From Hayes to McKinley*, 333–34; Samuel W. McCall, *The Life of Thomas Brackett Reed* (Boston: Houghton Mifflin, 1914), 118, 128, 138; Harry Thurston Peck, *Twenty Years of the Republic: 1885–1905* (New York: Dodd, Mead, 1917), 198–201.

3. Morgan, *From Hayes to McKinley*, 331–32; Peck, *Twenty Years*, 195–205.

4. Peck, *Twenty Years*, 208–12; Morgan, *From Hayes to McKinley*, 349–53.

5. Margaret Leech, *In the Days of McKinley* (New York: Harper & Brothers, 1959), 40; Peck, *Twenty Years*, 215–16.

6. Lewis L. Gould, *Grand Old Party: A History of the Republicans* (New York: Random House, 2003), 110.

7. Morgan, *From Hayes to McKinley*, 462; Steven R. Weisman, *The Great Tax Wars: Lincoln to Wilson—The Fierce Battles over Money and Power That Transformed the Nation* (New York: Simon & Schuster, 2002), 131–61; William Lasser, "Income Tax," in Kermit L. Hall, ed., *The Oxford Companion to the Supreme Court of the United States* (New York: Oxford University Press, 1992), 425–26; Loren P. Beth, "*Pollock* v. *Farmers' Loan & Trust Co.*," Hall, *Oxford Companion*, 655; Paul Studenski and Herman E. Krooss, *Financial History of the United States* (New York: McGraw-Hill, 1963), 222–24.

8. William A. Robinson, *Thomas B. Reed: Parliamentarian* (New York: Dodd, Mead, 1930), 321; Allan Nevins, *Grover Cleveland: A Study in Courage* (New York: Dodd, Mead, 1964), 651.

9. H. Wayne Morgan, *William McKinley and His America* (Syracuse: Syracuse University Press, 1963), 116.

10. *The Autobiography of William Allen White* (New York: Macmillan, 1946), 294; H. H. Kohlsaat, *From McKinley to Harding: Personal Recollections of Our Presidents* (New York: Charles Scribner's Sons, 1923), 96.

11. Leech, *In the Days of McKinley*, 69; Morgan, *McKinley and His America*, 170–73.

12. Morgan, *McKinley and His America*, 183–96; Kohlsaat, *From McKinley to Harding*, 30–31.

13. Morgan, *McKinley and His America*, 197.

14. Kohlsaat, *From McKinley to Harding*, 30–37.

15. *National Party Platforms, 1840–1968*, comp. Kirk H. Porter and Donald Bruce Johnson (Urbana: University of Illinois Press, 1970), 108.

16. Morgan, *From Hayes to McKinley*, 496; Paolo E. Coletta, *William Jennings Bryan*, vol. 1: *Political Evangelist, 1860–1908* (Lincoln: University of Nebraska Press, 1964), 91–92.

17. Morgan, *From Hayes to McKinley*, 494.

18. Coletta, *Bryan*, 1:123; H. W. Brands, *The Reckless Decade: America in the 1890s* (Chicago: University of Chicago Press, 2002), 258.

19. William Jennings Bryan, *Selections*, ed. Ray Ginger (Indianapolis: Bobbs-Merrill, 1967), 38–46.

20. Coletta, *Bryan*, 1:141–46.

21. Ibid., 153–57; John D. Hicks, *The Populist Revolt: A History of the Farmers' Alliance and the People's Party* (Lincoln: University of Nebraska Press, 1961), 340–79.

22. Paul W. Glad, *The Trumpet Soundeth: William Jennings Bryan and His Democracy, 1896–1912* (Lincoln: University of Nebraska Press, 1960), 41.

23. Herbert Croly, *Marcus Alonzo Hanna: His Life and Work* (New York: Macmillan, 1912), 216–20; Morgan, *William McKinley and His America*, 228; Lewis L. Gould, *Grand Old Party: A History of the Republicans* (New York: Random House, 2003), 125.

24. Coletta, *Bryan*, 1:166–89; Brands, *Reckless Decade*, 276–85; Louis W. Koenig, *Bryan: A Political Biography of William Jennings Bryan* (New York: G. P. Putnam's Sons, 1971), 221–51.

25. Coletta, *Bryan*, 1:167.

26. Leech, *In the Days of McKinley*, 88–89.

27. Gould, *Grand Old Party*, 126; Morgan, *From Hayes to McKinley*, 523.

28. Koenig, *Bryan*, 249–50.

29. Brands, *Reckless Decade*, 286; Kohlsaat, *From McKinley to Harding*, 54.

CHAPTER 20: IMPERIAL DREAMS

1. Archie W. Shiels, *The Purchase of Alaska* (College: University of Alaska Press, 1967), 15–20.

2. Ibid., 46; Paul S. Holbo, *Tarnished Expansion: The Alaska Scandal, the Press, and Congress, 1867–1871* (Knoxville: University of Tennessee Press, 1983), 12–13.

3. Shiels, *Purchase of Alaska*, 182.

4. Holbo, *Tarnished Expansion*, 48–49. The case for bribery in the Alaska purchase is persuasive rather than conclusive. Congress investigated itself shortly after the purchase and found nothing criminal or inordinately unethical. The money trail proved impossible to follow. Historian Frank A. Golder, who pursued the matter to Russia, summarized his verdict in a sentence: "It is clear that congressmen were bought, but there is no direct and conclusive evidence in the Russian archives to warrant accusation of any congressman by name" ("The Purchase of Alaska," *American Historical Review* 25 [April 1920]: 411–25). This has remained the verdict of most historians; see Robert H. Ferrell, "Purchase of Alaska," *The New Encyclopedia of the American West*, ed. Howard R. Lamar (New Haven: Yale University Press, 1998), 28.

5. William Graham Sumner, *What Social Classes Owe to Each Other* (1883; Caldwell: Caxton Printers, 1952), 19–22.

6. *Social Darwinism: Selected Essays of William Graham Sumner*, ed. Stow Persons (Englewood Cliffs: Prentice-Hall, 1963), 137.

7. Sumner, *What Social Classes Owe to Each Other*, 104–05.

8. William Graham Sumner, "War," in *Essays of William Graham Sumner*, ed. Albert Galloway Keller and Maurice R. Davie (New Haven: Yale University Press, 1934), 1:143, 168, and "Earth Hunger, or the Philosophy of Land Grabbing," *Essays*, 1:188–89.

9. Albert Galloway Keller, ed., *War and Other Essays by William Graham Sumner* (New Haven: Yale University Press, 1911), 15–16; H. W. Brands, *What America Owes the World: The Struggle for the Soul of Foreign Policy* (New York: Cambridge University Press, 1998), 18–20.

10. John Fiske, "Manifest Destiny," *Harper's New Monthly Magazine*, March 1885, 578–90.

11. Josiah Strong, *Our Country*, ed. Jurgen Hurbst (1885; Cambridge: Belknap Press of Harvard University Press, 1963), 200–20.

12. *The Selected Letters of Theodore Roosevelt*, ed. H. W. Brands (New York: Cooper Square Press, 2001), 72.

13. A. T. Mahan, *Sea Power in Its Relation to the War of 1812* (1905; New York: Haskell House, 1969), 1:vi; Mahan, *The Interest of America in Sea Power, Present and Future* (1897; Port Washington: Kennikat Press, 1970), 217.

14. Allan Nevins, *Grover Cleveland: A Study in Courage* (New York: Dodd, Mead, 1964), 549–62. Merze Tate, *The United States and the Hawaiian Kingdom: A Political History* (New Haven: Yale University Press, 1965), provides background to Cleveland's dilemma; Thomas J. Osborne, *Empire Can Wait: American Opposition to Hawaiian Annexation, 1893–1898* (Kent: Kent State University Press, 1981), carries the story forward.

15. H. W. Brands, *TR: The Last Romantic* (New York: Basic Books, 1997), 326–27; Hermann Hagedorn, *Leonard Wood: A Biography* (New York: Harper & Brothers, 1931), 1:141.

16. Denis Brian, *Pulitzer: A Life* (New York: John Wiley, 2001), 231–25; David Nasaw, *The Chief: The Life of William Randolph Hearst* (Boston: Houghton Mifflin, 2000), 125–42; Ben Proctor, *William Randolph Hearst: The Early Years, 1863–1910* (New York: Oxford University Press, 1998), 115–34.

17. H. Wayne Morgan, *William McKinley and His America* (Syracuse: Syracuse University Press, 1963), 369.

18. Hagedorn, *Leonard Wood*, 1:141; Morgan, *McKinley and His America*, 333; Lewis L. Gould, *The Presidency of William McKinley* (Lawrence: Regents Press of Kansas, 1980), 75.

19. Gould, *Presidency of McKinley*, 67; Morgan, *McKinley and His America*, 342.

20. Morgan, *McKinley and His America*, 340–48.

21. Gould, *Presidency of McKinley*, 70.

22. Morgan, *McKinley and His America*, 356.

23. Ibid., 364–67. The destruction of the *Maine* inspired subsequent investigations. A joint army-navy board in 1911 concurred with the 1898 verdict that the explosion was external and deliberate, but the most authoritative study, conducted in the 1970s, concluded

the opposite: that the explosion was internal and accidental. See H. G. Rickover, *How the Battleship Maine Was Destroyed* (Washington: Department of the Navy, 1976).

24. Brands, *TR*, 299, 326.

25. Morgan, *McKinley and His America*, 367–70.

26. Ibid., 372; Margaret Leech, *In the Days of McKinley* (New York: Harper & Brothers, 1959), 185.

27. Morgan, *McKinley and His America*, 374.

28. Gould, *Presidency of McKinley*, 84–86.

29. Morgan, *McKinley and His America*, 377–78.

30. Brands, *TR*, 334; *The Letters of Archie Butt, Personal Aide to President Roosevelt* (Garden City: Doubleday, Page, 1924), 146.

31. Brands, *TR*, 338–40; *Selected Letters of Theodore Roosevelt*, 182–85; Roosevelt, *The Rough Riders*, vol. 13 of *The Works of Theodore Roosevelt* (New York: Charles Scribner's Son, 1923–26), 13.

32. Brands, *TR*, 340.

33. Roosevelt, *Rough Riders*, 92.

34. *Selected Letters of Theodore Roosevelt*, 206–07; 209–11.

35. Brands, *TR*, 356; Finley Peter Dunne, "A Book Review," in *Mr. Dooley on Ivrything and Ivrybody* (New York: Dover, 1963), 104–06.

36. H. H. Kohlsaat, *From McKinley to Harding: Personal Recollections of Our Presidents* (New York: Charles Scribner's Sons, 1923), 68. The story about pacing the floor of the White House wasn't published until January 1903, when it appeared in an article in *The Christian Advocate* by James Rusling, one of the missionaries at the interview with the president. The by-then-deceased McKinley obviously couldn't confirm or deny the account, but several others of those present corroborated Rusling's version. See Charles S. Olcott, *The Life of William McKinley* (Boston: Houghton Mifflin, 1916), 2:110–11.

37. Robert L. Beisner, *Twelve Against Empire: The Anti-Imperialists, 1898–1900* (New York: McGraw-Hill, 1968), 61, 76–79.

38. H. W. Brands, *Bound to Empire: The United States and the Philippines* (New York: Oxford University Press, 1992), 27–32.

39. Ibid., 32–33; *Congressional Record*, Jan. 9, 1900, 704–11. On the anti-imperialists see also E. Berkely Tompkins, *Anti-Imperialism in the United States: The Great Debate, 1890–1920* (Philadelphia: University of Pennsylvania Press, 1970).

40. John A. Hobson, *Imperialism: A Study* (New York: James Pott, 1902), 82–83; V. I. Lenin, *Imperialism: The Highest Stage of Capitalism* (1917; New York: International Publishers, 1933).

41. On the annexation of Hawaii, see Julius W. Pratt, *Expansionists of 1898: The Annexation of Hawaii and the Spanish Islands* (Baltimore: Johns Hopkins University Press, 1936). Cleveland is quoted in Alyn Brodsky, *Grover Cleveland: A Study in Character* (New York: St. Martin's Press, 2000), 303. On the Open Door policy and other aspects of U.S.-China relations, see Michael H. Hunt, *The Making of a Special Relationship: The United States and China to 1914* (New York: Columbia University Press, 1983).

42. Ernest R. May, *Imperial Democracy: The Emergence of the United States as a Great Power* (New York: Harper & Row, 1973), offers an insightful discussion of the tensions between imperialism and democracy.

CHAPTER 21: THE APOTHEOSIS OF PIERPONT MORGAN

1. Richard Zerbe, "The American Sugar Refinery Company, 1887–1914: The Story of a Monopoly," *Journal of Law and Economics* 12 (1969): 339–75 (quote from 341); Charles W. McCurdy, "The Knight Sugar Decision of 1895 and the Modernization of American Corporate Law, 1869–1903," *Business History Review* 53 (1979): 304–42.
2. *United States* v. *E. C. Knight Co.*, 156 U.S. 1 (1895).
3. *Historical Statistics of the United States* (Washington: Bureau of the Census, 1970), 1:211.
4. Hamlin Garland, "Homestead and Its Perilous Trades: Impressions of a Visit," *McClure's Magazine*, June 1894, 3.
5. Burton J. Hendrick, *The Life of Andrew Carnegie*, vol. 2 (Garden City: Doubleday, Doran, 1932), 22–23.
6. Margaret G. Myers, *A Financial History of the United States* (New York: Columbia University Press, 1970), 216; Allan Nevins, *Grover Cleveland: A Study in Courage* (New York: Dodd, Mead, 1964), 657.
7. Herbert L. Satterlee, *J. Pierpont Morgan: An Intimate Portrait* (New York: Macmillan, 1939), 285–86.
8. Ibid., 288–92; Nevins, *Cleveland*, 661–63; Ron Chernow, *The House of Morgan: An American Banking Dynasty and the Rise of Modern Finance* (New York: Simon & Schuster, 1990), 73–77; Jean Strouse, *Morgan: American Financier* (New York: Random House, 1999), 342–45.
9. Nevins, *Cleveland*, 663; Strouse, *Morgan*, 348.
10. H. W. Brands, *The Reckless Decade: America in the 1890s* (Chicago: University of Chicago Press, 2002), 78–79.
11. Chernow, *House of Morgan*, 154.
12. Strouse, *Morgan*, 397–400; Joseph Frazier Wall, *Andrew Carnegie* (New York: Oxford University Press, 1970), 665.
13. H. W. Brands, *Masters of Enterprise: Giants of American Business from John Jacob Astor and J. P. Morgan to Bill Gates and Oprah Winfrey* (New York: Free Press, 1999), 78.
14. Hendrick, *Carnegie*, 2:136–39; Wall, *Andrew Carnegie*, 787–89.
15. Chernow, *Titan: The Life of John D. Rockefeller Sr.* (New York: Random House, 1998), 388–93; Allan Nevins, *Study in Power: John D. Rockefeller, Industrialist and Philanthropist* (New York: Charles Scribner's Sons, 1953), 2:267–73; Wall, *Carnegie*, 764; Strouse, *Morgan*, 404–05.

EPILOGUE: THE DEMOCRATIC COUNTERREVOLUTION

1. Maury Klein, *The Life and Legend of E. H. Harriman* (Chapel Hill: University of North Carolina Press, 2000), 226–34; *New York Times*, May 9, 1901.
2. Ron Chernow, *The House of Morgan: An American Banking Dynasty and the Rise of Modern Finance* (New York: Simon & Schuster, 1990), 88–94; Jean Strouse, *Morgan: American Financier* (New York: Random House, 1999), 431–34.
3. *Historical Statistics of the United States: Colonial Times to 1970* (Washington: Bureau of

the Census, 1976), 1:224, 240; Eric Foner and John A. Garraty, eds., *The Reader's Companion to American History* (Boston: Houghton Mifflin, 1991), 104, 855.

4. *Historical Statistics*, 1:402.
5. Ibid., 1:369, 379, 382.
6. Ibid., 1:383.
7. Arthur Wallace Dunn, *From Harrison to Harding: A Personal Narrative, Covering a Third of a Century, 1888–1921* (New York: G. P. Putnam's Sons, 1922), 335.
8. Margaret Leech, *In the Days of McKinley* (New York: Harper & Brothers, 1959), 592–601.
9. H. W. Brands, *TR: The Last Romantic* (New York: Basic Books, 1997), 415–18.
10. Ibid., 427–28.
11. Ibid., 437.
12. Ron Chernow, *Titan: The Life of John D. Rockefeller Sr.* (New York: Random House, 1998), 541.
13. W. E. B. Du Bois, *The Souls of Black Folk*, ed. David W. Blight and Robert Gooding-Williams (1903; Boston: Bedford Books, 1997), 62–72.
14. Louis R. Harlan, *Booker T. Washington*, vol. 1: *The Making of a Black Leader, 1856–1901* (New York: Oxford University Press, 1972), 311–24; Brands, *TR*, 421–24.
15. *The Selected Letters of Theodore Roosevelt*, ed. H. W. Brands (New York: Cooper Square Press, 2001), 273.
16. Stanley Karnow, *In Our Image: America's Empire in the Philippines* (New York: Random House, 1989), 191.
17. H. W. Brands, *Bound to Empire: The United States and the Philippines* (New York: Oxford University Press, 1992), 84.
18. H. W. Brands, *Woodrow Wilson* (New York: Times Books, 2003), 35.
19. Maury Klein, *The Life and Legend of Jay Gould* (Baltimore: Johns Hopkins University Press, 1986), 484; Joseph Frazier Wall, *Andrew Carnegie* (New York: Oxford University Press, 1970), 1042.
20. Chernow, *Titan*, 571–90.
21. Ibid., 674.

INDEX